Pre-Georgian Lewes
c890-1714
the emergence of
a county town

COLIN BRENT

Colin Brent Books

Publisher: Colin Brent Books
Printing: Biddles Ltd., Kings Lynn
Design: Andy Gammon, Lewes

2004

ISBN 0 9522423 1 1

Every effort has been made to acknowledge
correctly and contact the source and/or copyright holder of each illustration, and Colin Brent Books apolo-
gizes for any unintentional errors or omissions which
will be corrected in future
editions of this book.

Contents

List of illustrations

a view south-westward from the summit in 1778. WC. *James Lambert senior*.
LEWSA 1997.7.4

10 Saint Lewinna depicted in a 12th-century manuscript. Povey 285

11 A Saxon sundial at Bishopstone. Anon 1856 322

12 Grave-slabs from St John's church. D. *James Lambert senior*. LEWSA 1997.7.16

13 Silver pennies struck at Lewes for king Aethelstan by Eadric. Museo Nazionale Rome;
and by Wilebald. Brighton Museum. *Andy Gammon*. King plate 29

14 A gold penny struck at Lewes for Aethelred II by Leofwine. British Museum. King
plate 59

15 St John's church: the Saxon doorway. WC. *James Lambert*. LEWSA 1997.7.14

16 St John's church: the Magnus inscription. WC. *James Lambert*. LEWSA 1997.7.14

17 A silver penny struck at Lewes by Oswold for Edward the Confessor. Ade 39

18 Finding the remains of Gundrada and William of Warenne. *D. Mossman & W.E. Baxter*
1845; their display in Southover church. *R.H. Nibbs & F.W. Woledge* 1845.

19 Lewes castle: entrance to the bailey. *Bob Chaplin*

20 A Kufic coin from Lewes castle. Drewett 1992 88

21 The castle from the Wallands. *James Basire*. 1785. WC. *James Lambert senior*

22 Two keeps: Conisbrough. *James Basire* in Watson 1782 1: plate facing p. 32;
Lewes about 1775. *James Basire*. WC. *James Lambert*; an arrow-loop at Lewes keep
(reconstruction).Figg 1861 20

23 An arrowhead from Lewes castle. Drewett 1992 97

24 A brass steelyard weight. Lower 1845 317

25 The effigy of a knight found at Southover priory, now in Southover church.
Figg 1848 43

26 A seal of a John, earl of Surrey. ESRO PDC 17

27 An effigy at West Walton church in Norfolk. BL Add MS 23061 f. 137

28 Southover priory: blind arcading from the south-west tower. *Freda Anderson*

29 Southover priory: the great church - the ground-plan; the south elevation.
Andy Gammon

30 Southover priory: a fragment from the lavatorium. Spurrell plate 1

31 Southover priory: sculpture - a dove. LEWSA 1980.48.17 *Freda Anderson*; scenes from
the life of saint Peter. Mantell 1846b 435; a griffin and a 'screeching bird'. Kingston
Manor. *Andy Gammon & Freda Anderson*; a squirrel feeding and a lion with a cub. LEWSA
1980.48.208-9. *Freda Anderson*; 'a leaf man'. Lyne 1997 137

32 The tomb slab of Gundrada in Southover church. Horsfield Lewes plate 8; a detail.
Tom Reeves

33 Southover priory: the remains of the infirmary about 1762. WC. Attributed to
Francis Grose in Farrant 2001 269. LEWSA VR 3590

34 Southover priory: the ruined great oven in 1737. *Samuel & Nathaniel Buck*

35 Southover priory: the great gate; a view from the north-west in 1788. WC. *James
Lambert*. LEWSA 1997.7.12; a ground-plan. Godfrey 1926a 5; details of its decoration.
D. *D.T. Powell* 1845, SAS Library ACC 9089; Spurrell plate 3

36 Mote Park and Plashett Park about 1800. ESRO SAS/ACC 1236

37 An ivory crucifix found in Eastport Lane Southover in 1857. Now in the British
Museum.Lower 1865 337

71 Reticulated tracery at Southover church in 1778. WC. *James Lambert*. LEWSA 1997.7.12

72 The brass of prior Nelond, now in Cowfold church, West Sussex. Davidson-Houston 1936 150

73 A length of cornice from Southover priory. LEWSA 1980.48.206. *E.C. Curwen*. Godfrey 1955b plate 22

74 The pigeon-house at Southover priory. *James Basire*. Mantell 1846b 431

75 The remains of St James's hospital. Horsfield Lewes 1: plate 24

76 Partition screens at Swanborough 'grange'. Godfrey 1936c 12

77 Langney 'grange'. Toy 126. BL Add MS 5671 f. 56

78 John Deward's drawing of Malling Deanery. Copy by *Andy Gammon* of ESRO SRA 6/13/2

79 Two grotesques from Malling Deanery. Turner 1852 141

80 All Saints church in 1780. WC. *James Lambert junior*. LEWSA 1997.7.36

81 The brass of John Braydforde in St Michael's church. Davidson-Houston 1937 109

82 Late-medieval Lewes, a partly conjectural view. Godfrey 1953.

83 The brass of Bartholomew Bolney in Firle church. Davidson-Houston 1936 175

84 The 'founder's tomb' in St Anne's church. *Andy Gammon*

85 The French raid on Brighton in 1514. Horsfield Sussex 1: plate facing p. 119. BL Cotton MS Aug. 1, i, 18

86 The indent of a brass of a mitred prelate at Priesthawes near Westham. D. *Jerome Bertram*

87 The prior's lodging at Castle Acre in Norfolk. Hope 1895 152

88 John Deward's drawing of the Lord's Place at Southover. Copy by *W.H. Godfrey* of ESRO ACC 2187

89 A plaque with prior Ashdown's initials at Southover church. WC. *James Lambert senior*. LEWSA 1997.7.13

90 The exterior of the south aisle at Southover church. *Andy Gammon*

91 A buckle-plate from the friary. Gardiner 1996a 112

92 The brass of Richard Iden, formerly rector of St Andrew's. Davidson-Houston 1936 148

93 Gabriel hanging in the Market Tower. *Andy Gammon*

94 A grave-slab dug up in Malling churchyard. D. *John Elliot*. SAS Library ACC 3717

95 The remains of 'St Peter Westout' in 1773. WC. *James Lambert senior*. LEWSA Reeves 22/1

96 Ten Protestant martyrs at Lewes in 1557. *Frederick Colvin*, published 1853

97 The undercroft below the *Star.* Rouse plate 72

98 Thomas Sackville first earl of Dorset. ESRO PDB/S1

99 The Lord's Place Southover: John Deward's drawing. Copy by *W.H.Godfrey* of ESRO ACC 2187

100 Tin-glazed majolica tiles from the Lord's Place. Horsfield Lewes 1: plate 16

101 'Renaissance' sandstone pieces, possibly from the Lord's Place. LEWSA 1980.48.278 & 283. *Freda Anderson*

102 The 'Renaissance' doorcase at Fairhall in Southover. *Andy Gammon*

103 The spiralling path on the Mount at Southover. *Samuel & Nathaniel Buck*

104 Closet windows at Fairhall in Southover. *Andy Gammon*

Preface

Perspectives and problems

I believe few people have any idea of the cost of truth in these things; of the expenditure of time necessary to make sure of the simplest facts, and of the strange way in which separate observations will sometimes falsify each other, incapable of reconcilement, owing to some imperceptible inadvertency. I am ashamed of the number of times in which I have had to say, in the following pages, 'I am not sure', and I claim for them no authority, as if they were thoroughly sifted from error, even in what they most confidently state. Only, as far as my time, and strength, and mind served me, I have endeavoured, down to the smallest matters, to ascertain and speak the truth.
The Stones of Venice (1851)

Like the pages of John Ruskin's strenuous study of Venetian Gothic, my own are tiresomely strewn with equivalents of 'I am not sure'- ranging from 'conceivably' and 'possibly' , by way of 'quite possibly', 'maybe', 'arguably', 'perhaps' and 'probably', to 'doubtless' and 'almost certainly'. The reason is partly lack of evidence. Historians chronicling the Wealden iron industry or the Civil War in Sussex can embellish their narrative with apt and vivid detail drawn from a hundred localities, whereas the historian of Lewes is confined within its streets, its orchards and crofts. Any reference to 'Lewes' is itself a problem, for besides the walled Borough and its suburb at Westout, there were by the 12th century quite separate communities at monastic Southover and riparian Cliffe. Tediously, therefore, 'Lewes' or 'the town' should be invoked only when all three can be treated as an urban nucleus, loosely united.

As for evidence, Lewes invites a wealth of questions which archaeology, archives and its townscape cannot answer. Yet its history is of great interest. Arguably the Lewes spur was a focus for pagan ritual. Certainly the strategic value of the 'hilltop' site, commanding a crossing of a tidal estuary, caused the layout there, soon after 890, of a Saxon fortress-town. This soon housed a prolific mint, and by 1066 water-borne carriage of merchandise along the estuary, and the exchange of agrarian produce from the South Downs and the Weald, had rendered the fortress a thriving market and port - exemplifying the wealth of Greater Wessex. But the Saxo-Danish State, despite its administrative prowess - the steady supply of silver pennies for instance - lacked the political unity to withstand a double assault from Norway and Normandy. William the Conqueror imposed that unity. And typical of the war-lords delegated to enforce it was William of Warenne who made Lewes borough and its castle the focus of a rape organized to police the Saxon peasantry and guard a route to Normandy. He also founded a brilliant dynasty, interlocking by marriage with the Plantagenets, and fighting their battles in England, Wales and Scotland, most memorably the Great Battle of Lewes in 1264. At Southover William and his wife, Gundrada, founded a priory staffed by Continental monks willing to intercede for their Salvation and that of their knights. These Cluniacs grew rich from estates in Sussex and East Anglia, and a 'new town' was laid out at Southover to service them. The archbishops of Canterbury meanwhile built a palace at Old Malling and fostered commerce at Cliffe. So, in the 12th and 13th centuries, seigneurial and sacerdotal wealth reinforced the town's core economy, its trade in Southdown corn, Wealden livestock and merchandise brought up the estuary.

But thereafter the town and its hinterland were beset by bad weather, rising water-levels and recurrent plague. Calamities also arose from the decay of the Norman-Plantagenet State, founded on a Conquest which severed the ruling class from the folk. Locally the Crown failed to defend coastal communities against French raiders, or to persuade local seigneurs to do so. Typical were the Fitzalans, Lords of Lewes from 1361, immensely rich and usually absentee. This failure helped to fuel the Peasants' Revolt in 1381 and Cade's Rebellion in 1450.

From the 1460s a 'New Monarchy' was built up by Edward IV and Henry VII, which curbed the seigneurs and forged strong links with the 'gentry', with landowners of moderate wealth, anxious to serve a credible royal government. Moreover, being rooted in their shire, they were willing, as justices of the peace, to govern, and to defend it - at the Crown's command. In the three eastern rapes of Sussex, Lewes became their administrative focus. They tolerated the Crown's Dissolution of religious houses. At Lewes the Cluniacs and Franciscans, and at Malling the canons, were disbanded. The town also witnessed a doctrinal see-saw - Catholic, Lutheran, Calvinist, Catholic; Protestants were burnt at the stake there under Mary. However an Anglican Church took root under Elizabeth and James I, strengthened by a threat from Continental Catholicism, embodied in the Spanish Armada which 'came along by New Haven'. Meanwhile local gentry increasingly came to the town, to attend quarter sessions and militia musters, to see their lawyers and to socialize. The Sackvilles, Court aristocrats and Lords Lieutenant, often consulted the Lewes bench and kept a mansion at Southover. From the 1460s till the 1620s political stability was also reinforced by a national economic revival enriching farmers and landowners. Moreover London's rapidly growing population increased demand for corn from the South Downs and fat livestock from the Weald, where the New Monarchy pioneered the casting of cannon. Markets and wharfs at Lewes were re-vitalized.

Among the townsfolk, however, a Calvinistic Puritanism was taking root, which dominated its civic life till 1714. When the 'Popish' policies of Charles I provoked a civil war in England, most of them, in collaboration with local Puritan gentry - with Pelhams, Morleys and Shelleys - helped to secure Sussex for Parliament. During the 1650s many worshipped as Presbyterians or Independents, a few as Baptists or Quakers. After the Restoration the majority became Dissenters from the Anglican State Church. Control of the Borough's civic life was handed to a Cavalier-Tory minority till 1689. Dissenters responded by fostering a 'Bonfire' tradition and by aiding the election of Pelhams and other Whig gentry as Borough MPs between 1679 and 1714. Despite civil and religious strife, however, the town sustained, indeed diversified, its role as a market and port.

As a focus of shire self-government in a remarkably decentralized State, as a bastion of the Puritan Conscience, as an emporium for a diverse and prosperous hinterland, Lewes prospered after the accession of George I. These functions had consolidated its status as a county town, and were part of a widespread practice of Liberty which fostered England's maturing as a Democracy.

Yet though Lewes witnessed so much that was formative in the nation's growth, the historian is often denied that 'minuteness' of detail which Charles Baudelaire believed should be his reward for 'burning patience'. Archaeology, so far, has failed to elucidate the origin or purpose of the pagan mounds, or the layout of the Saxon fortress and the circuit of its wall, or the scale of the Warenne state-rooms in the castle bailey, or the evolution of successive monastic churches at Southover, or the extent of the archbishop's palace at Old Malling, or the date of the causeway carrying the High Street at Cliffe. In Lewes borough only one securely-dated pre-Conquest habitation has been unearthed. Refuse-pits routinely yield prosaic sherds, charcoal and bones, 'Saxo-Norman' in date, or slightly later - some from 'a shifting suburb' near North Street.

Information, moreover, from archives is usually sparse. Whether generated by Warennes and Fitzalans, by bishops or archbishops, they throw little light on the medieval town. As for the charters from the priory, the earliest are suspect as 'forgeries', and their topographical detail is meagre. Moreover, Lewes borough never achieved corporate status, so there are no lists of mayors, jurats and freemen. Parish records are poor and no chronicles of Dissent survive prior to 1689 - except from the Quakers, implacable in their paperwork, as in so much else. Only a handful of inventories listing furniture or merchandise occur. No detailed written surveys of the Borough, Cliffe or Southover exist - though by strange coincidence two 'platts' of the town were made in 1620, by John Deward and George Randoll. Even philology offers no certainty - the beguiling theory that the place name, 'Lewes', derives from the Old English *hlaewes*, meaning pagan burial mounds, has been massively refuted.

Yet the historian does stumble into patches of medieval light. John Bleach has discussed the pagan mounds; Jill Craddock and Gabor Thomas, artefacts from Saxon cemeteries; Caroline Dudley, the Saxon mint; John Houghton, the layout of burgage tenements; L. E. Whatmore, the fate of saint Lewinna's bones - until the battle for Dunkirk. Peter Drewett has excavated the castle's south-west keep, and Mark Gardiner, St Nicholas's Hospital and the Franciscan friary. Malcolm Lyne has written up the work done at the priory by Richard Lewis, on the site of the first monastic church and the great latrine blocks, and Freda Anderson has catalogued the precious sculptural remnants from the precinct. C. T. Clay has written on the Warenne dynasty, David Carpenter on the battles of Lewes and Evesham, R. A. Pelham on cross-Channel trade in the 14th century. David Jones has edited the *Life* of saint Richard of Chichester.

For the post-medieval period Malcolm Kitch has explored the Reformation in Sussex; Jeremy Goring, the rise of Puritanism and the Borough's Elizabethan civic elite; Anthony Fletcher, Sussex 'at peace and war' between 1600 and 1660; Henry Cleere and David Crossley, the Wealden iron industry. Cases at assizes and coroners' inquests in the county, calendared by J. S. Cockburn and R. F. Hunnisett, offer glimpses of Lewes life. So do the records of Lewes quarter sessions and, more obliquely, the surviving port-books of Newhaven. And spanning the medieval and post-medieval are the mighty tomes of the *Victoria County History of Sussex* and of the *History of Parliament*; also a myriad of notices by Walter Godfrey and Louis Salzman, on such topics as the castle, the parish churches and timber-framed buildings, Sussex miracles, a litigious anchorite, and dissolved Cluniacs.

I would like to thank John Bleach, David Jarman, Malcolm Kitch, Malcolm Lyne, Gabor Thomas, Kathleen Thompson, Pamela Tudor-Craig and Heather Warne for reading drafts of chapters. The late Freda Anderson, John Farrant, Eric Fernie, Anthony Freeman, Michael Leppard, Daniel Power, Andrew Rudebeck, David Rudling and Tony Way put themselves out to give me useful information. Elizabeth Houts sent me drafts of forthcoming articles on Gundrada and the Hide Chronicle. Edward Hussey threw light on John Twine's *De rebus Albionicis*. David Godfrey alerted me to the implications of William Green's plan of St James's hospital. Besides reading drafts, Christopher Whittick - Archivist Extraordinary - plumbed the darkest depths of the National Archives at Kew to recover shining fragments of data. With his usual flair, Andy Gammon has given the book its design and layout, orchestrated the illustrations and drawn the maps. Jim Hicks donated and disciplined several personal computers. And my wife, Judith, has proved a Tower of Strength, researching and transcribing, checking and correcting, calming and fortifying.

As for the illustrations, I must thank the following for permissions freely given: Millicent Godfrey , to use many plans and drawings made or commissioned by the late W.H. Godfrey; the late Freda Anderson, Bob Chaplin, Les Davey, E.S. Eames, Andy Gammon, David Gregory (and LAG, Norlington Lane Medieval Pottery Production Centre Project), Malcolm Lyne, Tom Reeves, David Rudling, Gabor Thomas, and Luke Barber, Peter Drewett and Mark Gardiner (Field Archaeology Unit of University College London), to use photographs or drawings, made or commissioned by them; Jerome Bertram, Ralph Corfield, Andrew Rudebeck, Jane Russell, Colin Sloley, G. Wicks and Robin Williams, the British Library, the Royal Pavilion, Libraries and Museums (Brighton and Hove), the East Sussex Record Office, Lewes Town Council, the Lewes Priory Trust, Pelham House Associates, and especially the Sussex Archaeological Society, to use photographs of objects or buildings, documents, drawings or watercolours, in their ownership or custody. I must also acknowledge the permission of the British Museum, English Heritage, and the Alexander Turnbull Library, Wellington, New Zealand, to use illustrations. Through the generosity of Ralph Corfield the Kingston capital is being given into the care of the British Museum. My thanks as well to the staff of the East Sussex Record Office and of the Library and Museum at Barbican House.

R E Y

to Darking   to Ryg   to L

Warnham   Ifield   Crawley   Worth   E. Grin
Rusper   Wakhurst   31
Surrey   St Leonards   Park   Forrest
Hill   Tilgate Forest   Row
Hill Pl.   Horsham   39   Forest   Balcombe   W. Hoathly
nfold   Slaugham   Horstead
hingfield   Den Park   Sedgwick Park   Coopers   Ardingley   Kayns
Nuthurst   Ae
linghurst   Cowfold   Cuckfield   41   Danh ill Str.
Grinstead Park   Bolney   Lindfield   Flete
Chipley   Nep Cas.   Butters Green   Ouse R.
Hookland   W. Grinstead   Wevelsfield   U
ton   Shermanbury   Nenick
Warminghurst   Twineham   Keymer   Chailey
shington   Hurstpierpoint   Clayton   Chittington
Ashurst   Hendfield   Albourne   Barcombe
Washington   Woodmancote   S   Ditchling   Westmiston   Plumpton
Wilton   Newtimber   Hamsey
Steyning   Edberton   Poynings   Piecomb   Sammer   Lewes
Bramber   34   Beeding   Hangleton   51
Buttolphs   Blatchington   Patcham   Falmer
Coombs   Old Shoreham   Portslade   Preston   Kingstone
W. Tarring   N. Shoreham   56   Hove   63   Ifford
Broadwater   Brighthelmstone   Rodmel   B
Ovingdean   Southease
Rottingdean   Telscomb
Newha   ven
Adur R.   Newha

P.1 The hinterland of Lewes [1785]

Scale of British Statute Miles.

2   4   8   12   16

K

E

Stoneland Park

Buckhurst

Withyham

Waterdown For.

Frant

Goodhu

n 43

Cr

Wadhurst

rtfield

Hanover Hall

Stocksbury Hill

Tyshurst

Collenden Str.

Rotherfield

R. Rother

Duddleswell

Mayfield

Echingham

S. B

Nutley

Burwash

Sad

Maresfield

Burwash Downs

Brightling

Munfiel

Buxted

Frantfield

Heathfield

field

Waldron

Bails Park

Warbleton

Dallington

field

Lit. Horstead

Rushlake Green

Penhurst

S

E. Hoathly

Shinlake

Ashburnham Ally

Whar

5

Brayl Park

Hellingley

Gardners Str.

Catsfield

E

Ringmer

Ripe

Chittingley

Horsebridge

Hurstmonceux

Nenfield

thover

Glynd

Chalvington

Hailsham

58

Wartling

Boreham Str.

Silmiston

Pevensey Level

Hove

Bech

dingham

Eirle

Alciston

Arlington

Westham

Pevensey

Sluce Haven

arring

Alfriston

Bernwick

Wilmington

evensea Harb.

Teighton

Lullington

Lymington

Pevensea Bay

Bishopstone

W. Dean

Willingdon

Batten

Langney Pt.

Seaford

60

Frieton

E. Bourn

64

E. Dean

S. Bourne

Langney Pt.

The Seven Cliffs

Beachy Hd.

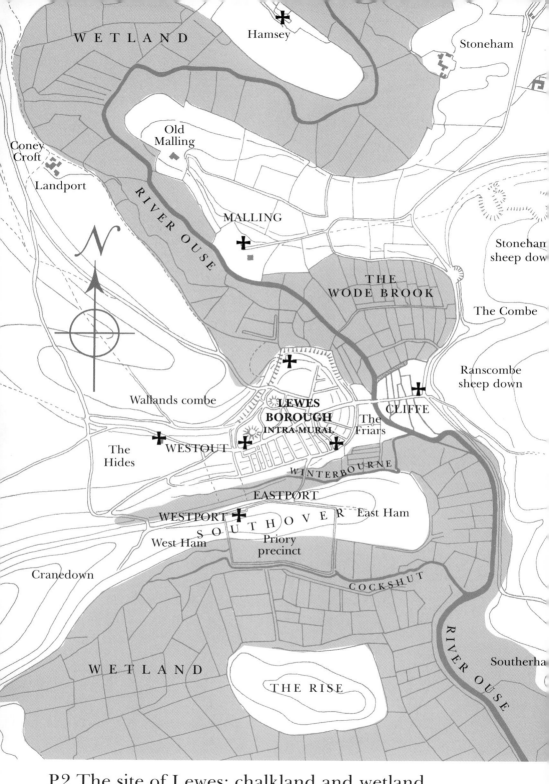

P.2 The site of Lewes: chalkland and wetland

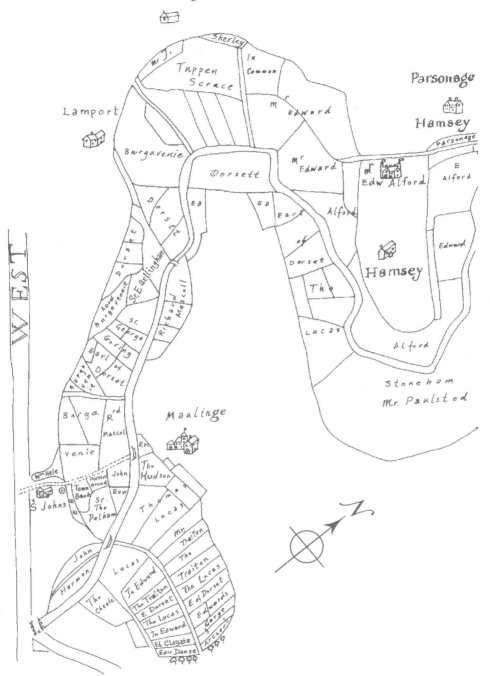

P.3 Water-meadows above Lewes in 1620.

1

Before the burh: mounds and minsters

But its population, its trade, its government, and the extent or situation of its straw-covered buildings in those dark and distant ages, are all equally difficult to be ascertained. Paul Dunvan's lament in 1795.

Lewes is first recorded as a Saxon burh, one in a network of garrisoned strongholds, devised by Alfred the Great (871-899) to defend Greater Wessex from invading Danes. The fortress was laid out on a spur of chalk, dominating fords across the tidal estuary of the Ouse. Down the spur to the river descended an ancient highway which followed for many miles the east-west ridge of the South Downs. Lewes was among the larger burhs, being designed to accommodate refugees, market-traders and a mint, and the vitality of the mint by the 930s suggests that commerce quickly buttressed its urban status.

Archaeology has still to clarify earlier activity on the spur. From Neolithic times the South Downs east of the river Adur had formed a highly farmed cul-de-sac, sandwiched between shifting coastal shingle and sour Wealden clay, and fragmented by the estuaries of the Ouse and the Cuckmere. These 'Lewes Downs', easily accessible only from the west, were perhaps ruled by the Atrebates in the late Iron Age. Their leader, Commius, had carved out a kingdom in Sussex and Hampshire, because Julius Caesar, after his expeditions to Britain in 55 and 54 BC, forced them to evacuate their homeland in northern Gaul. (A gold coin, struck about 55 BC by the Ambiani, has been found near the Caburn, so maybe that Gallic tribe had hired British mercenaries to fight against Caesar.) Until the invasion launched by Claudius in 43 AD the sons of Commius ruled the Atrebatic kingdom, though after losing much of Hampshire to the Catuvellauni they fixed their capital and mint near Selsey. On that fertile coastal plain they lived in affluence, their coins, ornate metalwork and wheel-thrown pottery all modelled on Roman

1 The gold coin

1

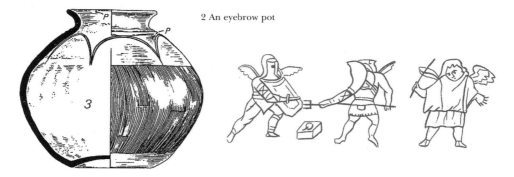

2 An eyebrow pot

prototypes. Affluence, though, was less apparent among the peasant farmers east of the Adur. The handmade pots, characteristic of their 'East Sussex' ware, were bucolically adorned with 'eyebrows' and chevrons.[1]

Sometime before 43 AD Verica, a son of Commius, 'fled' to Rome, perhaps to seek help against the aggressive Catuvellauni. And maybe, during the Claudian invasion, his tribe offered the legionaries a harbour at Fishbourne from which to subdue the Isle of Wight and the West Country. Certainly the Atrebates - now styled the Regni, 'the proud ones' - blossomed under Roman rule. Close to a chic new tribal capital at Chichester their leaders dwelt in sumptuous villas - a mosaic at Bignor depicts cupids engaged in gladiatorial combat. They also retained a king, Tiberius Claudius Togidubnus. As an 'Imperial Representative in Britain' he dedicated a temple at Chichester to Neptune and Minerva. His perhaps was the 'palace' at Fishbourne, with a recessed chair-of-state in a vaulted audience chamber.[2]

East of the Adur, arable farming intensified. Villa-estates were established along the scarp foot at Plumpton, Beddingham and Eastbourne; another lay by the middle-Ouse at Barcombe. And army veterans, maybe, cultivated a grid of fields at Ripe and Chalvington. The iron ore of the Weald was also exploited. The building of a bath-house near a works at Beauport north of Hastings required over 1300 tiles stamped with the letters CL BR - evidence that production was managed by the Roman navy in Britain, the *Classis Britannica*. Smaller in scale were three iron-making bloomeries on Ashdown Forest near Hartfield. Even the peasant-farmers on the chalk land of the Lewes Downs gained in refinement; at Houndean a Samian bowl bearing an image of Jupiter was broken; at Ranscombe below Mount Caburn oysters, mutton and mussels were munched from a Terra Nigra platter.[3]

3 Jupiter

The Romans also used some 35,000 tons of cinder-slag when they linked the Lewes Downs with London by driving a road through the Weald to the scarp foot near Stoneham in Malling. Wheel-tracks are still visible at Holtye near Hartfield. From Camp Hill on Ashdown Forest a

4 Cupids in gladiatorial combat

last alignment took the road through Shortbridge, Isfield and Barcombe Mills. There a Greensand Way led westwards through Streat to join another trans-Wealden road from London at Hassocks. Above Stoneham, on the Southdown chalk, a track continued south-eastwards, past Mount Caburn, to flint-paved fords at Glynde Reach. And beyond, a road along the scarp foot reached Pevensey through Wick Street and Stone Cross. Also linking with the London-Stoneham road was a flint-metalled track running almost east-west through Malling [just south of Church Lane], past a group of Romano-British cremation burials, and making, presumably, for a ford across the Ouse. Its alignment, if extended westwards, would skirt the site of St Michael's church at Malling. (Map 2.1) A drainage ditch near the track has yielded Romano-British pottery and tile, perhaps from a farmstead set amid arable acres later cultivated for canons and archbishops.[4]

Pottery and tile, a quern-stone and coins struck for Tiberius, Antoninus Pius and Domitian, have also been found on the site of the medieval walled town on the Lewes spur. Moreover a ring of post-holes in the grounds of School Hill House may be linked to pottery, possibly Romano-British, discovered near by. Further west, 'several singular pits' were disturbed in 1834 when a water-tank was dug beyond St Anne's church; shells of oysters and of *Helix Pomatia*, a snail relished by the Romans, were found among the ashes, charcoal, animal bones and boars' tusks littering these 'habitations'. Similar pits were uncovered at St Anne's Hill when the grammar school was rebuilt in 1851. Below the spur, in Southover, Mountfield Road has yielded a coin of Gallienus.[5]

Despite a paucity of finds, antiquarians confidently located a thriving Romano-British town on the Lewes spur, which they knew the Saxons and Normans had fortfied. Thomas Horsfield saw it as 'the key to the south-eastern district of the Regnian province'. For Paul Dunvan it was 'a major mart and thoroughfare, a most convenient emporium for the trader, whether Roman, Gaul or German', perhaps with a fleet of fishing boats, 'Corracks or Coracles', bobbing bravely on the Ouse. They searched Classical geographers for a likely name - John Elliot selected 'Trisanton' from Ptolemy. Horsfield preferred 'Mutuantonis' from Pancirollus. To be fair, their instinct that, without a Roman Lewes, Roman Sussex east of the Adur lacked an urban focus was reasonable - in Lowland Britain major Roman market towns were usually not more than thirty miles apart. Maybe one did exist, perhaps near the cemetery by the crossroads at Hassocks, or long submerged off Portslade, Brighton or Seaford. Unless of course the Roman transport network sped Southdown grain and Wealden iron to Chichester, London and Gaul without much need for exchange east of the Adur.

Dunvan also strove to rivet a Roman Lewes onto a major Roman road. The *Itinerarium Curiosum* (1724) of William Stukeley, who publicized the Druids, had traced a 'Hereman-street' through Newhaven and Rodmell ('road-mell') to Lewes, and then along an authentic stretch of the Stoneham-London road through Isfield and 'Sharnbridge' [Shortbridge]. Dunvan, however, re-routed Stukeley's Hereman-street north of Lewes, past Mount Harry and through Streat - 'so called by the Saxons for standing on or near this strata via' - to join another London road at Hassocks. More intrepid was Elliot's surmise that the street-plan of medieval Lewes retained the layout of a Roman legionary camp. Its *via principia*, he believed, had underpinned the High Street between the west gate and Fisher Street Corner, a distance of just over a thousand feet, a length recommended in Roman military manuals. South of the High Street the twittens that made a disciplined descent to the medieval town wall had demarcated a barracks for 12,000 foot and 1800 horse. Watergate Lane had also led to a postern gate, beyond which Elliot envisaged, not 'Coracles', but great ships of the *Classis Britannica*, serenely sheltering from equinoctial storms at a quay by the Winterbourne stream in 'East Port'. North of the High Street, an area occupied by the forum and quaestorium, the camp deviated from the usual parallelogram, to utilize the steep slopes above the Wallands combe.

Elliot was aware, of course, of the mighty rampart still looming over Westgate Lane and Keere Street, where an excavation in 1972 left its origin unresolved. It followed, perhaps, the line of a pre-Roman bank dividing the Lewes spur from ground rising to the west. Also visible in Elliot's day was an entrenchment where Gideon Mantell picked up 'imperial' coins. It formed the southern boundary of St John's churchyard and glebe, which occupied a natural bluff rising from wetland by the Ouse. Elliot believed the site had constituted a *castra aestiva*, a snug 'summer camp' where dusty legionaries could enjoy Rest and Recreation. A Roman origin is also assumed by a tablet affixed to The Fosse, a terrace of houses built in 1903 just south of the 'camp'. Archaeologists, meanwhile, have dated the entrenchment to the 12th century, possibly to king Stephen's troubled reign, though it may have obliterated an earlier bank and ditch. (Map 2.2)[6]

From about 250 AD the *Pax Romana* in Sussex was disturbed by 'Saxon' raiders who disrupted Southdown villa estates and Wealden ironworks, causing a hoard of coins to be buried at Newhaven. Imperial troops were deployed to repel the raiders, but were used by Carausius (288-93) and Allectus (293-6) to set themselves up, briefly, as rulers of Britain. Coins struck for them have been found near Mount Caburn. The disruption caused a coastal fortress to be built at Pevensey and

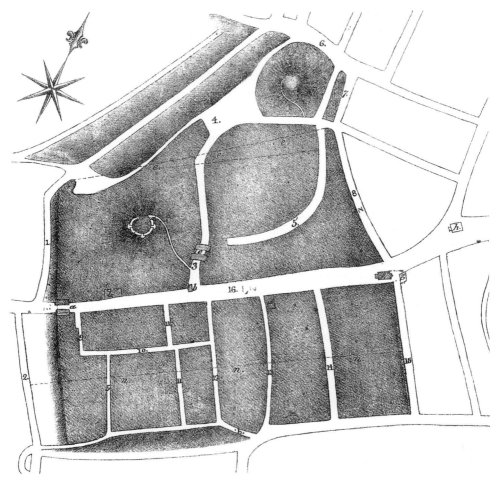

5 Elliot's Roman camp

bastions were added to the walls of Chichester. Thereafter Britain was often denuded of troops while would-be emperors led botched expeditions into Gaul, until the Roman army finally withdrew soon after 400.[7]

According to the *Anglo-Saxon Chronicle* it was in 477 that Aelle, a Saxon warlord, landed at *Cymenes ora* - possibly near Selsey - killing Britons or driving them into the Weald. He defeated them again in 485 at a battle beside a stream called *Mearcredes burna*, the 'frontier river', and slaughtered many more in 491 at Pevensey, *Andredes cester*. Though the precise dating is debated, Aelle's conquest of a kingdom gained him the title of *Bretwalda*, 'overlord' of the English. Certainly by about 500 his South Saxons were settled along the South Downs, from Ocklynge Hill at Eastbourne to Apple Down at Compton in the Mardens. Maybe his invasion was preceded by Saxons settling by agreement with the British. This might account for pottery found in a 'shrine' at Beddingham Roman villa and for sixty or more wooden buildings uncovered at Bishopstone. But though Aelle was styled *Bretwalda*, no pedigree links him with later kings of Sussex. So perhaps his dynasty perished, possibly when Aurelianus routed the Saxons near Mount Badon on the chalk hills of Wessex a decade or more after 500, halting any Saxon advance for fifty years. Moreover, if the barrow on the Southdown ridge above Firle, called Males Burgh, was the grave of Maegal son of Port, it could be this war-lord, unrelated to Aelle, ruled sometime after his death.[8]

By 607, when the British threat had become so remote that Saxon Sussex could war with Saxon Wessex, two pagan cemeteries had been dug near the Lewes spur. At Malling Hill a re-alignment of the turnpike road in 1830 uncovered more than twenty skeletons - 'even the young fellows', noted Gideon Mantell, 'had teeth worn down like Iguanodons'. Recently five graves near by have yielded iron spearheads, knives, swords and a shield-boss; also female accessories - buckles, and beads of glass, stone and amber, and a gilt saucer-brooch of copper-alloy set with a garnet. Over thirty skeletons were also disturbed when Saxonbury House was built at Southover End in 1891. The grave goods included a bronze button brooch bearing a fierce mustachioed face, a wrist-clasp decorated with animal heads, the bronze cap of a leather scabbard, and a Roman green glass bottle.[9]

6 The saucer brooch   7 The button brooch

The Lewes spur itself, from the site of the Crown Courts, has yielded only a throwing-axe dated to about 500, and a prestigious 'seax', a long single-bladed sword made about 700. So maybe it was not from any major settlement there that corpses were carried to Malling Hill or Southover End. Yet possibly the spur was fortified - or re-fortified. An abiding threat from Wessex prompted king Aethelwalh of Sussex to pay tribute to the king of Mercia in the 670s. And perhaps the Lewes Downs east of the Adur, restored by a rapid decay of Roman roads to being a cul-de-sac beset by salt water and Wealden mud, became a safe haven of sorts for his dynasty. At Mount Caburn, which the Saxons named *ceald burh*, 'the cold earthwork', strong defences were raised to protect the northern approach in post-Roman times, though the date is debated.[10]

But though there is no solid evidence for early-Saxon settlement on the spur, it may have been a focus for ritual practice. Earthworks at Mount Caburn, once viewed as enclosing 'a classic hill fort', are now interpreted as defining a 'sacred mount'. A grove of yew, dark and dense, covered the hilltop till the late Bronze Age. Then the site was cleared, ringed with a bank and ditch, and more than a hundred small pits dug inside. They were not filled with random domestic rubbish, but with weapons, knives, razors and loom-weights, often deliberately damaged, and with human and animal remains, carefully kept apart. Moreover the bank and ditch were placed not to obscure, but to 'monumentalize' the interior, and the area encircled included spaces visually segregated from each other, forming 'an arena for the public display, at a … distance, of private ritual acts'. Clearly no Second Legion led by Vespasian had cause to storm the 'camp' in 43 AD, as early excavators fondly imagined.[11]

This evaluation of the Caburn as a sacred mount has caused the Lewes spur to be reconsidered. It is known that Gideon Mantell disturbed evidence of Romano-British ritual when he built a retaining wall in his garden at Castle Place [166 High Street]. Cutting into 'the natural undisturbed chalk-rock' forming the base of the castle mound, he uncovered a pit some six feet deep. Descending layers within it contained ash,

A Loam, ashes, &c.
B Wood, resembling surturbrand.
C Loam, lime, &c.
D Decayed wood and charcoal.
E Muscle and oyster shells, in blue clay.
F Grinders and bones of a horse.
G Skeleton of a boar.

Urn containing the bones of a cock.

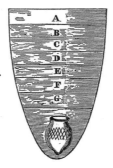

8 Mantell's urn

wood, charcoal, mussel and oyster shells, the bones of a horse, the skeleton of a boar, and at the bottom a Romano-British urn of dark-brown unglazed pottery, now in the British Museum. It was coarsely rayed on the surface, about thirty inches in circumference, with a small base; inside were the bones of a cock, its legs and spurs still perfect. And quite close to Mantell's garden, near the top of St Martin's Lane, a 'Roman' urn enclosing the bones of a cock was also unearthed, in 1838. Both birds, it seems, had been votive offerings. More problematic is the human skeleton found 13 feet below a back-yard on the north side of Brack Mount; adjacent were 'the bones of a large boar's head'.[12]

Recent scrutiny, however, has focused on four mounds, now vanished, elsewhere on the spur. Two were in St John's churchyard, at the south-east and south-west corners. The first was levelled in 1779 when its soil was used to raise the floor of the nave and to fill up 'the hollow of the old prostrate Chancel'. The impressive bulk of the other is shown in a view published by James Rouse in 1825; earlier James Lambert senior had sketched sheep and a cow on its summit. It was demolished in 1839 to make room for a new church, dismissed by Sir Stephen Glynne as 'very ugly quasi-Gothic'. The advance of the workmen towards the centre of this 'ancient British barrow', 'a site for Druidical sepulchres', was obscurely reported in the *Sussex Agricultural Express*:

> they came to large piles of chalk, so arranged as to afford spaces or cists for a human skeleton each, which were protected by a wall of chalk and filled up with ditch clay; presently they came to what the workmen termed an 'oven', or a rude construction of a steined vault; and when they reached the centre of the crown of the Mount they exposed a circle of burnt earth, of two rods in diameter, around the sides of which were a few burnt human bones and a large quantity of boars' and other animal bones also burnt. On the east side an urn of baked clay was found, and also a spearhead or iron weapon.[13]

There was a third mound, 'of colossal dimensions', 'within fifty yards' of the second - perhaps where Abinger House now stands. With woeful imprecision Mark Anthony Lower recalled that its clearance in the 1840s revealed 'several singular interments' and 'remnants of antient pottery'. Moreover, a little to the south a fourth mound overlooked the Wallands combe. Marked on James Edwards's map in 1799, it made way for the *Elephant and Castle* in 1838. Maybe it served as a gallows mound. It stood at the south end of 'Gallows Bank' and in 1800 the *Town Book* noted that 'Malefactors' had been hung thereabouts. 'Hangman's acre' lay a few yards to the south-west. From Saxon times pagan mounds elsewhere, with bracing views, were often chosen to locate and advertise a gallows. It could also be that the Normans enlarged two existing mounds to create the mottes which guarded the bailey of their castle - normally they were content with one. Sadly no date can be confidently ascribed to the 'artificial mix', the man-made compound of chalk-rubble and rubbish, which Mantell observed above the Romano-British pit he excavated.[14]

The 'singular interments', the 'steined vault', the 'antient pottery', found in the vanished mounds, were never precisely dated. Elsewhere the grouping of massive burial mounds spanned several cultures. Six at Treyford in West Sussex, 'the Devil's Jumps', were built in the Bronze

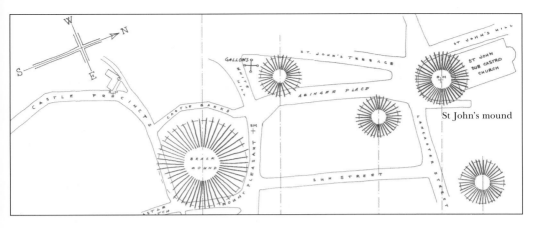

St John's mound

9 St John's mound: its site;
a view in the churchyard;
a view south-westward from
the summit in 1778

Age. Seven at Ashdon in Essex, 'the Bartlow Hills', have yielded splendid enamels owned by 'high Romano-British dignitaries'. Eleven or more at Sutton Hoo in Suffolk loomed above an estuary, like those near St John's; one sheltered the burial ship and treasure of an Anglian king. Such a span invites speculation. Were the Lewes mounds a prestigious necropolis for Bronze Age warlords, for Atrebatic princes or for South Saxon dynasts - among them, perhaps, king Aelle, Bretwalda of the English? Did the course of the rampart above Keere Street define a site more charged with ritual even than Mount Caburn?

The enigma of the mounds has rekindled a venerable debate on the origin of the place-name 'Lewes'. Laurence Nowell in his *Vocabularium Saxonicum*, compiled about 1570, derived it from the Old English *hlaew* meaning 'hill'. This was approved by the English Place-name Society: early Saxon settlers used *hlaew* to describe 'the prominent hill' on which Lewes stands, a plural form being adopted later to embrace the 'other hills just across the Ouse, at the gates of Lewes so to speak'. Yet *hlaew* could also mean 'barrow', so maybe the Saxons were describing a spur dominated by mounds - an extremely seductive derivation. But apparently not. In a massive monograph, Rune Forsberg has denied that the Old English word underpinning the place-name could have lost an initial 'h'. He also claims the noun in question was singular till Anglo-Norman scribes gave it a plural form, just as they substituted *Londres* for *Lunden*. Moreover they muddled *Laewe*, a common form of the place-name, with the Anglo-Norman *ewe* meaning 'water', rendering it into Latin as *Latis Aquis*, 'the broad waters', and coining a resonant adjective, *Latisaquensis*. Richard Coates, a fellow place-name expert, agrees, and suspects that the name was spoken as two syllables to avoid confusion with a word meaning 'pigsty'.

Having rejected *hlaew*, Forsberg derived the place-name from the Old English *laew* meaning 'wound, incision or gash', a word very 'apt' to describe the site of Lewes, set above 'the narrowest part of the great gap in the South Downs'. Such a use was rare and disappeared 'fairly early' perhaps, but its presence 'among the earliest place-names of Germanic origin in Sussex' accorded with the pagan Saxon cemeteries near 'the gap'. Coates deems this derivation 'phonologically perfect' but 'semantically questionable'. He argues instead for *lexowia*, a word from Brittonic, the language used in Sussex before the Saxons came, a word cognate with Welsh *llechwedd*. It means 'a slope' or 'slopes', and describes maybe 'the South Downs in general or the Adur-Ouse block in particular'. He concedes, though, that Celtic name-survival in Sussex is otherwise 'virtually non-existent'. Forsberg has challenged this derivation. A Celtic name had been canvassed by Elliot, reinforced by Horsfield, both anxious to promote a Roman Lewes. Blind to the perils of 'etymological conjecture', they united *Leaw*, 'hand', and *Ys*, 'water', to form 'the hand running into the water'- a reference to the 'claws' of upland intruding into the estuary between Hamsey and Southover: the name of the Hebridean island, maybe, had similar roots.[15]

Heathen ritual prospered locally till Sussex was converted by saint Wilfrid in the 680s, with the backing of king Aethelwalh. A few years before, after three harvests had failed, men desperate to placate the gods had joined hands and jumped from high cliffs into the sea. And in 664, when a gale drove onto a Sussex shore a shipload of Christians escorting Wilfrid to France, they were menaced on the beach by men 'fierce and stubborn as Pharoah', urged on by a chief priest who 'set himself upon a high mound like Balaam', and cursed steadily, till a Christian brained him with a sling-stone. Prudently Wilfrid's party then retired to their ship, casting anchor safely when 'God sent the tide back sooner than usual'. Maybe the chief priest had fulminated from a *hlaew* on the Lewes spur high above the tidal estuary.[16]

It was also perhaps about 670 that pagans near the estuary of the Ouse martyred a pious Christian virgin named Lewinna. After the Conversion of Sussex, her cult flourished. Indeed bishop Eadhelm of Selsey caused her bones to be wrapped in red cloth and displayed in a coffin in a church dedicated to saint Andrew built near the place where she died. Its walls were soon covered with sheets of parchment recording the miracles of healing credited to her. However on Easter Sunday in 1058 a monk from Bergues near Dunkirk, Balger by name, a seasoned relic-hunter, landed near 'Seaford' and glimpsed the church three 'leagues' inland. Learning of Lewinna's sanctity, he stole all but three of her bones, carrying them in triumph back to Bergues. Only a piece of rib survived a Calvinist assault on the abbey in 1558 and that perished during the battle for Dunkirk in 1940. Still extant, though, is a 12th-century drawing of her. It seems unlikely she perished amid the *hlaewes* on the spur. Lewes and Lewinna are not linked etymologically, and though a St Andrew's church stood there in the 12th century, her shrine was probably at Bishopstone, perhaps in the

10 St Lewinna from a 12th-century manuscript

11 The sundial

11

porticus still served by a Saxon sundial.[17]

How Christianity reached mid-Sussex in the 680s is uncertain, though it may have been soon after the Conversion that the archbishop of Canterbury received an estate at Wootton in East Chiltington, two miles north of a *hearg*, a pagan 'sacred place' located on Mount Harry. Just possibly, saint Wilfrid set up a missionary base on the bank of the estuary at Southover. When in the 1070s Cluniac monks settled there, they used and enlarged a once wooden church dedicated 'from old time' to saint Pancras. Pagans who converted swore to renounce the heathen gods, and oaths sworn on relics of Pancras were especially binding. Saint Augustine indeed dedicated to him a church outside the walls of Canterbury. So perhaps the Cluniacs adopted the former wooden church, and its dedication, because Wilfrid had used it to convert pagans 'fierce and stubborn as Pharoah', loath to forsake sacred places on the spur above. The church's 'island' site was similar to that of Wilfrid's first missionary base, soon to be the seat of the South Saxon bishopric. Otherwise hemmed in by water and marsh, Selsey was reached from the west, along a strip of land 'about a sling's throw in width'.

Moreover, recent excavation of the Cluniacs' first church has revealed traces, not only of a 'wooden' edifice, probably Saxon in date, but of an earlier, even simpler, post-built structure. Within this, and serving also as a focus for the later building, was a square vertically-sided

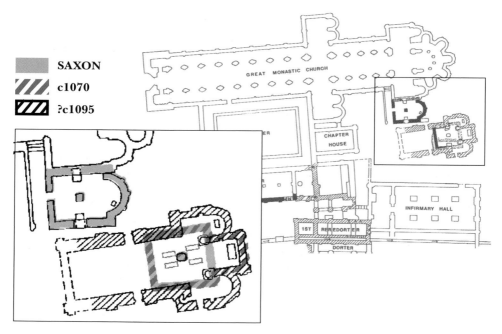

SAXON

c1070

?c1095

GREAT MONASTIC CHURCH

CHAPTER HOUSE

INFIRMARY HALL

1ST REREDORTER

DORTER

1.1 Possibly the site of a wooden church and *sacrarium*

shaft almost 12 feet deep. At the bottom fish bones were found, and a piece of handmade cooking-pot, dating perhaps to about 650. Possibly the pit was a *sacrarium*, a repository for remnants of consecrated fish meals, first eaten perhaps during Wifrid's mission. A few yards to the north-west, in 1845, a 'well', about 22 feet deep, was discovered in the centre of a square 'crypt' with an eastern apse and three entrances, which led perhaps to an ambulatory. The crypt served no obvious purpose in the Cluniac monastery and also dated back, maybe, to the Conversion. Wilfrid built crypts at Ripon and Hexham to display relics brought from Europe. Any mission church at Southover presumably became a 'minster', a base for a group of priests with pastoral care of a territory round about.[18]

Sussex after its Conversion remained an ally of Mercia, though perhaps two dynasties, represented by Aethelwalh, Athelstan and Athelberht, and by Osmund, Oswald and Oslac, were sharing sovereignty or had divided the kingdom between them - maybe with the river Adur as a boundary. However, king Offa of Mercia reduced Sussex and Kent to mere provinces, on his own authority granting an estate at Bexhill to the bishop at Selsey in 772. But though Offa styled himself *rex Anglorum*, 'king of the English', Wessex remained independent and Egbert, its king, after a victory over Mercia at Ellendun in 825, annexed Sussex and Kent to create a Greater Wessex.[19]

Egbert it was who granted 'land at Malling in Sussex' to the archbishop of Canterbury in 838 - quite possibly the 'manor of South Malling' recorded by Domesday Book in 1086. It stretched from the South Downs through the Weald to the border with Kent, from Glynde, Malling and Ringmer, through Isfield and Framfield, Buxted, Mayfield and Wadhurst. Its demesne lands alone supported some 250 peasant-farmers and cottagers; five water-mills rendered 2000 eels a year. By the 1280s the manor serviced a 'palace' at Old Malling used by the archbishop on stately progresses from Canterbury to his estates in western Sussex. Not till the Reformation was this immense manor wrenched away by the Crown. And till 1845 the parishes within it formed a Peculiar - their priests subject to the archbishop, not to the bishop of Sussex.[20]

Also by the 1280s the priests serving the Peculiar staffed a college of canons at Malling for part of the year. It stood on the site of the modern Deanery overlooking the Ouse, sheltered by a fertile river terrace. According to Domesday Book 'the canons of St Michael' already had an estate within the manor of Malling in 1086, and as 'the canons of South Malling' also held of the archbishop a Southdown estate at Stanmer, with Wealden appendages at Wivelsfield and Lindfield, and at Burleigh on the Surrey border. Their earlier history is obscure, for a charter dated to about 765 granting 'Stanmer' to priests 'serving Saint Michael' may be suspect. Yet possibly as early as the 840s the archbishop entrusted his Peculiar to the canons and built them a 'minster' church at Malling.[21]

If so, perhaps they tussled with demons still haunting the *hlaewes* which loomed on the Lewes spur - near a heathen mound at Crowland in the Fens a Mercian prince turned ascetic, Guthlac by name, parried with his blood-stained scourge the attacks of devils chattering in the 'British' tongue. Possibly, to counter such nuisances, a church was built on the spur in the 8th or early 9th centuries. The patron saint of St Michael's church, which stands near the castle mound, close to where votive urns were buried, was an Archangel and Captain of the Heavenly Host with relevant battle experience in High Places. The church of St John's, though, is a likelier candidate. It was close to three *hlaewes* - indeed Rouse shows its medieval west tower nudging the lower slopes of one. A powerful 'common spring' bubbled in the wetland below and its patronal festival, on 24 June, had replaced a midsummer rite of fire and water. Moreover the church probably had a strong subterranean dimension. The removal of its ruinous chancel in 1587 left a large 'Hollow'. And until 1779 the west door of the nave opened onto 'a Deep Descent' of seven or eight steps, two formed by massive reversed medieval grave-slabs. There were two more steps before the altar-rail was reached - a Cyclopean route to the Lord's Supper occasioned perhaps by the collapse of a crypt.[22]

There are also affinities between St John's and the church at Bampton in Oxfordshire, which by the 10th century stood within a long-established Christian cemetery, near three Bronze Age barrows, its site enclosed by a ditch, reminiscent of John Elliot's *castra aestiva*. And might St John's have been a minster church, like Bampton? Its medieval parish extended well beyond Lewes Borough - a possible remnant of former pastoral outreach. And evidence of lavish pre-Conquest funding could be Domesday Book's reference to a church of 'St John', its location unspecified, which held land at Frog Firle near Alfriston and at Parrock near Hartfield. A relic perhaps of close links with the archbishop was 'a cottage adjoining the church yard', held of the manor of Malling in the 17th century. Two minsters close together west of the Ouse, one serving saint John, the other saint Pancras, might seem excessive. But maybe Danish raids in the later 9th century forced priests at the latter to re-deploy to a church amid the *hlaewes*. Significantly perhaps, soon after the Conquest, bishop Ralph gave to the Cluniacs, as one grant, St John's church and 'the chapel in the cemetery of saint Pancras' at Southover.[23]

If by Egbert's reign there was ecclesiastical activity on or below the Lewes spur - two minster churches perhaps, even an archbishop's 'palace', and if a royal estate at Ditchling, and perhaps at Beddingham, was visited by the king's household, they could have caused the shipment to the Ouse estuary of wine, oil and spices, metals and ceramics, dyes and fabrics, weapons, hunting dogs and millstones. That Christianity did stimulate commerce is shown by the origin of Steyning. Saint Cuthman, a native, it seems, of Chidham, while pushing his mother in a wheelbarrow, was guided by God to a Southdown spur above the wetland of the Adur estuary. There he built a stave-church, in which, near his shrine, Aethelwulf, king of Wessex, was buried in 858. A trading community duly sprang up by the river, a few fields away - the nucleus of Steyning. Whether before king Alfred's reign there were wharfs on the Ouse below the spur remains unresolved - though Lewes was one of very few towns described as an *urbs* on coins struck for king Athelstan about 930, a hint maybe of an earlier settlement of sorts. However Paul Dunvan's lament still holds: 'its population, its trade, its government, and the extent or situation of its straw-covered buildings [if any] in those dark and distant ages are all equally difficult to be ascertained'.[24]

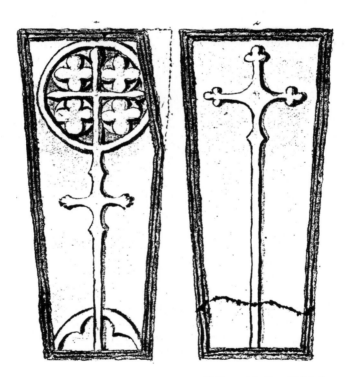

12 Grave-slabs from St John's

Overleaf St John's church: Saxon doorway

2

A Saxon stronghold
c890-1066

During those Danish ravages Lewes was rendered both by art and nature, the most eligible place of refuge for the inhabitants of the adjacent country, and a firm barrier against the invaders. Paul Dunvan 1795.

The Burgh of Lewes, in the time of King Edward, returned £6 and 4 shillings and 3 half pence for rent and toll. There King Edward had 127 burgesses in demesne. Their custom was: If the King wished to send his men, without going himself, to guard the sea, 20 shillings were collected from all men to whomsoever the land belonged, and they who took care of the arms in the ships had this money. Whoever sells a horse in the burgh gives a coin to the reeve, and he who buys, another. For an ox, a half-penny. For a man, 4 pence, in whatever place within the rape, he may buy him. Domesday Book.

Whatever rituals were enacted on the spur, the first evidence of urban settlement is the inclusion of 'Lewes' in an official list of burhs compiled about 918. Though a 'Great Army' of Danes had overrun most of England north of the Thames in 865-67, their war-lord Guthrum was defeated in 878 at Edington in Wiltshire by Alfred the Great, king Egbert's grandson, who also captured London in 886. To better guard Greater Wessex Alfred began building a network of strong-holds which his son, Edward the Elder, completed. Each burh was a place of refuge and the folk in its vicinity garrisoned and repaired it. The official list gives the number of hides for which the communities dependent on a burh were assessed - a hide being the land needed to support a peasant family. So the number allotted to each burh offers a clue to its strategic value - though details for Kent are missing. Lewes, with 1300 hides, was fixed securely on the geopolitical map, ranking just below Winchester, Wallingford, Southwark, Wareham, Chichester, Cricklade, Oxford and Wilton. Probably the town was laid out on the spur before Alfred died in 899 - a fruit of his 'discerning and original genius' as Paul Dunvan aptly expressed it. Already in 892 'Eorpeburnam', a small burh east of Hastings, was under construction, and in 894 marauding Danes were defeated by Saxons sallying from Chichester, where doubtless the Roman bastions had been repaired.[1]

A garrison entrenched on the Lewes spur could harass posses of Danes using the Southdown ridge way and intent on crossing the estuary of the Ouse. Quite where it was crossed is uncertain. In 1794 the canal engineer, Cater Rand, uncovered 'a causeway' and a bridge of 'gross piles' and planks in the water meadows between Old Malling and Landport farm. (Map 2.1) In 1775 John Elliot noted an 'Artificial causeway' which skirted 'the common spring' below St John's church to meet the riverbank opposite the Deanery - the destination maybe of the Roman metalled track through Malling, and the place where John Deward sketched a ferry boat in 1620. He drew another some 500 yards downstream, reached from the west by a bank known as Greenwall in 1457; brick makers found carriage-wheel marks six feet below a nearby water meadow in 1823. Repairs to Cliffe bridge in 1932 revealed a twelve-inch layer of small flints and ashes, ten feet beneath each bank - remains perhaps of an earlier roadway. And through 'the Hams' at Southover a track approached the riverbank opposite Southerham.[2]

Quite possibly too, in the 890s, seagoing ships navigated the estuary and docked below the spur, enhancing its strategic value. In 1086 Domesday Book cryptically recorded that the burh had rendered 'ship-service'. It was the custom, 'if the King wished to send his men, without going himself, to guard the sea, [that] 20 shillings were collected from all men to whomsoever the land belonged, and they who took care of the arms in the ships had this money'. This has been taken to imply that, if the king led his forces in person, the burh had to recruit at least one crewman.

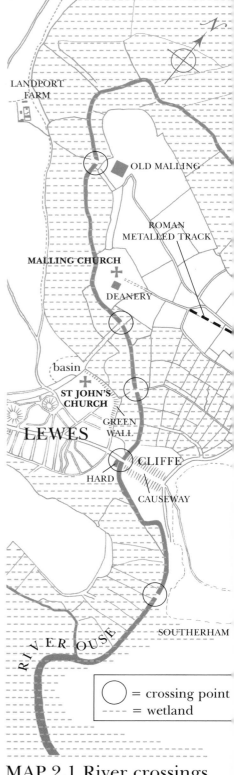

MAP 2.1 River crossings

18

Moreover it seems that in the 1080s fishing boats were beached along the estuary just below Lewes, for Domesday Book noted that folk living at Southease, Rodmell and Iford paid herrings, computed in thousands, as rent. Also in the 11th century there was an expanse of highly compacted flint-gravel forming a 'broad hard' on the Lewes bank of the Ouse [just south of Cliffe bridge]. And possibly a harbour 'basin' was sited to the west of St John's 'camp', now the vicinity of Toronto Terrace. In 1300 the fish ponds of earl Warenne were probably located there, though when soil from the railway tunnel was dumped, the aquatic character of the area ceased. (Map 2.1).[3]

If the burh's strategic value is clear, the location of its 1300 hides is not. To the west lay Burpham with 720 hides and Chichester with 1500. So maybe the settlements servicing Lewes extended to the river Adur, beyond which folk more easily rallied to Burpham on its Southdown spur above the Arun. To the east lay Hastings with 500 hides and 'Eorpeburnam' with 324, a burh tentatively placed either at Rye or at 'Castle Toll', an earthwork near Newenden. The allocation of a mere 500 hides to Hastings may suggest that settlements servicing Lewes stretched beyond the river Cuckmere to the limit of the South Downs at Eastbourne - though it has been argued that the 'Hastings' in the 918 list was in fact the Roman fort at Pevensey, where imperial bastions survived. Domesday Book recorded rural estates with burgesses, houses or 'closes' at Lewes, and others at Chichester, evidence perhaps of a duty, originating in the 890s, to man a garrison. But in the case of Lewes, all but two of the thirty or so estates lay between the Ouse and the Adur, so presumably links with estates east of the Ouse had broken before the 1080s, unless the nexus served a different purpose.[4]

Alfred's successors, Edward the Elder, Athelstan and Edgar, conquered England north of the Thames and preserved their kingdom from civil discord and invasion. The reign of Aethelred II (979-1013) witnessed renewed Danish incursions and massive payments of Danegeld. Stability was restored by Cnut (1017-35) who shaped the politics of Sussex till the Norman Conquest by granting an earldom encompassing Greater Wessex to Godwine, a Saxon thegn. His father Wulfnoth, who defected with twenty ships from the Saxon South-Coast fleet in 1009, was possibly descended from a royal dynasty in Sussex displaced by king Offa. Cnut also sanctioned Godwine's glittering marriage to Gytha, a daughter of Thorgils Sprakaleg, a Nordic magnate. Sprakaleg's son Ulf wedded Cnut's sister Estrith and their son Swein ruled Denmark from 1047 to 1074. Godwine's daughter Edith, moreover, married king Edward the Confessor (1042-66) and though he banished his over-mighty father-in-law in 1051, coastal henchmen of the earl gathered a fleet between Dover and Pevensey and secured his return - the South Coast being well supplied with merchant ships. In 1053 Godwine's son Harold inherited his earldom.

The Nordic Connection

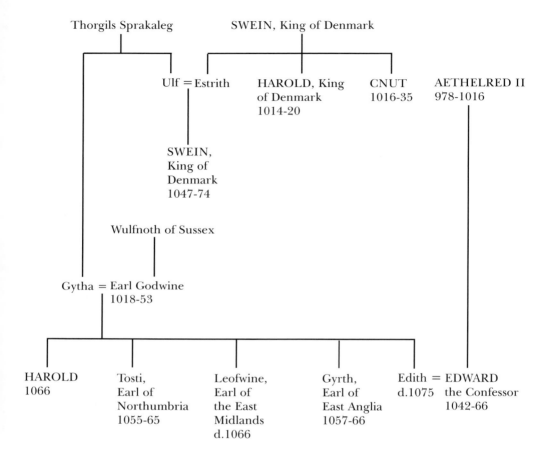

In Sussex itself Domesday Book reveals the scale of his family's influence. Between them in 1065 earl Harold, his widowed mother Gytha, and his three brothers, held about a third of the hides in the county. Moreover their estates in or near the ports of Pevensey, Brighton and Bosham were part of a maritime power-base stretching from Dover to the Solent. At Lewes king Edward had 127 burgesses paying him rent. But earl Harold shared the profits of the burh. And seventy 'closes' there were linked to his estates at Rodmell and Patcham, and 25 to lands at Barcombe and Plumpton held by vassals of his deceased father. Twenty-six burgesses were also attached to the Iford estate of Harold's sister, queen Edith, though maybe she had received it from the king.[5]

Amid these often turbulent politics Lewes put down abiding urban roots. The Saxon kings had made it a fortress, linked to a militia and a fleet, a focus of defence. But being a major burh, it was fashioned too as a hub of administration and trade. Its layout included a court house, a market place and workshops - as well as space for rustic refugees. Revenues from judicial business, market tolls and house rents were anticipated from the start, to recover the cost of building, repairing and manning the walls. Indeed because burhs were secure places under royal protection, positioned to control local road and river transport, all but trivial trading was quickly confined by law to their market places, and witnessed by officials. From the start Lewes was concerned with defence, administration and commerce, functions which were to underpin its status as a county town.[6]

Like other counties, Sussex was governed by a shire court at which the earl and the bishop, or their deputies, presided. It dispensed secular and ecclesiastical law, supervised taxation and organized a militia. Judicial activity at Lewes was noted in Domesday Book. 'A man who sheds blood pays a fine of 7s 4d'. 'A man who commits adultery or rape pays 8s 4d, and a woman as much'. 'From a fugitive, if he is retaken, 8s 4d'. Normally two thirds of any fine accrued to the king, a third to the earl; but in cases of adultery 'the king has [the penalty from] the man, the archbishop from the woman' - why the archbishop of Canterbury rather than the bishop of Selsey is unclear. That Lewes hosted sessions of the shire court is the likelier because it may be that Sussex, an elongated county, had for some administrative purposes been divided in two with the Adur as the boundary. In 918 burhs to its east were allotted 2124 hides, burhs to the west 2220, and again in 1065 communities to the east and to the west were assessed almost equally. The Normans were to use the Adur to define the rape of Lewes, albeit briefly, and the archdeaconry of Lewes, more permanently.[7]

Compelling evidence, moreover, that administration and commerce flourished at Lewes were the many silver pennies minted there, the only form of legal tender. King Alfred found time to reform the coinage, and by the 890s a mint somewhere in Sussex drew its die-stamps from Canterbury and Winchester. By the reign of Athelstan (924-939) the prosperity of Greater Wessex was such that twenty or so mints were at work there, mostly on or near the coast - testimony again to the power of the Saxon State. The king allotted six or more moneyers to London, Canterbury and Winchester, three to Rochester, two to Lewes, Southampton and Wareham, Dorchester, Shaftesbury and Exeter, one to Hastings, Chichester and other mints. Two of his moneyers at Lewes, Wilebald and Eadric, who struck pennies adorned with a Circumscription Cross, are the first townsmen known by name. A penny of Eadric ended up in a hoard buried beneath the forum at Rome, and one of Wilebald's bore the words 'LAE URB' - a recognition of 'urban' status accorded to only four mint-towns.

13 Silver pennies struck at Lewes

AEDELSTAN REX
Aethelstan King

EADRIC MONETA LAE
Eadric moneyer Lewes

AEDELSTAN REX TOT•BR•I
Aethelstan King of all Britain

PILEBALD M‾O•LAE•URB
Wilebald moneyer Lewes town

From 973 the mint's location, as well as the moneyer's name, appeared regularly on the obverse of each silver penny and, if surviving coins are a reliable sample, it seems that more moneyers were located in Lewes than in Hastings or Chichester, and worked more productively. Three moneyers are known about 973 - Goldstan, Sexbyrht and Theodgar; five in 979-85; 11 in 1009-17. Twelve struck Cnut's 'First Quatrefoil' penny between 1017 and 1023 - Leofwine, Leofnoth, Levifa and Aelfweard, Aelfwine, Ealdred, Edwerd, Liofsi and Wulfheh, also the Norseman Onlaf and the 'Germans' Godefrith and Godeman - whereas only five or six moneyers worked at Chichester and at Hastings. A mint, which opened at Cissbury 'camp', was moved to Steyning by 1029. Till the death of king Edgar in 975 the output of Sussex mints was probably a gauge of local prosperity. But under Aethelred II (979-1013) coining was driven in part by a demand for Danegeld - 97 of his pennies struck at Lewes have been retrieved from hoards in Scandinavia. After 1023, as

Danegeld dwindled, so did the number of moneyers. And from 1035 more frequent changes of coin type raised their overheads - Domesday Book noted that at Lewes 'when the money is renewed [the type changed], each moneyer gives 20 shillings; of these two parts were the King's and the third part the Earl's'. Even so, under Edward the Confessor, Lewes remained the busiest Sussex mint; three or four moneyers were the norm, though the striking of his 'small flan' penny employed Edwerd, Edwine, Osmund and Leofwine, Dirinc, Eadwig and Leofman.

The late-Saxon coinage remained centrally controlled, the die-stamps used in Sussex being cut at London or Winchester - two Lewes pennies have the king facing the wrong way. The mint was usually named as *Laewe* or *Laeve*, but such variants as *Lae*, *Lawa*, *Leawe*, *Laeew*, *Laewve*, *Laewwe*, *Laewenen*, *Laehwea* and *Laehwge* have fuelled the strenuous debate on its place-name. At Winchester moneyers also traded in bullion and redundant coin; they occupied separate workshops, with up to six forges in each; some had premises on its High Street.

Prestigiously sited at Lewes perhaps was Leofwine who under Aethelred II minted a gold penny found at Hellingly; one of only three late-Saxon examples known, it was struck maybe for ceremonial use. A penny minted by Aelfweard at London under Edward the Martyr (975-8), has been found at Landport.[8]

14 Leofwine's gold penny

The commerce at Lewes serviced by its prolific mint can be glimpsed in Domesday Book: 'whoever sells a horse in the borough gives to the reeve a penny and the buyer [gives] another; for an ox a half penny; for a man, wherever he may buy him within the rape, four pence' - Domesday Book listed over 400 slaves in Sussex. Long intervals of relative peace, and an improving climate, make it likely that local Southdown farmers had surplus oxen, sheep and wool, wheat, barley and legumes, to market at Lewes. Peasants at Southease in 1086 were expected to provide three pack-loads of peas as a yearly rent to their landlords, the monks of Hyde Abbey at Winchester. Their arable open fields lay among those flanking the estuary of the Ouse between Kingston and Meeching [Newhaven]. Another fertile 'slip' of arable followed the foot of the South Downs, from Hamsey towards Beeding, from Stoneham towards Eastbourne. Crops also flourished on the high chalk land near skilfully managed ponds, at Falmer, Stanmer and Balmer. After the harvest the arable was manured by the nocturnal folding of a sheep flock which served as 'a moving dunghill'. This closely integrated sheep-corn husbandry kept ten shepherds busy on earl Harold's estate at Patcham. In the 1770s the naturalist, Gilbert White, noted that Southdown sheep were horned and white-faced to the west of the Adur, but polled and black-faced to the east - the river, it seems, served again as a frontier.[9]

Domesday Book mentioned water-mills at Beddingham, Firle, Iford and Plumpton, driven by streams gushing from the Southdown chalk; also 'three and a half mills' at Barcombe, where a successor, beloved by Sunday painters, burned down in March 1939. Edwin Lutyens used the stream at Plumpton to fill a lake for the owner of *Country Life*. In 1121 the Cluniacs owned three mills at Southover, perhaps Saxon in origin since they were conveniently adjacent to Lewes market. Two were powered by the Winterbourne, the other by the Upper Cockshut. A charter, purporting to date from about 1089, described this mill as by a pond adjoining the priory's 'island' site, with a bondman attached, Lewin by name.[10]

Saxon Southdown farmers also exploited the forested Weald. Along drove-ways leading due north they dispatched cattle, sheep and goats to graze its rough pasture in summer, and pigs to fatten on its fallen acorns. They dug the wolf-pit which gave a name to Woolpack farm in Fletching. Indeed by 1065 Southdown estates near Lewes had dependent Wealden territories reaching right up to the border with Surrey and Kent. Moreover iron ore was mined. A 'forge' on a site near East Grinstead belonged in 1065 to the royal estate at Ditchling. About 1100 the vicinity of East Grinstead was also expected to supply the Cluniacs at Southover each year with four newly made carts, 200 beech boards and forty loads of logs. By then, presumably, bowls, spoons, arrows and casks were fashioned from Wealden timber. And possibly by 1065 livestock farmers, growing precarious crops of wheat and oats, were settled at Fletching and Horsted Keynes, high up near the Wealden watershed of the Ouse, for their churches display 'Saxo-Norman' features which may pre-date the Conquest. The corridor of the upper Ouse ensured Lewes was well placed to host any sales of Wealden iron, timber or livestock to Southdown farmers or even to out-county dealers.[11]

Perhaps Lewesians also preserved and barrelled sea-fish, for herrings and salt were almost certainly marketed in the town. Tenants at estates along the estuary of the Ouse, paying rents of herrings, have already been noted. They rendered 4000 a year at Rodmell, 16,000 at Iford, 38,500 at Southease, plus £4 in lieu of 'sea-pigs' alias porpoise. In 1086 tenants at Rodmell also worked eleven salt pans - shallow pits perhaps where water left by the ebbing tide could evaporate. There were four at Beddingham, eight at Ripe, sixteen at Laughton near the end of Glynde Reach. Certainly in the 11th or early 12th century Lewesians ate sea food and sea fish. As well as threshed grains of barley and bread wheat, and bones of oxen, sheep, goats, pigs and chicken, refuse pits excavated near North Street have yielded shells of oysters, mussels, winkles and whelks, and vertebrae of cod and mackerel, more rarely of plaice, black sea-bream, conger eel and thornback ray. The heads had been neatly sliced off, suggesting that fishmongers already acted as middle men. Upstream from Lewes a Domesday mill at Sheffield in Fletching rendered 500 eels annually.[12]

In late-Saxon Winchester the wool, hides, skins, bones and fat generated by its livestock trade gave work to weavers and tanners, to dressers of light leather, known as curriers, and to makers of shields, parchment and shoes. At Lewes the refuse pits near North Street have supplied evidence of textile making - a mudstone spindle-whorl, bone needles and clay loom-weights; also ashes, slag and charcoal from a bloomery, a primitive iron-making furnace. By the early 11th century some burhs, such as Steyning, were marketing wheel-turned pottery, fired by specialist craftsmen at kilns located within the wall or near clay deposits in the vicinity. But no such pottery, securely Saxon in date, has been found at Lewes, or indeed at Ringmer where kilns were at work by the 13th century. The North Street pits, however, have yielded fragments of a Pingsdorf wine-jar and of a quern made from Maya lava, evidence of trade with the Rhineland - the source too, along with northern France, of pottery found at Pevensey. Saxon Sussex certainly witnessed a sea-borne traffic in building stone. It was shipped from Quarr on the Isle of Wight, and from Caen in Normandy, to construct the pre-Conquest tower at Sompting church.[13]

As for the scale of judicial and trading activity, figures in Domesday Book suggest that in 1065 official revenue at Lewes - where 'the whole was worth £26', split equally between king Edward and earl Harold - exceeded that at Chichester which 'rendered' £15, with £10 to the king, the rest to the earl. This accords with the relative productivity of their mints. How the money accrued is not fully explained, though at Chichester 48s 11d came from 'closes' and 'crofts', at Lewes £6 4s 1d from 'rents and tolls'. The 'worth' of Lewes was the greater despite new rivals poaching on its commercial hinterland. Pevensey housed 52 burgesses, 24 on the king's demesne, and 35 shillings were derived 'from the harbour'. Steyning, the settlement near saint Cuthman's shrine, had a mint and 118 dwellings. Statistics in Domesday Book also allow Lewes's population in 1065 to be guessed at. A nucleus of perhaps 600 householders, children and servants can be deduced from the 127 burgesses who were king Edward's tenants. But what of the 53 burgesses, the 11 dwellings and the nearly 200 'closes' linked to rural estates, mostly between the Adur and the Ouse? If the burgesses and dwellings were each equivalent to a resident family, then maybe Lewes housed almost a thousand people. Of course if the closes each supported a family, the population was nearer 2000, but possibly they were warehouses or places of refuge.

Utterly problematic is the size of any Saxon community at Cliffe, on the east bank of the Ouse where most local wharfs were eventually sited.

A bridge was repaired at Lewes in 1159, and quite probably by 1065 a 'broad hard' of flint-gravel existed on the river bank to the south. So maybe, by then, the causeway existed which in 1159 carried the West Street of Cliffe, now the High Street, from the bridge, across the 'sea-sand and slub' of the flood plain, to solid chalk at Cliffe Corner. And perhaps this causeway served the settlement 'of the rape of Pevensey', which Domesday Book lumped in with the 'borough' of Lewes as '39 inhabited messuages and twenty uninhabited, from which the king has 26s 6d, and of these William de Warenne has half'. But if that warlord owned them in 1086, why a century or so later was Clifffe included in the archbishop's massive manor of South Malling? Were they removed from clerical control in 1066 because they formed a strategic bridgehead below Warenne's new castle? As for the uninhabited houses, had they been fired in 1066, perhaps to induce the burh to surrender, or were they new sites, signs of urban growth?[14]

Evidence of economic vitality, at Norwich, York and Winchester for instance, were the churches built by Saxon kings, prelates, thegns and merchants. At Lewes as many as ten churches may have existed by 1065, though none can be firmly documented till 1121 when eight belonged to the Cluniacs at Southover - St John's, Holy Trinity, St Nicholas, St Mary in the market place, St Andrew's, St Martin's, St Peter Westout and St Mary Westout, now St Anne's. (Map 2.2) All Saints was first recorded in 1148 and St Michael's, with its rugged round flint tower, in 1301. Yet both must have existed in 1121, for they were mother-churches, holding sway over Holy Trinity and St Nicholas, St Andrew's and St Martin's. And maybe the Cluniacs already owned their eight churches about 1089, though the relevant charter is unreliable. St Peter the Less was perhaps acquired by them after 1121, as a new foundation - 'the Less' being a recognition of St Peter Westout's seniority. And maybe Holy Sepulchre church, recorded in 1237, was founded by the third earl Warenne, who admired the Templars and perished on the Third Crusade in 1148. To 'St Swithens', mentioned as a street-name about 1624, no other reference has been found.[15]

In 1148 All Saints belonged to the bishop and was used perhaps as a base by his Saxon predecessors. Domesday Book noted in Lewes three burgesses and three 'closes' linked to episcopal estates at Henfield and Preston - presumably the tenements near All Saints included by 1330 in the episcopal manor of Bishopstone. The church had been eccentrically located, maybe to counter demons lingering near the Pin Well, a 'perennial spring' bursting from the chalk above the wet land beside the Winterbourne. Already 'enpounded' with a wall by 1280, public access to it was preserved in 1811 when 'waste' ground either side was enclosed. Also plausibly heathen was the 'old great stone', alias 'the great sandstone', standing in the churchyard in the 1670s - unless it was 'the great sand Tombstone' recorded in 1682. Only a 15th-century west tower survived a drastic rebuilding of the medieval church in 1806.[16]

St Michael's belonged in 1301 to Christ Church priory at Canterbury whose superior was the archbishop, and Domesday Book recorded 21'closes' in Lewes linked with the archbishop's manor of South Malling. So maybe a Saxon primate conveyed St Michael's to the monks, just as the revenues from the Wootton estate north of Mount Harry, first given to the archbishop, were diverted to swell their clothing fund. The archangel Michael, who captained the Heavenly Host against Satan's rebel angels and appeared to mortals in high places, was a likely guardian for a hilltop church in a Saxon stronghold, close to pagan *hlaewes* and scenes of Romano-British augural rites.[17]

Only relocated rubble survives from St Peter Westout. Dedicated to the keeper of the Heavenly portal, it stood outside the west gate of the burh and served maybe a Saxon suburb at Westout. In the 12th century its extensive medieval parish encompassed land at Houndean and a sheep run and a chapel at Smithwick alias Ashcombe. And possibly the parish of St Mary Westout was a small enclave carved out within it. Like All Saints, St Mary's church was eccentrically sited. The bulk of it stood just outside the post-Conquest Borough. Indeed folk beating the bounds climbed in and out of lancet windows in the chancel. Yet money was found for ambitious re-building in the 12th century. Perhaps the money - and the location - was due to the proximity of a holy well, dedicated at some date to saint Anne.[18]

That St John's church possibly predated the burh has already been mooted, because of its subterranean character and its location within an entrenched 'camp' near pagan *hlaewes* above a 'common spring'. From the medieval church, demolished in 1839, survives a doorway thought to be late-Saxon, composed of three undecorated semi-circular shafts of Quarr stone, with 'a slab across all three' instead of capitals. Also preserved are 15 stones which, according to the Jacobean antiquary, John Rowe, formed 'the circumference of the Chancel door' till 1587. A chancel arch, a mere eight feet wide, may well have been Saxon in origin. However a blocked 'pointed' arch terminated the nave in 1826, so maybe the door had opened into a porticus, a Saxon side-chapel. John Elliot noted other archaic features - 'pilaster-strips' and 'ancient mean Lights or Windows, near the Roof'. Possibly too the west tower had opened into a north and a south 'transept', a most unusual ground-plan, but similar to the 'westwork' at the Saxon cathedral in Sherborne.[19]

15 St John's church: Saxon doorway

Presumably it was a pre-Conquest church which housed the Danish anchorite celebrated by the Latin inscription on the stones forming 'the Chancel door'. Carved in Lombardic characters and renewed in John Rowe's time, the two concentric lines of 'good quantitative hexameters' have been edited to read:

> *Clauditur hic miles Danorum regia proles;*
> *Magnus nomen ei, magnae nota progeniei.*
> *Deponens Magnum se moribus induit agnum;*
> *Perpete pro vita fit parvulus annacorita;*

and translated as:

> *There enters this cell a warrior of Denmark's royal race;*
> *Magnus his name, mark of mighty lineage.*
> *Casting off his Mightiness he takes the lamb's mildness,*
> *And to gain everlasting life becomes a lowly anchorite.*

This immured Prince of Denmark, pondering 'the undiscovered country from whose bourn no traveller returns', has intrigued antiquarians. Elliot identified him as king Harold, smuggled to Lewes after Senlac, wounded but alive. Dunvan cast him as Harold's son, driven to renounce

16 St John's church: the Magnus inscription

the World by the cruel preference of a thegn's beauteous daughter for a comely Norman knight. A link with the Godwines cannot, of course, be ruled out, for Harold was a grandson of Thorgilds Sprakaleg and a cousin of king Swein.[20]

That St John's had possibly taken over the minster status of the wooden church at Southover dedicated to St Pancras has also been mooted. After the Conquest bishop Ralph gave both St John's and 'the chapel of saint Pancras' to the Cluniacs there. And perhaps the late-Saxon church had been well endowed, a sign of minster status. In the 12th century its extra-mural parish included Landport, much of the Wallands, and a detached enclave and chapel at Allington west of Hamsey. (Map 2.7) Moreover Domesday Book twice mentioned a church of 'Saint John' to which queen Edith 'gave' eight hides at Frog Firle near Alfriston, and from which her brother Harold 'took away' a virgate at Parrock near Hartfield. Was the earl being rapacious, or merely adjusting an endowment agreed within the Godwine family? After the Conquest the count of Mortain granted the hides at Frog Firle to the foreign abbey of Grestain, and many Saxon minsters also had their lands appropriated to fund new Norman monasteries. And maybe the fields near St John's which the Cluniacs acquired formerly belonged to its minster priests.[21]

That St John's was the principal church when the burh was first laid out is suggested by its matriarchal status described in 1337. Corpses were carried to its churchyard from houses on the north side of School Hill, in Fisher Street, in St Mary's Lane [Station Street], and in part of the High Street to the west - a generous segment of the medieval Borough, whereas corpses were delivered to All Saints from a cramped south-eastern quadrant, and to St Michael's from a narrow western sector.[22]

Despite the vitality of the burh, its topography remains uncertain, including the circuit of the wall which protected the spur. (Map 2.2) Nonetheless an 'embankment of some magnitude', once faced with 'chalk stone', still looms behind Keere Street and Westgate Lane - a rampart, like the Saxon earthwork at Burpham, designed to frustrate an assault launched from rising ground. Grants from the 'deep and wide fosse' below the rampart, formerly 'waste' of the manor of Lewes Burgus, had extended gardens in Keere Street by the 1630s and made room for an orchard in Westgate Lane. Maybe too a medieval round tower once stood at each end of the embankment, which was pierced by a handsome west gate before 1350. If this rampart did guard the burh, then the wall must presumably have veered north-eastwards, to command the steep slopes which still descend to Hangman's Acre and the Wallands combe. Part of these Castle Banks remained Borough waste in 1789, challenging terrain where dragoons tested their riding skills.[23]

Paul Dunvan believed that the circuit of the 'town wall' extended beyond Castle Banks to St John's 'camp', because in his day the slopes there above the Wallands combe were still guarded by two 'very high and

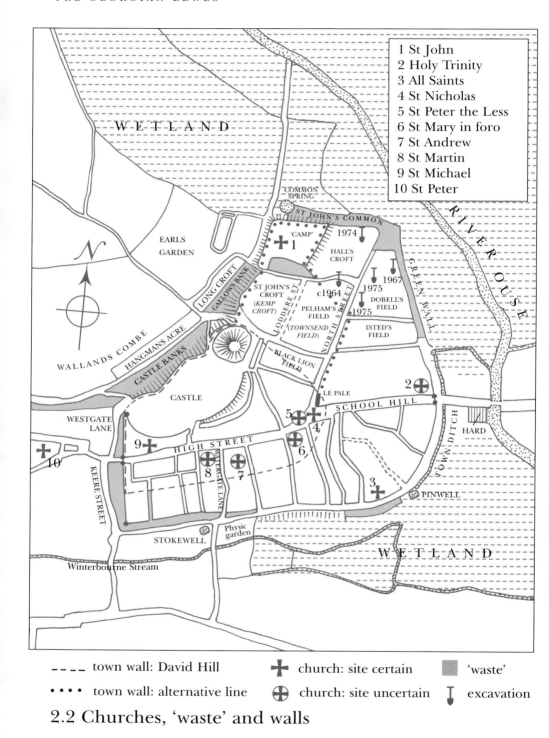

1 St John
2 Holy Trinity
3 All Saints
4 St Nicholas
5 St Peter the Less
6 St Mary in foro
7 St Andrew
8 St Martin
9 St Michael
10 St Peter

WETLAND

COMMON SPRING

ST JOHN'S COMMON

EARLS GARDEN

'CAMP'
1

1974

HALL'S CROFT

1967

LONG CROFT
GALLOWS BANK

ST JOHN'S CROFT (KEMP CROFT)

c1964

1975

DOBELL'S FIELD

PELHAM'S FIELD

1975

(TOWNSEND FIELD)

ISTED'S FIELD

WALLANDS COMBE

HANGMANS ACRE

CASTLE BANKS

BLACK LION FIELD

CASTLE

LE PALE

2

WESTGATE LANE

9

HIGH STREET

5

4

SCHOOL HILL

HARD

10

KEERE STREET

8

7

6

3

PINWELL

STOKEWELL

Physic garden

WETLAND

Winterbourne Stream

RIVER OUSE

GREEN WALL

NORTH STREET

LODDERE ST

WATERGATE LANE

TOWNDITCH

---- town wall: David Hill

•••• town wall: alternative line

✝ church: site certain

⊕ church: site uncertain

'waste'

⬇ excavation

2.2 Churches, 'waste' and walls

strong lines of vallation', which were separated by a ditch, 'a Middle Highway' [roughly the line of St John's Terrace]. The upper rampart formed Gallows Bank, waste on which the Borough pound was re-sited about 1799; the lower sloped down to a field, perhaps the Long Croft shown on George Randoll's map in 1620. Dunvan also noted that the upper vallation merged with the western rampart of St John's 'camp', Elliot's *castra aestiva*, which had clearly been a bastion of great strength, defended to the north and east by 'a natural bulwark', 'abrupt and lofty', rising from meadow ditches 'constantly full of water'. In 1614 and 1675 stretches of a southern rampart, zoned as Borough waste, had been granted away.[24]

Dunvan also believed that, beyond this bastion, the wall had skirted the wetland beside the Ouse - eastward to 'the northern end of Green Wall', then southward along the Wall to 'the ancient site of the East-gate' at the bottom of School Hill. Thereafter he thought it followed 'the side of Friars-wall' [Friars Walk], then skirted the wetland along the Winterbourne stream, westward under All Saints Church, and finally mounted 'the bank at the end of Water-gate'. Such a circuit above the water margin was the more plausible because in 1478 the Eastgate of Lewes was said to be 'by the Friars', and later John Rowe described it as 'anciently' standing between the Green Wall and 'the friars wall'. Dunvan's circuit also coincided with a ribbon of Borough waste. In 1799 Saint John's Common stretched from 'the common spring' below St John's camp to the north end of Green Wall, where a tan-yard was built on waste granted to Thomas Trayton in 1609-10. The Green Wall was occupied in common 'by the whole town' about 1570 and 'a fine row of elms' shaded a public foot way along it till the winter of 1778-9. Waste bordering the wetland below Friars Walk was granted away in and after 1727 - though public access to the Pin Well was preserved. The 'bank at the end of Water-gate' [overlooking the Grange gardens] was sold off in 1750 and 1797, though most of it, as far as Bull Lane, was acquired in 1854 by the Borough Improvement Commissioners and landscaped. In 1846 Gideon Mantell recalled the bank as 'a steep glacis' with traces of 'ancient ramparts' at the top, beneath which 'the town ditch or fosse' had been filled up; on the bank still flourished the evergreen *Anchusa semper-virens*, 'spangling with its bright blue flowers the dense foliage around'.[25]

But though an east gate stood at the bottom of School Hill in 1478, Dunvan's circuit above the water margin could be that of a wall built after the town had overrun its Saxon defences, or constructed to combat rising flood water. An excavation in 1967 concluded that the Green Wall began as an artificial earth bank of 'Middle-Saxon' date, but the findings may be 'ambiguous'. Another in 1974 seeking traces of a defensive earth-work at Brook Street was inconclusive. A wall skirting the water margin would have measured some 6400 feet, whereas 5362 feet of wall needing to be manned can be inferred from the allocation of 1300 hides to Lewes burh in 918. But the short-fall can be explained if the protection offered by wetland reduced official estimates of the manpower needed to guard the circuit. At Chichester, for example, the presence of the marshy river Lavant can reconcile the 6187 feet of wall derived from the 918 allocation with the 7800 feet of Roman wall which encircled the burh.[26]

David Hill, an authority on burghal defences, has recently rejected Dunvan's circuit beyond Castle Banks. He opts for a wall which excludes St John's camp and keeps well above the water margin, running south-eastward from Brack Mount to the crest of School Hill, and then south of the High Street to Keere Street, commanding slopes still very apparent below Pelham House and Steward's Inn Lane. It may be that subsequent settlement has erased any trace of such a circuit. (Map 2.2) However it falls well short of the 5362 feet of wall derived from the 918 list and allows little space for refugees from the South Downs.[27]

But a circuit of 5362 feet is compatible with a wall located lower down the spur, but still well above the water margin, running from Brack Mount via St John's camp to the crest of School Hill, and then to Keere Street along Hill's suggested route. This route might also mean North Street and Market Street began as intramural ways serving the wall. Moreover, near the crest of School Hill, there was in 1570 a strip of Borough waste called 'le pale', some ten feet wide and sixty feet long, forming the boundary of what is now 193 High Street where it borders Market Street, a relic perhaps of a burghal wall. An east gate near the crest of School Hill makes tactical sense. And maybe thereabouts stood the 'lesser' church dedicated to saint Peter, who kept the keys to the gates of Heaven and Hell. 'The Broken Church', on the site of the War Memorial, was referred to in 1592 as 'the church of St Nicholas, decayed and ruined'; but John Rowe noted it as 'Where the Town bell hangeth anciently called Little St Peters'.[28]

An east gate thereabouts might also explain the course of a now vanished Pinwell Street, first recorded about 1280. (Map 2.3) Defined in 1702 as a 'pedestrian way leading from a certain well called Pinwell to a certain lane called Church Lane', it was then blocked by Doctor Tabor who owned the land either side. Its likely course can be traced on James Edwards' map published in 1799. Church Lane quitted School Hill a few yards below the junction with Walwer's Lane, so possibly Pinwell Street began as a short cut from an east gate down to a powerful perennial spring. Walwer's Lane itself was an old-established twitten - a tenement called 'The Walewere' existed in 1329. However the name may stem, not from 'wall', but from a verb meaning 'to trundle'. Brooman's Lane, recorded in 1353, left School Hill some yards below the junction with Church Lane, and also ran south-eastward, 'bending downward towards the Fryers wall' as John Rowe put it.[29]

Certainly the Pinwell spring was a powerful source of fresh water. Perhaps when the burh was laid out, the stream gushing from it was partly

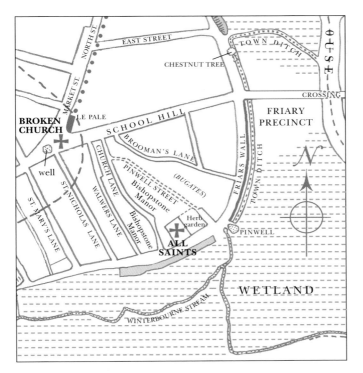

2.3 Pinwell Street, Town ditch and public well

diverted from the wetland by the Winterbourne and channelled north-ward into a Town Ditch, which crossed the bottom of School Hill and turned eastward at the southern end of the Green Wall through the wet-land and into the Ouse. In 1244 the Franciscans included the Ditch in their new precinct, arching it over to preserve the flow of water, though later they filled in part of it and sent the water through a culvert to the Ouse. In the 1620s the surviving stretch, north of East gate, needed to be thoroughly scoured three times a year 'to keep the Town sweet and free from annoyances'. It was much used perhaps for washing clothes. A chestnut outside Safeways marks the site of a last remnant, filled in about 1806.[30]

Access to a powerful spring beyond the wall may also have deter-mined the site of 'the gate of Watergate', outside which lived Norman de la Walle about 1230. (Map 2.2) A 'Stokewell' bubbled up somewhere to the south-west in 1512, possibly the 'common well or spring' near the tan yard polluted by Richard Eason in 1657 with 'filth and sullage'. Reliant perhaps on its spring water was the physic garden [at the east corner of Garden Street], supervised by the almoner of Southover priory in 1408 and by Thomas Fissenden apothecary in the 1690s. A herb garden was also tended just north of Pinwell in 1549. And possibly coeval with the burh was a public well sited by the Broken Church in 1761, 'exactly opposite the *Crown*'. It was choked with debris that year when the church was pulled down, prompting schemes to pipe its 'fine' water to a public pump.[31]

Being a major burh, allotted 1300 hides, Lewes was planned to accommodate refugees. Elsewhere this entailed the laying out of *hagae*, large hedged enclosures ready to receive families, carts and livestock. Perhaps a relic of such an area was the grid of pastures which sloped gently towards St John's church and Green Wall in the 17th century, consisting of St John's Croft, Pelham's Field alias Wood Croft, Black Lion Field, Hall's Croft alias The Lynke, Dobell's Field and Isted's Field. (Map 2.2) In the 1770s these pastures were still 'bounded almost on every side by narrow Carriage roads'. The area would have been almost entirely protected by the water margin, whether within the burghal wall or without. The grid itself, though, could have begun as a layout of residential streets, possibly post-Conquest. But dating back to the burh maybe was the line of 'Loddere Street' which in 1257 seemingly separated what became St John's Croft and Pelham's Field, and led from Fisher Street to the south-east corner of St John's camp. Thereabouts perhaps was a gate - possibly 'the barrs of St John's' recorded in 1498 - allowing access to 'the common spring' and to a causeway and ferry which connected with the Roman metalled track through Malling.[32]

The layout of the burh's commercial sector was probably the one widely used in large towns like Winchester, where the High Street had two parallel back-lanes and regularly spaced side-streets at right-angles to it. These delineated blocks of 'development' land granted to lay or ecclesiastical proprietors, and then subdivided into long narrow tenements running back from the High Street. Road surfaces at Winchester consumed many tons of flint cobbles. As already noted, tolls and fines gathered in a market-place and a court-house everywhere augmented the revenue from burgage rents. Much depended on meticulous layout; the re-planning of London in 898 was approved in person by king Alfred, the begetter of burhs.[33]

If the High Street at Lewes ran from the site of the medieval west gate to an east gate near the crest of School Hill, the building of the Norman castle would have obliterated most of the Saxon street pattern north of it - at Lincoln scores of pre-Conquest tenements were destroyed. But south of it narrow lanes called 'twittens' still lead due south, towards the likely circuit of the Saxon wall. (Map 2.4) John Rowe had listed 'St Swithens lane alias Stewards Inn'. St Martin's Lane alias 'Snellinges lane' was recorded in 1457-8, the alignment of Watergate Lane about 1230, St Andrew's Lane in 1343, St Mary's Lane [Station Street] before 1300. A saffron garden bordered St Nicholas Lane in 1523. John Elliot, who

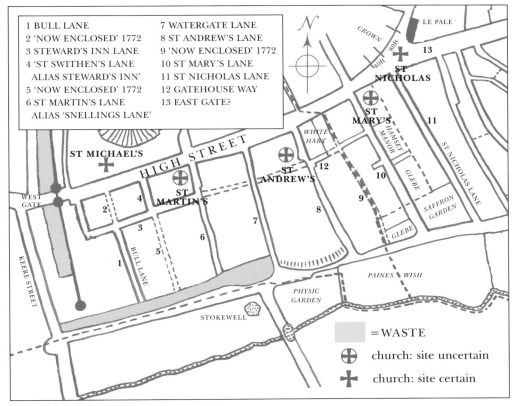

1 BULL LANE
2 'NOW ENCLOSED' 1772
3 STEWARD'S INN LANE
4 'ST SWITHEN'S LANE
  ALIAS STEWARD'S INN'
5 'NOW ENCLOSED' 1772
6 ST MARTIN'S LANE
  ALIAS 'SNELLINGS LANE'
7 WATERGATE LANE
8 ST ANDREW'S LANE
9 'NOW ENCLOSED' 1772
10 ST MARY'S LANE
11 ST NICHOLAS LANE
12 GATEHOUSE WAY
13 EAST GATE?

= WASTE

church: site uncertain

church: site certain

2.4 The twittens

interpreted this regimented layout as the residual ground-plan of a legionary camp, also noted stretches of twitten lost before his time. Bull Lane, which abutted Mr Michell's garden on the west, had once continued to the High Street. The course of St Swithun's Lane, southward beyond the back-lane, 'once the second lane of the [Roman] camp', had been fenced off. And a twitten formerly descended 'in a straight line from the East end of the *White Hart Inn* down through the stables to the South Rampart', roughly coinciding with a parish boundary. It was perhaps 'Olde scolestrete' recorded in 1316 or Tollers Lane mentioned in 1511.[34]

John Houghton has recently argued that - despite some slight topographical warping since - these Lewes twittens were embodied in a Grand Design, a layout using a plot with a High Street frontage of twenty feet (more or less), similar to that employed at medieval Southampton, Farnham and Chichester. He notes that 900 feet separate the west gate from the lost twitten descending through the *White Hart*; that St Swithun's Lane and Watergate Lane divide this distance at intervals of

35

300 feet; and that St Martin's Lane and St. Andrew's Lane sub-divide two of these intervals 'somewhere near the middle' [just as Bull Lane, if it formerly extended to the High Street as Elliot claimed, had sub-divided the third]. By allotting a width of ten feet to each lane, Houghton concludes that each sub-division provided space for seven house frontages, each twenty feet wide. Beyond the *White Hart* entry, he conjectures, were eight frontages, four each side of St Mary's Lane, bordered to the east by a twitten now lost. His theory might also explain why, north of the High Street and east of Fisher Street - an area untouched by the creation of the castle - the Old Bank commands a frontage of 40 feet, the New Bank with the *Crown*, of 80 feet.

As for a back-lane, Houghton notes that in medieval Southampton the High Street plots averaged somewhat less than a hundred feet in depth - at Lewes roughly the distance between the High Street and Steward's Inn Lane, a back-lane bordered by 'le scholehouse' in 1462. He also identifies a fragment of back-lane east of St Andrew's Lane. This 'narrow way', called the Gatehouse Way in 1558, the Common Street in 1581, bounded the gardens of what are now 57-59 High Street. Other stretches had perhaps disappeared into the grounds of 'Mr. Parker's great house' [the *White Hart*], and what became George Goring's new mansion [Pelham House]. That the back-lane once extended eastward, across St Mary's Lane, is suggested by the boundary of a medieval freehold held of Hamsey manor. Observing that Gatehouse Way ran 138 feet south of modern frontages in the High Street, Houghton explains the extra 38 feet as an encroachment onto a 'market area', citing structural evidence at 53 High Street for such a trend in the 16th century.[35]

At Southampton the modest size of the standard plot was compensated for by access to 'common fields', and 'the burgesses of Lewes' had formerly held the land at 'Crandona' [Cranedown], which the Cluniacs at Southover possessed by 1147 - quite probably the Fifteen Acres, a piece of rough pasture skirted by the Juggs Way. (Map 2.6) Maybe William of Warenne, the monks' great benefactor, had wrenched the pasture from the townsfolk after the Conquest. If he also created a hunting park on the Wallands below his castle, perhaps he seized their arable fields as well. At Battle, the Conqueror's new town, where no provision was made for common fields, the tenements were larger than at Lewes, an acre or more, enough land for 'a cow, a calf, a pack-horse'.[36]

John Houghton also suggests that the 900 feet between his lost twitten, east of St Mary's Lane, and the bottom of School Hill had at some time been divided into three equal blocks, accommodating 42 frontages, twenty feet wide, though he accepts that existing twittens offer no obvious framework. Such a layout also makes no provision for a burghal bank and ditch. However, if seventy feet are allowed for these below an east gate near the crest of School Hill, the frontages of the tenements on the north side, now 196-200, 201-6, 207-9 and 210-14 High Street, which

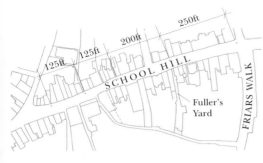

can be traced back to the 1620s, measure 125, 125, 200 and 250 feet. So could it be that they date back to tenements beyond the wall allotted a more spacious frontage - perhaps 25 feet or more? If East Street was their original back-lane, they always enjoyed a depth of over 250 feet. On the south side of School Hill the frontages of 11-19 High Street, below Fuller's Yard, also occupy 250 feet. Higher up, a standard plan was perhaps frustrated by Brooman's Lane and Pinwell Street 'bending' resolutely south-eastward.[37]

It could also be that a frontage of 125 feet was used to delineate the undoubtedly extra-mural tenements on St Anne's Hill, in the suburb of Westout outside the west gate. (Map 2.5) About a thousand feet separate

2.5 Westout

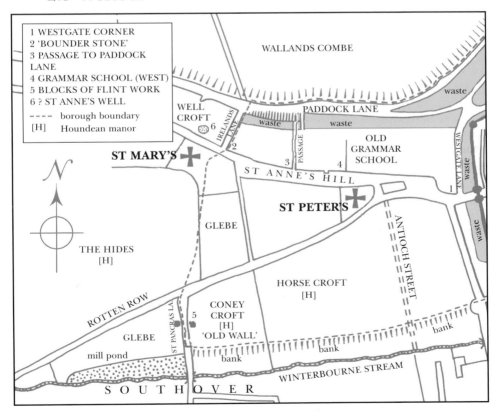

Westgate Corner, beyond the burghal ditch, from the west corner of Ireland's Lane, close to where the Borough 'bounder stone' stood in 1624. The distance from that corner to a former public 'Passage' to Paddock lane [a doorway beside *Millers*] is about 375 feet. Moreover, the distance from the Passage to the west boundary of the Old Grammar School is about 250 feet. In 1624 these tenements on the north side of the Hill were also at least 250 feet deep, abutting a bank of waste above Paddock Lane. On the south side ancient tenement boundaries are too uncertain to allow speculation - though, if Antioch Street was a late intrusion, some 250 feet were allotted west of Rotten Row for St Peter's church and cemetery. By the 890s Rotten Row was already perhaps a main road to Brighton, via Winterbourne, Haredean Gate and Ashcombe.[38]

And maybe Westout was planned with an eye to defence. The thousand feet between Westgate Corner and the bounder stone at Irelands Lane carried the suburb to the crest of St Anne's Hill, a tactically sound terminus. To the north lay the tongue of waste commanding the Wallands combe. To the south the terrain sloped to a 'bank' above the Winterbourne stream. Identified in 1587 as the boundary with Southover, the bank ran westward [the line of Grange Road] to the south-west corner of Coney Croft. Thereabouts in 1861, either side of St Pancras Lane, were two blocks of 'ancient flint work', regarded by the antiquary, William Figg, as remnants of a 'west port', a west gate. That a rampart once bordered Coney Croft on the west - a vulnerable stretch if it was a defensive perimeter - is suggested by the alias 'Oldwall', given to the croft in 1587.[39]

As yet, however, a Saxon origin for tenements on St Anne's Hill and School Hill, though plausible, has not been proved. The 'Saxo-Norman' pottery yielded by refuse pits in the vicinity of Walwers Lane, Broomans Lane and Friars Walk may not predate the 12th century, and though the site of 210-14 School Hill was partly occupied in 1570 by a 'church house' reputed to be a relic of Holy Trinity, that church, like St Peter Westout and St Mary Westout, is not securely recorded till 1121. The eccentrically sited All Saints church may have been built to guard the Pin Well spring rather than to serve a suburb on School Hill. Moreover, as already noted, the burgesses and 'closes' linked by Domesday Book with the bishop's estates at Preston and Henfield were probably located close to All Saints.[40]

Few clues to the built-up area of Saxon Lewes are supplied by other Domesday Book data about burgesses, houses and 'closes' there linked to rural estates. Twenty one closes in 1086 belonged to the archbishop's manor of South Malling, seven to the Stanmer estate of the canons of South Malling. Later rentals of the manor mention a cottage by the church yard of St John's and a house in Fisher Street. Moreover a 'tithe-barn' near the end of Fisher Street, 'belonging to the Deanery of Malling', was destroyed by fire in 1732. But of the secular estates listed

in Domesday Book, only Clayton manor was later credited with tenements in Lewes Borough, being High Street premises opposite St
Michael's. Other premises were linked to Southover, Kingston and
Withdean Cayliffe, ecclesiastical manors formed after the Conquest, or to
Portslade and Plumpton, Hamsey and Hurstpierpoint, 'head' manors of
knight's fiefs also post-Conquest in date, or to Houndean, a manor
retained by the 'lords of Lewes', the Warennes and Fitzalans.[41]

As for the Saxon estate from which the burh was carved, and onto
which extra-mural suburbs may have spread, it coincided perhaps with a
'Greater Houndean', later occupied by the site of Lewes Borough and
the medieval parishes of St John Without, St Peter Without and St Mary
Without. (Map 2.6) These stretched northward to Landport and westward through Houndean to Ashcombe - a territory first vested perhaps
in Saxon minster priests at St John's. Also coinciding with most of it in
1615 were the demesne lands of Houndean manor. Its 1200 acres of
arable and sheep-run encompassed Landport, the Wallands and 'the
Fludds', now the Nevill estate, also Houndean, Winterbourne,
Haredean, Sheeplands, Lane End and Little Down. Its demesne water
meadows bordered the Ouse from Landport down to the causeway below
St John's church. In Lewes Borough the freehold, now 207-9 School Hill,
was held of it, also Coney Croft, Horse Croft and Parsonage Croft, on the
slopes below St Anne's Hill. The Hides, further west, had probably been
detached from it by the Fitzalans, when endowing Holy Trinity Hospital
at Arundel. Filling that part of the parish of St Peter Without, not otherwise occupied by Houndean manor in 1615, was the manor of
Ashcombe-Smithwick. Its 700 acres of arable and sheep-run at Ashcombe
and Breadnore lay within Ashcombe Farm in the 1820s, and were probably the lands at Ashcombe held as two hides by Cola in 1065. Earlier
these acres may well have been detached from a Greater Houndean
estate, for around the hamlet of Ashcombe the territory of the two
manors intermingled.[42]

Quite possibly the lands forming the medieval parish of Southover
had also belonged to a Houndean estate in 1065. Its name can been
interpreted as 'southern bank' and its core, a narrow upland between the
Winterbourne and Cockshut streams, could well have formed the southern margin of a larger estate - a tract roamed by fishermen and herds-
men, its remote wooden church cherished perhaps as a relic of saint
Wilfrid's mission. Moreover, belonging to Houndean manor in 1615,
were water meadows beside the Ouse which swept through Southover
from the Friars estate to Pulbar, just short of the Iford boundary. Also
held of the manor were Dock Wish and 'the Rishy brook', wetland by the
Winterbourne south-west and south of the Friars estate, itself a watery
site probably detached from the manor about 1240. It seems likely, therefore, that soon after the Conquest the lord of Lewes rape, William of
Warenne, and his son, detached from Greater Houndean the lands in

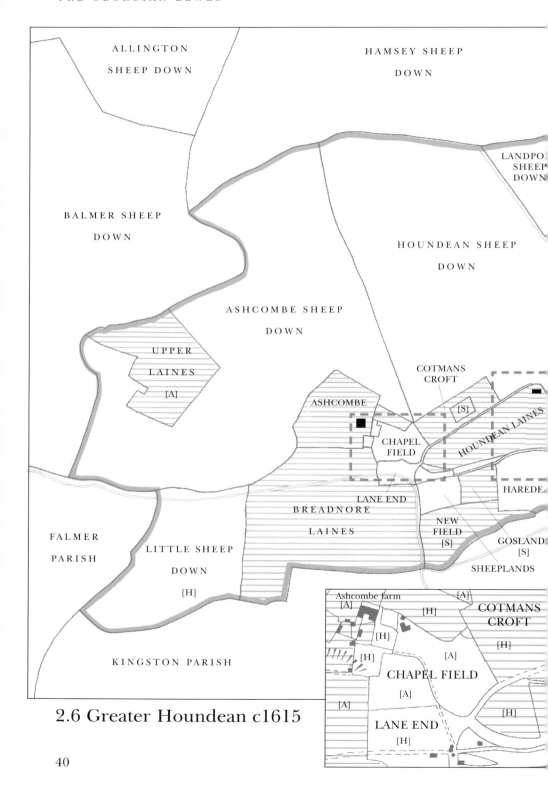

2.6 Greater Houndean c1615

ALLINGTON
SHEEP DOWN

HAMSEY SHEEP
DOWN

LANDPO
SHEEP
DOWN

BALMER SHEEP
DOWN

HOUNDEAN SHEEP
DOWN

ASHCOMBE SHEEP
DOWN

UPPER
LAINES
[A]

COTMANS
CROFT

ASHCOMBE

[S]

HOUNDEAN LAINES

CHAPEL
FIELD

HAREDE

LANE END

BREADNORE
LAINES

NEW
FIELD
[S]

GOSLAND
[S]

FALMER

PARISH

LITTLE SHEEP
DOWN
[H]

SHEEPLANDS

KINGSTON PARISH

Ashcombe farm
[A]

[A]

[H]

COTMANS
CROFT

[H]

[H]

[H]

[H]

CHAPEL FIELD

[A]

[A]

[A]

LANE END
[H]

[H]

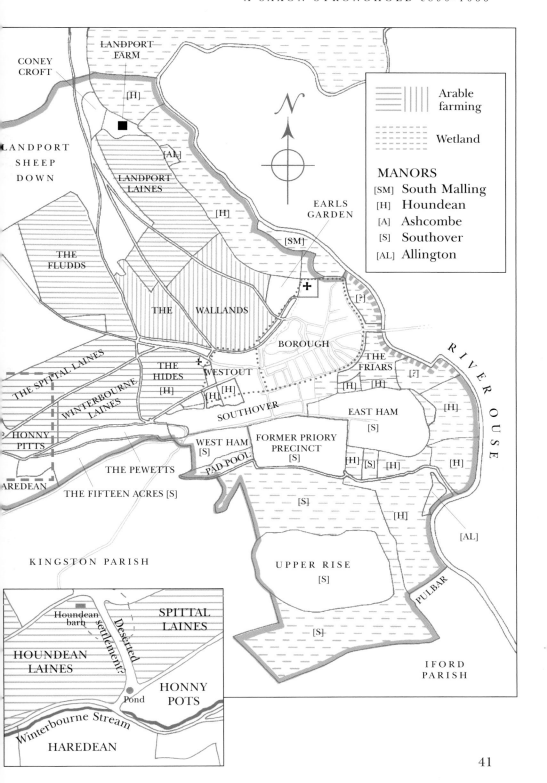

LANDPORT
FARM

CONEY
CROFT

[H]

LANDPORT
SHEEP
DOWN

[AL]

LANDPORT
LAINES

[H]

THE
FLUDDS

EARLS
GARDEN

[SM]

THE   WALLANDS

BOROUGH

THE SPITTAL LAINES

THE
HIDES

WESTOUT

THE
FRIARS

[?]

[?]

WINTERBOURNE
LAINES

[H]

[H] [H]

[H]   [H]

[H]

HONNY
PITTS

SOUTHOVER

EAST HAM
[S]

[H]

HAREDEAN

THE PEWETTS

WEST HAM
[S]

PAD POOL

FORMER PRIORY
PRECINCT
[S]

[H] [S] [H]

[H]

THE FIFTEEN ACRES [S]

[S]

[H]

[AL]

KINGSTON PARISH

UPPER RISE
[S]

PULBAR

[S]

IFORD
PARISH

Legend

	Arable farming
	Wetland

MANORS

[SM] South Malling
[H] Houndean
[A] Ashcombe
[S] Southover
[AL] Allington

R I V E R   O U S E

Inset map

Houndean
barn

Deserted settlement?

SPITTAL
LAINES

HOUNDEAN
LAINES

Pond

HONNY
POTS

Winterbourne Stream

HAREDEAN

41

Southover with which they endowed the Cluniacs, along with Cotman's Croft, New Fields, Goslands and the Fifteen Acres, in the parish of St Peter Without. Seemingly too, the 'Southover' lands, along with the chapel 'in the cemetery of saint Pancras', had been committed to the pastoral care of Saxon priests serving St John's, just as Houndean and Ashcombe may once have been.[43]

As for settlements in Greater Houndean in the 890s, it could be that peasant families clustered at Landport and the Wallands, at Winterbourne and Houndean, and at Ashcombe where a chapel stood in the 12th century. Doubtless large scale sheep-corn husbandry later caused the depopulation which left only a farmstead at Landport and at Ashcombe by 1615, only a house and cottage at Winterbourne, only a barn at Houndean and at the Wallands. John Rowe spoke of former copyhold tenements at Landport and the Wallands which by 1615 had 'long since escheated' and were 'now parcel of the Lords Demesne'. On some Saxon estates with three or more hamlets it seems that a centrally-placed settlement had emerged to service them, at Ringmer and Firle for example. Houndean Bottom, where ancient drove ways met, was a central site which gave its name, 'the valley of the hounds', to the puissant post-Conquest manor. It still shelters an elongated 'green' covered with nettles, evidence maybe of abandoned houses. Perhaps the site was down-graded when the laying out of Lewes burh provided a new focus for commerce and worship in Greater Houndean - and maybe Ashcombe alias Smithwick ceased to be 'the place of metal workers'.[44]

In 1065 it may be that all the lands of Greater Houndean belonged to king Edward. Linked to Cola's two hides at Ashcombe was a Wealden acreage at Brambletye, south of East Grinstead, which Cola held of the king, so doubtless he held Ashcombe from him too. Despite its imposing bulk, the manor of Houndean was not identified in Domesday Book, though by 1086 the manor was probably the 'home farm' of William of Warenne, whose chamber in the castle bailey doubtless enjoyed a fine view of the Wallands. But Domesday Book does divulge that Eldeid held from William a hide at Winterbourne, a hamlet within Houndean manor, and that Edeva had the same hide from king Edward, so probably the whole manor was the king's in 1065. Quite probably too in the 890s Greater Houndean had belonged to king Alfred, the begetter of burhs. To the west of it in 1065 lay the sheep down of Balmer, part of the Falmer estate belonging to Wilton abbey, and to the south the sheep down and arable fields of Kingston, probably a component of queen Edith's Iford estate.[45]

It may be, too, that Greater Houndean itself had a parent estate. To the north its sheep runs bordered, or approached, others attached to Allington and Hamsey, settlements at the scarp foot. Both were royal estates in 1065, though Hamsey, where a royal council was convened in 961, was much the larger. So perhaps the sweep of scarp foot and down-

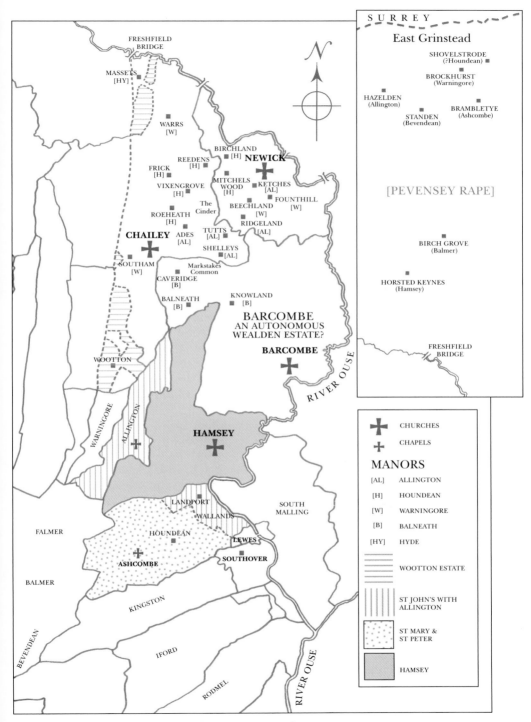

Map 2.7 Settlement - Wealden outreach

land from Allington through Hamsey to the Wallands had once composed a Greater Hamsey, with upland dependencies at Ashcombe, Houndean and Winterbourne. This might explain the water meadows, near Landport farm and south of the Cockshut in Southover, which were held of Allington manor, but marooned among those of Houndean. (Map 2.6). And could it be that a Saxon minster at St John's had once held sway over a Greater Hamsey? Its rectors in the 12th century controlled a chapel serving Allington, Beachwood and Wickham, the scarp-foot core of Allington manor, between which and St John's Without the parish of Hamsey was neatly intruded. (Map 2.7) [46]

What Domesday Book does make clear, with untypical precision, is that before 1065 folk from Allington, Ashcombe and Hamsey had been closely associated in exploiting Wealden territory south of East Grinstead, at Hazleden, Brambletye and Horsted Keynes. Others from Warningore, Balmer and Bevendean had a stake in Brockhurst, Birchgrove and Standen. No mention is made of 'Houndean', but a hide of land at Sholvelstrode had no parent estate assigned to it. Though these outliers were lost after the Conquest, others south of the upper Ouse, in what became Lewes rape, were kept. Indeed later rentals reveal that in the 1840s Houndean manor incorporated farms at Reedens, Roeheath, Birchland, Mitchelswood, Frick and Vixengrove, and Allington manor farms at Ades, Shelleys, Tutts, Ridgeland and Ketches, territory which focused on a shared Common at the Cinder. Moreover, Allington manor shared Markstakes Common with Balneath, a manor created after the Conquest to administer Wealden lands granted to the Cluniacs at Southover, including woodland near the Common at Caveridge, Balneath and Knowland which had belonged perhaps to Houndean manor - as a tenement near Knowland still did in 1615.[47]

Presumably this swathe of Wealden territory had been allotted to the estates of Allington and Houndean in Saxon times. Certainly the western boundary of Southam and Massets, lands dependent on the manors of Warningore and Hyde-in-Kingston, a boundary running due south from Freshfield bridge on the upper Ouse to the scarp foot west of Warningore, was respected by stretches of the Wootton estate based at East Chiltington, territory granted to the archbishopric of Canterbury before the Conquest - perhaps indeed in the 680s.[48] And possibly these lands allocated to Allington and Houndean, to Iford and Warningore, had been detached in early Saxon times from a massive royal estate at Ditchling extending eastward to the Ouse. Owned by king Edward and earlier by Alfred, it stretched in 1065 through Ardingly and Balcombe towards Crawley Down and East Grinstead. Curiously, in 1624 the only Wealden outlier attached to the manor of Lewes Borough - two houses near Ardingly church - formed an enclave within it.[49]

So despite its evident strategic importance and the productivity of its mint, the layout of Saxon Lewes remains a matter for speculation -

likewise its relationship with the great estates which surrounded it. William the Conqueror, however, redefined the town as the military and judicial focus of a rape: a function swiftly embodied in a massive castle precinct. He also restructured land-holding in the South Downs and the Weald to sustain a military occupation - radical surgery that Domesday Book convincingly describes. Moreover, the piety of his Norman warlords caused the planting of Cluniac monks at Southover whose charters throw a fitful light on the churches and topography of Lewes Borough in the 12th century. Whether archaeologists will reveal a sharper picture of the Saxon burh, only time will tell.

17 Silver penny struck at Lewes by Oswold (Ospold) under Edward the Confessor

Overleaf: the first earl Warenne

45

Willus Com: Warren, primus, ex Cod: M: S: Philp: Ebor: in Coll: Armor:

3

The Warennes 1066-1304

1264. This year, on the 14th of May, and on the day of the translation of the Holy Martyrs Victor and Corona, there was a deadly battle between King Henry and Simon de Montfort and the barons, and so it was, that the greatest part of the king's army was utterly overthrown between prime and noon. Firstly, the king was much beaten by swords and maces, and two horses killed under him, so that he escaped with difficulty, and his brother Richard, king of Germany, was soon captured. Edward, the king's son, [was] delivered over in hostage to Simon de Montfort, and many of the greatest men of England, who held with the king, [were] wounded in their heads and bodies even to death, the number of which dead is reckoned at 2700, more or less.

1286. This year, on June 30, was born the first-begotten son of Sir William de Warenn, by his wife, daughter of the Earl of Oxford. He was baptized and called by the name of John, on the 7th of November, with immense rejoicing; but, alas! as the prophet testifies, 'our joys are extinguished, lamentation possesses us'; for in the same year, on the first Sunday after the feast of Thomas the Apostle, the father of the aforesaid youth, concerning whom our gladness had been, expired, and, oh sadness! he in whom flourished entire nobility, generosity, and honesty, and the beginning of the glory of all knighthood, now lies buried and covered with stones. The annals of Southover priory.

Though England in 1066 was well cultivated and endowed with market-places and merchant ships, and its administration and mints were highly organized, the military and political resources of the Saxon monarchy proved too weak to survive the defeat at Hastings. Perhaps it was panic in mid-Sussex, after the Norman victory, which caused a hoard of newly minted Saxon pennies to be buried at Offham. And pillage may have accounted for a sharp fall in the value of many Southdown estates recorded in Domesday Book, pillage perpetrated by Norman soldiers advancing towards Winchester, there to reunite with king William, after his marauding march through Dover, Canterbury and Guildford. Possibly the lands of the Godwines were singled out; Rodmell was worth £60 in 1065, only £20 soon after, whereas Southease next-door maintained its value. That Cliffe was sacked to intimidate the fortress-burh across the river - as Southwark was burned to terrorize London - might explain Domesday Book grouping with Lewes in 1086 39 inhabited houses, and twenty uninhabited, 'in the rape of Pevensey'. And could such tactics pinpoint more precisely the burial of 13 young males in an 'execution pit' on Malling Down overlooking Lewes, sometime between 980 and 1150? Certainly there was administrative disruption, for the mint at Lewes, the busiest in Sussex in 1065, closed down. King Harold's 'Pax' penny was struck there and at Chichester, Steyning and Hastings, but king William's 'Profile-Cross Fleury' penny, issued before January 1067, only at Hastings and Chichester.[1]

Once Sussex was subdued, the Conqueror heavily policed it, to safeguard ports and roads now crucial to traffic between Normandy and London. He kept for himself Harold's harbour at Bosham. The rest of the county he sliced into four 'rapes' - north-south corridors, each with a harbour and a castle - and granted them to henchmen he trusted. Hastings went to Robert count of Eu, Pevensey to Robert count of Mortain, Lewes to William of Warenne (created earl of Surrey in 1088), Arundel to Roger earl of Shrewsbury. At first the river Adur divided the rapes of Lewes and Arundel, as it did the archdeaconries of Lewes and Chichester, also created after the Conquest. But this left the Adur 'gap' unprotected, so about 1073 a fifth rape was formed and granted to William of Braose who built a port and a castle at Bramber. William of Warenne also ceded the land between the upper Ouse and the Surrey border to Robert of Mortain, depriving Southdown estates like Ashcombe and Allington of Wealden pasture and woodland they exploited in 1065.[2]

Though Warenne's father was an obscure Norman knight whose forbears came from Varenne, a hamlet near Arques, his mother was perhaps a niece of Gunnor, the wife of duke Richard I of Normandy, the Conqueror's great-grandfather. Remote kinsman or not, Warenne remained loyal to William during his beleagured early years as duke, being rewarded in 1054 with the castles of Mortemer and Bellencombre. He helped to plan the invasion of England and fought at Hastings. As joint-justiciar of England with Richard of Clare he crushed the rebel earls of Hereford and Norfolk in 1075. Fighting the Conqueror's enemies in Maine, he was wounded at the siege of Sainte-Suzanne. After the king's death in 1087, he supported William Rufus, though many magnates, Robert of Mortain among them, rallied to his elder brother, Robert Curthose, now duke of Normandy. Indeed Warenne died on 24 June 1088 from an arrow-wound in the leg he received while besieging Mortain's castle at Pevensey. This battle-scarred career secured his reputation as 'a bellicose man famed for his boldness and energy', a role for which his physique also fitted him. After re-assembling his bones, discovered crammed into a small lead coffin at Southover in 1845, Dr Pickford of Brighton calculated he was six feet two inches tall. Still treasured in

1278 was an 'ancient' sword which, the seventh earl claimed, Warenne had wielded at Hastings. It figures formidably in Watson's *Memoirs of the Ancient Earls of Warren and Surrey*, in an engraving which depicts him anachronistically arrayed in a 'checky' surcoat. (See chapter opener)[3]

18 Finding the remains; their display in Southover church

Mistakenly Warenne's wife was long thought to have been a daughter of William I, or of his Flemish queen, Matilda, by an earlier husband. Gundrada, though, was indeed Flemish, her father being the lord of Oosterzele-Scheldewindeke, and she perhaps came to Normandy in Matilda's entourage. Her brothers both served the Conqueror. Gerbold became earl of Chester and Frederick perished in East Anglia fighting Hereward the Wake. His lands there were then granted to Warenne, who by 1086 was the fourth richest magnate in England, after bishop Odo of

Norman KINGS

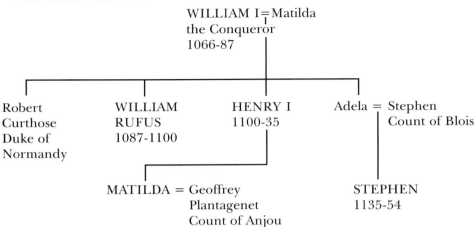

Bayeux, the count of Mortain and the earl of Shrewsbury. Warenne's estates spread into 13 counties; his castles loomed at Lewes, at Castle Acre in Norfolk, at Sandal and Conisbrough in Yorkshire. Moreover, just before Warenne died, William Rufus made him earl of Surrey and gave him lands in and around Reigate, where he built a castle guarding a Lewes-London road. His wealth largely funded the Cluniac priory at Southover in which Gundrada was buried after dying at Castle Acre on 27 May 1085. Warenne was interred beside her in 1088.[4]

In 1088-9 the count of Mortain and the earl of Shrewsbury had joined the revolt against William Rufus, underscoring the threat to the Crown now posed by the mighty lords of the Sussex rapes. Both were pardoned, but the next generation was less fortunate. In 1095 William of Eu, Robert's son, was blinded and castrated for offering Hastings to Robert Curthose as a bridgehead for an invasion of England. Rufus appointed two royal officials, recruited from local knights, to police the castle and the rape. His successor, Henry I, disinherited William of Mortain and Robert of Belleme in or soon after 1102, for adhering in their turn to Curthose. After he acquired Normandy Henry granted Pevensey rape to Gilbert of Laigle, a knight with lands guarding the frontier of that duchy. But the king retained Pevensey castle and the rich manor of Eastbourne.[5]

Warenne's son William, the second earl of Surrey, was lucky to survive this drastic royal surgery in Sussex. Not only did he join the rebellion against king Henry in 1102, earlier he had sought to marry Edith/Matilda, a Scottish princess descended from king Alfred, and became petulant when she married Henry instead. He also mocked Henry's love of hunting, calling him 'Harts-foot'. Yet Henry restored his estates in 1103 and offered the earl his bastard daughter as a bride - a

Norman **earls**

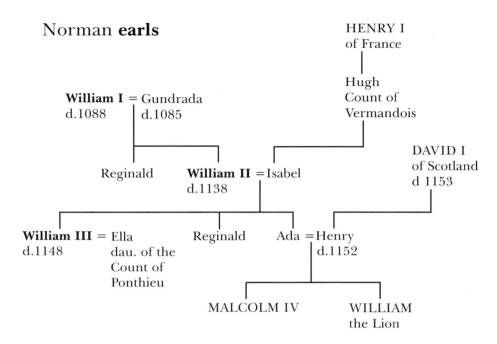

union archbishop Anselm blocked as consanguineous: William being the great-great-grandson of the father of Gunnor. In 1106 the earl, now firmly loyal, fought at the battle of Tinchebrai which delivered Robert Curthose and his duchy into king Henry's hands. At the battle of Bremule in 1119 William volunteered to fight in the front rank and experience 'the full shock' of combat. After Tinchebrai Henry granted to the already affluent earl the duchy estates of his deceased younger brother - Reginald - also the castle of Saint-Saens, and in England the rich manor of Wakefield. When the king died in Normandy in 1135 the earl escorted the corpse to Rouen to be embalmed. Shipped from Caen, it was buried at Reading abbey, which Henry had founded in 1121, recruiting the monks from Cluny and Southover. Hugh of Boves, the archbishop of Rouen who attended the king's embalming, had left Southover to be Reading's first abbot.

Dying on 11 May 1138, 'the fiftieth year of his earldom being unfinished', William was interred at Southover near his parents. His widow, Isabel of Vermandois, bought a lamp for his tomb, and to fund the upkeep of a perpetual flame, she gave to the monks a farm at Barcombe and Ordric, a serf who tilled it. Isabel, a granddaughter of king Henry I of France and a descendant of the emperor Charlemagne, had wedded the earl in 1118 - they eloped, it was claimed, while her first husband lay on his death-bed. A daughter, Ada, married Henry, the son of king David of Scotland, and though Henry predeceased his father, Ada's sons ruled Scotland, as Malcolm IV and William the Lion.[6]

Amid the 'anarchy' after king Henry's death, the second earl supported king Stephen against Henry's daughter, the empress Matilda. So did his son William, the third earl of Surrey, whom a hostile chronicler, Henry of Huntingdon, deemed 'a manifest adulterer and distinguished lecher, a faithful follower of Bacchus, though unacquainted with Mars, smelling of wine, unaccustomed to warfare'. Perhaps the perils of civil strife caused him to convert his seat at Castle Acre from a 'country house' to a massively fortified keep. During sporadic fighting in Sussex Arundel was besieged in 1139 and Pevensey in 1147. Earthworks at Clayhill in Ringmer may have been a defence improvised by an archbishop of Canterbury, others at the Caburn a watch post and beacon manned from Lewes castle or by soldiers hoping to assail it. Perhaps some such tactic inspired the construction - or enlargement - of the ditch and bank on the south side of the 'camp' within which St John's church stood. Their crumbling condition in the 13th century suggests by then they were obsolete. The Saxon ditch, noted earlier at Bampton, which had protected a minster, was re-fortified during the civil war.[7]

Yet earl William abruptly distanced himself from any strife seething round Lewes or Castle Acre, by taking the cross on Palm Sunday 1146 and departing in June 1147 on a Second Crusade led by his distant cousin, Louis VII of France. During his absence his immense estates were protected by the Church Militant. But he was risking their integrity, for his only child was Isabel, a most desirable heiress, now in the care of his wife Ella, a daughter of the count of Ponthieu, and already promised in marriage, it seems, to king Stephen's younger son, William of Blois. Maybe, despite Henry of Huntingdon's strictures, the earl had always longed to help liberate the Holy Places in Jerusalem. About 1139 Payn of Montdidier, Master of the French branch of the Military Order of the Temple of Solomon, had visited Lewes to witness William grant to the Order forty shillings a year from his rents there. Soon after, the earl founded at Thetford a priory dedicated to the Holy Sepulchre. And possibly he endowed, and gave to the Templars, the church of the Holy Sepulchre at Lewes, first recorded in 1237. His impending departure 'for Jerusalem' prompted valedictory rituals at Southover priory in April 1147. To sanctify gifts to the Cluniacs by the earl and his brother Reginald, hair was cut from their heads at the high altar by the king's brother, Henry of Blois, an illustrious bishop of Winchester.[8]

Earl William, though, never saw the Holy Sepulchre. With the rear guard of the Crusading army he was enveloped by Saracens in the mountains of Laodicea south of Antioch. It seems he died in the battle or in captivity soon after. A chartulary, compiled at Southover priory in 1444, gives 13 January 1148 as the date of his death, 'the Holy Land' as his burial place. But there has been speculation that his organs were piously borne home, for in 1845 near the bones of his grandparents was found an earthen jar within a lead vessel, packed with 'viscera, lungs and stomach'.

19 Lewes castle: gateway to the bailey

A more likely relic of crusading zeal, recently dug up at Lewes castle, is a late 10th-century Near-Eastern bronze coin adapted as a brooch; its Kufic inscription proclaims Muhammad to be the Prophet of God.[9]

20 The Kufic coin

By 1148 the Warennes had long used Lewes castle as the administrative focus of their rape, though the evolution of its plan is obscure. After the battle of Hastings palisaded timber forts were probably improvised at Arundel, Chichester and Lewes, the last consisting perhaps of a small bailey with a motte to the north-east [Brack Mount], sited on a natural spur with wide views across the estuary and the Weald - a vantage point later for Shelley & Co., the London-Lewes carriers. And possibly not till the 1090s was the bailey extended and a second motte built to the south-west. After all, it was in a lightly fortified 'country house' at Castle Acre that Gundrada died giving birth in 1085, a site that has yielded glimpses of gracious living - gilded pendants, decorated bone pins, buckles made from copper alloy. But what if two mounds already stood on the site that became Lewes castle, looming relics of the spur's pagan past? Did the Normans adapt Brack Mount first, and the other when the bailey was extended? Or did they link both to a central bailey, without improvising a smaller fort first?[10]

However the castle evolved, its medieval perimeter probably existed by about 1100. 'Early Norman' flint work, laid in robust herringbone fashion, occurs in the gatehouse of the bailey, in the curtain wall to the west, and in the shell keep on the south-western motte. This motte rises 65 feet above the High Street, twenty feet higher than Brack Mount, and was built, or heightened, by using chalk blocks which perhaps incorporated the foundations of the shell keep as they rose. The keep's roughly elliptical interior measures some 85 by 75 feet; its parapet platform is 22 feet above ground; the battlements have lost their ashlar coping. Inside it were 'chambers' built against the wall, a 'kitchen' with a hearth, and across a courtyard, an open 'hall' perhaps, with a solar attached. On Brack Mount, where viscount Torrington found a fragment of 'old wall' in 1788, George Randoll's map showed a second shell keep in 1620; a chalk-lined cistern or well survives.

The bailey forms an irregular oval, some 450 by 380 feet, still defined on the south and south-east by stretches of curtain wall and by a bank and dry moat, partly filled in. There are traces of a square tower which overhung the wall and guarded maybe a stairway up the south-western motte. The gatehouse to the castle bailey - comparable to one at Arques near Mortemer, measured internally 32 by 22 feet. It retains its southern and most of its eastern wall, with masonry eight feet thick, and also its monumental entrance - two arches, each of two orders, with quoins of Caen stone. The domestic range in the bailey - the hall, solar,

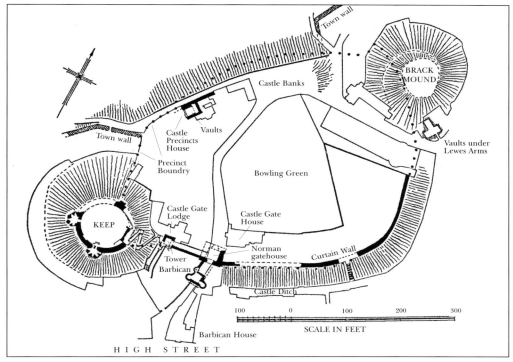

3.1 Lewes castle: plan of the bailey and the two mounds

21 View of castle from the Wallands c1775

55

chapel and kitchens - were probably on the north side, where Castle Precincts House now stands, and were doubtless as well-appointed as 'the country house' at Castle Acre. Views drawn in the 18th century depict a beetling crag of ragged masonry, a hundred feet long, looming above Castle Banks.[11]

From the castle were managed the manors in the rape which the first earl had kept in his own hands. His estates at Kingston and Iford, Northease and Rodmell, Piddinghoe and Meeching, formed a secure corridor along the Ouse from the castle to the sea - Northease and Rodmell remaining with the 'the lords' of the rape till sold by the marquis of Abergavenny in 1919. The harbour at Seaford Warenne shared with the earl of Mortain. Further west lay the Southdown manors of Balsdean and Rottingdean, Patcham and Ditchling, the last a former royal domain with tracts of forest and pasture reaching to the Surrey border. Also in the Weald were the manors of Cuckfield and Worth, the latter given by William Rufus in 1088. And stretching away below the castle, to Landport and almost to Ashcombe, was Houndean, a demesne manor first recorded in 1240, yet a 'home farm', presumably, supplying Warenne's household.[12]

Other manors in the rape Warenne granted to henchmen in return for military service. Robert and Godfrey came from Pierrepont near Falaise, William from Watteville near Rouen, Ralph from Quesnay in the Cotentin. Each vassal-knight received a scatter of estates, perhaps to ensure they collaborated closely when policing their Saxon peasantry, and these fiefs fixed the seigneurial geography of the rape for centuries. On the principal estate of each fief, at Hamsey and Hurstpierpoint, Portslade and Poynings, arose a spacious manor house; also at Plumpton, after a fief was assembled for Reginald, the third's earl brother. And to each of these estates, except Poynings, belonged premises in Lewes Borough, a 'town-house' convenient for a knight attending the rapal court at the castle. (See footnote reference) The fief of Poynings, however, included Ashcombe, only half a league from Lewes.[13]

Military expediency had caused the Conqueror to delegate near-sovereign powers to the lords of the Sussex rapes. Each became equivalent to a shire. Its sheriff, chosen by the lord, convened the court of the rape, which usually assembled every three weeks, except maybe in the harvest month of August. It dealt with all secular litigation, even that reserved elsewhere for royal justiciars. The vassal-knights, or their spokesmen, attended to transact business relating to their fiefs and to report on 'all things which may happen within the hundreds or barony', for the rapal court had absorbed the business and suitors of the now defunct hundred courts and shire court. To increase surveillance the sheriff toured the hundreds at Easter and Michaelmas. Two of these puissant officials held land at Kingston, close to Lewes. Peter gave an acre for 'the making of a church' there, a gift later confirmed by Hugh. A third sheriff, Warin, owned tithes there. A memento of the court, perhaps, was Hangman's Acre, mapped in 1618 by John Deward and a perquisite in 1690 of the Borough's crier. Nearby Gallows Bank was noted in 1799 as the place where 'Malefactors were hung, when such punishments were inflicted here'.[14]

That Lewes castle would remain a major seat of a glittering dynasty grew uncertain though, after the third earl's death in Laodicea, for about 1148 his only child, Isabel, did marry William of Blois, king Stephen's younger son, and when his elder brother, Eustace, died in August 1153, he became England's crown prince. In November, however, Stephen ended the civil war with Matilda by accepting her son, the future Henry II, as the heir to his throne. Nonetheless the sweeteners showered on William - the lordships of Mortain and Boulogne, Eye and Lancaster - still threatened to downgrade Lewes as a seigneurial base. But the fourth earl died without issue in 1159, fighting for Henry II near Toulouse. He was buried at Montmorillon in Poitou, rather than with the Warennes at Southover priory, to which his benefactions were few.[15]

Henry II, of course, insisted that a close kinsman of his should marry the widow Isabel, still countess of Surrey in her own right, the immensely rich mistress of citadels at Lewes, Reigate and Castle Acre, Sandal and Conisbrough, Mortemer, Bellencombre and Saint-Saens. Indeed he chose William of Anjou, his brother and boon-companion. But William was a second cousin of Isabel's deceased husband, and archbishop Becket vetoed the match as consanguineous, causing William to die of grief, it was said. Certainly his henchman, Richard Brito, while murdering Becket in 1170, claimed he was avenging his master. Isabel meanwhile had accepted king Henry's half-brother Hamelin, a bastard of Geoffrey, count of Anjou. The royal treasury paid £41 10s 6d towards the cost of her wedding clothes in April 1164. The advent of Hamelin ensured the autonomy of the Warenne estates, indeed reinforced it, for he exchanged his meagre inheritance, some lands near Chinon in Touraine, for the prosperous borough of Thetford. And maybe it was soon after the marriage that the bones of the first earl and his wife were buried in lead coffins beneath a new chapter-house at Southover. Over Gundrada's was laid a splendidly carved slab of Tournai marble - re-affirming the prestige of the dynasty. (Isabel's great-uncle, Simon of Vermandois, who perished with her father on the Second Crusade, had been bishop of Tournai.)[16]

Hamelin was himself a bitter foe of Becket during the archbishop's violent quarrel with Henry II. Losing his Plantagenet temper, the earl denounced him as a traitor, and the prelate retorted: 'Were I a knight and not a priest, this hand should prove thee a liar'. Isabel's uncle Reginald, by then a royal justiciar, also harassed Becket - conduct which monastic chroniclers later contrasted with his brother's sanctified death in Laodicea. All in all Hamelin's Borough of Lewes might have seemed a safe haven for Becket's murderers, and a picturesque legend does have them fleeing to his palace at Old Malling and heaping their blood-stained weapons on a table which twice shook off so abominable a burden. A slab of Sussex marble, reputedly a piece of the table, preserved at Malling House in the 19th century, now reposes at Anne of Cleves museum in Southover. However, after Becket's rapid canonization in 1173, Hamelin swiftly became a devotee; indeed a pilgrimage to the Blessed Martyr's shrine cured him of an eye infection. Uncle Reginald, meanwhile, renounced the World in 1179, to enroll with the Cluniacs at Southover where the Martyr was already revered.[17]

The pugnacious Hamelin was also a patron of sophisticated fortification. At Conisbrough stands his circular keep, ninety feet high, faced with ashlar and strongly battered at the base. From inside its six massive buttresses archers could direct a raking crossfire against assailants. Built about 1180, its design and its geometry influenced maybe the '13th century', semi-octagonal, two-storeyed, angle-towers grafted onto the south-western shell keep at Lewes. They were defined externally by three carefully spaced string-courses and a boldly battered base. Each storey was pierced by five arrow-loops.[18] Hamelin also valued his creature comforts. The solar in his keep at Conisbrough boasts a hooded fireplace, a dainty wash basin, a garderobe en suite. And maybe this influenced the updating of facilities in the shell keep at Lewes. After the angle-towers were added, a new 'hall' was built attached to the formerly free-standing kitchen, with a room in the north-western tower acting perhaps as a solar. Fireplaces, backed with re-used tiles, were set into the wall of the keep to serve the kitchen and the 'hall'. On the north side of the courtyard (newly cobbled with beach-pebbles) two rooms were built against the wall - possibly a

22 Two keeps: Conisbrough; Lewes; an arrow-loop at Lewes (reconstruction)

chapel and 'annexe', to judge from the 'fine finish' of the green-glazed floor tiles, whitewashed plaster and red-painted window glass retrieved there. Maybe too the north wall of the keep was pierced for a postern gate to link it with the bailey. Nothing is known of the domestic range in the bailey, except that the 'hall' and 'chamber' there were described as 'old' in 1240.[19]

Despite his eye trouble, Hamelin proved a dependable pillar of the Angevin empire. He supported Henry II against his rebellious sons in 1173; helped to frustrate the intrigues of prince John while Richard I was away on the Third Crusade; and carried a sword of state at Richard's second coronation in 1194. In Sussex he deployed his daughters to buttress his prestige, marrying Matilda to Henry count of Eu, lord of Hastings rape - the family had been reinstated - and Isabel to Gilbert of Laigle, lord of Pevensey rape. His devotion to Thomas the Martyr, notwithstanding, he quarrelled bitterly with the Cluniacs at Southover over the selection of their prior - pursuing his rights as 'founders' kin'. So possibly he chose a monastery at Rouen as his burial place in 1202, Isabel being interred beside him a year or so later - though the great chartulary of the Cluniacs, copied out in 1444, claimed both were buried in the chapter house at Southover.[20]

Just as Hamelin adhered to Richard I, so his son William, the sixth earl of Surrey, clung fast to king John, his hyper-active Plantagenet half-cousin. When the loss of Normandy seemed likely, John confiscated Hastings rape in 1201 from Alice, the earl's niece, and her husband, Ralph of Lusignan. After the French overran the duchy in 1204 John dispossessed the earl's brother-in-law, Gilbert of Laigle, who salvaged his Norman estates by swearing fealty to king Philip. Earl William, however, chose to forfeit Mortemer, Bellencombre and Saint-Saens. John, who stayed five days at Lewes in February 1205, right-royally compensated him, with the bustling boroughs of Grantham and Stamford, with custody of Gilbert of Laigle's estates, and 'for the sake of his name' with a grant of 'free warren' in Lewes rape, the sole right to hunt every kind of game. Very different was the fate of William of Braose. By dogged royalism his forebears had kept the lordship of Bramber rape. But despite serving John in Normandy, Wales and Ireland, William fell from favour in 1207. After his wife died in royal custody - starved, it was said, in a dungeon at Windsor - he fled to France. John was keeping greyhounds at Knepp castle near Bramber when he visited Lewes on 31 May 1209.[21]

The earl clove to John - almost to the bitter end. The king was at Lewes on 24-25 April 1213 and then darted to Dover, where William witnessed him deliver the realm into the custody of the papal legate. In May 1216, with prince Louis of France poised to land at Thanet and claim the English crown, John entrusted the earl with the strategically crucial Cinque Ports. Only when Louis captured London did William desert his half-cousin. Yet after John died in October 1216 he was slow

Warennes and PLANTAGENETS

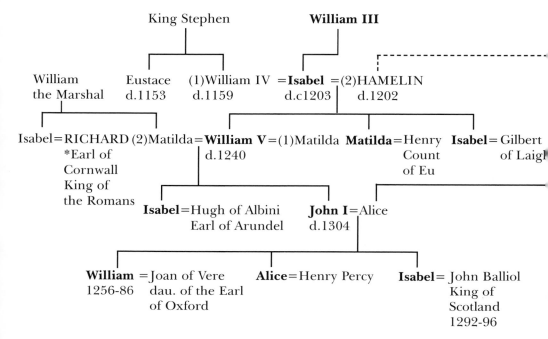

to join the patriots rallying to the nine-year-old Henry III. Their leader, William the Marshal, supported by men from the Cinque Ports and the Weald, sallied from Dorking in February 1217 and forced Louis to retreat by ship from Rye. On 2 March the Marshal signed a safe-conduct at Lewes, before advancing through Shoreham to capture the castles at Knepp and Farnham. Not till April did earl William seek to join the patriots, a reconciliation cemented maybe by king Henry visiting Lewes on 17 August 1217. Seven days later - according to a sketch made by the chronicler, Matthew Paris - the earl watched from the cliffs at Dover the royal fleet vanquish a French armada led by Eustace the Monk.[22]

The earl's re-charged patriotism paved the way for his marriage in 1225 to the Marshal's eldest daughter, Matilda, the widow of Hugh Bigod, earl of Norfolk. And when in 1231 her sister, Isabel, wedded king Henry's brother, Richard earl of Cornwall, the Warennes and Plantagenets were further entwined. Like Hamelin before him, earl William now acted as a royal anchorman in Sussex. He oversaw the re-instatement of Gilbert of Laigle, took custody of the castles at Bramber and Knepp, and married his daughter, Isabel, to Hugh of Albini, earl of Arundel. The earl also thrived as a royal justiciar and envoy, treating with Welsh princes and pacifying Oxford university. And like Hamelin, he negotiated, fruitlessly, with the papal curia for a greater say in selecting

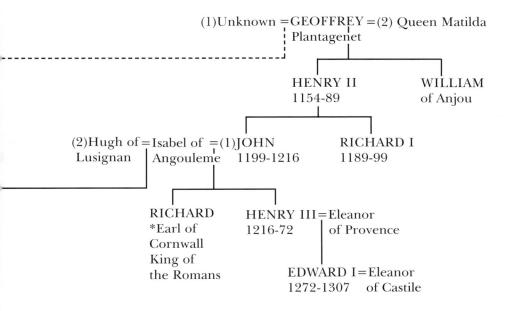

the prior at Southover. Nonetheless, after his death on 27 May 1240, he was buried 'in the middle of the pavement' before the high altar there. Presumably king Henry attended the stately funeral, for during a stay at Lewes on 23-25 July he sanctioned the late earl's gift to the monks of the South Rise. Its rents were to fund them 'celebrating' the anniversary of his death. The heart of his countess, Matilda, was buried beside him in 1248, her other remains resting at Tintern abbey near her mother. (A shadowy first wife, also Matilda, lay 'alone' in the chapter-house.)[23]

Born in 1231, the earl's only son, John, became a royal ward, which allowed king Henry to interlock the Warennes and Plantagenets even further by securing John's marriage to his own half-sister, Alice of Lusignan, in August 1247. At Christmas tide he bought 'two extra robes' for the gilded bridegroom, much as Henry II had purchased wedding clothes for countess Isabel in 1164. After bearing two daughters, Alice died on 2 February 1256 giving birth to a son. With Adelmar, bishop-elect of Winchester, as a witness, she was interred before the high altar at Southover, beneath 'a marble stone carved in the fashion of a dragon with branches coming out of its mouth'. Earl John never remarried, devoting a long life to High Politics and War. A close friend of king Henry's eldest son, prince Edward, he accompanied him to Castile in 1254 for his wedding to princess Eleanor; both were knighted by

Alfonzo X. (Before Edward's birth in 1239, John's father had pledged lands worth £10 a year to any messenger bringing news of so happy an event.)[24]

In 1257 earl John escorted his uncle, Richard earl of Cornwall, to Germany, to be elected King of the Romans. Two years later the annals of Southover priory recorded him twice crossing the sea 'for the sake of a tournament'. More serious, though, was a combat which began in April 1264 when king Henry challenged his dissident barons by assaulting Northampton, in the Midland power base of their leader, Simon of Montfort, earl of Leicester. Because Montfort also held London and Dover, the king dispatched earl John to garrison Reigate and Rochester. Whereupon Montfort united with Gilbert of Clare to besiege Rochester - John being inside the mighty keep with a supply of Lenten fish. But when Henry pushed south to Croydon, Montfort and Clare retreated to London, and earl John rejoined the king. While the royal army then marched south through the Weald, the king's cook was killed by an arrow at Flimwell, for which - it was said - Henry had 315 local archers beheaded, despite their assembling under the protection of his 'peace'. At Winchelsea, where his troops plundered the wine cellars, he pondered whether to besiege Dover or advance on London. But learning that Montfort, reinforced from the Midlands, was marching south to do battle, king Henry led his soldiers to Lewes - deer in the park at Herstmonceux being slaughtered en route. The royal army arrived on the 10th or 11th of May, in time for the feast of saint Pancras.[25]

Whether or not earl John had pleaded that his rape be the setting for the hoped-for destruction of Montfort, the choice of Lewes as a royal base made tactical sense. To the east and south lay the Ouse and estuarine marsh. To the north near Hamsey, the London road was easily defended where it ran along a ledge between chalk cliffs and the river. So Montfort's army, once it traversed the Weald, was likely to approach across the chalk land sloping towards Lewes from the west. But this required a stiff climb onto the ridge of the South Downs, a hazardous tactic if the royal scouts kept alert. Moreover, should the unthinkable happen and the king be defeated - once the Ouse was safely crossed - his castle at Pevensey guarded an escape-route by sea.

The more hot-blooded royalists - prince Edward, Hugh Bigod and several Marcher lords, joined earl John in his castle. King Henry and Richard, King of the Romans, settled themselves into the priory. But the feast of saint Pancras on 12th of May was disturbed soon after dawn when Montfort's scouts were sighted below the Southdown ridge. Overnight his army had rested at Fletching, his manor in the Wealden woods eight miles to the north. The royalists duly advanced along the ridge towards Blackcap, scrutinized the scouts and returned to Lewes about noon. Meanwhile a foraging party led by earl John skirmished 'in a valley near the hill'- perhaps in Coombe Hollow south-west of Offham, for at some

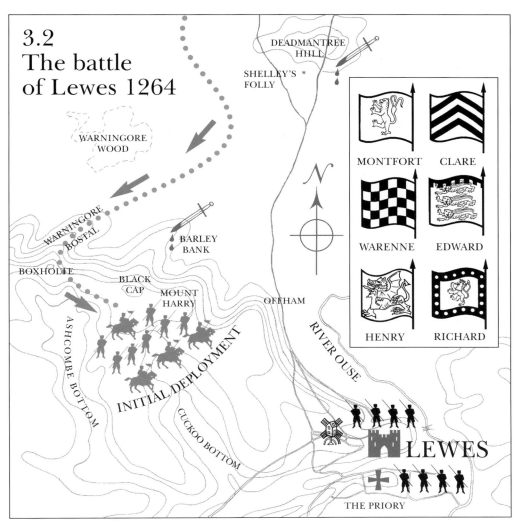

3.2
The battle
of Lewes 1264

DEADMANTREE
HILL

SHELLEY'S
FOLLY

WARNINGORE
WOOD

MONTFORT   CLARE

WARENNE   EDWARD

HENRY   RICHARD

WARNINGORE
BOSTAL

BARLEY
BANK

BOXHOLTE

BLACK
CAP

MOUNT
HARRY

OFFHAM

RIVER OUSE

ASHCOMBE BOTTOM

INITIAL DEPLOYMENT

CUCKOO BOTTOM

LEWES

THE PRIORY

RIVER OUSE

LONDONERS

CUCKOO BOTTOM

BATTLE JOINED

CASTLE

BURIAL
PIT

THE PRIORY

stage the earl's men seized 25 sheep owned by the chaplain of Hamsey. In the afternoon a posse of prelates and friars emerged from the Weald armed with a peace plan drawn up by Montfort. This the king rejected. Indeed prince Edward demanded that the 'rebels' surrender with halters round their necks, ready for a traitor's death. Next day Montfort's army moved closer, to a 'wood by Lewes' - perhaps at Warningore. And after a final exchange of threats, its leaders annulled the homage and fealty which they owed the king.

On the morrow, the 14th of May, Montfort consolidated 'his European reputation' as a daring, resourceful commander. A carefully researched account by David Carpenter suggests that before the sun rose at 4 a.m. he moved his soldiers onto the Southdown ridge, perhaps up the Warningore bostall north of Blackcap, and regrouped them at 'Boxholte', just north of the wood now called Ashcombe Bottom. He then advanced to the south-eastern side of Mount Harry and deployed them for battle just out of sight of Lewes - where the race course now curves southward. On the east flank were foot-soldiers from London, screened by cavalry led by Nicholas of Seagrave and Henry of Hastings. The centre was commanded by Gilbert of Clare, John fitz John and William of Munchensy. The west flank Montfort entrusted to his sons, Henry, Simon and Guy. He remained with the troops kept in reserve. To the south-east the chalk land sloped steadily towards Lewes. Some chroniclers claim that Montfort also snatched the moral high ground - that he thrilled his men by affirming God and Justice were on their side, whereupon they prostrated themselves with arms extended, confessed their sins, and donned white crosses to proclaim the sanctity of their cause. If so, Sussex would not see the like again till Colonel Herbert Morley marched local Puritans to the siege of Basing House.

The royalists, meanwhile, having failed to patrol the ridge in strength, perhaps even to post sentinels, were dividing their army into three divisions. Maybe this took time, for one chronicler stated that 'seven hundred evil whores' had debauched the troops - rampant lewdness spilling over even into the priory church. Eventually prince Edward, earl John, Hugh Bigod and several Marcher lords sallied forth from the castle onto the Wallands. From the priory precinct the King of the Romans probably advanced across the Hides past the church of St Mary Westout, while king Henry toiled up the slope further west, towards where the prison now looms. On a battle banner borne before him fluttered a menacing red dragon with jewelled eyes and flickering tongue - like the royal *oriflamme* of France it threatened 'rebels' with speedy extinction. But before the royalists could ascend much higher, Montfort's men thundered downhill, to precipitate the first pitched battle in England since prince Louis's forces were routed at Lincoln in 1217.

Though Montfort had seized the initiative, his mounted troops were heavily outnumbered. The king had perhaps 1500 knights and auxiliaries to his 500. Yet this advantage was thrown away by prince Edward, earl John, Hugh Bigod and the Marcher lords, whose troops were reputed to be 'the flower of all the army'. They speedily brushed aside the cavalry on Montfort's eastern flank and put the Londoners to flight. But instead of wheeling westward to attack the troops commanded by Clare, they pursued the Londoners for several miles to the north-east, slaughtering as they went - to avenge, it was said, an insult prince Edward's mother had suffered in their city. Tradition marks Deadmantree Hill, north of Shelleys Folly at Hamsey, as a place where cockneys were cut to pieces. And a relic of the 'killing field' could be the five skeletons of male adults found at Barley Bank below Mount Harry in 1938. One had been decapitated, one wounded in the head, and two speared 'with lance points'.

Prince Edward's blood-lust lost his father the battle. Clare's men smashed through the force led by the King of the Romans, obliging him to take refuge in a windmill - quite possibly sited west of St Mary Westout, where stood Snellings mill in 1343 and 1535, and Inkersolls mill in 1574. His capture was a gift for anti-royalist rhymesters who joked that he mistook the mill for a castle, its sails for a siege catapult, and tried to sharpen his sword on the mill post. To the west king Henry's division was also thrown back, once Montfort added his reserve troops to those commanded by his sons. Henry himself, claimed the annals of Southover priory, was 'much beaten by swords and maces', and a charger was twice killed beneath him. Moreover Clare's troops near Westout mill were now blocking any escape routes across the Ouse to Pevensey castle. So the battered king had perforce to retreat into an ill-fortified priory precinct.

By then it was midday and prince Edward reappeared with 'the flower' of the royalist army to learn that uncle Richard was a prisoner and his father a fugitive. In his fury he plundered Montfort's baggage train, located perhaps near Mount Harry, and killed, it was said, some royalist Londoners, penned in an iron coach as hostages. However, he judged it fruitless to attack the walls of Lewes, now in Montfort's hands. Instead he and several Marcher lords made for the priory, while Earl John and Hugh Bigod peeled off towards Pevensey castle. Montfort meanwhile attacked Lewes castle with burning arrows - the south-western keep has yielded 42 arrowheads of 13th century date, slender enough to pierce gaps in chain mail. But the garrison mounted a 'vigorous' defence, using maybe the well-sited arrow-loops so reminiscent of Conisbrough. The unearthing near the castle gateway of human bones and of a brass steelyard weight close by, bearing the double-headed eagle of the King of the Romans, caused Mark Antony Lower

23 Arrowhead from the keep

24 The weight

to fondly imagine Richard's steward busily measuring out scanty rations to his Cornish troops, and faithfully clutching the weight, 'even in death', when struck down in the fighting. Before nightfall Montfort also laid siege to the priory, briefly setting the church on fire - the whereabouts of the 'seven hundred evil whores' is unrecorded.[26]

On the morrow, Thursday the 15th of May, a settlement known as 'the Mise of Lewes' was brokered by mediating friars. The king ceded his sword to Clare and grudgingly accepted constraints on his authority already embodied in an earlier 'mise', the Provisions of Oxford: contentious details were to be resolved by arbitration. To widen support for the new agreement Montfort convened a parliament in January 1265, at which 'knights' from the shires and men from selected boroughs sat together for the first time.

On the 15th of May also began the burial of the dead - some 2700 men, 'more or less', according to the annals of Southover priory. Most were lightly armed infantrymen, though Montfort's standard-bearer and a royal judge were killed. A pit near the site of the leper hospital, a likely vortex of the battle, yielded 'a great quantity of human bones' in 1770, some of these, all from adult males, were re-discovered close by in 1994. Three pits slightly further west, beyond the crossroads, each contained 'quite five hundred bodies' when disturbed in 1810. And railway builders in 1845 encountered a mass of bones crammed into a pit, 18 feet deep and ten feet wide, near the former cemetery at the priory. Resourcefully they were removed in 13 wagons to underpin an embankment near Southerham Corner. But no skeletons as yet confirm a claim in the Lanercost chronicle that royalist knights, fleeing across Cliffe bridge or nearby fords, were forced onto the mud of the estuary, and either sank from sight or stuck fast till horse and rider were engulfed by the incoming tide.[27]

Anti-royalist rhymesters also rejoiced at earl John's flight from a battle lost a sling's throw from his own ancestral citadel, though maybe he carried the king's treasure safely overseas. After a spell in France and Flanders he returned to share the crushing royalist victory at Evesham in August 1265, being rewarded with houses confiscated from 'rebel' Londoners. Later he gave premises at Southwark, 'formerly Henry Gerlaund's', to Southover priory. However in June 1270 an ugly incident at Westminster Hall debarred him from another martial adventure. During the hearing of a land dispute between himself and a royal judge, Alan la Zouche, John fell into a rage and a henchman stabbed Zouche, fatally. The ensuing uproar, disgrace and heavy fine precluded the earl setting out in August on the Seventh Crusade which took prince Edward to Tunis, Cyprus and Acre.[28] After a decent interval, of course, John was pardoned, the fine forgotten. King Henry died in 1272 and John acted as a Guardian of the Realm till Edward returned home and feasted with him at Reigate castle. To the coronation he led a hundred knights who flamboyantly set free their horses as gifts to a gaping populace. Though deprived of his Crusade, the earl fought tirelessly in Edward's wars against the Welsh. His spoils included the lands of Bromfield and Yale in Denbighshire, where on the banks of the Dee he caused a 'new town' to be laid out with a market-place, a church and a grid of streets. Like king Edward's New Winchelsea, Holt mirrored the 'bastide' towns recently planted in Gascony. Its pentagonal castle was designed perhaps by Master James of Saint George.[29]

Perhaps the earl's irritability grew worse after his only son William was killed in a tournament at Croydon in December 1286. The annals of Southover priory elegized William's 'entire nobility, generosity and honesty, the beginning of the glory of all knighthood'. His father-in-law, the earl of Oxford, and Roger Bigod, the Earl Marshal, attended his solemn funeral at Southover which archbishop Pecham conducted. He was interred before the high altar 'on the left side near his mother', Alice of Lusignan. William's widow, Joan of Vere, who died in November 1293, was also buried before the high altar 'in a lofty tomb'. Perhaps this also bore his effigy, maybe the one unearthed near by in 1845 and now in Southover church. Fashioned from Purbeck marble in the 'late 13th century', the headless figure is arrayed in a surcoat and chain mail, the rings set edgeways. A baldric and a hip-belt secure a sword, its pommel placed high up near his left armpit. A kite-shaped shield, much damaged, covers that arm. The other is bent upon itself, the hand flat on the breast. The left leg passes over the right, the lower parts are missing. There are traces of blue on the surcoat, scarlet on its lining, gilt on the chain mail, vermilion on the hip-belt. A small yellow and gold cross, outlined in black, adorns the base of the surcoat. Though a device of the Braose family, John, the lord of Bramber rape from 1232 to 1290, was interred at Sele priory, his dynasty's usual place of burial. Besides, the cross also appears on the Borough arms of Lewes, associated with the coats of Warenne and Fitzalan. In June 1299 king Edward donated 5s 5d during a memorial mass for William at the priory.[30]

25 The effigy

In the 1290s Scotland much preoccupied earl John. His daughters, Alice and Isabel, had married the puissant Northern magnates, Henry Percy and John Balliol. The latter indeed, who was descended from the second earl's daughter Ada, the mother of Malcolm IV and William the

Lion, inherited the Scottish throne in 1292. But angered by Balliol's alliance with France, Edward I persuaded earl John to lead an invasion army across the Border in 1296. Soon after, Edward occupied Edinburgh, deposed Balliol, declared himself king and returned south with the Stone of Scone. He left the earl behind as Keeper of the Scottish Realm, parrying his plea that mists were bad for his health with a right-royal jest: 'When you get rid of a turd, you do a good job'. So it was a reluctant Keeper who, outside Stirling in September 1297, sent the van-guard of his army across a narrow bridge to assault a force led by William Wallace ('Braveheart'). After the vanguard was cut to pieces, the rest of the army fled, carrying the Keeper with it. When the English won at Falkirk a year later, he commanded the rearguard. Yet he dauntlessly endured mist and demotion. And during the siege of Caerlaverock castle in 1300, with his grandson, Henry Percy, beside him, he charged at the enemy who fled 'like hares before greyhounds'.[31]

The impact on Lewes rape of so fearsome an earl can be imagined. When a royal commission enquired by what 'warrant' he held his many franchises, he brandished - it is said - the 'ancient' sword of his ancestor, William of Warenne. And indeed the Norman Conquest had occasioned the wide jurisdiction still vested in his rapal court at Lewes, where the business of vassal knights, such as wardship and relief, mingled with cases of debt and robbery, false weights and breach of covenant. There was bitter complaint in 1275 that its officials fined bed-ridden men for not attending it; loaded fees on bakers and brewers, butchers and tanners; distrained livestock without cause and seized merchandise stranded on the sea-shore. Savage fines were levied too on farmers who killed rabbits and hares to protect their crops. Indeed archbishop Pecham, a native of mid-Sussex, felt duty-bound to deplore the havoc wrought by the earl's swarming game.[32]

Complaint was also made in 1275 that the earl had obliged his vassal knights in Surrey to help pay for 'the enclosure of Lewes with a stone wall', though in 1286 he released the tenants of Hyde abbey at Southease and Telscombe from the burden. Probably the town's defences sustained severe damage in May 1264. Certainly in 1266 king Henry authorized new market tolls at Lewes for three years to fund the build-ing, or repair, of a wall.[33]

The judicial powers of the Crown, however, now set limits to the earl's freedom of action. The complaints in 1275 were made to royal commissioners. Though he seized an estate at Bevendean from Hawise, the widow of John of Gatesden, a wealthy lawyer-diplomat - falsely claim-ing she had sided with Montfort - she clawed it back in through the royal courts. And when Robert Aguillon, a landowner married to an aunt of queen Eleanor, chose to hunt on his own estate at Fulking, and the earl's henchmen chased his servants to Henfield and bore them captive to Lewes castle, they were freed by the king's sheriff appearing in person, armed with a royal writ for their release.[34] Rapal sheriffs meanwhile had faded away. Indeed, already in 1130, Hugh of Warelvilla was acting for the Crown in Sussex, receiving royal writs and collecting royal revenue. Earl John's officials, it was plausibly claimed, obstructed the royal sheriff when he toured the hundreds in Lewes rape. At Ditchling his groom was beaten up by the earl's park-keeper and robbed of an iron gorget.[35]

The sheriff also presided at a county court which met every three weeks and drew suitors from across Sussex - an early example of that 'self-government at the king's command' which was to foster English liberty. 'The men of Sussex' were summoned there to elect two knights of the shire to sit in parliament, and 'the whole county' to choose its coroners. The court sessions also brought profit to local traders, and to the local seigneur. Richard earl of Cornwall was lord of Chichester rape in January 1254 when a royal command ordered the court to convene at Chichester, its 'ancient meeting place', and no longer alternate between Lewes and New Shoreham. Folk in eastern Sussex duly complained at its removal so far to the west.[36]

Coroners were established in 1194 and like sheriffs were recruited from the knightly or 'near-knightly' class. William of Worth, accused in 1275 of extorting money in Lewes Borough, held Bolebrook manor near East Grinstead. He acted, it seems, in the eastern rapes. And maybe Gilbert Sikelfoot, who held Piddingworth manor and was displaced as a coroner in 1306, also served as an adviser to the Cluniacs. A namesake topped the tax assessments at Southover in 1296 and witnessed, there and at Westminster, conveyances of their property. Coroners could be hampered. In 1262 the prior of Southover refused access to a waterwheel which had occasioned a death.[37] The increasing activity of royal judges also eroded the power of the rapal court. Posses of justiciars took to touring the shires, ruthlessly punishing infringements of royal rights and other misconduct. They were at Lewes in 1148, 1194, 1214 and 1220. 'Assize' judges also began holding regular yearly sessions in the county to hear civil and criminal cases, visiting Lewes in October 1229, October 1248, June 1260 and April 1269.[38]

Spokesmen for Lewes Borough did not swell the complaints about the earl's officials made in 1275 by jurors less firmly under his thumb. They merely lamented the misconduct of William of Worth - and the reluctance of royal tax collectors to receive money the burgesses had ready! What measure of municipal self-government the Warennes allowed them is unknown. Reginald, acting for his brother, the absentee third earl, had 'restored' to them a 'merchant gild' about 1148, 'with all the customs and privileges which belong to it', in return for twenty shillings a year paid to 'the provostry' of Lewes - the earl's reeve presumably. A gild might oversee the market, supervise craft production, indulge in corporate brewing and feasting, or purchase masses for the souls of deceased members. In the 13th century royal writs to Lewes

Borough were addressed to 'the bailiffs' and to the 'good men' or to the 'burgesses'. The bailiffs perhaps were officials of the earl rather than senior townsmen. A Borough 'court' of some kind existed in 1266, for a case of trespass was removed from the rapal court and heard by the burgesses 'in parochia eorum'.[39]

Yet a slight erosion of his local powers did little to diminish the earl as a mighty magnate, a life-long companion of Edward I, though the king's visits to Lewes owed much perhaps to its location midway between the shrines at Canterbury and Chichester of two cherished English saints, Thomas the Martyr and Richard of Droitwich. In May 1276 he stayed four days, along with queen Eleanor and 'many nobles'. On 15 August 1281 he dubbed there two knights, 'born in the country of Burgundy'. He returned on 28-29 May 1297 and again on 24-25 June 1299, having caused serious damage 'with his own hand' at the Uckfield house of Master Arnald who supplied the royal party with 82 gallons of beer. At Lewes in more genial mood he gave two cloths of gold to the Cluniacs and money for three days' supply of food; the prior countered with two oxen, three pigs and six sheep. On 13 September 1302 he sealed a writ there to prorogue parliament.[40]

Earl John finally expired at Kennington, his Surrey manor near London, on 27 September 1304. His last days were perhaps soothed by his musician, Master John, summoned to repair a royal organ at Kings Langley in 1303. The earl was buried after Christmas before the high altar at Southover; archbishop Winchelsey officiated. The 'flat tombstone on the flat pavement' was as suitably austere as the slab soon to be laid above the corpse of king Edward at Westminster. The terse epitaph warned: *Vous q'passez ove bouche close/Priez pr cely ke cy repose/En vie cum vous estis iadis fu/E vous tiel serretz cum ie su/Sire Johan Count de Gareyn gyst ycy/Deu de sa alme eit mercy.* His only known gift to the Cluniacs was a house at Southwark, though with Purgatory in mind he amassed indulgences promising 390 days' remission. For over fifty years he grasped a massive inheritance and served his Plantagenet kin; he battled at Rochester and Lewes, Evesham and Caerlaverock; won lands in Wales; was Keeper of the Realm of Scotland. As valorous and irascible as king Edward - and perhaps as ruthless - Sussex never knew his like again - its last full-blooded feudal warlord.[41]

26 A seal of a John earl of Surrey - note the rabbit warren

Overleaf: A smiling woman

4

Cluniacs, prelates and Franciscans 1066-1300

About ten years after his establishment in that town, the review of a sanguinary life filled this nobleman [Warenne] *with compunction, which he resolved to allay by pilgrimage, the fashionable atonement of those days for the blackest crimes. A visit to Rome, to Palestine, or some other centre of misguided devotion, was considered an ample reparation for the most atrocious offences against society.* Paul Dunvan.

1268. William Foville, prior of Lewes, died on the eve of Saint Michael, and left the convent in good condition and without debts. He assigned to the convent a gold cup, with five precious gems, and a gilt cup for the eucharist, and four capes for the choir of the best, and a silver pall in the choir for the Easter candle. Also he bequeathed for the benefit of the convent 100 pounds sterling in money for tunics, to be bought in the second year, when they do not receive fur cloaks from the chamber. Also for completing the two towers in front of the church, 200 pounds sterling. Also 100 marks to the Treasury. He governed the Lewes church eleven years from the feast of Saint Laurence to the said day. Also in the refectory a gilt cup; also in the infirmary his own silver goblet.

1282. On the day of the Apostles Peter and Paul, the lord archbishop of Canterbury, namely John de Peckham, of the order of Minors, was at Lewes, and a procession of the convent [was] *made, in which took part the said archbishop, clothed in his pontifical robes, that he might display his affection to the convent of his love ... the procession being completed, he pointed out the word of life to the people, preaching in the great church ...* [then he] *ascended to the great altar, where, for the solemnization of so great a festival, he sang the mass. Whence, when the hour of refreshment came, certain Friars Minor and a few secular priests simply accompanying him, he entered the refectory, where he ate with the convent, that he might the more openly and clearly demonstrate the emotion of his love towards the same convent.*
The annals of Southover priory.

A necessary part of the Norman Pacification had been a drastic over-haul of the English Church, spearheaded by Lanfranc, the new archbishop of Canterbury. In Sussex Chichester replaced Selsey as the site of its cathedral. Archdeacons were appointed, based eventually at Chichester and Lewes, the Adur serving as a boundary. Ecclesiastical courts were set up, answerable in the diocese to the bishop and the archdeacons, in the Peculiar of South Malling to the archbishop and the dean of Malling. They dealt with Church matters, with tithes and heresy, wills and administrations, disorderly clerics and loose-living laity.

The Pacification also entailed the planting of Norman and 'French' prelates to police the Saxon clergy, and of Continental monks to intercede, night and day, for the immortal souls of the new Norman overlords. And it was Lanfranc - according to a narrative contained in a charter of Southover priory transcribed in 1444 - who urged William of Warenne to fund a colony of Cluniacs in Lewes rape. The narrative also tells how Warenne and his wife Gundrada, with Salvation very much in mind, crossed the Channel to visit the shrine in Rome of saint Peter, the Keeper of the Keys. But war in Italy [between pope Gregory VII and emperor Henry IV] halted them at Cluny, an abbey in Burgundy dedicated to saint Peter and much in favour with the Holy See. Impressed by the piety and liturgical skill of its monks, they enquired if three or four brethren might be spared to launch a daughter-house at Southover, offering as a base the church 'dedicated from old time to saint Pancras', which they had converted from wood to stone. They also promised enough land to support twelve monks, an apostolic minimum. Abbot Hugh of Cluny was absent - if it was January 1077 he was busy reconciling the pope and emperor amidst the Alpine snow at Canossa. On his return he agreed to sanction this first Cluniac priory in England, provided king William approved it and the endowment was guaranteed. This done, he sent over [sometime between 1078 and 1081] 'Sir Lanzo and three of his fellows' - later recorded as Hugh, Lanzo's deputy, and two brothers, Conan and Walter Abeman. During the delay the Warennes had thought of applying to Marmoutier abbey near Tours whose monks had staffed the Conqueror's foundation at Battle.

This narrative may broadly be true, though the charter copied in 1444, despite purporting to be late 11th-century in date, was concocted sometime after. King William did issue a charter at abbot Hugh's behest, which approved the priory's foundation and endowment - revealing indeed that three carucates of land to be given at Falmer belonged to Gundrada. Other sources confirm the narrative's comment that king William tried in vain to recruit twelve Cluniacs to fill key posts in his 'reformed' English church. But it probably overdid the providential nature of the Warennes' arrival at Cluny. That illustrious Benedictine abbey, which Lanfranc admired, already ruled scores of Continental daughter-houses. Moreover by 1077 Gundrada's brother, Gerbold, had enrolled as a monk there, to repent at leisure killing his feudal overlord, the young count Arnulf of Flanders, at the battle of Cassel in 1071. Indeed the Warennes' foundation was intended maybe to expiate his crime - Gundrada's epitaph, which survives at Southover, hints that its endowment atoned for unspecified sins.[1]

As for the 'wooden' church, rebuilt in 'stone' by the Warennes soon after the Conquest, recent excavation in the priory precinct, on a site long known as the infirmary chapel, did find traces of a single-celled structure, partly built of lath and plaster, and perhaps late-Saxon in date. This was indeed rebuilt in 'stone' as the nave of a church to which a rectangular presbytery was added. The nave had chalk-rubble walls and a rammed chalk floor. Beneath it was a redundant 'ritual shaft' filled with debris. A wooden pipe, in the foundations of the presbytery, served perhaps as a drain for a vanished piscina near the high altar, the base of which was also found. Quite probably this was the 'stone' church received by the Cluniacs. Two

The re-build by the Warennes

graves, dug there before it was later enlarged, contained skeletons of aged men - one had been laid on a bed of charcoal, the other on a nailed wooden bier; their heads rested on pillows of stone. A third grave, formed from chiselled chalk-rock and Greensand slabs into the shape of a boat, reminiscent of Scandinavian ship-burials, had at one side a small recess. So maybe it was made for Gundrada, who died giving birth in 1085. Her husband William was buried near her in 1088 - under 'a white stone', a chronicler recorded - and remnants were found of a floor tomb, symmetrically placed near the third grave.[2]

Lanzo proved a resourceful, indeed charismatic, prior. By 1089 there were Cluniacs enough at Southover for him to supply monks to a daughter-house at Castle Acre founded by Warenne and his son, the second earl. In 1104 Lanzo sent monks to launch a priory at Thetford endowed by Roger Bigod, earl of Norfolk, and abbot Hugh of Cluny asked him to keep a paternal eye on them. Moreover, William of Malmesbury, no great admirer of Cluniacs, credited to him the reputation for charity and zeal achieved at Southover before his death in 1107; indeed the chronicler copied out an account of his passing, probably composed at the priory:

Being entreated by the brethren to be mindful of them with the Lord to whom he was going, he affectionately assented. He beckoned for the crucifix to be presented to him, which adoring and clasping with his hands, he kissed with joy and affection. When the moment of death was near he was carried, yet alive, into the presbytery of the church, before the altar of saint Pancras. Here he departed to Christ, pure and freed eternally from every evil.[3]

At some time the 'stone' church was itself enlarged, almost certainly by Lanzo. Transepts were built, with apsidal chapels extending eastwards to flank the presbytery, creating an unusual ground-plan. The altar-stone of its north chapel survives. The south chapel was paved with Horsham stone and in its south-west corner a spiral staircase led, perhaps, to a bell turret. The nave was extended westwards, with matching doors almost half-way down. Its massive walls, which carried maybe a tunnel or barrel vault, were relieved externally by shallow pilasters and largely faced with Quarr limestone, stretches of which remain. Possibly before the mid 12th century, eleven graves were dug in a row, in and between the transepts. One yielded an abraded sherd from an Egyptian amphora, 9th-century in date or earlier, a memento perhaps of a Near-Eastern pilgrimage.

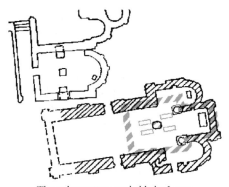

The enlargement, probably by Lanzo

Typically, the Cluniacs adorned their enlarged 'stone' church with costly frescos. Fragments of wall plaster survive, painted with figure subjects and geometric borders. Expensive pigments were used - scarlet derived from cinnabar, ultramarine from lapis-lazuli, brought from Afghanistan and more precious than gold. The colours were mixed and layered with great skill onto damp plaster, a sophisticated 'true fresco' technique. These fragments have enriched a debate as to whether a 'workshop' of artist-craftsmen, based at the priory, either painted or at least deeply influenced the style, or subject matter, of majestic schemes, executed in true fresco, at Clayton and Plumpton, Coombes and Hardham. At Clayton, for instance, were the frescos done when the mighty chancel arch was built, perhaps about 1050, or do such episodes as Christ giving the keys to Peter, and angels unveiling an empty Cross, point to a liturgical impulse very plausibly Cluniac? The priory at Southover was patron of the churches at Clayton and Hardham by 1121.[4]

Maybe Lanzo found more than a 'stone' church dedicated 'from old time' to saint Pancras. As already noted, just north of its probable site, in 1845, railway builders swept away a 'crypt' which had a shallow apse at the east end, thresholds for three doorways elsewhere, and a well at its centre some twenty feet deep. If Saxon in date, had it been used by priests serving the 'wooden' church nearby, and did Lanzo adapt it as a chapter house? - a passage to the west, also unearthed in 1845, serving perhaps as the east walk of his cloister. A Saxon date too has been mooted for the northern half of a south-facing wall, 147 feet long, some 200 feet to the south-west. At some date this wall was incorporated into a monastic refectory, possibly by Lanzo. However, that a pre-Conquest wall could fit so neatly into a later monastic layout has been queried. Moreover, a Saxon origin is derived, controversially, from the wall being pierced by windows with internal north-facing splays formed by clumsy stone voussoirs of Greensand stone.[5]

There is stronger evidence for a latrine block by Lanzo. Excavation has confirmed it as something of a showpiece, a very early example in England of what became the standard monastic latrine, a row of cubicles set in an inner wall above a sewer, fed in this case by the Upper Cockshut - a layout in use at Cluny maybe by 1000. Lanzo's latrine block was 83 feet long, with a western chamber identified as a possible bath-house by a fragment of Devon slate perforated for a faucet. Remnants survive from four of perhaps ten recessed latrine cubicles, each with a hole discharging into the sewer. Also extant are three handsome Romanesque windows, their bases just above floor level, that ventilated the room into which the cubicles faced. The arches were mostly of Quarr stone, the walls of Greensand stone. (Illustration 62)

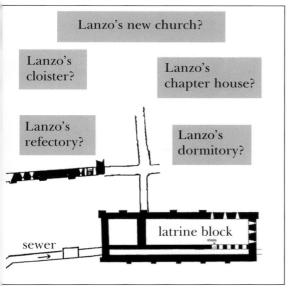

If this ambitious latrine block, and a dormitory to the north, were in situ before Lanzo died in 1107, maybe to their north by then also stood an equally ambitious new monastic church, itself rebuilt in and after the 1140s. A church was indeed dedicated sometime in the 1090s by three bishops, Ralph of Chichester, Walkelin of Winchester and Gundulf of Rochester, but some historians have viewed this as a rededication of the enlarged 'stone' church, regarding it as the only monastic church on the site till the mid 12th century. Maybe, however, it had been superceded by 1107, but was preserved as the successor to the former 'wooden' church because it was sacred to Pancras, just as the *vetusta ecclesia* at Glastonbury, built it was believed by Joseph of Arimathea, was venerated. At Cluny itself, the apse of the second monastic church, on the site of the first, was

preserved when a third basilica was built near by in 1130. Though trans-
ferring from faraway Burgundy, Lanzo and his Cluniacs adopted Pancras
as their guardian. Like Peter and Paul, he was a patron saint of Rome,
the seat of the Papacy, their powerful protector. Perhaps, too, the 'wooden'
church had links back to saint Wilfrid's Mission. Moreover the Hyde
Chronicle, a 12th-century narrative which highlights the Warennes,
affirmed that the relics on which earl Harold swore his oath of allegiance
to duke William were those of Pancras - a potent reason for that family
wanting his memory cherished.[6]

Abbot Hugh chose a Southover monk, Eustace of Beauvais, as the
second prior - presumably honouring his promise to Warenne, recorded
in the foundation narrative, that Lanzo's successor would be of high calibre. Clearly talented was the third prior, Hugh of Boves, a former prior
of Limoges, who trained at Laon, a prestigious theological school. In
office by 1120, he departed in 1123 to be abbot of Henry I's new foundation at Reading which was staffed with monks from Southover and
Cluny. In 1130 Henry made him archbishop of Rouen, and from there
in 1135 he and the second earl Warenne dispatched the king's embalmed
corpse to Reading for burial. Prior Ansger, who followed prior Ralph
about 1126, was talented enough to replace Hugh as abbot at Reading in
1130. But his successors are shadowy figures. Hugh of St Margaret died
in 1143. Aymer was in office by 1145 and while visiting Norwich sought
to secure for Southover the corpse of William, a skinner's apprentice,
murdered, it was said, by local Jews, and credited with miracles of healing. But Aymer's efforts alerted the bishop who swiftly installed it in his
cathedral. A prior William died in 1159. A second William was recorded
in 1170-1, and an Osbert about 1176, a former manager maybe of the
convent's wide estates in Norfolk. A very high-flier, however, was Hugh
III. Installed at Southover by 1182, he departed in 1186 to be abbot of
Reading, resigning in 1199 to reign at Cluny itself.[7]

By Lanzo's death in 1107 there were other Cluniac priories in
England at Lenton, Montacute, Thetford, Wenlock and Daventry,
Pontefract, Northampton, Bermondsey and Barnstaple. All were subject
to Cluny or to her daughter-houses at La Charite sur Loire and St Martin
des Champs in Paris. Between 1112 and 1142 Southover itself acquired
daughter-houses at Stansgate and Prittlewell in Essex, Monkton Farleigh
in Wiltshire, Clifford in Herefordshire and Monks Horton in Kent. With
Castle Acre they formed a dependent 'family' ruled from Southover.
There are other glimpses too of continuing vitality. Henry of Blois, bishop
of Winchester, abbot of Glastonbury, and himself a Cluniac, chose a
Southover monk, brother Robert, to restore discipline at Glastonbury,
and then secured his election as bishop of Bath and Wells in 1136. Abbot
Warner of Battle, who resigned in 1138, retired to Southover because it
was 'very notable for its religious life'. And about 1150 Gilbert Foliot,
bishop of Hereford, claimed that many poor and disabled people, ship-

wrecked mariners and pilgrims, found refuge there.[8]

After Hugh III's departure to Reading in 1186 the priors become shadowy once more. William III occurs in 1191 and 1196, Alexander in 1201, Humbert in 1202-3 and 1209, Stephen in 1218 and 1220, Hugh IV in 1224-5 and about 1234. Prior Albert disputed the patronage of Bignor church with Hugh Sanzaver in 1237, and his may be the fine, if mutilated, Purbeck-marble effigy of a priest at West Walton church in Norfolk. Guichard of la Osaye took office on the vigil of saint Pancras in 1245, but left quite quickly, after withholding tithes due to Cluny. William Russinoll, who reigned between 1249 and 1256, never returned from a journey to the Holy Land, though his chaplain, brother Cuckfield, did. His successor, William of Foville, a former prior of Northampton, 'left the convent in good condition and without debts' at his death in 1268, despite damage done during the battle of Lewes, and by a great wind which devastated the apple orchard. He also weathered a conspiracy involving the sub-prior and nine monks.[9]

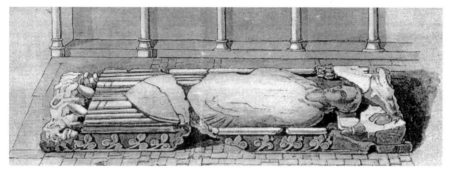

27 Possibly prior Albert at West Walton

Among other bequests Foville left £200 to 'complete the two towers at the [west] front' of the church, though in 1538 Thomas Cromwell's demolition contractor was to mention only one 'steeple ... set upon a corner of the forefront'. The legacy nonetheless must allude to a late stage in the building of a church whose immense ground-plan was eventually enclosed by 1512 feet of external wall. In 1147 Henry of Winchester and Robert of Bath and Wells had joined with archbishop Theodore of Canterbury and bishop Ascelin of Rochester in a service of 'dedication'. Himself a great builder, bishop Henry stood at the altar and cut hair from the heads of the third earl and his brother Reginald, to publicize endowments they were making before the earl departed 'for Jerusalem'. Whether this ceremony was inaugurating the re-building of an existing church, or the building of a grandly conceived new church, at last superceding the enlarged 'stone' church to the south-east, has yet to be resolved. Sadly the only architectural fragment to survive in situ - a stretch of blind arcading at the base of the south-west tower - cannot be securely dated to the 1140s, when such ornament was used 'to excess' at Castle Acre; it could be earlier or later. Once begun, however, construction was on a massive scale. Adam of Poynings about 1170 gave to 'the work' on the church the tithe of cheeses yielded by his Southdown sheepflocks. Imposing capitals, perhaps from the choir, have figure-sculpture carved maybe in the 1160s. A Purbeck marble plinth was positioned at the entry to the north side of the nave about 1200, and two free-standing figures were possibly fashioned about 1205 to flank a west portal. Caen stone 'for the church' was imported through Seaford in 1225 and maybe a Lady Chapel was completed in 1229 - there are finely carved Early English capitals compatible with that date. From the 14th century or later few fragments remain.[10]

28 The blind arcading

The church which prior Foville endowed was to retain till 1538 a Romanesque ground-plan broadly modelled on the third church at Cluny, the largest in Christendom when dedicated in 1130. Both plans provided for two west towers and a long processional nave. At Southover its arcades were perhaps eight bays long, the pillars 18 feet high and five feet in diameter, the vault 63 feet above the pavement. Southover also aspired to the soaring spaces and spectacular silhouette of Cluny's compressed eastern end. First came a crossing tower (galleried maybe) carried on four piers 42 feet high and seven feet in diameter, flanked by transepts, each with two chapels to their east. There followed a short choir, perhaps four bays long and 63 feet high; then a second crossing tower, flanked by apsed transepts; and finally a climactic high altar, set within a semi-circular arcade carried by four round columns, with maybe a gallery and half-dome above - a space which at Cluny blazed with a vast fresco of Christ in Glory. From an ambulatory behind the altar radiated five chapels. The distance from the west portal of the nave to the terminus of the easternmost chapel was 420 feet .

Cluny, though, managed to exceed Southover's spatial drama and aerial ebullience. The choir was compressed into a mere two bays and each western transept carried a tower, whereas at Southover they sported a turret at most, though the crossing towers, 147 and 135 feet high, made a mighty landmark. Cluny's internal spaces were also mathematically marshalled in the best Vitruvian manner by an exact relationship of major and minor units, shaped by sacred numbers, harmonic theory and

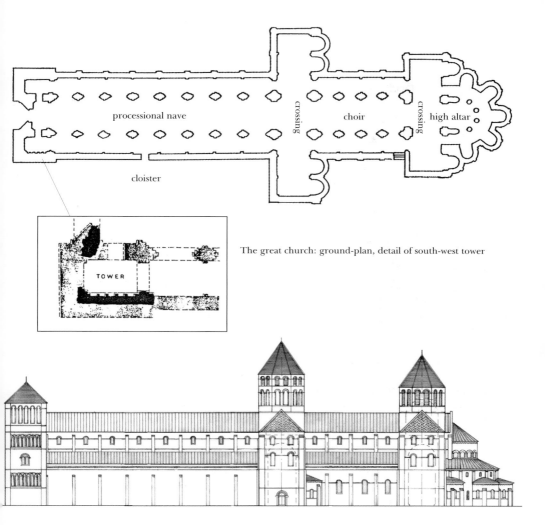

processional nave

crossing

choir

crossing

high altar

cloister

TOWER

The great church: ground-plan, detail of south-west tower

29 The great church: south elevation - conjectural

Biblical reminiscence. Thus the width of the nave, 153 feet, recalled the 153 fish miraculously caught by Peter, Cluny's patron saint. At Southover, fortuitously perhaps, some measurements in feet recorded in 1538 - 420, 147, 63, 42 and 14 - were divisible by seven, a sacred number.[11]

Masons were busy too, about 1150, at the enlarged 'stone' church. Its chancel was given a rib-vaulted roof with red floral decoration. Internal walls were refaced with Caen limestone and imitation masonry was outlined on them, also in red.[12]

The architectural pieces surviving from the new 'great' church were probably carved from blocks of Caen limestone on the site. Capitals, imposts and voussoirs, friezes, brackets, string-courses and corbels display common Romanesque decorative motifs - cable, chevron, fret and lozenge, scallop, pellet, 'ravioli', sawtooth and nailhead, though a Cluniac preference might explain a profusion of billeting, and a patera formed as a stylised petalled flower. A capital displays a dove with wings outstretched. Another, perhaps from the sanctuary, depicts saint Peter being called by Christ, fishing with saint Andrew and healing a crippled man - 'monumental' scenes comparable to those from the lives of Christ and saint Nicholas on the font at Brighton church, whose patron was the priory. More dynamic are the images on two other capitals. On one a lion and a griffin are poised either side of a stylized Tree of Life, their heads turned away. The lion, 'bursting with ferocity', could be tearing at its roots, a symbol perhaps of Mankind's rejection of Christ the Saviour. The other capital carries a grotesque creature with goggle eyes, gaping mouth, a deeply creased neck and wings strongly veined. Such highly charged work was prefigured maybe at Moissac in southern France, a Cluniac house on a busy pilgrim route to Compostela.

Sculpture carved somewhat later, perhaps in and after the 1180s, displays greater naturalism - a squirrel feeding; a lion grasping a cub, and a 'leafman', damaged but still vibrant. As for the battered crowned heads from two free-standing figures, the woman has almond-shaped eyes, the man a drooping moustache and a flowing beard divided into long straight curls. If they were made about 1205, that was the year the Cluniacs granted to William of Kent, 'sculptor', a house near the great gate. About 1300 Master Helias 'carver', a London tenant of theirs, witnessed the gift to them of a sluice by their mill at Seaford.[13]

30 A fragment from the lavatorium

Doubtless the 'great' church could absorb the hundred monks that earl Warenne claimed were resident in 1240, as many as at Reading, Gloucester and St Albans. By then other facilities had been expanded. Probably before 1170 a new chapter house and cloister were built, the latter an impressive 100 by 150 feet. (See 4.2) Surviving bases suggest that the cloister arcade had alternate single and double columns made from Tournai marble, a pattern also adopted at Moissac. Of Tournai marble too are fragments from a lavatorium, nineteen feet in diameter, where the monks washed their hands and faces. It stood near the refectory, towards the south-west corner of the cloister. The water descended maybe

31 Sculptures from
the priory

from a central basin fitted with small taps. In 1172 the abbot of Battle left money for a 'marble' washing place in his cloister. Also carved from Tournai marble, and now in Southover church, was a tomb slab placed in the chapter-house when the bones of Gundrada were transferred there. Its superbly chiselled decorative motifs - stylised lion-heads and heart-shaped palmettes - echoed those on capitals in the cloister at Reading and on pages in the Lambeth and Winchester Bibles illuminated about 1155. Perhaps the Cluniacs were alert to the merits of Tournai marble because of links with St Bavon's abbey in Ghent which guarded relics of saint Pancras and was built 'almost entirely' of it. Some carving perhaps was done on site, supervised maybe by Flemish masons, for 'practice' pieces seem to survive.[14]

32 Gundrada's tomb slab

As for an enlarged refectory, north of the 'Saxon' wall, square stone bases for eight, or possibly six, pillars were found in 1845. They, like the wall, belong to the undercroft of a post-Conquest refectory - the monks eating in an upper hall, as the Bayeux Tapestry shows king Harold doing at Bosham.

The dormitory probably built in Lanzo's time was also enlarged and extended southwards, to absorb the upper storey of the trail-blazing latrine block and to cover out-houses and cobbled yards resting on land reclaimed earlier from estuarine marsh by dumping chalk, flint and rubble-stone. The use of Sussex marble suggests the dormitory was remodelled sometime after 1175. It probably had two upper storeys and a lead roof resting on four central wooden pillars. Certainly it needed to be robustly underpinned; windows were blocked and piers built in the

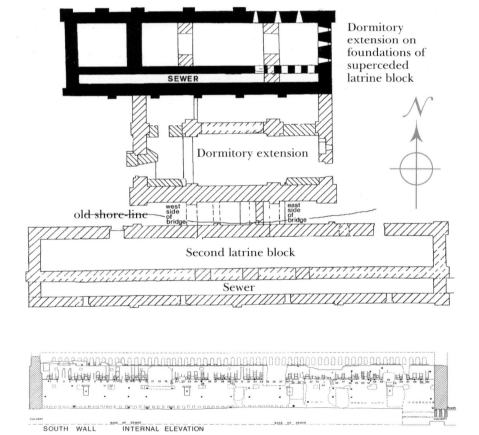

Dormitory extension on foundations of superceded latrine block

Dormitory extension

old shore-line

west side of bridge

east side of bridge

Second latrine block

Sewer

SOUTH WALL   INTERNAL ELEVATION

4.1 The extension of the dormitory and the second latrine block

redundant latrine, and a new undercroft to the south was heavily buttressed and divided by a sturdy triple-arched arcade.[15]

A stone bridge, perhaps carrying green-glazed ceramic water-pipes, linked the dormitory to an equally ambitious latrine block newly built even further south. It measured 34 by 168 feet, longer than Christ Church priory's at Canterbury, though the longest in Christendom, of course, was at Cluny. Because it trespassed so far into the marsh, the thick, heavily buttressed walls of its undercroft massively reposed on layers of Greensand stone, chalk, flint rubble and bedding mortar, underpinned - as at Pevensey's Roman fortress - by closely packed oak saplings driven into the sub-soil. In the lower part of the south wall of the latrine are still traces of four ventilation windows, and above them of sixty arch-springers which carried a tunnel vault across a new sewer leading from the Upper Cockshut, and above them of the sills of closely spaced squints which lit a corridor resting on the vault. Facing this corridor were latrine cubicles, perhaps 59 of them, recessed into the vanished north wall of the chamber, their shutes emptying between the arch-springers into the sewer. A similar layout can still be admired in the cathedral precinct at Worcester. Perhaps the chamber also housed a laundry, for a conduit and a box drain there led to a stone tank in the sewer, maybe to trap things accidentally lost. Caen limestone was freely used for windows, doors, arches and buttresses.[16]

Conveying water to the precinct needed bold engineering, though not quite the 3200 feet of lead piping which linked a conduit head outside Canterbury with five settling tanks and a water tower in Christ Church priory. The Cockshut stream flowed from a powerful chalkland spring at Well Green near Kingston Street, and reached the precinct along a diversion, the Upper Cockshut, which may have driven a pre-Conquest mill. West of the precinct it fed 'the Padpool', a reservoir and settling tank, linked apparently to the Winterbourne stream by an underground conduit still traceable in the 18th century. (Map 5.2). On the sewer dug to cleanse the new latrine block an oak sluice-gate controlled fresh water flowing eastwards from the Upper Cockshut, and salt water surging westwards at high tide from the estuary. How fresh water reached the upper precinct is uncertain. Possibly 'the Lantern', a subterranean Domed Chamber with a corbelled roof, still in situ below the site of the lavatorium, served as a pump house - unless it was reserved for disobedient monks.[17]

A ground-plan recovered by excavation also reveals a spacious infirmary. The roof of its hall rested on two stone arcades, each four bays long. To the east a fragment of masonry retains two niches, remnants perhaps of an aumbry and a piscina in the chapel. Their mouldings (preserved in old photographs) are compatible in date with a 'great infirmary' which the priory annals recorded - though not without ambiguity - as completed in 1218. A drawing made about 1775 shows a great mass

33 The remains of the infirmary about 1762

of masonry still standing. As for the refectory, it was perhaps modernized on an existing undercroft. At some date too a great kitchen oven was built. Sir William Burrell in 1772 noted its remains, also apparent in a Buck print published in 1737. It was 17 feet in diameter, with a roof composed of 'Tyles set perpendicularly' and with air vents in its walls, 'square spiracles' which the credulous believed the Cluniacs had used to stage 'juggling tricks or miracles'.[18]

By prior Foville's time the guesthouse was perhaps on the west side of a spacious courtyard just south of the great gate. From its kitchen, about 1270, Robert of Glyndele's widow could collect, each day, 'a loaf of convent bread, and a loaf of knight's bread, and a gallon of the best ale'. The guest rooms were sufficiently spacious in 1308 for Sir William Etchingham, his wife and household servants, to stay 'in the priory' for three days,

34 The ruined great oven in 1737

35 The great gate: view from the north-west in 1788; ground-plan, and details of decoration.

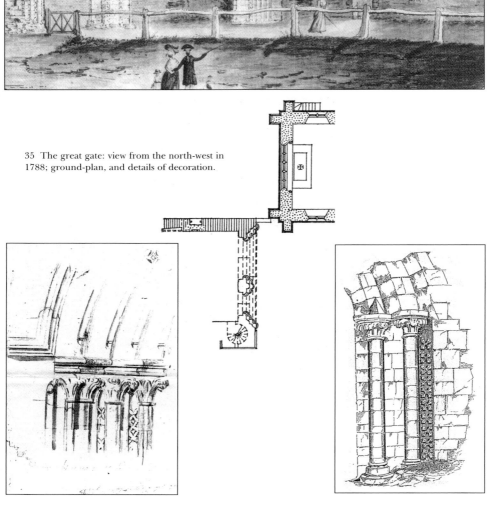

four times a year, and hear mass and eat breakfast on the fourth day. William could also opt to be bled by the monks.[19] About 1200 a gate house was erected, worthy of the ambitiously rebuilt precinct within. Its west-facing show facade sported a stair-turret and two round-headed archways, about five and ten feet wide. Their orders were elaborately moulded and adorned with stiff-leaf foliage and descending bands of nail-headed quatrefoils, carved from Sussex marble. When the gate was removed in 1832, 'the pillars and arch of the porter's lodge' were re-erected near by.[20]

Sometime too, perhaps in the later 12th century, a separate lodging was built for the prior and his staff. Most likely it adjoined the south-west tower of the church and faced across the courtyard to the great gate. In 1278 five servants of prior John of Dwyanges chose to abjure the realm - Guichard a serjeant, Hugelin a porter, Janin a bottler, Emery a palfrey-man and Reynold a cook. Suspected of murdering two bailiffs sent to arrest their drinking companion, a monk called John of Acres, they had taken sanctuary in the church. Besides using the guesthouse, Sir William Etchingham was entitled to place a servant in the prior's kitchen 'to learn the business of cooking banquets' - also a charger or palfrey in his stable, and two hounds in his kennels till they were a year old. Probably, too, the prior needed a treasury and muniment room. In 1237 he was trusted with the marriage portions of four daughters of Sir Godfrey Waleys of Glynde, and about 1250 legal papers, deposited with him by Hugh of Folkington, were produced at the county court.[21]

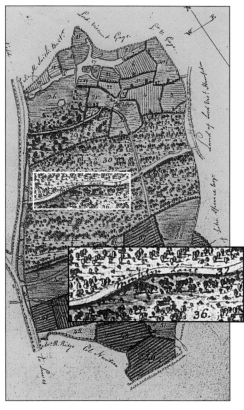

In the late 11th century the priors were allowed to hunt 'within the park' of the Warennes. But by 1300 a park was being expanded at Little Horsted, its nucleus rented from the archbishop of Canterbury. In the 1530s two hundred acres of pasture were stocked with bucks and does, and 200 acres of woodland yielded cartloads of fuel; indeed in 1309 firewood was already being fetched from 'Monkenewode' in Horsted. In 1563 the park's southern boundary

36 Mote Park and Plashett Park about 1800

4.2 The priory and its precinct about 1300

■ Masonry still standing in 1844

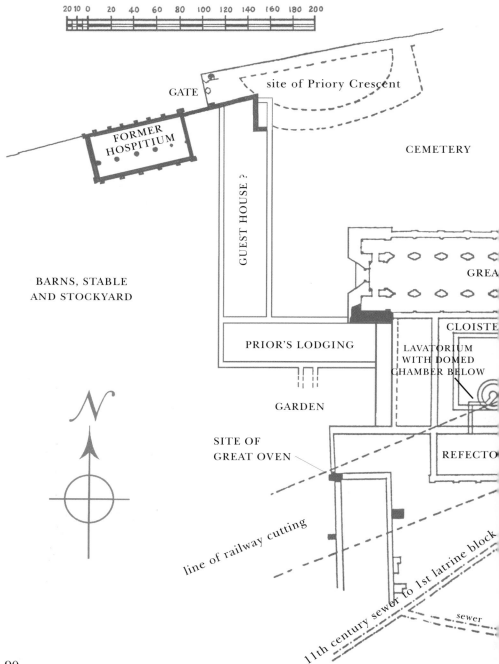

GATE

site of Priory Crescent

FORMER HOSPITIUM

CEMETERY

GUEST HOUSE ?

BARNS, STABLE AND STOCKYARD

GREA

CLOISTE

PRIOR'S LODGING

LAVATORIUM WITH DOMED CHAMBER BELOW

N

GARDEN

SITE OF GREAT OVEN

REFECTO

line of railway cutting

11th century sewer to 1st latrine block

sewer

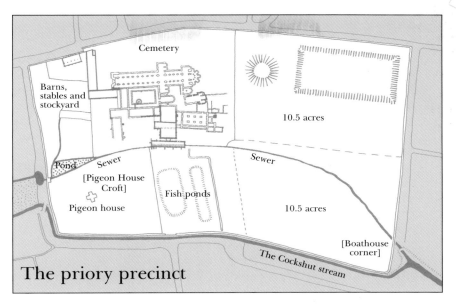

The priory precinct

In the early 1530s, probably in the eastern precinct (21 acres), wheat, barley, mustard, saffron, onions and garlic were grown in the 'vine garden' and the 'convent garden', and in the Lower Croft and the Upper Croft. There were also apple and pear orchards and hemp plots. (see p.197.)

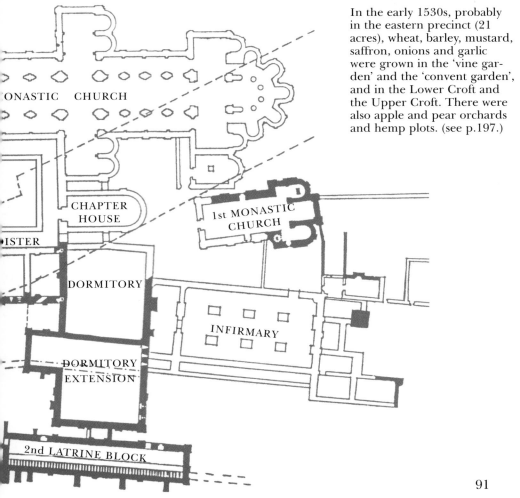

91

towards Plashett park was still known as 'Monken lane'; it led westwards from 'Monken gate'. Stretches of the pale survive.[22] The prior also acquired a London base. About 1175 a householder near the church of St Thomas the Apostle, in Vintry Ward, agreed to keep 'a well considered hospice' for prior Osbert and his monks, 'provide them with fire and water and salt and sufficient utensils and wait upon them'. In 1272 Salvagius of Florencia undertook to reserve them 'lodgings' there. However in 1278 earl Warenne granted them a house at Southwark, where Battle abbey, St Augustine's abbey and Christ Church priory held property. Perhaps this was the spacious house south-east of London bridge, beneath which until 1832 was a large 12th-century stone-vaulted undercroft supported by a central column with a scalloped capital.[23]

The energies of the spaciously re-housed monks still focused, of course, on the gorgeous rituals enacted amid the soaring spaces of their great church - a strenuous round of solemn procession, disciplined psalmody and chanted prayer, which justified Cluniacs receiving ampler rations than other Benedictines. Bequests by prior Foville in 1268 confirm this liturgical splendour - a golden cup set with five precious gems, a gilt cup for the eucharist, four capes for the choir, a silver pall for the Easter candle - also a gilt cup for the refectory and a silver goblet for the infirmary.[24]

Jubilantly celebrated was the feast of saint Pancras on 12 May. The priors of the six daughter-houses attended, though in 1313 Farleigh's pleaded illness. Through the great gate thronged tenants with their rent - the chaplain of Kingston brought a pound of incense, John of Benfield ten shillings for his windmill at Hangleton. But it was also a day for largesse. Miller John passed the time 'at the cost of the prior' and took home a cheese worth fifteen pence. Robert of Glyndele's widow received money for clothing, and a fur garment every other year. By 1363 a 'saint Pancras fair' catered for the crowds. To keep candles blazing before his image on the high altar, the keeper of his 'light', John of Trymyngham, drew a house-rent from Avery Street at Southover in 1314.[25]

Another great feast was Pentecost. In 1247 'the faithful' in Sussex were reminded by Richard, their bishop, of a duty to travel with their parish priests to Chichester at Whitsun, to pay dues to him and his cathedral chapter, confess their sins and receive absolution. A year later he conceded that folk in the three eastern rapes could resort to Hastings or Lewes instead. And indeed in 1249 a diocesan agent was collecting money at Lewes on 'Procession Day', on Whitsun Tuesday. He also recompensed a widow from Lindfield for entrusting a cruciform reliquary to the bishop, which 'the frailty of her sex' rendered her unfit to retain. A visit at Whitsun to 'the Church of Lewes', 'with banners and processions', by folk from the archdeaconry of Lewes, was still demanded in 1409 by bishop Rede. Perhaps they paid their dues at All Saints, the episcopal church. But they also thronged the priory church, for in 1400 the pope authorized the prior and ten priests to hear confessions during Pentecost from visitors viewing the relics and swelling the fabric fund. The immense nave, moreover, could channel any united 'procession' of the faithful on Whitsun Tuesday. Doubtless for their carnal delight, the great fair evolved in Lewes borough, recorded as 'the Whitsun fair' in 1440. In 1603 it was busiest on the Tuesday. A Town Fair was also held on Whitsun Tuesday at Hastings.[26]

The reverence paid to saint James the Great reflected maybe the taste for battle of the seigneurial class. His shrine at Compostela flourished as the crusade against the Moors intensified and the empress Matilda donated his hand-relic to Reading abbey. His altar at Southover was endowed about 1145 'for the soul' of John of Poynings. In 1262 John of Gatesden was buried before it. A diplomat and chamberlain to queen Eleanor, he gave land at Wantley in Henfield to the priory. And perhaps George 'of Antioch' had an altar, a saint conspicuous among the Heavenly Host seen by Crusaders before they captured that city in 1191. About 1290 a tenant at Antioch Street in St Peter Westout gave the Cluniacs a pound of wax, possibly to keep a light burning for him. Martin of Tours, the soldier saint adored at the Conqueror's abbey in Battle, was also patron saint of a church near Lewes castle.[27]

Naturally, a cult of Thomas Becket, killed in 1170 and canonized in 1173, took rapid root. Indeed, a day or so after the murder, a deceased colleague revealed to a dreaming Cluniac that Christ had already raised the archbishop 'from the ranks of the Martyrs to that of the Apostles'. Former foes, like earl Hamelin, became devotees. And to Thomas the Martyr, perhaps, was dedicated the enlarged 'stone' church, from which by 1173 the altar of saint Pancras had been removed to the great church. Edward I gave a cloth of gold to the altar of saint Thomas, and in 1375 the earl of Arundel's will distinguished between his chapel in 'la dite maison' [the priory] and the Lady Chapel in 'la grande esglise'.[28]

In 1375 the Lady Chapel stood 'on the north side' of the great church, as it did at Castle Acre. Fifty years earlier, house-rents in Southover were funding a 'St Mary's light'. Three were from Avery Street, a corruption perhaps of Ave Maria Street - Geoffrey atte Sermerye was a Southover resident in 1314. About then the altars of saint Mary and of the Holy Cross shared John of Nottingham as 'a keeper' of their lights. Maybe both were on 'the north side', where a 'picture of the Crucifix' had just been painted in 1374 when William Laxman asked to be buried before it. In 1250 a crippled man, 'his arm and both knees as it were contracted', was cured near 'the holy cross of saint Pancras at Lewes'. Perhaps this cult was the stronger by then because pilgrims were flocking to Bromholm priory, a daughter-house of Castle Acre, to adore a piece of the True Cross deposited in 1223. Linked with this cult was a plaque carved from walrus ivory, late-Saxon or Anglo-Norman in date, discovered at Eastport Lane in 1857 and now on show at the British Museum.

37 The ivory crucifix

It depicts the hand of God descending to touch the head of a slender, elongated crucified Christ, partly encircled by a mandorla.[29]

Intersecting with the great feast days was a daily round of Cluniac prayer that by the 11th century included skilled intercession for the souls of the Departed, which the priory's seigneurial benefactors hoped to harness. And confident indeed was the epitaph on the founder's 'white' tombstone, recorded by a chronicler: 'Earl William in this place your fame is kindled. You built this house ... a gift freely and gladly given to the poor of Christ. The saint himself, Pancras, who guards your ashes, will raise you to the mansions of the blessed. Saint Pancras give, we pray, a seat in heaven to him [the founder] who for your glory, gave the house'. The epitaph of Gundrada, still preserved at Southover, also invoked 'holy Pancras', indeed adopted him: 'She makes you her heir; you in your mercy acknowledge your mother'. It also conflated Mary of Bethany and Mary Magdalene who anointed the crucified Christ, when it declared that Gundrada 'brought to the English churches the soothing ointment of her goodness' and after death shattered the alabaster [of her body], 'the part of her that was like Martha died; the finer part that was like Mary survives'. Several English Cluniac houses were dedicated to Mary Magdalene; in 1263 she was also joint patron, with John the Baptist, of Southover's parish church.[30]

Vassal-knights in Lewes rape also endowed the priory in return for intercession and burial near its relics. William of Pierpoint, giver of land at Rottingdean, was promised prayers 'for his soul'. Ralph of Plaiz, the donor of Iford church, was interred in the chapter house. Ralph of Clera, who gifted the manor of Atlingworth, was enrolled in the confraternity, sharing 'all its benefits'. Bristelm and Ormar, Guy of Menchecurt and Reginald of Warenne eventually became monks, to better prepare to meet their Maker. Benefactions also flowed from knights in Pevensey rape where the counts of Mortain founded no fully fledged monastery. When William of Keynes gave Horsted Keynes church, he was assured the Cluniacs would feed 300 paupers for a year on his behalf. In return for a fishery at Langney, they agreed to intercede 'ceremoniously' for the soul of Eustace of Boulogne. And even in a rape dominated by Battle abbey, Rainald of St Leger donated 2000 herrings a year and a bondman called Olaf, the Cluniacs pledging to 'make' a monk in Rainald's name. Because Salvation was at stake, Guiscard Laident's charter allotted 'the lowest place in Hell with Beelzebub, the Prince of the demons', to any person seeking to frustrate his gift.[31]

On 3 May 1297 the annals noted the death of Nicholas the 'circator' - so exhausting was the sumptuous Cluniac liturgy that a monk patrolled to detect drowsiness among his brethren. Cluny abbey was famously equipped for worship; a seven-branched candlestick stood eighteen feet high; a jewelled corona-wheel blazed with 120 hanging lamps. At Southover the sacrist, as master of ceremonies, guarded the gilt chalice, the gold cup set with five gems and the pall of silver, bequeathed by prior Foville, also the cloths of gold given by Edward I - though a gold chalice and paten were stolen about 1299. Also costly was an ornate finger-ring of beaten gold, heavily adorned with bosses, pellets and pearls, 'found at Lewes Priory' sometime before 1887. Like the ivory crucifixion plaque, it is late-Saxon or Anglo-Norman in date - and on show at the British Museum.[32]

The precentor oversaw the worship and service books - the psalters, missals and copies of Scripture. Monastic libraries elsewhere also included texts allowing the liturgy to be better understood - Biblical commentaries by Jerome and other Early Fathers, books of grammar and rhetoric, theology and canon law, even of medicine and astronomy. In the Bodleian Library is a psalter used at Southover in the 12th century, but compiled about 1025, probably at Crowland abbey. And the Fitzwilliam Museum owns a small breviary-missal composed 'according to the custom of Lewes', with the names of Pancras, Thomas of Canterbury and Richard of Chichester picked out in letters of gold; its three parts were separately penned and illuminated in France between about 1265 and 1315. The precentor also supplied the prior's secretary with parchment in 1319 and doubtless presided over Southover's scriptorium. Penned there in the 12th century were brief entries on two obituary notices of deceased clerics, sent from monastery to monastery - the scripts, though, were not especially assured and

38 An illustration from the breviary-missal

in one the word 'faithful' [*fidelium*] was at first omitted.[33]

Also compiled at Southover were two sets of annals, one now in the Vatican Library, the other in the British Library. Facts in the first are few and spare, but entries in the second, for the years 1218 to 1304, are more circumstantial, though remarks on a great infirmary (1218-19), a lady chapel (1229) and 'new work' at the church (1243) may not relate to Southover. Topics included priors misbehaving at Castle Acre and Monkton Farleigh; a cripple cured at 'the holy cross of saint Pancras'; an October gale devastating the precinct gardens and orchards; archbishop Pecham eating in the monks' refectory 'that he might the more openly demonstrate his love towards the convent'; the fraught funeral of the seventh earl's only son, a paragon of 'nobility, generosity and honesty, now buried and covered with stones'; and the 'deadly' battle during which 'the greatest part of the king's army was utterly overthrown between prime and noon'.[34]

As in the case of William of Keynes, the Cluniacs also proclaimed the Glory of God by charitable gifts of money, food and clothing, which sometimes promoted too the Salvation of lay benefactors. In 1535, 'for the souls' of the founder and his kin, the almoner still dispensed 2s 10d to the poor each Sabbath, also doles at Pentecost, Shrove Tuesday and Maundy Thursday totalling £5 3s 8d. About 1150 bishop Gilbert Foliot praised the priory as a 'refuge' for the poor and disabled, for pilgrims and ship-wrecked sailors. Thirty years later bishop Seffrid of Chichester declared that the 'sweet and renowned odour' of its charity 'filled the country round about'. Walter, its 'pious hospitarius', died in 1136 and revenues from St Olave's church in Southwark were assigned about 1205 to 'the refreshment of guests'.[35]

As for a late-12th-century hospitium, a remnant may survive in the parish church just west of the great gate. Four drum-like piers there carry three plain semi-circular arches, part of a Romanesque arcade originally at least five bays long, which perhaps divided the men's ward from the women's. Possibly, the wards had altars to John the Baptist and Mary Magdalene, 'hospital saints' who shared the dedication of the parish church opened on the site between 1257 and 1263.[36]

4.3 St John the Baptist Southover: ground-plan

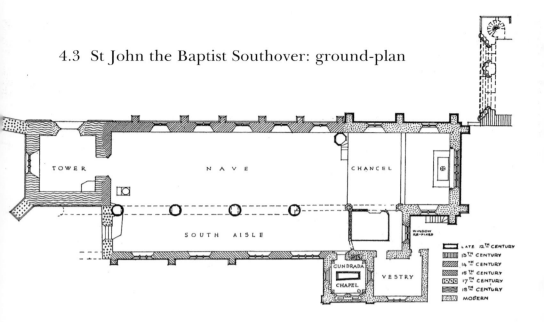

TOWER

NAVE

CHANCEL

SOUTH AISLE

WINDOW RE-FIXED

GUNDRADA CHAPEL

VESTRY

	LATE 12ᵀᴴ CENTURY
	13ᵀᴴ CENTURY
	14ᵀᴴ CENTURY
	15ᵀᴴ CENTURY
	17ᵀᴴ CENTURY
	18ᵀᴴ CENTURY
	MODERN

Was this hospitium west of the great gate abandoned by 1264 because St James's hospital, just across the road, had been enlarged? Quite probably the hospital did already exist, for the site has yielded a column base of Sussex marble dating from the 12th century. In 1535 the Cluniacs still paid £16 10s a year to thirteen 'poor brothers and sisters' there who prayed 'perpetually' for the soul of William 'the founder', and maybe he was the first earl. If the hospital was enlarged to take the local 'sick poor', who were gathering in its 'great hall' about 1300, was this 'the new work of our church', noted by the annals as begun in 1243 on the anniversary day of 'earl William'? William, the sixth earl, who died in 1240, gave the Cluniacs the revenues of Stoke-by-Guildford church to benefit pilgrims, and also visited the shrine of saint James at Compostela. The final ground plan of St James's was similar to that adopted in the 1290s for St Mary's hospital at Chichester where a 'great hall' still leads into a 'chancel' chapel. A survey of St James's in 1772 plotted the foundations of a 'nave' and aisle, forming a spacious sickroom, 110 by 36 feet. This opened into a 'chancel', 34 by 15 feet, still extant, and recently turned into a private house. These measurements, repeated by Horsfield, if accurate, would suggest that the hall stretched westward across what is now St James Street - part of its west wall still embedded perhaps in number 12. (See map 5.2) To the north of the chancel in 1772 were foundations of 'Cells', 60 by 18 feet, and to the south in 1582 'a gatehouse' and 'old kitchen', at the west end of Thomas Saunders' house.[37]

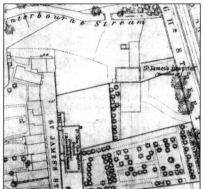
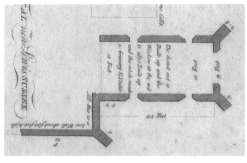

39 St James's hospital: the remains in 1782; part of William Green's ground-plan, and the site in 1874

Also in 1535 'thirteen poor brethren and sisters' at the former leper hospital of saint Nicholas in Westout were receiving £5 10s a year from the Cluniacs, a charge on their revenues authorized, it was said, 'by the first founder of Lewes priory'. Warenne perhaps followed the example of archbishop Lanfranc who founded a leper hospital dedicated to saint Nicholas at Harbledown, north-west of Canterbury, about 1084. Pieces of late 11th-century pottery have been recently recovered from pits on the Westout site dug to extract chalk and lime during the hospital's construction. And buildings there, now vanished, but sketched in 1772 , were described as 'Norman' in 1861. In 1535 some income accrued to the hospital from 'ancient' charges - levied on the manor of Ditchling, on 'the Lord's Houses' in Westout [St Peter's Place], on garden plots in St Martin's Lane and Rotten Row - rents first authorized, presumably, by the earls Warenne. The site at Westout, of course, was suitably isolated, though quite close to a powerful 'well', perhaps associated with saint Anne.[38]

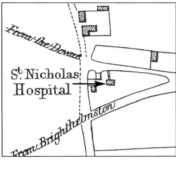

40 St Ncholas's hospital: the remains viewed
from the north-west in 1772

Only two of 103 skeletons excavated at the hospital's cemetery in 1994 were certainly of lepers. The leg of another had a 'manacle' attached, and the hands of a fourth were crossed behind the back and the vertebrae displaced. Some showing head or leg wounds were perhaps the remains of men slain during the battle of Lewes which raged around the *domus leprorum*. The Cluniacs' involvement in its funding reflected a wider monastic commitment. Walter of Lucy, a mighty abbot of Battle (1139-71), regularly washed and kissed the hands and feet of lepers. And about 1250 the Cluniacs were linked to a leper house at Southover, 'opposite the Lortepool', the pond of the west mill on the Winterbourne - an outstation of Westout perhaps. Roger of Ash, who founded a leper house at Seaford before 1169, was also a benefactor of the priory.[39]

There are glimpses of the rations sustaining the Cluniacs. The kitchen of their guesthouse baked 'knight's' bread and 'convent' bread and brewed 'convent' ale. The Warennes allowed them fish from seigneurial waters near Lewes and a tithe of eels caught in Yorkshire. Rents paid to them included six sorel pears, half a pound of cummin, and beans brought from Coates in the Adur valley and from Langney near Eastbourne. Olive stones and grape seeds have been found near a skillet discarded in their latrine. Vines were grown in, or near, the precinct and they owed 100 marks to vintners in 1279. The tastier meals were reserved for festivals, for 'great' guests and for the infirmary, where monks relaxed after their regular bleedings and often 'revealed to each other the secrets of the heart'. Also sustaining during worship on winter nights were the fur cloaks issued by the chamberlain every other year - prior Foville left £100 for 'tunics' to be distributed in the years between. The chamberlain also authorized a tenant to fell trees at Imberhorne near East Grinstead in 1273, so perhaps he guaranteed too a supply of fire wood.[40]

The priory's revenues coped reasonably well, it seems, with its re-building campaign. Clearly funds were buoyant at the time of the 'dedi-cation' ceremony in 1147, for the Cluniacs paid 100 marks to John of Chesney for half his lands at Brighton and agreed to occupy the rest rent-free for seven years as 'interest' on an earlier loan. They also allowed William Malfed, captured at the siege of Pevensey, twenty marks towards his ransom. There were debts to Jewish lenders in 1200, and again in 1234, but the convent was free of them by Foville's death in 1268.[41]

Undoubtedly by then the revenues were substantial. Most of the endowment held at the Dissolution in 1537 was already in place - the last major land grant, eighteen Wealden virgates at Wantley in Henfield, was made about 1240. This being also the case elsewhere, the valuations of monastic income in the *Valor Ecclesiasticus*, a national survey made in 1535, are some guide to relative wealth 300 years earlier. With a gross revenue of £1091 (£ 921 net) Southover narrowly missed being among the 23 houses (4% of the total) with a disposable income of over £1000. In south-east England only Christ Church Canterbury, St Augustine's Canterbury and Merton priory were wealthier. In 1291 Southover's net income was assessed at about £944. Just over half came from 'spirituali-ties' - from tithes, appropriated rectories, 'pensions' paid by parish clergy; in 1535 these accounted for about 47%. Among the manors in the convent's portfolio of 'temporalities' in 1535, the jewels were Swanborough (£48) and Falmer (£98) in Lewes rape, Langney (£43) in Pevensey rape, and Heacham (£69) and Walton with Walpole and Walsoken (£126) in Norfolk.[42]

By 1291 the priory was the patron of over a hundred churches and chapels, including a majority of those serving Lewes rape, where it built a chapel at Balsdean and perhaps the church at Kingston dedicated to saint Pancras. These advowsons, though, were somewhat unstable assets - Poynings was returned to the local seigneur about 1180, and Portslade exchanged for Harthill in Yorkshire in 1191. By the early 13th century, moreover, the pope had required diocesan bishops to ensure that the priests were all either rectors paying a fixed 'pension' to the monastery or vicars enjoying a secure tenure and income. About 1250 this caused a bitter quarrel with bishop Richard, who established 'sufficient' vicarages at Rodmell and Brighton, but transferred their advowsons from the pri-ory to his own cathedral chapter - only after lengthy arbitration did the Cluniacs cling on to Brighton. Seemingly, about then, to document an early date for their title to advowsons and tithes, they forged charters crediting the grants to remote benefactors.[43]

In 1535 the Cluniacs also received £24 from 'the tenth penny of Lewes barony', a relic perhaps of a pledge by the third earl in 1147 to give to them a tithe of all produce from his demesne and of all rents paid by his tenants, in Sussex and elsewhere - his grandfather's income from these in Lewes rape in 1086 was £232. In 1323 this 'tithe' also accrued from Warenne lands in Yorkshire.[44]

Initially the close ties between the Warennes and the priory caused no friction between them and the abbot of Cluny. Once chosen by him, the priors were hardly constrained by his remote paramountcy, though he received the breviary, cope and palfrey of any who died in office. In his presence, however, all novice monks 'professed' obedience to the Order, which entailed an arduous journey or a long wait, for abbots rarely crossed the Channel - Peter the Venerable did in 1130 and Hugh, the ex-prior of Southover, in 1200. The convent also paid an annual tribute of fifty shillings to Cluny, increased before 1201 to a hundred - a token of dependence, a silver mark, was paid to the priory, on the feast of Pancras, by its daughter-house at Farleigh.[45]

The near-autonomy of its priors, though, was eroded somewhat in the early 13th century. The Cluniac houses in England were grouped into a province, and the priors of Cluny's daughter-houses there had now to attend, at least every other year, a general chapter convened at Cluny on the third Sunday after Easter. This issued binding decrees and sent visitors to each province to inspect the discipline, fabric and finances of each house. At Southover they noted debts and disrepairs, and in 1266 a 'conspiracy' for which the sub-prior and nine monks underwent prolonged penance elsewhere. On the feast of Pancras the prior presided over his own chapter of subordinate priors, whom he could appoint and demote at will. Stansgate, Clifford and Horton were too poorly endowed to achieve a full monastic life. But Farleigh, Prittlewell and Castle Acre, with net annual incomes in 1535 of £153, £155 and £306, maintained their 'statutory' establishments of 14, 20 and 26 monks. The 'family' offered a career path. Mainer, the chamberlain at Southover, departed to rule Farleigh in 1191. So, later, did Thomas, the guestmaster, but he so 'vexed' the house with lawsuits that John of Newcastle, the gardener, replaced him in 1300.[46]

But the prior's power within the 'family' had limits. Castle Acre itself ruled four daughter-houses, including Bromholm priory which thronged with pilgrims, once a piece of the True Cross, pillaged from Constantinople, was deposited there in 1223 - indeed abbot Ivo of Cluny came to adore it in 1260. Anxious perhaps to cash in, the prior of Southover challenged the right of Castle Acre's prior to appoint Bromholm's prior. However after Castle Acre's prior appealed to the abbot of Cluny, it was decreed that 'Bromholme is to Acre, as Acre is to Lewes, and Lewes is to Cluny'. Even so, the relic encouraged maybe the cult of the Holy Cross so apparent at Southover.[47]

Cluny's paramountcy had been valued by the first earls of Surrey. The skilled intercession of 'French' monks had much to offer expatriate Norman warlords steeped in slaughter. However, the bond between a Continental Church and a Norman Nobility, exemplified by the third earl's death in Laodicea, fractured somewhat during Henry II's quarrel with Becket. And earl Hamelin, though he gave Conisbrough church to the priory, as well as lands at Balsdean and Ovingdean, and eels in Yorkshire, now demanded that the abbot of Cluny recognize his right, as founders' kin, to influence the selection of priors at Southover. Indeed about 1197 the earl rejected abbot Hugh's choice of brother Alexander, and after the pope sided with Hugh, Hamelin froze the convent's revenues in Norfolk and set guards at Southover to turn away messengers. When Hugh came to England to meet mediators appointed by the pope, Hamelin's men barred him from Southover and Castle Acre. In 1201 a compromise was patched up - at future elections two proctors of the earl, and two Southover monks, would choose at Cluny one of two monks nominated by the abbot. As a result, brother Alexander was installed. Pope Gregory IX, however, annulled the agreement in 1228 as prejudicial to Cluny, and so it was that archbishop Pecham wrote to the abbot in 1285 urging him, out of gratitude and 'without offence to God', to consult the seventh earl before choosing a new prior.[48]

Pecham, whose 'great love' for the monks caused him to eat with them in 1282, also complained to the abbot of a sharp deterioration at Southover since Foville's death in 1268. Priors had enriched themselves, appointed 'robbers' to benefices, let prayer and charity decay. And indeed Foville's successor, Miles of Columbiers, who departed in 1274 to be abbot of Vezelay, did leave the convent 4000 marks in debt, equal perhaps to three years' income - a debt only slightly reduced by Peter of Villiaco who quitted in November 1275 to be prior of St Martin's in Paris, and by John of Dwyanges who moved on in 1285. The debt was despite a sharp fall in numbers. A hundred monks exercised 'almost indiscriminate charity' in 1240; but by 1263 the roll had fallen to 55, by 1279 to 50, by 1288 to 39. Pecham also urged that the next prior, however chosen, should be English (less likely, perhaps, to be an asset-stripping carpet-bagger). No Englishman, it seems, had held the office, though John of Northampton did become prior of Prittlewell in 1260, and William of Shoreham prior of Castle Acre - but he, after being degraded for malpractice in 1282, defiantly clung to office, helped by soldiers from the castle.[49]

The abbot of Cluny's choice was John of Avignon, a Venetian by birth, formerly prior of Bermondsey, of Northampton, and of Wenlock. It was said that he wrecked the finances of all three while trading in land and wool, being hand in glove with a corrupt Exchequer official, Adam of Stratton, and hoping to purchase a bishopric with the proceeds.

Installed at Southover by 1285 he borrowed heavily from agents of merchant-bankers based in Lucca, Florence and Siena, and was often overseas on urgent personal business. In 1294 the convent's debts stood at over 9000 marks; at his death in 1298 they probably approached the 22,000 marks reported in 1301. Small wonder the seventh earl withheld his 'tenth' or that a Cluniac was imprisoned at Lewes castle in 1293 for poaching. In 1298 the abbot of Cluny finally heeded Pecham's advice. The 1201 agreement was revived and the earl's proctors joined in selecting the convent's English sacristan, John of Newcastle.[50]

Doubtless these three decades of corruption damaged the spiritual prestige of Southover's Cluniacs, at a time when intermittent war with France was exposing all the houses of an 'alien' Burgundian Order to a rising tide of xenophobia. Indeed had John of Avignon been born in 'France', a royal edict might have deported him from the 'sea coast' in 1295. It must have seemed that the priory's Golden Years were over.[51]

Yet whereas from the 1270s the Southover Cluniacs were immersed in liturgical routine, corporate finance and careerism, the Franciscans had emerged as a mendicant Order which preached to lay folk, heard their confessions and buried their dead. These Grey Friars arrived in England, at Dover, on 10 September 1224 - just before saint Francis received the stigmata on Monte La Verna - and had settled in some forty towns by 1241. In October that year a group of them at Lewes received ten marks for their clothing, and the following May ten oaks for their friary, by order of Henry III, the guardian of the sixth earl's heir. Their low-lying precinct bordered the busy road between the 'east gate' and the bridge - a site well placed for a mission to the laity. In July 1244 they were seeking to wall over the Town Ditch. They used the ground towards the river-bank and the Winterbourne stream for pastures, orchards and fishponds. Formerly perhaps it was demesne land of Houndean manor, given maybe by the sixth earl who died in 1240. The friars quickly attracted other gifts, such as the mullet 'miraculously' netted at the bridge in the presence of bishop Richard, who also bequeathed them twenty shillings in 1253, and a book of Gospels, 'namely Luke and John'. The seventh earl and the prior of Southover gave annual doles of wheat. Edward I in 1299 allowed them 24 shillings for three days' supply of food - at four pence per head per day enough to sustain 24 friars.[52]

Recent excavation has revealed that their humble church, cloister, chapter house and kitchen were sited as far from the river as possible, yet adhered to a standard Franciscan plan. Only a narrow graveyard lay between the busy road and the church, and perhaps a passage from the road to the cloister always ran through it, separating the chancel from a nave into which lay folk could crowd to savour the sermons. A 'Chapel' on the site, demolished in the 1830s, had 'traces of Early English work'. An engaged capital in that style has been found, also fragments of grisaille window glass with stiff-leaf fleur-de-lys and other formalized floriated

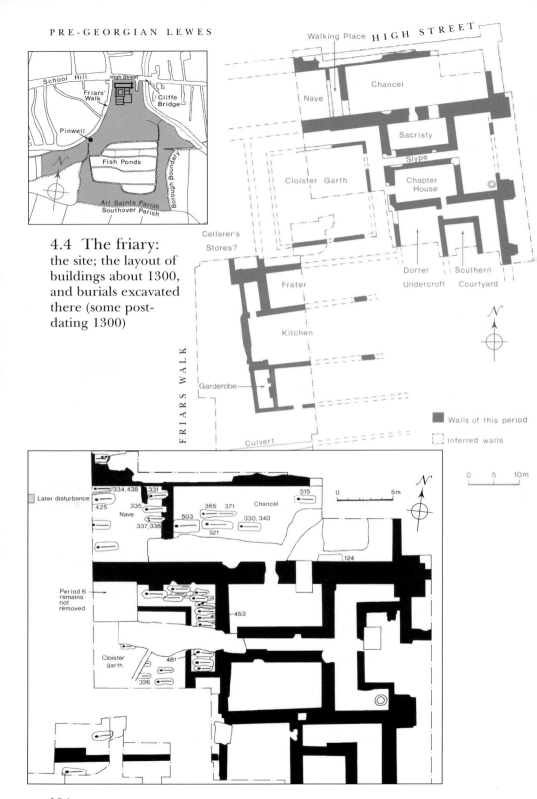

4.4 The friary: the site; the layout of buildings about 1300, and burials excavated there (some post-dating 1300)

motifs. Yet the church remained a small, heavily buttressed, two-cell structure, lacking even a belfry maybe. The clunch walls were faced externally with knapped flint. At some date the interior plaster was decorated with red and black lines imitating masonry, and the roof covered with 'blue' West Country slate. Lay folk sought burial in the precinct and there was, it seems, a pecking order. Skeletons found under the church and the cloister garth were decently spaced and mostly in coffins, and those in the chancel rested in graves lined with well-cut chalk blocks; but those under the cloister walk were crammed together, protected only by shrouds.[53]

41 The friary: window glass

Quite apart from the Cluniacs and Franciscans, the archbishops exercised considerable local influence. Doubtless Pecham, who trained as a Franciscan, favoured them as he did the Cluniacs. Quite probably he was born at Patcham, where lay their Withdean estate, and the monks, he acknowledged, had been 'kind' to him in his boyhood. Nostalgia perhaps reinforced his frequent visits to the 'palace' at Old Malling, the hub of his great manor of South Malling. On progresses through Sussex, usually between Mayfield and Slindon, he paused there to transact a stream of business. He stayed two or three weeks, in June, July or August, in 1279, 1281, 1282, 1283 and 1288, and again in January or February, in 1282, 1284, 1286, 1287 and 1289. Twice in St Mary Westout church, moreover, he conferred holy orders on several score priests, deacons, sub-deacons and acolytes. And twice he made emotionally charged visits to the priory - to eat with the monks as a token of his 'love', and to bury before the high altar the seventh earl's only son, 'on the left side near his mother'.[54]

A detailed survey of Pecham's estates, compiled in 1283-5 by a Sussex man, John of Iford, reveals tenants in South Malling manor being mobilized to ensure that his entourage could lodge at his 'court of

Malling' for 'fifteen days in winter' and 'fifteen days in summer'. They prepared his 'privy chamber'; fenced or hedged the 'burghyard'; repaired the stable, the baking-oven and great gate. They supplied hay, rushes, wood, lead, kitchen skewers, and a trough made from alder. They carried provisions from Lewes market and conveyed baggage westwards as far as Sele near Bramber bridge. They fetched yeast for brewing, threshed corn and carted it to mills at Wellingham. Pecham's three local foresters also attended him. Most years his successor, archbishop Winchelsey - a native of Sussex presumably - managed two stays at Old Malling. He came for at least two weeks in August 1296, April 1300 and April 1309. In December 1304 he buried the seventh earl in the priory, 'under a flat tombstone on the flat pavement'. Slowed down by illness, he lingered at Old Malling in January and February 1311, then at Mayfield till the end of April.[55]

Earlier archbishops can be glimpsed. At the palace in 1121 Ralph confirmed to the Southover Cluniacs a portfolio of spiritualities, in 1175 Robert consecrated Odo abbot of Battle. Legend has it that Becket 'often ate' in the great hall, at a table topped with Sussex marble. Probably by Pecham's time the residence was substantial. In 1595, some decades after the archbishops were dispossessed, John Norden noted 'the walls and ruins' of a 'stately ancient house', though in 1620 a sketch by John Deward shows only a farmhouse. The site has yielded late 12th-century carved stones, some of Purbeck marble, and on it still stands a fragment of flint wall with blocked windows. Adjoining this in 1772 was a round-headed gateway, and near to it, a ruinous pigeon-house, the nesting boxes open to the sky.[56] In 1620 Thomas Trayton rented the farmhouse, along with sixty acres which fitted snugly into a sharp bend of the river Ouse. (Map 5.5). These included 26 acres of water meadow which in the 1530s lay within archbishop Cranmer's land at 'Old Malling', and per-haps all sixty acres had been used with the palace. A hundred acres of adjacent water meadow formed part of Cranmer's Stoneham estate. In 1283 this great demesne farm, like the palace, was a focus of labour services by tenants in South Malling manor. These fell most heavily on those outside 'the Wood', but virgaters living in the Weald at Wadhurst were obliged to harvest wheat, barley and oats, and repair the barley grange - for his part the archbishop laid on an annual 'Gutfelling' feast.[57]

As John Norden also noted, the 'stately ancient house' had been 'the head house of the hundred of Loxfylde', which included the entire manor of South Malling. In the 13th century its court met every three weeks to transact all secular litigation in this 'liberty' - the equivalent indeed of the court of Lewes rape. Among its suitors was the prior of Lewes, for 250 freehold acres at Little Horsted, the nucleus of his deer park. As elsewhere, by the 1290s royal justices might enter the liberty and try the graver cases, but the archbishop's servants collected the money if fines were levied, and the chattels if convicts were hanged. On the chalk

42 Old Malling palace : two views of the remains in 1772

heights above Cliffe there was still a field called 'Hangmans Acre' in 1641, perhaps near to the 'execution pit' on Malling Down where the skeletons of 13 young males were discovered in 1973.[58]

The archbishops also appointed the priests who served the churches and chapels within the manor of South Malling - at Wadhurst, Mayfield, Framfield, Buxted and Uckfield, at Isfield, Ringmer, Cliffe, Southerham and Glynde - parishes which constituted the Peculiar of South Malling, that endured for over a thousand years till 1845. At Buxted Pecham installed John of Lewes who built the handsome Early English chancel there. Within the Peculiar the archbishops had a spiritual jurisdiction enjoyed elsewhere in Sussex by the bishop of Chichester, though by Pecham's time these powers had been delegated to the dean of the collegiate church at Malling. So like the bishop's deputy, the archdeacon of Lewes, in his spiritual court the dean could adjudicate 'in causis matrimonialibus, testamentariis, in fidei lesionibus, diffamationibus, divorciis'; he also inspected and punished peccant priests and lay folk in the Peculiar.[59]

The early links between the archbishops, the Peculiar and a community of priests at Malling are unclear. In 1086 'the canons of South Malling', who held from the archbishop a pre-Conquest endowment in

43 Collegiate seal

Stanmer, Lindfield and Burleigh, were it seems also the 'canons of saint Michael', who held from him four hides in the manor of South Malling. So maybe priests based at a Saxon 'minster' at Malling had already served the massive Peculiar of South Malling for a century or more. Certainly by the 1290s the collegiate church of St Michael at Malling did function as a 'mother-church'. Parishioners in Cliffe, Southerham and Ringmer buried their dead in its churchyard, though archbishop Pecham licensed burial at Ringmer if access to Malling proved 'impossible'. Until the Dissolution the college kept two sextons on its pay-roll. The church also received a dribble of offerings from elsewhere in the Peculiar - payments for wax, for example, from Isfield and Glynde. A battered collegiate seal, with an image of saint Michael, survived in 1826. A vicar at Cliffe, John of Arundel, was first recorded in 1320, but the square plan of the small chancel there suggests the church dated back to the 12th century. An Early English lancet window survives at the west end of the north aisle. Sometime after 1172 the building was dedicated, naturally enough, to Thomas the Martyr.[60]

Perhaps as part of a wider, national, reform, with an eye to discipline, worship and finance, archbishop Theobald about 1150 reshaped the community at Malling as a college of canons regular, obeying a tight common Rule, with himself as their nominal head. Maybe too his reform fixed the establishment as a dean, three resident canons, a penitentiary and a sacrist. He granted, or confirmed, to the canons certain tithes and pannage rights, and 'consecrated and dedicated' their church of saint

4.5 St Thomas at Cliffe: ground-plan

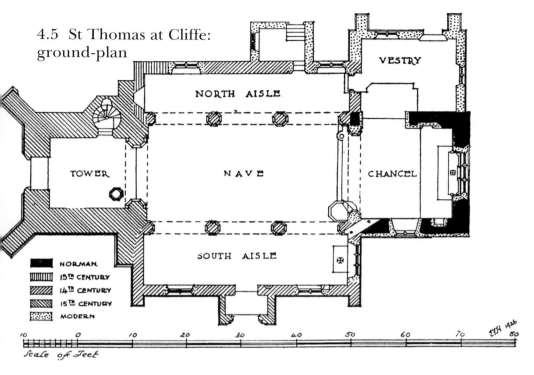

VESTRY

NORTH AISLE

TOWER

NAVE

CHANCEL

SOUTH AISLE

- ■ NORMAN
- ▥ 13ᵀᴴ CENTURY
- ▨ 14ᵀᴴ CENTURY
- ▧ 15ᵀᴴ CENTURY
- ░ MODERN

ETH 1926

Scale of Feet

Michael - as he did the priory church of saint Pancras in 1147. A 'fair' collegiate church, demolished in the 1550s, was remembered in John Norden's day. On its site in the 1620s a parish church was built, which William Figg's map of 1824 shows occupying the vanished chancel of a once cruciform structure. The parish church retains two stiff-leaf capitals and a tower arch of 14th century date.[61]

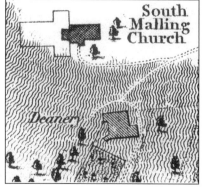

44 The once cruciform structure

The bishops of Chichester also progressed through Sussex - William of Malmesbury spoke of Luffa (1091-1123) touring the diocese three times a year to preach. In 1086 the bishop held estates at Bishopstone, Henfield and Preston near Brighton; in Lewes Borough three burgesses were linked with Henfield, three 'closes' with Preston. By 1329 all episcopal tenants in the Borough, it seems, owed suit to Bishopstone manor. They mostly lived near All Saints, a church probably founded by a Saxon bishop of Selsey. (Map 2.2). Its possession by bishop Hilary was confirmed by pope Eugenius III in 1148.[62]

By Hilary's reign - if not earlier - the bishop had delegated to an archdeacon 'of Lewes' a jurisdiction in the diocese east of the river Adur similar to that enjoyed by the dean of Malling in his Peculiar. The archdeacon presided over a 'spiritual' court and inspected the clergy and laity. About 1225 he and two deputies, the deans of Lewes and Selmeston, appointed a priest - pro tem - to the benefice at Ripe, while the prior of Lewes and William Malfed disputed the right of patronage in a royal court. In a 'Chapter' held at Lewes in 1246 parishioners from Old Shoreham accepted his ruling that they should pay five shillings a year to Sele priory. Archdeacons, though, might also serve as royal judges or diplomats. Eustace crossed the Channel in 1226, entrusted with 500 marks for the count of Poitiers. Robert Passelewe was a specialist in forest law. Henry III gave him a set of 'gold-wrought' vestments and promoted him, after a brief spell as archdeacon of Lewes, to the bishopric of Chichester in April 1244. But archbishop Boniface, and pope Innocent IV, set him aside in favour of Richard of Droitwich, a canon lawyer and ex-chancellor of Oxford university, who was denied access to Chichester and its revenues by a furious king till 1246.[63]

Once in office, Richard proved a fearsome champion of the local Church Militant. When a posse of Lewesians dragged out and hanged a thief who took sanctuary in a church, the bishop made them carry the putrefying corpse back to it for burial. He made a local knight, who imprisoned a priest, carry on his shoulders into Lewes market-place - 'like a beast of burden bearing its yoke' - the heavy wooden stocks used to fetter the sacerdotal feet. In more genial mood Richard blessed the nets that fishermen were fruitlessly casting from Lewes bridge; whereupon they caught four fine mullet - sea-fish not usually found upstream. These they gave at his request to the nearby Franciscans. Doubtless Lewesians listened intently when he toured Sussex preaching a crusade to avenge the army of saint Louis lately engulfed in Egypt. Soon after, he died at Dover, in April 1253. And doubtless they gazed at his corpse, 'dressed in his robes and placed in a casket', while it was borne slowly back to his cathedral, amid tolling bells, lamentation and tearful psalms. Richard was duly canonized in 1262. Beforehand, Isabella, the widowed countess of Arundel, earl Warenne's sister, encouraged a Dominican friar at Chichester, Ralph Bocking, to compile a *Life*. This included a 'miracle' witnessed at Lewes castle while Isabella was there with her half-brother Hugh Bigod, the Justiciar of England. His son fell gravely ill and everyone in the castle despaired of his life, save Joanna, a resourceful girl of noble family. Recollecting his baptism by the deceased bishop, she measured the boy with a length of lint and prayed that Richard in Heaven would entreat the Blessed Virgin to heal him. The boy instantly recovered, and a candle, the length of the lint, was sent to light Richard's grave at Chichester.[64]

As for the parish churches in Lewes borough, little impressive

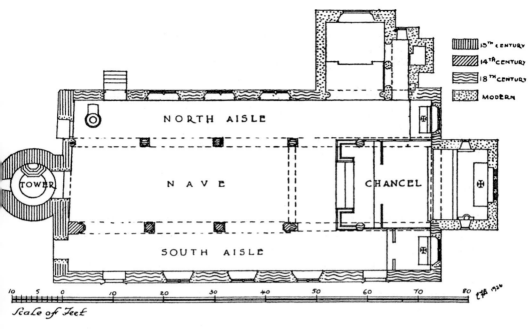

15ᵀᴴ CENTURY
14ᵀᴴ CENTURY
18ᵀᴴ CENTURY
MODERN

NORTH AISLE

NAVE

CHANCEL

TOWER

SOUTH AISLE

Scale of Feet

4.6 St Michael's church: ground-plan

Romanesque or Early English fabric survives. At All Saints only a late 15th-century west tower escaped the rebuilding in 1806. At St Michael's, a mother-church whose patron was Christ Church priory Canterbury, a 13th-century west wall and round west tower remain. From St John's, a mother-church pulled down in 1839, only an 'Anglo-Norman' portal and an arch bearing the Magnus inscription are left. Substantial grave slabs, unearthed there in 1779, were carved perhaps for rectors with incomes

45 St John's: grave slabs

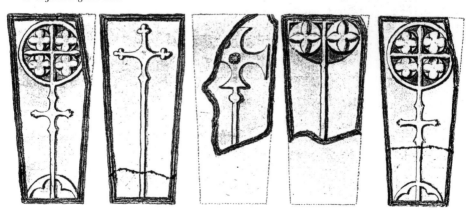

swollen by burial fees. Maybe, in the later 13th century, two short 'transepts' were built, north and south of the west tower - though possibly they were a re-building of earlier, perhaps Saxon, work. Southover priory was patron of St John's and of the seven daughter-churches in the Borough, apart from Holy Sepulchre which maybe the Knights Templars owned. The locations of Holy Sepulchre, Holy Trinity, St Martin's and St Andrew's are all uncertain, and though 'the Broken church' was described in 1592 as 'the church of St Nicholas, decayed and ruined', John Rowe seemed to imply it was formerly the bell tower of St Peter the Less. St Mary in the Market perhaps stood on the site of 49 High Street, for in 1778 a house there retained a stone door and a window with two lights, 'apparently of the 13th century'.[65]

46 Possibly the remains of St Mary in the Market, depicted in 1776

Southover priory was also patron of St Peter Westout and St Mary Westout. From the former only a few displaced stones, possibly 'Norman', survive. However St Mary's - now St Anne's - incorporates a post-Conquest building remarkably assured and generous in scale. The west tower, the nave and south transept date from the early 12th century. But the doorway of the nave was probably composed from Norman fragments in 1775 by Robert Austen, a rector with a taste for Antiquities. The south aisle and the 'wonderful' nave arcade, with its stiff-leaf capitals and sprays, were in situ by 1200, also the quadripartite rib-vault of the

4.7 St Mary Westout: ground-plan

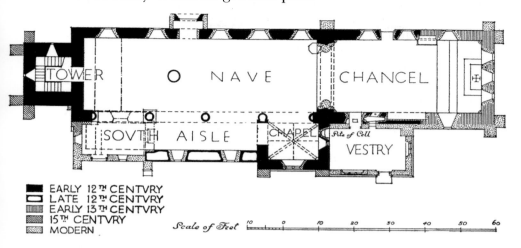

TOWER

○ N A V E

CHANCEL

SOVTH AISLE

CHAPEL *Site of Cell*

VESTRY

- ■ EARLY 12ᵀᴴ CENTVRY
- ▢ LATE 12ᵀᴴ CENTVRY
- ▦ EARLY 13ᵀᴴ CENTVRY
- ▨ 15ᵀᴴ CENTVRY
- ▩ MODERN

Scale of Feet 10 0 10 20 30 40 50 60

47 St Mary Westout: stiff-leaf capital and font

transept, and the drum-shaped font with its robust basket-weave decoration. The chancel was re-built in the 13th century, though not vaulted as first intended.[66]

But how came the church to be so lavish and so eccentrically placed? Its parish, it seems, was a mere enclave within St Peter's, and only the east end of the chancel lay within the Borough boundary in 1624. Suggestive perhaps was a tangle over the church's dedication. In 1537 it was spoken of as 'saint Anne's', though its patron was the Blessed Virgin Mary, believed to be her daughter. In 1588 the ambiguity was blamed on an 'image' or 'idol' of Anne, which till the late 1530s had attracted adoration and 'offering'. As for her cult, she was much venerated as a patron of healing wells, especially after the capture of Jerusalem in 1099, for a house there, thought to have been hers, stood near the sheep-pool of Bethesda, whose waters were credited in saint John's gospel with healing powers. Wells dedicated to her, at Caversham and Chertsey, Malvern and Buxton, were suppressed in 1538. And in 1540 Julian Chaloner, the rector of St Mary's, had recently vacated a garden in 'Westout' *cum fonto aquatico*, 'with a well of water'. If parson Chaloner was the final custodian of a healing well, a predecessor perhaps was Henry, a rector of Balcombe, a living in the priory's gift, who surrendered back to it about 1240 a property called 'Esdewalle' in St Mary Westout. And it could be that 'offering' at her well funded the building near by of St Mary's and that her image stood in the vaulted south transept.

As for the well's location, the Cluniacs owned a field near St Mary's, known in 1712 as Wellcroft, a strip of land south of the Wallands, now bounded by Western Road, De Montfort Road and Ireland's Lane. In 1533-4 they repaired 'le damme versus le Walends', which presumably penned water somewhere in Wellcroft. In 1624 an alias of Ireland's Lane was 'Buckettwin', 'the way by the bucket'. All this suggests the presence of a healing 'well' close to St Mary's, perhaps opposite the church, near the present public toilets. a change of use which Pugin might have deplored in his *Contrasts*. Complaint was made in 1639 that what is now Western Road was 'in decay', 'for want of taking in the water' from adjacent land. A powerful spring could also help explain the proximity of the early-Norman leper hospital. Moreover, surviving maybe from a wellhead and conduit, are a mid-Gothic corbel fashioned as the face of a smiling woman, now in Anne of Cleves museum, and three blocks of Quarr

48 The smiling woman

stone, late-Norman in date, with a hole pierced through their centre, which were found about 1990 built into a barn within the former Wellcroft, opposite the church.[67] All Saints church, of course, was sited near the 'perennial' Pinwell spring, and maybe the Cluniacs oversaw it, for in the 1530s they owned 'Pinwell', a house and garden bounding the churchyard on the west - its rent probably accrued to their refectorer.[68]

Also at St Mary Westout, a narrow 'cell' was discovered in the 1920s, in the right-angle formed by the south transept and the chancel, now the site of the vestry. Below the floor were the remains of a woman, 'past middle age' - quite possibly the anchoress, 'the female recluse of the Blessed Mary at Westout', bequeathed five shillings by bishop Richard in 1253. Revealed too was a squint with a view of the high altar, its sandstone cill worn down, presumably by arms and hands composed for prayer; also a well-worn seat below a small hatch - its iron door-pins in place - opening into the transept.[69]

An immured anchoress, a canonized bishop Richard, a compassionate archbishop Pecham, zealous Franciscans preaching the Word, even Cluniacs struggling with corporate finance, reveal a society still robustly Catholic, just as the pomp and martial exploits of the seventh earl Warenne and his companion, king Edward, show it still securely seigneurial. But Worship and High Politics were themselves sustained for over two centuries after the Conquest by a vigorous English economy, and the contribution to this of folk at Lewes Borough, the Cliffe and Southover must be examined.

49 The Kingston capital

Overleaf: an aquamanile

5

A market and port serving mid Sussex 1066-1300

I Hugh de Fokyntun have given to God and Blessed Mary and the church of St Pancras at Lewes and the monks for the welfare of my soul and of my ancestors and successors a plot of my land in Bevenden [near Falmer] lying beside my well on the south, containing 4 perches in length and 2 in breadth; to hold in free alms, with free entrance and egress and with the easement of drawing water in my well. Cluniacs facilitating their sheep farming in the South Downs (about 1230).

In the year 1273 on Sunday after the feast of the Translation of St Thomas the martyr, it was agreed between Brother Miles, Prior of Lewes, and the Convent of the same place ... and Ralph Bruneman ... that the Prior and Convent granted, demised and gave to farm to Ralph for his life all their land which they had in demesne at la Stone with the woods meadows and pastures pertaining , to have and to hold as aforesaid for 26s. payable at Imberhorne. Provided that Ralph shall at his own cost marl all the land there not already marled, within five years of the commencement of this agreement. Cluniacs improving their soil in the Weald.

For every cart load of corn ... every horse and mare, ox or cow ... every hide of a horse and mare, ox or cow, fresh, salt or tanned ... ten sheep or hogs ... ten fleeces ... for every cart load of sea fish ... of brushwood ... of hay ... of salt ... of cloths ... for every cask of wine and potash ... of honey ... for every sack of wool ... for every cart load of iron ... of lead ... of tin ... for every tumbrel of squirrels ... for two thousand of onions ... of herrings ... for every load of garlic ... for every load of planks ... for every mill-stone ... for every dozen of cordovans. Commodities marketed at Lewes in 1266.

Inevitably the Norman Conquest disrupted the economy of mid-Sussex. Saxon landowners were dispossessed; the value of many estates fell, selectively ravaged perhaps by Norman troops; possibly the Cliffe was set ablaze. At Lewes Borough no moneyers made the first pennies issued by the Conqueror; commercial space was cleared for a castle - in a similar exercise at Lincoln 166 tenements perished; and the burgesses lost land at Cranedown formerly held 'in common'. Domesday

Book, however, shows that in the nearby Borough of Pevensey economic activity soon exceeded pre-Conquest levels: 52 burgesses resided in 1065, 27 when the count of Mortain acquired it, and 110 in 1086; moreover, revenue from tolls there rose four-fold. Pevensey, of course, was the focus of a newly established rape, with a rehabilitated fortress and harbour. Yet Domesday Book also suggests an increase of roughly a third in the fiscal value of Lewes Borough - in king Edward's time it had 'rendered' £6 4s 1½ d from rents and tolls, and was 'worth' £26; by 1086 it rendered 38 shillings more, and was worth £34.[1]

Also a sign of renewal was the swift resurrection of its mint. Early in 1066 king Harold's Pax penny was struck at Chichester, Lewes, Hastings and Steyning; but the Conqueror's first penny, issued before January 1067, only at Hastings and Chichester. Soon after, however, Saxon moneyers, like Winraed, Oswold and Aelfric, were again working in Lewes, and so in the mid-1090s were Winraed, Brihtmaer and Aelfwine. Thereafter, though, royal management of the coinage degenerated and the productivity of mints ceases to be a useful guide to local trading vitality. At Lewes only Edmund is recorded till about 1133 when Edmund, Brihtmaer and Aelfric, Oswold and Winraed, Herrevi and Osbern, struck a penny for Henry I. In the mid 1140s Herrevi, Osbern, Aelmar and Hunfrei were active. Hunfrei minted Stephen's 'Awbridge' penny, and two unnamed moneyers the 'Tealby' penny for Henry II about 1170. Subsequently the only Sussex mint to operate was at Chichester under king John - two farthings of his, found in Lewes, were struck in London and Ipswich. Mints had opened at Pevensey in 1077, at Rye in 1135, at Bramber in 1150, doubtless promoted by their rapal overlords and usually with one moneyer only. At Hastings nearly all the pennies struck between 1068 and about 1130 bore the name Dunninc. These four mints ceased production in the 1150s.[2]

Presumably the commerce of Lewes borough quickened as its seigneurs, the Warennes, grew steadily wealthier. To the lands granted by the Conqueror and William Rufus were added the boroughs of Grantham and Stamford, 'rebel' property in London, and terrain in north Wales. Their visits to Lewes borough, of course, were intermittent. The provenance of pottery discarded by their household reveals it journeying resolutely from castle to castle - some found at the keep at Lewes was made in London or near it; some came from a kiln at St Neots which also supplied Castle Acre in Norfolk; pots fired in west Sussex were broken at Sandal castle in Yorkshire. Provisioning the earls, their knights, esquires and pages, chaplains, officials, soldiers, musicians and menials, also mobilized local resources. More demanding still were royal visitors: in 1299 the immense entourage of Edward I included a butler, a marshal, an almoner, keepers of hawks and foxhounds, clerks to supervise scullions and farriers and poultry, a chandler, a barber, a fisherman, a letter-carrier, a saucemaker.[3]

Though the domestic range in the castle bailey remains unexcavated, the keep has yielded such traces of seigneurial high-life as a brooch, a pin and several buckles, made from copper alloy and sometimes silvered. Animal bones discarded there also suggest an up-market diet. Mutton was plentiful in a Southdown citadel. Even the mendicant Franciscans at Lewes ate more mutton than beef,

50 A buckle

unlike those at Oxford, Leicester and London; sheep bones predominated too in the refuse pits of 'the shifting Saxo-Norman suburb' at North Street. However in the keep the bones of pig far exceeded those of cow and poultry, rabbit and deer, and pig was decidedly a seigneurial delicacy - in 1326 packhorses carried dead hogs to Pevensey castle from Plumpton and Battle; in 1343 eight boars were 'sought out' near Lewes and their pickled heads sent to the royal larderer at Westminster Palace.[4] Rabbits, of course, were introduced into England late in the 12th century as a seigneurial delicacy. Indeed the seventh earl employed a 'warrener' and four assistants based at Lewes. One warren maybe was at the north end of Landport laines, where in 1618 John Deward sketched a low grassed mound, some 250 feet long, in an east-sloping field called 'Connycroft'. (Map 2.6) Being bounded by farm buildings, sheep pasture and water meadow, it was desirably isolated from the arable laines, for seigneurial rabbits near Ovingdean, so it was said, once 'annihilated' a hundred acres of crops. (There is still a similarly sited Warren Field next to Hamsey Place farm). In 1618 a second 'Connycroft', south-facing and also part of Houndean manor, sloped down from Rotten Row to the Winterbourne stream.[5]

51 Landport warren

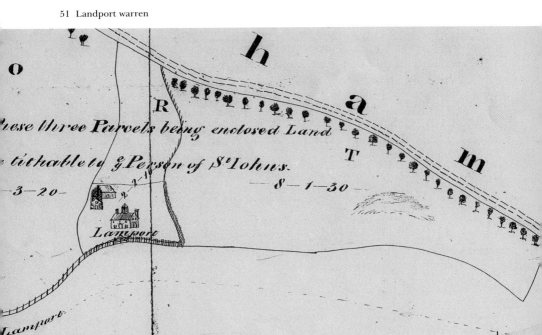

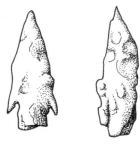

52 The arrowheads

In the 1140s the Cluniacs had leave from earl Warenne to take venison 'within the park, or without', for the benefit of sick monks. In the keep at Lewes castle barbed arrow heads have been found, of the kind used for hunting. A deer park lay close to the rapal castles at Bramber, Arundel and Hastings, and maybe one also occupied the ninety or so acres in the Wallands combe, which by 1615 were arable laines within the demesne of Houndean manor. (Map 2.6) Defined as 'Wallandes', they were leased out separately from the demesne farms of Landport and Houndean. If they began as a park, sheltering perhaps a hundred fallow deer - a park given up perhaps after 1361 by absentee Fitzalans - this might explain why no grazing rights on the manorial sheep runs were linked to them in the 1615 survey. Their status, moreover, was to puzzle the Court of Chancery in 1896. A deer park needed a pale, a kind of 'wall', and Dunvan noted 'traces of an extensive encampment' on the 'wall-lands' - built, he believed, by Danes blockading the burh. Perhaps seigneurial horses also grazed there, and at 'Horsecroft', a part of Houndean manor lying south of Rotten Row, between Coneycroft and Antioch Street. In 1304 the main stud farm of the earls was at Ditchling. When Edward, Prince of Wales, bought the horses there from the seventh earl's executors, he kept on the trainer, John of Ditchling, as Master of his Colts. Also the site of a capacious deer park, Ditchling probably served the Warennes as a 'retreat' from seigneurial duties at Lewes, much as Laughton and Crowhurst did the lords of Pevensey and Hastings rapes.[6]

Salmon and trout were also eaten in the castle keep, as were pond-bred carp and bream. An upsurge in nocturnal theft from the seventh earl's ponds, fisheries and swanneries at Lewes and Iford, Rodmell and Piddinghoe in the 1290s was attributed to his absence in Wales and Scotland. Already in the 1140s the third earl's 'keeper of the water at Lewes' was overseeing the Cluniacs privileged to catch fish for their 'great feasts', 'great guests' and 'sick brethren'. A royal command, in June 1305, required the seigneurial 'gardens and copses about the stew-ponds' at Lewes to be repaired with 'green turves and other materials', and the fish replenished if need be. This shady pleasaunce was perhaps located at the eastern end of the Wallands combe, into which water from the Ouse could be diverted - the site of Allcroft's Saxon 'harbour'. In 1594 it was a six-acre copyhold called 'Earlesgarden', presumably the demesne 'garden called Earlesgardyne' leased out in 1457-8, and abandoned perhaps as a pleasaunce once the absentee Fitzalans inherited in 1361. (Map 2.6) About 1770 Henry Shelley planted osiers and fruit trees there, and maybe revived some silted stewponds when he dug a 'canal' to store fish in. The Cluniacs had a swannery near by, 'under' [on the north side of] St John's church - possibly at 'the common spring', later the Horse Pond.[7]

Quite apart from the intermittent presence of the Warenne household, the three-weekly session of the earls' rapal court attracted business to the town. The Warennes, moreover, sponsored a prestigious priory at Southover, where Cluniacs expended a massive revenue drawn from lands, tithes and churches in several counties. By 1240 perhaps a hundred monks were spaciously housed. Their altars and relics also attracted tourists and pilgrims, often with money to spend, as well as the parishioners from the deaneries of Lewes and Pevensey who processed to 'Lewes' each Whitsun - a by-product, presumably, being the great 'Pentecost' fair held in the Borough on Whitsun Tuesday. Other clerics too stimulated local trade - the canons at Malling, the visiting archbishops, bishops and archdeacons. Even the Franciscans, humbly settled by the bridge, drew crowds to their sermons. Among the hearers were peasants from the South Downs and the Weald, who increasingly came to markets in Lewes borough to sell produce, securing thereby the cash to pay their rents.

Until the loss of Normandy in 1203 regnal and seigneurial ties between England and the duchy reinforced the strategic role of castles and harbours in Sussex which controlled communications between London and Rouen. The Gough map, drawn about 1340, shows the castles linked by a highway from Southampton to Winchelsea, through Havant, Chichester, Arundel, Bramber, Lewes, Boreham Bridge and Battle; a branch road, described as 'old' in 1252, followed Roman alignments through Glynde and Stone Cross to Pevensey. More difficult - thanks to the irredeemable decay of another Roman road - were overland links between Lewes and London through the 'bottomless' clays of the Low Weald and the bleak sandstone uplands of Ashdown Forest. After acquiring Reigate the Warennes perhaps promoted a highway to the west of the Forest, down which maybe Montfort's army marched to Fletching in 1264. A road to the east of the Forest, through Uckfield and Tonbridge, skirted a tenement near Isfield about 1170, and passed the palaces of the archbishops at Malling and Mayfield. Doubtless the planting of East Grinstead as a 'new town' in the mid 13th century encouraged a direct route to London across the Forest, through Wych Cross, Felbridge and Godstone. The perils of road travel were such that in 1299 the king's Master Foxhunter hired 17 guides when Edward I journeyed from Dover to Chichester and then to Canterbury.[8]

Harbours, of course, had commercial as well as strategic value, and doubtless hopes of revenue from harbour tolls also prompted the first Norman overlords to promote cross-Channel commerce with their native duchy. By 1086 Pevensey was a busy port. Exploiting the river Adur, the Braoses developed a harbour at Bramber, and then at New Shoreham. And quite possibly by 1086 there was a 'broad hard' for beaching ships on the Lewes bank of the Ouse, south of the Cliffe crossing - later buried by rubbish and river sediment. A wooden bridge at the crossing was repaired in 1160 and probably by then, between the bridge and Cliffe Corner, the chalk blocks and rubble had been dumped into the flood plain which still underpin Cliffe High Street. (Map 5.4) The nature of earlier settlement at Cliffe, though, is obscure. The upper layers of compacted chalk, north of the church, have yielded sherds of 13th-century green lead-glazed pottery, but lower layers were too water-logged to excavate. The church's oldest feature is a blocked Early English window, though the plan of the small square chancel may date from the 12th cen-

53 The Romanesque arch

tury - likewise a fragment of a carved figure found in the fabric. However, three stones decorated with 'volute-like' ornament, built into 1 Malling Street, and an arch adorned with chevron moulding, sketched at the *Swan* in 1774, could be debris from Malling College or the palace at Old Malling.[9]

Whether the first Warenne was involved with Cliffe hinges on an enigmatic entry in Domesday Book. Under 'Lewes' it divulges that in 1086 he held '39 inhabited messuages and twenty uninhabited' in Pevensey rape. If these were in Cliffe, had the 'uninhabited' houses been devastated in 1066 to help terrorize the burh, or were they new, as yet unoccupied, tenements, in a suburb being expanded by Warenne to tap sea-borne commerce? Either way, how was it that Cliffe belonged to him in 1086? Had it been wrenched from the archbishop's manor of South Malling because of its strategic value as a bridgehead - only to be reunited with that manor before the 1280s?[10]

Probably, till at least the early 13th century, the estuary of the Ouse up to Lewes was plied by sea-going merchant ships. The burh had paid a 'ship-tax' under Edward the Confessor. The 11 saltpans at Rodmell, and the 38,500 herrings 'rendered' each year at Southease, suggest the river was tidal in 1086. Moreover, about 1167, and again in 1207, timber cut in the Weald by royal command was delivered to 'Lewes' for shipment downstream. Nonetheless Seaford, at the mouth of the Ouse, had achieved Cinque Port status as a 'limb' of Hastings by 1229 - its mariners enjoying privileged access to North Sea fishing grounds and to the fish fair at Yarmouth. How soon, and how fully, sea-borne traffic at Lewes was diverted to this upstart out-port depended presumably on the progress of silting along the estuary which rendered navigation ever more tortuous. Seaford probably began as a joint initiative by the overlords of Lewes and Pevensey rapes, to quicken sailings to Normandy and generate revenue. In the 1140s earl Warenne granted market privileges 'at Saford' to Southover priory and in 1275 his bailiffs allegedly orchestrated there the illicit export of local wool. In 1348 a market held on Warenne 'soil' sold corn, another on Pevensey 'soil' fish and bread. In 1563 the premises held from the 'Pevensey' lordship were clustered between the church and quay near the courthouse. That the out-port was in being by the 1080s would accord with the character of its Romanesque parish church - St Leonard's was a severe, aisleless, cruciform structure, like those built at Westham and Bramber in or before that decade. Moreover, in Domesday Book, wedged between entries for Lewes and Iford, is the comment, 'In the rape of Pevensey William of Warenne has 12 messuages, 7 inhabited and 5 not. [They belong] to Laughton, a manor of the count of Mortain'. If an-outport then under construction, Seaford might indeed have been linked with Laughton, the 'country retreat' of the count of Mortain.[11]

The outreach of sea-borne commerce at Lewes is revealed by the provenance of the stone and 'marble', the slate and tiles, used to build the priory and the castle. In Lanzo's time malmstone was brought from beds of upper-Greensand - perhaps from the coastal quarry at Eastbourne, the source of facing for the Roman fortress at Pevensey; and a limestone, briefly fashionable in south-eastern England, was shipped from Quarr on the Isle of Wight. A fragment found in the first 'stone' church came perhaps from earl Warenne's 'white marble' tomb-slab. For Battle abbey the Conqueror ordered Norman limestone quarried east of Caen near the river Orne. Fine-grained and coloured yellow, with a crystalline sparkle, 'Caen' made a splendid ashlar. It was used about 1100 at Lewes castle for the entrance to the bailey gatehouse, along with flints laid herringbone fashion, and extremely lavishly at the priory in the 12th century and after. The Cluniacs imported a cargo through Seaford in 1225 and 42 blocks were bought to repair Pevensey castle in 1288-9.[12] A fashion in the later 12th century for 'colour' also caused the Cluniacs to import 'marble', from Tournai in Flanders, from the Isle of Purbeck in Dorset and indeed from the Weald, 'Sussex marble' being mined at Laughton and elsewhere. Some masons' marks from the priory survive: a fish, a five-pointed star, two triangles joined at the apex (similar to one at Canterbury cathedral) and a capital 'A', possibly carved by Alwin, a 'cementarius' who witnessed priory deeds about 1150.[13]

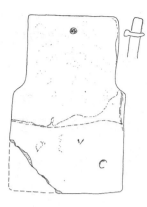

54 The shouldered tile

Progressive roofing techniques were also employed for the Cluniacs. Of high-quality, and used maybe for the 11th-century dormitory, was a 'shouldered' type of ceramic tile; fine-sanded and fairly hard fired, it overlapped two-thirds of the tile below and its bottom third was glazed green to brown. Three tiles thick and secured with iron nails, the roof was bedded in mortar to stop the wind rattling it. The kilns perhaps were at Ringmer, a likely source too for the thin peg-tiles which covered, quite possibly, the late 12th-century latrine-block, where slates from the West Country made an early appearance. Quarried in south Devon, especially along the Kingsbridge estuary, they proved popular in the South-East, being used at Eltham palace and Colchester castle, at Lewes castle, the friary and Old Malling palace, and higher up the basin of the Ouse, at Laughton Place and Hamsey Place, Wapsbourne and Buxted Old Place. Mostly grey, though sometimes lilac or green, they silvered after rain - indeed in 12th-century Caen their equivalents 'shone like marble'. More prosaically, some roofs at the castle and the friary were mended with oyster shells. Remnants survive too of 'Sussex' chimneys, with a main vent at the top and apertures at the side - a green-glazed louver from the friary being exuberantly pierced with circular holes and rectangular openings.[14]

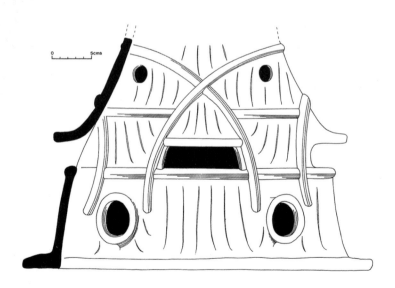

55 The green-glazed louver

About 1265 the Cluniacs repaved the nave and north transept of their enlarged 'stone' church. At first they used glazed 'Wessex' tiles, perhaps made in Hampshire, some fashionably decorated with patterns picked out in white clay. A thinner cheaper sort were laid at the friary. But soon after, perhaps because of a cash shortage, the Cluniacs themselves bought some inferior tiles to finish the job. They were ill made, with stock Gothic motifs feebly designed - stags leap stiffly and disjointed peacocks confront a potted lily. Two of the motifs - a stylized fish within a pointed oval and an encircled rosette with eight petals, also occur on tiles found at the friary and the castle keep. If made at Ringmer, the white clay used was drawn perhaps from the Fairlight Beds.[15]

Alongside stone and 'marble', slate and tile, shipped from a distance, Wealden sandstone was used for door jambs and window tracery, Southdown flints for external walls, and blocks cut from the Lower Chalk, and water-rolled pebbles gathered on the beach, for footings and internal work. Thirty-five chalk blocks, each incised with a Roman numeral to guide the mason, formed three courses of a wall, probably medieval in date, found at a site near Eastgate Corner. And on a chalk cylinder, unearthed at the friary, are what seem to be two overlapping representations of a gable wall. By the late 13th century there were 'limepits' at Southover End and at Cliffe where Robert Lymbernere, and Thomas 'his fellow', rented a kiln 'under the cliff'. (Maps 5.2 and 5.4) Many oak saplings from the Weald were felled to underpin the Cluniacs' second latrine-block, but sparingly used, perhaps for coffin wood, was pine timber derived from the Baltic.[16]

56 The inferior tiles

Generally in the 12th and 13th centuries the cost of seigneurial and ecclesiastical building was sustained by buoyant revenues extracted from an expanding economy. In Sussex agriculture along the South Downs and the coastal plain grew ever more intensive. By 1100 peasant farmers were already sowing nitrogenous legumes which restored fertility to the soil: they sent three measures of peas each year from Southease to Hyde abbey at Winchester, and 36 loads of beans from Pagham to Southover priory. Crops of wheat and barley filled the great aisled barn built by Battle abbey at Alciston. Surplus grain was shipped away to victual Plantagenet armies. When Henry II launched his Irish expedition in 1171, Sussex sent wheat, and handmills to grind it. Over 600 bushels were carried by packhorse to Shoreham from the archbishop's farm at Stoneham by Malling, to supply Edward II's troops gathered at Newcastle in 1319. Seaford was also a focus for corn exports. In 1260-1 the townsfolk complained that earl Warenne's agents had raised fourfold a levy on 'grain-bins' shipped from their harbour.[17]

As for a grain trade at Lewes, the presence at Southover in 1121 of 'two ponds and three water mills' owned by the Cluniacs suggests that the corn market in the Borough was already thriving. Another, rather suspect, charter stated that by then they also possessed 'two tenants-at-will beside the mill at Lewes and beside them a meadow'. At some date they did acquire a 'meadow', later called Well Croft and located close to 'Sknellyngs mill'. Mentioned in 1343, and leased by Richard Audeley in 1535 and by John Inkersoll in 1587, the mill was quite possibly where Richard King of the Romans received his come-uppance in 1264. But a windmill at work in 1121 would have been remarkably early.[18]

There was certainly an increasing trade in fleeces shorn from short-woolled Southdown sheep. An agile breed, they readily scrambled from thyme-scented pastures on the ridge down to wattle pen-folds on the stubble below, where they deposited invaluable dung. By 1340 many thousands grazed the 26 miles of downland between the river Adur and Beachy Head, and indeed, about 1402, the burgesses of Lewes very plausibly claimed that most wool in Sussex was 'grown' within ten leagues (15 miles) of their town. Doubtless the keen interest shown by bishop Ralph Nevill (1222-37) in his flocks at Bishopstone and Preston was shared by the Warennes who could exploit immense demesne sheepwalks. Complaint was made in 1275 that their bailiffs orchestrated the illicit export of wool from Seaford. In 1310 the clip from the Beddingham estate of Sir William Etchingham - who could opt to be bled by the Cluniacs - was sold to Roger of Ely, elected an MP for Seaford in 1322. By then the value of Southdown wool - though only middling in quality - had been increased by demand from weavers in the Netherlands and northern France.[19]

At Southover at least one dead Cluniac was shrouded in layers of cloth skilfully woven from high-quality fleeces, quite probably 'grown' on one of many Southdown estates enterprisingly amassed by the monks. The first grants by Warenne were perhaps the arable fields and sheep runs noted on tithe maps in the 1840s as formerly owned by them and tithe-free - 542 acres at Swanborough farm, 1616 acres at Falmer Court farm and 553 acres at Withdean farm. Adjacent land was acquired, probably before the 1130s - at Kingston and Iford, at Moulscombe, Hodshrove and Patchway, Balmer and Housedean, and at Withdean. Large flocks were doubtless kept on demesne land there, for in 1535 it was estimated that 400 sheep could graze at Swanborough, 2600 at Falmer, 700 at Withdean. About 1175 earl Hamelin granted land at Balsdean near Swanborough, and at Ovingdean, near St Wulfram's church - estates with pasture for 600 and 800 sheep in the early 16th century. Hamelin's gifts suggest that the Cluniacs were active sheep ranchers, like bishop Nevill and the Battle Benedictines at Alciston. Presumably, Hugh of Folkington granting their shepherds access to his well at Bevendean, about 1230, allowed more intensive grazing of their nearby sheepwalk on Heath Hill Down in Falmer manor. And a relic maybe of their enterprise are the foundations of two massive timber-framed barns at Falmer Court farm. In 1279 the Cluniacs failed to deliver wool worth a hundred marks to unspecified dealers.[20]

The amount of wool shipped overseas from Sussex, and its destination, can be glimpsed in official returns for 1287-8 and 1289-90 (Easter to Easter). Through Seaford were exported 259 sacks of wool and fleeces, through Chichester 295, through Shoreham 677 - at Seaford 13,690 wool fells were included. Most cargoes from Seaford and Shoreham went to northern France, to Rouen, Fecamp, Abbeville and St Omer, often in freighters based at Cherbourg, Fecamp, Dieppe, Treport and Calais. Of the fifty or so merchants exporting through Seaford between Easter 1286 and Easter 1292, six from Saint Omer and one from Fecamp transacted 13% of the trade. The rest were from Sussex, 17 from Seaford. By contrast at Shoreham 17 merchants from Rouen and Fecamp accounted for 62% of the trade, Richard 'Gwydechun' & Co. of Lucca for 7%, two traders from Sandwich for 19%; the rest was shared by small dealers from Dieppe, Calais and Haarlem, Wales and Dunstable, Bramber and Steyning, Shoreham and Hove. Wool was also shipped to Sandwich for delivery to the Netherlands, the usual terminus for cargoes from Kent. Two Seaford merchants recovered wool confiscated at Sandwich by royal officials, and at Shoreham a vessel of Middelburg (on the isle of Walcheren) loaded 63 sacks for John Brech of Sandwich.

Most of the wool-dealers, identified in these Seaford accounts as 'of Lewes', traded on a small scale. William Bruman, Robert Tympan and Ralph the Palmer shipped fewer than three sacks, so did Martin, convolutedly described as 'from the Cliff of Malling'. Robert Tote, Nicholas Petyt, Robert Mose, Ralph Petit, William Bukele and William 'from Southease of Lewes' dispatched between three and 17 sacks. But the Warren Scot, who sent away 28 sacks, perhaps rented sheep-pasture, for in 1296 a man of that name was taxed in Swanborough Hundred which included Warenne sheep-runs at Houndean and Ashcombe-Smithwick. Moreover, Adam 'of Pyecombe', trading eight sacks, could be the dealer, Adam 'of Smithewyk', taxed in 1327 at Pyecombe and Westout. And William 'of Northease', shipping over a hundred sacks, was also very well-placed to rent demesne pasture, from earl Warenne.[21]

Evidence of cloth making in Lewes borough are the spindle whorls of chalk or mudstone, the bone needles and baked-clay loom weights, excavated there. Though the type of cloth made is uncertain, much wool in Sussex was woven into rather coarse 'kerseys'. The local clothing trade in the later 13th century employed Robert the weaver, William the dyer, Adam the girdler, John the hatter and Robert the wimpler - all witnesses to property transactions at Southover. Lewes became famous for its wimples - a 'Keuerchef of Lewes' being stolen from Margery Chelsham at Ashburnham in 1374. A prosperous tailor, Wulnoth Parmenter, had rented houses in the Borough given to the Cluniacs in the early 12th century.[22]

As well as ventures on the South Downs, the Cluniacs' quest for corn and sheep caused them to assemble an 800-acre estate at Langney, southwest of Pevensey. By 1150 they owned perhaps 300 acres of upland stretching from Stone Cross and Thorne eastwards across Ranging Hill and 'Hothleigh', and southwards for two miles through Friday Street to the shingle beach at Langney point. Near by they held desolate marsh-girt 'Entenie' - now Antony Hill - reminiscent perhaps of the remote fort at Pispir in Upper Egypt where a saint of that name fought off extreme Temptation. Below this upland the monks reclaimed some 500 acres of salt marsh - much as they drained and walled fenland in East Anglia at West Walton, Walpole and Walsoken - helping to transform Pevensey 'level' into a fertile plain crammed with corn and fat livestock, like the Biblical land of Goschen. Richard the Soper, a tenant at Reddyke near Thorne, had to render three bushels of beans each Lent, a sign of good husbandry. Doubtless too, the Cluniacs collaborated with the earls Warenne, the lords of Houndean manor, to reclaim marsh land near the convent and around the Rises.[23]

Draining salt marsh was paralleled by piecemeal clearance of Wealden woodland and scrub which reached almost to the gates of Lewes, and was the former preserve of the 'swineherd, woodcutter, charcoal-burner, honey-gatherer, hunter and hawker'. By the mid 11th century pioneers, many from Southdown manors, were consolidating small farms on more amenable patches of clay and sand. Because yields of grain, mostly oats and wheat, were much lower than at Alciston or Swanborough, Wealdsmen inclined towards livestock farming, though their dairy produce was little regarded - before Edward II visited Robertsbridge the abbot sent for cheeses from Rudham in Norfolk. Nor was their cider outstanding, supplies from Normandy being imported through Winchelsea in the later 13th century. Yet Wealdsmen did use skins from their livestock, and local reserves of timber and clay, iron ore and water power, to develop a variety of crafts. They became quarriers of sandstone and Sussex marble, carpenters, coopers and turners, weavers and dyers, tanners and glove-makers, iron-workers and potters, charcoal-burners and wood-cutters. And in the weeks before their own corn grudgingly ripened, they helped gather in the Southdown harvest.[24]

The Wealden lumber trade is the most easily glimpsed. To build a palace at Winchester and a nunnery at Amesbury, Henry II had timber shipped from 'Lewes' to Southampton. In 1207 king John required local landowners to facilitate the carriage of timber to 'Lewes', possibly for the repair of Dover castle. Beams cut and squared in Maresfield park were used to roof a hall at Pevensey castle in 1302. From Winchelsea 129 foreign merchants transported timber, oak bark and wood fuel to the Netherlands and northern France in 1307-8. As for craftsmen, in South Malling manor about 1285 Peter at Strode of Wadhurst made 300 platters a year 'from three alder trees'; other Wealden tenants fashioned casks, troughs and hurdles. Moreover, eight potters based at Wellingham in Ringmer dug clay from Broyle Common to make tiles and lopped branches from fallen trees to fire their kilns; at Uckfield two freeholders each rented a fulling mill. Previously, Domesday Book had noted a 'forge' near East Grinstead, and by 1300 the power of local iron makers was such that London ironmongers complained of 'the smiths of the Weald'. Iron from northern Spain, though, was unshipped at Winchelsea about 1270.[25]

By 1147 the Southover Cluniacs had been amply endowed with land in this industrious Weald by the Warennes. (Map 5.1 overleaf) The core of their manor of Ditchling Garden - 'a garden and land between two roads with a wood belonging' - survived in 1842 as 147 tithe-free acres at Court Garden farm and included a Muntley [?Monken] wood. Also in the manor were tenements at the East End of Ditchling near the medieval market-place. But this Low Wealden bridge-head was dwarfed by the Cluniac manor of Balneath, which sprawled disconnectedly across several thousand acres and made further Wealden endowment in Lewes rape superfluous. The woods closest to the convent, on the manor's southern fringes at Caveridge, Balneath, Knowland and Great Homewood, were largely left uncleared - the Homewood in 1842 included 327 tithe-free acres. Further north as far as the upper Ouse, the small farms existing in Victoria's reign had first been cleared, quite probably, in the 12th and 13th centuries - Furzley and Furzegrove near Markstakes Common; Bromfield and Homewoodgate near Chailey South Common; and skirting Chailey North Common, Newhouse, Broadstone and Woodcroft, Longridge, Hole and Breens, Townings, Wildfield and Great Noven, Leylands, Leighwood, Teagues and Plumtree. On the North Common, 'in the middle of Sussex', still stands Balneath's windmill. Overspilling into Lindfield parish were Pellingbridge and Little Pellingbridge; Inces and Chapel Land by Hendfield Common; Nash, Wallhouse and Pegden; and most northerly of all, Ham, beside Blackhouse Common near Freshfield bridge. These farms formed an enclave in Lindfield served by a chapel at Pelling; to control it the Cluniacs fought off in the Church courts the canons of Malling.[26]

Surfeited though they were in Lewes rape, the Cluniacs pieced together the immense manor of Imberhorne beyond the upper Ouse, using gifts from the lords of Pevensey rape and their vassal-knights. The

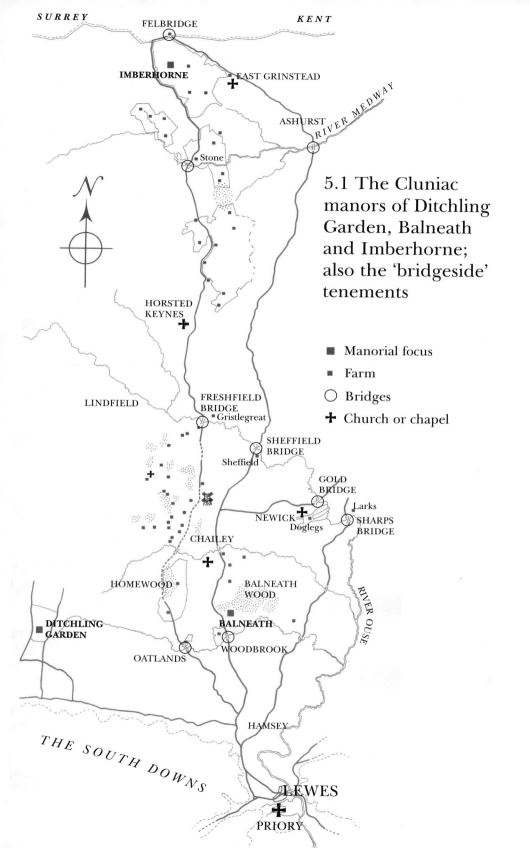

SURREY · KENT

FELBRIDGE

IMBERHORNE

EAST GRINSTEAD

ASHURST

RIVER MEDWAY

N

Stone

HORSTED
KEYNES

LINDFIELD

FRESHFIELD
BRIDGE
Gristlegreat

5.1 The Cluniac
manors of Ditchling
Garden, Balneath
and Imberhorne;
also the 'bridgeside'
tenements

■ Manorial focus

■ Farm

○ Bridges

✝ Church or chapel

SHEFFIELD
BRIDGE
Sheffield

GOLD
BRIDGE
Larks
NEWICK   SHARPS
Doglegs   BRIDGE

CHAILEY

HOMEWOOD

BALNEATH
WOOD

DITCHLING
GARDEN

BALNEATH

OATLANDS   WOODBROOK

RIVER OUSE

HAMSEY

THE SOUTH DOWNS

LEWES

PRIORY

manor formed a discontinuous tract in the High Weald, over seven miles long and about 3000 acres in extent, beginning four miles beyond Freshfield bridge, at Broadhurst just north of Horsted Keynes church, and reaching the Surrey border at Felbridge west of East Grinstead and north of Imberhorne. Its demesne in 1597 encompassed almost 700 acres at Imberhorne and Ridge Hill. In the 1840s its customary farms and small estates, medieval in origin, included, just west of East Grinstead Borough, Chantlers, Newlands and Killicks; further south, along the headwaters of the infant Medway, Brook House, Hill Place and Butlers, Imberley Lodge, Kingscote and Hurley, Fenn Place, Stone and Hollybush (by Philip Webb's Standen), Monkshill and Charlwood; and further south still, beyond Plaw Wood, skirting Ashdown Forest and forming an outlier of West Hoathly parish, Plawhatch Hall, Dallingridge Place and Courtlands, Wickenden, Balcombe and Restlands, Birchgrove, Warren House and Broadhurst.[27]

Maybe the Cluniacs painstakingly assembled Imberhorne manor to restore ties with their Southdown lands, for three hides beyond the upper Ouse had been severed from their Falmer estate and given to the count of Mortain. In 1065 other lands along the infant Medway, near Imberhorne, had been linked with estates near Lewes: Burleigh with Wootton, Hazleden with Allington, Standen with Bevendean, Brambletye with Ashcombe. Certainly the Cluniacs were persistent. Sometime before 1150 they received Imberhorne farm from William Maufe, 'Pliege' (Plawhatch) and 'Buntesgrave' (Birchgrove) from Alvred of Benedeuilla, 'Healdeleya' from William count of Mortain. They exchanged 'the land of Wiresteda and of Lefsi of Haseldena' for 'the woods of Vluehola and la Hamoda'. They acquired the churches of East Grinstead and West Hoathly.[28] The Balneath and Imberhorne lands soon became a source of timber, grain and livestock. 'Healdeleya' in 1106 already rendered to the priory 200 beech boards and forty cart loads of logs. A condition of leasing Stone farm to Ralph Bruneman in 1273 was that he spread marl within five years on any acreage needing to be fertilized - he was also admitted to the Cluniacs' confraternity and promised, in due course, a daily dole of bread and ale at the priory. The Wealden field pattern too was taking an enduring shape - the 18 acres near Imberhorne rented by Warin the Bat in 1258 reappear in 1826 as the pasture east of Brook mill called Battsfield. North of the upper Ouse, moreover, trading local produce was quickened by the market borough which Gilbert of Laigle, lord of Pevensey rape, planted before 1225 at East Grinstead.[29]

Involvement with the transport of Wealden produce might explain the Cluniacs owning, within their Wealden manors, small farms located near strategic bridges along two major roads threading northwards to the Surrey border. (Map 5.1). The eastern road crossed the Bevern stream near 'Woodbrook', the Ouse near 'Sheffield', and the Medway near 'Ashurst Wood', south-east of East Grinstead. After 'Woodbrook', moreover, it crossed the Longford stream near 'Bineham alias the Chapel lands', possibly the 'twenty pennyworths of land' at Binham given by Ralph son of Warin to the priory. The western road, heading at first also towards Lindfield, crossed the Bevern stream near 'Oatlands', the Ouse at Freshfield bridge near 'Gristlegreat', and passed Horsted Keynes church to reach Imberhorne, negotiating the Medway below Stone farm which Ralph Bruneman agreed to marl. The roads united at Felbridge on the Surrey border and continued to Southwark passing near the Cluniacs' churches at Horne and Bletchingley.[30]

Clearly the transport of Wealden produce by road could be onerous. Sixteen pack horses were used to convey the carcasses of 45 Wealden hogs to Seaford for shipment to Dover castle in 1326. So maybe the Cluniacs used some bridge-side farms as depots for water carriage. On the banks of the upper Ouse, as well as 'Gristlegreat' and 'Sheffield', they owned 'Doglegs' near Gold bridge in Newick and 'Larks' at Sharps bridge in Fletching. By 1357 a wharf at the latter was perhaps linked to others at Cliffe and Southover, for John Sharp's 'Bregghous' there had been inherited by his youngest sister, the wife of a John Smith at the Cliffe. Water carriage could explain the use of easily fractured West Country slate to roof farms at Wapsbourne near Sheffield bridge and Buxted Place east of Sharps bridge.[31]

Doubtless, quickening activity in the Weald stimulated commerce at Lewes. Wood and fuel were much in demand along the South Downs and a wood market, subject to seigneurial decree, existed in the Borough by the 1140s. The Cluniacs were granted 'the first choice of logs for making their wood pile on Tuesday, Thursday and Saturday, from Whitsun to Lammas'. Wealden oak for timber-framing was also welcome in a town where the 'stone house' of Nicholas the Butler was an obvious rarity about 1250. Wealden cattle maybe were traded at the Borough fair in Whitsun week, which probably dated back to the Whitsun processions promoted in the 1240s by bishop Richard. Pelts and hides were stripped by the skinners, Edward and Arnold, who lived near the Lortepool in Southover; others perhaps worked at the Pells, the water meadows below St John's. Heavy cattle hides and Wealden oak-bark were used by the tanner, John of Iford, who rented land at Eastport in Southover in 1297, somewhere between the Borough wall and the Winterbourne stream. Curriers used oil and tallow to render tanned leather supple, and one, William by name, lived at Lewes in 1291, next door to a tenement called 'le Flay'. To prepare light leather, tawers treated with alum the skins of sheep, pony, goat and fox. These leathers were supplied to cordwainers, glovers and saddlers in the town. At Battle 'heavy, inelegant' waterproofs, shoe-soles, leggings and gloves had a steady sale.[32]

During the 13th century iron-ore, quite probably from the Weald, was smelted in clay-sealed bloomery-furnaces set up during building work at the castle keep, the friary and Friars Walk, which left charcoal, bloomery slag and vitrified furnace-linings as debris. Discarded too in the keep were iron nails, studs and hooks, staples, braces and hinge-pivots, also superannuated chain mail, used maybe to polish armour, and 48 socketed arrowheads - a reminder that Montfort attacked the castle with burning shafts. Pre-eminent as a worker of Wealden iron, moreover, was Master Henry of Lewes. As the chief smith of Henry III, with the very high wage of three shillings a week, he purchased 406 iron rods 'in the Weald', supervised the making of 50,000 crossbow bolts, and worked at Westminster abbey on the king's exquisite tomb, its slabs of red porphyry being secured by foliated iron clips. Master Henry also cherished his Sussex links; in 1291 he left property at Lewes borough to his daughter Joan, and at Seaford to her sister Margery; smiths at the royal armoury in the Tower of London witnessed his will.[33]

Doubtless Lewes borough was a convenient market for potters at Ringmer who by the 1280s were digging clay on the Broyle. They satisfied a demand for cheap ready-made wares, which extended to Selmeston and down the Ouse to Meeching [Newhaven] and Seaford. Possibly they supplied the coarse handmade pots, jars and pitchers used by the Cluniacs at Southover in the late 11th century, and the wheel-turned wares, fired black or orange, sometimes splashed with glaze and decorated with cream slip-bands, bought a century later. From Ringmer too, or from kilns near Marchants farm at Streat, probably came the coarse sandy wares discarded in the castle keep and the friary about 1300. However, 'wasters' from a kiln reveal that by then superior ceramics were made at Ringmer. They include pieces of jug of a very fine fabric, mostly glazed green or brown, and a spout formed as a ram's head, part perhaps of an aquamanile. A robust anthropomorphic jug, green-glazed with white slip, was used at the friary. More remotely 'Wealden', if fired at Limpsfield in Surrey close to the Lewes-Felbridge-London road, was the late 12th-century near-stoneware pottery found at the priory.

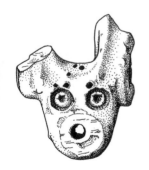

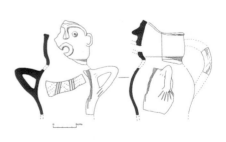

57 The ram's head   58 The anthropomorphic jug

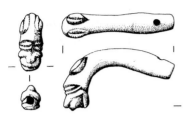

59 The zoomorphic spout

Resolutely zoomorphic by contrast was the grooved face decorating the spout of a copper alloy tap found at the friary, perhaps from a lavatorium near the refectory.[34]

The quickening of its economy caused market-places to be established in the Weald by seigneurs anxious to tax the exchange of goods. Michael of Poynings, so it is said, gave king John 'a good Norway Goshawk' in exchange for a licence to hold a Friday market at Crawley. Other markets emerged at Horsham, East Grinstead, Hailsham, Cuckfield, Ditchling and Uckfield. Nonetheless in the 1250s the market-place at Lewes borough remained the 'navel', the primary focus, of the diocese of Chichester - just the place for a peccant knight to do public penance with a heavy log on his shoulders. These new markets, moreover, were held on weekdays, between Monday and Friday, whereas in 1406, and probably much earlier, the Borough's was kept on a Saturday. As for its location, the church of St Mary-in-the-Market, if it stood at what is now 49 High Street, may have been islanded within it, for in the 16th century the site of 53 High Street encroached forward 38 feet, and so presumably did its neighbours. (Map 2.4)[35]

There are glimpses too of Lewes as an emporium for commodities arriving by sea carriage, though Seaford, it seems, served increasingly as an out-port. Lewesians bought a variety of seafish, mostly cod and mackerel, but also plaice, black sea-bream, conger eel and thornback ray. The skeletons discarded were headless, so maybe fishmongers had sold the fish already smoked or salted; entire skeletons unearthed at Seaford were probably of fish freshly caught. Cod cured at distant Aberdeen were shipped from Shoreham to provision a fleet at Portsmouth in 1294. Lewesians also ate lots of oysters - less prestigious molluscs, such as mussels, whelks and cockles, accounted for under 7% of those consumed in the castle keep.[36] As for salt, though in 1086 much was boiled very locally - 39 of the 300 or more salterns in Sussex lay along the estuary of the Ouse - maybe, later on, some arrived from salt works which the Cluniacs owned by 1121 in the Adur estuary below Bramber castle, and near Langney, where Brihderic was the tenant.[37] Certainly brought by sea was the pottery made at Rye and Winchelsea, used in the Borough by the mid 13th century. And fashioned maybe at Scarborough was an aquamanile in the

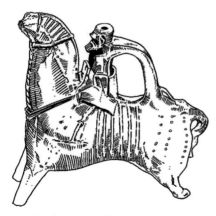

60 The aquamanile

form of a horse and rider, discovered when the railway tunnel was dug west of Watergate Lane. 'Newcastle' coal from Tyneside was also delivered to Sussex ports. A cargo at Seaford was forwarded to Willingdon and burned to make lime for the repair of Pevensey castle about 1289.[38]

Norman overlords at Lewes borough and Burgundian monks at Southover also strengthened a demand for Continental fare. Olive stones and grape seeds were found near a clay skillet discarded in the Cluniac latrine-block used till the late 12th century. Some grapes were home-grown, for by then grants to the priory had included 'two fields beside Saint Pancras and a garden in the vineyard'; in 1533 the larderer grew onions in a 'vine garden'. But local sources had been outstripped by 1279 when the monks owed a hundred marks for wine, perhaps to a vintner called William, resident near their gate in 1291. Doubtless quantities were quaffed at the castle, six tuns being ordered from Seaford before Henry III's visit in 1240, though two were sent on to Cuckfield, perhaps to slake the royal thirst in its deer park. At Seaford a mid 13th-century vaulted undercroft survives as the Crypt Gallery. Similar to cellars at Southampton and Winchelsea used by wholesale wine importers, it has grapes and vine leaves carved on a sandstone roof boss.[39]

The Continental vineyards supplying wines to local importers can be roughly located from the origin of the storage jars used to ship them. Sherds of Normandy white ware and of Pingsdorf and Andenne ware, found at Lewes or Seaford, reveal the popularity of wine from northern France and the Rhineland in the late 11th and 12th centuries. But by the late 13th century, fragments of jars from Normandy, notably from Rouen, are far exceeded by those from the Saintonge region near Bordeaux, reflecting a new reliance on Gascon wines from the duchy of Aquitaine, by then the only 'French' province under English control. About 1258 John le Beure 'of Lewes' invested eighty marks in trade with Gascony and hired a ship at Seaford with a crew of thirteen.[40] As for other Continental luxuries, in the 1330s, and doubtless earlier, raisins, figs and dates were unshipped at Winchelsea by traders from Lisbon and north-west Spain; also unloaded were Irish hose, woollen cloth from Malines and Louvain, linen cloth and canvas from Normandy, masts, pitch, oil and plaster, mirrors and copper cups, onions and garlic. Similar merchandise, presumably, was delivered to Lewes. Certainly employed there were querns made from lava dug at Mayen and Niedermendig in the German Rhineland, also hones fashioned from Norwegian mica-schist - the worn molars of local Cluniacs resulted maybe from particles of grindstone in their bread.[41]

Mill-stones were mentioned when Henry III authorized market tolls to be levied in the Borough, to pay for repairs to the town wall soon after the battle of Lewes. Indeed the commodities listed in 1266 probably reflected local trading well enough - the horses and mares, oxen and cows, sheep and hogs, the fleeces and hides -'fresh, salt or tanned'- the corn and hay, honey and wool, onions and garlic, the brushwood and plank, seafish, salt and potash, the iron, lead and tin, the mill-stones and wine - even the tumbrels of squirrels and the cloths from Cordova.[42]

A growth in freight carriage and sea fishing might explain why the Southover Cluniacs markedly increased their coastal footholds in Rottingdean, Brighton, Portslade and Seaford between 1140 and 1175. Before departing 'to Jerusalem' the third earl Warenne gave them half his lands at Rottingdean - probably fields on the west cliff near the harbour, and houses in the village street. The monks paid John of Chesney a hundred marks for half his lands at Brighton and also received two virgates there in exchange for a mill at Meeching [Newhaven]; on sites formerly theirs stood many of the houses at North Street in the 1620s. The manor of Atlingworth, given them by Roger of Clere, included land in Portslade and Aldrington. At Seaford Robert of Thorne (near Langney) gave them seven houses; a constable of Pevensey castle also promised them property there. Possibly their stake survived in 1600 as a manor of 'Seaford', containing the Dan and the Cheker on the west of the town, also the vicarage garden and 'the house with the hand'. At Meeching, a place with little maritime life, the Cluniacs gave up the mill but kept premises near the ferry. (See p. 270) [43]

Seaford seems to have enjoyed a modest prosperity, though the loss of Normandy in 1204 dislocated cross-Channel trade and reinforced piracy. About then its merchants paid £13 as a tax compared with £712 at Southampton, £62 at Winchelsea, £23 at Chichester, £20 at New Shoreham, £11 at Rye. As already noted, by 1229 it enjoyed Cinque Port status as a 'limb' of Hastings, which gave its mariners privileged access to North Sea fishing grounds and to the fish fair at Yarmouth. In the 1290s its merchants and ship-owners dominated the dispatch of wool from the port to northern France; it first sent two burgesses to parliament in 1298, and in 1301 it was granted a fair on saint James's day.[44]

61 A pilgrim

Besides its trade in local and sea-borne produce, Lewes profited from a burgeoning traffic in pilgrims. In 1276 the body of the canonized bishop Richard was moved within Chichester cathedral to a glittering shrine, where a Welsh harpist, Walter Luvel, was stationed to sing of his sanctity. After attending the Translation, Edward I made the first of several visits to Lewes while journeying between Chichester and the shrine at Canterbury of Thomas Becket, canonized in 1173. In the treasury at Battle abbey Edward may also have admired William II's gorgeous coronation robe and the sword wielded by the Conqueror at Senlac. And Lewes burh indeed must have serviced pilgrims using the Southdown highway as a route to adore the relics of Saxon saints at Winchester - Birinus the apostle of Wessex, Swithun the rain maker, Judoc whose hair grew steadily after his death, Ethelwold who built England's mightiest organ which employed 400 pipes and 36 bellows. Along the highway stood the shrine at Steyning of Cuthman, a Saxon shepherd, born perhaps at Chidham by Bosham, who built a church at Steyning on the spot where the barrow in which he was wheeling his aged mother broke down. And till purloined by Balger in 1058, the remains of the martyred Lewinna rested 'three leagues or so' from Seaford, probably at Bishopstone. By the 13th century healing waters and revered recluses also punctuated the highway. At Eastbourne a Holy Well bubbled near saint Gregory's chapel; at Steyning sparkled saint Mary's spring. And though immured in the church at Steyning, Miliana sued the prior of Hardham in 1272 for thousands of loaves, cooked meals and draughts of ale, which she claimed he had unlawfully denied her for 18 years. Less litigious anchoresses, at Stopham and Houghton, were remembered by bishop Richard in his will.[45]

Lewes itself had much to beguile the passing pilgrim. Bishop Richard left five shillings to 'the female recluse of the Blessed Mary' at Westout. Her cell opened into a church which by the 1530s housed a much venerated image of saint Anne, placed there perhaps to serve visitors thronging a healing well near by. The Southover Cluniacs, maybe, helped to manage it, and two other springs - the Pin Well below All Saints and 'the common spring' below St John's. The latter church preserved the cell of prince Magnus, the Danish anchorite. And though the Cluniacs failed to secure the corpse of saint William at Norwich or the piece of the True Cross at Bromholm, their annals recorded in 1250 the curing of a cripple near 'the Holy Cross of saint Pancras', in a church crammed with altars and graven images, lamps and frescos, costly fabrics and 'high' tombs. Doubtless the Franciscans treasured the book of Gospels that bishop Richard left them - even perhaps the four fine mullet 'miraculously' netted near by after his intercession. Maybe too a legend solidified that a table-top of Sussex marble at Old Malling palace had twice shaken off the bloodstained weapons of Becket's murderers.

As well as toiling through Canterbury, Battle and Lewes, Steyning, Chichester and Winchester, the pious increasingly embarked at Sussex ports for the shrine of saint James the Great at Compostela in northern Spain. Earl Warenne went in 1223 and a party from Ticehurst about 1275 - while away they were fined for not attending a seigneurial court.

At Westham church near Pevensey 15th-century glass depicted the saint as a bare-footed pilgrim with a broad-brimmed white hat and palmer's staff. A hair shirt and comb, once his, were displayed at Wisborough Green in western Sussex. Possibly the Southover Cluniacs, like their Continental brethren, helped to organize the Compostela pilgrimage. Certainly by 1300 a spacious hospital dedicated to saint James stood near their great gate.[46]

Clearly the commerce of Lewes was variously sustained between 1066 and 1300. Money was spent there by earls and archbishops, Cluniacs, Franciscans and pilgrims, by folk attending its secular and Church courts, and this quickened the sale of peasant-produce from the South Downs and the Weald, and of merchandise brought upriver. A glimpse of the town's population and wealth in 1296 is given by a tax on moveable goods. The assessments for Lewes borough, Southover and Cliffe with Malling amounted to £19 10s, and perhaps some 500 or 600 people lived in the households of the 114 taxpayers. Of these, 16 were at Cliffe with Malling, where a rental listed in the 1280s at least 45 houses, tenements and 'cots'. If two in every three householders did indeed escape the tax, then a population of between 1500 and 1800 seems plausible for the whole town. Its assessment, £19 10s, was close to the £19 17s 10d levied at New Shoreham, and exceeded Seaford's, a mere £8 16s 5d, but that total excluded maybe the Duchy of Lancaster's tenants there.

At Lewes borough twenty of the 65 householders were assessed at over four shillings. This commercial elite included Nicholas Tannator, Henry Braciator [brewer], John Marshall, Walter Mercator and William le Haftere. Henry of Burn, Geoffrey Kucku and Thomas of Sheluyng were assessed together for twenty shillings. None except William Selverleg (5s) served as a Borough MP between 1295 and 1301, though Reginald Combe (3s), Roger Coppyng (1s) and Richard Palmer (1s) did. Surnames among the 45 less heavily assessed point to employment as a clerk, a spicer, a baker, a cook, a comber, a girdler, a cutler, and a painter - Roger Tympan played a kettledrum perhaps. At Seaford the more heavily assessed householders included two shipmasters, John the Packere and Henry the Strong, and three wool merchants, John Bosse (£1 1s), Ralph Prime and Richard of Burn. Margery of Ely (£1 2s) was perhaps a wool dealer, for in 1312 a clip at Beddingham was sold to Roger of Ely, a Seafordian.

At Southover many householders, 29 out of 33, were assessed at four shillings or less, so perhaps they included many artisans servicing the monks or utilising the waters of the Winterbourne stream. Among them were John le Hattere, Nicholas Pellipar [skinner], Robert Vitrear [glazier], Thomas Vitrear, Godfrey le Tayllur, William Carpenter and Philip de Pistrin ['from the bakery']; also Simon Helpusgod - a holy fool perhaps. A tanner, John of Iford, paid 4s 10d, but the two most heavily assessed, John Serle (£1 7s 1d) and the clerk Gilbert Sykelfot (14s 1d), were it seems legal advisers to the Cluniacs. At Cliffe and Malling John of Radmelde (£1 2s) and Walter of Piecombe (8s), seemingly of Southdown origin, were wool traders maybe - Martin of Cliff (2s) certainly was. Other householders included William Dier, Geoffrey Carnifice [butcher], William Molend [miller] and John Pistor [baker] - Helewise atte Watre leased a ferry perhaps.[47]

Though population estimates for Lewes borough, based on the Domesday survey and the 1296 tax, are too tentative to confirm any trend after 1086, scraps of topographical evidence suggest that the Borough was heavily built over by the 13th century, and remained so till the the Black Death arrived in 1348. It seems the sunny slopes south of the High Street were quite thickly settled, whereas they were not in the 1620s. Refuse pits near Friars Walk and upper Broomans Lane have yielded pottery dating from the 12th to the 14th century. So have others beneath the new Lewes library, pits possibly associated with houses 'between Pinwell Street and Brooman's Street' held in 1353 by William Stodewold and Robert Aumbler, houses due west of crofts bought by Richard Blake in 1358-9 from John of Pierpoint. In 1353 John Reygate, chaplain, had given the house, later Aumbler's, to the Brotherhood of saint Sebastian. On the west side of Pinwell Street, about 1280, the premises of Agnes of Pinwell lay between William Bune's house and the curtilage of William the Scuitor. (Map 2.3) Five tenements, three curtilages and 'a place acquired from the tenement of the Walewere', all held in 1329-30 from the bishop of Chichester, were mostly situated, it seems, to the east of Walwers Lane, where 13th and 14th-century pottery has been found.[48]

'Olde scolestrete', tentatively identified as the lost twitten dividing the parishes of St Andrew and St Mary-in-the-market, was also built up. In 1316 a house on its east side, belonging to the wool dealer, Adam of Pycumbe, was bounded to the south by John Tebaud's house, to the north by William the Hafter's curtilage. (Map 2.4) Outside the Borough's west gate sherds of 13th-century pottery have been found at the west side of Westgate Lane, and in 1345, on the eve of the Black Death, Agnes of York granted to Robert Harewode part of a house-site in Keere Street with a street frontage of 15 feet and access to a common well. About 1290 a pound of wax, given to Southover priory, was funded from a house-rent in 'Antiokstrete'. This traversed St Peter's parish west of, and parallel to, Keere Street, but was 'enclosed' sometime before 1595. (Map 5.3)[49]

Altogether devoid of houses in the 1620s - though overlooked by a tanyard and some cottages under one roof near St John's church - was the grid of pasture-crofts stretching north from the back lanes behind the High Street, now Market Lane and East Street. The grid, though possibly occupying space set aside for Saxon refugees from marauding Danes, was seen by John Elliot as a framework for residential streets: 'each field being bounded [in the 1750s] almost on every side by narrow Carriage roads ... formerly streets of Communications'. In his day, though, no such 'road' formed the boundary between Kemp's Field and Townsend Field which ran due north from the end of Fisher Street. (Map P.2) But maybe the boundary had been the 'Loddere Street' in which John Eustace gave a house to Southover priory about 1260. If so it gave convenient access to the mother church of St John's. Excavation has shown that areas of the grid were residential in the 12th and 13th centuries. Refuse pits at the Naval Prison site [in Townsend Field] yielded 'much early Norman material' and from others near North Street came evidence of 'a fairly short-lived suburb' abandoned in the 14th century - as was a furnace for smelting copper or bronze discovered near Edward Street. 'Tis handed down to us', John Elliot also divulges, that 'the Well in the Field near the Green Wall was the Town Well, and of course near the Residence of the Major Part of the Inhabitants', and that 'the Old Fish Market was about the North End of Fisher Street beyond the Bray Mount (or rather in the Field a little behind where the Old Barn now stands)'.[50]

At Southover, too, pockets of 13th-century topography suggest a tightly packed population in the 'new town' built between the Winterbourne and Cockshut streams to serve a spacious Cluniac precinct which housed perhaps a hundred monks by the 1240s. At Benedictine Battle Norman administrators had clustered in the Sandlake quarter near the great gate of the abbey, while Saxon craftsmen and traders were spread along a High Street reaching westward to the market-place - a layout which segregated the monks from Worldly bustle while satisfying a need for goods and services.[51] At Southover by the 13th century an 'Eastport' and a 'Westport' had also emerged. Each was anchored by a rectangle of roads, and by 1600 the two localities were separated by the site of St James's hospital, by two acres of wetland south of the Winterbourne called 'the North Brooks', and by a tongue of pasture descending, west of Cockshut Lane, to the Westham. (Map 5.2) Perhaps hospital, wetland and pasture had served as 'green belt', insulating the walled precinct and Eastport from an overtly commercial Westport.[52]

The new Southover had no market-place. Instead its monks enjoyed privileged access to those at Lewes borough and Seaford. However there was a fair on the feastday of saint Pancras, recorded in 1363-4 and in 1533-4, and possibly held at 'the cross of Southover'. This was described about 1240 as adjacent to 'an acre of land opposite the marl pit to the south' - presumably the pit recorded about 1147 as 'outside the vill, with the land and meadow in Crandona', and again in 1533-4 as 'the limepits and quarry' leased out by the priory's master of works - its face still beetles above Juggs Close, just north of Juggs Lane. So 'the cross', it seems, was the staggered junction at Southover End still formed by the High Street, Bell Lane, Juggs Lane and the Newhaven Road, remote enough from the precinct to stage the saint Pancras fair. Near 'the marlpit', about

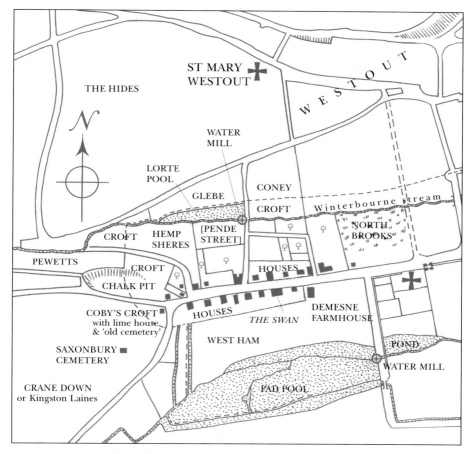

5.2 Westport Southover about 1600

1200, lived Snelingius, a fisherman gifted to the monks' infirmary, along with his house and orchard - a reminder that Southover End lay close to navigable water. Boats used the Cockshut stream to dock near the quarry in 1533-4 when ditches abutting the Westham and 'leading to the mine', and to a lime kiln in Mr Coby's croft, were cleaned. (Map 5.2)[53]

In the croft, which Mr Coby rented from the master of works, was also 'the old cemetery'. This was again described in 1540, as 'the old churchyard alias le old Lyghten' - a corruption perhaps of the Saxon word *lictun*, meaning 'the lying-in enclosure' or cemetery. Probably the name referred to the pagan Saxon burial ground, badly disturbed in 1891 when Saxonbury House was built, slightly further west. Just possibly, though, the Cluniacs built a church to serve 'Saxon' Westport, which was abandoned once a parish church was established in the former hospitium by the great gate.[54]

The core of Westport was the rectangle of roads apparent today as St Pancras Lane, the High Street, Potters Lane and The Course (called Gold Street in 1414). By 1600 all the houses there fronted the High Street, except the parsonage, which still faced onto Potters Lane when roofed with Horsham stone about 1560. In 1300, however, there were perhaps at least five houses on the west side of Avery Street, now upper St Pancras Lane - two 'belonging' to the Light of the Blessed Virgin Mary; also at least three houses in Lortepole Street, later corrupted to Lurpole or Ludport Lane, in what is probably now lower St Pancras Lane - the Lortepool being the pond-head of the west mill by 'Pancras' bridge. And there were three or more houses in Pende Street on the south side of the pond; one was partitioned between the four married daughters of Robert Lambe deceased. Besides driving the mill, the Winterbourne stream was useful to craftsmen. Householders thereabouts included Robert the weaver, Bartholomew the cobbler, Jordan the plumber, Peter the painter, Edward the skinner and Arnold the skinner. South-west of the mill pond in 1600 lay 'the hempsheres', the location maybe of four parcels of hemp-plot rented in 1371. The houses standing south of the High Street in the late 13th century testify to Westport's vitality, whereas the spacious free-hold-plots, orchards and crofts occupying their sites by 1600 point to depopulation - caused perhaps by the Black Death, or by the priory's dissolution in 1537.[55]

It was through Westport that wheeled traffic approached the priory's west-facing gate and Eastport itself, both from Juggs Lane and from Rotten Row and 'Pancras' bridge. Possibly James the farrier worked a smithy in 1342 at the south-east corner of Avery Street. Unless they negotiated steep inclines such as Antioch Street and Watergate Lane, vehicles could otherwise reach Eastport only via Eastgate and the Friars Wall, and then use the the bridge called Bowyers bridge in 1512 - for in 1699 it was confirmed that the bridge by the pond-head at Watergate mill had been 'from time immemorial used by horses' only.[56]

At Eastport a rectangle of roads is apparent today as Southover High Street, Priory Street 'under' the former precinct wall, Garden Street which led to the physic garden beyond Watergate mill, and Eastport Lane. As in Westport, there were spacious freehold-plots in Eastport by 1600 - also a sign perhaps of depopulation. Among them were two hop gardens called 'the Island', and the *Chequer*, an inn of uncertain origin - a namesake at Canterbury lodged Chaucer's pilgrims. (Map 5.3) More tightly packed were at least eight houses and gardens stretching from Eastport Lane to the Winterbourne stream. In 1315 four tenements in Eastport 'extended in length from the high street called Bromanstrete to the watercourse flowing to the mill called Watergate'. They were held by William the porter, William the brewer, Maurice the glazier and Saverie the 'lyneter', a measurer or surveyor - men who worked, quite probably, in the precinct. Presumably Bromanstrete was Eastport Lane,

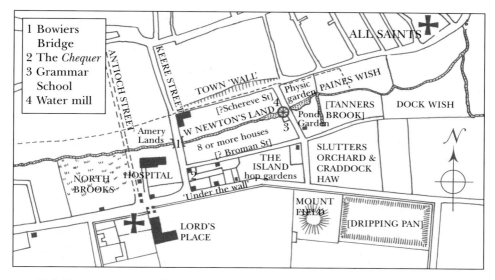

1 Bowiers
  Bridge
2 The *Chequer*
3 Grammar
  School
4 Water mill

KEERE STREET

ANTIOCH STREET

ALL SAINTS

TOWN 'WALL'

PAINES WISH

[?Schereve St]

Physic garden

[TANNERS BROOK]

DOCK WISH

W NEWTON'S LAND

Pond Garden

Amery Lands

8 or more houses
[? Broman St]

THE ISLAND
hop gardens

SLUTTERS
ORCHARD &
CRADDOCK
HAW

NORTH BROOKS

HOSPITAL

'Under the wall'

MOUNT FIELD

[DRIPPING PAN]

LORD'S PLACE

N

5.3 Eastport Southover about 1600

unless the tenements lay north of the stream, in which case it was Southover Road. By 1512 that area north of the Winterbourne formed part of what became the 'Grange' estate, though maybe in 1297 the tanner John of Iford, John Dun, John of Becherswold and William of Acres held adjacent premises there, south of 'the path under the town wall of Lewes'. Certainly by 1300 the vicinity of Watergate mill was more built up than in 1600. In 1282 two sisters gifted to the Cluniacs' granator premises beside the mill between those of Richard Bishop and John Fukkebegger; and about 1290 John of Reygate and Thomas the glazier owned property off 'Watergate Street' [now Garden Street?], between the mill and 'Schereve Street' [maybe Southover Road].[57]

How tightly packed settlement at Cliffe had become by 1300 is uncertain. (Map 5.4 overleaf) Doubtless the first houses there abutted the chalk slopes below the sheepdown belonging to Ranscombe manor, from which the Mill Field had been carved by 1571. Presumably though, by 1300, a causeway connected the bridge and Cliffe Corner [West Street], broad enough to support timber-framed houses. The antiquarian, Thomas Woollgar, noted that they rested on 'made grounds raised from a Marsh formerly overflowed by the River as appears from the Slub and Sea sand found beneath in sinking wells'. Excavation in the Fair Place, north of the church, has found deposits of compacted chalk, possibly laid down in the 13th century or earlier, and maybe the causeway incorporated the 'sewers' which by 1600 connected a deep channel dug north of West Street with the river sweeping south-eastwards. Doubtless the work was funded by the archbishops of Canterbury. The survey made in the

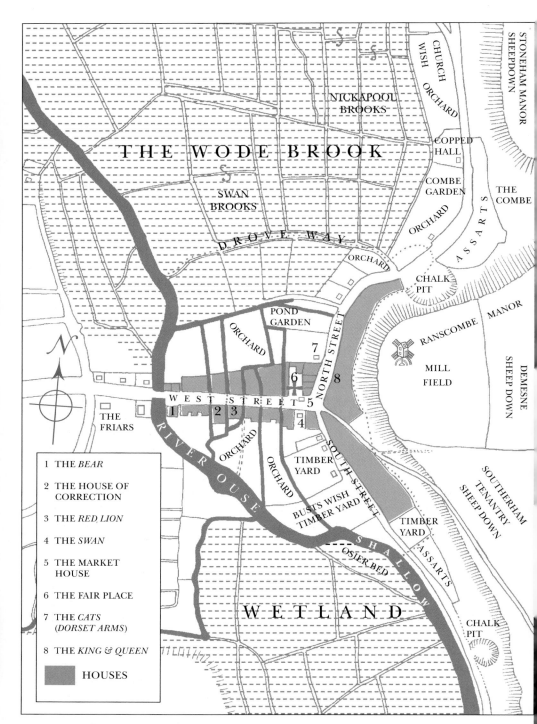

STONEHAM MANOR SHEEPDOWN

CHURCH WISH

ORCHARD

NICKAPOOL BROOKS

COPPED HALL

THE WODE BROOK

COMBE GARDEN

ORCHARD

THE COMBE

SWAN BROOKS

A S S A R T S

DROVE WAY

ORCHARD

ORCHARD

CHALK PIT

POND GARDEN

ORCHARD

NORTH STREET

RANSCOMBE MANOR

7

6

8

MILL FIELD

DEMESNE SHEEP DOWN

WEST STREET

5

N

1 2 3

4

THE FRIARS

ORCHARD

ORCHARD

TIMBER YARD

SOUTH STREET

SOUTHERHAM TENANTRY SHEEP DOWN

R I V E R   O U S E

BUSTS WISH TIMBER YARD

TIMBER YARD

ASSARTS

SHALLOW

OSIER BED

1 THE *BEAR*

2 THE HOUSE OF CORRECTION

3 THE *RED LION*

4 THE *SWAN*

5 THE MARKET HOUSE

6 THE FAIR PLACE

7 THE *CATS* (*DORSET ARMS*)

8 THE *KING & QUEEN*

HOUSES

W E T L A N D

CHALK PIT

5.4 Cliffe in the 17th century

1280s for Pecham reveals that by then 'the Wode brook', almost seventy acres of marshland north of Cliffe, had been drained.

There was as yet no market-place. If Pecham visited Old Malling palace, provisions were fetched from 'Lewes' market. Neither his survey, listing about fifty premises, nor a rental for 1305-6, give much topographical detail - 'a plot next the bridge'; 'ten acres on the downs', perhaps part of the Mill Field; 'a kiln under the cliff', rented by Robert Lymebernere and Thomas 'his fellow', probably at the end of North Street. A second kiln, with other property, was held by John Marescall, maybe also a freeholder in Uckfield and the archbishop's hereditary head forester, and a third by Adam of Rising, whose name recurs as a tenant at Southerham and at Greenhurst near Uckfield. If they did own kilns and Wealden land, perhaps they traded lime upriver. Gilbert Sikelfoot, a coroner and a legal adviser to the Southover Cluniacs, rented two 'shops'; and the Lewes widow, Juliana Dodd, went to law in 1276 over five houses and 70 acres in Beeding, Ringmer and Cliffe. The canons of Malling held considerable property, including five houses and two shops bought by a vicar of Ringmer to endow a chantry in his church, but 'appropriated' by the archbishop and bestowed on their sacrist.[58]

The survey also reveals a teeming peasantry just beyond the borders of Cliffe. Towards the end of South Street loomed the sheepdown of farmers tilling arable fields at Southerham. Between them, 24 virgaters there ploughed some 14 yardlands, each 'containing about 12 acres'; moreover, about fifty acres of downland, of 'terra montana', had recently been converted to arable. The virgaters also ploughed, reaped and threshed for the archbishop on his demesne at Ranscombe and united their 'milk' sheep and 'milk' cows with his at certain seasons. Much smaller on average were the holdings at 'Malling' of thirty or so free tenants, cottars and 'porters' - Simon the tinker appeared in each category. The cottars reaped and threshed the archbishop's grain; the porters carried supplies to his palace from Lewes market and drove his animals as far as Uckfield and Framfield. Chune at Bote rented a boat 'for carrying men across the water' - perhaps to a causeway below St John's church. Probably their holdings were sited on upland east of the palace, bounded on the north-east by the demesne of Stoneham, and on the south by 'Wode brook'. Formerly all tenants had grazed their milk cows on these water meadows, but recently they had been rented only 'to certain of them'. (Map 5.5 overleaf) Sadly no survey survives of the peasants clustered at Landport, Winterbourne and Houndean, cultivating customary virgates and the demesne of the earls Warenne. In the 1620s John Rowe alluded to copyholds there long discontinued. One substantial farmer within the manor of 'Huntingdean', however, was John le Beure of 'Lewes', who also traded with Gascony; unthreshed grain and 16 oxen were seized from him by the earl's bailiff about 1258.[59]

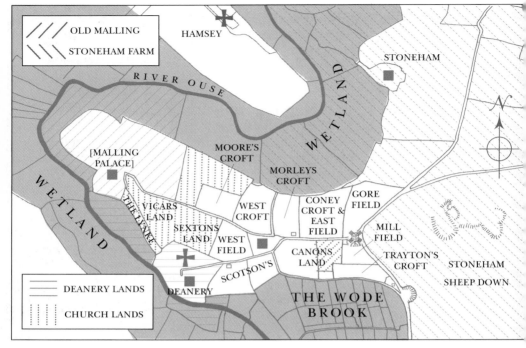

5.5 Malling about 1650

Clearly in the 12th and 13th centuries Lewes borough and Southover, along with Cliffe and Malling, shared fully in the golden years of medieval England. They accommodated a confident seigneurial and sacerdotal culture - a glittering half-Plantagenet dynasty, a sprawling castle, a puissant rapal court, a majestic Cluniac precinct, an archiepiscopal palace, a bishop soon to be enshrined at Chichester, and Franciscans in the first flush of fervour. The Borough also focused much of the commerce of mid-Sussex. Its corn market was hailed as 'the navel' of Sussex. Men dealt in wool and fleeces from sheep flocks thickly grazing the Downs. Unloaded there (or at Cliffe) was Caen stone from Normandy, 'marble' from Tournai, slate from south Devon, wine from Gascony, querns from the Rhineland. In 1300 few would have predicted that so vital a culture, so pulsating an economy, could falter, even fracture.

62 Windows in the priory's first latrine block, arched with voussoirs made of imported Quarr limestone.

Overleaf: plague (*pestilencia*) erupts into the account rolls of Alciston manor, 1425-6 and 1440-1

147

Summa xxj li. x s. x d.

Summa lij li. ix s. iiij d.

6

Converging calamities: pillage, commotion and plague 1300-1461

The prior of Southover's men fought with great courage, especially one of his French servants, 'who fought so stoutly, fiercely and persistently against his fellow Frenchmen that his stomach was pierced by their swords and his bowels dropped to his feet. Disregarding this injury, he pursued the enemy, trailing his intestines far behind him'. An episode during the Rottingdean skirmish.

John Wryther merchant, John Chamberlayn yeoman, Thomas Podey senior yeoman, Andrew Somer glover, William Cheseman yeoman, Richard Cole chapman, William Bourehunte smith, Richard Benet sherman, Thomas Cheseman chapman, John Worth yeoman and all of the township. Cliffe residents pardoned after Cade's Rebellion.

The plague carried off so vast a multitude of people of both sexes that nobody could be found who would bear the corpses to the grave. Men and women carried their own children on their shoulders to the church and threw them into a common pit ... There was so marked a deficiency of labourers and workmen of every kind that more than a third of the land was let to lie idle. The Black Death in Kent in 1349.

Between 1300 and 1461 Lewes borough, Southover and Cliffe suffered many misfortunes. The Borough ceased to be a major focus of seigneurial power. From 1361 its lords were Fitzalans who preferred their castle at Arundel, and from 1439 the lordship was fragmented. Intermittent hostilities with France solidified into the Hundred Years War in 1336, and though French plunder enriched some Sussex knights, the fighting disrupted cross-Channel trade and exposed coastal communities to repeated pillage by French raiders. Local seigneurs, along with the agents of a deteriorating monarchy, offered scant protection. Indeed official ineptitude, and rapacity, stoked unrest in southeastern England which fuelled the Peasants' Revolt in 1381 and Cade's

Rebellion in 1450. The war also nourished a xenophobia injurious to the Cluniacs at Southover who secured a grant of naturalization from Edward III and then became part of an English province, independent of Cluny, during the Great Schism in the Catholic Church. By 1300, moreover, the population of England, urban and rural, had grown too large; food supplies became insecure, malnutrition and unemployment mounted, until, beginning with the Black Death in 1348, epidemics of plague scythed away perhaps a third of the population, severely depressing the English economy for over a century.

That Lewes borough ceased to be a major focus of seigneurial power in 1361 owed much to the turbulent love life of John, the eighth and last earl Warenne, whose childhood was perhaps unhappy. Six months after his birth, his father was killed at Croydon in December 1286. His mother, Joan of Vere, died in 1293. When his formidable grandfather expired in 1304, he became a ward of Edward I. While lodging at Lewes castle on 23-27 June 1305, that tireless king licensed two knights to go crusading, settled the arrears of 19 Brabantine mercenaries for services in Scotland, filled a prebend in his Free Chapel at Hastings castle and rode out to 'Horsted', perhaps to hunt the prior of Southover's deer. Tarrying at Lewes too was the king's heir, Edward of Caernarvon, in disgrace for insulting the royal Treasurer. Earl John received his immense inheritance on 7 April 1306. Soon after, he attended the feast at Westminster Hall into which were carried two massive effigies of swans, laced with gold - symbols of Fidelity which prompted the revellers to swear vengeance on the Scots for crowning Robert Bruce. Three days later, John married Edward I's ten-year-old granddaughter, Joan, whose father was Henry count of Bar. The royal treasury paid for the minstrels, the fly-past of royal falcons, a cloth of gold for the chaplain and chariots for the newly weds. And in February 1307 the dying king graciously forgave John his grandfather's massive debts to the crown - including the fine, still unpaid, for the manslaughter of Zouche in 1270.[1]

Yet despite immense wealth and a glittering Plantagenet bride, the earl's passions drove him to impair his patrimony. By 1314 he was living apart from Joan, claiming she had been forced upon him. Moreover, his mistress, Maud of Nerford, though nominally the wife of Sir Simon of Derby, swore that John had contracted to marry her before he wedded Joan. Though the pope refused him a dissolution, the earl never reunited with Joan and never fathered a legitimate heir. After acquiring a new 'compaigne', Isabel of Holland, who inherited his plate and jewels and half his livestock, he tried to have his marriage annulled as consanguineous, by swearing that before it, he seduced Joan's aunt, the long-dead princess Mary - in her nunnery. Clement VI, however, let him off with a penance - a lead bulla of that pope being found in 1845 under a skull near the high altar at Southover, close to which the earl was buried in 1347.[2]

The extinction of the legitimate male line

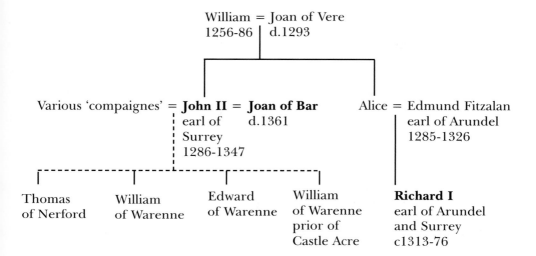

William = Joan of Vere
1256-86 | d.1293

Various 'compaignes' = **John II** = **Joan of Bar**   Alice = Edmund Fitzalan
                      earl of   d.1361   earl of Arundel
                      Surrey   1285-1326
                      1286-1347

Thomas   William   Edward   William   **Richard I**
of Nerford   of Warenne   of Warenne   of Warenne   earl of Arundel
                                              prior of   and Surrey
                                              Castle Acre   c1313-76

John did beget bastards, and he gained Edward II's consent to their advancement by agreeing that after his death Grantham, Stamford and his Yorkshire lands would pass to the crown - the rest going to his only sister Alice, the wife of Edmund Fitzalan, earl of Arundel. The king visited Lewes on 1-4 July 1324 and because of John's loyalty to him, the earl only narrowly survived Edward's murder by queen Isabel and earl Mortimer in 1327. Thereafter he became fruitlessly involved in Scotland, once the death of Robert Bruce in 1329 tempted his cousin and former ward, Edward Balliol, to claim its throne. When Balliol granted him the Palatine earldom of Strathearn (modern Perthshire), John ordered a splendid head-dress spun with gold and a sumptuous seal four inches wide; on one side a serene bearded figure is seated on a pinnacled throne, while rabbits feed and a hart nibbles an oak; on the reverse a heavily armoured warrior gallops through shallows studded with swans - chequered drapery swirls from his charger which sports a fearsome head-piece. But Balliol's cause fizzled out and in 1343 David Bruce granted Strathearn to a loyal Scotsman. As chimerical maybe as John's Palatinate was a 'vast treasure' allegedly found in a cave on his Welsh estate by a Saracen physician.[3]

The earl employed his bastards in Lewes rape. Indeed in 1338 William 'of Warenne' abducted Sir John of Waleys from Glynde and detained him for eight weeks at Lewes castle. And there in 1339 the earl sealed a deed witnessed by his bastard, Thomas of Nerford, for whom he finessed the manor of Saddlescombe from the Knights Hospitallers.

Other knights, meanwhile, from families long entrenched in the rape, were showing new poise and independence. Geoffrey of Say built a spacious hall at Hamsey measuring 60 by 30 feet, with two fireplaces. Simon of Pierpoint enlarged his park at Danny, keeping animals there, 'wild or otherwise'. John of Radynden served Edward III as a diplomat. And three paladins rode forth from Poynings. Michael was slain at Bannockburn in 1314. His son, Thomas, was killed near Cambrai in 1339. Thomas's brother, Michael, fought at Sluys and at Crecy. To the siege of Calais in 1347 he led a retinue of two bannerets, eight knights, 23 esquires and 12 archers. The knights included John Waleys and Roger Dallingridge of Fletching. William Mareschal of Lewes and Ralf atte Doune of Seaford were foot soldiers whose valour he attested. A Brotherhood of saint Sebastian, an archers' gild perhaps, had premises south of Brooman's Lane in 1353.[4]

As a precaution against the French, Edward III ordered Lewes castle to be 'securely guarded' in 1336 and quite possibly the earl complied by building the barbican. But like his Palatine seal, the spectacular gatehouse, with its double portcullis, had a touch of fantasy. The thin walls were hardly siege-proof and the facade is decidedly alluring: the portal has moulded orders; the twin bartizans repose on elegant corbel-

63 The barbican

tables; the cruciform arrow-loops swell suavely at their base; a trefoiled ogee adorns a solitary window beneath arched machicolations; and chequered squares of knapped flint and greensand-stone replicate, maybe, the Warenne coat of blue and gold. Such stylish fortification set a fashion followed at Michelham, Bodiam and Herstmonceux. Perhaps the earl also modernized the castle's domestic range, inserting the massive first-floor window shown in an 18th-century view (see illustration 21) of the craglike masonry above Castle Banks.[5]

64 The arcading

Directly facing the lofty barbican are remnants of an ambitious timber-framed building of 'mid 14th-century' date, forming part of 74-6 High Street. The delicate arcading on its east side above St Martin's Lane - similar to church screens at Eastbourne and Playden - formerly extended also along the front. Was this conspicuous structure perhaps built by earl John as the court-house of the rape, described as 'beyond the [draw] bridge' when re-tiled about 1458? Possibly, though, the court was held at La Peryne, a 'stone house' in the earl's hands in 1341. It stood north of the High Street, some doors east of St Michael's, maybe at 165-6 High Street, the site of the *White Horse* in 1624, which had two large vaulted cellars below.[6] In 1334 a royal grant of murage, valid for five years, was made to the bailiffs and 'good men' of Lewes, which perhaps funded a new west gate. Unlike the barbican it was a squat prosaic structure, 68 feet wide and 30 feet deep. The semi-circular facades of its twin west towers were faced with greensand-stone and flanked a gateway ten feet wide. Its archway was removed 'for a wager' in 1763.[7]

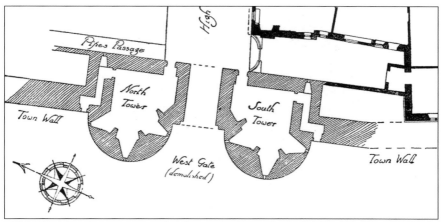

6.1 West gate: ground-plan

65 The remains of the west gate about 1779

Though in 1342 'age and infirmity' excused the earl from a tournament at Dunstable, he served on a Council of Regency while Edward III
campaigned abroad, but died on 29 June 1347 at Conisbrough castle,
part of the Yorkshire estate which then reverted to the crown, along with
Grantham and Stamford. Unlike his grandfather's 'flat tombstone on the
flat pavement', his was to be 'lofty', on the left of the high altar under an
arch 'already prepared'. He also planned a funeral at Southover as conspicuous as his Palatine head-dress, or the golden chalice studded with
pearls which he gave to saint Cuthbert's shrine at Durham. Though his
wrangles with the Cluniacs had been frequent, even violent, he wished
them to have the trappings used at the solemn obsequies - the cloths of
gold and drapes of silk; the two armoured war-horses that were to precede his corpse; the weapons carried by the retainers who led them; the
leather canopy which deflected the wax dripping from candles above the
bier. Sussex notables thronged this flamboyant farewell to the Warenne
dynasty. The abbot of Battle was there, Michael of Poynings, Thomas of
Pashley and John of Waleys - who then set about sueing William, the late
earl's bastard, for abduction nine years before.[8]

To that same William the earl bequeathed his jousting armour, his glittering Palatine head-dress and a hundred marks. William's brother, Edward, received £20. From one of them descended, maybe, the 'warrior of the noble house of De Warren' whose brass survives in St Michael's church. The headless knight is clad in plate armour of about 1430 and though the inscription is lost, a dexter shield remains, bearing quarterly I and IV 'Checky', II and III 'paly of four'. When the coffin beneath the brass was opened in 1828, Gideon Mantell observed 'a tall slender corpse' in a linen shroud, embedded in moist sawdust, made of cedar apparently. 'The outline of the face', covered by the thin wet linen, 'was eminently beautiful'. To a second William, a bastard born at Conisbrough, who was a monk at Southover and became prior of Horton and then of Castle Acre, the earl left a bible compiled in France.[9]

66 The headless knight

After the eighth earl died Lewes borough ceased to be a major seat of a great seigneur. Edward III acquired Grantham, Stamford and the Yorkshire manors. Moreover the earl's widow, the countess Joan, leased out the Welsh lands to her nephew and heir, Richard Fitzalan, earl of Arundel, whose mother Alice was the late earl's only sister. And it seems unlikely Joan had any affection for Lewes itself. In the 1350s she was often 'overseas'; grain was shipped abroad through Seaford to supply her household in February 1361, and after she expired six months later, she was not buried 'in England'. However she was at Lewes castle in March 1360, insisting that her steward obliged local tenants of the bishop of Chichester to attend her courts, as they had done 'time out of mind' till 11 March 1348. Her steward was Roger Dallingridge, a veteran of the Crecy-Calais campaign, whose splendid brass survives at Fletching. His son, Sir Edward, built an elegant ashlar castle at Bodiam in the 1380s. Being a Plantagenet, Joan was, quite possibly, tough-minded. She

67 Roger and his lady

was a close friend in 1326 of Isabel, Edward II's queen, when that 'she-wolf' plotted the destruction of the king and of Joan's brother-in-law, the earl of Arundel. Over thirty years later the dowager-queen still welcomed the dowager-countess to Hertford and London; Joan was given a fur coat and summoned to Isabel's sick-bed before she died.[10]

Though the wars with France afforded plunder to local paladins, the anarchy that ensued in the English Channel deeply disrupted the commerce of mid Sussex. Between 1325 and 1328 foreign wool merchants deserted the ports, and armed local freighters were kept on standby 'in case malefactors [from] Normandy and Poitou' should appear. Shipments of corn from Seaford to Norman and 'other hostile ports' were banned in 1344; 'hostile ships' drove back a Seaford vessel freighted with wool for Flanders in 1347. The wars also exposed coastal communities to relentless pillage. In 1339 French raiders burned 52 houses at Hastings. By 1340 coastal farms near East Dean and Friston lay deserted and Seaford had been 'repeatedly destroyed', its men 'badly wounded and killed'. It lacked a defensive wall, though a trebuchet was in place by 1334. Seafordians claimed in 1356 that the town had again been burned, as well as desolated by plague - buildings, still intact, were being dismantled and carted away, and indeed in 1352 French raiders 'from Seaford' had stolen six ewes at Alciston.[11]

Its obvious failure to co-ordinate coastal defence undermined confidence in the political establishment, in local seigneurs and Crown officials - moreover seigneurs in eastern Sussex became increasingly absentee. Lewes rape passed in 1361 to Richard Fitzalan, now earl of Surrey and of Arundel. Immensely wealthy, he stored £60,000 in hard cash at Arundel castle, his favourite Sussex residence. Yet despite the threat from the French, the neglect of Lewes castle was such that local malcontents easily 'captured' it in 1381. By the mid 1370s Bramber rape belonged to the Mowbrays whose power-base was Norfolk, Hastings rape to John of Montfort, duke of Brittany, and Pevensey rape to Edward III's second son, John of Gaunt - who kept the castle unrepaired, it was rumoured, to impress his nuisance value on the Crown.[12]

Unprecedented disaster duly struck in 1377. The French burned Hastings and Rye, and were repulsed at Winchelsea only because the valorous abbot Hamo of Battle led its defence, cross-bow in hand. When they came ashore at Rottingdean, they were confronted by the 'extemporised regiment'of John of Charlieu, a vigorous prior of Southover (perhaps Burgundian by birth), who went hunting at Laughton with the earl of Oxford in 1375. His lieutenants included Thomas Cheyne, sometime constable of Dover castle, John Fallisle whose marriage to Elizabeth of Say was to bring him the manor of Streat, and John Brocas, a landowner in Selmeston and a great-nephew of Katherine Peverell, Richard Fitzalan's sister. But the prior and these lieutenants were defeated with heavy loss, and held captive in France, till ransomed. A prisoner in 1379

The advent of the Fitzalans

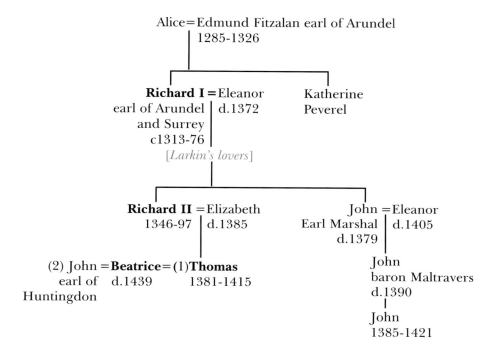

Alice=Edmund Fitzalan earl of Arundel
1285-1326

Richard I = Eleanor
earl of Arundel | d.1372
and Surrey
c1313-76
[*Larkin's lovers*]

Katherine
Peverel

Richard II = Elizabeth
1346-97 | d.1385

(2) John = **Beatrice** = (1)**Thomas**
earl of   d.1439   1381-1415
Huntingdon

John = Eleanor
Earl Marshal | d.1405
d.1379

John
baron Maltravers
d.1390

John
1385-1421

was William Horsham, a Southover tanner. French casualties were heavy enough, however, for the raiders to retire without assailing Lewes borough or the priory - the Cluniacs there had received a licence to crenellate in 1360. But the French did burn the churches at Rottingdean and Ovingdean, the prebend house at Sutton, and probably nearby Seaford as well - in the 1380s its taxes were rescinded because of 'irreparable' losses. Burgesses at Winchelsea, meanwhile, were moving to Battle where the monks fed a multitude displaced from the coast.[13]

Prior Charlieu's heroism was highlighted by a rumour concerning Richard Fitzalan II, who succeeded his father as earl of Arundel and Surrey in 1376. It was said that when the French landed at Rottingdean, he took flight and then, from a safe distance, agreed to find 400 lances for the defence of Lewes - if the Borough would bear the cost. Certainly his unpopularity was such that Lewes castle was sacked in June 1381, while peasants from Kent and Essex were converging on London to demand an end to poll taxes, heavy labour services and seigneurial corruption. William Grete of Lewes and William Wodeland of Cliffe were among the insurgents prosecuted by the earl for breaking the castle's gates, doors and windows, tearing down its masonry, drinking or destroying ten casks of wine valued at £100, carrying off chattels worth £40 and burning manorial records. Maybe too a house near St Andrew's church was levelled to the ground. Violence elsewhere in eastern Sussex was slight, though two knights who helped levy the poll tax were assaulted. Perhaps affection for abbot Hamo and prior Charlieu ensured monastic property was untouched. By contrast, at Lambeth Palace, men broaching wine barrels, clashing kitchen plates and crying 'a revell, a revell', avidly burned the archbishop's court rolls and rentals. Some related perhaps to his mighty manor of South Malling where in 1359 archbishop Islip had vigorously enforced labour services. Summoning John and Robert atte Broke from Framfield to Old Malling palace, he obliged them to confess their villein status, swear fealty to him, kiss his pectoral cross, and agree to publicize their bondage when the manorial court next met at Uckfield.[14]

For his part, earl Fitzalan doggedly pursued through the courts the looters at Lewes, naming 21 ring-leaders in 1386. Not all were townsfolk. William Shortport came from Ringmer, William Mot from Herstmonceux. And not all were *hoi polloi*. Richard atte Gate, Robert Wodeland and John Bucher had paid the poll tax at the Borough in 1379 - and 'Thomas' was 'the rector of the church of St Michael at Lewes'. Was he an ideologue, using the failings of local seigneurs to subvert faith in their authority - or merely a rogue, like the rector of St John's pardoned in 1397 for stealing a chalice from Hamsey church, as well as a brass pot, 16 tin vessels and nine bushels of malt from Henry Brigge in St Nicholas's parish? Perhaps no local John Ball was needed to convince townsfolk that the basic feudal contract, defence in return for tribute, lay in tatters. And maybe the beheading at Lewes of John atte Hothe of Maresfield in June 1391 for 'insurrection and sedition' was staged as a warning to a turbulent Borough.[15]

Possibly the looting did persuade Fitzalan to better equip the castle for defence. The armoury there, inventoried by royal officials after his beheading for conspiracy in 1397, consisted of two kettle-hats, 11 breast-plates, 17 head-pieces for cavalrymen, 17 pairs of gauntlets, twenty leather coats sewn with small iron plates, six crossbows, four guns, and a 'springald' - a machine akin to a giant crossbow. And possibly plans were afoot to repair the castle, for sawn timber, roofing lead, 3000 slates and 2000 old stone slabs were stored in the chapel. There was little else of any value - two buckets, two bronze jars, two bronze dishes, a 'furnace', a vat, a cauldron, a cistern, two sets of worn-out iron fetters - chattels which contrasted starkly with the sumptuous trappings listed at Arundel, Reigate and London: a silk bed-canopy worked with the arms of Fitzalan and Warenne; a red velvet cloth 'for the chapel' embroidered with angels and archangels; tall silver candlesticks 'for supper in winter', their battle-mented rims hung with armorial pendants; an enamelled gilt cup with a stag on its cover - and piles of hard cash.[16]

The earl's execution typified the factional politics which beset a monarchy in decline. He and his fellow Lords Appellant in 1386-7 had used parliamentary pressure, and military force, to cripple the power of Richard II and control the machinery of State, until the king struck back in 1397. And clearly several Borough MPs elected between 1383 and 1397 were willing to support Fitzalan's agenda. To Stephen Holt (1383 and 1388) the earl had granted land at Oving in 1378 worth £5 a year. Richard atte Gate (1388), though an 'insurgent in 1381, swore to support the Appellants. So did Walter Gosselyn (1388) and John Maryot (1395 and 1397). Maryot, moreover, bought a royal pardon after Fitzalan's execution, as did William Chepelond (1393 and 1399) who was a butcher. Some other MPs dealt in cloth or wool, some being 'customers' in Sussex, officials weighing wool for export - a commerce over which Fitzalan exerted some influence.[17]

After the earl's execution, his son Thomas fled to France to join the exiled Henry Bolingbroke. In 1399 they docked briefly at Pevensey castle, before landing at Ravenspur in Yorkshire and overthrowing Richard II. After Bolingbroke's coronation as Henry IV, the re-instated earl fought Owen Glendower in north Wales, before expiring of fever during Henry V's siege of Harfleur in 1415. French raids into mid Sussex, meanwhile, continued. On saint Bartholomew's day in 1403 marauders reached Selmeston - where John Hendyman had just broken his left leg playing football. Thomas Fitzalan died childless, leaving the earldom and rape of Arundel entailed to a second cousin, John baron Maltravers, but the rape of Lewes with the Reigate lands to his widow Beatrice, a legitimized daughter of king John I of Portugal, with remainder to his three sisters as co-heirs. After a 'magnificent' wedding in 1405 Beatrice had received the order of the Garter in her own right. She re-married in 1433 - John earl of Huntingdon being the king's Lieutenant in Aquitaine - and died at Bordeaux in 1439. It seems unlikely she passed much time at Lewes's semi-derelict castle. Her local administrators there included two Borough MPs: William Northampton became her castle bailiff about 1416, and Thomas White, a coroner, impounded some casks of wine washed onto her manorial beach at Seaford in 1421.[18]

In 1439 Lewes rape was duly divided between the heirs of Thomas Fitzalan's three sisters - John Mowbray, duke of Norfolk, already overlord of Bramber rape; Elizabeth, wife of Edward Nevill, later baron Bergavenny, based at Birling in Kent; and Edmund Lenthall whose father had been Master of the Wardrobe to Henry IV. Each held a third of Lewes castle and of the rapal 'forests' and 'fisheries', and received a third of the revenues from the Borough's burgage rents and manorial courts, from its Whitsun fair and Saturday market, and from the rapal court. As for the demesne manors, John was allotted Clayton, Pyecombe, Middleton, Allington, Brighton, Seaford and Meeching; Elizabeth received Ditchling, Rodmell, Patcham, Rottingdean and Northease; to

Thomas Fitzalan and his sisters

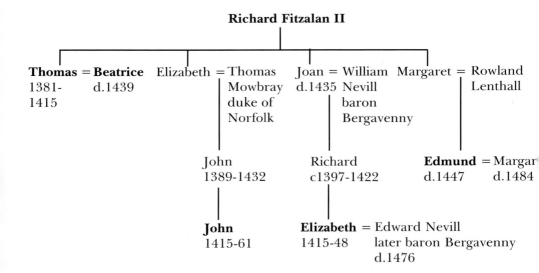

Richard Fitzalan II

Thomas = **Beatrice**	Elizabeth = Thomas	Joan = William	Margaret = Rowland	
1381- d.1439	Mowbray	d.1435 Nevill	Lenthall	
1415	duke of	baron		
	Norfolk	Bergavenny		

John 1389-1432   Richard c1397-1422   **Edmund** = Margar d.1447   d.1484

John 1415-61   **Elizabeth** = Edward Nevill 1415-48   later baron Bergavenny d.1476

Edmund accrued Houndean, Keymer and Cuckfield. Lenthall died childless in 1447, but his widow survived till 1484.[19]

Local men, meanwhile, were consolidating a grip on eastern Sussex. In 1417 king John of Portugal had requested Sir John Pelham of Laughton, as a 'noble and prudent' man, to give protection to his daughter, the widowed countess Beatrice. Pelham's father and grandfather were obscure Sussex coroners. But John was constable of Pevensey castle when Bolingbroke and Fitzalan docked, and rose dizzily thereafter, as a trusted Lancastrian, to become Treasurer of the Realm in 1411. He acquired the franchises in the rapes of Pevensey and Hastings, once vested in John of Gaunt and the duke of Brittany, and was repeatedly elected as senior knight of the shire for Sussex. An unofficial Royal Jailer, he detained at Pevensey castle a duke of York, a king of Scotland, and an alleged necromancer - Henry V's step-mother, Joan of Navarre.[20] Other men also deployed royal favour, war booty, legal office or mercantile wealth to acquire local power. The paladins from Poynings profited from the French wars. Sir Edward Dallingridge built Bodiam castle in the 1380s. Sir Roger Fiennes, Treasurer to the King's Household, raised an elegant brick mansion at Herstmonceux sixty years later.[21]

That 'new men' could pose as great a menace to social order as 'old' seigneurs became clear during the faction-ridden reign of the feeble-minded Henry VI (1422-61). Amid simmering unrest in 1443, John Oddeshole, a 'soldier' from Lewes, joined malcontents at Isleworth in Middlesex planning to capture the king and his advisers. Then came the loss of Normandy, of Rouen and Harfleur, in 1449. French raiders re-appeared, burning Rye and Winchelsea; at Tarring in west Sussex folk feared to venture to market. The anguish in south-eastern England was such that in June 1450 cohorts of peasants marched from Sussex to Blackheath, to unite with others from Kent led by Jack Cade. They occu-pied London, presented their grievances, extracted official pardons and marched home for the harvest.

Most pardons issued to communities in Sussex were collective, but some named individuals, men active perhaps in the revolt. West of the Adur, many of these resided in a string of parishes between Steyning and Rusper, the path perhaps of a contingent of Wealdsmen making for the Surrey border. In eastern Sussex Wealdsmen were named in the vicinity of manors held by Sir Roger Fiennes, the Treasurer, and by baron Hoo, a hated ex-Chancellor of Normandy. Downsmen too were listed, at Folkington and Alfriston, Milton and Litlington, communities wide open to raiders. At Seaford, where a patent to fortify, awarded in 1442, remained a dead letter, ten burgesses were noted.

Pardons were also issued to the high constables of Lewes borough, John Cook and John Bekwith, and their burgesses; to the constable of Southover, John Stempe, and his burgesses; to prior John Daniel with his 'convent and all the men and servants of the same'; and to 'all and sin-gular of the township' of Cliffe. A pardon was awarded as well to John Forger of All Saints and 'all and singular of the same parish'. Was this double indemnity needed because episcopal tenements there had been pillaged? Somewhat earlier, bishop Moleyns of Chichester, a much hated royal minister, had been killed at Portsmouth by soldiers with pay badly in arrears. At Southover a cooper, a husbandman and four yeomen were singled out; at Cliffe a merchant, a glover, a shearman, a smith, two chap-men and four yeomen; at Westout a weaver, a carpenter and a tailor; at Iford five husbandmen and labourers; at Hamsey Richard Profit 'gentle-man' and five yeomen.[22]

Maybe some unrest in Lewes borough spilled over from the realm of High Politics. Its 'lords', the duke of Norfolk and baron Bergavenny, opposed the clique around the king, a conflict partly waged in parlia-ment. John Southwell, elected at Lewes in 1449, 1450 and 1453, was Norfolk's salaried servant and rented perhaps the pigeon-house at 'the Steward's inn' in the Borough. His fellow MP in 1450, John Bekwith, had earlier sat for Shoreham in Bramber rape where Norfolk had influence. He was bailiff and janitor of Lewes castle in 1458, and after Edward IV siezed power in 1461, he received a customs post in East Anglia.[23] Thomas Best and William Delve, chosen as MPs for 'Lewes' in 1447 and 1449 respectively, were perhaps the same men who were singled out for pardon at Southover. A Thomas Best served as an 'auditor' on the prior's council in the 1460s, a William Delve was his tenant at Eastport. Their sitting for 'Lewes' may have resulted from a protocol, reaffirmed in 1553 as long-established, which required that at every other election burgesses in Southover should choose one of the two MPs for 'Lewes'. If so, doubtless the prior's wishes were decisive, and in the 1440s prior Daniel probably looked to the 'lords' of Lewes for leadership.[24]

Though Henry VI's ministers ignored the grievances which sparked Cade's rebellion, later unrest in Sussex was largely confined to Wealdsmen intoxicated by communistic or millennial fantasies. In October 1450 men 'in the woods' near Hastings voted to depose the king and 'hold all things in common'. In Worth Forest the talk was of the king being overthrown by 'a marvellous and terrible man of the ancient royal race', bearing on his coat of arms 'a red lion and a white lion'. In May 1451 a shingler from Rotherfield was among several men hanged at Lewes; Stephen Strode, who gave King's evidence, claimed they had plotted to elect a dozen 'peers' to rule the land. A month later Henry VI himself arrived from Tonbridge with the duke of Somerset and a posse of judges. They learned that two Brightling men in open market had mocked the king as a 'a natural fool' who 'would oft times hold a staff in his hands with a bird on the end, playing therewith as a Fool'. When Henry moved on to Chichester, men seeking his mercy stripped to the waist and lay prostrate before him.

A strange twist in this saga of unrest was the conduct of Robert Poynings, a son of Robert lord Poynings. In London he served, it was said, as Cade's adviser - as his 'carver and sword-bearer', and in 1453, from his abode at Chinting near Seaford, he fomented a popular uprising which fizzled out at North Cray in Kent. He was pardoned, nonetheless, in 1458. Maybe his maverick career caused the name 'Poynings Town' to become associated in the popular mind with Chinting.[25]

In a quite separate sphere, the Hundred Years War with France placed severe strains on the English province of the Cluniac Order. Even during the spasmodic hostilities before 1336, if the prior happened to be a native of France, the assets of the convent at Southover were at the mercy of the Crown, often abetted by an eighth earl Warenne exploiting his shadowy rights as 'founder's kin'. In 1314, during the reign of John of Monte Martini, a former prior of Prittlewell, the earl authorized 'armed men' to enter the priory; in 1321 his 'custody' of its assets alarmed the visitors sent by the general chapter at Cluny. Edward II, meanwhile, insisted that retired royal servants should be quartered there.[26]

In 1324, after Martini's death, the king wanted as prior either James of Cusancia, prior of Prittlewell, or his brother John, prior of Bermondsey, former monks at Southover and Burgundian by birth. But contact with the abbot of Cluny proving difficult, the pope intervened to appoint Adam of Winchester, who placated the king by granting away rich advowsons at Dewsbury and Wakefield to a current royal favourite.[27]

Edward II's downfall, however, and a papal change of heart, caused Adam to be set aside in favour of a 'Frenchman', Peter of Joceaux, also a former monk at Southover, who arrived to find the refectory stripped of its plate. In 1335 he was praised for paying off £10,755 of debt - the £1856, still owed, included large sums to London vintners. But after the Hundred Years War began in 1336, Peter's 'alien' status meant he could retain the priory's secular assets only by paying an annual 'charge' to Edward III; its advowsons and tithes were 'entrusted' to the eighth earl. Probably debts mounted again, for Walter Prest of Melton Mowbray was owed 2000 marks in 1340.[28] Peter resigned in 1344, and though Edward III cautioned the abbot of Cluny against nominating any 'alien person suspect and defamed for dilapidation', he chose another 'Frenchman', John of Jacourt, who retrieved the position, nonetheless, by rendering the king 'good service' on diplomatic missions to Sicily, Austria and Hungary.[29]

Troubles at Southover coincided with grave indiscipline at its daughter-houses. About 1314 the prior of Horton brazenly defied the visitors sent by the general chapter at Cluny. In 1319 William of Averno refused to step down as prior of Prittlewell. In 1334 Peter of Joceaux pungently warned his subordinate priors that monks, sentenced to life imprisonment, should be closely confined, 'lest they return to their offences, as dogs to vomit'. In 1335 the prior at Clifford was rumoured to be a leper. In 1336 the prior of Farleigh had 'betaken himself to remote and unknown places'. At Castle Acre - doubtless disrupted by plague - the monks had dwindled in 1349 from 36 to 13, and two ex-monks were roaming the vicinity. But at Southover the visitors merely censured some inmates for neglecting the tonsure or engaging in secular business.[30]

In 1351 John of Jacourt's successor, Hugh of Chyntriaco, managed to secure from Edward III a decree conferring English status on Cluniacs resident at Southover. The first such decree granted to an alien house, its price was five advowsons worth 200 marks a year. The monks at Southover's daughter-houses were naturalized in 1373, and all other English Cluniacs by 1406. The Order, though, remained supra-national. Indeed abbot Ardruin of Cluny, in person, received the profession of 32 monks in the Lady Chapel at Southover about 1355.[31]

Besides securing the decree, prior Hugh acted as a papal chaplain and as a legal adviser to the dowager-countess Joan; after his departure overseas in 1362, 'the great bell' was always gratefully rung on his anniversary. His successor, Gerald Rothonis, formerly prior of Montacute, served as a papal nuncio to the king and as the abbot of Cluny's vicar-general in England. And the stalwart John of Charlieu (c1364-97), an ex-prior of Bermondsey, spectacularly displayed his patriotism at Rottingdean in 1377. Yet though priors became officially English, from 1365 they were not summoned to parliament, Edward III claiming that they had attended only since 1310-11, 'only at intervals', and not 'by right'.[32]

From 1378 the xenophobia encouraged by the Hundred Years War reinforced a Great Schism in the Church injurious to the Cluniac Order. English clergy acknowledged Urban VI at Rome as pope, while French clergy, and the abbot of Cluny, recognised Clement VII at Avignon - an appalling fracture in Catholic Christendom. Pope Urban instructed the priors of Thetford and Bermondsey to convene an English Cluniac chapter to replace the Order's defunct general chapter, and to elect two 'presidents' to exercise the powers forfeited by Cluny's 'schismatic' abbot. Because Urban ignored Southover's status as the 'senior' English house, John of Charlieu, along with the priors of Montacute and Lenton, held aloof and vainly protested to Rome when the priors of Thetford and Bermondsey were elected presidents. Thereafter a 'national' chapter met at Bermondsey to issue decrees, appoint visitors, vote money and fill vacancies. But Charlieu merely served as one of three key-holders, unlocking the chapter's treasure-chest.[33]

Charlieu was followed in 1397 by John Oak, formerly prior of Castle Acre, whose prestige was such he was asked to resolve a bitter land dispute within the Waleys family. In 1403 he lent to a monk, John Burgherst, a glossed copy of a summary of the Bible in blank verse composed in 1393 by a Franciscan, John Vasco. Burgherst, a native perhaps of Burwash in the Sussex Weald, succeeded Oak in 1409 and when the Great Schism ended, the abbot of Cluny, back in control of the English province, made him his vicar-general in England and Scotland with power to hear professions, install priors and forward money. But Burgherst complained that English houses, not founded directly from Cluny, rejected his authority. Moreover, though countess Beatrice warmly supported his schemes to have the priory elevated to the status of an abbey, they were blocked by the general chapter at Cluny. Frustrated on two fronts he resigned in 1417 with a pension of £20 a year, though he later claimed to have acted under duress.[34]

That Southover was becoming a very English, indeed South-Eastern, house is suggested by the surnames of inmates ordained at Malling church in 1419 - Thomas Feversham priest, Thomas Wynchelsea, Thomas Mallyng and William Hertefeld deacons, William Wynchelsea acolyte. Burgherst's successor, Thomas Nelond, was perhaps from the Weald, for his brother John, resident at East Grinstead, bought the manor of Bevendean near Falmer in 1416. Prior Nelond, prior Robert Auncell (1432-45) and prior John Daniel (1446-64), also officiated as vicar-generals of an increasingly autonomous English province - with power to act in Ireland as well as Scotland. In 1452 Daniel was licensed to travel for three years - though in 1458-9 his authority was briefly suspended while an emissary from Cluny vainly tried to salvage the abbot's ebbing authority.[35]

The priory also lost its role as the sepulchre of the lords of Lewes, though at first the Fitzalans chose to be buried there. After the funeral in

1372 of Eleanor, his 'most dear' wife, earl Richard I ordered two 'high tombs' from the royal Master Mason, Henry Yevele. In January 1375 they were loaded at Poole onto the *Margaret* of Wareham for delivery to London. The following December the earl stipulated he was to rest beside Eleanor in the priory chapter-house beneath a tomb no taller than hers. He wanted none of the 'bombance', the armed men and war-horses, which dramatized the last earl Warenne's funeral - five large wax candles merely were to illuminate the hearse. If the effigies on Yevele's 'high tombs' reached Southover, they may now repose, somewhat battered, in Chichester cathedral - removed there, tradition asserts, at the Dissolution. The lion rampant on the knight's surcoat suggests a Fitzalan;

68 Larkin's lovers

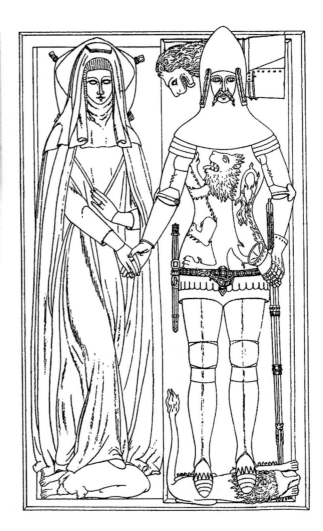

his armour resembles the Black Prince's at Canterbury carved in the 1370s. But the clasping hands of the husband and wife, which so engaged Philip Larkin, though a gesture fashionable at that time, date from a restoration of the effigies in the 1840s.[36]

It was at Arundel that earl Richard II founded a college of secular canons and a hospital dedicated to the Holy Trinity. Perhaps to endow the hospital, which did eventually receive it, he assembled the manor of 'Kingston' near Lewes, listed among his estates in 1397. It included what is now 87 High Street and the Hides, the fields south-west of St Mary Westout, which he detached maybe from Houndean manor. But for his burial Fitzalan was promised by prior Charlieu a prestigious space behind the high altar at Southover, which his deceased wife, Elizabeth, would share. The cost of their monuments was to equal that of his parents' 'high tombs'. Fitzalan's execution, however, meant a hasty interment in London, and Elizabeth remained in her grave south of the high altar.[37]

Other Fitzalans were buried at the priory church. In 1375 Katherine Peverel, the sister of earl Richard I, left the site to prior Charlieu's 'discretion'. In 1379 Richard II's brother John, the Earl Marshal of England, opted to rest under an arch between two small chapels in a south aisle - though an early-Tudor herald recorded him 'under a plain stone' in the chapter-house, next to William, Richard's first son who died in 1385. Wherever John lay, his widow Eleanor chose to join him in 1405. Like his father, the Marshal wanted no funeral 'bombance', no mourners wearing black; the remnants of the five wax candles and forty torches were to be sent to local churches. Adherents of the Fitzalans were also interred at Southover. In 1374 William Laxman, a retainer of the Marshal at Reigate, asked to lie near a crucifixion scene painted 'on the north side'. He left a coat of mail and a vizor to John Brocas, prior Charlieu's companion-in-arms at Rottingdean. Lady Joan St John in 1385 was laid to rest in the Lady Chapel near her husband Edward. And in 1392 Sir John Fallisle, who also fought at Rottingdean, chose to lie in the crowded sanctuary, 'on the left of the image of saint Pancras'.[38] The Fitzalans, moreover, enriched the furniture of the church and multiplied the acts of intercession. John the Marshal endowed the altar next his tomb with a 'daily' and a 'festival' missal, with a chalice and a pair of cruets, a blue silk vestment and a cross carried by three angels. His father left £200 for two monks to each chant daily 'in perpetuity' a mass to shorten his soul's time in purgatory. The Marshal's wife preferred a blitz of intercession, a thousand masses to be sung 'en tout hast qe poet est estre'.[39]

However in the 15th century the church ceased to be a seigneurial sepulchre. Earl Thomas, who died at Harfleur in 1415, was buried in the choir of his father's collegiate church at Arundel, where his tomb, 'ornate and competent', survives. In 1439 the dowager-countess Beatrice was laid beside him. Thereafter the joint-lords of Lewes rape still exercised in rotation the rights enjoyed by 'founders' kin'. Edmund Lenthall sponsored John Daniel as prior, after Nicholas Benet, the abbot of Cluny's choice, chose to remain at Castle Acre. Yet they preferred to be buried elsewhere, as did local knights, for chantry chapels in parish churches were coming into fashion. Blanche, Lady Poynings of Slaugham, it is true, was interred at the priory in 1409, but she had drifted from her family to become a 'particular favourite' of king Richard II. More typical was Richard Weyville, a minor landowner at Rodmell, who opted in 1417 to repose 'under the processional way'. In 1437 John Nelond sought a space near the tomb of his brother, prior Thomas.[40]

The town of Lewes faced other misfortunes, apart from absentee seigneurs, the disruption of sea-borne commerce, the pillage of its outport, and troubles at its priory. Even before the Black Death in 1348, its commerce was damaged by falling grain yields and widespread livestock disease along the South Downs, the result of exhausted soil and a wetter, colder climate. At Hangleton near Brighton the Great Plague was but 'the culminating blow' to a community in decline. Rising sea levels, moreover, were drowning coastal and estuarine acres in Sussex. Old Winchelsea was abandoned in 1287. A 'great flood' was recorded in 1331-2 and tidal damage along the Lower Rother ended the water carriage of goods to Salehurst market place. At Lewes - though the date is unclear - a causeway across water meadows near St John's was abandoned to flood-water. At Southover the Cluniacs built six massive buttresses against the south wall of their latrine-block to combat subsidence. The impact on the estuary is unclear, though in 1377 it was still possible, perhaps, for a French fleet to anchor 'within sight' of the town.[41]

The plight of parish churches in Lewes borough also suggests a shrinking revenue from commerce. By 1319 the rectors of St Nicholas, Holy Trinity and St Peter the Less could no longer pay 14 shillings a year to the priory's precentor. Indeed the two latter churches were 'entirely ruined beyond repair by storms and gales'. In 1337, in a fruitless bid to solve a cash crisis, the bishop of Chichester proposed to suppress the seven intra-mural daughter-parishes - St Mary in the Market, St Peter the Less, St Nicholas, Holy Sepulchre, Holy Trinity, St Andrew and St Martin. 'Trustworthy men' had assured him that their revenues, and those of All Saints, were inadequate, and that the livings had suffered a 'prolonged vacancy', leaving their flocks unattended, a prey to 'the cunningly [devised] wiles of the enemy of the faith'.[42]

No coherent picture of the town's wealth can be gleaned from taxation levied in 1327 and 1340. In 1327 59 taxpayers, in the Borough, Southover and Cliffe, paid £8 0s 8d - but Southover's total was distorted by William Darnell's £1 2s 9d. At Seaford 23 townsfolk paid £4, but its status as a Cinque Port perhaps exempted some residents. At Chichester

48 citizens paid £10 17s 8d, but in 1340 the moveable goods of 121 citizens were valued at £182 11s, at Lewes Borough those of 27 townsfolk at £19 2s 6d - a worrying discrepancy.[43] Darnell's affluence, though, is a reminder that some men prosper in difficult times. Listed in 1351 among wool merchants owed money by the Crown, he witnessed the conveyance of Cluniac property and endowed the monks with premises at Balsdean. Moreover, Robert the Spicer, a taxpayer in the Borough, held over 100 acres at Barcombe and Ringmer in 1318; he owed £10 to John Ive of Winchelsea in 1320, served as a Borough MP in 1322 and 1323 and sold to the bishop of Chichester for £20 a house, a ferry and four acres near Seaford in 1326. Just possibly a house at the top of School Hill, described in 1337 as sometime his, included the rectangular cellar beneath the present Town Hall, ascribed to the early 14th-century. It has a plain barrel vault of neatly-dressed clunch and a flight of steps from the street.[44]

The manifold ills of eastern Sussex in the earlier 14th century help to explain the paucity of its Decorated architecture - though the splendid, heavily cusped, church of St Thomas at New Winchelsea was a result of rising sea levels overwhelming Old Winchelsea. From the priory at Southover very few Decorated architectural pieces survive. But in the first monastic church a new east window, almost 11 feet wide, was filled with sophisticated stained glass; fragments carry border designs, drapery patterns and sharp Lombardic lettering. Also found, displaced perhaps from a floor tomb, were two Lombardic 'D's made of copper alloy and a cusped brass quatrefoil depicting the lion of saint Mark. Moreover four single-light Decorated windows, with ogee heads and trefoil cuspings, survive in the 'chancel' of St James's hospital.[45] And decorated with intricate interlace and robustly drawn figures were the well-made floor-tiles, perhaps early 14th-century in date, which the Franciscans laid in their church: a shaven-headed man points his tongue; phoenixes stretch their ragged wings, and griffins cavort - part lion, part eagle, and in this case, part 'domestic goose'.[46]

Work was also done at the parish church of Southover, which had previously served perhaps as

69 The 'D's and the lion of saint Mark

70 The floor-tiles from the friary

71 The reticulated tracery

the Cluniacs' hospitium. Into the north wall of the nave and the chancel were inserted windows with fine reticulated tracery, the circles at top and bottom drawn into ogee shapes. At some date, moreover, perhaps to make room for a bell-tower, at least one western bay of the Romanesque arcade was demolished and a new west wall and entrance built. (Ground-plan 4.3) In 1698 the 'old decayed steeple' collapsed, 'in lieu of which' a new tower was begun in 1714. Long vanished, though, is a font noted by Sir Stephen Glynne in 1826 as a good Norman specimen, 'of square form supported upon a round central pillar, and at the angles octagonal shafts with square bases and rude Norman capitals' - if authentic, its provenance remains obscure.[47]

But more disruptive even than bad weather or flooding was the bubonic plague which struck England at the close of 1348. Its impact in rural mid-Sussex can be gauged on Alciston manor. In Edward I's time just over a hundred tenants were spread between East Blatchington, Lullington, Tilton, Alciston and Hellingly. In the first eight months of 1349 almost eighty died. The plague struck first at Blatchington by Seaford, then moved up the Cuckmere valley and into the Weald. The monasteries at Battle and Southover were hard hit, and at Michelham by 1353 only five of the 13 canons survived. A sudden depopulation might explain why in March 1352 the Cluniacs warned John Norman not to demolish a house in Southover they were renting to him, and why episcopal tenants were suddenly absent from 'the courts at Lewes' of the dowager-countess Joan. Between Michaelmas 1348 and 1350, moreover, no merchants exported cloth from Sussex. Plague again swept Sussex in 1361-2, 1387 and 1396, and was blamed in 1425-7 and 1440-1 for a shortage of labourers at Alciston manor. (See chapter opener)[48]

Because the population in mid-Sussex, as in the rest of England, fell heavily between 1348 and 1400, and stagnated long into the 15th century, the impact on agriculture was profound. Arable acres in the Weald were abandoned to rough grazing. Along the South Downs many large, labour-efficient farms were formed, replacing peasant family-farms - a depopulation which speeded the decay of parish churches at Excete and Sutton-by-Seaford, Aldrington and West Blatchington, of chapels at Northease and Balsdean, Balmer, Ashcombe and Southerham. Farmers still contended, moreover, with cold wet weather, harvest failure, and rising sea-levels. The Battle Benedictines and the Southover Cluniacs evacuated flooded arable near Barnhorne and Langney. Along the Ouse estuary and Glynde Reach the drainage of 6000 acres of water-meadow, above and below Lewes, became disrupted - by 1405 many 'walls, dykes and gutters' between Isfield and the sea were reported to be broken, and in 1421 a Commission of Sewers was set up to restore the banks down-stream from Fletching. Yet in the 1530s winter floods below Lewes could linger 'all summer long', and water-meadows at Southover and Swanborough might yield only thatching reeds.[49] A loss of agrarian vitality accounts for the dwindling annual revenues from fairs in Lewes rape noted at its court after 1400 - at Cuckfield, West Hoathly and Ardingly they fell to 'nothing'.[50]

Landowners now faced soaring labour costs and falling income. The Benedictines at Battle saw theirs slump by a third - permanently - and maybe the Cluniacs at Southover did so too. Yet in 1391 their annual 'worth', if reliably recorded as 1600 marks (£1066 13s 4d), was still considerable, close to the £1091 gross and £921 net officially estimated in 1535, when only 23 English religious houses enjoyed a 'clear' revenue of over £1000. At Battle the number of monks dropped from 52 in 1347 to perhaps twenty in 1403 - a cost-cutting exercise maybe. At Southover the fall was much less rapid - there were forty monks in 1294, 33 in 1306, 40 in 1381, 48 in 1391, 36 in 1405 and 1450, and 23 in 1479-80, 13 of them priests and ten novices.[51]

The Fitzalans and their adherents still made benefactions to the Cluniacs; so did Sir John Philpot, a Lord Mayor of London who defeated French raiders in the North Sea. But from the early 15th century they largely dried up. To raise cash, the priory began annexing rectories and probably, like the Battle Benedictines, it leased out much manorial demesne, though in 1433 and 1496, it rented Wootton manor in East Chiltington, an estate close to Balneath, from Christ Church priory at Canterbury.[52] The Battle Benedictines also drew rising rents from property in Southwark, a suburb crammed with hostelries, bordellos and bear-gardens, servicing a metropolis which thrived, though the kingdom languished. Rather unwisely, the Cluniacs had exchanged the tithes from St Olave's at Southwark for an annuity of £4. However in 1373 they commissioned a local carpenter, William Wintringham, to build two rows of jettied shops each side of the approach to their town-house in Tooley Street, already perhaps 'the great house built of stone with arched gates' that John Stow noted at Southwark in the 1590s.[53]

Maybe priors became more managerial. Thomas Nelond wiped out a debt of 3200 marks incurred by John Burgherst - indeed the epitaph on his sumptuous memorial brass, preserved at Cowfold, has him uniting the practical skills of a Martha with the 'heavenly wisdom' of a Mary. However, it was reported to the general chapter at Cluny in 1429 that he was trading benefices for cash and allowing discipline and hospitality to slide. And indeed parishioners at West Hoathly, Patcham and Ditchling, where rectories had been annexed, did complain that their churches were unrepaired, their pastoral care neglected.[54] As for Nelond's funeral in 1432, John Mason Neale, author of *Good King Wenceslas*, concocted a shamelessly bogus account of the music - 'soche ravishynge melodye made of organs; and soche swete harmonye companied therewith of voyces that I dide almost thynke I was in hevynly felicite' - and of the cortege setting out (which it never did) for Cowfold - 'fyrste wente sixteene Priests, chauntyng; aftyr hem twayne pursuivantes atte armes; thanne was the coffin

72 Prior Nelond

drawne by four mulys upon a lowe charett, and over hit was borne the herse [by] eighte monkes'; last came 'a raskell rowte of menne, women and childryn'.[55]

Prior Auncell was managerial enough to order a massive chartulary of priory deeds to be compiled in 1444. Pressmarks on them reveal that their cataloguing had passed through several stages. The earliest endorsement, the grantor's name, was written in a 'fine, bold hand', probably in the 12th century. Thirteenth-century scribes often added the name of the manor, the county or diocese. Then about 1400 the deeds were re-arranged by donor, hierarchically, into 19 sections, with the Roman numeral written in a deep black ink; popes were allotted i and ii, kings iii and iv, Warennes v and vi, archbishops vii, bishops viii and ix; then the deeds of lesser mortals were grouped under diocese, rape or county. Prudent prior Auncell also ensured that a daily mass for his 'wholesome estate' on earth, as well as for his soul's salvation, was offered

171

daily during his life-time, and 'for ever' after his death, at the altar of saint Mary Magdalene, before which he chose to be buried. His successor, John Daniel, had been the convent's chamberlain, a key administrator. While immersed in his duties as Cluniac vicar-general in England, Scotland and Ireland, he was licensed in 1452 to travel for three years. Henry VI commended him for his 'religion, honesty and conscience'.[56]

Architectural fragments from the priory do not suggest any major rebuilding during the century after the Black Death, though there survives a length of cornice carved in very high relief, which depicts an armoured warrior in separate combat with a dragon, a devil and a wild man of the woods; each contest is framed within sprays of oak-leaves and acorns.

73 The cornice

Also post-dating the Black Death, perhaps, was the bold cruciform pigeon-house with recesses of hewn chalk for 3228 pairs of doves; its arms were about eighty feet long, with openings under each gable-end.

74 The pigeon-house

172

At St James's hospital the chancel-chapel received a bold Perpendicular east window with three lights.[57]

75 The bold east window

There is greater evidence of the Cluniacs building elsewhere. The 'grange' at Swanborough was stylishly remodelled, perhaps about 1400. An upper room, inserted earlier into the late 12th-century hall, was given a handsome single-frame wagon roof, two delicately traceried partition screens, and an elegant quatrefoil oculus affording a view of the chapel. A two-storied gatehouse was also erected.

76 The partition screens

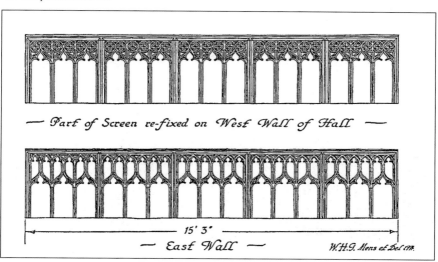

— *Part of Screen re-fixed on West Wall of Hall* —

— 15' 3" —

— *East Wall* —

W.H.G. *Mens et Del 177.*

At Langney 'grange' a chamber and fireplace were constructed above an enlarged chapel, and the south facade was chequered with blocks of green sandstone and narrow panels of cut flints. Maybe the prior hunted from these 'granges', much as the abbot of Battle roamed the thyme-scented sheepwalks above Alciston and the coastal marshes near Barnhorne. The priory's 200-acre park at the Mote in Little Horsted was stocked in 1535 with bucks and does. A chapel existed there in 1312 at the hunting lodge, from which out-lying farms were administered. In June 1538 the 'pretty house' there called 'the Motte' was larger than Swanborough 'grange', big enough indeed to absorb the household of Thomas Cromwell's son. Its island site is under investigation. A mound of uncertain date stands on the edge of nearby woodland, ideal for potting deer with crossbow or arquebus.[58]

77 Langney Grange

The Franciscans at Lewes still partially relied on charity, on doles of corn from the manors of Glynde and Beddingham, on cheese from the abbot of Battle - though at some time they did acquire tithes at Houndean and elsewhere. Possibly their kitchen was made smaller after the Black Death, so their number may have fallen. However a range at the west side of the precinct was extended, perhaps to provide guest quarters or a warden's lodgings - fragments of large complex windows have been found. The extension straddled the Town Ditch, so the water was diverted through a barrel-vaulted chalk culvert which doubtless flushed the latrine-block before debouching into the Ouse.[59]

Certainly scaled back, if their sealing of documents is any guide, were the visits paid by archbishops to Old Malling palace. Henry Chichele (1414-43) came most years till 1424, staying at least a month in July-August 1421; he returned in 1428 and 1433. A new oratory on the south side of the chapel was ceiled, plastered and floored in 1426-7. William atte Beche, 'roofer' of Lewes, William atte Welle mason and John Snayton glazier, repaired the chapel, hall and archbishop's chamber, the kitchen, buttery and larder, in 1432-3. Yet after 1433 Chichele sealed nothing at Malling, and very little at Slindon or Mayfield. Thomas Bourchier (1454-86) sealed in Sussex only at Mayfield, in October-November 1479. Perhaps his building a vast mansion at Knole discouraged progresses through Sussex. Old Malling, though, was kept in repair. The keeper of the archbishop's quarry at Horsham sent six cartloads of stone to the palace in 1456.[60]

It seems likely that a tolerably lavish life-style was sustained by the deans of the college of secular canons at Malling. William of Swanton (1302-26) served archbishop Winchelsey as chaplain, steward of his household and executor of his will. Roger of Stratton (1330-37) was chancellor of Oxford university, where John of Etchingham (1357-71) resided till graduating as a Doctor of Theology in 1365. Thereafter he 'lived the life of a country gentleman', litigating with his neighbours and hunting the abbot of Battle's game. Archbishop Courtenay briefly bestowed the office of dean on his 14-year-old nephew in 1395. The sybaritic William Piers (1406-39), a former archdeacon of Exeter, bequeathed a fur-lined gown, two silver salt-cellars, a coral rosary adorned with a silver Agnus Dei, and two pet horses called Deghenet and Sorel. His *Summa Confessorum* was to be stoutly chained in the choir of the collegiate church and inscribed with a curse damning anyone who removed it. A receipt signed by John Urry (1453-58), for cash sent from his rectory farm at Lindfield, was found in 1947 in the wall of a High Street bakery there.[61]

An order made by archbishop Winchelsey required the three canons - the precentor, chancellor and treasurer - to each reside at Malling for forty days a year. In 1366 each had a 'dwelling' there and a garden stretching down towards the Ouse. Though the college was secularized in 1545, a sprawling south-facing range, with a tower, sketched in 1620 by John Deward, could be interpreted as three 'dwellings', with a commodious wing on the east, very fit for a dean. In 1622

78 Deward's sketch

175

the complex was described as 'fairly and strongly built', with a gatehouse, two stables, three barns, a dovecote, three gardens, two orchards and a court. A late-Stuart mansion on the site retains a '16th-century' two-light stone window and a 'Tudor' doorcase, its oak spandrels carved with grotesque details. Sometime after 1795 a 'refectory', long used as a barn, was demolished and 'ancient fishponds within the bank of the river' filled up, though a dove-house was spared.[62]

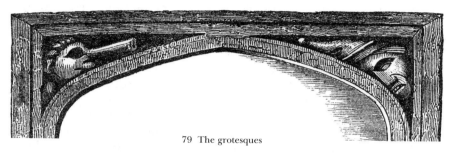

79 The grotesques

Quite apart from absentee seigneurs, disruption to coastal trade, civil commotion, a recession in agriculture and retrenchment by Cluniacs, the economy of Lewes borough suffered from the refusal of the Crown to make it a steady centre of shire administration, despite its being in the middle of Sussex. Litigants, jurors, witnesses and attorneys, it is true, were drawn to the rapal court which still transacted a mix of Honorial and Hundredal business. In 1356-7 this included the wardship of John Lyvet; the relief due on four and a half knights' fees; the over-pricing of bread; the false use of a measure, known locally as a 'lyncer'; the theft of gold from a merchant; the breach of a contract to cart tithe-corn at Pyecombe, and a debt of 8s 3d owed 'since the Pestilence'. But hardly ever was the county court of the sheriff held at Lewes. As the agent of royal justice, he empanelled juries and collected fines. His court met on a Thursday every four weeks to publish writs, declare outlawries, adjudicate crimes, settle major debts and stage the election of coroners and knights of the shire by the county's freeholders. Royal commands in 1254 and in 1336 confirmed its location at Chichester, in the extreme west of the county, close to the Hampshire border. After a violent quarrel between the sheriff and civic leaders, it was removed to Lewes in June 1378, but only briefly. The sheriff also officiated in Surrey, and prisoners from Sussex were detained for trial in a common gaol which he oversaw at Guildford castle.[63]

Royal assize judges, however, who resorted to Sussex ever more frequently, did usually sit at Lewes or East Grinstead. About 1387 Sir William of Etchingham expended 17s 8d at Lewes while attending a sessions. There too, after Whitsun 1400, Henry FitzJohn was charged with murder; he appeared with his attorney at East Grinstead in December, and was found guilty at Lewes in the fourth week of Lent 1401. More crucial still for its growth as an administrative centre, landowners known as Keepers of the Peace were authorized in 1368 to try felonies committed in their shire, and they held some of their 'quarter' sessions in the Borough. Lawyers took local root. The coroner Thomas White, five times an MP for 'Lewes' between 1420 and 1435, served the dowager countess Beatrice. John Stempe, constable of Southover in 1450, resigned as a coroner in 1440 because royal business in Sussex preoccupied him. John Delve, an 'attorney of London' who paid the 1379 poll tax in Cliffe or Malling and witnessed local conveyances, may have acted for John of Gaunt in 1366. John Harold, the steward of the Etchingham family's estate at Beddingham, lived at Cliffe in 1379. At Lewes too was trained a literate elite. In 1308-10 the Etchinghams paid for a youth from Barcombe to be taught there by 'master Henry'. 'The schoolmaster of Lewes' was owed six pence by a priest at Westout in 1405. Even earlier, in 1248, the Cluniacs had appointed their 'beloved clerk, Lucas, schoolmaster of Lewes' to represent them at Rome - he also witnessed a grant of land to them at Wantley. John of Hampton, 'master of Lewes school', was ordained an acolyte at Malling collegiate church in 1285.[64]

Despite the encircling gloom, commerce in Lewes and mid-Sussex struggled on. Warfare could be a brief stimulus when soldiers were supplied. In 1346 corn from Southdown granaries near Seaford was sent to the army besieging Calais, so were twenty 25-foot scaling ladders made at Thakeham by Wealden carpenters. To sustain the new English garrison at Calais in 1349, a cask of cider was dispatched from Clayton, via Shoreham. A Wealden smithy near Horsham provided crown-agents with 1000 horse-shoes in 1327, with 150 sheaves of arrows in 1347. Two oaks from Worth Forest were used for the beams of a 'great engine' built at the Tower of London in 1337.[65]

Piracy in the Channel, moreover, fed a shabby trade at Seaford in plundered merchandise. A Sandwich-based privateer docked in 1338 laden with the goods of Norman traders seized from a Flemish freighter. Pillage on offer in 1352 included 132 hides and 150 tons of 'ashes', loaded in Flanders by a Genoese merchant - many of the ashes were bought by a Lewes blacksmith, James Ferour. But the cargo of a Flemish ship, seized between Southampton and Sandwich in 1455, belonged, it transpired, to London fishmongers. 'Wrecking' of course was a constant pastime, abetted by vicious currents in Seaford Bay. In 1387 the agents of earl Fitzalan and prior Charlieu were reluctant to release seven 'tons' of Gascon wine, claiming they had been 'stranded' on their manorial beaches.[66]

As for the cross-Channel export of Sussex wool from the county's ports, which averaged 300 sacks a year between 1307 and 1336, its disruption by the Hundred Years War might account for the clip from the Waleys estate at Glynde being supplied in 1348 to weavers at Canterbury, and for wool from Alciston being drawn in wagons by 16 oxen to Wych Cross and to East Grinstead in 1355 and 1356, perhaps for delivery in London. From 1353, moreover, the pattern of shipments from Sussex was distorted by regulations requiring wool exported from England to be weighed and taxed at a 'staple' port, before being shipped to Calais as a first destination, and by the choice of Chichester to serve the whole of Sussex - even though, as Lewesians were at pains to point out, most wool in the county was 'grown' within 15 miles of their town, and its carriage so far westward was expensive and often perilous.[67]

The regulation, though, was relaxed after Richard Fitzalan became earl of Surrey in 1361. He inherited demesne farms in Lewes rape on which over 8000 ewes, wethers and rams were grazed in 1397. (His predecessor, Earl Warenne, in 1338 had sold 200 sacks of wool to Edward III for delivery to his Italian creditors, 'the Societies of the Bardi and the Peruzzi'.) So maybe Fitzalan's influence at Court secured the order made in 1365 authorizing customs officers based at Chichester to weigh and tax wool at Lewes, before its export through Seaford or New Shoreham to Calais. In 1380, for instance, 'the balances' were brought over to weigh sixty sacks belonging to Richard Fitzalan II, and between 1382 and 1397 customs officers like Walter Goslyn, Stephen Holt and John Mariot were officiating at Chichester and at Lewes. Indeed in 1397 Fitzalan's neglected castle itself housed 'a beam' and 13 bronze weights for measuring wool. In the year ending at Michaelmas 1384 368 of the 511 sacks sent overseas from Sussex passed through Lewes, and all of the 150 sacks shipped away in the year ending Michaelmas 1397. Vessels based at Dordrecht, Middleburg and Zeeland received several cargoes, which suggests that the Netherlands was a frequent destination. 'A man of Brabant' loaded uncustomed wool into a Dunkirk vessel at Seaford in 1365. Another smuggler, John Russell of Lewes, shipped three sacks one night in 1394 from Goring in west Sussex ; they had been hidden in the premises of William Green, elected an MP for 'Lewes' in 1406.[68]

Seemingly the role of Lewes as a staple port prompted wool exporters to redeploy there from Seaford and Shoreham. Whereas twelve can be identified at Chichester in 1323-26, seven at Shoreham, six at Seaford, but only one at Lewes, between 1378 and 1398 eight Borough residents were leading exporters from Sussex. Five were described in the 1379 poll tax as 'buyers of wool' - Henry Werkman, Robert York, Robert Hore, Nicholas Uppehous and William Tynnott. The others were Andrew Blake, John Bedford and Roger Gosselyn. Henry Werkman leased a third of Ovingdean manor about 1371 and set up a 'stall' on a plot of land 'below' St Andrew's church with Robert York. Roger

Gosselyn bought the clip from the Battle abbey flock at Alciston in 1375-6 and rented pasture for 800 sheep near Seaford. John Bedford shipped away 120 sacks in 1378, mostly in the *Margaret* of Shoreham. And in 1397 Robert Hore and Andrew Blake bought wool worth £100 from Richard Fitzalan II. Other leading exporters were Richard Vyne at Cliffe and Thomas Norris at Southover. Assessed there in 1379, along with a 'wool packer', Norris leased four curtilages in the 'Hempsheres' at Westport, and sat at least seven times as an MP for 'Lewes' between 1363 and 1391 - perhaps indeed for Southover, if the protocol, re-affirmed in 1553, already applied. Taxed in Lewes borough in 1379 as 'cloth merchants' were William Downing and William Smyth, Richard atte Gate and Robert Draper.[69]

From March 1397 till Christmas 1400 the export of wool overseas through Lewes continued to be authorized. Thereafter, though, a royal licence was needed and was issued only to a favoured few, to the London merchant, Richard ('Dick') Whittington, in 1409, to Sir Robert Poynings in 1422 - whereas John Parker, an MP for 'Lewes' in 1417, was fined for shipping fleeces to Zeeland without one in 1418. However in October 1444 it was acknowledged that no revenue had recently accrued to the king from the beam for weighing wool located at Lewes from 'old time', and consequently, for the next three years, 'native' merchants were to be allowed to have their wool customed there, for export to Calais through Shoreham or Seaford. It seems this concession was extended, for in 1453 wool from Seaford, destined for Calais, was diverted 'by fraud and negligence' to Normandy and Brittany, and in 1456 to Zeeland. But by the 1460s the export of wool overseas from Sussex had ceased, replaced by small shipments of rather coarse kersey-cloths, probably woven in the county - a traffic nothing like as lucrative as the trade in wool.[70]

Wealden timber and firewood were still supplied to communities in deforested areas of northern France and the Netherlands. The bulk was dispatched through Winchelsea, but at Seaford were loaded the timber and oak-bark shipped away by Henry Bastard of Calais in 1327-8, and the firewood diverted, along with wool, to Zeeland in 1456. Other local produce was also sent away through Lewes and Seaford. In 1370 John Criour of Brighton was licensed to convey 800 bushels of malt to Southampton. In 1388-90 the 'Lewes' MP, William Chepeland, a butcher with a pasture on 'the banks' near Watergate, exported a medley of mead and candles, peas and oats, butter and cloth, salted beef and bacon. Though the output of salt from coastal works in Sussex was dwindling, two bondsmen from Bramber in the Adur estuary delivered four bushels to Leigh near Reigate in 1345.[71]

Doubtless, wine was still regularly brought from Gascony. There, in the service of the Black Prince, in 1364, resided William Crouge of Lewes, perhaps the merchant of that name at Bordeaux owed money by John Kent of Lewes in 1387; a William Croughe also rented premises on

School Hill. More prosaic imports - herring, garlic and onions - were carried in two Dutch ships bound from Zeeland to Seaford in 1403, but driven by a storm into Sandwich. The cargo belonged to the 'Lewes' MP and wool merchant, Andrew Blake, who part-owned the *Margaret of Hoke*, impressed at Southampton for royal service in 1402. And doubtless it was often via Southampton, Winchelsea or London that exotic commodities arrived upriver from Seaford - figs, raisins, almonds, dates, leather and wax from the Mediterranean, hose from Ireland, linen cloth, mirrors, canvas, fish and Caen stone from Normandy, woad from Picardy, woollen cloth from northern France and from Malines and Louvain in Flanders, masts, pitch and oil from the Baltic. Debts to Londoners included £10 owed by Adam Crek of Cliffe to a fishmonger in 1329, 56s 3d by a Borough chapman, Thomas Larks, to a linendraper in 1417, and 86s 8d by Richard Brasyer, a 'Lewes' MP, to a pewterer, also in 1417. Robert Cousin, a spicer of Lewes, killed a man at Stoneham in 1392.[72]

Among the articles on which the murage grant of 1334 authorized tolls to be levied at Lewes borough were linen thread and canvas, Irish cloth and worsted, silks from Cyprus, cloths of gold and satin, alum and copperas, verdigris and argol [a tartar derived from grape juice], stockfish and Aberdeen fish, fresh and salt salmon, lampreys 'for sale before Easter', mill-stones and steel rods, sheaves of garlic, casks of wine and potash.[73]

Building materials also came by sea. Roofing slates were still delivered from south Devon. Floor tiles fired in Normandy, glazed brown and yellow, and decorated with fleur-de-lis and vine tendrils, were laid at the priory, possibly in the dormitory, and at Poynings church which was rebuilt about 1368. Well made and easy to handle, they were also shipped to distant Dublin and York. Flemish bricks, unloaded at Winchelsea and Seaford by the early 14th century, probably arrived as ballast.[74]

Perhaps till about 1400 Lewes could still be reached by sea-going ships. Malt was loaded there in 1370, sacks of wool in 1384-6. French raiders sailed to 'within sight' of the town in 1377 and Adam Melle voyaged in a 'Lewes' boat from Seaford to Calais in 1386. But soon after maybe, and certainly by the 1530s, the estuary became too choked with 'slub' to be navigated other than by barge. As for the upper Ouse above Lewes, though it was not canalized till the 1790s, its use by 1300 for the carriage of commodities would explain the presence in its basin of easily fractured West Country slate. Possibly, too, 'the Bridge-house' near Sharpsbridge in Fletching was used as a depot, perhaps for Wealden timber. Formerly John Sharp's, it was granted in 1357 to John Smith at Cliffe; in 1417 Smith's grand-daughter married the Borough chapman, Thomas Larks, and in 1706 the Bridge-house and wharf, alias 'Larks', was held by Nicholas Longley, a Barcombe timber merchant with a yard at Southover, where three sawyers had paid the poll tax in 1379.

Moreover, in 1635, long before canalization, Barcombe mill was deemed a possible 'annoyance' to the passage of boats. Nonetheless, oxen were used to remove the '300 trees, half oaks, half beeches', at 'Sayshomwode' near Hamsey, bought by prior Charlieu in 1372 from Sir William Saye.[75]

After the Black Death markets closed at Hurstpierpoint, Lindfield and Alfriston, though others survived at Brighton and Ditchling, Eastbourne and Hailsham, East Grinstead and, probably, Cuckfield. Moreover, in May 1346, maybe to tap the resources of his Wealden manors, archbishop Stratford was granted weekly markets at Cliffe on Tuesdays and Fridays, and two annual fairs, on the feast of the Beheading of John the Baptist and on the feast of saint Catherine. Doubtless they soon fizzled out, but in 1409 archbishop Arundel secured a Wednesday market and two fairs, 'on the eve, the day and the morrow of saint Mark [24-26 April] ... and on the eve, the day and the morrow of saint Matthew [20-22 September]'.[76]

There are glimpses of the Borough's trading life. 'About the hour of vespers', on a Saturday in February 1399, John Swone was returning to East Hoathly across Broyle Common in Ringmer with victuals bought at the market, when he was ambushed under an oak tree by William Lenyng and silently dealt a mortal wound to the brain. In 1406 the butcher William Coterell was granted a piece of ground near the Borough pillory, six by seven feet, on which to set up a stall every Saturday. At the 'Lewes' fair in the 1360s the reeve of Beddingham bought a five-gallon container and sold some wether sheep. In 1440 it was held in Whitsun week, probably to cater for the Pentecostal processions, first authorized in 1248 by bishop Richard. At Whitsun in 1400 visitors were offered a desirable indulgence if they visited the relics at the priory, gave to its repair fund and were shriven by the prior and ten assistants. In the 1360s the Beddingham reeve also sold wethers and lambs at the 'saint Pancras fair' in Southover, as well as wheat, barley and fleeces to John Harold at Cliffe, and wool to William Morris there, a trader too in wheat.[77]

Purchased at Lewes, and carried away, were a cask of honey to Battle abbey, chalk to Mayfield, malt to Heighton St Clere, three cows to Chalvington and to Alciston a pipe of wine, wheels for a plough and a wagon, a barrel of salted eels, and barrels of tar to combat sheep-scab. Between 1464 and 1479, churchwardens at Arlington bought a bell rope, a gallon of oil, and nails to fix tiles and shingles. They also hired carpenters from Lewes to construct an upper floor in their tower and hang two bells. In 1432-3 William atte Beche, 'roofer' of Lewes, did repairs at Malling palace, to which William Bohunte of Cliffe supplied locks and keys. Simon Orloger, clockmaker, was a Borough resident in 1352. A Lewes glasier, William Pende, was party to a recognizance of £100 in 1430. A Lewes goldsmith, Walter Hales, was sued, 'touching £20', by the parson at Ripe in 1371, whereas the action brought by prior Oak against

Richard Shareshulle, goldsmith, in 1404 involved 'the detention of a chalice'. Six aliens from Flanders, Brabant, Holland, Zeeland and Gelderland, probably craftsmen, were authorized to reside in 1436, among them Iselbert Deson, cordwainer. Among four 'fishermen' listed at Cliffe in the 1379 poll tax was John Blacche, who supplied the Waleys household at Glynde with sea fish. From the archbishop's fishery close by, on the Ouse below Ranscombe, pike, bream, tench, perch, roach and eels were carried to Canterbury in 1435 and to Lambeth palace in 1444. Engines called 'warenettes', for taking eels, were located in the river.[78]

In many towns a fall in population, caused by plague and commercial decline, resulted in the 'decay' of houses and churches. On the edge of Battle, for instance, the sites of cottages and shops were converted into gardens. In Lewes borough too, houses were abandoned on the sunny slopes south of the High Street. Messuages and crofts between Pinwell Street and Brooman's Lane, recorded in the mid 14th century - among them the premises of the Brotherhood of saint Sebastian - had been merged by 1582 to form Bewgates, a two-acre croft rented by John Holter butcher - medieval pottery from rubbish pits there pre-dates the 15th century. About 1330 perhaps eight tenants, some of them house-holders, were occupying the bishop of Chichester's land east and west of Church Lane; in 1552 only three tenants were named, all renting garden 'plats'. And possibly 'Olde scolestrete', which had been partially built up in 1316, was the twitten descending between St Andrew's Lane and St Mary's Lane, which was abandoned before 1624. A similar fate befell Antioch Street, officially confirmed as 'nowe enclosed' in 1595.[79]

As already noted, the antiquarian, John Elliot, interpreted the grid of pasture fields south and east of St John-sub-castro - an area devoid of houses by 1620 - as an erstwhile framework for lost residential streets, where tradition sited 'the Town Well' and 'the Old Fish Market'. Recent excavation has revealed a 'shifting suburb' there, around North Street, abandoned before the 15th century. In 1488 John Coke rented as 'pas-ture' a disused lane in St John's parish, 'anciently called Laddereslane'; about 1260 John Eustace had given a house in 'Loddere Street' to the Cluniacs. (Map 2.2) This led perhaps from Fisher Street towards the east corner of St John's churchyard and maybe abutted west on the house and dovecote of Roger Seman, still in situ in 1466. A lane in the Borough, called 'Medellane', its location unknown, was granted out in 1436. A loss of houses in the vicinity of St John's church may have hastened the decline of its fabric. In 1587 the chancel was pulled down, and in 1826 it was deemed a 'very mean structure, 'much curtailed of its original dimensions'.[80]

There are also hints of 'decay' in a Borough revenue account com-piled in 1457-8 for the dowager-countess Beatrice. Though 4s. 2d. was spent on repairs to the pinfold 'at Westout', to the bridge 'at the end of the town of Lewes', and to the court house 'beyond the [draw] bridge', a waning of seigneurial involvement is apparent in the renting out of the 'Earlsgardyne', of long stretches of the castle ditch and of the town ditch behind Keere Street and east of 'Watergate'. Moreover, allowance was made for the 'decayed' rents of 'various tenements and vacant plots'. In addition 'shops' in Fisher Street were lying empty, and nothing accrued from the 'tolnet', the toll booth, 'next the Friars Minor', because 'nothing happened in the time of this account' - though the 'tolnet of Westout' yielded eight pence.[81]

As early as 1337, the staffing and repair of seven 'intra-mural' daughter churches in the Borough had become so burdensome that the bishop of Chichester sought to close them and transfer the parishioners, and assets, to his church of All Saints. Maybe self-interest tempted him to exaggerate the crisis. Yet no more is heard of St Martin's, St Peter the Less, Holy Sepulchre and Holy Trinity, or of St Nicholas after Henry Turmur was presented in 1410 - its alleged remnants, the 'Broken Church', housed a smithy in 1572. By then tenements on School Hill, once served by St. Nicholas, Holy Sepulchre and Holy Trinity, had been absorbed into All Saints parish. Its church was much used for episcopal business. In 1409 clergy from the Lewes and Pevensey deaneries met there. In 1415 the bishop of Caithness ordained 33 'tonsurati' there - acolytes and subdeacons, deacons and priests, drawn from religious orders in eastern Sussex. For ignoring a summons there, the rector of Catsfield was excommunicated in 1425. And doubtless it was used by the archdeacon's officials, among them John Bagot of Lewes, pardoned for unspecified 'trespasses' in 1444. The church received a sturdy 'late 15th century' west tower, and Perpendicular east windows of three lights in the chancel and a flanking north chapel, perhaps known as 'our ladies' chapel' in 1616.[82]

80 All Saints church

81 Vested for Mass

Nothing can be known of any rebuilding during this period at St Peter Westout, St Andrew's or St Mary in the market place. But St Michael's acquired a chamfered '14th century' arcade between the nave and south aisle, and was deemed larger and 'more beautiful' than St Andrew's in the 1540s. Its rector, John Braydforde, was memorialized in 1457 as a brass demi-figure vested for Mass. At St Mary Westout a two-light '15th century' window was inserted in the south chapel which housed perhaps an image of saint Anne.[83]

A 'decay' of houses in the Borough might explain the rather small population that can be plausibly extracted from the 1379 poll tax return, which asessed 105 heads of households - six buyers of wool, six cloth merchants, four hosiers, eight butchers, three bakers (including Alice, Thomas Strode's wife), three cobblers, two smiths, the Constables, John Peyntour and James Ferour, and 71 other married townsmen, also 19 male and 22 female servants. These 105 households, with their bread-winners, spouses, children and servants, accounted perhaps for between 400 and 500 people, so even allowing for paupers, tax evaders and the clergy, a population below a thousand seems probable, smaller than that teased by some historical geographers from data in Domesday Book.[84]

As for Southover, though John Norman was warned not to demolish a house there in 1352, the timing of subsequent 'decay' is less straightforward. Houses recorded before the Black Death in St Pancras Lane [Avery Street], and near the west mill [Pende Street] were abandoned before the early 17th century, but this perhaps resulted, in part, from the priory's dissolution in 1537. At Cliffe, because trading space was so cramped, vacant sites were maybe never empty for long. The grant of a market and two fairs in 1409 testified to archbishop Arundel's concern for its commerce. St Thomas's church was remodelled in the 14th century, when the existing nave arcades with their hollow chamfered arches were erected. About 1450 the living became a rectory and by the 1540s the church was the focus of a well endowed Brotherhood which funded perhaps the massive Perpendicular west tower, adorned with gargoyles as robust as the foliage in the spandrels of its doorway. There is too a stylish squint framed by a 'broad foiled ogee arch'.[85]

In the 1450s the South-East was still nursing the grievances which had fuelled Cade's Rebellion. In particular the coast lay undefended. Indeed in February 1458 a visitor to Southover priory reported that '60 sail of Frenchmen' were 'keeping the sea' off the Sussex shore. Given the local unpopularity of Henry VI, it is not surprising that Sandwich was chosen in 1460 for the landing by Yorkist nobles which led to his over-throw. The duke of Norfolk, who fought 'like a second Ajax' at the decisive battle of Towton, acted as Earl Marshal at Edward IV's coronation in June 1461. Yorkist too was his fellow 'lord' of Lewes, baron Bergavenny. Doubtless rejoicing was heartfelt when the newly anointed king visited Lewes on saint Bartholomew's Eve 1461, and his reign, moreover, was to prove a turning point in the fortunes of the kingdom.[86]

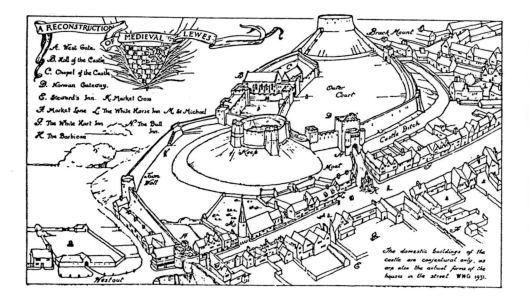

82 Late-medieval Lewes, partly conjectural

Overleaf: remains of Southover priory

7

The impact of a 'New Monarchy' 1461-1558

At Lewes I found corruption of both kinds, and what is worse, treason, for the sub prior has confessed to me treason in his preaching. I have caused him to subscribe his name to it, and submit himself to the King's mercy. I made him confess that the prior knew of it, and I have declared the prior to be perjured. ... That done, I laid unto him [the prior] concealment of treason, called him heinous traitor in the worst names I could devise, he all the time kneeling and making intercession unto me not to utter to you the premises for his undoing, whose words I smally regarded, and commanded him to appear before you at the Court on All Hallows Day, wherever the King should happen to be, and bring with him his sub prior. When I come to you I will declare this tragedy to you at large, so that it shall lie in your power to do with him what you list. Richard Layton to Thomas Cromwell, October 1535.

By 1461 the calamities experienced by the English since the Black Death had inspired a widespread yearning for political stability, and this a reinvigorated monarchy was soon to deliver. Edward IV restored royal authority: he restrained over-mighty peers, husbanded Crown revenues, revitalized its administration, and parried the threat from France. A spasm of turbulence under Richard III (1483-5) ended at Bosworth Field, and Henry VII resumed Edward's policies to such effect that Henry VIII (1509-47) was able to make or break magnates at will, and partially dismantle the Catholic Church in England. The powers vested in the Crown survived Edward VI's minority, to be fully deployed by Mary (1553-8).

With Edward IV's accession the Yorkist 'lords' of Lewes duly prospered. John Mowbray succeeded his father, the 'Ajax' of Towton, as duke of Norfolk in 1461; George Nevill, knighted after the Yorkist victory at Tewkesbury in 1473, became second baron Bergavenny in 1476. Though Mowbray's chief seat was at Framlingham in Norfolk, and Nevill's at Birling in Kent, doubtless they ensured the election at 'Lewes' of MPs acceptable to themselves and to the Crown. After Norfolk died in 1476, his only child, Anne, was married to Edward's IV's second son, Richard

The fragmentation of the Mowbray share

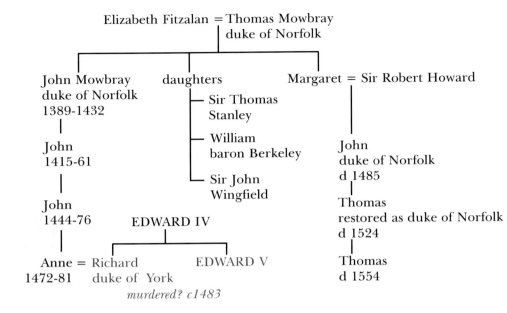

duke of York, who became earl Warenne and duke of Norfolk. But Anne Mowbray died in 1481, and a year or so later, her husband, and his brother, Edward V, were murdered, maybe, in the Tower by Richard III. Anne's half share of Lewes rape was divided between John Howard, now duke of Norfolk, William lord Berkeley, Sir Thomas Stanley and Sir John Wingfield. When Howard (Shakespeare's 'Jackie of Norfolk'), a trusted servant of Richard III, perished at Bosworth Field in 1485, his titles and estates were forfeited. The Yorkist, George Nevill, however, kept his patrimony intact, and in 1492, as 'founder's kin', chose to be buried in a tomb, already prepared, south of the high altar at Southover priory - a brazen bull's head, a Nevill badge, was found thereabouts in 1845. His son George, the third baron, shone in a royal tournament at Westminster Palace in 1494, when his small black horse 'did marvels', jumping high off the ground. In 1497 he fought doughtily against Perkin Warbeck, who claimed to be Richard, duke of York. Also loyal to Henry VII was Thomas Howard, the late attainted duke of Norfolk's son. Indeed in 1507 the pragmatic king restored to him Bramber rape and the Howard eighth of Lewes rape; he acquired the Berkeley eighth in 1512.[1]

Another assiduous agent of king Henry was the barrister, Edmund Dudley. After his downfall in 1510, the rumour was spread that his father had been an itinerant carpenter from Dudley, employed at the priory, and that the charitable Cluniacs sent his boy to Oxford university. In sober fact his father, an MP for Arundel, was a son of John, baron Dudley, which could explain why young Edmund was elected for 'Lewes', possibly six times, between 1483 and 1491. Thereafter, as a puissant Privy Councillor, he sat for Sussex - as the parvenu Lord Treasurer, John Pelham, had done. He also bought the manor of Hamsey, and his will acknowledged that 'M[istress] Morley and her feoffees' should receive £20 a year from it, in return for £400 already paid to him. With this annuity in 1512 widow Agnes Morley endowed a master and usher to staff a grammar school in Southover. Agnes was related to John Ernley of Sidlesham near Chichester, and he probably owed to Dudley his appointment in 1507 as attorney-general.[2]

Because Dudley became widely hated for levying taxes and feudal dues on the Crown's behalf, Henry VIII had him executed in 1510, an early example of a callousness that boded ill for older-established notables. In 1521 the duke of Buckingham was beheaded for 'conspiracy' - his real crime being his descent from Edward III. Baron Bergavenny, his son-in-law, and Chief Larderer at Henry's coronation, was also arrested and only just escaped execution - 'leaving his feathers behind' as the French ambassador put it. In 1525 the baron lay very low while Wealdsmen near his Eridge estate noisily protested at the impending closure of Bayham abbey - Thomas Wolsey wanted its funds for his new Cardinal College at Oxford. Henry did, however, restore Thomas Howard as seventh duke of Norfolk in 1514. His son, also Thomas, succeeded in 1524 and doggedly served as Lord Admiral, Lord Treasurer, Earl Marshal and Lord High Steward. Doubtless he secured the election for 'Lewes' in 1529, along with John Batnor mercer, of Sir Edward Bray, the captain in 1513 of Norfolk's flag-ship, the *Mary Rose*, which was to sink so memorably off Southsea in 1545.[3]

Meanwhile, Lewesians had acquired John Gage as a neighbour at Firle. He married a daughter of John Bolney, Henry VII's Controller of the Household, and being blessed with 'wisdom, personage and hardiness', became in the 1520s commander of Guisnes, a fortress near Calais, Vice-Chamberlain of the Household, and a knight of the shire for Sussex - a sure sign of royal favour. His estate at Firle had been assembled by his maternal grandfather, Bartholomew Bolney (c1405-77), a thrusting lawyer. As a kinsman of William of Wykeham, he was educated at Winchester College. He acted for many years as steward to Battle abbey

83 The thrusting lawyer and his wife

and advised prior Attwell and archbishop Stafford. Also a busy justice of the peace and local commissioner, he reported on contraband wool, coastal flooding, and the sale of plundered merchandise at Seaford. His memorial brass in Firle church presents him as an esquire in flamboyant 'Yorkist' armour, sword and dagger at his side.[4]

Lawyer, land-purchaser and JP, Bolney's career typified the consolidation of a shire 'gentry' whose members were often eager to serve a New Monarchy, itself very pleased to employ them. Such men were elected as MPs for 'Lewes'. Christopher Furnes (1473), was a customs collector at Chichester in 1455, who served Edward IV as a 'yeoman of the bottles', and ended up a royal pensioner at Windsor castle in 1481. Thomas Lewknor from west Sussex (1468), the younger son of a knight, acted locally as a tax collector, JP and commissioner of array. More rooted in Lewes borough was the Sherman family which supplied three MPs. In 1474 John Sherman (1468) left to his wife Joan a garden there, once his grandfather's, as well as a silver goblet and premises near St Andrew's church. Wealthy and spiritually self-confident, he founded in the graveyard of St Peter Westout a chapel dedicated to the Virgin Mary, where 'for a hundred years' an 'honest' chaplain was to be paid ten marks per annum to offer masses for his soul. John's brother Thomas (1459), though Clerk of the Peace for Sussex, was accused of fraudulently acquiring the Hides in Westout, and goods in Cliffe rightfully the archbishop's. He was buried in John's chantry chapel in 1494, having bequeathed it £40 and lands near the town. Thomas's son, John Baker alias Sherman (1478), also a lawyer, served locally as a JP and a commissioner of array.[5]

84 The Founder's tomb

When the chantry chapel was discontinued in 1547, maybe John Sherman's tomb was carted up to St Mary Westout, now St Anne's. In its chancel is the 'Founder's monument' so described when the artist Grimm drew it in 1787, though no 'Founder' is linked with the church. Sir Stephen Glynne noted the 'Altar Tomb' in 1826: the 'fine' Perpendicular panelling; 'the vestige of a brass new torn off'; the ogee canopy enriched with crockets, finial and double feathering; the flanking buttresses each with a crocketed pinnacle.[6]

The eagerness of a shire 'gentry' to serve a New Monarchy was matched by an expanding role for JPs in shire administration - a form of 'self-government at the king's command'. Already in 1368 they had been authorized to hear and try felonies. In 1461 they took over judicial work from the county sheriff. Later statutes required them to concern themselves with wage rates and vagabonds, riots and unruly magnates, poor relief and bridge repair. Annually they assembled four times at 'quarter sessions', at New Year, Easter, Midsummer and Michaelmas, and quite soon, because of the extreme length of Sussex, an 'eastern' bench of JPs drawn from the rapes of Hastings, Pevensey and Lewes, sat separately, usually at Lewes, and united with a 'western' bench, recruited in the rapes of Bramber, Arundel and Chichester, only at Midsummer. Thus in 1489 the vicar of Hollington informed the Lewes bench that, after suffering a vicious assault, he had prayed to the 'martyred' Henry VI and received back his speech, and the sight in one eye. From 1504 Lewesians could also observe the sheriff's county court in action, publicizing royal commands, proclaiming outlaws, adjudicating debts, summoning freeholders to elect coroners and knights of the shire. Since 1378 the court had met at Chichester, but from 1504 its three-weekly meetings alternated between Chichester and Lewes. So it was at Lewes, on 31 August 1525, that a friar and a Church official were outlawed for rescuing a man from a gallows at Broyle Heath near Chichester, after the weight of his body broke the rope.[7]

A petition to parliament in 1487 had also pleaded that a 'common jail' be established at Lewes, a 'convenient place', because the use of Guildford castle as the only royal prison in Sussex and Surrey endangered the transport and custody of 'great murderers, errant thieves, misdoers, breakers of the King's peace'. Some such request was granted, for a horse thief, who escaped from a prison at Lewes in 1508, was outlawed there on 27 February 1516. Doubtless the jail was in the castle, one eighth of which was in the king's hands in 1487. A setback, however, to the build-up of administration in the town was the loss of occasional sessions of the Lent and Summer assizes. After July 1477 the royal judges from London refused to toil across Ashdown Forest, halting instead at Horsham or East Grinstead.[8]

Better shire government brought more effective coastal defence. When in 1514 the French landed from a fleet armed with 'basilisks and other great artillery' and assaulted Brighton, beacons lit on the Downs summoned a swift counter-attack. Many of the raiders were killed and their commander wounded, though the damage was such that Brighton was exempted, at least initially, from a tax levied in 1524. Quickly repulsed was a French landing at Seaford on Saturday 25 July 1545. Militia men from Kent, reaching Uckfield on the Sunday night, learned they were no longer needed. Local resistance was led by Sir Nicholas Pelham, whose epitaph in St Michael's church proclaims:

WHAT TYME YE FRENCH SOUGHT TO HAVE SACKT SEAFOORD
THIS PELHAM DID REPELL THEM BACK ABOORD.

How different to the seigneurial shambles preceding the skirmish at
Rottingdean in 1377.[9]

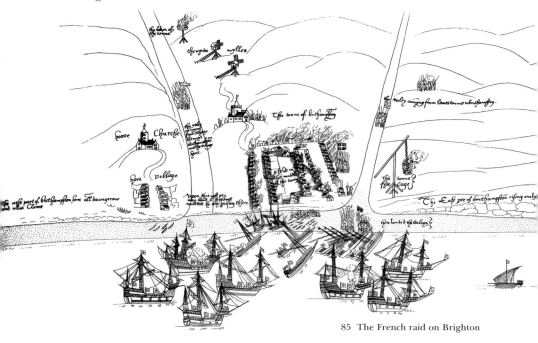

85 The French raid on Brighton

The Crown's new capacity to wage war had become very apparent in
Sussex in 1496-7 when immigrant French artisans built England's first
water-powered iron furnace at Newbridge in Ashdown Forest. It manufactured cheap cast-iron shot for the king's carefully budgeted conflict
with Scotland. They also erected a water-powered forge, to hammer out
the wrought iron needed to bind the stocks and wheels of royal
ordnance. By 1506 the Newbridge furnace was casting barrels and chambers for two-piece cannon, and a Wealden armaments industry had been
securely established. This initiative indeed was part of a wider economic
renewal, apparent from the 1460s, which nourished a sense of well-being
among the propertied classes - and even a grudging tolerance of royal
taxation.[10]

In the 1530s, however, the new prestige and resources of the Crown
dislocated English Catholicism. Southover priory indeed had already felt
the weight of royal authority. In 1465 the abbot of Cluny, as desired by
the 'lords' of Lewes, chose its chamberlain, Thomas Attwell, to be its
prior. He was also made vicar-general of the English province, and insti-

tuted a prior at Northampton in 1473. But the 'alien' link was disliked by Edward IV and his bishops. So when Anne Mowbray, married Edward's IV's second son, Richard duke of York, and he became earl Warenne and duke of Norfolk, the Crown's new stake in the lordship of Lewes prompted it to sever the fraying bond between the priory and the abbot of Cluny. At the request of prior Attwell and his monks, of Edward IV and his queen, and of 'Richard, duke of York and Norfolk, founder of the said priory in right of his wife' (Anne Mowbray), pope Sixtus IV in 1480 placed it under direct papal jurisdiction, leaving it 'free' to choose its superior - in return for 13s 4d paid each year to the papal collector in England. Sixtus also showered privileges on prior Attwell and his successors - they could confer minor orders, consecrate chalices, bestow solemn benediction and assume the trappings of a bishop - the gloves and sandals, the dalmatic and tunicle, the mitre and staff. Final separation from the abbot and general chapter at Cluny came in 1490 when Innocent VIII placed the English province under the archbishop of Canterbury's jurisdiction. Royal and nationalistic pressure had ended the supra-national status of the Cluniac Order in England, a part of its Catholicity.[11]

By then, of course, the priory was very English, its inmates often recruited from the vicinity. John Lewes and Thomas Lewes, George Horsted, John Framfeld and George Goodherst were novice monks in 1479. John Ashdown, who followed Thomas Attwell as prior before March 1508 and died about 1525, was perhaps a native of that Forest. His successor, Robert Peterson alias Crowham, was probably born at Westfield near Battle. In 1534-5 the 28 monks and novices included Anthony Bolney and David Framfeld, John Symson [Selmeston], John Wynchelsea and William Nutley; among the 'boys in custody' were Tristan Dychening and William Firle.[12]

The severance of the English Cluniac province from Cluny was followed in 1534 by the separation of the English Catholic Church from the papacy. The parliament, to which Sir Edward Bray and John Batnor were elected in 1529, confirmed Henry VIII as Supreme Head of an Anglican church, and set the scene for the Crown to confiscate the wealth of the monasteries. The smaller were suppressed in 1536, the others between 1537 and 1540. Already, in 1526, Southover's daughter house at Stansgate had been closed - its assets, like Bayham's, went to fund Cardinal College. In 1535 a Crown survey of monastic income was carried out. Southover's was calculated as £1091 gross, £921 net. Twenty or so other houses enjoyed a disposable annual income above £1000, including St Augustine's abbey (£1431) and Christ Church priory (£2423), both at Canterbury.[13]

King Henry's main purpose was to acquire cash. Since his theology was still Catholic, he could hardly object to the daily cycle of monastic prayer. At Southover in the 1530s, the five boys 'in custody', who shared

24 pounds of candle with the junior monks, probably sang in the choir. And Robert Inglonde, a 'singing man' at Cliffe in 1553, may have been the priory 'servant' listed in 1537. Christmas was joyously celebrated - one year, 19s 4d was spent on a Great Candle - to pay the man who made it, and to buy rosin, verdigris and 34 pounds of wax. During the last week of Advent a senior monk sang an antiphon at each daily vigil, its words sometimes echoing his official duties. '*O key of David and sceptre of the House of Israel, Who openeth and no man shutteth*', was sung by the granator who kept the store rooms; '*O root of Jesse, who standeth for an ensign of the people*', by the procurator who supervised the gardens. But the hosteler, not the master of building works, sang '*O king of the nations and their desire, O Corner Stone, who maketh both one*'. Each celebrant was allowed 6s 8d to spend on wine and 'treats' for the brethren - maybe figs, raisins and cakes. Sadly no list survives of the relics sanctifying the many altars. Among those adored at Wisborough Green in west Sussex were the cloak worn by Becket during his martydom, a hair-shirt used by saint James the Great, a stone cast at saint Stephen, and 'a little quantity of Our Lady's milk'.[14]

The elaborate cycle of the Cluniacs' daily prayer mingled with their memorial masses to shorten the sojourn in Purgatory of the souls of founders and benefactors - an intercession still approved by king Henry, and still attracting bequests. In 1492 baron Burgavenny left 200 marks for a daily mass 'at the altar where my body shall be buried', and for 'mine obit or anniversary' to be kept yearly 'for ever'. Humbler folk at Arundel and Beeding, Hangleton and Eastbourne, gave smaller sums, and at Hamsey Edward Markwick, 'a brother' of the priory's lay fraternity, bequeathed forty shillings to the 'treasurer' for 'a remembrance to pray for my soul'. John Thatcher at Ringmer in 1526 made provision to reimburse the monks, novices, singing men and bell ringers officiating in the priory church at his 'burying day', his 'month day' and at his 'year's mind' - and to fund 1000 masses at the 'Grey friars'. But he chose to lie in a chapel he attached to the chancel of Ringmer church, where a priest was to pray for his soul 'continually' - the endowment to be the £200 loaned by him to the late prior Ashdown. The 'great' bell, one of five in the western crossing tower at Southover, was also wrung on the 'anniversaries' of deceased priors and donors; 'wastel' bread too was baked from the finest flour.[15]

There could be little criticism either of the lengthy academic study undertaken by some monks. John Ashdown, for example, after seven years at Cambridge, went on to qualify as a Bachelor of Canon Law at Oxford in 1506. In 1336 pope Benedict XII had required each major English Benedictine house to send a monk to study theology or canon law at a university, and the Southover Cluniacs quickly forged a link with the Cambridge college founded in 1348 by Edmund Gonville, steward to the Norfolk estates of earl Warenne. Before 1354 they pledged to endow it with the advowsons of churches at Fouldon and Wilton in Norfolk. The link endured into the 1530s. Ex-students of Gonville included prior Crowham, sub-prior Anthony Bolney, the master-of-works William Aderolde, Doctor John Senock and Nicholas Orell. During nine years there, Senock bought the works of the third-century theologian, saint Cyprian, whose writings were studied at Cluny during Lent in the 11th century. And Orell purchased some high-powered Renaissance criticism - an edition by Erasmus of saint John Chrysostom's *In epistolam ad Galatas*; works by Melanchthon on Rhetoric and Dialectic, and his edition of Cicero's *De officiis*.[16]

Benedict XII also decreed that in major houses a master should teach the novice monks basic grammar, logic and philosophy, a task performed at Southover perhaps by Doctor Senock. Little evidence, though, of a lively intellectual life is to be found in the sketchy annals compiled, it seems, by William Horton, who entered the priory in 1475 aged twenty. Uniquely he noted the three monks who arrived with prior Lanzo from Cluny - his deputy Hugh and the two Abeman brothers. Otherwise he gives the covering dates of priors between 1324 and 1465, and a few scraps of narrative: windmills struck by tempests; John Vatte possessed by demons; the slaying of Richard III.[17]

But what made the monasteries an easy prey to king Henry's greed was perhaps their lack of spiritual impact and pastoral outreach. The life-style within them had grown too secular, eroding the letter and the purpose of the Rule. In the 1530s, for instance, each monk enjoyed a weekly wage - to spend on books or rosaries, spices or sweets. The sub-prior received thirty pence, priests twenty pence, deacons five pence, sub-deacons two pence, boys 'in custody' a penny. An annual clothing allowance was less minutely graded: £2 18s 8d to the sub-prior, £1 9s 4d to each of the other monks. Tailors worked within the precinct. The procurator paid for white and coloured thread, for candles when they stitched at night, for the repair of scissors. He also bought canvas, to be made into napkins for the infirmary, and for a 'shearing house or barber surgeon's house'. Robert Swift, a priory 'servant' in 1537, was presumably the Robert Swift who oversaw the wills of two ex-Cluniacs living at Southover in 1544, and also the barber of that name who died in 1550, resident near the great gate. As well as a wage and a clothing allowance, the sub-prior and seven 'senior' monks shared a small sum for 'recreation' - expended maybe during the period of rest after their blood-letting.[18]

The Cluniacs' diet was even more starkly at variance with the Rule. This required fish to be eaten on Fridays and Saturdays, on the vigil of certain feast days and during Lent. Accordingly, in the year ending at Michaelmas 1534, their larderer accounted for 10,217 smoked red herrings, 30,071 dried white herrings, 2576 'salt fish', 2900 'stock fish' (mainly cod), 164 hake and 237 ling; also for river fish, mostly bought from John Hyve of Lewes - two lampreys, four pike, five trout, eight bream, 24 salmon in a barrel, thirty young pike, 302 tench, and eels of various size, including 4950 'grasslyngs' which cost a farthing for ten. He leased 'the fishery' along the Ouse from the bailiff of 'earl Warenne' and paid men to catch eels, knot hemp into nets for bream and tench, and drag the river for mullet during a three-day period when extra kitchen staff were employed. As manager of the precinct's capacious fish ponds, he bought iron for a net-house, a padlock and key for a 'room' in the 'pond garden'; he had the 'moat' dredged and a boat built to sail on it. He also supplied the 'household' with butter and honey, oil, salt and vinegar, green peas, 24,893 eggs and 181 cheeses.[19]

Lavish spending on fish perhaps accorded with the letter of the Rule, but an immense consumption of meat and poultry did not. In that same year the larderer supplied 787 sheep, 15 lambs, 69 oxen, 29 cows, 139 calves, 115 pigs, 172 piglets, 643 rabbits (bred on the Upper and the Lower Rise), 122 geese, eight ducks, 135 capons, 47 chickens, 137 pullets, 942 pigeons, 18 swans and 36 quails. He also sold 216 'tithe conies'. 'Various guests' ate another 17 swans, and 'various fowls' were bought in London to set before baron Bergavenny and the earl of Wiltshire - queen Anne Boleyn's father. New sets of pewter were also needed, because archbishop Cranmer, official Visitor of the English Cluniacs, was expected. By-products of the kitchen included skins, hides and offal, 273 gallons of skimmed fat and 4495 pounds of tallow, much of it made into candles. The larderer also repaired three dovecotes, in the precinct, at Swanborough and at Falmer, and managed six swanneries - at the mill-pond in the precinct, at the Padpool, in the Limebrooks near the priory, in a water-meadow near St John's, at Rodmell and at Falmer. And he supplied the almoner with the three bushels of beans fed to the poor each Maundy Thursday.[20]

The granator, meanwhile, facilitated a convivial flow of bread and ale, by supervising the bakery, the brew-house and the mills in the precinct. During the year ending at Michaelmas 1533 he accounted for 5560 bushels of wheat and 3592 bushels of barley. He bought 100 pounds of hops and six barrels of 'double' strength beer, and sold 27 barrels of convent ale to the priory's warrener. He employed two bakers, two malt makers, a brewer, a cooper, a wood cutter and women to prepare oat flour. He purchased cords for the bakery pumps, straw malt-baskets, and a base for a mashing vat. He equipped the cooper with an axe, an adze, a nail wimble and hazel hoops. He managed the precinct pigs and their keepers, buying a lock and keys for the sty and linen to caulk a basting cistern. He oversaw the growing of mustard seed 'at the Rise' and its feeding to the quails. He installed a new horse-mill for use in summer if water-power failed - about 1530 five carpenters had 'framed' a new water-mill in the precinct. He received rents from the mills at St Pancras bridge, Watergate and Barcombe, and from the windmill on Cranedown.

He supplied the almoner with the corn and bran distributed 'outside the doors' of the priory.[21]

Barns, byres and stables, sties and yards, were located in the precinct's north-west corner, an area bounded to the south by the mill pool - 'a watering-place' which the larderer kept 'cemented'. The buildings probably included the 'great barn' dismantled after 1668; its walls abutting Cockshut Lane and the High Street were left standing to a height of eight feet, as depicted in a Buck print published in 1737. A 'great stable' lower down the Lane was also listed in 1668 for demolition - though a large building was sketched thereabouts in 1762, later torched during the Swing Revolt in November 1830. Elsewhere in the forty-acre precinct, ground was productively used in the 1530s. Onions and garlic grew in the 'vine garden', mustard and saffron in the 'convent garden', apples, pears, onions and hemp in the hosteler's garden, wheat in the upper croft, barley in the lower croft. Ewes grazed in the orchard and in the cemetery and 'the great garden' next to it. Trees in the 'oriel' garden were lopped for firewood - at St Alban's abbey meat was eaten in an 'oriole' chamber separate from the refectory, to preserve the letter of the Rule.[22]

Constant repair of the precinct buildings in the 1530s brought more secular intrusion. Masons installed windows in the malt house, an oven in the bake house, and a 'causeway' in the pond garden; 'a layer of Horsham stone' mended a roof. The master of works supplied shoes to a plumber, a glazier and sub-glazier, to a smith and his mate. He bought an ox hide to make a bellows, ewe pelts to make aprons, 1060 shingles for the chapter house, 'brick stones' and ridge tiles from kilns at Ringmer - also paving stones, 'marble' stones and grave stones, rope, tow and oakum, pitch and tar, plain glass, locks, keys and hinges. Some nails he received from a London armourer, though in one year the precinct smithy produced 988 horse shoes and 7052 shoe nails, besides hooks, hasps and latches, staples and hoops. He employed men to cut down elms at Barcombe, saw up boards in Horsted Park, split lathes at Rotherfield by Sheffield bridge, cut fuel in the Homewood and at Balneath - all for delivery to the precinct. And doggedly he accounted for a tithe of cheeses at Pangdean, a grant made about 1170 to fund work on the monastic church, though nothing accrued because 'no dairy' existed.[23]

Financial control in 1533-6 largely lay with John Councister, the chamberlain - an office held earlier by John Daniel and Thomas Atwell. He allowed some £300 a year to the larderer, granator and master of works, the bulk of their income, and almost £200 towards farming costs at Southover, Falmer and Balneath. He accounted for sales of wool, hides, grain and ale. He received the 'pension' money - often badly in arrears - which Nicholas Jenny collected from clergy in Chichester archdeaconry. He was assisted, though, by a secular staff. When in 1526 he authorized a new rental of Falmer manor, he was joined by John Stempe 'auditor', John Cotmot surveyor, and Richard Otlye clerk of the court. Some fifty years earlier a similar 'council' included Bartholomew Bolney steward, Alan Scras and Thomas Best 'auditors' and John Thatcher surveyor.[24]

Seemingly the families of these officials intermarried. Margaret, daughter of a Thomas Best, wedded a John Thatcher who owned property in Southover, Ringmer and Southwark and left £6 13s 4d to prior Attwell in 1502, 'to do with after his discretion'. In 1499 Thatcher's

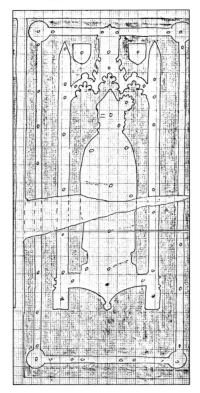

86 The indent

'cousin', Richard Benjamin, had bequeathed 300 marks to erect a new high altar, leaving the place of his burial to Attwell's discretion. His will also conveyed to Thatcher's son, Thomas, a lawyer of Gray's Inn, all the 'enrolments' in his chamber, 'for that he [Thomas] must often resort to ... business' concerning the priory. This business probably extended to 'a cellar' and loft in New Shoreham called 'Malappynnys'. A Southampton merchant sold the warehouse to Benjamin in 1498, but it was described in the 1540s as formerly owned by the prior of Lewes. Quite possibly, Thomas Thatcher rescued from the priory at its dissolution in 1537 the brass of a mitred prelate with a crozier, the indent of which survives at Priesthawes, his mansion near Pevensey - both Thomas Attwell and John Ashdown were entitled to episcopal trappings. In 1539 Thatcher's very Catholic will specified that eight black-gowned mourners armed with torches should grace the dirges and masses at his funeral. His daughter Agnes married John Ledes, a landowner at Piddinghoe, possibly the John Ledes 'gent' listed as a priory 'servant' in 1537. Both families became firmly recusant under queen Elizabeth.[25]

John Ledes probably held an honorary post in the prior's household, where the Rule was spectacularly by-passed. Richard Benjamin in 1499 bequeathed a gold ring with a turkey [stone] to the 'master chamberer' and 6s 8d each to three yeomen of the chamber- members of Attwell's entourage. The prior's 'lodging' was deemed 'convenient' enough to house the king in June 1538. Earlier, three beds were made for prior Crowham's chamber there, his new kitchen was improved and his garden walls repaired. 'At his table' he was privileged to consume 'meat, butter, etc.' throughout the year. The Cluniac lodging at Castle Acre included on the first floor a chapel linked by a spiral stair to the south-west corner of the church, a great chamber, a study snugly fitted out with fireplace, bay window and latrine closet, and a gallery connecting the study with guest quarters. At Southover a lease of the lodging in 1540 suggests a similar layout. On the first floor, above wine cellars, a storehouse and 'the Chequer', were a chapel and annex, with steps 'downwards through the west door of the church', an outer chamber, a great chamber with steps down to a garden on the south side, and 'a gallery with the new buildings above and below on the north end and west of the great chamber'. The Lord's Place, as sketched by John Deward in 1620, may have incorporated such a layout - an east-west range on the south side of a courtyard, facing the great gate, and linked at its west end to a range between the courtyard and the churchyard - the 'new buildings' perhaps - converted maybe from the former guesthouse. Possibly John Ashdown had been a patron of 'new' work, for his initials and the letters D E were carved on a stone plaque, which was placed, sometime after 1698, on the tower of Southover church. Was it retained when the lodging was demolished soon after 1668, and did D E stand for 'Domum Edificavit or Erexit'?[26]

The statutes in 1534 affirming Henry VIII as Supreme Head of an Anglican church, and making criticism of him a treason, ushered in a regime of State Terror, as well as an Age of Plunder. Bishop Fisher and Thomas More duly perished, but Doctor Senock at Southover wisely refused to join the vicar of Pevensey's protest at the 'diminishing' of papal authority. As a prelude to the confiscation of monastic wealth Thomas

87 Castle Acre: the lodging

88 The Deward sketch

89 The Ashdown plaque

Cromwell, the king's all-powerful Secretary, sent forth Commissioners to gather evidence of monastic ignorance, vice and sedition. In August 1535 the odious Richard Layton, a skilled State inquisitor, claimed to have uncovered all three at Farley, a daughter-house of Southover. He found 'a great comb called Mary Magdalene's comb' and 'a book of Our Lady's miracles, well able to match the Canterbury Tales'. He found 'unspeakable abominations' which, 'as appears by the confession of a fair young monk late sent from Lewes', festered at the mother-house too. And he found evidence of treason, 'sufficient to bring the prior of Lewes into great danger - *si vera sint quae narrantur*'. Forearmed, Layton reached Southover in October 1535. There, so he gloatingly wrote to Cromwell, he quickly unearthed, 'corruption of both sorts' [fornicators and sodomites], 'and what was worse, treason' - for Antony Bolney, the sub-prior, confessed to 'treason in his preaching' and alleged the prior had 'counselled it'. Thereupon he challenged Crowham and 'laid upon him concealment of treason, called him heinous traitor with the worst words I could deliver, he all the time kneeling, making intercession unto me not to utter to you the premises of his undoing'. Spurning this, the reptilian Commissioner had ordered him, and his sub-prior, to attend Cromwell at Court on All Hallows Day, 'wherever the King should happen to be'.[27]

Yet Layton's letter ended flippantly: 'When I come to you I will declare this tragedy to you at large, so that it shall lie in your power to do with him [the prior] what you list'. Since Crowham and Bolney survived, maybe the plan was to terrorize them into serving a Secretary with his sights already set on their priory's assets. Cromwell was badgering Crowham for a lease of Swanborough manor in 1536, when he snapped up Michelham priory. Among other small monasteries 'dissolved' that year were Southover's daughter houses at Farley and Clifford, Horton and Prittlewell. Well before 16 November 1537, when Southover became the first major house to 'surrender' to the crown, the king had reserved its Sussex estates for Cromwell and its East Anglian lands for the duke of Norfolk. Crowham meanwhile had received a prebend at Lincoln and, it was said, a promise from the duke of a share in the priory's assets.

Crowham's 22 monks united with him to affirm that they surrendered the priory 'with unanimous assent', voluntarily and of their own accord. Doubtless their resolve was stiffened by memories of Layton's visit, and by the payment of pensions and the prospect of benefices. Also pensioned, at Norfolk's command, was the ex-chamberlain, John Councister, who quitted the cloister in October 1537 for a rich living at Cuckfield - presumably he had served the ducal predator well. As for benefices, Crowham became treasurer of Chichester cathedral and dean of South Malling, sub-prior Bolney sacrist of Beverley collegiate church, William Aderolde rector of St John's Walbrook in London, Doctor Senock rector of Kemsing in Kent and a canon of Rochester. Others received livings in mid Sussex. Thomas Chamberlain at Piddinghoe left

6s 8d for the casting of a great bell. David Michel at Horsted Keynes was to combat the onset of Protestant doctrine under Edward VI. John Peverell settled at Southover and perhaps assisted George Morley and Richard Ball, who both died there in 1544. Morley wanted six priests to officiate at his burial, 'month's mind' and anniversary.[28]

Cromwell chose the prior's lodging - thenceforth called the Priory House or the Lord's Place - as the focus of his new power-base in mid Sussex. Servants of his, all too aware in December 1537 of the ironwork, doors and window glass being stolen from empty buildings in the precinct, suggested that his son Gregory, newly married to a sister of queen Jane Seymour, should celebrate Christmas there. In April 1538 Gregory confirmed that the 'commodious house' greatly pleased his wife, and in June a Yeoman of the Guard judged it 'convenient' to receive the king and his entourage - a visit cancelled because of a lingering outbreak of plague. Such by then was Cromwell's local influence that the authorities at St Mary Westout agreed to bury there the plague victims who died at Southover, where the refurbished lodging stood close to the churchyard. In August 1538 the Secretary was busy at the Place with his correspondence.[29]

To demolish the great church, prior Lanzo's church and some domestic buildings, Cromwell used Giovanni Portinari, an Italian military engineer who later fortified Berwick on Tweed. With 17 men at work, he reported their methods in March 1538. Two smiths, two plumbers and a man who 'kept the furnace' melted down the roofing lead. Nine labourers, starting at the east end of the great church, broke up the wall vertically into sections and dug trenches beneath them. Three carpenters shored the foundations, posting and propping them. The props on one side were then burnt with fire or with powder, and the walls brought to the ground. The remnants of Lanzo's church testify to these methods. Excavation there has also revealed the desecrating plunder unleashed by near limitless royal power. Besides ripping up floor-tiles and memorial brasses, Portinari's men pick-axed through grave stones in search of chalices and lead coffins. They overlooked a jewel of rock-crystal, possibly from a reliquary or book-cover, and left behind a dice and counters, which they deployed while resting from sacrilege. In 1539 Cromwell's agents received over £700 from the sale of lead, bells and salvage.[30]

The priory's toppled masonry long remained a quarry. Local buildings were 'rudely ornamented with the fragments of its grandeur'. A carved capital of superlative quality was taken to Kingston, a shaft of Tournai marble to Rodmell church, sculptured stone to Clayhill House in Ringmer parish. Tradition states that the flint and stone chequer adorning the aisle of Southover church, once visible from the Lord's Place, came from the priory, also the nave roof at St Mary Westout with its tie-beams, king-posts and curved struts. The indent of a mitred

90 The chequer at Southover

prelate rests at Priesthawes and the brass of prior Nelond at Cowfold, where in 1557 John Warde wished to be buried 'under the marble stone' he had brought from Lewes. Maybe, too, the 'high tombs' of earl Fitzalan and his countess repose at Chichester.[31]

Cromwell also enveloped the Franciscans of Lewes in the toils of 'treason'. Even in 1533 his agent, Thomas Folks, had kept him informed that John Parker, their warden, had 'lent' a chalice to a smith at Framfield. On 9 December 1537 he was alerted by another agent, John Milsent, that the warden, awaiting Cromwell's 'pleasure', had imprisoned a friar Richard. This friar had told friar Longe and friar 'Black Herry' that the king was dead, claiming his source to be a summoner who kept an alehouse near the friary gate. In the event at least two Franciscans were disciplined, for the Secretary learned that 'the friars' had taken very penitently their 'punishment' at Lewes on a Saturday, market day. Soon after this flurry, the mendicant orders were disbanded. In December 1538 a Commissioner confiscated Lewes friary 'to the king's use'. Apart from tithes at Westout and Kingston, Plumpton and Barcombe, the pickings were few. The value of the implements, altars and bells, the windows and gravestones, did not cover debts amounting to £15 4s, and the 77 ounces of plate were mostly 'abroad in pledge'. The library, which included works printed at Nuremburg and Cologne, received no mention. Till their dispersal, the friars were sought as intercessors, especially by folk in Pevensey rape. Thomas Thatcher at

Priesthawes left them 33s 4d for a hundred masses. But no strings were attached to the large brass pot and plain table cloth bequeathed by Margaret Apsley of Buxted. Their precinct too remained popular as a place of burial. Both John Rundell in 1517 and John Peterson in 1524 asked to be interred 'before the chapel of saint Barbara'. As already noted, there was a hierarchy of sepulture - skeletons in the chancel rested in graves lined with well-cut chalk blocks; those in the nave and the cloister garth were decently spaced, mostly in coffins; those under the cloister walk lay crammed together, protected only by shrouds. The church, of course, was looted, the graves ransacked; skeletons were crushed and littered with shattered slate and floor tile, stained glass and window lattice - the debris included an enamelled buckle-plate bearing a griffin with a human face.[32]

91 The buckle-plate

The Crown's desire for hard cash - rather than hostility to 'superstition' - also provoked an order that all 'feigned images abused with pilgrimages or offerings' be destroyed. This triggered the plunder in December 1538 of saint Richard's shrine at Chichester, hitherto widely revered: the jurats of Hastings sent it pieces from the embroidered canopies they carried at coronations; St Andrew's parish at Lewes gave money to the saint's 'head and crozier', which were separately adored. The 'disgarnishing' of the shrine yielded 112 images of silver and gilt, 82 rings and jewels set with stones and pearls. The image of saint Anne at St Mary Westout also perished. Witnesses were to testify in 1588 that because her 'idol' there had attracted so much 'offering', the church was still widely known as 'saint Anne's'. Some evidence for a nearby healing well, under her protection, perhaps opposite the church in Well Croft, has already been noted. Thereabouts by 1540 John Kyme rented a garden *cum uno fonto aquatico* [with a well of water], the previous tenant being Julian Chaloner, rector of St Mary Westout. If the *fons* had been a healing well, Chaloner perhaps was its final custodian.[33]

Though images not 'abused with pilgrimages or offerings' were spared, votive candles were also forbidden in 1538, except before the chancel rood, the high altar and the Easter sepulchre. Previously in St Andrew's church 'lights' had flickered elsewhere, at the font and before images of saints Andrew and Ursula, Roch and Nicholas. One year, a candle for Nicholas absorbed ten pounds of wax, a 'taper' for the patron saint only three. Perhaps his cult transferred there when the church dedicated to him (the 'Broken Church') had closed. Maybe as the guardian of sailors and unmarried girls, merchants and pawnbrokers, apothecaries and perfume sellers, Nicholas attracted many 'offerings' in a busy market Borough.[34]

A prompt destruction of Anne's 'idol' was the likelier because at the priory's closure Thomas Cromwell, a zealous 'reformer', became patron of all the churches in the Borough, except St Michael's and All Saints. In 1538 bishop Sampson of Chichester readily deferred to his influence there. 'He never meddled about Lewes', so the bishop assured the Secretary in 1538, when rebutting a rumour, spread by 'some at Lewes and Rye', that he [Sampson] favoured 'the bishop of Rome'. And maybe Cromwell instigated the uniting of St Mary-in-the-Market with the parish of St John's in 1538, and of St Peter Westout with St Mary Westout in 1539. St Mary-in-Foro was duly pulled down in 1543-4. But despite the pooling of resources, so was the 'ruinous' chancel of St John's in 1587. And though St Peter's also closed, the western bay of the aisle at St Mary Westout continued to crumble. The Crown became patron of St Michael's sometime before 1542, and the union of its parish with St Andrew's came in 1545. The poverty of St Michael's prompted the merger, but it was St Andrew's church, smaller and less 'beautiful', that was demolished in 1548. Masonry, roofing lead and three altars of 'alabaster' were sold, also plate and brass work, copes, vestments and altar cloths, 25 old books and 'other stuff', fetching £19 11s 7d.[35]

92 Richard Iden: priest at St Andrew's c1490-1500

93 Gabriel

Already partly ruinous by the 1530s was the Broken Church, described in 1592 as formerly St Nicholas's. By 1571 its bell-loft belonged to the Borough and hanging there in 1690 was a curfew bell called Gabriel, now in the Market Tower. The largest pre-Reformation bell in Sussex, it was cast by John Tonne, a Frenchman perhaps, who supplied at least seven bells to churches there between 1529 and 1536. The great bell bears a figure of saint Catherine, a medallion of Henry VIII and the inscription GABRIELIS MENTI DEDENS [?DEDUS] HABIO NOMEN, which may mean 'Yielding to the mind I have the name of Gabriel'. It seems unlikely any parish church in Lewes could have afforded so large and costly a bell, so perhaps it was cast for the priory and sold by Cromwell to the Borough, or donated even.[36]

Despite his destruction of shrines, 'idols', religious houses and Papal authority, Henry VIII remained very Catholic in his theology. Indeed when in 1534 John Hoggesflesh of Westout, a pioneer 'protestant', challenged the sacrament of the mass and the value of Confession, he was referred from the Church court at Chichester (presided over by dean William Fleshmonger!) to archbishop Cranmer, then to the duke of Norfolk and finally to the king, who found against him. The now 'famous heretic' was forced to recant his 'detestable' opinions in the market-places at Chichester, Midhurst and Lewes. However, a decision promoted by Cromwell, to make Scripture more accessible to the laity, caused St Andrew's parish to spend 15 shillings in 1539 on an authorized English translation of the Bible. Peter Flusher, a local merchant, also left 40 shillings to fund eight sermons 'setting forth God's holy word'. But after Cromwell's execution in 1540, the king's Catholic orthodoxy hardened. Indeed in 1543-4 St Andrew's parish bought three books expounding that orthodoxy, vetted by Henry himself. As for the townsfolk, between 1540 and 1544, 13 out of 19 testators at Lewes left money for masses to be said for their souls, suggesting a belief in Purgatory, as a prelude to salvation, was still widespread. Robert Bradfield and Thomas Kayforth specifically wanted memorial masses linked to 'the worship of the five wounds of Christ'. At Rye only 12 out of 36 testators made such provision. 'Protestant' opinions had surfaced at that crowded fishing port in the late 1530s; the mass was derided as 'a juggler's making', and divine service sung in church dismissed as of no more effect than the bleating of a cow to her calf.[37]

A late spasm of Henrician spoliation in Sussex was the suppression of the college of canons at Malling. The deed of surrender, dated 10 March 1545, bore the 'somewhat shaky' signature of dean Robert Peterson alias Crowham, the late conniving prior of Southover. Adding his compensation, an annuity of £100, to other emoluments, he rode out a Protestant surge under Edward VI, ending his days as warden of St Mary's hospital at Chichester. Most previous deans had also flourished as bureaucrats. Thomas Hanwell (1458-73) was archdeacon of Lewes; Thomas Edmonds, chaplain to archbishop Bourchier; Robert Brent (1481-1515), almoner to queen Elizabeth of York; John Piers, household steward to archbishop Warham; Thomas Heritage (1536-7), surveyor to Westminster Palace. Nicholas Heath left in 1539 to become bishop of Rochester.[38]

Under dean Brent, it seems, discipline had languished. Archbishop Warham intervened in 1515 to require that the sacrist and the three 'competent' vicars, who assisted or deputized for the canons, should lead a more regulated life, in a 'suitable manse' to be built near the churchyard at his own expense - instead of lodging in unbuttoned fashion some distance away, perhaps in Cliffe. Was this manse, perhaps, the venerable cottage with an arched stone entrance and iron-guarded door, which afforded viscount Torrington a refuge from the rain in August 1788? Perks of the sacrist were the 'white vests' and half pennies given by women at their Purification. In his custody in March 1545 were a chalice and green velvet cope, an altar cloth and Lent cloth, three silk curtains and four candlesticks, which were salvaged after the college's closure, and given to Cliffe church in March 1555 - though a sanctus bell went

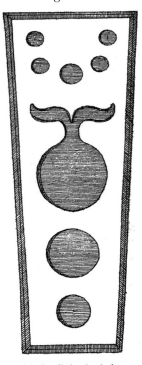

missing. Also salvaged was a case for a pair of organs, a reminder that a sub-deacon there, of 'upright character' and qualified as a singer, was paid for in 1414 by the rector of Buxted, a canon who held the 'chanter's prebend'. Once a chanter at Malling, perhaps, was William Sumers, a parish clerk buried at Buxted church in 1558 'beside where the organ [had] stood', and 'a very rare singer when the organs were up'.[39]

The decay of the 'fair' collegiate church after March 1545 was revealed by a survey made in 1554 before its demolition. Lead and Horsham stone had been stripped from the chancel roof and from the 'embattled' tower where six bells still hung. Rotting shingles covered the nave and aisles, the vestry and porch. Remaining were the sandstone pillars and buttresses, and the flint walls, rough-cast with sea-sand mortar, and lined inside with chalk. Farm animals trampled the pavements. Floor tiles had been ripped away, and brass 'images and scriptures' removed from 29 'marble' gravestones. One of these perhaps, with distinctive indents, was dug up in the 18th century. Dean William Piers had chosen to be buried before 'the high cross' in the church,

94 The distinctive indents

Ingelram Bedyll before the statue of Blessed Mary, dean John Piers before the image of Thomas Becket. Fittings sold off in 1555 included a font, a stone seat by the high altar and a window from the steeple. The Lady Chapel ceiling was carted to Cliffe church. Malling folk meanwhile worshipped as best they could, resorting in 1595 to Hamsey or elsewhere'.[40]

During these years of royal Terror and Plunder all magnates in Sussex remained at risk. Baron Bergavenny survived, and sensing perhaps that the priory's days were numbered, chose to be buried at Birling in 1535. But his brother, Sir Edward Nevill, was beheaded for 'conspiracy', and though his son Henry, the fourth baron, weathered a royal visit to the family's hunting lodge at Eridge near Frant in 1538, the king secured the execution of Henry's brother-in-law, baron Dacre of Herstmonceux, after Dacre's servants slew a gamekeeper at Hellingly. The duke of Norfolk, despite the fate of his niece, queen Catherine Howard, was convicted of treason only in 1547, but escaped the block because the king expired first.[41] Sir John Gage withdrew from the Court in 1533, troubled it was said by the divorce of Catherine of Aragon. He reappeared, however, to serve as Controller of the Household, Constable of the Tower and Chancellor of the Duchy of Lancaster, and to fight at Solway Moss and the siege of Boulogne. Locally he acquired the Duchy manor of Maresfield and the ex-ecclesiastical manors of Alciston and Ranscombe. Dean John Piers left him a great double chest covered with red hide. He also acted for Anne of Cleves, who was granted the Sussex estates of Thomas Cromwell, to sweeten the annulment of her marriage. She chose to reside at Hever castle in Kent rather than at the Priory House.[42]

Because the returns for 'Lewes' are lacking for Henry's reign after 1529, the influence exerted by local magnates, or the Crown, on the choice of MPs is unclear, though deference to the duke of Norfolk caused the High Constables in 1541-2 to spend 17 pence on wine and a pair of rabbits for his 'Officers'. In 1542-3, though, they paid the parliamentary expenses, some 63 shillings, of a John Kyme. He was either the affluent Borough householder of that name or his son, a trusted servant of William Petre, the Crown agent who received the surrender of the priory. The father, probably, was the priory 'servant' listed in 1537. A John Kyme owned in 1540 the house with 'the spring of water' in Westout, and bought the reversion of the site of the friary in 1544.[43]

In 1549 a John Kyme also bought Sherman's chapel in the church-yard of St Peter Westout, along with the chantry house (on the site of the car-park of *Shelleys Hotel*) and lands near Lewes, all valued at £11 5s 9d a year. The Crown kept a ten-ounce chalice priced at 36s 8d. This new Plunder was a by-product of the ecclesiastical 'reform', now driven by explicitly Protestant doctrine, which gathered pace during the minority of Edward VI (1547-53). Once Purgatory was officially rejected in 1547, the assets of chantry chapels accrued to the Crown. Sherman's chapel, built in the 1470s, was still standing in 1570 and James Lambert senior depicted a possible fragment in 1773 - a Perpendicular doorway and window, an outhouse to St Anne's rectory. The artist believed it was a remnant of St Peter Westout. But maybe that church had been incorpo-rated into the rectory which William Inians occupied in 1600; large worked stones of 'Romanesque' date were found about 1870 just to the south. St Peter's was closed in 1539 'for want of competent maintenance', so perhaps it was never embellished in a Perpendicular style. The sup-pression of the Okehurst chantry in Chichester cathedral also brought the Crown a freehold garden near lower Antioch street - a part of that chantry's endowment.[44]

95 Sherman's chantry?

Also confiscated were the assets of a Brotherhood at Cliffe dedicated to Thomas the Martyr, the parish's patron saint. In 1514 William Batnor had bequeathed a house there 'for the augmentation of a priest to sing [masses] for the brothers and sisters of the said fraternity'. And perhaps there was a Fraternity House, a focus of conviviality. A remnant maybe was 'a Chimney piece with the Arms of Thomas a Becket upon it', revealed when buildings were pulled down 'almost opposite' the church in the late 18th century. South-east of it, the *Swan* still retained in 1773 a Romanesque arch adorned with chevrons. But the inn was not among the nine houses listed in 1631 as formerly owned by the Brotherhood or by Malling college, though 'ground' on the north side of the Fair Place was. Perhaps the Brotherhood embellished the church with its stylish squint and massive west tower. The piety of members was stiffened, presumably, by a local miracle recorded in July 1498. Joan Reynolds, though sewn up in her shroud after dying of plague, was restored to life when her mother prayed to the 'martyred' king Henry VI. An obscurer fraternity was patronized in 1521 by Henry Coby who left money for a priest to pray at the altar of saint Catherine in Southover church for 'the brothers and sisters of the Brotherhood of Colyn'.[45]

Not suppressed in the 1540s, however, was the grammar school at Southover, launched in 1512 by the will of Agnes Morley, a childless wealthy widow whose treasures included a 'coconut cup', silver spoons with acorn heads, and rosaries with beads of coral and gold. She left premises near Watergate mill to house a school, a schoolmaster, and an usher to teach basic grammar. The prior of Southover was to select the master, and the master the usher. Their wages, fixed at £10 and £5 a year, were to be paid from a £20 annuity, a charge on the Hamsey manor of the freshly beheaded Edmund Dudley. The master, being a priest, was to pray regularly in Southover church, in the chapel of saint Erasmus - the patron of sick children - for Agnes and the feoffees who guarded the school's assets. The annuity was also to fund the chapel's upkeep, and the wine, wax and 'other things necessary for a priest to sing with'.[46] In April 1536, at prior Crowham's special insistence, 14 new feoffees had been recruited - mostly local gentry, headed by the ill-fated Sir Edward Nevill. They helped perhaps to ensure that, after the priory closed, the king acquired, and exercised, 'the right of the late monastery of Lewes' to appoint the master - who in 1544 was duly receiving £10 a year, and that the school survived the assault on the chantries. When Anthony Stringer, a Crown agent, visited about 1547, all was in order, with £72 stowed in the school chest and a clear annual revenue of £19 6s 8d, though the post of master was vacant. Noting that the inhabitants of Lewes, 'a populous town [with] much youth', wished a learned man to fill it, he suggested Thomas Otley, the parson of Ripe, a former lecturer in logic and Greek at Oxford. But he became vicar of Burwash in 1549.[47]

The upkeep of the town's two hospitals had also been accepted as a legitimate charge on Thomas Cromwell, the new owner of the priory's assets in Sussex. After entrusting to his servants a book recording 'the gift and grant of their founders', the 13 brethren and sisters at St Nicholas's were promised charitable alms 'as of old time'. Peter Tompson pressed the claims of the 'poor bead folk' at St James's - 13 men and a woman. About 1547 ten women and 16 men at the two hospitals were each allowed 13s 4d a year, a sum which the earl of Dorset was still paying in 1628 to 26 poor alms folk. Dorset owned the Priory House, where Thomas George, an inmate at St James's in 1592, had been a porter. The will of William Bossom gives a glimpse of communal life in 1559 at St Nicholas's, the 'upper spital': he left money for its repair and for bread and drink at his funeral, and asked to be interred 'in the common burial' within it. There were bequests to the hospitals till at least 1617, but in time they became mere parish poor houses. The churchwardens repaired St Nicholas's in 1712, and 'the last of the Spittal houses' at Southover was sold about 1730.[48]

After Purgatory had been disposed of, successive Prayer Books, issued in the name of Edward VI, set forth ever more radical Protestant doctrines. The Eucharist became a commemoration of the Last Supper, rather than a bodily sacrifice of Christ. Faith in his Atonement was now the only path to salvation. Good works, and the good-will of saints, were of no account. This theology now shaped the preambles to wills made in Lewes. Before 1547 most townsfolk had entrusted their souls to Almighty God, the Blessed Virgin and the Glorious Company of Saints. In Edward's reign most dispensed with the Virgin and the Saints, confining themselves to Almighty God 'maker and redeemer', to Jesus Christ 'saviour and redeemer', or to the 'merits' of his death and passion. As a guide to the new official theology, the king's council issued an edition by

Nicholas Udall of the *Paraphrases* of Erasmus - the scholar, not the protector of sick children. When the churchwardens at St Michael's paid 11 shillings for it, they complained that the parson should have shared the cost. A copy at Cliffe was kept with Henry IV's market charter.

Protestant doctrine now demanded the destruction of 'monuments of idolatary and superstition' - sacrificial stone altars, images of saints, pictures painted on wood, walls and glass - a panel depicting the Day of Judgement had been left to St Mary Westout in 1405. At St Michael's church three stone altars were removed, and a glazier, John Harman, 'defaced' two windows. Seats in the chancel, formerly used perhaps by a deacon and sub-deacon, offices now defunct, gave way to a pew and a desk for the rector, and a window near the pulpit was newly glazed - preaching the Word needed maximum light. Fifteen pence were spent on a wooden communion table, 12s 10d on furnishing it with an altar cloth and four yards of 'carpet'; soon after, a new table was bought for 4s 4d. Candles were only for illumination. Doubtless at Southover images of Catherine and Erasmus were smashed.

There was a final surge of State Plunder in 1552. Churchwardens were required to hand over to the Crown their plate, jewels and vestments, except for a great bell, a sanctus bell, a surplice, some linen for the communion table, and a chalice - or two, if the parish was populous. At St Michael's they had already sold some broken silver, and converted an old cope into a carpet, but a list was duly delivered to JPs, and royal agents bagged up the loot in 1553. The treasures at St Andrew's, its demolished daughter-church, had included a silver pyx and basin, a silver censer and cruets; four chalices; a cross of copper and gilt; twenty brass candlesticks and a 'branch'; four banner cloths and a streamer; five copes; a vestment 'for saint Nicholas'; others of red silk, one adorned with a blue cross and stars of gold, one with a cream-coloured cross and white favours. Protestant doctrine, however, did require at least one new fitting, 'a poor men's box'. John Batnor of St Michael's left forty shillings to it, to be distributed in 'time of sickness or need' - a targeting of charity intended to replace the cash, the bread, cheese and beer, the salt and candle tallow, indiscriminately doled out at funerals.[49]

During Edward's minority the Borough's former Catholic patrons lost influence. Norfolk languished in the Tower - his Sussex estates mostly going to the king's uncle, baron Seymour of Sudeley. Sir John Gage kept a low profile, and baron Bergavenny traded mere courtesies with the High Constables - sending them a buck-deer, perhaps from Eridge, and receiving a present of fish. So probably Edward's Protestant advisers nominated the Borough's MPs. Elected in 1547 were Sir Anthony Cooke, one of the king's tutors, and Walter Mildmay, a senior royal official, and in 1553 John Southcote, a barrister of the Middle Temple. None had local links. But seemingly Thomas Gravesend, elected in 1553, did. A Thomas Gravesend was listed as a priory 'servant' in 1537, held property at Southover, owned the Marlipins warehouse at New Shoreham, and about 1546 acquired Sherman's chapel in Westout from its chaplain, Christopher Dugdall, allowing him a pension. In 1550-1 the High Constables, 'in the name of the whole town' spent 18 pence on wine for 'Mr Gravesend'. As already noted, before the 1553 election, the Boroughs of Southover and Lewes agreed to observe an ancient practice whereby the Constable, burgesses and inhabitants of Southover had elected a member to each alternative parliament. So maybe Gravesend was their choice.[50]

The immense power of the New Monarchy was revealed when Mary became queen in July 1553 and swiftly restored the government of Sussex to Catholics. Released from the Tower, the aged Norfolk died in August 1554. It was a troupe of players patronized by his grandson, the fourth duke, which the High Constables rewarded in 1557-8. Sir John Gage re-entered public life as Lord Chamberlain. Zealous Catholic priests took charge of Chichester diocese, among them Richard Brydley, a former Cluniac prior at Horton, who became archdeacon of Lewes. Catholic worship was reinstated. St Michael's church acquired two stone altars, a crucifix, a tabernacle, an Easter sepulchre and a 'form' for votive candles. Thomas Neale painted the saints Mary and John on a new rood screen - more obscurely, he obliterated the 'balance' and 'the devils' from a picture of saint Michael. Worship at Cliffe was enriched with articles already noted as somehow salvaged from the collegiate church at Malling. And maybe vestments, which were sold by churchwardens at Southover after Elizabeth's accession, had also been piously preserved - the 'children's' copes of red and black Bruges satin, the cope of green damask, the 'suit of blue silk with birds'. Also restored there was a 'palm cross' in the churchyard, which Margaret West recalled in 1567- the focus for an elaborate procession on Palm Sunday.[51]

The influence of Catholics was quickly apparent at 'Lewes' elections, which also yield a plausible sequence of MPs chosen for Southover (marked with an asterisk). Sir Henry Hussey and George Darrell, a Kentish lawyer, were elected in October 1553, Darrell and Robert Gage*, Sir John's third son, in April 1554. Hussey had led a company recruited from Norfolk's estates in Sussex when the duke invaded Scotland in 1542. Darrell's father had acted as legal adviser to Sir John. The return in November 1554 of John Morley merchant and John Stempe rentier respected government advice that boroughs should choose resident townsmen who were 'grave' and 'catholic'. The Borough duly bore their expenses of a shilling a day. Morley's 'catholicism' was hardly ingrained, for in 1563 he entrusted his salvation to the merits of Christ's passion, 'without any other act or acts of men'. Stempe, the son of a priory official, had appeared on its pay-roll and was a zealous feoffee of the grammar school. The advice to elect residents was not repeated, and in 1555 William Devenish, a landowner from Hellingly, was chosen. He was so firm a Catholic, he was singled out as a 'misliker of godly orders' by a Protestant bishop of Chichester in 1564. His fellow MP, Thomas Gravesend*, who soon after became an official at the royal mint, was left money by Sir John Gage who died in April 1556. Doubtless Gage's son and heir, Sir Edward, sponsored the return in 1558 of John, his own eldest son. Also chosen was William Peterson, a London haberdasher with Lewes property, who oversaw in 1555 the will of his brother Robert, last prior of Southover and dean of Malling. Returned to Elizabeth's first parliament, in 1558-9, were George Goring and Thomas Saunder*, a Southover resident.[52]

That the Borough flexibly conformed to official thinking, whether Protestant or Catholic, might explain the continuity of its civil government - the same men served as High Constables under Edward VI and Mary, and under Mary and Elizabeth. Moreover, the bequests that the townsfolk made to fund masses for their souls suggest they tended to re-embrace Catholic doctrine under Mary, like householders at Battle and Chichester where overt Catholic influence was strong. Residents at Rye, Hastings and Horsham made fewer such bequests. Indeed at Rye a powerful faction in the mid-1550s elected an MP, and then a mayor, with 'Protestant' views highly offensive to the queen's Privy Council.[53]

The will of Sir John Gage reveals the material splendour encompassing the puissant Lord Chamberlain at Firle in 1556: furs of sable and lynx, suits of black velvet and Bruges satin; 'Burgundian trimming' and 'parchment lace of gold'; Turkey carpets and testers of damask and silk; a walnut bedstead and chairs of Spanish manufacture; a standing cup 'gilt after the antique fashion' and a small salt-cellar adorned with 'antique heads'. His blue and white saddle cloths were 'set full of rams embroidered'; the Garter encircled his coat-of-arms. His 'outfit for the field' (pitched perhaps at Solway Moss and the siege of Boulogne), comprised seven tents - for a commander, for his captains and a surgeon, for a buttery, a kitchen, an 'outlet', and a stable with mangers. And he made very Catholic bequests. Selected paupers were to share the proceeds from the sale of his 'Garter collar of gold'. A chantry priest was to be funded in the church at Firle. He also advised his son Edward to maintain 'hospitality and household' at the mansion there - a largesse extended no doubt to voters at 'Lewes'.[54]

Certainly Edward's influence did secure his eldest son's election there in 1558. And in 1557 he and six other feoffees pledged to increase, from their own purses, the funds of the school at Southover 'which now flourishes'. John Stempe, their 'chief doer', had fended off Treasury inquiries about its assets; buildings had been repaired, and the master and usher reimbursed (rather belatedly) for 'meat and drink' previously available at the priory. Doubtless the tuition was firmly Catholic, for Gabriel Fowle, the master who died in 1555, wanted ten priests, 'if they can be got', to celebrate masses for his soul. He left his manuscript mass-book to Southover church, his printed book of antiphons to Ringmer church. Five shillings were to be shared among five senior pupils 'for their diligence about me', and forty pence were to furnish a penny each to others who had been with him at least 'a quarter of a year' - if fewer than forty qualified, the senior five could claim extra pennies.[55]

But Edward Gage's Catholicism had a darker side. In August 1554 the Privy Council admonished JPs in Sussex to punish Protestant dissenters, 'evil disordered persons' who 'rail upon the mysteries of Christ's religion'. Those subsequently detained mostly lived east of the Adur, where Gage's influence as a landowner and a Crown servant was strongest. As a deputy-sheriff he oversaw arrests at an illicit prayer meeting in Brighton. As high sheriff he supervised the burning of 13 Protestants. When Richard Woodman was betrayed at Warbleton by relatives, it was to Firle that he was led - 'in a dog harness'. Gage was also singled out as 'an extreme persecutor of the gospel' by John Trewe of Hellingly. Because Trewe 'persuaded the people from going to mass', Gage ordered that his ears be cropped and that he be set in the pillory, at Hailsham and at Lewes.

Most Protestants detained east of the Adur were from the Weald. As Henry VI had discovered after Cade's rebellion, its dense woods, waterlogged roads, sprawling parishes and remote family farms made it ideal terrain for discontent - like the Brittany Balzac portrayed in *Les Chouans*. In 1556, for instance, the Privy Council informed baron Bergavenny that folk at Rotherfield and Frant, near his seat at Eridge, were 'out of order, especially in matters of religion'. Indeed some local families may have cherished Lollard heresies first current in the 15th century. Perhaps Richard Hosmer of Rotherfield, whose son was burned in 1557, believed he belonged to a company of 'saints' on earth, for he bequeathed his soul to God in 1540, hoping 'to have an habitation among his holy saints in Heaven'. And presumably the theology of Margery Morris of Heathfield, also burned in 1557, was ultra-radical, for she even boycotted the Protestant communion service in Edward's reign. Wealdsmen, moreover, debated theology in prison. Thomas Avington and Thomas Read from Ardingly, incarcerated in the King's Bench for leading 'a lewd tumult' at Waldron, stubbornly defended the doctrine of Free Will against Protestant inmates expounding Predestination.

In Sussex the first Protestants were burned in July 1555. John Launder perished at Steyning, Thomas Iveson and Richard Hook at Chichester, Dirck Carver at Lewes - a stark warning to the entire county. Carver was a brewer from Flanders who settled at Brighton to help satisfy a growing demand for beer. An edifying account of his death - the details may be pure invention - was given by John Foxe, the Protestant propagandist, in his *Acts and Monuments*, published in 1563 and better known as a *Book of Martyrs*. Carver, he narrates, was led to the stake near the sign of the *Star* [in the market-place] on 22 July. While he knelt in prayer, his [heretical] 'book' was tossed into the fire-barrel. When he clambered in, he threw it into the crowd. But the sheriff [John Covert] had it tossed back to burn with him. Carver affirmed his faith in 'God's Gospel', and his belief that Catholics would 'burn in hell perpetually'. Covert challenged him to call upon his God to 'deliver' him, or to strike Covert down 'to the example of this people'. Carver called on God to forgive Covert such blasphemy. The faggots were then lit: 'The fire came to him, he cried Lord have mercy upon me, and sprang up in the fire, calling upon the name of Jesus, and so ended'.

Probably, subsequent burnings were all staged east of the Adur - three at East Grinstead, four at Mayfield, at least 16 at Lewes. Thomas Harland carpenter and John Oswald husbandman, both from Woodmancote, and Thomas Avington and Thomas Read, the 'freewillers' from Ardingly, died there on Saturday 6 June 1556 - market day; Thomas Mills and Thomas Wood a 'minister', both from Hellingly, a fortnight later; and ten 'in the same fire' on 22 June 1557 - the county's fiercest holocaust. Alexander Hosmer, Margery Morris, her son James and Richard Woodman were joined by 'George Stevens, W. Maynard, his 'maid' Thomasina Woode, Denis Burgys, Ashdon's wife, Groves' wife' - folk scrappily listed by Foxe and otherwise unknown.[56]

96 The ten Protestant martyrs

By the early 19th century tradition linked these 'martyrs' with the vaulted medieval undercroft of the *Star*. 'In all probability', Horsfield surmised, 'they were immured in the dark damp cell and brought from that dismal abode to the faggots which blazed before it' - till recently the chamber had 'every apparatus and appearance of the gaols of those days'. Mark Antony Lower noted 'a curious piece of iron frame-work' there, believed to be a rack or gridiron on which Protestants were stretched, or partly broiled, before being fed to the fire above - he thought it more suited to 'the stowage of good liquor'.[57]

If the influence of the Gage and Howard families steadied Catholic conviction among some townsfolk, the summer burning of Protestants in the market-place doubtless encouraged others to conform. Residents lacked, it seems, the visceral zeal nurtured in the Weald. The only 'martyr' among them was the shadowy Christian Grover of Lewes - place of execution unknown, whereas a pewterer there, a strong 'Gospeller' under king Edward, was mocked by Richard Woodman for having ostentatiously returned to Rome. Yet so fluid was religious belief, and so powerful the New Monarchy, that the accession of Elizabeth was to transform, yet again, the political and ecclesiastical establishments in Sussex.[58]

97 The undercroft below the *Star*

Overleaf: a female caryatid from Pelham House

8

A thirst for Order: 1558-1625

LEWES BURGUS: - Articles concluded & agreed upon to be observed & kept by the Inhabitants of the said Boroughe for the better ordering & government of the same ... confirmed & subscribed at A generall assemble in the Townhouse upon Whitson daye the viii[th] of June in the yere of our lord 1595...
9 Item that the xxiiii[tie] shall always be chosen in the Townhowse upon Whitsondaye after evening prayer and not anye more to be chosen in the Castle, for the avoyding of further disorder.
10 Item that the hedboroughes shall diligentlye & in reverent manner attend with there staves upon the Constables at all tyme, when they shalbe called to doe anye service belonging to there office...
16. Item for the better ordering & government of the Towne in suppressing & punishing of malefactors & disordered persons, that the Constables or one of them and two of the Fellowship ... & others to ayd them shall everye weeke at the least & oftener if nede shall so require in the night time from the first of October to the last of Marche make diligent serche in all Innes alehouses & other suspected places where anye badd & disordered rule is thought to be kept for the fynding out of lewd persons and all suche disorders as they shall fynd in there discretions to see dewlye punished according to the quallitye of the fault.

On 15 January 1559 the coronation of Elizabeth enthroned a consummate politician. Endowed with her grandfather's pragmatism and her father's intellect, she maintained the New Monarchy as a bastion of Order, the linchpin of national security and social peace. She also imbued it with Glamour and a touch of Glory - an achievement which James I (1603-25) did not entirely dissipate. Her first task was to establish an Anglican State Church with bishops amenable to the Crown, a liturgy tinged with ritual, and dogmas loosely defined. So there was no room for the Calvinistic iconoclasts who despoiled Hailsham's parish church in March 1559, or for stubbornly Catholic clergy. Glaringly 'papist' fittings were also removed from churches. At Southover 'a great wooden cross' and two stone altars were sold, along with linen rochets and silk cushions, two silver clasps and an ivory box.

At St Michael's two stone altars and some 'latin books' were disposed of, and when the bishop visited and twenty pence were spent on 'plays', doubtless their scripts were acceptably Anglican. Some officially tolerated vestiges of 'papist' ritual did trouble the more ardent Protestants. Yet they moved ever closer to the Queen when Catholic militancy in France and the Netherlands culminated in the Saint Bartholomew Massacre and Alva's Council of Blood, and she became the focus of a febrile patriotism when Philip of Spain dispatched Armadas against England in 1588 and 1596 and landed troops in Ireland in 1601.[1]

To push her Church settlement through parliaments that assembled in 1559 and 1563, Elizabeth partially remodelled the political Establishment. In Sussex she appointed as Lord Lieutenant the astute Sir Richard Sackville, whose mother, born Margaret Boleyn, was her great-aunt. He was also elected its senior knight of the shire. As a base for his official duties, the queen granted him in 1559 the Lord's Place at Southover, which had reverted to the Crown when Anne of Cleves died. Richard's bequests in 1566 included a generous £100 to the poor at Lewes and East Grinstead. His son Thomas was created baron Buckhurst in 1567 - a signal honour, for Elizabeth rarely made new peers. From 1569 he served, almost continuously, as Lord Lieutenant, firstly with Anthony Browne, viscount Montague, and from 1586 with Charles baron

98 The Lord Treasurer

Howard of Effingham. In 1599 he was appointed Lord Treasurer. James I confirmed him in office and promoted him to earl of Dorset. He reinforced his power-base in mid Sussex with massive purchases of land, among them the manors of Swanborough, Kingston, Allington, and Ringmer which included Malling and Cliffe. He acquired the estates of Old Malling and Malling Deanery, also a quarter of Houndean manor, and in 1576 a quarter of the barony and Borough of Lewes from the earl of Derby, as well as Southover manor in 1582 from John Stempe - he already owned the Lord's Place there.[2]

As an able, energetic Lord Lieutenant and a local Colossus of wealth, Buckhurst grew to dominate mid Sussex. In 1580 he arbitrated between fishermen and landsmen at Brighton. He mustered the militia above Rottingdean in 1586 when a Spanish raid seemed imminent. He busied with guns and powder in 1588 when the Armada 'came along by New Haven' - a telling contrast to earl Fitzalan's indifference in 1377. During a time of 'famine', in 1597, he arranged a local distribution of cheap Baltic rye bought at Billingsgate. When the French governor of Dieppe arrived at Lewes from Newhaven with 'a 100 persons' in April 1600, Buckhurst sent from London the order which secured horses to convey them to the capital. He was often at the Lord's Place and seemed unperturbed when Elizabeth contemplated a visit in 1577, merely asking for time to ship provisions from Flanders - in the event a local outbreak of plague cancelled the royal progress, a re-run of 1538. Provisions from mid Sussex for the Place included conies, 'good', 'sweet' and 'well killed', from Telscombe Down, pigeons and capons from Milton Street, fat calves and steers from Parrock, wood and charcoal from Newick. At his death in 1608 the Lord Treasurer left armour and household 'stuff' at the Place. He also considered, it seems, stocking a granary at Lewes with grain to be sold to the poor 'in dear years' at a subsidized price - a project never realized.[3]

Being deeply versed in Renaissance culture, Elizabeth also valued her 'cousin' Buckhurst as a polished courtier well grounded in the Classics, who collaborated with Thomas Norton to write *Gorboduc*, a very early English tragedy, acted in 1561 and printed in 1565. Possibly he gave the Lord's Place a Renaissance make-over, some time after William Newton renounced a lease of rooms there, perhaps in 1570. As already noted, John Deward in 1620 sketched an L-shaped mansion, south of the great gate, within a walled enclosure. The site has yielded pieces of elaborate 'Elizabethan' plasterwork, also 'Dutch' tiles of tin-glazed majolica, depicting a ram and a dog. Moreover, two pieces of Caen-stone carved with Renaissance strapwork, are also preserved, at Anne of Cleves museum. Their provenance is unknown, but they have segments of a 13th-century string-course on their reverse, which

99 Deward's sketch

suggests they were salvaged from the priory and re-used at the Place. Also preserved are sandstone pieces, similarly carved and possibly from the mansion. Two fit together to form a square-edged tympanum adorned with strapwork, with a plain rounded arch beneath, and a fluted overhang above. Three display a double-lined lozenge within a rectangular border, with a base or capital attached. So maybe Buckhurst gave the Lord's Place a modish facade, akin to that at Somerset House or Slaugham Place.

100 The 'Dutch' tiles

101 Sandstone pieces

102 Fairhall: the Renaissance doorcase and its Classical detail

And maybe Buckhurst installed at the Place the Renaissance stone doorcase now at Fairhall in Southover - a resident there, William Lane, was involved with the Place's demolition soon after 1668. The doorcase - surely too grand for its present site - is embellished with robust Classical detail: two cherubs either side of a blank tablet regard splays of weaponry radiating from a cuirass and tunic, and from a quiver and helmet.[4]

Maybe Buckhurst also landscaped the precinct due east of the Place, creating the Mount and the arena beyond, now called the Dripping Pan - both are built of chalk brought from elsewhere. The Mount existed in June 1604 when a cow strayed into the 'Mount garden', a squarish enclosure intact till the railway came in 1845. (Map 5.3) No such garden was recorded by the Cluniacs in the 1530s, though it has been argued that they erected it as a Calvary. Doubtless Buckhurst valued the views of the estuary and the Downs; a path spiralling up it is shown on a Buck print dated 1737. Probably in 1604 its 'garden' was already bordered to the east by the arena, a likely setting for the bull baiting and bowling, if not the cards and dice, which beguiled the third earl of Dorset in May 1616. Mounts were a feature of formal Elizabethan gardens, as laid out by Sir Thomas Tresham at Lyveden, the earl of Northumberland at Petworth and viscount Montague at Cowdray.[5]

103 The spiralling path

A tradition ascribing 'the Tumulus' to the Sackvilles was relayed by Robert Austen, a local parson and antiquarian, to Francis Grose in 1772: 'It is said to have been raised by one of the Earls of Dorset, between whom and a brother of his Living at Lewes, a Difference arose on the Account of being over looked by each other'. Absurd, of course, yet the 'brother' may be a confused reference to Henry Sackville, Buckhurst's second son, a comely youth, whose 'rare curled head' attracted the 'very special liking' of queen Elizabeth. His marriage to Alice Colson in 1592 brought him estates at Bexhill and Heathfield. But from June 1597 he suffered 'a distraction of his senses'. After three years of fruitless therapy in Germany, he was escorted to Padua, but again to no avail. Quite possibly this deranged brother of the second earl had been lodged at the Place, for Henry died on 22 May 1635 at the house on School Hill of the physician, John Panton, and was buried in the chancel at Southover.[6]

Buckhurst's prestige and wealth allowed those he favoured to flourish. His first cousin, Bartholomew Garway, left him a cup with a silver cover in 1607 as a token of 'duty and affection'. He was already managing

104 Closet windows

estates for Buckhurst's father in 1560 and probably enlarged Fairhall at Southover into a 'modest urban mansion'. A northward extension of its east wing included a ground-floor kitchen with a massive fireplace, and a 'high-quality' chamber in a jettied storey above, lit by a projecting north window; its doors and wall plaster were painted to simulate oak panels and strapwork. A new west wing contained a parlour below and a chamber above, similarly heated and lit. Small windows opened onto the new courtyard from first-floor closets set in the massive brick chimney breasts.[7] Garway left Fairhall to a nephew, Paul, who was probably living near by, in a 'Gatehouse' complex, once part of St James's hospital. In 1608 Paul paid £50 for barley grown on the 'the Rises and Hams', demesne fields near the Lord's Place; in 1609 he shipped 640 bushels of oats to London. Quite possibly the wider Garway family also traded corn grown on other Sackville manors in mid Sussex - a Henry Garway dispatched barley and wheat through Newhaven to Messina in 1607. Paul's daughter Anne married a London mercer, Thomas Browne. Their son Thomas, born in 1605, remembered 'when I was very young and I think but in coats, my mother carried me to my grandfather Garawaye's house in Lewes'. After his father's early death Thomas saw little of his mother - a deprivation the future author of *Religio Medici* shared with John Evelyn, also the grandson of a 'Lewes' merchant.[8]

However, another affluent Southover resident, William Newton, was not planted there by the Sackvilles; the tradition that he served as Buckhurst's 'steward' seems groundless. He arrived from Cheshire about 1540 and resided for some thirty years at the 'dissolved monastery' - in rooms at the Lord's Place - latterly as the inheritor of Nicholas Jenny's 50 year lease of the priory site and demesne. This lease he gave up before rebuilding the mansion now called the Grange, where his initials and the date 1572 survive on a fireplace. He already owned East Mascalls at Lindfield which still displays 'Cheshire' timberwork, and so does Clayhill House at Ringmer, acquired by him before 1575. In its walls are pieces of carved Caen stone from the priory, so doubtless the stone used for the gabled wings and linking hall at the Grange was also carted from the precinct.[9]

from the south-east

The north range

The Newton shield

The Tudor stables

From the west

An author himself, Buckhurst was a patron of scholarship. In 1580 he presented Thomas Underdowne to the rectories of St Mary Westout and St John's, two of the many local advowsons he bought up. Underdowne had dedicated to him a translation of *Ovid his Invective against Ibis*, because of Buckhurst's 'good affection' for his father Stephen, a yeoman at Chiddingly. In 1587 he translated *An Ethiopian Historie* by Heliodorus. In 1596 Buckhurst also sponsored the admittance to the College of Physicians of his medical adviser, Dr Thomas Twine - another author. Twine had taken his MA at Corpus Christi College Oxford in 1568 and then studied medicine at Cambridge. Equally versed in astrology, he knew the great magus, Dr John Dee. Twine's translations included *A dialogue of witches* (1575), *The wonderful workmanship of the world* (1578) and *A new counsell against the pestilence* (1578). When his tiresome son Brian was born in 1579, he was resident at Lewes, perhaps in All Saints parish where his servant, Robert Drake, was buried in 1582. After composing *A short and pithy discourse concerning the engendering tokens of earthquakes*, he rendered Books XI-XIII of Virgil's *Aeneid* into English verse. He also edited in 1590 his father's treatise on British history, *De rebus Albionicis*, which advocated the study of place-names and geology, instancing how the river-mouth below Lewes had silted up since earl Warenne built his castle. The dedication to Buckhurst's son Robert, who read the work with enthusiasm, was penned from 'Meridionali traiectu Leuisensi' - 'the southern crossing of Lewes', alias Southover.[10]

By 1602 Twine resided in the Borough, just outside the west gate. On his memorial brass in the chancel of St Mary Westout 14 lines of mannered Latin hyperbole precede the information that he died at Lewes, A.D. 1613, 1st August, in the climacteric, 70th. year of his age. The sense of the hyperbole seems to be:

Hippocrates had looked upon Twyne lying effaced by death and his bones under their thin (covering) dust buried in the earth. Now, says he, there shall be dust for me from this sacred dust for the alleviation of diseases and troubles; this dead man shall drive out sickness when transformed into medicine, and these ashes shall prevail against ashes, thus he speaks. Now that the physician is no longer here disease is all powerful on every side and rejoices in the absence of its avenger. For so it is; here Twyne is buried, who was our foster-son; alas, here he lies, the flower and pride of his generation. Bereft of her physician Sussex languishes; and in this nearly fatal year in which he passed away, she perishes. Believe me, scarcely can any future age produce a physician and man so famous in his accomplishments as this one has borne.

Above the inscription is a shield surmounted by an arm and a hand grasping two snakes entwining.[11]

The author perhaps of this convolution was Brian, who entered his father's college in 1594, graduated as a Master of Arts in 1603, but then

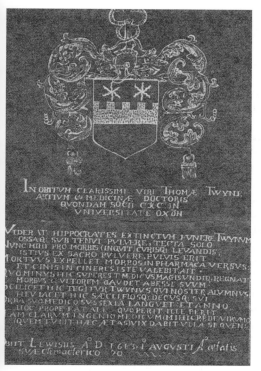

IN OBITVM CLARISSIMI VIRI THOMÆ TWYNI
ARTIVM & MEDICINÆ DOCTORIS
QVONDAM SOCII C & C IN
VNIVERSITATE OXON

VIDERAT HIPPOCRATES EXTINCTVM IVNERE TWYNVM
OSSAQ SVB TENVI PVLVERE, TECTA SOLO
IVNC MIHI PRO MORBIS (INQVIT) CVRISQ LEVANDIS,
ISTIVS EX SACRO PVLVERE, PVLVIS ERIT
MORTVVS EXPELLET MORBOS IN PHARMACA VERSVS:
ET CINIS IN CINERES ISTE VALEBIT, AIT
VO MINVS HIC SVPEREST MEDICVS MAGIS VNDIQ REGNAT
MORBVS & VLTOREM GAVDET ABESSE SVVM
DCILICET HIC TEGITVR TWYNVS QVI NOSTER ALVMNVS
HEV IACET HIC SÆCLI FLOSQ DECVSQ SVI
RHA SVO MEDICO SVS SEXTA LANGVET ET ANNO
IIOC PROPE FATA ALI QVO PERIT ILLE PERIT
AM CLARVM INGENIO MI DIC VM MIHI CREDITE VIRVM
QVEM TVLIT HÆC Æ TAS VIX DABIT VLLA SEQVENS

BIIT LEWISIIS A D 1613 1 AVGVSTI Æ ætatis
VÆ Climacterico 70

106 The Twine memorial

stayed on. His letters home meanwhile were tactlessly condescending. He resolved to deport himself as a 'Gentleman' scholar and study only those non 'empirick' precepts 'for whose sake your Physick is counted among the sciences'. And he pestered relentlessly, for money, for Holland cheeses, for cloth to make a gown (preferably 'peach' in colour), yet never condescended to pawn his lute, worth £5 10s. In February 1605 came a withering paternal riposte: 'You take no course to live of yourself, but linger and loiter still in Oxford. When you come [to Lewes], come not altogether in your worst and most tattered clothing according to your wont, in hope to have new here. You are still a child, and will be, though you live to be as old as Cupid. You busy your head about toys that bring no profit; and do somewhat resemble Hannibal, that often overcame the Romans, but still sent home to Carthage for money. I would I had your years, and you my mind'. Fortunately, soon after, Brian secured a fellowship at Corpus Christi, and graduated as a Bachelor of Divinity in 1610. When in 1614 the third earl of Dorset found him the vicarage at Rye, Brian installed a curate in that Puritan seaport, preferring to lecture at the university, gather notes on its history and help archbishop Laud draft new statutes.[12]

In December 1605 Thomas Twine acquired, albeit briefly, a mildly illustrious neighbour - if the Nicholas Yonge, who bought 'a garden with a house lately built called Caprons' at the bottom of Keere Street, was indeed the London-based singer and music editor of that name. In 1607 Yonge was licensed to sublet for seven years, but appeared at court leets in 1609 and March 1612, before selling the premises in December. Yonge had fed a fast-growing English enthusiasm by publishing in 1588 and 1597 two volumes of *Musica transalpina*, anthologies of Italian madrigals with English texts; many of the lyrics were later reset by English composers. Between 1594 and 1618 he also sang in the choir at St Paul's cathedral, dying in London a year later. His purchase of Caprons is plausible because of the claim that he was born at 'Lewes', perhaps into a clan of aspiring South Down yeomen. A Nicholas Yonge (his father perhaps) was left forty shillings in 1549 by Nicholas Jenny of Southover; so

107 The charming memorial

108 The alabaster effigies

were the daughters of John Yonge 'late of Malling', quite possibly the executor to whom John Piers, the dean of Malling, bequeathed two cows and 12 lambs in 1536. Malling College, of course, was a focus for Church music. Less plausible is a role for Buckhurst as his patron - the 1588 anthology was dedicated to Gilbert Talbot, later seventh earl of Shrewsbury. A charming memorial now graces the Grange gardens.[13]

Though they amassed local manors and advowsons, the Sackvilles played no conspicuous part in 'Lewes' elections till the 1580s, despite the Gages falling from royal favour in the early 1560s, and the duke of Norfolk's execution in 1572. Sir Edward Gage, the heretic-hunter under Mary, and a stubborn Catholic, was excluded from the Lewes bench of JPs and died in 1568 at Firle, where he sheltered the ex-Cluniac David Michell, lately evicted as rector of Horsted Keynes. Gage's son John, the former 'Lewes' MP, proved an unflinching recusant, often in custody during the Armada years. In 1592 his servant, Henry Collins, was accused of plotting to kill the queen - in 1599 a namesake rented 157 acres of demesne arable at Firle. Beleaguered though John was, he proclaimed his family's former prestige by engaging a fashionable Flemish sculptor, Gerard Johnson, to design a sumptuous memorial at Firle to his grandparents. The 'telling' alabaster effigies of the Lord Chamberlain and his Lady still recline on a richly ornamented tomb-chest, the Garter below his knee. The Fleming also designed less conspicuous memorial brasses to John's parents, and to John himself and his two wives - John wanted them shown with French hoods and loose gowns, 'not girded'. His successor in 1598, a less militant nephew, preserved a Catholic enclave at Firle till his death in

1633, despite treasonous talk by a tenant, John Isaac. A former Marian archdeacon of Lewes, Robert Taylor, was still living in 1592 at Bentley in the household of John Gage's relative, Edward, whose monument at Framfield carries a quotation from the Roman breviary.[14]

Less immediate was the duke of Norfolk's eclipse in mid Sussex, for he seemed at first to accept the new regime. Indeed William Cantrell, elected an MP at 'Lewes' in 1563, had served under him against the Scots four years before. But the duke forfeited his life and estates in 1572 for allegedly conspiring with Mary queen of Scots. His son Philip - canonized in 1970 - died in the Tower in 1595, and not till 1610 did a grandson re-possess the Norfolk quarter of Lewes Borough and barony. By contrast Elizabeth allowed the 'loyal' Catholic, viscount Montague, to share the Lord Lieutenancy with Buckhurst till 1585, and he greeted her with elaborate ritual in 1591 at Cowdray House, where the male servants were marshalled in 37 ranks, from the steward down to the junior scullions.[15]

Meanwhile, a new dynasty was entrenching in Lewes borough. George Goring, a lawyer favourable to Elizabeth's religious settlement, was elected for 'Lewes' in 1559 and 1563. His father, a former Gentleman of Edward VI's privy chamber, owned an estate in West Sussex, but locally George's wife, Mary Everard, had inherited half of Ovingdean manor, and a fourth share of the demesne manors of Lewes barony allotted in 1439 to Edmund Lenthall - though all were settled on Edward Bellingham, her son by a former marriage. Goring's cousin, Edward Fenner, a lawyer from Crawley, was elected for 'Lewes' in 1571, and his step-son, Edward Bellingham, in 1572. Chosen with Fenner was William Morley, a graduate of Cambridge and Padua, who in Mary's reign had joined John Knox's Calvinistic congregation at Geneva. He built an austere inner quadrangle at Glynde manor-house in 1569, owned ironworks at Hawkesden in Mayfield, and was an active JP till his death in 1597, but never sat in parliament again.[16]

109 The austere quadrangle: a doorway

Whether Morley was Goring's political ally is unclear. But John Shurley, elected with Bellingham in 1572, probably was, for he was Goring's second cousin and Edward Fenner's nephew - though his marriage also reinforced his local influence. A product of Queen's college Cambridge and the Middle Temple, he become a serjeant-at-law (a senior barrister) in 1603. Like Goring, he was the second son of a Court official - Edward Shurley of Isfield Place had been Cofferer to Henry VIII. John married a coheiress of Richard Kyme, High Constable of the Borough in 1556-7. Richard and his brother John had served the powerful Court official, Sir William Petre. In 1544 John Kyme bought the Friars estate which he leased to his nephew-in-law, William Covert, while Covert was High Constable in 1576-7. But John Shurley was probably installed by 1580, for his brother Thomas died there on a visit from Isfield Place. In 1605 he purchased the manor of Broadwater in west Sussex.[17]

George Goring, meanwhile, was expanding a local power-base. Between 1575 and 1582 he bought an eighth of Houndean manor from the earl of Derby and the manors of Hurstpierpoint, Streat and Westmeston from baron Dacre, Buckhurst's brother-in-law - as well as premises west of St Andrew's Lane in Lewes borough. In 1583 his elder brother, Sir Henry, whose wife, Dorothy Everard, also inherited half of Ovingdean manor, paid £180 for the *Bull* inn near the west gate. Maybe George's lavish purchases were funded by loans secured because the lucrative post of Receiver-General at the Court of Wards was soon to be his - it reverted to him in 1584. Before his death in 1594 he spent perhaps £4000 on remodelling the Dacre mansion at Danny Park in Hurstpierpoint, and £2000 on building 'in stone' a mansion in St Andrew's Lane, now Pelham House. Its two southern angle-pavilions survive. So does fine oak panelling dated '1579', on which two achievements of arms, framed by fluted pilasters and rayed tympana, record the marriages of George and Henry to the Everard sisters. Elsewhere, on pedestals adorned with strapwork and masks, stand undraped, 'almost bacchanalian', caryatid figures, crowned by baskets filled with fruit and

110 The Goring achievements of arms

111 A caryatid

112 The carpenter

IHON⸱HATHOR

flowers. There is too a trimly bearded man, wearing a broad-brimmed hat and open-necked high-collared coat, who clasps a jar with IHON HATHORN inscribed on it. The high quality suggests a metropolitan craftsman, and though a John Hathorne, citizen and carpenter of London, died in 1577, '1579' could be the year the panelling was installed. Two crouching satyrs carved in oak, one female, one bearded, decorate a porch probably built after Henry Goring bought the *Bull*.[18]

By October 1584, however, George Goring was in conflict with Buckhurst who, backed by viscount Montague, sponsored the election for Sussex of his son, Robert Sackville, along with Sir Thomas Shirley of Wiston. Goring unsuccessfully opposed this, aided by Herbert Pelham, the head of a minor branch of that family at Warbleton. That same year, Buckhurst also asserted himself at 'Lewes'. Returned there were his first cousin, Thomas Pelham, and a more distant relation, Richard Browne, a Surrey landowner. In 1586 Browne was again chosen, and also elected, 'for Southover, a member of Lewes', was Buckhurst's 'cousin' and close friend, Francis Alford, a civil lawyer whose scruples as to the fate of Mary Stuart prevented him writing an official history of Elizabeth's reign. Thenceforth one 'Lewes' member was always Buckhurst's nominee - in 1588 his son, Robert Sackville, in 1593 and 1597 his son-in-law, Sir Henry Glemham, a Suffolk landowner who married Anne Sackville at Southover in 1585, and Goddard Pemberton from Herefordshire, the friend of a friend of Buckhurst in 1601. Also chosen at Peterborough, Pemberton was replaced by Buckhurst's neighbour, Percival Hart of Lullingstone in Kent. Though Alford's election for Southover in 1586 is a reminder that one MP in four sat for that 'member of Lewes', the sequence is uncertain after the return in 1559 of Thomas Saunder, a Southover 'yeoman' who left a gold ring in 1581 to his 'singular good lady', Buckhurst's wife.[19]

113 The Pelham monument

Thomas Pelham, elected in 1584, was probably an ally of Buckhurst. His father, Sir Nicholas, had married Anne, a daughter of John Sackville, Buckhurst's grandfather. Though seated at Laughton, Sir Nicholas was buried in 1559 at St Michael's in Lewes. His mural monument shows him kneeling in armour facing Anne across a draped prayer-desk. Below them are six sons and five daughters confronting an hour-glass, and a bold cornice terminating in elaborate strapwork. Above the parents an entablature resting on Corinthian columns frames an inscription flanked by cherubs and martial insignia, which a rustic verse seeks to justify:

> HIS BRAVE EXPLOIT IN GREAT KING HENRY'S DAYES
> AMONG THE WORTHYES HATH A WORTHIER TOMBE:
> WHAT TYME YE FRENCH SOUGHT TO HAVE SACKT SEAFOORD
> THIS PELHAM DID REPEL-EM BACK ABOORD.

The swift repulse of the landing on Saturday 25 July 1545 has already been noted; militia men from Kent, reaching Uckfield on the Sunday night, learned they were no longer needed.[20]

Thomas Pelham, the MP, was the second son of Sir Nicholas. A graduate of Queen's college Cambridge, he practised law. In 1568, with his widowed mother, he bought 'Mr. Parker's great house', which they already occupied - now the *White Hart*. There, in an upper chamber in a south-facing wing, the initials T P were carved on a stone fire-place (now removed). They also acquired five cottages in St Mary's Lane, a Tenter Garden off St Andrew's lane, meadows near Watergate mill and St John's, and crofts to the south of St John's called 'the Pepercorn' and 'the Woodcroft'. In 1584 Thomas purchased High Street premises [53-4 & 56-9] either side of the 'great house'. But Thomas's status was transformed when he inherited the Laughton estates from a nephew in 1586. Indeed that year he was returned for Sussex in place of Sir Thomas Shirley, who was soldiering, and peculating, in the Netherlands. Thereafter, like the Morleys of Glynde, the Pelhams of Laughton took little part in 'Lewes' elections for several decades.[21]

Returned in 1593, however, with Glemham, Buckhurst's son-in-law, was Goring's eldest son, George. Quite probably the Gorings had reached an accord with Buckhurst, for their finances were foundering. George senior died intestate in March 1594 owing almost £20,000 to the Court of Wards. The son clung on to his estates, hoping to recoup by prospecting for iron in Munster. He was again returned for 'Lewes' in 1601, but died in February 1602. An alabaster tablet displaying his coat of arms, taken to Eastgate stoneworks when his elaborate tomb in St Michael's was dismantled in 1748, was restored to the church in 1924. Horsfield, morover, published an engraving of two broken effigies from the tomb - a son bare-headed, a daughter chicly bonneted - and recorded a thoughtful verse incised on its black marble:

114 The Goring tomb: the tablet and the effigies

> *Dies mortis, aeternae vitae natalis est,*
> *Sementis mors est, unde vita pullulat,*
> which can be translated as:
> *The day of death is the birth of eternal life,*
> *Death is a seedbed from which life grows abundantly.*[22]

Maybe it was as an ally of the Goring family that John Shurley, the barrister at the Friars, re-emerged to be elected in 1588, 1597 and 1604, along with Buckhurst's nominees. Chosen with him in 1604, after James I's accession, was Sir Henry Nevill, the son of baron Bergavenny. Though his family's stake in the barony and borough of Lewes was long established - in 1563-4 the High Constables had paid twenty shillings for one month's board for Bergavenny's huntsmen - Sir Henry was also married to Buckhurst's daughter Mary, and from 1595 he and Buckhurst's son, Robert, had controlled a syndicate exploiting a royal patent to export cannon. The families owned Wealden ironworks, at Eridge in Frant and Sheffield in Fletching. Their guns were shipped to France and the United Provinces through Newhaven.[23]

Buckhurst was created earl of Dorset by James I, and died, still Lord Treasurer, in 1608. His son Robert, the second earl, expired a few months later. Robert left £80 for the poor of 'Lewes' and funds for a 'Sackville College for the Poor' at East Grinstead. He also forbade excessive solemnity at his funeral, which would merely enrich 'the heralds and drapers'. But his son Richard, the third earl, lived in magnificent style. Residing chiefly at Knole near Sevenoaks and Dorset House in London, he starred in the costly masques and archaic tournaments which delighted the Jacobean Court. In mid Sussex, where he served as a Lord Lieutenant from 1612, his prestige, of course, was considerable. The diary of Anne Clifford, his talented wife, notes a visit he paid in May 1616 to the Lord's Place at Southover, along with 'Tom Neville, J. Herbert and all that Crew, with Wat. Raleigh, Jack Laurie and a multitude of such company. There was much Bull Baiting, Bowling, Cards and Dice, with such like sports to entertain the time'. In August 1617 the earl's 'Crew', assembled there, was again 'very gallant, brave and merry', and in March 1619, when he inspected a muster of the rapal militias,

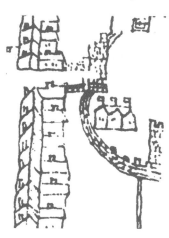

Anne records how warmly 'the county' showed 'their affection to him' - also the fireworks put on by 'the town'. But she also noted 'great play between my lord of Hunsdon, my lord of Effingham and my lord who lost them £200' - profligacy which was impairing the Sackville fortune. Maybe the fireworks were staged in the Dripping Pan, or in the castle bailey where John Deward depicted in 1620 what seems to be a two-storeyed pavilion with flags fluttering bravely from three gables.[24]

In 1614 Dorset's prestige was apparent when 'Lewes' returned Christopher Nevill, the brother of his uncle, Sir Henry, along with Richard Amherst, the 'high steward' of

Deward's pavilion

the Sackville estates in Sussex. Amherst was also elected in 1621, Christopher Nevill in 1624. When his son was baptised as Sackville at St Mary Westout in June 1610, Amherst was probably living at the former *Vine* inn - now *Shelleys Hotel* - which Buckhurst had bought in 1588 from the brewer, Thomas Pelland. Like John Shurley, Amherst was a successful barrister, becoming Treasurer of Serjeants Inn at Chancery Lane in 1626. He advised Anne Clifford on freeing her jointure from debts, and also acted for queen Henrietta Maria. He joined the Lewes bench of JPs in 1625 and died in 1632 owning local pastures at Horse Croft and Winterbourne, an iron-making furnace at Oldlands in Buxted and a coach with all its 'furniture'.[25]

Elected with Amherst in 1621 and with Christopher Nevill in 1624 was George Goring whose debt-burdened father died in 1602. Young George, by a career at Court, had mended the family fortune where it had first been made, for he served as a Gentleman of the Privy Chamber to Henry prince of Wales, and then to king James. And doubtless his marriage to Mary, a daughter of Edward Nevill, baron Bergavenny, also helped to renew his family's influence in Lewes borough.[26]

Also serving king James, as an 'esquire to the Body', was Ambrose Trayton, whose family had prospered serving the Sackvilles. His grandfather Thomas was a carpenter who dabbled in commercial malting and rebuilt in stone the west wall of his house on School Hill. Ambrose's father, Thomas II, had prospered as a Sackville factotum. In 1607 he repaired Dorset's houses at 'Lewes' and distributed £10 among the local poor at Christmas. In 1613, perhaps with malting in mind, he paid £299 15s for 3592 bushels of barley supplied by 'farmers and tenants' of the third earl. From him Trayton also leased demesne land at Ovingdean and the defunct palace at Old Malling. By 1624 he owned a string of houses on School Hill [210-14]. His will made in 1635 itemized a basin and ewer of 'china mettall', and a shoal of silverware - spoons, beer-bowls, wine-bowls, a sugar-box, a candle-cup, a salt-cellar. Being socially aspiring, he placed his eldest son, Thomas III, at Christ Church college Oxford in 1604, under the care of Brian Twine at Corpus Christi. But Brian's father was soon to denounce him as 'a runnagate accursed from his father's mouth, & like pitch defiling, or like a viper hurting, all that have to do with him'. Nothing more indeed is known of Thomas III. But his younger brother, Ambrose, married a daughter of John Sackville of Chiddingly in 1611 and served the person of king James.[27]

Trayton

The prestige enjoyed in mid Sussex by the Sackvilles, the Nevills and the Gorings, stemmed from their territorial weight as landowners, from the official duties delegated to them by the

Crown, and from a growing veneration for Elizabeth, in which as Courtiers they bathed. As fears grew of a Catholic invasion of England - or Ireland - 'Gloriana' became the guarantor of national security. Excommunicated by Pius V in 1570, she allied (reluctantly) with Calvinist Protestants in the Netherlands and France battling against Philip II of Spain and the Catholic League. 'Popery' meanwhile was now reviled as a deadly threat to 'true' religion and to English identity. In 1588 a joyous firing of the field-guns parked in Lewes castle celebrated the dispersal of 'the spanish fleet [that] came along by New Haven'. In 1600 the defiant remark at Cliffe of an itinerant Irish labourer, Philip Browghowe - 'I love not the Queen, nor yet her laws, but I love the pope and his laws with my heart' - caused him to be whipped and pilloried 'with a paper containing his words'. And though the crushing in 1602-3 of Catholic resistance in Ulster, its last Irish stronghold, allowed James I to make a swift Peace with Spain, the failure of Guy Fawkes to blow up parliament in 1605 was hailed as a further Deliverance from Popery. In 1618, moreover, Europe drifted into thirty years of devastating religious war. And though Catholics in Lewes were few - Richard Bowater and Agnes Spencer in the Borough, Robert Dennis and Joan Copper at Southover, were the only recusants recorded in the 1580s - nonetheless the Gages at Firle and Bentley sparked agitated gossip from time to time.[28]

The popular veneration which Elizabeth earned, and king James inherited, allowed them to ignore sporadic pleas for a 'Puritan' reform of the Anglican State Church - the purging from its liturgy of residual Catholic rites; an explicit commitment to the Calvinist belief that Salvation was confined to an 'elect' elite enjoying predestined grace'; the down-grading, or abolition, of bishops, archdeacons and Church courts. In the 1560s, though, the task had been to firmly establish an Anglican State Church. In 1564 bishop Barlow of Chichester singled out Lewes and Rye, Hastings and Brighton, as its bastions in a still 'Catholic' shire - towns 'governed with such officers as be faithful favourers of God's word' - a judgement hopefully unaffected, as far as Lewes was concerned, by the wine, costing four shillings, which the High Constables gave him. Barlow's stress on civic officers reveals perhaps how many clergy had opted out of the State Church - or succumbed to a recent devastating influenza. In 1563 St John's and St Mary Westout each had a rector, and St Michael's a curate, but All Saints, Cliffe and Southover had no incumbent. At Lewes borough at least two of Barlow's 'faithful' officers already showed Puritan leanings. The merchant John Morley, a Constable in 1562-3, hoped in 1565 to be forgiven his sins by the merits of Christ's passion 'without any other act or acts of man'. John Stempe, a Constable in 1563-4, and a busy grammar school trustee under Mary, later orchestrated a testimonial for a Puritan curate. After Stempe died in 1594, aged eighty, his epitaph celebrated his charity and pure faith, and his new status as 'a joyful tenant of the skies'. Local Puritan gentry in the 1560s included

William Morley of Glynde and John Pelham of Laughton, both lately returned from voluntary exile at Calvin's Geneva.[29]

In 1569 Sussex was still deemed 'very blind' for want of teaching - 'except it be about Lewes and a little in Chichester'. Popish ornaments were treasured, 'ready to be set up for mass again'; old Latin primers were thumbed during Anglican services. In the 1570s, however, a posse of learned ministers, led by bishop Curteys, toured the diocese inveighing inclusively against Machiavells and Papists, Libertines and Atheists. Thomas Drant, the archdeacon of Lewes, also issued his *Wailings of the prophet Hieremiah done into English verse*. Classified perhaps as a Libertine was David Thickpenny, a curate at Brighton, supended in 1576 by bishop Curteys, for being 'a favourer of the Novel Doctrine of the Heretics called the Family of Love' - a sect, Continental in origin, which sought guidance only from the Holy Spirit. But Archbishop Grindal found Thickpenny 'well learned', with 'a very good Testimony' from his parish, and reinstated him, provided he renounced the Novel Doctrine. Continuing to officiate with scant regard for the Prayer Book, he moved from Brighton to Lewes borough, where children of his were baptised in 1576 and 1579. When in 1580 he was in trouble for preaching without a licence, John Stempe affirmed that he was 'zealous in good religion', his life 'a spectacle of honest living to others'. Stempe also secured him a testimonial 'under the town seal of Lewes', subscribed with the hands of the Twelve - the Borough's civic elite. John Batnor, the senior Constable in 1579-80, himself fathered a Puritan preacher, and along with Thickpenny witnessed a will in St Michael's parish in 1577.[30]

Others in the Twelve were citing Puritan doctrine in preambles to their wills, trusting to find a place in heaven among 'the elect' or the 'saints'. George Cockey commended his soul to Christ 'who appeased the wrath of God his father towards me and all mankind'. William Claggett called on his Redeemer to assist him at the hour of death 'with his holy spirit, the comforter'. Robert Aware wanted a 'godly sermon' at his burial, and his children to be trained in 'godly exercises'. Parson Thomas Underdowne, the translator of Ovid, also displayed Puritan scruples, hesitating in 1583 to subscribe unreservedly to the Book of Common Prayer and the Thirty-nine Articles. He resigned in 1590 when required to wear a surplice, make the sign of the cross in baptism, and pray for archbishops and bishops. In the Weald of Sussex meanwhile there was a sudden fashion for 'godly' Christian names, as borne by Renewed Wisberry of Hailsham, Kill-sin Pemble of Withyham, More-fruit Fowler of East Hoathly, Faintnot Bachelor of Burwash, Aid-on-high Vinall of Warbleton, Stand-fast-on-high Stringer of Crowhurst, and Fight-the-good-fight-of-faith White of Ewhurst. Flie-fornication, a 'base son of Catren Andrewes', was baptised at Waldron. Lewes could muster Joy-in-sorrow Bailey, Repentance Avis and Weep-not Billing, but their native parishes are unknown.[31]

Whatever its merits as a compromise, Elizabeth's Church settlement did nothing to improve the funds available to local clergy. In 1603 it was estimated that £30 a year was needed to attract an educated man to a parish living. Yet in 1650, after a steep rise in prices, All Saints was valued at £8 a year, Southover at £11, St Michael's at £14. Till the 1620s all three were usually served by curates. St John's and St Mary Westout were each valued at £50, but were held in plurality by Thomas Underdowne, and later by William Innians. At Cliffe the rector was excused a clerical levy in 1613, the benefice being 'mean and his substance not much', though lay trustees held property once owned by the Brotherhood of saint Thomas and by Malling college. Church fabrics also decayed. Though at St John-sub-castro in 1586 the churchwardens had merely noted that its walls might be beautified with sentences from Scripture, in 1587 the chancel was demolished. The antiquarian William Camden later observed the site, all desolate and beset with briars and brambles. At St Mary Westout the western bay of the aisle arcade had fallen into ruin. At Malling, because their church had been pulled down, folk resorted to Cliffe or rowed across the Ouse to Hamsey. Moreover, at Old Malling, John Norden noted in 1595 the walls and ruins of the once 'stately ancient house' of the archbishops of Canterbury. By 1547 Cramner had ceded to the Crown large segments of his manor of South Malling, at Mayfield and Ranscombe, but he clung on to Ringmer, Cliffe and Malling. These, though, were 'exchanged' with the Crown early in Elizabeth's reign, ending a once powerful lordship, and causing the 'stately' palace, now redundant, to quickly decay.[32]

Because the State Church of Scotland was strongly Calvinist, the accession of James I raised hopes of a Puritan reform in England. Indeed 27 gentlemen in Sussex petitioned him to that end, 'as the women of Samaria did [king Jehoram of Israel] in a great famine (2 Kings vi. 26)'. With an unctious lack of realism they asked that each parish should have a godly and learned pastor to instruct the people, 'with sufficient maintenance'; that pluralities and non-residence be ended, 'unpreaching', ignorant and ungodly ministers be removed; that pastors should subscribe only 'to your Majesty's supremacy' and to articles defining the true faith, doctrine and sacraments; that 'the hot urging of ceremonies' repugnant to godly ministers should cease - doubtless they had in mind the sign of the cross in baptism, the giving of a ring in marriage, kneeling at communion. They wanted too a government of the Church according to the precept of God's word, but avoided specifics, trusting in king James as the children of Israel did in the wisdom of Solomon. But a less mincing petition, from 'the commonalty' of Sussex, coupled Church Courts and 'insufficient ministers' as twin evils 'that continually haunt us', a 'gulch' choking the realm with 'loathsome smoke'.[33]

Among the 27 gentlemen-petitioners, and doubtless grieved by the king's swift rejection of any Puritan reform of the State Church, was

William Newton of Southover, whose father had built the Grange and whose uncle Lawrence signed David Thickpenny's testimonial. A graduate of Magdalen Hall Oxford and a barrister of Gray's Inn, William died in 1648, aged 84 years, bemoaning the earthly 'grievances' that flowed from his many sins and entrusting his salvation to 'God's mercy in Christ apprehended by faith'. The Crown's prestige, nonetheless, still muted Puritan discontent. Not till the late 1620s were ungovernable tensions provoked by the religious wars in Europe, and by a new Anglican theology which denied the doctrine of 'election'. Englishmen, meanwhile, acquiesced in the wisdom of their Solomon and respected his aristocratic entourage.[34]

Lewesians of course were familiar with 'the loathsome smoke' of the archdeacon's court, staffed by civil lawyers, versed in canon law. To it churchwardens submitted quarterly reports on church fabric and furniture, graveyards, parsonage-houses and glebes; the licensing of schoolmasters, surgeons and midwives; cases of adultery, whoredom and incest, drunkenness and swearing, ribaldry and usury; the disruption, neglect or boycotting of divine service. The court cleared a widow and her daughter at Hove of being 'notorious' witches. It heard rival claims to a pew at Ditchling, bitterly argued by the minister's wife and the late minister's widow. It excommunicated a Northiam man for abusing his rector, on the public highway, as 'old Fool, old Ass, old Coxcomb'. Its officials proved wills, issued letters of administration and settled disputed tithes. Difficult cases were referred to the bishop's lawyers at Chichester. On its behalf in the 1590s, John Kidder of Lewes, an 'apparitor', carried paperwork to and fro, serving citations in the deaneries of Hastings and Pevensey. Churchwardens at All Saints Hastings paid the fees of a 'summoner' each quarter. At Berwick in 1619 they listed the sums due to the bishop and paid to his 'collector' at Lewes, the tenths, procurations and synodals. There was a parallel bureaucracy, answerable to the archbishop, in the Peculiar of South Malling.[35]

Townsfolk could also observe the secular bureaucracies which allowed landowners of modest wealth, without personal ties to the Court, to play an ever greater role in the government of the shire - a role which soothed maybe those with Puritan leanings. The Lord Lieutenants selected deputy-lieutenants and captains to oversee the weapons and musters of the county militia. In 1587 Buckhurst chose Lewes borough as the place to store the county's arsenal of guns and ammunition, for the town, being in the middle of a shire 'more than seventy miles naked to the sea', was fittest to be its military headquarters. From 1604 the Peace with Spain somewhat slackened vigilance. When musters were resumed in 1614 arms and expertise were woefully lacking - no powder, no coats, the few guns 'unfit for defence'. But largely thanks to the earl of Dorset, by 1618 each rape had recruited a company of 50 horsemen and four companies of foot soldiers - two 'select', two 'unselect' - each with 168 men. The non-commissioned officers were drawn, it was hoped, from 'the most able and active freeholders'. After the harvest, at the end of August, infantry men from each eastern rape were separately mustered for two days, at Battle, Alfriston and Ditchling; their united cavalry men were deployed at Uckfield on 15 September. For his 'store' at Lewes, Dorset bought 6 cwt of gunpowder made at Battle.[36]

As Justices of the Peace local landowners attended the assizes, which were mostly held at East Grinstead, though sometimes in summer at Horsham. There the royal judges tried cases of felonious killing, grand larceny, sedition, witchcraft and perversion. William Hunt, a Cliffe labourer, was convicted of breaking his wife's neck, and Thomas Atherton, a Ringmer 'gentleman', of fatally stabbing his spouse at Southover. In March 1603 a Lewes saddler, William Fletcher, was set in the pillory for chattering that 'king Henry [VIII] swore the nobles that no foreign Prince should inherit the Crown; if they did, they were perjured' - dynastic twaddle at a delicate juncture. John Cox, though, was acquitted of killing Thomas Drapier by throwing him onto 'the stall' of a house in the Borough market-place. The royal judges did venture through the Weald to Lewes in August 1565. From seats which cost the High Constables 13s 4d they sentenced men to death by hanging, for a murder at Rye, sheep-stealing at Fittleworth, the theft of a chalice at Warbleton. For causing 'two toads to suckle a red cow so that it died within three days', a spinster from Battle was pilloried twice. When the judges returned, in July 1580, the cases included bestiality at Rusper, sodomy at East Grinstead, and the killing with a goad of a shepherd at Eastbourne. The JPs sitting with the judges were headed by Sir Richard Sackville in 1565, by his son Buckhurst in 1580.[37]

Convenience demanded that, almost invariably, JPs from the eastern rapes assembled in Lewes borough for their sessions at Michaelmas, Epiphany [New Year] and Easter, though a joint Midsummer session with the western bench was held wherever the assize judges were sitting. Most cases involved alleged burglary or larceny - beef stolen from the Lewes butcher, Edward Bastard, russet cloth and Devonshire kerseys from the Cliffe draper, Richard Motlie; sheep taken from the common fold at Kingston by John Pomfret, a Southover labourer, from the Tenant Down at Ditchling by Thomas Robinson, a Cliffe miller. Like the assize judges the JPs also tackled a flood of 'rogues, vagrants and idle wandering persons', the result of a rising population and a plunge in the value of real wages. Somewhat sanguinely, though, in 1613, JPs from the Wealden part of Lewes rape claimed to be free of them, largely because in April 1608 Thomas Trayton (the Sackville factotum) had been authorized to build a House of Correction at Cliffe, just west of the *Red Lion* in West Street [the High Street]. The site, bounded on three sides by drainage ditches, cost the ratepayers of Lewes and Pevensey rapes £240. The gallows, moreover, was to be 'set in his old place where it was wont to be'

- on Gallows Bank perhaps. Scandal erupted in 1617 when the Master of the House was accused of 'foul abuse', of whipping a single mother 'to make her confess an other father' - the man she named three years before had run away to avoid the charge of the child.[38]

Single mothers were of concern because JPs had a duty to oversee the machinery of Poor Relief imposed on parishes by the great statute of 1598 which aimed to rehabilitate the deserving pauper. Also to foster Public Order, they were empowered, if a scarcity of grain drove up the price of bread, to regulate the local movement and sale of corn. Among the dealers they licensed was John Bexhill, a Lewes miller. And they could prune back alehouses, to conserve barley stocks. Five keepers of unlicensed houses at Cliffe were indicted at the Midsummer assizes in 1598, and from January 1599 new licences in Lewes borough needed the consent of the Justices and the town authorities - Thomas Clark being singled out as a publican 'notoriously known to be most disordered' - a man of that name was clerk of the Borough corn market in 1579-81. Public Order also required that Lewes Bridge be rebuilt in 1561 at the joint charge of Lewes and Pevensey rapes; the surveyor of the works was John Chatfield, senior Constable in 1558-9.[39]

A bureaucracy also sustained the sheriff's county court which alternated every three weeks between Lewes and Chichester. At one or the other, depending on the timing of the writ, the forty shilling freeholders of Sussex converged to elect two knights of the shire. At Lewes in August 1656 their choice was made 'in the open castle'. Though the sheriff's county gaol was at Horsham, the castle was also used as an out-station. Its keeper in 1561 was William Grynder and when the assizes were held in the Borough in July 1580, Buckhurst solicited the post for a faithful retainer. A Ditchling grocer, accused of recusancy, died at the castle in 1573; William Fisher, a Lewes barber suspected of murder, made his escape in 1615. At St Michael's in 1594 the churchwardens paid 2s 8d towards a county rate 'due' to the gaol at Horsham, 'being 20 years behind unpaid'.[40]

Doubtless a reverence for Monarchy was reinforced at Lewes by the respect for Precedent engrained in its resident lawyers who were enticed there by its civil and Church courts - a respect exemplified by John Rowe. An assistant to John Shurley at the Friars in 1583, and high steward of the Bergavenny manors in Lewes rape between 1597 and 1622, he bought from the Sackville estate in 1614 a spacious property [143 High Street] outside the west gate. Believing that 'continuance of time may obscure that to posterity which yet is manifest and well known to many aged persons', he compiled a massive record of manorial tenures and hundredal organisation in Lewes rape - though when dealing with the common fine of Newick tithing, he omitted details possibly prejudicial to tenants, because 'the escheators and feodaries of these times have Argus Eyes, piercing into all conveyances'. He was unable to record any details

115 John Rowe

of Portslade manor because 'Mr. Snelling [its lord] would not have them entered; not willing, as I suppose, that any should know his tenants tenures, but himself'. Rowe also collected data about Lewes borough - its civil government and benefactors, public buildings and street-names. For its benefit he conveyed to trustees two acres of water-meadow near St John's. And he tracked down the deeds relating to Blunt's charity, 'in the lxxviith year of mine age (after I had given over my practice at law) perusing over my old paper books'. Doubtless he was among 'the lovers and favourers of Antiquities', whom he commended for saving from the destroyed chancel of St John's the inscribed stones celebrating the anchorite Magnus.[41]

The Borough's civil government, of course, was embedded in yet another bureaucracy, for the barony court still convened at Lewes every three weeks to supervise hundredal business and to settle civil actions 'not exceeding 39s 11d'. The bailiffs of the lords of the barony also presided at the court leet of the manor of Lewes borough on the Monday after Michaelmas, at which a jury - 'the Twelve to enquire for the crown' - reported householders suspected of common assault or drunkeness; of selling bread or beer by short measure; erecting 'foul' chimneys; failing to fasten cellar-covers; polluting the streets with blood and filth, fishwater and ashes; cluttering them with casks and timber, carts and sties; allowing pigs to roam, gutters to gush, privies to leak. Once appropriate fines had been imposed, the jury, alias the Twelve, elected from its ranks a senior High Constable, and then adjourned for a celebration supper. To its cost, from barony revenues, the bailiffs contributed ten shillings, as well as 6s 8d to the crier of the court, and to St Nicholas's hospital.[42]

John Rowe was anxious to spell out the autonomy enjoyed by the Constables and the Twelve within this seigneurial structure. The 'elder' Constable was chosen from the Twelve 'by course according to his seniority'. He in turn selected the junior Constable, with the consent of a majority of the Twelve, 'out of such of that society as were never formerly constables'. And the Constables, 'with consent as aforesaid' and 'without any contradiction or alteration by the [seigneurial] Stewards', chose two headboroughs and other officers. In 1614 these were a pound-keeper, a scavenger, a sealer and a searcher of leather, a clerk for each of the markets dealing in corn, fish, 'butchery' and textiles, also an ale-taster for each of the Borough's four parishes. The Twelve, moreover, being 'never so few as 12 nor more than 24', filled by majority vote vacancies in their ranks caused by death or resignation, recruiting from an inferior company called the Twenty-Four.[43]

Yet though autonomous, the Constables and the Twelve did not constitute a corporation of aldermen elected by freemen, delivering justice at their own quarter sessions, collecting royal taxes, able to sue or be sued - as did the jurats at Hastings, at Rye, and even at Seaford. As the itinerant poet, John Taylor, later put it, they had

.... *no power themselves to hang or draw*
Or on offenders to inflict the Law,
But to a Justice of the Peace, or Coram
They bring the parties, and their case before 'em.

As far back as 1372 Constables had been chosen at a Michaelmas court leet. But there are no clear links with the merchant gild restored in the 1140s by Reginald of Warenne, or with a request made by the burgesses of Lewes in 1266 that a plea of trespass be removed from the barony court and be heard instead before them 'in porchiam eorum'. As for the medieval bailiffs of the Borough, they seem to have served the seigneurs - in 1477 Henry Rake was made porter of the castle and bailiff of both castle and Borough. The castle precinct itself constituted a separate 'parish' and 'liberty'; Thomas Stowell 'of the Castle', shoemaker, was suspected of stealing twenty ewe sheep from the Wallands in 1632.[44]

Though without 'power themselves to hang or draw', preserving Public Order much concerned the Constables and the Twelve. They detained suspected law-breakers in the west gate, which the lords of the barony made available 'for the suppressing of disorders & restraint of offenders'. A lock and two keys for a cell there figure in a Borough inventory made in 1577. Suspects were sometimes pursued, Henry Key being paid in 1578-9 to carry a precept of Hue and Cry to the Constable of nearby Swanborough Hundred. Articles agreed in 1595 stipulated that once a week or more, from the first of October to the end of March, at least one Constable and two of the Twelve, with others to aid them, should diligently search inns, alehouses and other likely places 'for the finding out of lewd persons' - a response perhaps to a flood of winter vagrants. In 1598 the Constables were assured by local JPs that new public houses would be licensed only at their request. They also oversaw the punishment of offenders, paying for the 'Carting and Whipping of diverse lewd persons' in 1567-8 and for repair of the Borough's pillory, cucking stool and stocks. In 1617 they ensured that a beggar, 'born as he saieth at Halden in Kent', was properly whipped, before being conveyed there with a testimonial, which carried presumably the impress of the seal 'for vagabonds' listed in 1576 - perhaps the smaller brass matrix, bearing the arms of the Borough and inscribed SIGILLUM BURGI DE LEWYS, now in the Town Council's care.[45]

The Constables had also to supervise the Borough's militiamen. An article in 1595 specified that on the afternoon of Whit Monday the burgesses were to display 'in serviceable manner all such furniture of Armour and Weapon as they stand charged with' for the queen's service, and either in person, or by deputy, to attend upon the Constables and the Twelve 'in the Queen's Watch & walking according to the ancient custom and order'. In 1577 the Borough inventory included an 'Aunsyent' [an ensign of silk], a drum, two drumsticks and a partisan - a broad double-edged halbard, given in 1557 by Thomas Slutter for the senior Constable to carry. In 1588-9 it was entrusted to Andrew Crane 'at his going into France and by that means Lost'. A 'Town' drummer, Nicholas Locke, was buried at St John's in 1621. To keep their militiamen exercised the Constables repaired the archery butts in 'the fields' outside the west gate - on the Hides perhaps or the Wallands. They also equipped Andrew Crane and others for active service, paying for 'the furniture, apparelling and setting forth' of 12 soldiers in 1557-8 and for sending a man 'into the Queen's ships' in 1569-70.[46]

Because Buckhurst as Lord Lieutenant deemed Lewes ideally placed to be an arsenal 'for the defence of the most dangerous parts of this coast', the Constables also took charge of government artillery, powder and shot. In January 1588, after 'Goram's hoy' docked at Newhaven, they received six cast-iron field guns - two sakers, two minions, two falcons - also gun carriages and wheels, horse harness and bridles, sponges, ladles and five dry vats of match. In February 1588 captain Goram unloaded 42 barrels of gunpowder, six powder boxes with skin covers, 12 axle-trees and a quantity of cast-iron shot and raw lead. An engine 'to hoist great ordnance' also arrived. The gunpowder, it seems, was mostly stored in the town house which was newly lofted over. When in July 1588 'the spanish fleet [the Great Armada] came along by New Haven', twenty barrels of powder were released to Lord Buckhurst and one to Brighton. In 1588-9 a barrel was given to a captain shipping supplies to Dieppe for soldiers sent over to aid Henry IV of France; another was consumed 'in shooting of the great pieces in the Castle at the Rejoicing day for the overthrow of the Spanish navy'. Powder was also spent testing the pieces till in July 1597 Buckhurst dispersed them; two went to Brighton and four to Newhaven, along with their carriages, shot, horse harness, barrels, ladles and sponges. These were the guns deemed utterly unfit for defence in 1614.[47]

The Constables also supervised the Borough's deserving paupers and 'impotent people', till the statute of 1598 shifted this duty to parish overseers. In 1547-8 they bought sheets and blankets for a woman called Bridget; in 1557-9 they paid for 'the bringing up of certain poor children', in 1567-8 for apprenticing John Leyward to a cutler for eight years. They received the 7s 6d collected in local churches to assist Nicholas Browne during his sickness and gave a shilling to Sevenoak's wife when her husband contracted smallpox. They also administered funds for charitable purpose. In 1585 John Kyme, who owned the Friars estate, left them £20 to lend out, for up to two years, to six young residents in the town, then to another six, 'and so to continue for ever'. In 1611 Thomas Blunt left them £20 to similarly 'set up' young tradesmen, and Abraham Edwards £20 more in 1615. And to safeguard a charity, the Constables deposited in their Town Box in 1586-7 a copy of the will in which Richard Kykherst left to trustees four houses in Westout, 'now called rotten row' - three to shelter poor people, the other to be let to fund repairs. The Constables also guarded against conflagration. They paid men to 'watch' when a great fire raged at Westout. Their inventory in 1577 included 12 leather buckets and two long poles with chains which ended in great iron hooks - for tearing down burning thatch and timber. Twelve mattocks and 12 shovels were acquired before 1589, but eight of the latter were soon lost during a fire at Stewards Inn.[48]

Because Lewes borough was 'a shire town' the Constables had custody of an official set of standard weights and measures. They paid three shillings to the usher in the Office of the Exchequer at Westminster in 1579, 'for three times opening the treasury door' when a brass measure of a quart, a brass weight of a pound and an iron ell, 45 inches long, were collected. In 1588-9 they bought a branding iron to mark bushels, and an iron beam and scales to use with the town weights. Also in 1588 the parliamentary return for the Borough was made by the Constables and ten named burgesses - possibly the rest of the Twelve. In 1571 the Constables had paid 16 pence for the writing of an election indenture, though a succession of 'gentleman' MPs spared the Borough the payment of parliamentary 'wages'.[49]

The Constables and Twelve also owned real estate. In 1571 they leased to a blacksmith, Robert Stuckell, a waste plot of ground within the walls of the Broken Church under the bell loft, where by 1589 hung 'the common bell of the town', perhaps the one newly cast at the Constables' expense in 1554-5, and doubtless a convenience for market traders. Presumably in 1624 the loft also housed the Borough clock - its keeper by then was paid 40 shillings a year. There was too 'a common brook', a water-meadow lying near St John's, which the Twelve leased in 1573 to widow Eleanor Dopp for ten years, on condition she kept the ditches scoured. In 1667 'ancient custom' sanctioned the use of its rent to fund the Michaelmas 'feast'. These leases bore maybe the impress of a seal first recorded, like the vagabonds' seal, in 1576 - perhaps the larger brass matrix, bearing the arms of the Borough and inscribed SIGILLUM COMUNE BURGI

116 The seal

Randoll's market-house and sessions-house. (a modern copy)

117 The arms

DE LEWYS, also in the Town Council's care. In 1634 the arms of the Borough were certified to be of great Antiquity and a copy was added to its archive. They have since been officially defined as Checky Or and Azure a sinister Quarter Gules seme of Cross Crosslets Argent thereon a Lion rampant Or.[50] The sessions-house, where seats for the assize judges were set up in August 1565, was also used by the Twelve as a town-house - two chests for storing Borough records stood there in 1576. George Randoll depicted it in 1620, islanded in the High Street west of Fisher Street Corner, with a stair to an upper story, below which by then the Twelve rented out 'shops'. And they kept in repair the market-house just west of Castlegate Corner. After receiving a bequest of £10 towards its building from Widow Alice Holter in 1564-5, they raised a further £10 by subscription; they paid 40 shillings to Richard Jeffery for 'certain stones' - possibly he was leasing the former Cluniac 'grange' at Swanborough - and maybe Ralph Hogge of Buxted supplied 75 tons of timber costing £10.[51]

Whitsun was the climax of the civic year. Elections to the Twelve were held on the Sunday. On the Monday the militiamen paraded and the Constables held a 'feast' for the Twelve. By Tuesday the Borough fair was in full swing. To help fund the feast John Cotmot bequeathed eight shillings in 1558, to be spread over four years. From 1611 the board was graced by a silver bowl 'double guilt', given by the barber-surgeon Thomas Blunt. In 1550, and perhaps every year, the inferior company, the Twenty-Four, feasted separately.

The Constables' manifold expenses obliged them to levy an annual rate. The amount needed fluctuated sharply - £4 or £5 in some years, but £42 13s 6d in 1562-3 and £43 16s 3d in 1583-4, years in which the Borough contributed to rebuilding the western half of Lewes Bridge, and £32 4s 7d in 1596-7, when soaring wheat prices required heavy spending on poor relief. After 1597, with poor relief now a parochial charge, the rate stabilised at below £20, till rebuilding the bridge in June

1624 drove it up again. If any burgess refused to pay the rate, levied as it was for 'the public good and common use of the whole borough', his goods could be distrained. On leaving office the Constables submitted accounts and handed over 'all necessary things concerning the town'; one had custody of the town box, the other of the town key.[52]

John Rowe claimed that the Twelve were co-opted from 'the wealthier and discreeter sort of the Townsmen'. Their affluence is confirmed by a tax return made in 1572. As to discretion, in Elizabeth's reign the average age on entry was about forty and since Senior Constables rotated 'by course', some were elderly - Thomas Huggins being over eighty during his second term. An episode in 1585, however, hints at a current of violence just below the carapace of civic Order. At the archery ground some townsmen wounded Abraham Edwardes, a junior Constable in 1582-3, and killed a servant of Richard Cheney, a gentleman living in Westout. When an inquest jury returned a verdict of manslaughter, rather than murder, Cheney accused Thomas Trayton I carpenter, Richard Kidder wheelwright and John Stempe of perverting the course of justice by helping to pack the jury with tenants and 'friends' of Lord Buckhurst. All three were leading members of the Twelve. So was William Lane, an attorney who acted for Buckhurst's son, Robert, in 1598. Thomas Trayton II, moreover, was soon to begin a lucrative career as Buckhurst's local factotum. That a faction loyal to him, and protected by him, dominated the Twelve by the 1580s would not be surprising.[53]

Faction-based strife may have caused the 'stubborn' stances within the Twelve, and the 'disorder' outside it, which required articles to be enacted on Whit Sunday 1595 for the 'better ordering & government' of the Borough and for 'the better increase & continuance of perfect peace and unity' - articles confirmed and subscribed to by a general assembly held at the town-house. (A previous assembly 'for the common weal of the town' had met in 1550.) The Twelve were enjoined to attend meetings punctually and diligently; to wear a gown and 'other sad decent and comely apparel fit for ancient Townsmen'; and to accept majority decisions with good grace - 'stubborn' behaviour might lead to a fine or exclusion.

Relevant to 'disorder' outside the Twelve were articles touching the company of the Twenty-Four from which they were chosen. Its members were not to exceed 27 and were to be nominated by a majority of the Twelve and then by a majority of the Twenty-Four. But promotion to the Twelve was not by seniority. Article 2 spelt out that a burgess, to be chosen, need only have been a member for 'a year' and have 'walked' with the Twenty-Four 'in the Watch' the previous Whit Monday. This was not new, but the article added that if a burgess had 'borne the office of a Constable or some other office of more countenance or credit in some other place', he could by-pass the Twenty-Four altogether. Article 9 also broke with tradition. It required new members to be chosen in the town-house upon

Whit Sunday after evening prayer and not any longer in the castle, 'for the avoiding of further disorder'.[54]

As already noted, the 1590s witnessed acute social strains as 'dear' bread and rising unemployment swelled the cost of poor relief and the fear of vagabonds. Elsewhere in Sussex, at Rye and Hastings, Arundel and Chichester, the more affluent burgesses were also tightening their grip on civic oligarchies, and at Hastings the election of the mayor was removed from the open Hundred Place to the court hall, a 'more decent, apt and secret' location. At Lewes recruits to the Twelve between 1594 and 1604 included an unprecedented clutch of affluent 'gentlemen' - John de la Chambre; William, son of John Stempe; Ambrose Comporte, Trayton II's brother-in-law; Thomas Colt who wedded a daughter of queen Elizabeth's Clerk of Jewels; and also of 'gentlemen' lawyers - the wealthy public notary, Thomas Dawson; the attorney William Thomas, a future Clerk of the Peace; John Rowe, steward to baron Bergavenny. Nicholas Jefferay was perhaps the graduate of Clare College Cambridge ordained a deacon in 1605, while Edward Newton, though a mere draper, was a cousin of William Newton, the Southover barrister.[55]

De la Chambre

Yet these 'gentlemen' recruits did not achieve civic unity. Maybe indeed the machinery of Borough government partly broke down. In the civic year 1595-6 the names of the headboroughs recorded in the Town Book were later struck through. No totals for receipts and disbursements were recorded in 1595-6, 1597-1600 or 1601-2. For the years 1603-5 no totals and no civic officers are given, apart from Mr Nicholas Jeffray, a Constable noted in 1603-4, - his Christian name altered from 'Richard'. That this apparent disruption was not mere slovenly record-keeping is suggested by a note in the Town Book that the Monday after Midsummer day 1605 was 'appointed for the meeting of both companies of the Borough of Lewes to consult & advise on divers questionable matters between them for the better government of the town, the advancement of the king's service and the formation of unity'. But 'unity' perhaps was not quickly achieved. No headboroughs were recorded in the Town Book for 1606-8, so maybe the Twelve and the Twenty-Four were still at odds.[56]

Was the apparent lack of headboroughs in 1595-6, 1603-5 and 1606-8 a by-product of the civic discord? Their duties were onerous - to gather the annual rate, render 'a true account', escort suspects to the west gate prison, set malefactors in the stocks, publicize militia business, summon the Twelve to meetings and attend the Constables 'diligently and in a reverent manner', bearing their staves of office. And their status was low - article 14 enacted in 1595 menaced them, if refractory or irreverent, with the west gate prison or the stocks. It is true these tiresome tasks often preceded election to the Twenty Four - its 25 members who subscribed to the 1595 articles included 17 ex-headboroughs. Yet only four members of the Twelve in 1595 had held the office. And because of fast-track promotion, only six, out of the 25 members subscribing, later joined the Twelve, and only two, Thomas Darrington and Thomas Blunt, were among the 17 ex-headboroughs. So maybe a failure to promote ex-headboroughs, and a by-passing of so tiresome an office by most of the Twelve, fed the lack of civic 'order' and 'unity' recorded in 1595 and 1605.[57]

Seemingly however this state of affairs was partially rectified after Midsummer 1605. In September the ex-headborough, Thomas Darrington, a butcher who bequeathed a brown 'stubhorn' cow, became junior Constable, to be followed in 1606 by William Carter saddler, a member of the Twenty-Four in 1595. Moreover the choice as headboroughs in 1605 of William Dodson goldsmith and Thomas Snatt draper, and in 1608 of Benjamin Holter butcher and the affluent Thomas Oliver, suggests that the mercantile elite were now prepared to perform tiresome duties as a prelude to high office - all four, except Holter, became junior Constables. This trend continued. By Whitsun 1618 nine of the Twelve, just over half, were ex-headboroughs, among them the recently recruited Thomas Snatt, Gerson Bailey shoemaker, John Mathew butcher and Richard Newton grocer. Civic drudgery was now a recognized route to civic honour.[58]

And there was other evidence of a search for 'unity'. Abraham Edwardes, soon to acquire a stake in the manors of Portslade and Atlingworth, returned to the Borough he had quitted after the fracas in 1585. He rejoined the Twelve, became senior Constable in 1608 and left £20 to the Twelve in 1615 for the 'benefit of young tradesmen or decayed artificers'. A similar bequest had been made in 1611 by Thomas Blunt, a veteran ex-headborough chosen into the Twelve that year. The barber-surgeon also left £3 a year to the grammar school, and a silver bowl double gilt, worth twenty nobles, to the

118 A headborough's staff

Twelve, 'as a pledge of my love of the townsmen of Lewes'. Both men, it seems, were hoping to promote a more integrated civic life. Moreover, by 1611, the lawyers Dawson, Rowe and Thomas, though still resident burgesses, had withdrawn from the Twelve. Had their presence been unproductive, because provocative, or was it no longer needed, a sign that civic tensions were being addressed?[59]

However, at Lewes, as elsewhere, such local tensions - civic, social or doctrinal - were easily contained within the massively stable political Establishment created by Elizabeth and manned by her Courtiers, Buckhurst, Burghley, Howard of Effingham - a stability that endured under king James. And it was surely to celebrate this that the church-wardens of Cliffe set up the queen's arms in 1598. Of solid plaster, vigorously modelled in high relief, the rampant leopard and the fiery Welsh dragon are penned between Ionic columns below a sturdy pediment - another framework of Order.[60]

119 The silver 'bowl'

120 The queen's arms

Overleaf: Deward's survey of water-meadows along the Ouse (a modern copy)

249

9

A focus of economic recovery 1461-1625

Lewes .... a plentiful market town ... standeth in a most fertile place for corn, pasture, wood, fish, fowl, sheep and health. John Norden's verdict in his Description of Sussex 1595.

Full of iron mines it is in sundry places, where for the making and fining where-of there be furnaces on every side, and a huge deal of wood is yearly spent, to which purpose divers brooks in many places are brought to run in one channel , and sundry meadows turned into pools and waters, that they might be of power sufficient to drive hammer mills, which beating upon the iron, resound all over the places adjoining. William Camden's impression of Wealden iron-making 1586.

Item one great drawing table ... one great wrought chair ... sixteen high stools of Turkey work ... one black velvet cushion ... one pair of brass andirons ... two pictures ... a map ... one great basin and ewer .. two saltcellars ... one trencher salt ... one sugar dish with a spoon ... one tablecloth of damask ... one dozen and a half of damask napkins. The luxuries of William Thomas, Clerk of the Peace.

The success of the New Monarchy owed something to its coinciding with a period of sustained economic renewal. Between the 1460s and the 1620s England's population probably doubled to about five million. A rising demand for food encouraged farmers to produce surpluses for the market. To that end they enclosed 'waste' land, drained swamps, spread fertilizers and tried new crop rotations. Farmers in mid Sussex also supplied meat, grain and beer to London's population, which grew especially fast and came to rely for its sustenance on producers in the Home Counties, East Anglia and the South East. Farmers could concentrate on wheat, barley and sheep along the Southdowns, on beef cattle and hops in the Weald, on fatstock in Pevensey Level. There was rising demand too, in London and elsewhere, for Southdown wool and for Wealden leather and iron, glass and timber. This buoyant trade in local produce revivified the markets and fairs at Lewes. Moreover, its wharfs and warehouses received groceries, wines and textiles from London and from ports in the West Country and the Netherlands, along with mounting cargoes of coal from Tyneside. The luxuries unloaded were sought by local landowners and yeomen benefiting from the agricultural boom, and by resident lawyers and doctors, clergy and gentlefolk - consumers who also patronized the town's diversifying band of skilled craftsmen.

However, employment opportunities failed to keep pace with a growing army of labourers, and prices began to outstrip wages. As already noted, paupers and 'vagabonds' increased, to the intense agitation of local civic officers and JPs. And despite the ambitious Poor Law statute of 1598, poverty, malnutrition and disease were checking population growth by the 1620s. But there was no Black Death, no dramatic demographic collapse - rather a gentle stagnation till the late 17th century, then a slow rise.

Southdown husbandry in the 1460s was already efficient. The sheepfold served as 'a moving dunghill', helping to fertilize an arable soil which William Camden described as 'a fat chalk or kind of marl' that yielded corn 'abundantly'. Very typical were the crops rotated in the early 1530s on the small 'home' farm used by the Cluniacs. The arable comprised the West Ham above the Pad Pool, Newfield and Goslands to the north of Juggs Lane, and to the south the Thirty-Three Acres scattered in strips below Cranedown mill. (Map 2.6) About thirty acres were sown with wheat, slightly more with barley, and small parcels with beans, peas and vetch. Camden's fellow topographer, John Norden, commended the Downs between Lewes and Bramber for their 'admirable' pasture. Over 3000 sheep were kept on the manor of Falmer at Michaelmas 1530; over 2500 were tended in and around Firle and Exceat by the shepherds of John Gage in December 1578. Also abounding were Southdown rabbits. The warren on the South Rise at Southover was leased for an annual rent of £14 and fifty dozen conies in 1566. On Coney Croft, just west of Landport farm, a pillow mound was depicted by John Deward in 1618. Pigeons too were tended. A Cliffe tailor was accused of robbing a dovecote at Ringmer, John de la Chambre of erecting one at Rodmell without authority. The great cruciform columbarium, built by the Cluniacs at Southover, still stood in 1714.[1]

The productivity, and profits, of Southdown husbandry were being increased by the 'engrossing' of family-farms. When the Michelbornes bought up almost 500 acres of arable at Stanmer between 1608 and 1639, they displaced perhaps twenty peasant households. This depopulation was matched by a scarcity of local blacksmiths, carpenters, wheelwrights and weavers of canvas and fustian, linen and broadcloth, though John Yokehurst at Firle owned a loom and a wooden shuttle, a warping bar and a pair of yarn winders. Such craftsmen were hampered by high fuel costs and lack of running water. But quarrymen did increase, as farmers in the Weald took to sweetening their acid soils with Southdown chalk and lime. A pit by the Ouse at Southerham, rented by Richard Mead of Cliffe in 1620, had eaten into three acres of tenantry sheep down. Moreover peasants near the sea coast, or along the estuary of the Ouse, could combine farming and sea fishing. William Camden noted that such 'Amphibious Creatures' in Kent were 'quick and active in both employment'. Nonetheless a growing scarcity of householders sapped some communities. At Southerham the hamlet withered. At Combe in Hamsey, after 'the chapel of ease' was allowed 'to run to ruin', Edith Bedford tried in 1638 to retrieve the bell which her uncle had given it. At Iford Stephen Ridge, an energetic engrosser, was the only farmer affluent enough to be Constable in 1614. At Piddinghoe men could not be found to 'watch' by the beacon at Brighton. Gathering the harvest, moreover, needed an influx of labour. Fishermen from Brighton toiled at Moulescoomb, a tailor from Lewes at Kingston Buci. While her brother was away 'at harvest in the downs', a girl at Rotherfield succumbed to fornication. Two sisters at Southover earned money for clothes by gleaning wheat. But despite the engrossers, some peasant farmers survived. Sheep from the common fold at Kingston were stolen in 1559, and again in 1681, by an under-shepherd from Glynde.[2]

Timber and wood fuel continued to be brought to the virtually treeless South Downs from the Weald. After unloading chalk at Laughton, a boatman carried wood back along Glynde Reach to Cliffe in 1599. A travelling 'cole man' exchanged charcoal for barley at Rottingdean in 1574. And prices on the South Downs soared as Wealden iron-making boomed. In 1549 a jury at Lewes claimed they had more than doubled in 15 years. The Borough gave forty shillings in 1562-3 to promote a bill in parliament to preserve 'great timber' in the Weald, and in 1581 its use for iron-making was forbidden within four miles of the Downs between Pevensey and Arundel. Yet wood fuel sold at Lewes in 1649 was denounced as 'excessive dear'. The plight of coastal fishermen was more eloquently pleaded: 'when the whole night in the sharp winter is spent in painful travail and toiling in the seas with vehement endurance of the cold and wetness of the water, these men are only comforted with hope of fire at their return'.[3]

Whereas peasant households grew fewer in the Downs, they increased in the Weald. Family farmers there kept dairy cows, sheep and poultry; worked cider presses and apple mills; grew enough wheat, peas and oats, in a good year, for their needs, and relied on sales of beef cattle to pay the rent. They took to spreading their acidic soils with lime or marl, and by the 1560s were tending hop gardens. They also enclosed common 'waste', though in 1614 the 12,000 acres of Saint Leonard's Forest were still 'full of unwholesome shades and overgrown hollows', the alleged haunt of a 'monstrous Serpent' spitting a strong and violent poison, though its wings had yet to sprout - perhaps giant fossilized bones

Hic iacet Petrus Scwt Glouer
cuius aie[?] pricietur deus Amen ?

121 The gloves

had been discovered, of the sort later found by Mrs Gideon Mantell. Without question, Wealden commons were roamed by stealers of sheep. John Worsell of Southover rustled them at Mayfield, Framfield and Waldron in 1658.[4]

Cheap fuel and abundant winter water-power in the Weald facilitated craft production by tanners, curriers and glovers, weavers, fullers and dyers, carpenters, joiners and shinglers, makers of baskets, sieves and saddle-trees, of bricks, tiles and pots, of charcoal, glass and iron, nails and edge tools. At Fletching, about 1480, gloves were inscribed on a memorial brass. Thomas Upton, 'a glover, a joiner, a carpenter, an instrument maker, a curious workman for jacks, clocks, stoves and vices for glaziers', was dubbed the Archimedes of Wadhurst in 1638. Some craft workers also kept livestock on a small holding or loosely-stinted common. Indeed large-scale enclosure of common 'waste' could provoke a violent response - John Norden noted that 'people bred amongst woods' were 'naturally more stubborn and uncivil' than those raised in open 'champion' country like the South Downs. During Edward VI's reign 'certain rebels' - doubtless local commoners - burned down hedges newly planted around sixty acres at Ditchling, part of a wider unrest which caused soldiers to be sent over from the English garrison at Boulogne. Anger, sparked by enclosure, also erupted at Chailey in 1624.[5]

Lewes, of course, was well placed to service these buoyant local economies in the South Downs and the Weald. Indeed the catchment of the Borough's Saturday corn market widened as its rivals decayed. The market at Alfriston ceased before 1595, though the stump of its cross still stands. Alehouse licences at both Cuckfield and Ditchling were restricted in 1613 because their markets had been 'discontinued'; in 1654 a Lewes tailor bought two bushels of beans grown at Ditchling before they reached the Saturday market. At Eastbourne market trading did not long survive the riotous tearing down of the royal arms in the 'famine' year 1591. Hailsham market closed soon after the winter of 1633-4 when 'impassable' roads made access problematic. And at the Saturday market in 1662 a Piddinghoe farmer recognized a bag of meal stolen from his barn, which suggests he traded there rather than at Seaford, a Cinque Port deemed 'a poor miser-

122 The stump of the cross

254

able village' in 1743.[6]

South-west of Lewes, though, lay Brighton. Yet John Ogilby described it in 1675 as 'indifferent large and populous, chiefly inhabited by fishermen ... with a reasonable good harbour' but only 'a small market on Thursdays'. Deep-sea fishing had impelled its growth from 200 households in 1565 to 'near 600 families' in the 1650s. By then the annual fleet making for the North Sea herring grounds might number fifty sail, crewed by 600 masters and men. Yet the port's 'indifferent' [proletarian] character precluded its shops becoming a serious rival to those at Lewes. Indeed such was the Saturday market's prestige by 1558 that William Everett, a farmer at Malling, offered £8 towards a market cross. In the event a legacy of £10 from Widow Alice Holter for a market house was matched in 1564 by members of the Twelve and by Richard Kitson, a Church lawyer. In 1636 the Borough spent 3s 2d on its repair and when it was rebuilt in 1648, maybe the market area was extended.[7]

Some corn sold at the Saturday market, especially barley, was bought by Wealdsmen, though a husbandman from Framfield purchased wheat in 1645, so he said. Grain was also barged down-river and shipped away. In 1610 spokesmen for Hastings and Rye, both populous fishing-ports, affirmed that 'the west country about Chichester, Arundel and Lewes' was a major source of their corn. Through Newhaven in the 1560s wheat was also shipped to London, malt to London, Devon and Dorset, barley to Sandwich and Dover, where it was malted to supply the capital. And after bountiful Southdown harvests grain, especially wheat, was sent overseas under licence - to Venice in 1592, to Seville and Marseilles, Leghorn, Messina and 'Barbary' in 1605-7, to the Canaries in 1640. One cargo, dispatched to Seville in 1607 aboard a Newhaven boat, the *Blessing of God*, was 'ventured' by John Slade, a weaver at Southover.[8]

Because Lewes borough hosted a bench of JPs as well as a busy corn market, the town hummed with official activity when a shortage of grain sent prices sky-high. The Sackvilles, too, exerted their influence. In 1597, 'a time of the greatest scarcity that ever we did know', Lord Buckhurst sent down from London 'Danske' rye from the Baltic, bought at Billingsgate; in 1608 he authorized wheat stored at his mansion, the Lord's Place, to be sold at half the going rate. Baltic rye was the bread-corn of last resort. Over 10,000 bushels arrived at Newhaven in 1609; more in 1623, from Dieppe, Middelburg and Flushing. Poor relief in times of 'scarcity' drove up the parish rate levied in All Saints from £4 3s 6d in 1618 to £30 14s 9d in 1631 and £68 5s 4d in 1650. During the 'scarcity' in 1631 the JPs tightly regulated the Saturday market: no corn could be sold before eleven o'clock, before people from remote parishes had arrived, and only in small quantities till one o'clock. One merchant was ordered to sell barley rather than ship it to Kent. In 1638 the JPs probed claims that Daniel Shoulder scrivener and other townsmen had illicitly barged wheat down-river.[9]

In 1649 it fell to the Borough's High Constables to persuade local maltsters to keep enough barley in hand 'to serve all the poor if they require it'. They also named local millers who took 'much more toll in these dear times than is their due'. William Willat, Widow Fox and Thomas Baldy had windmills at Cranedown, Malling and Cliffe, Widow Verrall and 'Goodman' Jeffrey water-mills at the Lord's Place and Watergate. The west water-mill at Southover was defunct by 1609; the site of its pond nourished a productive kitchen garden in 1767.[10]

The provisioning of Londoners, who multiplied from 35,000 in 1450 to 400,0000 in 1650, also attracted hops, livestock and wool from mid Sussex, as well as iron and timber, some of which was marketed at Lewes. Though in 1567 Nicholas Mascall of Plumpton imported Flemish hops from Middelburg into Newhaven, their cultivation was spreading across the Weald. In 1581 'a stranger using the trade of making hop gardens' died at Mayfield; in 1592 hop poles were carted from Balneath Wood to Ditchling; in 1619 two '[hop] gardens' were tended on the Island at Southover. By 1588 Andrew Stone, a merchant at Cliffe, was shipping 'English' hops from Newhaven to Dartmouth. Thereafter Plymouth was often supplied, also London in 1609, Ireland in 1638. But most hops grown in mid Sussex and destined for London were carried overland through East Grinstead and Croydon.[11]

Access to hops, to Southdown barley and to water from the chalk, encouraged commercial brewing and malting at Southover, at Cliffe and at low-lying premises in the Borough. At Southover in the 1530s the Cluniacs turned barley into ale and sold 'convent' beer; in 1617 Edward

Hart paid £150 for a house [Gables Cottage], a 'long malting house' and two acres of meadow called the North Brooks; John Gill maltster was suspected of smuggling away wheat in 1638, a 'famine' year, and William Adams of supplying beer to an unlicensed alehouse at Offham in 1649. Spirits were also concocted - George Baker left two stills and eight gallons of *aqua vitae* to his wife in 1588. And it was a Southover brewer, Thomas Pelland, who added a stylish porch to the *Vine* in 1577. At Cliffe Richard Adam leased a brew house and 'brewing vessels' in 1576; Robert James owned malting vats and a brewing furnace in 1599; William Swan sold beer to a joiner from Brighton in 1617; and Richard Faulkener, though a tailor, left malting utensils in 1619, and

123 The stylish porch

a shilling to each of the 'the poor women porters' who 'carried barley' for him. As for the Borough, the Cluniacs bought barrels of 'double' beer from John Crowden of 'Lewes' - a Widow Cobden was an ale brewer there in 1539. Thomas Trayton II on School Hill employed a brewer called 'Gregorie' in 1615. The output of the Borough's four maltsters in 1649 was reckoned to be about 2080 bushels, whereas 3200 were stored in William Augur's malt house at Southover in 1687. The Cluniacs also bought an adze for their cooper, Simon Michell, perhaps the householder on School Hill who owned working tools and timber in 1556, and defined his garden boundary by reference to a walnut tree.[12]

Doubtless, trading at Lewes and Cliffe also facilitated the increasing flow of cattle and sheep, reared or fattened in mid Sussex, to London's meat market at Smithfield. A butcher from Mitcham in north-west Surrey, abetted by two labourers from Cuckfield, stole 38 sheep at Lewes in 1590. During the Borough fair on Whitsun Tuesday in 1595 the churchwardens at St Michael's were paid 2s 4d rent for 'standings' against their wall; 15 runts were bought by John Everenden of Sedlescombe in 1606, ten 'beasts' by John Millward of Pevensey in 1636. Henry IV's charter granting fairs at Cliffe, on saint Mark's Day (25 April) and saint Matthew's Day (21 September), was preserved by its church-wardens, along with the *Paraphrases* of Erasmus and the *Commentary* of bishop Jewel. In September 1629 they blamed a very rainy day for a poor return, a mere 3s 4d. At the 'Spring' fair in 1632 two working oxen were sold from the Pelham estate at Halland. Some cattle fattened in mid Sussex were 'Scottish' or 'Welsh' in origin. William Prother and William Thomas, both drovers from Breconshire, allegedly 'wronged' a metal-worker's daughter at Brightling in 1646. In that shire too lived relatives of Hugh Edwards, who lodged in 1643 with Robert Stapley, a butcher in All Saints. Also brought from afar, from Ireland, was a cargo of beef and pork unloaded at Newhaven by a local shipmaster in 1616.[13]

Besides closes in Fisher Street and crofts on sunny slopes below the High Street, prominent butchers in the Borough occupied pastures and 'farms' in the Weald, in order to fatten livestock, as well as slaughter it. Richard Holter, with lands at Hamsey and Chiddingly, left money to repair the Offham to Chailey road in 1518, and to paint a 'crucifix', and an image of saint Anne, in St Mary in the Market. His widow, his four children, a grandson and a sister, Emma Smythe, were among 19 Borough residents assessed at £20 or more for the 1524 tax. His son Robert had an impressive spread of pastures, in Denton and Bishopstone, Laughton, East Hoathly and Chiddingly. Robert's widow, Alice, bequeathed a featherbed with 'a coverlet of imagery work', £10 to build the market house and £10 to repair 'the west part' of Lewes Bridge. Robert Acton butcher held pasture at Barcombe in 1598, John Holter a farm at Hamsey in 1601. John Matthew owned land in several manors in 1630, along with the *Cat* in St Michael's. To his wife he left 'the high bedstead' in the hall chamber with its curtains and rods, and to his sister £100 - 'unless she marries Barnard Bourne of Battle'; his two worst cloaks and 'a russet suit', worn every day, he allotted to his dogsbody, Richard Grisbrook. Matthew's wife was a Bodle, a family of wealthy graziers in Pevensey Level, where prime fattening ground became a valued investment, as the pace of livestock trading quickened. The Cliffe merchant, John Stansfield, had seventy acres at Hooe; Sir John Colbrand, who farmed at Southover, employed a 'looker' to oversee his livestock at Wartling.[14]

As for wool, the 'Lewes' Downs yielded it abundantly. The Cluniacs received 3494 fleeces from flocks at Falmer and Bevendean in 1530. No details survive of sales at the Borough's wool market. Its clerk, Daniel Johnson, accused a local butcher of killing ewes unfit to be eaten in 1588. By then some local wool was destined for the Weald of Kent, for between 1592 and 1617 the clip from the Pelham flock at Bishopstone was sold to cloth makers at Cranbrook and Staplehurst. Shipment of wool through Newhaven was so burdened by regulation that only a single cargo - to Weymouth in 1572 - occurs in extant port books. There was smuggling down-river, of course, though in 1622 Edward Paine of Eastbourne denied colluding with Ralph Akehurst of Cliffe to dispatch it abroad.[15]

Weavers never settled in force locally, whereas in the 1540s salesmen from London bought cloth woven at Steyning, Midhurst and Petworth. Moreover, weaving in the Pennine dales around Halifax meant its rectory-manor was worth £130 6s 8d to the Cluniacs in 1535. Nothing came of a report in 1538 that the occupier of Thomas Cromwell's demesne lands at Southover was minded to make cloth and 'would beg as many trees [at Balneath] as would make a fulling [mill]' - to harness the Cockshut stream perhaps. James Hale at Westout kept a journeyman in 1618, but most local weavers were in Southover. The looms of John Auger stood in his hall; John Slade also 'ventured' wheat into Spain, and Thomas Hunter built a house on vacant land 'under the priory wall' in 1612; in February 1769 a Thomas Hunter there advertised for a journeyman, promising 'constant work' till the harvest. Partly destined for Lewes, presumably, were cargoes of hemp and flax shipped to Newhaven from Holland and London; from the capital too in 1629 came two wooden frames for weaving serge. Less welcome to local weavers maybe was the Norman and Breton canvas received from Dieppe. A nearby fulling mill was Robert Mackrell's at Shortbridge in Fletching. When Curtis Gooden, a 'cloth worker' at Malling, sent nine yards of white cloth there in 1649, they were stolen and the weaver's mark removed. Dyers, though, resided in the town. In 1588, the year he became senior Constable, William Butcher of All Saints dyed red the petticoat of a woman from Fletching. Also active in All Saints, a parish with wetland along the Winterbourne, was Edward Godman, commended in its burial register as 'an honest and devout old man'. In 1619 he left £130 to his younger son Roger, who studied medicine at Leiden university. Dyes unloaded at Newhaven included madder from London, fustic wood from Southampton, English woad from Gosport.[16]

Though cattle from the Weald reached London, probably dairy produce did not, despite a local traffic. When hawking stolen butter and cheese at Lewes in 1649, William Larking claimed that some came from four cows he kept near 'Tarble Down' in East Hoathly, and some he bought in Mayfield. But William Newton, the Puritan barrister, noted that good cheese in Sussex was 'scanty', while praising a Banbury cheese as very meet to be set before welcome guests. How much leather from the Weald reached London is uncertain. In Lewes borough sales of hides tapped a wide Wealden hinterland. Between 1616 and 1652 the Searchers and Sealers who supervised the sales - usually shoemakers - impounded as 'insufficiently tanned' hides brought from Hurstpierpoint and Wivelsfield, Rotherfield and Waldron. Illicitly by-passing the market, George Withers from Steyning bought 'rough' hides direct from Lewes butchers in 1654. The shipment of hides, as of wool, was strictly regulated. One 'Parkhurst', suspected of smuggling them from Mayfield into France in 1630, was perhaps the Francis Pankhurst who sent hops overseas through Newhaven. Dealers in the town did export other by-products of local slaughter-houses - sheep skins and calf skins, ox bones, ox horns and horn plates - mostly to Dieppe.[17]

The town itself attracted processors of heavy leather - tanners, curriers who rendered hides soft and waterproof, shoemakers and saddlers. Thomas Jones tanner lived at Cliffe in 1601. Later a tannery was built above the water-meadows at the north end of Green Wall, on 'waste' granted in 1609-10 to Thomas Trayton II, the Sackville factotum. Five half-hides were stolen in 1575 from the currier, Michael Pullen. A shoemaker at Westout, John Browne, bequeathed boot-trees and a hammer in 1560, also debts to a tanner and a currier. In 1580 Richard Rice, a Borough shoemaker, owned a Wealden tenement at Fillpots in Horsted Keynes, a source perhaps of 'rough' hides. John Bayley owned another, at Chailey, in 1637. He also bequeathed books, £100 in cash, a 'birding piece' and a musket with a rest and bandoleer. John Beard shoemaker, who died in 1601, bought the *White Horse*, a few doors from St Michael's church; he desired his executors to keep the deeds in a chest with three locks. The saddler, William Carter, purchased the *White Lion* on School Hill in 1597. And John Forde cut a bachelor dash in 1644, with his rapier and gold rings, his sword hilts of damask and silver-gilt, his 'white gay doublet, jerkin and breeches'. Less glittering perhaps was a bellows maker, Charles Massey, resident in 1606.

A whitetawer, Lawrence Warden, was robbed in 1589 of twenty sheep and calf skins, the kind he converted to the light-weight leather used by glovers. Doubtless his trade absorbed some of the Rhenish alum shipped to Newhaven from Dartmouth in 1573. Glovers, like tanners and dyers, could exploit adjacent wetland. Samuel Walter, senior Constable in 1601-2, had 'a warehouse' at the south end of Green Wall by the Town Ditch. William Reade, Constable a decade later, leased a 'workhouse' in a water-meadow near the Friars; a William Reade, 'aged 5 or 6', drowned in a glover's pit in 1629. Edward Browne of Cliffe occupied 'a little water house and yard' below Ranscombe in 1614, and Haman Hardiman bequeathed wainscot and window glass in several houses at Cliffe.[18]

The town was also a depot for Wealden timber, for oak, alder, hazel and beech, ash, maple, willow and birch. Doubtless much of it arrived by water. Wood bought by Abraham James of Cliffe was boated along Glynde Reach from Laughton in 1599, a time when oak and beech timber, some already fashioned into posts, rails and spokes, was sent to the town from the Vert Wood there. Further east, at Folkington and Wilmington, trees were selected for 'Lewes' in 1613. Wood also arrived from locations near the upper Ouse. Laths delivered to the Cluniacs at Southover were cut in Rotherfield Wood by Sheffield bridge in 1533-4. Ralph Hogge, an iron master at Buxted, supplied 75 tons of timber for 'the Sessions house'. John Gallop, a miller at Malling, owned timber stacked at Little Horsted, already 'framed for a barn', in 1596, and Nicholas Foster of Southover, three tons of wood lying at Isfield in 1600. Doubtless somewhere upstream were the 400 oaks which Thomas Paris of All Saints had bargained for in 1557. Near the headwaters of the Medway, at Hartfield, lay the wood, 'cleft and cut out', which the Cliffe maltster, Daniel Prior, bequeathed in 1638. And just to the north, at Hever and Edenbridge, were the Kentish freeholds owned by Richard Kidder, the wheelwright on School Hill. A Wealdsman from Maresfield, he served as Constable in 1585-6 with his neighbour, Thomas Trayton I, the carpenter-cum-maltster.[19]

Presumably Lewes was also a depot for Wealden wood shipped out through Newhaven. Cargoes sent overseas, though, were dwindling. The jury, which bewailed in 1549 the rising price of wood, instanced a slump in supplies from Sussex to English garrisons at Calais, Guisnes and Boulogne. By the 1560s only small quantities of laths, ship boards, barrel boards, elm logs and wood ash left Newhaven, for Flushing and Dieppe, Saint Valery and Fecamp. And once the accompanying cargoes of iron dried up, only wood ash was shipped. But dispatched to English ports, including London, in or after the 1560s, were laths, boards and planks, a house frame and window frames, 'arrow' timber and shovel 'trees', hoops and alder poles, wheel spokes and felloes, and tan extracted from Wealden oak bark. Usually these cargoes accompanied iron or guns, though some to Plymouth, Sandwich, Dover and Maldon did not. Oaks were also sent to the royal shipyards in the Thames estuary - in 1573 the Privy Council ordered 1000 loads of plank and timber from 'the Wode' of Sussex. Exported too through Newhaven were 'osier rods'. In 1588 the clerk of the Borough market dealing in 'spars and withies' was

Edward Dawby; in 1636 a thatcher of that name, living on School Hill, occupied two acres of water-meadow in Malling. In 1619 the house of a basket maker at Southover, Lancelot Lennard, stood near the Pad Pool, which supplied 'white' thatching reeds to Falmer in the 1530s.[20]

As for iron-making in the Weald, the New Monarchy itself sponsored a dramatic change in its technology. In order to cast cheap iron shot for Henry VII's war with Scotland, artisans from northern France built England's first water-powered furnace in 1496-7, at Newbridge in Ashdown Forest, along with a water-powered forge which hammered out the wrought iron needed to bind the stocks and wheels of royal ordnance. By 1506 the furnace was casting barrels and chambers for two-piece cannon. Another breakthrough came in 1543-4 when the first single-piece muzzle-loading iron cannon was cast at Buxted by Peter Bawde, who had previously made bronze guns for the *Mary Rose* at a royal foundry in Houndsditch. William Levet, his business-manager, was soon supplying the new-style guns to batteries at Portsmouth, Rye and Eastbourne. Because of their tough casing and skilful moulding, their small calibre and great length, these Wealden cannon were highly popular in western Europe for almost a century. And domestic ironware became cheaper - Daniel Marret of Lewes proudly bequeathed an iron pot in 1552.[21]

The jurors at Lewes, who lamented in 1549 the rising price of wood, also estimated there were 53 new-style furnaces and forges in the Weald of Sussex - a number which almost doubled by 1574. Producers shipping iron from Newhaven between 1567 and 1575 included John French of Chiddingly, John Faulkenor of Waldron, John Relfe of Mayfield, Arthur Middleton of Rotherfield, William Relfe of Fletching and Edmund Challoner of Cuckfield. Between Easter 1574 and Easter 1575 some 900 tons of wrought iron were dispatched. Twenty-two cargoes went to London, 33 to West Sussex and Hampshire, 14 to the West Country, seven to Yarmouth and King's Lynn. Shipped away, too, that year, along with iron shot and 15 kettles, were 26 cargoes of guns, variously described as minions and sakers, falcons and falconets. Cannon were also sent to the royal armoury at the Tower of London, a traffic unrecorded in the port books. Gun-making especially thrived once Wars of Religion convulsed western Europe. In the 1590s, to sustain embattled Protestants in Germany, the Netherlands and France, ordnance left Newhaven for Hamburg and Amsterdam, Rotterdam and Flushing, Cherbourg and Saint Malo, Quimper and La Rochelle.[22]

In 1595 Abraham James of Cliffe was overseeing at 'Lewes' the 'shipping' of guns cast by founders in the pay of Henry Nevill, and indeed the town had long been a useful depot for the dispatch down-river of ordnance and wrought iron. In March 1577 Richard Andrews collected at Lewes, and conveyed to the Tower, almost 44 tons of shot, cast by Ralph Hogge at Buxted and carted to the riverside at Isfield. William Nutshawe

124 The plaque

of Southampton and John Martin of Torbay shopped in the town for guns in 1578. And at Widow Adams's premises 'by the bridge' 15 tons of wrought iron, 'well drawn into bars', awaited the London dealer, Giles Garton, in November 1579 - they came perhaps from Freshfield forge at Horsted Keynes. Ralph Hogge worked several furnaces in the Buxted area, and cast a self-mocking plaque which survives - unusually, too, he manufactured muskets. Besides being official supplier of iron shot to queen Elizabeth from 1559, he received in 1567 the sole right to ship abroad iron ordnance and shot surplus to royal needs. To protect this monopoly he made a bitter 'complaint' in 1573 that John Harman, who resided, like Widow Adams, near Lewes bridge, had colluded with gun founders at Wadhurst and Rotherfield to ship ordnance through Newhaven, ostensibly to English ports, but in reality to France or Flanders, a territory under Spanish control - so enabling 'enemy' ships to become as well armed as the queen's were. Harman, who trained as a glazier, shipped a variety of merchandise and twice served as senior Constable. But despite the 'complaint', in 1577-8 Hogge sold him 25 tons of small ordnance, 'pieces with Rings upon their nose', accepting a barrel of herrings in part-payment. By then, maybe, Harman was buying on the queen's behalf, though in 1591 the Privy Council investigated new claims that he was exporting guns illegally. Directly involved with iron-making perhaps was Robert Olyff, a resident on School Hill about 1570, for a man of that name was John Relfe's partner at Howbourne forge in Buxted.[23]

In the early 17th century, however, production of wrought iron upstream from Lewes declined. The 634 tons sent from Newhaven to English ports in 1633 went mostly to London - the westward trade had succumbed to competition from forges in the Forest of Dean. Exports overseas, mostly to Holland and northern France, amounting to 180 tons in 1623, petered out soon after. And ordnance production wavered once the European powers signed treaties or truces which held till 1618. Meanwhile Maresfield furnace was put to exotic use in 1608 when a Scottish goldsmith, paid by the royal mint, tried to extract silver from twenty tons of ore, 'traced with many small strings like unto hairs', brought upriver from the royal lead mines at Linlithgow. But despite 'many dangerous fits' in the furnace, too little silver was retrieved even to cover the cost. By 1614 cannon cast at Maresfield and Framfield were being exported without a licence by George Bindles of Lewes. Worse still, Stephen Aynscombe at Pounsley furnace in Framfield tried to ship guns to Spain using a counterfeit warrant - to that end, it was alleged, the Privy Seal was removed to Lewes. Certainly in 1619 the Privy Council ordered his furnace to be 'blown out' and any cannon found there to be auctioned on Tower Hill. Maybe the 160 tons of ordnance which Count Gondomar, the Spanish ambassador, was licensed to ship through Newhaven in 1620, were cast at Maresfield furnace. By then Sackville Crowe, who acquired the sole right to make and supply 'merchant' guns, probably worked it. Cardinal Richelieu sent an agent there in 1627 to entice away the skilled moulders. The sort of technology they employed was depicted on a fire-back cast by Richard Leonard at Brede furnace in 1636.[24]

125 The Leonard fire-back

No guns were cast at Lewes, but images of iron-making tools decorated two of the 19 church bells that Edmund Giles is known to have cast, or re-cast, there between 1595 and his burial at St Michael's in 1615 - the *Bell* in that parish was sold in 1587. His bells included a 'second' for All Saints and a treble for St Michael's; others were carried to Lindfield in 1598 and 1603, and to Mayfield in 1615. At that time his foundry was perhaps the only one in eastern Sussex. It was continued maybe by Thomas Giles from Chichester, who between 1615 and 1621 supplied bells to at least five local churches, among them Cliffe, where a re-casting in 1622 was also locally done. Thereafter the craft is unrecorded in the town till 1650 when John Palmer, bell founder of Lewes, accused John Lulham of practising it at Chiddingly, though a mere 'carpenter' - and indeed in 1649 Cliffe parish had spent heavily sending two bells to

'Lulham' for re-casting.[25]

Another Wealden product traded - albeit briefly - at Lewes was glass. French artisans, who settled in and around Kirdford in western Sussex, had updated its manufacture thereabouts in the 1550s. Forty drinking glasses were stolen at Cliffe in 1588, and 33 cases of 'English' glass were sent to Poole, Weymouth and Plymouth from Newhaven in 1589. 'A glass carrier', Lewis Jones, was based at Cuckfield in 1595 and 'a glassman', David Wakefield, was buried at All Saints in 1613. However the unloading at Newhaven of eight cases of 'Norman' glass from Dieppe in 1604 signalled the waning of Wealden production.[26]

Lewes too was a market for sea fish netted by fleets based in Sussex. Some of the herrings the Cluniacs ate in the 1530s had been gutted at Brighton or barrelled at Pevensey or Hastings. They also bought hake from Peter Flusher in the Borough. The fish market there was located maybe in Fisher Street, its clerk in 1593-4 being John Cooper. In the 18th century fishwives from Brighton, known as 'juggs', sold fresh mackerel and herring there, also whiting, plaice, sole and pilchards, dory, skate, turbot, sand-rays and shrimps. And there perhaps, as at Hastings and Brighton, fish were traded for Wealden geese. In the hinterland of Brighton they were also sold by itinerant 'rippiers' like William a Weeks of Keymer, who left money in 1568 to folk at Wivelsfield and Lindfield - former customers perhaps. From the sea shore at Pevensey oyster-catchers and lapwings were sent to the Lord's Place in 1604 to be fattened on bullock's liver - their eggs were counted a delicacy. The Ouse itself was

drag-netted by the Cluniacs in due season for mullet. Moreover, in 1531 Christopher Page of Cliffe leased the Broadwater water-meadows below Ranscombe, on condition he supplied 'great bream' weekly when the earl of Wiltshire visited Sussex or Kent. Two bargemen at Cliffe were suspected in 1636 of stealing eel-pots from Thomas White, a basket maker with osier-plots by the river - himself suspected of poaching fish 'with nets and unjust engines'. (As recently as 1942 'an old man of the name of Baker', living in South Street at Cliffe, owned a newly made three-pronged eel-spear.)[27]

The town's vitality as a distributive centre depended in part on the carriage of commodities, by water, to and from its outport. In the 1530s the Cluniacs used Thomas Colthurst to barge gravel, Caen stone and barrels of white herring up the Ouse from Seaford. Yet at that time the meadows along the estuary, and indeed as far upstream as Sheffield bridge, lay under water 'almost all the year'; indeed fishing nets were tied to hedges in the Broadwater 'brooks'. The flooding was largely due to eastward-drifting shingle blocking the river mouth at Seaford, and in the

126 The eel spear

1530s landowners in these water-logged Lewes and Laughton Levels, buoyed up perhaps by profits from agriculture, took bold remedial action. Earlier, the Cluniacs had won back from the sea a hundred acres near Pevensey, and prior Crowham it was who sailed to Flanders, 'at his own cost', and returned with two drainage experts. He also consulted another who had drained Saint Catherine's marsh near the Tower of London. The upshot, it seems, was the levying in 1537 of a water rate on land in the Levels, which funded, soon after, the cutting of a channel through the accumulated shingle below Castle Hill in Meeching. 'One of the earliest canalizations in England', it also created a 'New Haven' there, which became the outport for Lewes.[28]

At a stroke the flooding upstream dispersed. The Broadwater meadows were restored as rich summer pasture and the Town Brook below St John's church was let for a robust rent. Water carriage along the estuary also improved. In 1556 Sir John Gage at Firle owned a barge 'of three ton for the river'. And about then, the cost of carting lead from the disused church at Malling to the waterside was five shillings, its carriage by boat to Newhaven 13s 4d, its transport by ship to London £4. The town's barges were mostly moored at Cliffe. Two 'watermen' there, Edward Manning and Edward Dorridge, were accused in 1587 of stealing bell metal at Piddinghoe, and John Butler there, though he lived 'by husbandry most', also worked in the barges 'on the water'. But it was from a barge-house at the Lord's Place that wheat and oats, destined for Greenwich, were boated away in 1603-4, along with casks of eels, cucumber and saline samphire, the aromatic leaves

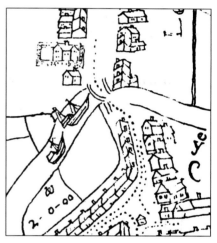

Barges at the bridge, drawn by Deward (a modern copy)

of which made an excellent pickle. Perhaps the Cockshut stream, between the barge-house and the Ouse, was scoured by Richard Tuppen, whose diking tools in 1613 included an old scaffold, a draw hook and a 'slubber'. More mysteriously, an All Saints man incurred debts prior to February 1567, 'whilst the walls were a making'- maybe the Green Wall was being improved as a flood defence? [29]

After a time, of course, the 'New Haven', created at Meeching by the 'new cut', itself began to choke with shingle, for the south-west wind still 'tyrannized' and 'cast up beach infinitely'. Flooding upstream also resumed. The summer of 1629 was a dry one, but the waters in Lewes Level remained high. And about then Lewes borough paid forty shillings to 'the Surveyor' at Newhaven - a prelude perhaps to the dredging privately funded in 1633 by Samuel Towers of Cliffe and other merchants.

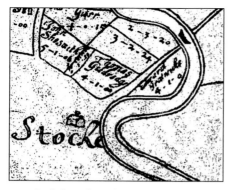

Stock ferry, drawn by Deward
(a modern copy)

Doubtless, though, the currents in the estuary were always perilous. Two shepherds and 58 sheep drowned in 1576 when the boat at Stock Ferry sprang a leak. Near by, the corpse of 'Parker' was retrieved at Christmas 1640, ten weeks after his barge sank.[30]

Yet whatever its capacity, the harbour at New Haven was little used by large freighters. The biggest recorded in its port books were of fifty tons - the *Mary Bennet* of Hastings loaded iron for Hull in 1567; the *Eleanor Stansfield* unloaded Spanish salt, sack wine and figs from Saint Lucas in 1606. And the fleet based there was small - 11 vessels perhaps in 1589-90, 16 in 1609 and 1620, 11 in 1633. The larger fleets at Hastings and Brighton combined freight carriage with deep-sea fishing. They dominated traffic at Pevensey and Shoreham, the delivery of coal from Tyneside, and much of Newhaven's trade with London and the West Country. Few fishermen settled in the outport, where access to a cramped harbour was often impaired by vicious weather in Seaford Bay, its waters lashed by south-westerly gales. The shelving rocks along the shore were sometimes strewn with anchors and masts, corpses and merchandise, washed from wrecked vessels. The harvest might include Purbeck marble, Irish cow hides, French wines, elephants' teeth and hangings of Spanish leather. Pilfering and plunder flourished. The Malaga wine of a Hamburg merchant was borne away in buckets. A local shepherd penned his flock and joined men swarming over a stranded ship; from a cabin in the stern he removed a silk garter, a silver-threaded glove and several 'knee-tops' lined with red taffeta.[31]

That timber and iron were carried along the upper Ouse, north of Lewes, would explain why Barcombe mill was queried as a possible 'hindrance' to boats in 1635, and perhaps why, from his mansion at Isfield Place, Sir John Shurley saw guns 'passing along' daily in 1615. Doubtless the river was a welcome alternative to the Wealden roads either side of it. The highway from Chailey to Offham was 'almost impassable' in the winter of 1604-5, while along the road from Plashett bridge to Malling 'the many dangerous holes and extreme dirty places' caused horses to 'stick fast in the mire' in October 1643. All Wealden roads were damned by a London barrister in 1690 as bad and ruinous beyond imagination. Rain quickly turned the 'bottomless' clays into a quagmire. 'Great waters' or 'a mighty flood' could postpone or divert a baptism. The droving of cattle wrought havoc. So did five carts laden with iron which Richard Comber of Horsted Keynes sent through Cooksbridge and Offham in the winter of 1653-4. And conscience perhaps prompted Richard Leeche, an ironmaster at Fletching, to leave £60 in 1596 to repair 'the ways' between Lewes and Godstone.

Doubtless these 'ways' connected Offham with Chailey, Danehill, Forest Row and East Grinstead, the route which John Ogilby, His Majesty's Cosmographer, mapped in 1675 as the Lewes-London road. John Paine, a carrier based at East Grinstead, probably used them in the 1530s when he delivered cod, salmon and sprats, loaded at Southwark, to the Cluniacs at Southover, along with Wealden charcoal. A likely depot at Southwark for Lewes-bound freight was 'the sign of the Tabrett', for its lease was held in 1564 by Widow Elizabeth Batnor of All Saints - in 1633 the *Talbot* was used by a carrier based at Buxted. Occasionally carried overland to London were goods stockpiled in Paris and shipped from Dieppe to Newhaven - though Rye was the usual port. In 1579 these included spectacles and burning-glasses, ivory dials and surgeons' cases, children's daggers and gloves from Valenciennes; carried down in return were Hampshire kerseys, Manchester 'cottons' and Devonshire cloths. Perhaps packhorses were used. In 1797 the first leg of their route from Lewes to London was through Hamsey, over Cobbs Green, down Hams Lane, to Barcombe mill.[32]

Busier, maybe, was the highway which hugged the Southdown ridge between Petersfield and Beachy Head, but descended to cross the Ouse at Lewes. Through the town trudged a variety of 'passengers' - tinkers and tailors, pedlars and 'decayed' merchants, gypsies and Irish folk, discharged soldiers and ship-wrecked seamen. More stylishly, in the summer of 1689, Sir John Ashburnham was to set forth from the *Star* in his calash coach 'over the Downs' towards Bramber, Winchester and South Wales. Beyond Beachy Head travellers could use the shingle shore of Pevensey Bay. Lieutenant Hammond traversed it in 1635, before savouring 'the holy quiet' of the *Lamb* at Eastbourne, and then ascending the South Downs to a mill 'that stood in the Clouds' with 'a fair Prospect' of the Weald. The bishop of Chichester, intrepidly intent on visiting his clergy around Hastings, crossed the 'seaside' shingle in June 1688.[33] Lewes Bridge was the busier because it was the only one between Barcombe mill and the sea. Till the Reformation, its massive stone counterpart at Bramber supported a chapel displaying an image of the Virgin adorned with rings and necklaces of silver. But the wooden framework at Lewes, shaken by heavy usage and by an often turbid Ouse, needed to be repaired or rebuilt in 1562-3, 1584, 1591, 1624 and 1652. The renewal in 1652 cost rate payers in Lewes and Pevensey rapes £80, provoking one of them to assault a collector at Tarring Neville. Doubtless the work was done more quickly than at Exceat where the bridge across the Cuckmere, though 'altogether clear down' in July 1609, was still 'altogether decayed and gone' two years later.[34]

Doubtless, until the 1530s, pilgrims to Chichester and Canterbury used the Southdown highway, and the capacious inns established along

127 'Medieval' pottery at the *Star*

it. In Lewes borough the Cluniacs had owned the freehold occupied in the 1550s by the *Star*, its sign emblematic of the Virgin and of Welcome. Its impressive 14th-century cellar survives, below the Town Hall, and stones carved with 'dog teeth' and diamonds were found when a kitchen was pulled down in 1891-2, also much 'medieval' pottery. And perhaps the *Chequer*, recorded at Eastport in 1618, had begun as a hostelry under Cluniac auspices - its sign depicted maybe an accounting frame, or the checky coat of Warenne. At the *Chequer* in Canterbury Chaucer lodged his immortal band. The *Vine* in Westout, which provoked a lawsuit in 1526, bore a sign possibly blending the sacred and the profane - likewise a house at Cliffe near the bridge, described as 'late the Lamb' in 1685. At Alfriston, where the Southdown highway crossed the Cuckmere, the

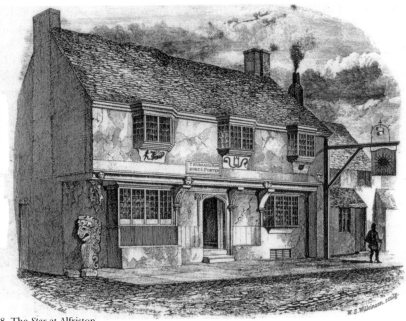

128 The *Star* at Alfriston

268

Benedictines of Battle had owned the *Star*; on its exterior in the 15th century were carved saint George with a dragon and saint Giles with a deer. At Eastbourne the 'holy quiet Lamb', savoured by Lieutenant Hammond, preserves a rib-vaulted medieval cellar, and at Battle, 'a town of wine and alehouses', the wife of the landlord at the *George* by the abbey gate took silver spoons etc. worth £4 when she ran off with John Saxon in 1460.[35]

In Lewes borough pilgrims could also adore an image of saint Christopher at St Mary in the Market. And maybe, in churches near the bracing Southdown highway, they encouraged a cult of saint Catherine, whose body, so it was said, was miraculously removed to Mount Sinai after her martyrdom on a wheel in Alexandria. Altars and images celebrated her at Southover, Ringmer and Arlington, bells at Edburton and Pyecombe, Iford and Jevington, St Mary Westout and All Saints, a wall painting at Alfriston. The highway was also served by founts of healing water. Saint Mary's spring bubbled at Steyning; the Holy Well gushed into the sea below saint Gregory's chapel at Eastbourne; the Pin Well sparkled near All Saints, and a cult of saint Anne flourished at Westout. There too, near the *Vine*, Thomas Hider rented a tenement called the 'hermitage' about 1570. Had it really been used by an eremite? Some favoured desolate places, like Winchelsea Beach or Seaford Head, but Richard Petevine was stationed near the west gate of Chichester in 1405.[36]

As well as being a market and depot for local produce, the town served as a warehouse for a wide range of merchandise brought upriver. London developed as a mighty emporium of English and foreign produce, and delivered from it to Newhaven were groceries, cheese, butter, white salt and hops, red and white herrings, sprats, spices, sugar, raisins, currants, prunes, almonds, figs and liquorice, wine, vinegar and *aqua vitae*, haberdashery, linen, canvas, hemp, Irish frieze and Welsh 'cottons', alum, madder, paper, bottles, pins, nails, starch, oil (from Seville, Canary and Candy), glue, bird lime, soap, pitch, tar, tallow from Muscovy, cordage, flax, hemp and turpentine, plaster of Paris, steel, brass ware, pewter, scythes and wire, glass, lead, shot, coal, 'deals' (softwoods), masts, mill stones and grave stones. Moreover, till shipments of Wealden iron to the West Country ceased, cargoes to Newhaven from Southampton, Poole and Weymouth, Exeter, Dartmouth and Plymouth, included tin and lead, woad, alum and kerseys, slates, burrs and mill stones, vinegar, raisins, prunes, cork and almonds, aniseed, figs, rice, sugar and molasses, pepper, ginger, cloves, cinnamon and liquorice, 'Brasil' wood, 'bank' fish from Newfoundland, Breton canvas, Guernsey cloth and Seville oil, salt from the Bay of Biscay, wine from Malaga, from Canary and Madeira.

Cargoes also reached Newhaven from northern France and the Netherlands. From Saint Valery, Fecamp, Rouen, Caen and especially Dieppe, came quilts, quails and feathers, prunes, hops and cider, teasels and walnuts, paper, canvas and thread, glass, wicker baskets, wool-cards and earthen platters, plaster of Paris, Gascon wine and Newfoundland fish; also such Gallic fripperies as playing cards, rattles, masks and puppets, girdles, petticoats and beaver hats, bangles, counterfeit rings and silver plate. Unloaded from Flushing, Middelburg and Rotterdam were goods reflecting the industry of the Dutch: hops, onions, cabbages and cheese, madder, starch and linen, stoneware pots, bricks and tiles, steel, frying pans, pins and iron rods - while the spices, sugar, 'bark' wood and wine, the deals, masts, spars, pitch and tar from the Baltic, testified to the scale of their entrepot trade. However, 300 deals were delivered directly from Norway to the Lewes merchant, William Peake, in 1617. Salt also arrived from the Bay of Biscay and 'sea coal' from Newcastle and Sunderland. The fuel was used by a Southdown blacksmith at Litlington in 1600 and imports into Sussex rose thereafter.[37]

Several merchants at Cliffe were active between 1604 and 1625, a time of comparative peace in the Channel. Peter Stone, like his father before him, shipped iron and planks, malt and hops to Dartmouth and Penryn. Henry Hale received consumer goods from London, salt from the Bay of Biscay, canvas from Dieppe; he died in 1629 leaving over £1900, a house at Eastbourne and lands at Plumpton and Fletching. Richard Mead, a grocer who dispatched wheat to Marseilles and Seville, also controlled a chain of taverns and a quarry near Southerham. Most enterprising perhaps was John Stansfield, born about 1550 in All Saints parish, though sprung from an 'ancient' family in Shropshire. He sent iron to the West Country, wheat to Marseilles, lead to Newfoundland; he received coal from Milford Haven, salt from La Rochelle, almonds from Malaga, stoneware pots from Rotterdam. And his, presumably, was the *Eleanor Stansfield* trading from Newhaven, where he owned extensive

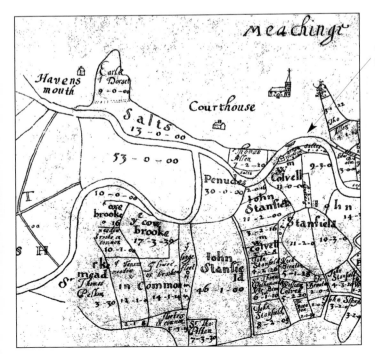

The site of the Cluniacs' tenement by the ferry

Stansfield's water-meadows east of the ferry, drawn by Deward (a modern copy)

water-meadows east of the ferry near the harbour. With his profits he bought the Malling Deanery estate, the manors of Denton, North Stoke and Preston Becklewin (in Beddingham), and fattening grounds at Hooe. His only child, Eleanor, married a Surrey magnate, Richard Evelyn of Wootton. Their second son, John, recalled in his *Diary*: 'her eyes and hair a lovely black; of constitution more inclined to a religious melancholy, or pious sadness; of a rare memory, and most exemplary life'. From 1625 John himself resided at Cliffe with his aged grandfather, whose lands he was to inherit, and attended his 'solemn' funeral at All Saints two years later. A drawing survives of the 'pious' monument (long dismembered) paid for by Stansfield's second wife, Jane. There were fewer merchants in Lewes borough, though

129 The 'pious' monument

the grocer, Richard Newton, imported wine, currants and prunes, sugar and spices, steel, hemp and vinegar from Holland in 1624. He also sponsored at St Michael's the baptism of his sixteen-year-old black servant, Mary Samboyce.[38]

Merchandise unloaded at Newhaven was sometimes distributed across a wide hinterland, which extended beyond the basin of the upper Ouse. Between 1565 and 1575 dealers at Lindfield and Alfriston, Rotherfield and Burwash, were supplied with candles, herrings and muscadel from Southampton, prunes from Caen, pitch and tar, alum, madder and Newfoundland fish from London. In 1640 Edward Green, a tailor on School Hill, carried 'stuffs and laces' to Cuckfield to make a wedding dress. In 1593 a doublet was stitched at 'Lewes' for a Pelham servant at Halland. Glass was sent to Lindfield church and lead to repair Bolney steeple. Wares worth £40 were also bought at Lewes in 1599 by a tailor from East Grinstead, a market town whose 'Inhabitants' were sufficiently well-disposed to Newhaven harbour to back a scheme published by Andrew Yarranton in 1677 to improve it.[39] Lewes was also a warehouse for wine. It was shipped from Southampton and Holland, Dieppe, Bordeaux and Spain by Samuel Towers and William Peake, Richard Mead and Thomas Oliver, who between them controlled in 1636 almost half the taverns licensed in mid and eastern Sussex, in 15 places extending from Beeding and Brighton to Westham and Burwash. Oliver, a son-in-law of the brewer, Thomas Trayton II, also owned the *White Lion* and the *Bull* in the borough.[40]

Itinerant pedlars based in the town included Robert Farden, robbed of two pieces of cloth in 1574; Richard ap Beaven who molested a local child in 1599, and Owen Powell, a seller of 'hard ware', 'knives, shears etc.', buried at St John's in 1620. On lengthy circuits from the town John Bromand stole clothing from houses at Udimore near Rye in 1589, and the tinker, Richard Rumney, fatally stabbed a man at East Grinstead in 1596. Salesmen also converged there. A pinner from Lambeth purloined a purse at Cliffe in 1588. The livestock fairs attracted them and maybe John Evelyn drew on childhood memories when he wrote of streets at fair time 'swarming with well-clad Lusty Boores and women of the Country'. The Whitsun fair in 1614 drew a tailor from Uckfield and a fisherman's wife from Brighton.[41]

Textiles and fabrics were stockpiled in the town, like the silk sarsenet and Spanish taffeta, the silk lace and velvet velour, stolen there in 1584, the Devonshire kerseys and russet cloths purloined in 1606. A furrier, Matthias Ware, traded in 1596, a tapestry weaver, Jeremy Croggett, and a silk weaver, Henry Goldam, in the 1620s. Widow Parnell Ive, keeper of a 'woollen shop' in 1540, left a kerchief to every poor women in St Mary's Lane. John Holmwood draper, worth over £1000 in 1586, probably paid for the massive oak frame visible at Barbican House; his initials, and his wife Mary's, were carved in 1579 on the spandrels of a sandstone chimney-piece, adorned with sprigs of flowers. William Clagget haberdasher owned the *Bell* near the market-house, also the defunct Steward's Inn with its pigeon-house and near-acre of orchard. In 1603 he bought land at Coneyborough in Barcombe. His daughter, Mary, married Henry Stonestreet mercer, owner of the *Kings Head* in Westout and premises at Hailsham and Salehurst. His son, Henry II, a Cambridge graduate, became rector of South Heighton. Tailors tended to be less affluent. Thomas Hayward bequeathed 'two best black jerkins, one cloth, one worsted' and 'a black cloth coat' in 1579. Widow Julian Cadman divided her 'seamstress ware' among her daughters in 1599.[42]

The raw materials available in the town also attracted metal workers. Nicholas Vaunt and John Lockyer, 'alien', supplied locks, keys and hinges to the Cluniacs in the 1530s. Ingots of copper alloy were smelted in the Friary precinct after the Dissolution. Robert Stukell blacksmith renewed the mechanism of the church clock at Southover in 1561-2. In 1571 he leased space under the bell loft of the Broken Church, which probably housed the Borough clock by 1624. By then two locksmiths near the Broken Church, Thomas Burkin and Lawrence Townsend, may have been making clocks, a craft previously confined to London. By 1636 a watchmaker-cum-schoolmaster, George Moth, was resident in the Borough, and so, on School Hill, was a gun maker, William Goring. Doubtless militiamen were among his customers; in 1637 John Bailey took pride in a musket, rest and bandoleer. John Inkersoll, the miller at Westout, already owned a 'fowling piece' in 1587.[43]

272

Lubricating the Borough's commerce were goldsmiths like Francis Fynson, who also sent skins and hides through Newhaven to Southampton in 1567, and John Symme, trading in St Michael's parish in 1596. By 1612 William Dodson was at Castlegate Corner, right next to the market-house. By 1643 he owned freehold land at Hamsey. In 1627 he gave a servant girl 14 shillings for a gold ring she had stolen at Ditchling; it had cost 'about thirty'. And maybe he made silver spoons of the small Seal Top type.[44]

By the 1620s there was a demand for luxury goods from a corps of professional men, strongly rooted in the Borough - barristers and attorneys, notaries public and scriveners, physicians and apothecaries. Bestriding its courts, civil and ecclesiastical, was William Thomas. Appointed Clerk of the Peace for Sussex in 1615, to deploy the paperwork at quarter sessions, he was also by 1619 the archdeacon of Lewes's registrar and the bishop's collector of revenue - a formidable portfolio. Francis Nedham, buried at All Saints in 1623, was one of several clerks in his employ - so was William Alcock, his successor as Clerk of the Peace. In 1603 Thomas paid £225 for a residence on School Hill [School Hill House]. He installed a massive dining table and a matching 'wrought' chair, a black velvet cushion, damask table cloths, stools covered with Turkey work, brass andirons, two maps, four pictures and books worth £50. With the profits of office he bought an estate at West Dean where his costly alabaster tomb towers in the chancel of the church. His descendant, Freeman Thomas, became Viceroy of India and Marquis of Willingdon. An earlier registrar, Stephen Stapley, also lived spaciously on School Hill [192-200]; his garden rails encroached onto the way 'from Green wall to Fisher Street' [East Street]. A Bachelor of Civil Law and former fellow of Magdalen College Oxford, he left a lease at Glyndebourne to his wife in 1596 and a best gelding to his brother.[45]

Legal expertise focused too on manor courts and customary tenures. Mention has been made of Richard Amherst, principal steward of the Sackville estates in Sussex, who owned a coach with all its 'furniture', and of John Rowe, steward of the Bergavenny manors in Lewes rape, whose silverware included tankards, a ewer, a candle cup and a dozen Apostle spoons. Also stewarding the Bergavenny lands were Christopher Blaxton and Nicholas Fitzherbert - the latter's ignorance of manorial custom was noted by the meticulous Rowe. In 1604 Fitzherbert's widow, Elizabeth, left a house on School Hill to her brother, Blaxton. Near by, on the Hill, was Edward Henshaw, steward to the earl of Arundel in 1615. And outside the west gate lived Harbert Springett, an active arbitrator and trustee, who presided at the manor court of Lewes Borough in 1600, and purchased Broyle Place at Ringmer. Resident meanwhile at Southover was the Bencher of Gray's Inn and Puritan devotee of Banbury cheese, William Newton. With perhaps undue pessimism, after starting up his practice in 1598, he complained of mixing with 'covetous men where nothing is to be had'.[46]

Essential to the legal process were the public notaries. John Otringham died in 1583, shaken by the cost of keeping two sons at Trinity College Cambridge, whereas in 1614 Thomas Dawson left over £600, and lands in east Sussex and Yorkshire; his set of *Statutes at Large* went to William Newton, his copy of Brook's *Abridgment* of the Year Books to Harbert Springett. In 1624 James Nott, a notary in All Saints, left a black mourning cloak to Edward Henshaw. Essential too were the scriveners. In 1619 the bequests of Henry Parker at Cliffe included a lease of land at Goring, his late wife's black silk gown and camlet petticoat edged with velvet, a 'birding piece', and twenty shillings to Ralph Briscoe, a 'writer' on School Hill, whose chest in London contained only 'waste papers' when he died in 1628. Briscoe's own 'birding piece', however, passed to Jeremy Croggett, the tapestry-weaver. So maybe Parker and Briscoe had potted wild fowl together in the local wetland - the water-meadows below Ranscombe were celebrated in the 18th century for their winter flocks of bald coots. An evidently affluent scrivener, William Foster, died in 1621 worth over £700.[47]

As for physicians, Thomas Twine's passing in 1613 left Henry Panton as the town's most eminent doctor. His brother Nehemiah, based at Brightling, charged heavily when treating the Pelhams at Halland. Henry was prestigiously buried at All Saints in 1630, 'under the great stone before the clerk's seat in the chancel' - Richard Mead, a mere grocer, made do with the churchyard, 'on the right hand as people pass in at the east gate'. Henry's son John, who graduated at St Alban Hall Oxford in 1622, took over the practice on School Hill, where his patient, the deranged Henry Sackville, died in 1635. Resident at Malling by 1621 was Thomas Scotson. Already licensed at Cambridge after leaving Trinity College in 1600, he denied needing the archbishop's permission to practise in the Peculiar. Apothecaries too were taking local root. Thomas Brooke became junior High Constable in 1631, the year in which his father-in-law at Southover, Nicholas Russell, left £350 to a younger son, Richard, already apprenticed to Brooke's friend, Robert Walker, a London apothecary. In 1634 Nicholas's widow left a silver salt to her daughter (Brooke's wife), also her 'furnace' and 'burning vessels' - used perhaps to distill herbal remedies. Richard Russell returned to found a medical dynasty that climaxed with his namesake, 'the father of modern Brighton'. By 1648 the reputation of local medicine was such that when the aches of captain Sheppard, stationed at Horsham, made him fear 'the Egyptians would make a drum' of his body, he pondered a journey to Lewes for physic.[48]

Doubtless local surgeons commanded less prestige, their craft being badly regulated and open to dabblers. In the 1590s an armourer at East Grinstead owned two treatises on surgery, as well as barber's tools and a herbal. Dubiously versatile too was Nicholas Wetherby saddler, parish clerk of St John's, who bequeathed 'a French book of surgery' in 1623. More securely founded perhaps were the skills of Thomas Blunt, the barber-surgeon whose bequests in 1611 were commemorated on his table-tomb in St John's churchyard: 'a cup to the Fellowship as a pledge of love, and three pounds to the poor, and as many to the masters of the [grammar] school, to be claimed by them annually in perpetual donation ... also twenty pounds to be advanced without interest to needy tradesmen'. A surgeon at Cliffe, Abel Bytott, attended a fatal stabbing at Newhaven in 1599, and built a 'fair' dwelling house near Malling church in 1611; he also constructed a malt house with 'three floors', an oast and a cistern, and planted apple and cherry trees.[49]

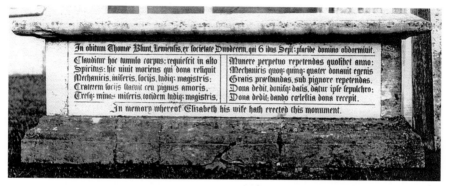

130 Blunt's tomb

School teaching also quickened, if marginally, the town's economy. In 1499 John Sherman agreed to board, feed and clothe Stephen Daniel's three sons and pay for their tuition. But the profession was not a path to affluence. The masters at the grammar school remain shadowy figures, apart from Gabriel Fowle, who bequeathed small sums to his pupils. Martin Citolin, the 'French Refugee' who taught writing and the rudiments of Latin to John Evelyn, was left a modest £12 by his mother in 1616. And though George Seager, a schoolmaster at Cliffe in 1605, became junior High Constable in 1625, he was by then a 'scriptor', often appearing in local wills as a witness or overseer - as such he failed, twice, to copy up the Borough accounts on time, forgetting or losing 'particular papers'. Nor were the town's clergy especially affluent, though John Chauntrell had panache enough to install a rector's seat at St John's in 1617 and proclaim the deed in white letters on a blue panel; in 1619 he preached at Knole House near Sevenoaks to his patron, the earl of Dorset, who 'sent for him purposely for that end'.[50]

Already John Stansfield and John Shurley have been observed using wealth amassed in the town to acquire land and secure their gentility. Somewhat earlier, so had John Colt. From his wharf by the bridge he traded iron to the West Country in the 1560s, in return for Bay salt, mill stones and wine, enterprise which allowed his son Thomas to marry a daughter of queen Elizabeth's 'Clerk of Jewels' and bequeath manors in Sussex and Kent to his son Edward, who entered Sidney Sussex College Cambridge in 1620. Also safely a 'gentleman' was Thomas, eldest son of Harbert Springett. He attended Oriel College Oxford and the Middle Temple, and was knighted at Wanstead in 1621. Inheriting Broyle Place at Ringmer, he acquired demesne lands in Southease and Plumpton and a mansion in St Michael's [Newcastle House]. Yet he cherished his local roots. Prompted by 'his birth and education' and by 'his love to the said town & Townsmen', he entrusted £100 to the Borough authorities in 1621, to support 'young beginners' apprenticed there, and 'ancient and decayed tradesmen'. In 1620 his younger brother Harbert, a lawyer, had given £100 to 'beautify' St Mary Westout, which paid for a handsome pulpit. There followed a bequest of £50 for 'young beginners' trading in the Borough , when Harbert died in 1622.[51]

In the early 17th century the town also attracted minor gentlemen, like William Overy at Westout who leased Ditchling Park and water-meadows at Rodmell and bequeathed £600 and a 'great' gold ring, or Thomas Burton on School Hill who held the 'parsonage' of Pevensey and fattening ground at Hooe. And several investors with property along the lower Ouse occupied spacious houses at Westport in Southover. John Codwell 'gent', who farmed the Lord's Place demesne and prized a saddle brought from Wales, had a malt house at Newhaven. Thomas Puckle held the 'parsonage' of Kingston and used premises in Westport to store the tithe corn. James Plumer possessed 'the tithes of Balsdean', Paul Garway the ferries across the Ouse at Stock and Newhaven, and Nicholas Russell the 'parsonage' of Piddinghoe. John Vinall, a rich farmer at Swanborough, bought and rebuilt a house, now The Croft. In 1599 John Saxpes added a porch, and possibly a west wing, to his residence, now

131 The porch at Anne of Cleves House

Anne of Cleves House, though his assets were at Ringmer, rather than along the Ouse valley. But why Robert Hassard 'of Carshalton' was buried in 1624 at All Saints is unclear. 'Forlorn little kneeling figures' remain from a wall monument which described him as the 'eldest officer' of king James's Jewel House. Perhaps he died in Malling, for his daughter was to marry Francis Polstead of Stoneham in 1634.[52]

That the demands of shire government had caused the Pelhams and the Gorings to maintain a town-house in the Borough, has already been noted. By the 1620s, moreover, John Stapley of Hickstead and Walter Dobell of Streat owned residences on School Hill. Dobell bought his [on the site of Albion Street] in 1608; he also acquired the manors of Streat and Westmeston. Appropriately, he faced his new E-shaped mansion, Streat Place, with squares of Southdown flint, for his forbears had prospered by leasing demesne lands at Falmer. Inside, carved emblems and adages alluded to the untimely death of Henry Prince of Wales in 1612. His own son, Walter II, attended

Dobell

Magdalen College Oxford and Gray's Inn. The Borough also attracted affluent widows. In 1613 Elizabeth Cheyney from Guestling, mother-in-law to Sir Thomas Culpeper, occupied a four-gabled house just below the *Vine*, which John Buckler sketched in 1830. Elizabeth sold it in 1629 for £120 to Widow Judith Heneage. She and her husband, who left her £500, had resided opposite, just above the rectory, in 1624. Some townsmen's widows also deployed spending power. In 1543 Katherine Parker

Grammar School at Lewes, Sussex. B april 5th 1830

132 The Buckler sketch

itemized various rooms in what became the Pelham town-house [now the White Hart]; her possessions there included a dress welted with tawny velvet, a silver piece called 'the lion piece' and a bowl painted with small flowers. In 1562 Elizabeth Batnor left money to her 'gossip' and to repair the road near Watergate mill, also a set of silver spoons 'with maiden heads' and a lease of 'the Tabrett' in Southwark. In 1612 Mary Batnor bequeathed leases of land at Westmeston; she also warned Edward and Alice Newton not to pester her executors about some 'old rotten and moth eaten lumberment' of theirs which she took in out of tender concern for their children. In 1629 Joan Batnor treasured a gold ring, an arras-work cover fit for a truckle bed, and a 'coral' with a silver whistle and silver 'hart' attached.[53]

Vital of course to Lewes's economy were its inns. And seemingly the trade they lost, when pilgrimages ceased in the late 1530s, was redressed by rising activity at the town's markets and fairs, its shops and law courts, for the inns were much resorted to by farmers and merchants, pedlars and carriers, scriveners, money lenders and litigants. Simon Michell kept the *Star* when Robert Holter's will was 'shown' there in 1554. Its host in 1593, William Burrell, left over £700, also silver table-ware and a gold ring 'with a ship upon it'. Arthur Bindles bought the hostelry for £240 in 1606, and by 1624 a barn in Fisher Street had been demolished to make way for a side entrance. Near it lived a cook, Edward Britten, a friend of John Chauntler butcher and of Edward Middleton who farmed at Landport - between them, perhaps, they supplied the *Star* with roast meat. And probably the carrier, Stephen Apps, also resided near the side entrance in the 1620s - a William 'Addis' conveyed 14 dozen pigeons to London in 1604. John Awood was landlord of the *White Lion*, near the top of School Hill, when he rented pasture in St Andrew's parish in 1541. Its 'decayed' premises were let by the heirs of a Southampton merchant to a cap maker, Thomas Slutter in 1557. Widow Slutter owned the lease in 1582, along with a 'best' cupboard, four chests, six wine racks and an orchard in Eastport. In 1621 Thomas Oliver paid £400 for the *Lion*, and soon after, an under-sheriff met JPs there, to mull over a riot at Barcombe.[54]

The *Bull* was bought for £160 in 1583 by Sir Henry Goring, who rebuilt the back as a rectangular stone-walled town-house entered through a timber-framed annexe, its doorway flanked by crouching satyrs. The front premises remained an inn, where Thomas Harman fatally stabbed a fellow brawler in 1594. Thomas Oliver paid £325 for the entire complex in 1615. Edward Homewood

133 A crouching satyr

gave short-measure in 1628, charging a penny for less than a quart of beer, and in 1641 William Vaughan, a goldsmith and bachelor, left money for five friends to enjoy a jovial wake there. Perhaps Homewood had also kept the *White Hart*, just north of the sessions house. John Kyme owned it about 1570, when 'the white horse' outside the west gate [143 High Street] was held by John Dopp. However the shoemaker John Beard bought land south-west of the castle barbican to improve stabling at a relocated *White Horse* [166] in 1600. It housed a 'sheriff's chamber' in 1644, and its ostler and two other male servants consorted there with John Forde, the saddler with the damask sword hilt.[55]

The signs of the *White Lion*, the *White Horse* and the *Bull* were tributes to the lords of the Borough. The lion and the horse supported the arms of the Howards, dukes of Norfolk. A white lion also graced the Borough's armorial shield. The bull was a device of the barons Bergavenny - so was the rose, the name in 1624 of premises just below their 'houses' in Westout [St Peters Place]. Baron Buckhurst, who acquired a quarter of the Borough's lordship in 1576, had wild cats flanking his arms, and a freehold near the market-house, called the *Cat*, was rebuilt in 1630 - Martin Citolin kept a school there in 1637. The *Bell*, a door or so to the east, was owned in 1587 by Edward Pelland of Cuckfield. But its sign alluded maybe to a market bell, or to the work of Edmund Giles. A 'black boy', displayed in 1591 at a house 'late' John Austen's, opposite Rotten Row Corner, celebrated perhaps a communal pipe of tobacco available there. James I, of course, was averse to the weed, and the sign of the *King's Head* swung there by 1630. And maybe the *Black Lion* [the *Crown*] advertised the family trade of Henry Townsend, the owner who tolerated 'tippling' there on the Lord's Day in 1649 - a smithy in the Broken Church, just opposite, was worked by a Henry Townsend in 1624. Entrusted with £7 by his journeyman, William Sanderford, the money was paid to Temperance Parris, William's bride to be, after his sudden death in 1629.[56]

These inns, except the *King's Head*, punctuated a busy stretch of High Street between the west gate and the crest of School Hill. At Cliffe the *Swan*, with its orchard and closes, stood just south of the market-house, at the Corner where traffic turned to funnel along West Street to the bridge. Owned in 1620 by John Edwards of Cuckfield, it was perhaps through its hall, parlour, three chambers and cellar that a burglar, Edward Moore, roamed in 1639 - observing maybe the round-headed doorway with Romanesque chevrons, sketched there in 1774. Further west, near the House of Correction, stood the *Red Lion*. William Reade was its landlord in 1603 and in a large upper room a petition was signed in 1628 asking that services be speedily resumed at Malling church, newly rebuilt 'upon the ancient foundation'. The swan was a badge of Henry IV, who granted the Cliffe its market charter, and the lion of Castile, a device of Henry's father, John of Gaunt, lord of Pevensey rape.

Southover had little through-traffic to cater for, especially after the Cluniacs and pilgrims departed, And two inns were sold by the earl of Dorset's agents about 1618. John Garway paid £55 for the *Swan* [17-19 High Street]. When the manor jury adjourned there in 1635, it was kept by Henry Sparkes, a brewer from Hampshire. Thomas Virgoe bought the *Chequer* at the west corner of Eastport Lane. Surviving from it perhaps were the carved stones and the remains of a bear found in 1985 at Dale Cottage.[57]

The *Vine* in Westout had ceased trading by 1625, despite the stylish porch added by the Southover brewer, Thomas Pelland, in 1577, its stone doorway framed by an entablature and Doric columns. Yet its Renaissance inn sign still hangs at Anne of Cleves House Museum - a rustic Bacchus brazenly astride a barrel, clutching a goblet and leather bottle, with clusters of grapes hanging below. And an upper room at *Shelleys Hotel* is still embellished with a Renaissance frieze depicting eagles and cupids (almost Ganymedes) romping merrily amid flowers and grapes, which also punctuate a robust trellis below. The artist is unknown, though probably he was not 'dape the painter' paid 10s 6d in 1594 to beautify St Michael's church with sentences of scripture. Painted hangings 'in both chambers' were fixtures in John Millesent's house in 1574, and Widow Savage itemized her 'painted clothes', along with a great spit and a cage to set meat in. At Antioch House West an early 17th-century wall painting of a hunting scene survives over a first-floor chimney-breast.[58]

134 Relics of the *Vine*: the frieze, the trellis and the sign

Doubtless the town's inns welcomed musicians. George Peirson was left ten shillings by an ex-innkeeper, George Smither, in 1625. Henry Trash and John French were sureties when their fellow musician, Richard Golding, received an alehouse licence in 1627 - in 1622 Henry Trash of Petworth had bequeathed a treble violin, 'a tenor violin' [a viola] and music books. And the William Britten, who inherited the family home near the side entrance to the *Star* in 1632, was probably the 'Mr Britten' paid £4 1s for giving lessons on the lute to the Pelham children at Halland in 1634. Perhaps musicians had been among 'the players of Lewes' who received two shillings by order of the mayor of Rye in 1526, a borough where amateur troupes from Sussex and Kent often acted scenes from the bible, the lives of saints, and folklore. At Lewes in the 1530s the churchwardens of St Andrew's paid for 'the labour and gloves' of a boy bishop on saint Nicholas's Day, and for a man to carry his crosier. At Hock-tide their wives 'kidnapped' parishioners, the ransoms swelling the church funds. But amateur players became less active once church ritual was curtailed. In 1559-60 St Michael's parish did lay out twenty pence for 'plays when the [ecclesiastical] visitors were here', but who the actors were is unclear. In the 1550s the High Constables had hired the duke of Norfolk's players, as well as a royal musician. Rye was visited till the 1570s by professional troupes, patronized by the 'king', the 'queen', the Lord Warden, baron Bergavenny and other notables. In 1598 a player, 'a stranger', died at Eastbourne, while on tour presumably.[59]

Doubtless Lewesians also enjoyed the sort of marvels recorded elsewhere in Sussex - the performing ape at West Harting, the two-headed calf at Petworth, the sword dancers, the camels and the 'stammering' minstrel at Rye - the Royal Bears were also paraded through the shire. A very local amusement was throwing the sledge on Snellings Mill Down below St Mary Westout. When in August 1575 a man from Iford stood too near the mark, he was fatally struck on the head. Also in Westout were the 'fields' used as an archery ground, and near by, in 1595, resided an arrow maker, John King. Abraham Edwardes was practising with his long bow at the butts when assaulted and cut about the head in August 1585. The miller at Westout, John Inkersoll, owned bows and arrows, as well as a sword, a dagger and a 'fowling piece', but despite this weaponry he was bludgeoned to death in 1589. Bowling too was a pastime. A Lewes draper indulged at Brighton in 1567. The earl of Dorset enjoyed bowls, as well as 'Bull Baiting, Cards and Dice' in May 1616. A bowling-green existed in the castle bailey by 1639 and both Deward and Randoll drew a small pavil-ion-like edifice there in 1620. And maybe there

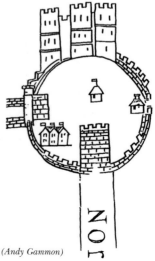

Deward's edifice (*Andy Gammon*)

North

was cricket of a kind. At Horsted Keynes in August 1624 a batsman on the village green, hoping to hit a ball a second time, accidentally killed a fielder trying to catch it. The laying of bets spiced the sports, the cards and the dice. From Lewes Francis Wilson, a young 'gent', wrote a specious letter to his father at Fletching: 'I do undoubtedly resolve in myself not to use that tormenting life of a gamester any more ... an unfortunate disaster - more my miserable destiny, and God's appointment, than any desire in me'.[60]

All in all it seems the town's economy was sufficiently diversified to ensure a measure of prosperity. As for its population, if wives, children, servants and apprentices are allowed for, the number of taxpayers listed in 1524 suggests there were maybe 1000 residents in the Borough, 500 in Southover and at least 250 in Cliffe. A calculation based on householders listed in the hearth tax return for 1662 yields 1200, 300 and 350 residents. These estimates, of course, ignore the households of those too poor to be taxed. However, totals derived from baptisms registered in 1611-40, give the Borough almost 1500 residents, Southover 400 and Cliffe 450. In each case they seem to suggest a fall in population at Southover, reflecting perhaps the loss of an opulent Cluniac community. Not all the priory's eighty 'servants' paid off in 1537 lived in Southover - for instance, John Amore, the beadle of Ditchling Garden manor, resided in Wivelsfield. But they did include at least 18 of the 106 taxpayers present in 1524, among them John Stempe 'auditor', Robert Swift barber, Henry Hirst rent collector, and John Reygate, bailiff of the grange farm. A shrunken population might explain two 'decayed' tenements 'under the priory wall' at Eastport; also the use of a house at Westport as a tithe barn; even the 'enclosure' of Antioch Street, sometime before 1595. By contrast, about 1613, in cramped, commercial Cliffe, Hamon Hardyman glover and Gargin Archer 'freemason' each owned a 'new' house built on a sub-divided tenement.[61]

The returns for 1524 also reveal that in Lewes borough about forty taxpayers were 'aliens', many of them craftsmen. There was a Herman Glasier, a Harman Couper, a Hans Paynter and a Charles Capper. 'Cornellus' was a mason, 'Gaskyn' a hat maker. John Lockyer supplied locks to the Cluniacs. Hans Legan was a churchwarden at St Andrews. Richard Margyn bequeathed a velvet nightcap, and John Peterson, assessed at £20, asked to be buried at the friary, in the chapel of saint Barbara. Among the native-born, John Ive (£30) owned a 'cider house garden', Christopher Kneller a copyhold at Fishbourne, and Peter Flusher (£40) land at Malling and a silver cup with 'a knopp' on its cover.[62]

Even if local commerce was harmed, albeit briefly, by the departure of pilgrims, Cluniacs and Franciscans, it seems surprising that an Act of Parliament in 1542 included 'Lewes' among three dozen towns disfigured by 'decayed' houses and 'desolate and vacant grounds ... with much uncleanness and filth, with pits, cellars and vaults lying open'. Some 'decay', of course, there was - of the castle's fabric, of clerical income, of market stalls. Because of a fading seigneurial presence, the castle by 1542 was near-derelict, neither a fortress nor a residence, and only fitfully a royal prison. The Brack Mount, it seems, had become a timber yard. In 1559 ground near the barbican [the Gun Garden] was granted away, and in 1567 much of the south-west mound as well, though 'the castle green' found no takers. In 1498 the stables of the *Steward's Inn* were let separately from its pigeon house; the inn itself was untenanted. But though a 'decay' of clerical income was blamed for the closure of three parish churches between 1538 and 1545, the timing was due maybe to Thomas Cromwell, rather than to a recent withering of revenue. And perhaps a change in retail methods caused tenements 'called St Mary's shops', in the market-place near St Mary's church, to be razed to the ground when the church was demolished in 1543-4, and 'workshops' in Fisher Street and near the market-house to stand empty. Elsewhere, at Battle for example, traders were deserting market stalls for permanent shops, open every day, with space for display, storage and processing. St Mary's shops had been small, if typified by a parcel of land near the belfry on the north side of the west door, granted in 1431, which measured eight by six feet.[63]

The town's diversified economy was largely shielded from the fluctuations experienced by communities very dependent on sea-borne commerce. The streets of New Shoreham, William Camden observed, were mostly 'ruined and under water', and the value of its harbour 'wholly taken away by the banks of sand cast up at the mouth of the river'. At Rye, too, the silting-up of its harbour was steadily eroding its sea-borne trade, and its fishing fleet. There were 530 householders in 1565, but only 281 in 1662, and of them, 141 were too poor to pay a hearth tax - moreover, 27 houses stood empty. At Brighton, though, till the later 17th century, the shingle beach proved adequate for its shipping, and despite French raids in 1514 and 1545, the town sent thereafter ever larger fishing fleets to the North Sea, and mushroomed as a result. But all local ports were rocked by outbreaks of plague, being in close maritime contact with London, a seed-bed of pestilence. Rye registered over 700 burials between August 1563 and July 1564. At Brighton 'many hundred' died in 1608. Chichester, like Lewes, was screened by an outport from sea-borne trade, yet 'one quarter of the population' may have perished in the winter of 1608-9. However in October 1609 Doctor Twine noted the end of an outbreak at Lewes, which the burial registers suggest was not unduly serious. The scale of earlier 'visitations' is unknown. In 1498, so it was said, a girl at Cliffe who died of plague and was sewn into a shroud, came to life when her mother prayed to the martyred Henry VI. In 1538, and again in 1577, an outbreak precluded a royal visit to the Lord's Place at Southover - in 1543 a local man mentioned a loan made 'since the time of sickness'. The town was wide open, of course, to influenzas. Indeed perhaps 7% of its population died between August 1638 and July 1639 - an 'infectious' time, according to a parish clerk in the Weald, 'especially in the Downs'. An earlier influenza in 1558-9 disrupted business at the archdeacon's court in the Borough for nine months.[64]

The town's broad-based economy also sustained a cohort of building craftsmen. In the 1530s the Cluniacs used the masons John Iden, John Corvill and Thomas Puckyll to erect an oven in the bake house, insert windows in the malt house, and repair walls round the prior's garden. A bricklayer, John Weston, improved the prior's kitchen, and a joiner, John Frenchman, made him a folding bed and a great wardrobe. A carpenter, Richard Draper, and two assistants, spent ninety days fashioning two 'rooms' in the monks' dormitory. But summoned from the Weald, perhaps, were Thomas Hosier, a 'layer of Horsham stone', who worked on the dormitory, and John Kenwood who covered the chapter house roof with 10,600 shingles - in 1630 a 'shingler' came from Warbleton to repair St Michael's church. As for materials, the Cluniacs bought 'brick stones' and ridge tiles from John Gyllott at Ringmer and John Randall at Hamsey, and collected eight loads of Caen stone at Cliffe bridge. They rented the archbishop's quarry at Cliffe and paid Thomas Colthurst to barge lime from it to their precinct - the quarry and lime kilns at Southover End they had leased to Thomas Hill. From 1537, of course, the precinct itself became a quarry. A superbly carved capital was used to build Kingston 'manor' house, and fragments of column to underpin premises at Westport. Flints were pillaged too from the near-derelict castle - that 'lover of Antiquities', John Rowe, sanctioned the removal of 78 loads to repair a wall. Bricks, still sparingly deployed, were used to enlarge the Garway residence at Southover.[65]

Builders needed ample workshop space, easily reached by boat along the river or through the water-meadows, so they tended to avoid the busy High Street between the *White Lion* and the west gate. At Cliffe George Shoulder mason occupied a 'lime house' by the quarry at North Street in 1637. Close by, it seems, near the Combe, stood the 'lead house' used in 1600 by Nicholas Foster, and later by Foster Whitebread, both slate layers. In 1613 Gargin Archer mason owned newly-built premises in West Street with rear access to the Ouse. At Southover in the 1630s lived Robert Holford mason and Robert Standen and Richard Harwood bricklayers. Richard Legatt bricklayer had bought a house at Westport in 1572 and John Weekes bricklayer owned 'Copthall' in 1580, a tenement 'under the priory wall'. Doubtless earlier craftsmen thereabouts had kept the immense Cluniac precinct in repair.[66] In the Borough, just above Eastgate Corner, resided Thomas Trayton I carpenter. He removed the bells from Malling church in 1555, and invited members of the Twelve to confirm that four inches had been left for an eavesdrop when the west wall of his house was rebuilt in stone. Opposite him on School Hill traded

Richard Kidder, the wheelwright with freeholds at Hever and Edenbridge. Close by, somewhat later, was Edward Bashford joiner, who left his daughters £120 in 1638. Thomas Jennings glazier was based at Keere Street in 1594. But he also had a 'shop' at West Street in Brighton and sold 'wood' at Pyecombe, Hamsey and Barcombe, so perhaps he distributed imported deals. Glass was still so highly prized that Alice Unson in 1583 made separate bequests of panes in her hall and chamber. David Lawrence carpenter used a barn 'near the pound' at Westout, and though on high ground, it was well placed for timber carted from the Weald. He left a bedstead to his grandson.[67]

When in 1635 Lieutenant Hammond deemed Lewes to be 'reasonably well built', almost all its houses, most probably, were still timber-framed. A surviving three-storied show-piece 'of Elizabethan date' stands at Keere Street Corner; its west wing projects above the High Street on curved oak brackets, its jetty towards Keere Street displays shaped oak joists. A drawing remains of a comparable twin-gabled house once sited between the *Star* and the *Black Lion* [190 High Street]. At Cliffe the open hall of a Wealden-style house in West Street [12-13] was floored over during the mid 16th century to create a hall chamber - an improvement typical of its time. Though it seems that few houses were built on crofts and orchards in the Borough between the 1560s and 1620s, 'Caprons' was erected on a 'garden' in Keere Street for Henry Giles of Southover about 1605. A prosaic need for stables and privies also caused nearly 400 feet of the castle ditch, east of the barbican, to be granted away between 1614 and 1634.[68]

135 The Fifteenth-Century Bookshop

136 Once the neighbour of the *Black Lion*

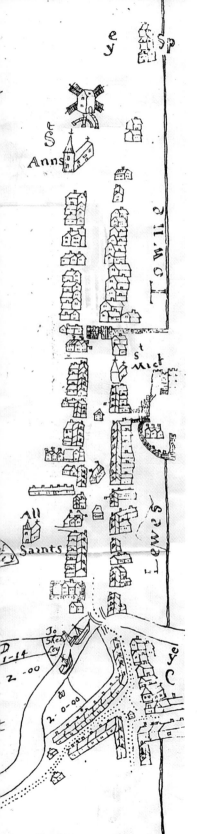

By a remarkable coincidence both John Deward and George Randoll depicted the town in 1620, showing the houses in the Borough hugging the High Street. Deward, 'an excellent surveyor of land' in Sussex and Kent, was buried at Eastbourne in 1625. He mapped Landport and Wallands in 1618. His depiction of Lewes is set within a massive survey of Lewes and Laughton Levels. (See chapter frontispiece) He showed barges by the bridge, public buildings and the west gate, the Friars and the Goring town-house, signs outside the *White Lion*, the *Star*, the *White Horse* and the *Bull*, also the mill and the 'spital' at Westout, and the spacious L-shaped Lord's Place at Southover, owned by the earl of Dorset, who paid him £10 for a survey of Framfield manor. George Randoll by contrast was a local man. In 1624 his house stood just west of St Martin's Lane, well placed for clients using the market-house - a George Randoll resided there in 1655. With Martin Citolin, John Evelyn's early teacher, he witnessed the will of William Crane barber in 1628. His detailed 'DESCRIPTION of the site of the Borough Town and Castle of Lewes' intrudes into a map showing, somewhat sketchily, the eighth part of Houndean manor owned by Sir Edward Bellingham in 1620. In 1621 he plotted the manor of West Ferring near Worthing.[69]

In his DESCRIPTION Randoll adorned some houses with gables, which can be correlated with affluent householders - with Edward Fitzherbert merchant, south of the bridge; Mistress Shurley at the Friars; Thomas Oliver, doyen of the drink trade, north of the bridge; John Harman merchant, towards Eastgate; then up School Hill - on the north side, with Thomas Trayton, the Sackville factotum; Walter Dobell 'gent', within a curtilage wall; Henry Panton physician; John Stapley 'gent'; and on the south side, with Thomas Colt 'gent', and William Thomas, Clerk of the Peace. Just above him appears the *White Horse*, and beyond the Broken Church, the *Star*. Between the sessions house

137 Deward's depiction
of the town (a modern copy)

and the west gate Randoll's gables are too crowded to allow any correlation, though the Goring mansion is shown. In Westout, however, the gables thin out. Across the bottleneck John Rowe looks over to Harbert Springett, his fellow attorney. Past Rotten Row, Edward Heaneage 'gent' faces Richard Amherst barrister at the former *Vine*; the gables of Widow Elizabeth Cheney, below him, are probably those sketched in 1830 by John Buckler. A problem, though, lurks in Randoll's side-streets. It seems he omitted Broomans Lane, but included the now vanished Pinwell Street, slanting up the slope east and north of All Saints church. 'THE CLIFT' is depicted less lovingly, yet maybe the gables of John Stansfield merchant, on the north, face those of the *Red Lion*.[70]

By the 1620s many decades of relative political stability and social order had strengthened the town's trading and professional elite. Their profits were spent on curtained bedsteads, window glass, silver salt-cellars and Apostle spoons, on Bibles and birding pieces. They invested in Wealden pastures and Southdown 'parsonages'. They set up trust funds for 'young beginners' in trade. Their own sons were trained for medicine and the law, or sent to Oxbridge to graduate as 'gentlemen'. Affluent, literate and pious, proudly urban yet socially aspiring, they were typical of townsfolk elsewhere. They were staunchly monarchist too, for the Crown was identified with Order: it defended their Realm, their Property, and True Religion . But their allegiance wavered in the 1630s. Indeed during the Civil War many embraced Rebellion, and drifted thereafter towards Revolution.

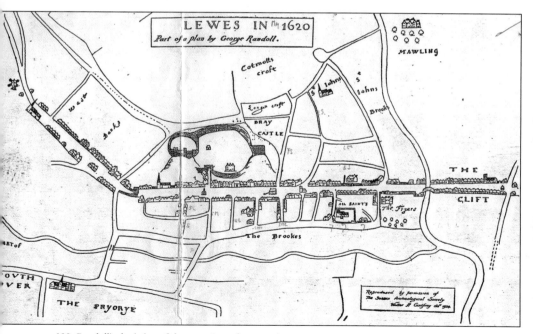

138 Randoll's depiction of the town (a modern copy)

Overleaf: Lunsford, the evil Cavalier

I'le helpe to kill, to pillage and deſtroy
All the Oppoſers of the Prelaƈy.
(My Fortunes are growne ſmall, my Freinds are leſſ
I le venter therefore life to have redreſſ
By picking, ſtealing, or by cutting throates.

10

The Great Rebellion
and its aftermath 1625-1662

*In full and sure hope of my salvation and my having a place in the eternal
kingdom of Almighty God, one in essence and three in persons, waiting for and
expecting the same my salvation with all the rest of God's Elect, of which number
I do assuredly persuade me to be one, condemning herein those accursed, hellish
and devilish blasphemies either of Pope or Arminius, assuring myself of the same
my salvation none otherwise either by merit of mine own or the works of
superrogation of any other Saint or Angel, but only by the alone, full and perfect
means and merits of the death and passion of Jesus Christ.*
The passionate Puritanism of John Batnor, rector of Westmeston, 1624.

*When we came to Arundel, we met with a most dismal sight, the town being
depopulated, all the windows broken with the great guns, and the soldiers
making stables of all the shops and lower rooms.*
The impact of civil war, January 1644.

*Nor could it be expected that a Testimony levelled both against the darling Vices
of the Laity, and the forced Maintenance of the Clergy, should meet with any
other than an unkind reception. The messengers of it were entertained with
Scorn and Derision, with Beatings, Buffetings, Stonings, Pinchings, Kickings,
Dirtings, Pumpings, and all manner of Abuses from the rude and ungovernable
Rabble; and from the Magistrates, who should have been their defenders, they
met with Spoiling of Goods, Stockings, Whippings, Imprisonments, and
Banishments, and even Death itself.*
The sufferings of the People called Quakers.

Beginning in 1618, the Thirty Years War in Europe did much to
destabilize politics in England, exposing the weakness of its armed
forces, stoking debate about the legal basis of war taxation, and
rekindling fear of militant Catholicism. In 1620 the defeat of the
Protestants in Bohemia was followed by the flight of their leader, the
Elector Palatine, and his 'Winter Queen', Elizabeth, the daughter of
James I - in 1629 Lewes was visited by their fellow refugee, a 'poor'
minister 'that came out of Bohemia'. To enlist Spanish support for his
displaced brother-in-law, Charles Prince of Wales journeyed to Madrid,

hoping to woo the Infanta. When this strategy failed, the Prince united with Parliament to promote a war with Spain in 1625. But an attack on Cadiz was bungled, and so were attempts to supply troops to Christian IV, the Protestant king of Denmark - in 1628 penniless soldiers 'out of denmark' drifted through Lewes. After Charles became king in 1625, he waged a futile war with France, sending the inept duke of Buckingham with an army to the isle of Rhe, to assist French Protestants under siege in nearby La Rochelle. Beforehand, many recruits from Sussex were billeted in the Lewes area, a chaotic 'general muster' observed by the young John Evelyn at Cliffe. The duke evacuated the isle in November 1627 - with nothing achieved. Instead, 140 of his diseased, disgruntled soldiers limped into Lewes, till bitter local complaint caused the Lord Lieutenant, the fourth earl of Dorset, to remove seventy or so. Destitute Irish seamen also appeared, who claimed that while 'carrying victual to the isle of Rea', they had been captured by 'Dunkirkers' based in the Spanish Netherlands. French privateers, meanwhile, bombarded Hastings and seized a ship at Shoreham harbour. Buckingham, widely reviled for the 'disgrace before La Rochelle', was assassinated at Portsmouth in 1628 - Evelyn was woken to be told the news. To fund its military fiasco, Charles's government imposed local rates and demanded 'loans' and 'free gifts'. But when the JPs, deputy-lieutenants and MPs from Sussex gathered at Lewes in August 1626, they offered a mere £120, for they shared a widespread distrust of 'arbitrary' taxation not authorized by a Parliament.[1]

The defeat of Protestants abroad fuelled fears of Catholic insurgency at home. The recusant Gages at Firle, so it was said, were hiding cartloads of weapons, and building a house near the sea shore - perhaps at Cuckmere haven - for a darker purpose than the storage of fishing nets. Renewed fear of 'Popery' also enflamed distrust of a novel doctrine being preached by some clergy in the Anglican State Church, with the approval of king Charles. Nick-named 'Arminian', after Arminius, a leading Dutch exponent, it was clean contrary to Calvinism, which taught that Salvation was reserved for a pre-ordained 'elect'. Arminian doctrine insisted that God's grace could reach all believers through the sacraments, especially the Holy Communion - a conduit regulated by ordained priests and prelates whose functions Christ himself had instituted. This doctrine of Free Will, reinforced by Sacred Ritual, was denounced by Puritan Calvinists as akin to 'Popery'. John Batnor, rector of Westmeston, bequeathed to a son-in-law in 1624 the living of Clayton which he had 'beggared' himself to buy; but warned him to preach 'the sacred word of God without any fantastical conceit and devilish belching either of Arminianism or any such other heretical and poisoned inventions of man's devising'. (His mother at Lewes had waxed vehement about 'some old rotten and moth eaten lumberment'.) By then the fluidity within the State Church was such that Batnor was followed at Westmeston by a militant Arminian, Thomas Barton. His father-in-law, Walter Dobell, presented him to the living, despite the 'gaming and unthrifty manner of life' he had pursued at Dobell's town-house on School Hill. Turning pamphleteer, Barton defended 'the Holy Mother Our Church' against charges of 'superstitious JESU worship' and attacked Puritan 'Zealots' who 'defy all external bowing at the Name of Jesu'. During the civil war he was congenially employed as chaplain to prince Rupert.[2]

The prospect, turmoil and expense of war caused four Parliaments to be elected between 1621 and 1626. Returned for Lewes at each was Sir George Goring, who rebuilt the family fortune, as his grandfather established it, by service at Court. A 'creature' of Buckingham, he accompanied the duke and prince Charles to Madrid in 1623. The other MPs were closely linked to the Sackvilles: in 1621 their legal adviser, Richard Amherst, was chosen; in 1624 Christopher Nevill; in 1625 and 1626 Sir George Rivers, a barrister from Kent who administered the third earl of Dorset's will. However, during the general election held in 1628, some Boroughs were enflamed by debate about billeting and martial law, 'prerogative' taxes and 'Papist' preaching, such that 'Countrymen' and 'Puritans' were at odds with 'Courtiers' and 'Arminians'. At Lewes, Goring was re-elected, though he was Buckingham's henchman and 'the greatest customs farmer in the land'. But Rivers was unseated by Anthony Stapley, a local landowner with estates at Framfield and Patcham. Perhaps Goring exerted a very personal influence from the family mansion in St Andrew's Lane - servants of his were buried at St

Michael's in 1615 and 1620. His sister, moreover, had married Anthony Stapley. Yet Stapley, who was to sign king Charles's death-warrant in 1649, was closely allied with local Puritans. In 1624 the high Calvinist, John Batnor, chose him to oversee his will, along with Robert Morley of Glynde, and the barrister William Newton, the lover of Banbury cheese. Stapley's tenant at Watergate Corner was Batnor's close friend, Richard Newton, the Borough grocer who sponsored Mary Samboyce's baptism. Stapley, moreover, was helping to fund at Lewes a 'lecturer', a full-time preacher unattached to any parish. Called Anthony Lapthorne, he was seemingly a Puritan, for when he moved to the North his message that sermons were 'the only means to salvation' duly outraged Arminians there.[3]

139 Stapley's town-house: western half

That Stapley, a local Puritan, was in conflict with Rivers, a Kentishman close to an earl of Dorset who was a 'Courtier' and a Lord Lieutenant, seems clear from a petition delivered to Parliament by Stapley's supporters after the election. It claimed that 69 votes for Stapley, and 42 for Rivers, were polled by the High Constables; that 20 other supporters of Rivers persuaded a clergyman, a spectator, to poll their votes separately, which the Constables allowed; and that '17 or 20 gentlemen' decided to 'number themselves' and polled for Rivers. The Stapleyites argued that these 'voices' were invalid and the relevant committee of Parliament agreed. They also accused the Rivers camp of 'foul play' - 'deceitfully' giving out that Stapley 'would not stand and would be sorry to be chosen'; threatening that his supporters would have 'soldiers sent unto them' and would 'smart for it'; and touting for votes when his friends were 'all together, fast', before going to the poll. Clearly his supporters were close-knit, and confident enough to suggest that the Lord Lieutenant might countenance punitive billeting. They were also happy to be polled by Constable Gerson Bailey shoemaker and Constable Henry Godman dyer, whereas many 'gentlemen' clearly were not. In another context, the barrister, Richard Amherst, remarked how 'irksome' it was for 'a gentleman to be abused by a clown'. Possibly, similar tensions had surfaced during the debates between the Twelve and the Twenty Four at Midsummer 1605. And perhaps there was a doctrinal dimension. Relatives of Bailey and Godman worshipped as Puritan Independents in the 1650s, whereas some 'gentlemen' in 1628 doubtless embraced Arminianism, with its emphasis on Authority and Deference, sacramental grace and priestly hierarchy, bowing the head and bending the knee. Sadly the petition is silent on the number and conduct of Goring's supporters. How did they cast their second vote? Did some boycott the Constables as returning-officers? Clearly, though, the electorate was broad-based, composed perhaps of all male householders paying the parish poor rate.[4]

Maybe the Rivers campaign was hampered by some decline in the local prestige of the Sackvilles, resulting from massive sales of property in mid Sussex, forced on the family by the profligacy of the deceased third earl - a portrait by William Larkin shows him bedecked with pompons, pearls and fine lace. When the earl visited the Lord's Place in 1619, his wife noted the 'great play between my lord of Hunsdon, my lady of Effingham and my lord who lost them £200'. The *Swan*, the *Chequer* and other premises at Southover were sold. John Vinall of Kingston bought Carter's Wish near the Rise. In Westout the Horse Croft, the Hides and pastures at Winterbourne passed to Richard Amherst, in lieu of legal fees. Sir Thomas Springett snapped up Southease manor, John Stansfield the Malling Deanery estate and the manor of Preston Beckelwin. The Sackvilles' own factotum, Thomas Trayton II, paid £600 for Chalvington manor. In 1624 the earl's widow, Anne Clifford, received a life-interest in the Lord's Place. But neither she nor her brother-in-law, the fourth earl, used it much, though Henry, the lunatic uncle, was buried at Southover in 1635. Anne's rich son-in-law, John Tufton, earl of Thanet, bought the reversion of her life-interest in 1637. Abraham Nicholls of Southover, an old retainer who oversaw the provisions at the Place in 1619, left his daughter £21, some silver spoons and a feather bed in 1638 - but no more, because the earl of Dorset had promised her 'the next place' at Sackville College in East Grinstead.[5]

Because it denounced 'prerogative' taxes, 'arbitrary' imprisonment and 'Papist' preachers, the Parliament elected in 1628 was dissolved in 1629 by Charles I, who then embarked on eleven years of 'personal rule', which included a thoroughly Arminian reform of the State Church directed by archbishop Laud. Central to this was the new reverence paid to the Communion table. Instead of languishing in the nave for use during a 'Lord's Supper', it was to be always at the east end of the chancel and protected by a rail - to ensure a seemly setting for a 'spiritual' sacrifice of Christ's atoning body and blood. Accordingly, in July 1635, churchwardens from the Peculiar of South Malling gathered in Cliffe church to hear Sir Nathaniel Brent, the archbishop's special envoy, praise

140 The spendthrift third earl

the 'very comely and decent' rail installed there by the rector, Anthony Huggett, a seasoned conformist who in 1615 had preached at Paul's Cross in London on the duty of 'true obedience'. Elsewhere reform was often more slothful or grudging. Indeed at St Michael's, after the bishop's Chancellor himself supervised the table's re-positioning 'north-south' at the east end, and warned that 'no man should presume to alter' it, a churchwarden, John Parmeley, moved it back. Though he was pardoned - the parish paying seven shillings for his 'absolution' - he was later indicted at the Church court for pre-marital sex. The incumbent, George Bunyard, himself had Puritan leanings: prone to extempore prayer, he was reluctant to bow at the blessed name of Jesus. But merely eccentric perhaps was Widow Devereux in St John's: scorning the eucharistic wafer as 'dry bread', she ate a piece of cheese with it.[6]

Besides its exemplary altar-rail,

Cliffe parish acquired other Arminian accessories in the 1630s: a font-cover, various 'screens' and 'crosses', a surplice of 'fine holland' (£3 4s) and a sheet under which Margaret James 'did penance'. And maybe the 'Painter', paid £4 14s in 1624 for 'stuff and work', had been the 'Mr Bugg of Lewes' paid thirty shillings in 1633 for painting a children's gallery, a font-canopy and 'scutcheons' - the royal arms perhaps - in Cuckfield church where the Laudian, bishop Richard Montagu, was patron. A William Bugge, a 'painter stainer', lived at Westout in 1632 and forfeited an alehouse licence at Cliffe in 1653 because of 'great misdemeanours' - doubtless the same 'Bugg' who painted a royal arms and a Ten Commandments there after the Restoration.[7]

Cliffites hostile to Huggett's Arminian novelties were duly indicted in the Church court of the Peculiar; William Pemell for keeping his hat on 'when the Creed, the Epistle and Gospel were read and the name of Jesus mentioned and during the communion'; Thomas Goldham, Simon Everenden and his mother-in-law, the widow of Henry Hale, for boy-cotting services and keeping their children and apprentices from cate-chism classes; Thomas Prior for 'unfitting speeches' during the classes. At a court session held in the *Red Lion*, John Cheale averred that if Huggett's 'tongue was out of his head, all the land would be the better for it'. Simon Everenden, a man of substance, supplied his brother at Sedlescombe with sugar, licorice and pepper, starch, prunes and spices; he shipped salt, sea-coal and groceries from London, and sent iron, ox bones and glovers' clippings to Dieppe. Linked to these dissidents was an earlier Puritan stalwart at Cliffe. John Stansfield, had died in his 76th year in 1628, expressing his faith in the 'only merits' of an 'all sufficient Saviour', and leaving £20 to 'honest preaching ministers' in Sussex, with a wife and children but 'no preferment or certainty of living'. In 1627 he had given £20 to support 'young beginners or aged tradesmen' at Cliffe and the six trustees he chose included Henry Hale, John Cheale, Richard Prior - father perhaps of the doubting Thomas - and John Adams, a glover who also invoked the 'only merits' of Christ. Thomas Goldham and Simon Everenden joined the trust in 1635. Clearly it was a Puritan bastion.[8]

Moreover, when Stansfield bought the rectory and tithes of Malling from the Sackville estate in 1623 and instituted an annuity of £20 to fund 'a fit and honest preaching minister' there, among the trustees he selected were Robert Morley and Anthony Stapley, already noted as the executors of John Batnor, a bitter foe of Arminians. After consulting 'the principal sort or greatest number' of the parishioners, the trustees chose as the curate, Mascall Giles, who later penned the Puritan pamphlets denounc-ing 'superstitious JESU worship' which the Arminian, Thomas Barton, strove to refute. Stansfield also promoted the rebuilding of Malling church 'upon the ancient foundation'. Its graveyard was still in use - indeed the headstone of Mrs Margaret Cheale, interred in 1610, survives. Though 8s 9d was collected at Cuckfield for the 're-edificing', some Malling folk - doubtless the 'ungodly' - balked at paying a parish rate. Apart from a small west tower and a porch with slight Classical detail dated 1628, the church formed a single space ideal for 'fit and honest' preaching, chastely lit by a large east window, reinforced with mullions and transoms. Stansfield's grandson, John Evelyn, laid 'one of the first stones' and his widow, Jane, later gave the parish a deep, unadorned, slightly bell-shaped communion cup of silver with a round stem. Ecclesiastical protocol delayed the consecration till May 1632.[9]

141 The re-edified church: the porch and the large east window

By then widow Jane had married Stansfield's executor, the widowed barrister, William Newton, and John Evelyn was living with them [at the Grange]. After he left for Balliol College in 1637, in what she deemed 'loose and declining times', Jane conveyed to him in a letter Newton's verdict on the Arminian clergy now entrenched at Oxford - 'as it was once said they had wooden chalices but golden ministers anciently, but now they have wooden ministers but golden chalices, so it may be said of your university, that you have glorious buildings and outsides far beyond those of old, but not such sound scholars as heretofore'. Jane added for good measure: 'If popery and altars increase among you, I doubt not but you will be courteous and sacrifice many knees, but nothing in god's worship is allowable which has not god's word to warrant it. All the glory of your university, take your crucifixes, altars, images, organs and what else you have, is nothing to the glory of the Temple of Jerusalem'. Newton himself wrote later: 'Care not for flaunting preachers, but resort to such plain teachers where the hope of grace may be wrought in one's heart. One drop of sanctified grace is worth all the world'. Yet, despite these admonitions, Evelyn embraced Arminianism.[10]

142 The pulpit Springett paid for

Another local Puritan, Sir Thomas Springett, died in 1639 confident that at the Day of Judgment his 'immortal and glorious body' would be 'clothed with the righteousness of his Saviour'. A Puritan too was his brother Harbert, who died of consumption in 1622. As already noted, the £100 he left to St Mary Westout was partly spent on the pulpit adorned with lions' heads still in situ there. His son William married Mary Proude and years later, when a Quaker matron, she recalled that, despite 'the dim light of that day', her father-in-law had been zealous against popery and usury, sober in discourse, constant in 'the exercise of holy duties'. Harbert's widow, Katherine, removed to Kent and achieved fame as a healer, intrepidly 'taking off cataracts and spots, burns and desperate cuts', 'taking out bones', concocting salves, balsams and syrups, purges, pills and lozenges. William she sent to Cambridge, 'more sober than Oxford', to Katherine's Hall, a Puritan college. His corpse passed through Lewes in 1644, on an ammunition wagon.[11]

Typically, Sir Thomas Springett mingled Puritanism with a sharp distrust of 'prerogative' action. Though a trained-band captain, he would not pay when the government imposed a tax on Sussex to fund 72 barrels of gunpowder deployed in the county. Also considered damaging to consumers, as well as legally dubious, were monopolies of commerce or production created by royal decree. People at Lewes and Rye, for example, complained in 1639 that their salt, now manufactured only in Scotland and South Shields, was much inferior to that previously brought from the Bay of Biscay. But of especial concern, as the period of 'personal rule' lengthened, was Ship Money. The lawyer, John Rowe, fondly hoped that an initial levy on Sussex in 1634 would foster an English 'dominion' of the seas, by paying for a royal navy able to destroy 'Dunkirkers' and other privateers in the Channel. Less trusting, in November 1635, were the churchwardens at St Michael's who paid ten shillings for 'counsel about the tax for ships'. However, a fourth annual levy was apportioned by the county's elite meeting at the *Bull* in 1637 and collected without much difficulty. But a crisis deepened in 1639 - though John Rowe and 19 townsmen still found time to secure John Standing a licence to sell beer at his house 'in the Castle' near the bowling-green. Opposition to a sixth levy now mingled with dismay at the king's persistent Arminian agenda - and at his quarrel with militant Scottish Calvinists. Indeed at Lewes in 1639, Anthony Stapley, the Puritan chairman of the bench, opened the Michaelmas quarter sessions by declaring that 'the altering of the communion table altar wise was an innovation detracting from God's glory'.[12]

The ritual of the State Church was no more the business of JPs than 'the tax for ships' was of churchwardens, but demarcations were breaking down. In January 1640 Edward Burton, a parson at Westham and himself a JP, warned Laud's chaplain that Anthony Stapley, John Baker of Mayfield, Herbert Hay of Glyndebourne and James Rivers of Hamsey formed a Puritan clique dominating the Lewes bench - men 'steered rather by humor and faction than justice'. He also warned that Lewes itself was so 'tainted' that Stapley and James Rivers were likely to be returned there at the impending election, even though the earl of Dorset and baron Goring [Sir George was ennobled in 1632] were lobbying for their 'creatures' - men partial, presumably, to altar rails and 'personal rule'. And so, the parson concluded, if the new Parliament proved as Puritan as were Stapley and Rivers, 'Lord have mercy upon our Church'. But the Lewes scene was blacker still, for Burton failed to mention Sir Thomas Pelham, a Puritan JP who spent Christmas with Stapley and Rivers and gave silver salt cellars to their wives. Indeed both men were in his coach, driving with him to divine service at Laughton in August 1633, when it was fired on by a disgruntled neighbour, Thomas Lunsford 'gent'. Though convicted of assault, Lunsford was pardoned in time for the king to make him governor of the Tower in December 1641; during the civil war hostile verses portrayed him as a child-eater.[13]

As Burton predicted, this Puritan 'faction' triumphed in March 1640 at an election reluctantly called by a king faced with Calvinistic Covenanters poised to invade England. Pelham and Stapley were returned for the county of Sussex: their joint bill for the 'treating' of freeholders who converged on Lewes to vote came to £130. Stapley was also returned for Lewes, with James Rivers,

I'le helpe to kill, to pillage and destroy
All the Opposers of the Prelacy.
My Fortunes are growne small, my Freinds are leß
I'le venter therefore life to have redreß
By picking, stealing, or by cutting throates.

143 Lunsford the evil Cavalier

but stood down. Whereupon Herbert Morley, a steadfast Puritan and hater of Popery, was chosen. Educated at Southover grammar school and Emmanuel College Cambridge, he inherited the Glynde estate in 1632 while still a minor, and his Puritan father, Robert, the friend of Batnor and Stansfield, had selected Pelham and Stapley as his guardians. King Charles swiftly dissolved what proved a 'fractious' Parliament, but was obliged to call another election in October 1640 when the Covenanters invaded England. Rivers and Morley were again returned for Lewes, and Pelham and Stapley for Sussex, their bill at Lewes being £193. When Rivers died of plague at London in June 1641, Henry Shelley, a local JP and a friend of Pelham, replaced him. He was leasing demesne lands at Southover in 1650, as his father had done in the 1630s.[14]

Clearly no longer in Sussex or in Lewes did an alliance between the Crown, the 'Courtier' aristocracy and the State Church inspire the trust on which the stability achieved under Elizabeth had depended. Moreover, that the members of the Twelve in 1640 mostly remained in office during the turmoil of civil war and its aftermath, suggests that the Borough's ruling elite was already committed to a Puritan agenda. Some members were long established - Edward Fitzherbert merchant, Thomas Oliver doyen of the drink trade, George Segar scrivener, Richard Kidder wheelwright. Newer recruits included William Claggett haberdasher, John Aylwin attorney, Richard Burdett grocer, Peter Pemell mercer, Edward Holmwood draper, Joseph Bailey shoemaker and William Peake merchant. As for Henry Godman dyer, William Dodson goldsmith, and Richard Newton grocer, who died during the war, Godman's son and Dodson's grandson both became Independent pastors, and Newton's widow survived to worship as a Presbyterian. As for local Monarchists, even the names of the 'creatures' sponsored in March 1640 by Dorset and Goring are unknown. But maybe a modest purge of the Twelve did mar the stately rotation of civic office. In July 1641 the Lewes bench of JPs ordered Henry Rose saddler and Richard Snatt, chosen as High Constables in October 1639, to hand over to their successors £5 14s of rate money 'unjustly detained'. Neither held office again. Of Rose's sons, Samuel was suspected in 1655 of being a papist and a royalist agent, and Henry was elected to the Twelve in 1663 as a sop to resurgent Cavaliers.[15]

The Long Parliament elected in October 1640 rapidly removed Laud's Arminian innovations, along with Church courts, and in February 1641 the churchwardens at St Michael's duly paid Robert Standin to pull down its altar rails. Moreover monopolies, Ship Money and other pre-rogative levies were declared illegal. But politics entered uncharted waters once the killing of Protestant settlers by rebellious Catholics in Ireland pushed fear of Popery to fever pitch. In February 1642 a petition from 'the gentry' of Sussex applauded the House of Commons for defending their 'consciences and livelihoods' from 'the violent cruelties' of the prelates and their courts, but also urged that English Catholics be disarmed and policed. Large collections for refugee Irish Protestants were made in the county. Yet at Westminster the Commons faced ugly dilemmas. Should Crown or Parliament control the army needed to pacify Ireland? Should bishops be abolished and the State Church reformed on Presbyterian lines? Or were 'riots' by Puritan apprentices in London a sign that reform had gone far enough? These dilemmas were unresolved and the nation drifted into civil war. In May 1642 the militia trained-bands in Sussex were mustered for the Puritan majority in Parliament by the Lord Lieutenant, the earl of Northumberland. His most active deputies were Sir Thomas Pelham, Anthony Stapley and Herbert Morley. The Puritan clique of eastern JPs now wielded military as well as political power, and would soon control a bureaucracy improvised to administer a county at war.[16]

At Lewes the High Constables presided over an expanding arsenal. In October 1639 they accounted for '5 halberds, 2 drums, one ensign, 15 barrels of powder, 9 sows of lead' - all stored it seems in the town-house. By October 1642 five pipes and one hogshead of 'match' had been added, also six 'great' ordnance - including two from Newhaven and two from Brighton. By October 1644 their inventory also listed bullets for musket and carbine, shot for various sizes of cannon, 32 soldiers' coats, 34 muskets and fowling pieces, 'certain old arms and many new arms'. Early on, Parliament's control of Sussex was reinforced when London's militia men suppressed royalists in Kent. But in November 1642, after an indecisive battle at Edgehill, as the king advanced on the capital, Edward Ford of Uppark was able to occupy Chichester, abetted by 'gentlemen' and clergy within its walls. Fearing Ford would advance eastward, Parliament alerted Herbert Morley to authorize Ambrose Trayton - the son of the Sackville factotum - to recruit 200 men for the defence of Lewes. In early December Ford and the earl of Thanet did indeed advance, hoping to seize and fortify the Lord's Place, the earl's sprawling mansion at Southover. Morley, however, 'a man of nimble apprehension and vigilant spirit', rushed down with troops from London and repelled the royalists at Haywards Heath. He then united outside Chichester with a force led by Sir William Waller, the city surrendering after artillery fire laid waste the extra-mural suburb of St Pancras. Anthony Stapley became its 'governor'; the cathedral plate and vestments were seized, and the estates of local 'rebels', alias 'delinquents', became subject to fines or forfeiture.[17]

Military control of Sussex by the Puritan faction focused at Lewes was also reinforced. Stapley now commanded a regiment of foot and Morley headed eighty horsemen and 100 dragoons. This 'small but efficiently managed' army, raised in the county, was quite separate from the militia. Morley, though, was a moody if 'nimble' commander, waxing furious when at West Hoathly fair his recruiting sergeant was punched and a drum-head punctured. After leading his men into Oxfordshire, he resigned because no attempt was made to rescue a dozen of them captured by prince Rupert. But he bounced back in December 1643 when royalists surprised and captured Arundel castle. They planned a new thrust towards Lewes, part of a general assault on London and the South-East. Known by then as 'the crooked rebel of Sussex', Morley deployed its 'eastern' militia men to guard the bridges across the Adur. The royalists were duly beaten back at Bramber, John Coulton from Rye rejoicing that they were 'welcomed with drakes and muskets, sending some eight or nine to Hell (I fear) and one of Captain Everenden's dragoons to heaven'. On 20 December General Waller, with troops from Hampshire, reached Arundel. Morley joined him and the castle swiftly surrendered. Grateful Lewesians presented the General with £50 and pealed their bells. Again John Coulton exulted: 'heaven begins to be gracious, the Lord awakes as a man from his wine'. (Local Puritans also identified the hand of God during 'a sad accident' at Lewes on Sunday, 16 April 1648. Some children, not at church to hear God's Word, 'pleased their foolish fancy' by playing with lighted coal-brands, setting fire to their house, and to others near by, 'the most profane in all the town'. One house, however, 'very famous for religion', escaped unscathed. Sadly the licentious locality was not divulged.)[18]

144 The monument

Sharing with Morley command of the captured castle at Arundel was Sir William Springett, whose father paid for the pulpit at Westout, and whose mother was famed for her surgery and lozenges. A passionate Puritan, when leading his Kentish regiment he never failed to slash 'superstitious' pictures with his sword. Wounded at Newbury he convalesced on 'candied green citron and biscuit'. But at Arundel he contracted a fatal fever and like Falstaff began to 'babble of green fields'. His wife Mary travelled post-haste through deep snow from London, though pregnant with Gulielma Maria Posthuma, the future bride of William Penn. She found Springett lucid and was greeted with sublime if stark Assurance: 'Let me embrace thee before I die; I am going to thy God'. On 3 February 1644 his officers laid his corpse on an ammunition wagon and escorted it to burial at Ringmer, where his cousins owned property. Doubtless godly Lewesians crowded to watch, and pray, as the Puritan cortege descended their High Street. And maybe widow Mary influenced the austerity of his mural monument: the sombre bust, the gauntlets, the helmet. His distaste for Popish pictures was shared by Herbert Morley who in 1644 misread Geralde de la Valle's *The betrothal of saint Ursula*: 'On the Pope's right hand stands the Queen [Henrietta Maria]; the King tenders his sceptre to the Queen, she accepts it not, but directs it to be delivered to the Pope. I look upon this picture as an hieroglyphic of the causes of our present troubles'.[19]

By June 1644 Morley had moved his troops to assist at the siege of Basing House in Hampshire, quartering his 'pikes and muskets' in the park. Briefly left in sole command, he thrust trenches to within a pistol shot of the immense half-shattered mansion and called on its owner, the Catholic marquis of Winchester, to surrender - only to receive a patrician response: 'It is a crooked demand, and shall receive its answer suitable; I keep the house in the right of my Sovereign, and will do it in despite of your Forces; your Letter I will preserve as a testimony of your Rebellion'. Morley resumed the assault and a bullet struck his shoulder, 'spoiling his clerkship' for ever. But the siege was abandoned when troops from Oxford led by Henry Gage drew near. During the retreat a colour flag, believed to be Morley's, was left behind, bearing what the marquis might have deemed a 'crooked' motto: *Non ab Aequo sed in Aequo* - [Victory] is not by Right, but in Right.[20]

The colour flag (*Andy Gammon*)

In January 1645 Morley and Stapley were stationed near the Hampshire border to block any advance by George Goring junior. But being repulsed at Christchurch, he chose to recoup at Salisbury till the spring. Meanwhile, his father, the Borough's former MP, now earl of Norwich, had pawned the queen's jewels in France. In March 1645 the civil war entered a decisive phase when Parliament required Sussex to supply 600 men, 'able, fully armed, and clothed in red coats faced with blue', for a New Model Army. In June the king's Midland forces were destroyed at Naseby. In October Oliver Cromwell stormed Basing House: 'We have had little loss; most of the enemy our men put to the sword, and some officers of quality'. Thereafter only a few royalist privateers in the Channel could menace Puritan Sussex, though George Goring junior, now in Paris, schemed to land French troops at Newhaven. In May 1646 the king 'surrendered' to the Scots, hoping to play them off against the English Parliament.[21]

By then the demands of civil war had created a new bureaucracy in Sussex. Parliament authorized a County Committee which met at Lewes. It recruited soldiers, mustered the county militia and defended the coast; it apportioned and collected a new monthly assessment, and managed the estates of 'delinquent' royalists, mostly in western Sussex; it collaborated with Committees in Surrey and Kent. Dominated by Sir Thomas

Pelham and Herbert Morley, it delegated routine work to sub-committees packed with Puritans. That for Lewes and Pevensey rapes included the aged barrister, William Newton, and Herbert Hay of Glyndebourne. Some of the Twelve were also cogs in this new machine - John Aylwin served as a treasurer for the assessment in 1644, Walter Brett grocer as a 'high collector' in 1647, Richard Burdett as a receiver in 1657. William Claggett managed 'delinquent' estates in 1650. Other members lent money to Parliament, expecting a share in lands yet to be confiscated from Ireland's Catholic 'rebels'; William Lane had committed a 'great sum' by 1644; decades later, Richard Barnard draper and Richard Russell apothecary bequeathed lands 'in Ireland'.[22]

Henshaw

Despite being the meeting-place of the County Committee, Lewes borough did not advance as a focus of routine shire government, though it still hosted the quarter sessions for the eastern division. Only once did the town welcome the assizes, in September 1644, when there was a heavy backlog of interrupted business. And the county gaol remained at Horsham, though in 1636 'western' JPs had deemed a location at Lewes 'the fittest place for the whole county'. When a gaoler - a drunken innkeeper accused of extortion, black magic and the brutal chaining of debtors - was dismissed in 1647 for refusing the sheriff entry, the under-sheriff was Thomas Henshaw, a trustee of Blunt's Charity, whose father owned the *Star*, where Thomas's clerk, Joseph Pellatt, died of smallpox in 1652.[23]

A bureaucratic void, of course, was created when Parliament abolished prelates and archdeacons, Church courts and their officials. These no longer disciplined the clergy, administered probate, resolved tithe disputes, licensed schoolmasters, medical men and midwives, or punished loose livers and profaners of the Sabbath. Robert Fell had been censured for baking bread at Lewes, Francis Verrall for working his water-mill at Southover, a butcher at Laughton for killing 'a porker' to sell at Selmeston fair on the Monday. The JPs on the Lewes bench now dealt with loose livers, though adultery was referred to the assizes. They also saw to the repair of churches and graveyards, and promoted sobriety. They banned a fair at Fletching and a 'church ale' at Hartfield. They joined with the Twelve to police alehouses, quashing the licence of a landlord who refused to lodge 'strangers'. But it fell to the County Committee to eject from his living any minister deemed guilty of political or moral 'delinquency'. Edward Burton at Westham was condemned as a 'smiter of Presbyterians' [godly Puritans], and Christopher Swale at Hurstpierpoint, a fellow JP, for preaching rank Passive Obedience, that 'subjects must bear what ever their sovereign please to lay upon them, though to the death'. Anthony Huggett, of course, was ejected from Cliffe. Had he not been seen in the royal army? Had he not denied the sacrament to a man too lame to kneel for it? Did he not so cruelly use Mistress Huggett that she miscarried? His delinquent 'screens' and 'crosses' were ejected too, and perhaps some 'idolatrous' stained-glass, for nearly £2 were spent mending the church windows and leads. When Richard Tanton was evicted from Ardingly rectory in November 1643, the dragoons involved were dispatched from Lewes by Captain Simon Everenden, the grocer previously cited in the Peculiar court for boycotting Huggett's services.[24]

More constructive was the Puritans' zeal for a well-funded preaching ministry, for the uniting and better endowment of benefices. Once death, rather than 'delinquency', had emptied the rectories of Southover and St Mary Westout, the livings were merged and the stipend boosted by £60 a year from the defunct cathedral at Chichester. In June 1646 the benefice was awarded to Benjamin Pickering, 'a godly, learned and orthodox divine', who transferred from East Hoathly, the home parish of Sir Thomas Pelham. Besides releasing funds, the dismantling of the Anglican hierarchy in 1643 provoked debate on the structure of a new State Church. With Pelham's backing, Pickering had joined other leading Puritan divines at Westminster to advise Parliament on this - a Presbyterian model being the preferred option. In 1644 he assured MPs they were 'engaged in the greatest work that ever lay upon the children of men'; 'the Lord has promised great things'; 'glorious days now hasten concerning his church'. Doubtless his transfer to Lewes, the seat of the County Committee, was carefully contrived. Sometime too, alongside his parochial work, he began ministering to a group of committed Presbyterians. Widow Joan Newton in St Michael's left forty shillings to the poor of his 'society' in 1657.[25]

Pressure for a Presbyterian State Church - ruled by ministers and elders answerable to synods - had increased once Parliament entered into a Solemn League and Covenant with the Calvinists now dominant in Scotland. It pledged both sides to set up a uniform State Church in England, Scotland and Ireland, shaped 'according to the Word of God, and the example of the best reformed churches'- which the Scots believed to be their own. In March 1644 the Covenant was signed by 54 parishioners at Newhaven; in September the churchwardens at Cliffe paid for its 'writing'. The Covenant also required an end to 'popery' and 'prelacy' - a war-aim justified perhaps to many Lewesians by the refugees they observed: the widower whose wife and five children 'had been slain and burnt by the rebels in Ireland'; the widow with four children from a village near York 'burnt to the ground' by Sir Thomas Glemham.[26]

By May 1646 however, when the king surrendered to the Scots, a victorious New Model Army was forming its own priorities. Its soldiers feared any resurgence of royal authority. And many had become Independents, believing that autonomous congregations of the 'elect' were the building blocks of organized religion, and that a State Church should embrace all 'godly' worship - though not, of course, 'prelacy' and 'popery'. But 'Toleration' was anathema to Scottish Presbyterians, and many Puritan MPs feared it would be socially subversive. They wanted a rigidly Presbyterian State Church, but less controlled by ministers and synods than Scotland's was. These cross-currents caused two years of sterile negotiation by the king, the Scots, the Parliament and the Army. Indeed in May 1648 popular discontent prompted the drawing up, 'at Lewes', of a petition from 'the knights, gentry, clergy and common-wealth' of Sussex. Lamenting 'the miserable effects of the Civil war', it wistfully asked for 'a safe and well-grounded peace, both in Church and Commonwealth', which would respect 'the just rights' of King and Parliament and 'the known laws of this Realm', and would allow the Army to be disbanded 'with all expedition', its arrears paid. These ano-dyne sentiments drew wide support; all 40 adult males at Malling signed, except John Scotson who was 'not at home'.[27]

Political realities were less tractable. The king, though now in Parliament's custody, was flirting dangerously with the Scots, hoping to exploit their hatred of English Independents whose power base was the New Model Army. Indeed he tempted a Scottish army to cross the Border, which Cromwell crushed at Preston in August 1648. Royalist uprisings occurred in Kent and Essex. And after a 'tumult' at Horsham,

145 The earl of Norwich by Van Dyck

its Puritan minister took refuge at Lewes where 'the well affected' were gathered. General Fairfax swiftly subdued Kent and captured Colchester after a stubborn siege. Its commander, George Goring senior, the earl of Norwich, was sentenced to death, but reprieved. His king was less fortunate. Their repeated victories had convinced Independents and radical Presbyterians, in the Army and in Parliament, that God desired his destruction. A petition to Fairfax from Puritan Rye, a garrison town, wanted those fomenting war to be punished. Suitably buoyed up, the Army leaders acted. Colonel Pride purged Parliament of 'moderate' Presbyterians like Sir Thomas Pelham. Henry Shelley withdrew voluntarily. The MPs remaining, the 'Rump' Parliament, authorized the king's trial and sanctioned his execution in January 1649.[28]

Anthony Stapley and Herbert Morley sat among his judges. Stapley also signed the death warrant, but Morley, guided perhaps by prudence, did not. Yet in the republican Commonwealth, ordained by the Rump, both served as Councillors of State, occupying furnished lodgings at Whitehall. Adept at managing Parliamentary business, Morley secured naval protection for Sussex fishermen when war broke out with the Dutch, though there was alarm at Lewes in August 1652 when Admiral De Ruyter cruised off Brighton with '80 sail'. And Richard Lawson of Westout, 'pressed from the town', left a widow and three small children when he was killed on board the *Little Charity*. In mid Sussex itself many Puritans were willing to serve a republican Commonwealth. Though Pelham withdrew from public life, Shelley remained on the Lewes bench, being joined by William Morley and the lawyers Thomas Springett and William Spence. Morley was Herbert's brother, and governor of Arundel when a fugitive Charles Stuart, glimpsing him in October 1651, 'did not much like his starched mouchates'.

Springett bought the family mansion in St Michael's [Newcastle House] from his elder brother Harbert. Usefully, he secured a reduction in the monthly assessment levied on Lewes borough and Southover, and died in 1652, leaving a silver watch and a lease of Plumpton 'parsonage' to John Vine, the Puritan minister there. William Spence, a native of Balcombe, resided at Malling by 1656, on land bought from Thomas Lucas - the nucleus of the Malling House estate. But already in April 1653 he gave £10 to St Michael's parish 'to set the poor to work'. A memorial brass at Malling described him as 'an ornament to his country, a patron of letters, a support to the poor'.

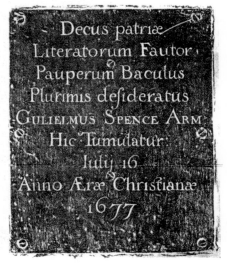

146 The memorial brass

Serving the county as Treasurer for Maimed Soldiers in 1652-3 was William Newton, the son of John Evelyn's Puritan mentor, and his executor in 1658 was a Puritan JP, his cousin Edward Polhill of Burwash. Moreover, despite Sir Thomas Pelham's withdrawal from public life, his son John gave £4 and a mourning cloak to Benjamin Pickering when that Presbyterian stalwart delivered a 'solemn panegyric' at Thomas's lavish funeral in 1654.[29]

While local republicans flourished, the aristocratic mainstays of royalism collapsed. With cold decorum, on 21 December 1648, just before the king's trial, the earl of Dorset, a joint Lord of Lewes, advised the 'Noble Gentlemen', Herbert Morley, Anthony Stapley and Henry Shelley, that the Borough's corn market should remain in its 'ancient place', reminding them, surely sardonically, that he - a defeated Cavalier - was 'altogether against Innovations'. The earl of Thanet never turned the Lord's Place into a second Basing House, but as a 'delinquent' peer he was heavily fined. The earl of Norwich, after escaping execution at Colchester, sold his mansion in St Andrew's Lane to pay his debts. The purchaser, Peter Courthope, a Puritan ironmaster from Kent, re-sold it to Sir Thomas Pelham who left it as a dower-house to Margaret, his 'very loving' third wife, in 1654, along with £1000 in cash, abundant plate and a coach with six horses. Her brother, Sir Henry Vane, a deep-dyed republican, was executed after the Restoration.[30]

Independents in particular were at ease with a republican Commonwealth, for their congregations were self-governing and 'tolerated' diversity in worship and doctrine. At Lewes Walter Postlethwaite became their chief pastor. He arrived at St Michael's in 1647, fresh from Emmanuel, Herbert Morley's old College, and married the widow of George Bunyard, its former minister - her assets included a 'whole *Book of Martyrs*'. His stipend was boosted by £32 a year from confiscated cathedral revenues and the living was later united with St John's. In April 1649 Mary Hills came from Southover to a service at St Michael's, a sign that people were over-spilling from their parish in search of sermons - though she marred the occasion by stealing a 'taffety sarsenet' scarf from a nearby pew. A year later Postlethwaite was also ministering separately to Independents, for Margaret Jorden left money 'to the church of Christ in Lewes whereof I am a poor member' and to Postlethwaite its 'pastor'. Doubtless his sermons were enlivened by his millenarian views: as a Fifth Monarchist he believed that 'the saints', the elect of God, were locked in a final struggle with 'Anti-Christ' - a coalition which included papists and royalists - and that victory would usher in the Great Day of Judgement. By 1650 Postlethwaite's St Michael's had no use for elaborate Communion plate and disposed of two silver bowls and four pewter flagons. The royal arms were also 'put out' at two places in the church.[31]

Three townsmen, Simon Everenden grocer, Thomas Fissenden apothecary and Edward Bailey shoemaker, who served as Captains in

Herbert Morley's regiment during the siege of Basing House, became Independents, so doubtless his 'small provincial army' had proved a seed bed for the sect - much as the New Model Army did. The daughter of Simon Everenden married Henry Godman an Independent pastor. Fissenden was recalled to the colours by Morley to lead a militia troop of horse in 1659. And in April 1661, after the Restoration, 'Captain' Bailey was defiantly chosen a churchwarden at St Michael's by its Puritan parishioners. Also from Lewes was the regiment's surgeon, Peter Ray, awarded a county pension in 1659. Moreover, the regimental chaplain, 'Mr Osborne', was perhaps 'Mr William Osborne', the Puritan preacher buried at St Michael's in January 1657, and the latter maybe was the 'lecturer' in the town whose sermons Committee men sometimes tasted - a William Osborne had entered Exeter College Oxford in 1640. Though Lewes was not a garrison town like Rye, two soldiers from Captain Elsmor's troop were buried there in February 1658, and Colonel Gibbon's regiment was quartered there in August 1659.[32]

The civil war, and then the Dutch war, stimulated armaments manufacture in the Weald, and presumably Captain Everenden, or his son, Simon II, was the Simon Everenden of Cliffe 'gent', who leased the appurtenances of Woodcock forge near Godstone on the Surrey border in 1652 and also petitioned to export 4800 bushels of malt. A 'Mr Everenden of Lewes' occupied an unidentified forge visited in 1649 by Ellis Wood, a Southover blacksmith, and was asked in August 1653 to supply the government with shot. Though his furnace too was unidentified, it may have been at Pounsley or Maresfield. Earlier, in 1630, Philip Burlamachi, a licensed exporter of 'military' guns, shipped 179 cannon from Newhaven to Rotterdam. Though his official supplier was John Browne, a gunfounder at Horsmonden in Kent, doubtless the cannon were cast locally. Also leasing out an iron forge in 1656, at Cotchford in Hartfield, was a 'Mr Pickering of Lewes' - perhaps the Presbyterian minister who bequeathed land in that parish in 1657.[33]

Some local Independents served the Commonwealth as administrators of 'delinquent' estates. When control was centralized at London in 1650, Thomas Fissenden, George Stonestreat and Jeremy Tompkins, a 'yeoman' of Ringmer, were made commissioners for eastern Sussex, with Thomas Crouch tailor as their agent. Stonestreat died in 1669 at 'Caprons' worth over £900 and owning an eighth of Houndean manor. His brother John, an Independent pastor, was ejected from Lindfield rectory in 1662 after the Restoration. That year too Crouch's nephew John cut short his studies at Magdalen College Oxford rather than conform to a reinstated Anglican Church. In 1673 he preached to Independents illegally gathered in Fissenden's barn near the *Star* - Jeremy Tompkins was among them. In 1670 Fissenden and John Crouch had also witnessed the will of William Alcock, whose assets included Old Malling farm and the Friars estate. As Clerk of the Peace for Sussex he accounted between December 1650 and September 1660 for monthly assessments totalling £253,167. That he was an Independent seems likely. His tenure of the Clerkship ended soon after the Restoration.[34]

From the mid-1640s, there was also a steady recruitment into the Twelve of men who clung to Independency after the Restoration. Richard Russell apothecary and Edward Homewood draper were joined by Stephen Botting baker, Nicholas Curle haberdasher, Robert Swan barber-surgeon, Richard Button, Thomas Fissenden, John Lopdell draper, Ralph Pope tanner and George Stonestreat. The only certain Presbyterian recruit was Thomas Mathew butcher, who reinforced Richard Barnard and Walter Brett. The sectarian allegiance of Stephen Snatt, John Savage, Richard Savage and William Peake, is unclear, though all clashed in the 1660s with the restored Anglican State Church.[35]

Doubtless local Independents rejoiced that Pickering and Postlethwaite each ministered to a parish and to a sect, embodying a pluralism within the Puritan State Church that endured till the Restoration. A sect also cohered around Zachery Montague, the incumbent at Cliffe by December 1644 and later at All Saints as well - in 1654 the parishes chose him as their joint registrar. It seems he also served 'a congregational church' in the Cliffe. When Mistress Panton, 'a Gentlewoman of good repute', applied 'to be admitted to the Sacrament', he required a written account of her faith, to 'produce before God's tribunal', if need be. She was probably Mary Panton, an active Independent after the Restoration, when her son John was ejected from a fellowship at All Souls College Oxford - and when pastor Montague conformed to the reinstated Anglican Church.[36]

After pastor Pickering died, in 1657, his Presbyterian son-in-law, Edward Newton, succeeded him at Southover and Westout - a reminder that though Independents were prominent in Morley's regiment, in the republican bureaucracy and the Twelve, Presbyterians probably outnumbered them in the town, to judge from rough estimates made by bishops and informers after the Restoration. In 1669 local Presbyterians were reckoned at 'about 500', and '500 common followers' were counted at an open-air service in Henge Lane below Mount Caburn in 1670. Whereas 'about 150' Independents were gathered at Fissenden's barn in 1673. Whatever the balance, the sects were still formidable, despite official harassment, and doubtless in the 1650s, a time of official favour, 'professing' Presbyterians and Independents, their number swollen by conformists, were a majority of the residents.[37]

By 1660 at least three native Lewesians were ensconced as pastors in the pluralist State Church - John Stonestreat at Lindfield, Henry Godman at Rodmell and Edward Beecher at Kingston. John Brett, moreover, was a fellow of Magdalen College and John Panton of All Souls; also at Oxford as students were John Crouch and William

Staninough. Many, if not all, must have been taught at the grammar school by Edward Snatt. Born in Rotherfield, he succeeded Mr Hallman in 1622, after leaving Emmanuel College, which Herbert Morley and Walter Postlethwaite later attended. One pupil, though, was suffered to be 'extremely remiss' in his studies; indeed John Evelyn moved on to Balliol 'rather out of shame of abiding longer at school, than for any fitness' - having wasted much time 'drawing and designing'. Perhaps Snatt was unusually indulgent to a boy whose father served as sheriff of Sussex and Surrey in 1633, attended by 116 retainers clad in doublets of green satin. Evelyn always kept in touch, sending Snatt a translation of Lucretius in May 1657. And maybe his ex-pupil, Herbert Morley, the powerful Committee man, secured him the living at Firle which he combined with his pedagogic duties. In 1659 he chose to be buried at Glynde, Morley's home parish. Afterwards, in May 1660, Walter Brett was authorized to spend £10 from county funds on 'the new building of the free school'. Benjamin Everenden from Sedlescombe was boarded and schooled in the town in 1647. Also a boarder, quite probably, at the 'Free School', between 1626 and 1631, was Nicholas Culpeper from Isfield. He published a famous Herbal in 1652 - a cheap manual for the layman. As an advanced Puritan, Culpeper believed that priests, apothecaries and lawyers preyed on the purses of ordinary folk.[38]

147 John Evelyn aged 30

As well as a pluralistic State Church, a system of civil registration was in force from August 1653: births and burials were notified to an official charging a standard fee. Burials at Cliffe became possible after a grave-yard was laid out below the chalk rock at North Street - it was 'new' in 1647-8 when the parish bought a lock, a key and a staple for the gate. Even so, Joseph West, a maltster in West Street, chose to be buried at Malling near his child; his corpse-bearers were to receive gloves and rib-bons, and 'the poor', cake and wine. As for civil marriages, due notice had still to be given, some being 'thrice published' in the Borough mar-ket-place. Couples then sought out a JP and exchanged vows of the sim-plest kind. In October 1655 Edward Langridge and Elizabeth Lidloe were united before Herbert Morley at the *Star*.[39]

There is evidence too that the Lewes bench embodied a Puritan belief that crime should be punished more systematically. The town was deemed a sober community by John Taylor in 1653. He found the 'moul-der'd ruins' of a once 'strong and spacious castle', but 'no Beggars, Scolds or Shrews':

For every one there lives in quiet state;
They quarrel not for wagging of a straw,
For each man is to himself a law.
They need no bridle (like the Horse or Mule)
Where every one himself can wisely rule.

The 'bridle', though, became very much the norm at Cliffe House of Correction. In October 1655 its Master, Nicholas Shelley, was required to whip once every month persons committed for one year, 'and at their coming and going out', and every fortnight those detained a shorter time; an 'officer' or 'person of quality' was to ensure this was 'well exe-cuted'. Perhaps an earlier attempt to discipline inmates by physical toil - reminiscent of the rasping of brazil wood at Amsterdam's Bridewell - mis-carried, for the stones of a 'great mill', being 'too great and unservice-able', were sold for fifty shillings in July 1652. The proximity of the House of Correction, moreover, failed to deter John Peckham, a net maker at Cliffe accused in 1651 of grievously assaulting William Storer, in 1658 of receiving a white buck ferret adept at killing rabbits on the Broyle, and in 1665 of stealing a 'cock boat' from William Kempe.[40]

Ironically, a threat to good order emerged from among the 'godly'. William Penn, the Quaker who married Gulielma Maria Posthuma Springett, recalled how a few Puritans, avoiding 'all visible churches and societies', had 'wandered up and down, as sheep without a shepherd, and as doves without their mates; seeking their beloved, but could not find Him'. Some became Baptists, and these mustered a few artisan house-holders at Lewes by 1660. Others, called Seekers, 'waited together in silence, and as anything rose in any one of their minds that they thought savoured of a divine spring, so they sometimes spoke'. A shoemaker, George Fox, shaped this silence into a theology for a new sect, 'the friends'. A Christian in contact with God needed no guide, not even Scripture; he owed no obedience to ministers in 'steeple houses' or magistrates on the bench; tithes were an abomination, also militia taxes, for violence was a sin. In March 1655 three of Fox's itinerant disciples, testifying in Horsham market-place, were stoned as 'madmen'. Soon after, though, one visited a group of Seekers at John Russell's house in Southover and 'convinced' Ambrose Galloway, his wife Elizabeth and Stephen Eager. In August 1655 Fox himself came to Russell's house and a 'Meeting' was established, the first of several in mid Sussex.

The disruptive radicalism of Fox's disciples enraged the orthodox godly, as a 'Book of Suffering' compiled by local Friends made abundantly clear. When a missionary was brought before the Lewes bench in 1655 he accused the Puritan JPs of upholding laws that 'maintained priests and false ways'. When in 1657 a Friend, indicted at Lewes for interrupting a sermon, refused to give sureties and was referred to the House of Correction, a 'Rude Rabble of Professors' [orthodox Puritans] dragged him from the Bar; when a bystander protested at such violence, they tried to toss him over the outer Bar. With some precision the 'Book' also narrates that after Mary Akehurst argued with 'an Independent priest' during divine service at St Michael's - with pastor Postlethwaite presumably - she was shackled by her husband 'in a close back chamber' at Cliffe, 'between two high bedsteads with a great chain much like a timber chain, containing thirty-five links'. Ralph Akehurst clearly was a man of action. Though suspected in 1638 of smuggling wheat down river; he traded legitimately with Dieppe and Calais, Waterford and London. His curbing of Mary caused Ambrose Galloway and two female Friends to post a protest at the market-house. They denounced his conduct as contrary to the laws 'of God and of the Nation' which gave 'every free-born subject' - male and female - 'their liberty'. Radical language indeed. The 'Book' also tells how 'very cruelly and wickedly' townsfolk molested Friends assembled for worship. 'Fire', water, dirt, cow dung and 'squibs of gunpowder' were thrown and windows broken. When they knelt in prayer at the Castle Green, 'the rude people, the sons of some of the Independents', armed with swords, guns and pikes, ran 'violently upon them' - an assault the Borough officers ignored. Well entrenched within the Twelve, the Independents had reason to be angry. Though more 'liberal' than Presbyterians, they feared subversive zeal would discredit the limited Toleration they had achieved.[41]

But though - Friends apart - the pluralistic Puritan State Church achieved some stability, the republican Commonwealth did not. The defeats inflicted by the New Model Army on Irish Catholics at Wexford and Drogheda in 1649, on Scottish Presbyterians at Dunbar in 1650, on Charles Stuart at Worcester in 1651, nurtured in Oliver Cromwell and his senior officers a sense of Divine mission. Indeed in April 1653 they expelled the Rump Parliament, believing its members preferred to cling on to power rather than draft a new Constitution for the Commonwealth. Thereafter, in effect, England, Scotland and Ireland were ruled by the Army. As soldiers victorious in a 'godly' cause they felt answerable only to a Puritan civilian constituency, on which Cromwell, whose authority within the Army was absolute, sought to build a Parliamentary system. To that end, his senior officers selected 140 persons, 'fearing God and of approved fidelity', from lists sent in by Independent congregations, and invited this 'Nominated Parliament' to frame a Constitution. From Sussex came three men closely linked to Lewes - Anthony Stapley, William Spence - already noted for giving £10 in April 1653 to St Michael's parish 'to set the poor to work - and Nathaniel Studley JP, a lawyer from Mayfield, with a residence on School Hill. However, attempts by an ultra-Radical minority to abolish tithes and the Court of Chancery brought the assembly's swift dismissal. Instead Cromwell chose to rule as a Lord Protector, sharing control of taxation and the Army with a Council of State and a Parliament. The parliamentary franchise was vested in males with an estate, real or personal, worth £200, and the seats were redistributed. Royalists and Catholics, of course, were excluded. At a general election in July 1654 nine members for Sussex were chosen at Lewes, among them Herbert Morley, Anthony Stapley and Sir Thomas Pelham. Henry Shelley was returned for Lewes borough, now a single-member seat. But resolute attempts by Morley and others to expand Parliament's allotted powers ensured another swift dissolution. The death of Pelham in August 1654, of Shelley in November, of Stapley in January 1655, rendered the politics of mid-Sussex even more uncertain.[42]

More destabilizing still, after a royalist rising in Wiltshire in March 1655, was the Lord Protector's decision to divide England and Wales into eleven districts, each supervised by a Major-General with powers to reform county militias, disarm suspect royalists and levy a decimation tax of ten per cent on their income from land. Major-General William Goffe, a regicide and 'godly' enthusiast, a veteran of Dunbar and Worcester, whose father had been a 'puritanical' minister at Stanmer, duly arrived at Lewes in November 1655 hoping to 'pacify' Sussex before moving on to Hampshire and Berkshire. He reported 'much good correspondence' when his officers dined with local militiamen (many, in both corps, were probably Independents), and recognized that 'the stress of this business', the policing of royalists, 'must lie upon the middle sort of men', upon radical Puritans of modest property. Nathaniel Studley 'of Lewes', for instance, would be a good militia commissioner, he thought. A courtesy call at Glynde confirmed Herbert Morley's hostility to the regime. But John Stapley, the regicide's eldest son, agreed to 'venture life and estate' for the Lord Protector, and his brother, Anthony, joined him on the Lewes bench. Goffe, a zealous sermon taster, also praised the 'moderation' of pastor Postlethwaite's preaching, though the minister had fears that the Protectorate was too like the Stuart monarchy and that God might jettison the English as his Chosen People, and 'set up the government of Jesus Christ [instead] among the barbarous places', in America or the East Indies. With the Millennium in mind, Goffe also reported that 'the generality of the professions of religion' in Lewes regretted the arrest in London of two prominent Fifth Monarchists whose fanaticism had disturbed the Lord Protector. Perhaps Goffe magnified such local sentiment, yet Joan Newton, a Presbyterian, cautioned her executors in 1657 that they 'must give an account to him that will shortly come to judge both the quick and the dead'.[43]

When Cromwell deemed 'pacification' complete, he called an election and in August 1656 nine members for Sussex were chosen at Lewes 'in the open castle'. Afterwards, Goffe glumly informed the Council of State that 'Colonel [Herbert] Morley ruled the roost, by the help of a disaffected party', pledged to frustrate the election of any 'soldier, decimator, or any man that hath [an official] salary' - 'much to the grief of the honest party'. Again Morley was elected, and again excluded. Those MPs remaining failed to strike a more stable balance between Protector, Parliament and Army before Cromwell's death in September 1658. Meanwhile John Stapley, a member for Sussex, and his brother Anthony, now MP for Lewes borough, - despite their previous protestations to Goffe - dabbled in a fatuous plot to prepare for a landing in Sussex by Charles Stuart. Perhaps their duplicity owed something to their parentage - their father a regicide, their mother a sister of the earl of Norwich. To save their skins, John confessed all to Cromwell in person and pledged to fight against Charles Stuart, 'though it be but in the capacity of a private trooper'. Also in the plot was Thomas Woodcock, a landowner at Newtimber related, most probably, to two brothers called Woodcock who assaulted a Puritan, John Pellet, at the *Bull* in 1657. They had derided the godly for going forth to battle praying 'Lord bless me' and the like, causing Pellet to retort that the Lord of Hosts had allowed the royalists to be 'trampled' by the Protector like 'mire in the street', and that any of them still 'irreconcilable' should be shipped away to work on sugar plantations in the West Indies. Thereupon the Woodcocks threw beer in his face and so battered him that 'two table-napkins were soaked in blood'.[44]

But despite trampling royalists like 'mire in the street', the failure of Puritans to achieve a stable political regime, after Cromwell died, triggered the Restoration of Charles Stuart in 1660. The Protector's death removed the victorious general, the rugged politician, the relentless seeker of scriptural truth, whose massive prestige had sustained an uneasy truce between Army officers and Parliamentarians. Richard, his son and successor as Lord Protector, was merely an amiable civilian. At a general election in January 1659 Herbert Morley was returned for Sussex and for Lewes, but chose the former. The Borough vacancy was filled by Richard Boughton. While a barrister based at Chichester, he administered 'delinquent' estates, becoming a JP in 1649 and a militia colonel-of-horse for the western rapes in 1650. According to Goffe he knew 'as much of the present temper of Sussex as any man that I am acquainted with'. In 1656-7 he briefly owned the *Star* and by 1659 he lived in a spacious residence [Antioch House] beyond the west gate.[45]

Boughton's views on Richard Cromwell are unclear, but Morley was hostile as ever to a 'monarchic' Protectorate. Under pressure from the Army, Richard dissolved Parliament in April 1659, and then abdicated in May. Thereupon an uneasy alliance of Army officers and civilian republicans recalled to Westminster surviving members of the Rump Parliament - Herbert Morley among them. A revamped Commonwealth was set up, with Morley as an elected Councillor of State. In Sussex he recruited John de la Chambre of Rodmell and John Hay of Glyndebourne to the Lewes bench. When royalist conspiracies were rife in July 1659 he placed his brother-in-law, John Fagge of Wiston, in control of the county militia, and gave Thomas Fissenden, the Borough apothecary, command of a troop of horse. (There was also talk that 5000 Fifth Monarchists had assembled for eight hours at Horsham.) But the restored Rump Parliament was soon at loggerheads with the Army. Indeed in October 1659 Morley stood in Palace Yard at Westminster, pistol in hand, in a fruitless bid to stop soldiers sent by General John Lambert from dissolving it. Some republicans then allied with General Monck, the Army commander in Scotland, who opposed this 'interruption'; Morley himself secured a pledge of support for the Parliament from the garrison at Portsmouth. This disintegration of Army unity induced its London-based officers to reinstate the Rump in December 1659 and Morley received the formal thanks of that much-molested assembly.[46]

Morley's republicanism, though, had been shaken. Indeed, in November, John Evelyn had urged him to work for a Restoration, assuring him that Charles Stuart would pardon his past excesses. Evelyn was already a royalist when he crossed 'into France' in 1643 - William Newton doggedly warning him to keep 'religious company', so as not to leap 'out of the dripping or frying pan into the fire'. Nonetheless, Morley, Evelyn's 'old school fellow', had shown him 'many kindnesses' when he returned from a Continental tour in 1652. Moreover in 1655 Evelyn sold him the manor of Preston Bekhelwyn at Beddingham, adjacent to Glynde Place. Yet though Morley was made Lieutenant of the Tower in January 1660, he could not openly support a Restoration. Instead he facilitated Monck's march to London with troops from Scotland and helped to persuade the Rump Parliament to recall members excluded, or self-excluded, before the late king's trial. Though many like Sir Thomas Pelham and Henry Shelley were dead, the influx resulted in the Rump's voluntary dissolution and the holding of a 'free' general election in April 1660 to choose a

'Convention Parliament', which would pave the way for Charles Stuart's accession.[47]

For the election the old constituencies and franchises were restored. John Stapley of Patcham and Nizel Rivers of Hamsey were returned for Lewes Borough, though whether they were opposed is uncertain. Puritans, of course, were strongly entrenched there. All the 22 members of the Twelve in May 1661 were later debarred from civic office by a royalist government purging local government of perceived enemies. Many thereafter refused to attend a restored Anglican State Church, so presumably they were 'professing' Presbyterians or Independents in the 1650s. But maybe these Puritans made do with Stapley and Rivers. Though Stapley flirted maladroitly with royalism in 1657-8, he was a regicide's son. And James Rivers, the brother of Nizel, had been the Puritan Borough MP who, together with Stapley's father, denounced Arminian altar rails from the Lewes bench in 1639. At the county election held in Lewes, Sir John Pelham of Laughton, the son of a stalwart Presbyterian, was chosen, along with Henry Goring of Highden; jointly they spent £505 treating freeholders at the *White Horse*, the *Bull* etc. - the cost had more than doubled since 1640.[48]

The Convention Parliament duly invited Charles Stuart to return, but without any binding pledges on his part as to the precise structure of a restored Church or State. He landed on 29 May, kept thereafter by Monarchists as 'Oak-Apple Day'. John Evelyn stood in the Strand and thanked God it was 'done without one drop of blood shed', a Restoration without parallel 'since the return of the Jews from their Babylonish captivity'. At Eastbourne the royalist landowner, William Wilson, paid for bonfires and freely flowing claret. Rejoicing among the godly at Lewes was perhaps more restrained. Indeed a merchant there owned the ship in which Richard Cromwell slipped away to France. The vessel was also used at the end of August 1660 by the regicide General, Edmund Ludlow. He recalled fleeing London and reaching Lewes at daybreak.

On the Tuesday following, a small boat being prepared [at Newhaven presumably] I went on board; but the wind blowing hard and the vessel having no deck, I removed into another [which] stuck upon the sands as she was falling down to receive me. After I had entered into her, the searchers came on board my small vessel to see what she carried, omitting to search that in which I was, because she was stuck upon the sands. But the storm still continuing, we continued in the harbour all that day and the night following. The master, who had used the ports of Ireland whilst I had been in that country, [inquired] if lieutenant general Ludlow were not imprisoned with the rest of the king's judges; to which I answered that I had not heard of any such thing. The next morning we set sail, and had the wind so favourable that we arrived in Dieppe that evening before the gates were shut.

Ludlow then made for Vevey in Switzerland, a sanctuary too for William Cawley, the Chichester MP and regicide.[49]

The regicides did well to flee, for those remaining were executed - the Restoration did not long remain 'bloodless'. Republicans, moreover, were steadily displaced from office. In Sussex Puritan JPs were removed, including Herbert Morley who paid £1000 for his royal pardon. William Alcock ceased to be Clerk of the Peace. More ominous was the fate of pastor Nathaniel Jones. Ejected from his rectory at Westmeston and indicted before the Lewes bench in January 1661 for preaching 'sedition', he was made to swear an oath of allegiance. He died in St Michael's parish in July 1662. Westmeston meanwhile was restored to the Arminian pamphleteer, Thomas Barton, prince Rupert's former chaplain. The hazards facing committed Puritans increased after the election in April 1661 of Charles II's first Parliament, which was so strongly Cavalier that the king kept it till 1679. At Lewes borough John Stapley, now a baronet, and Thomas Woodcock, newly dubbed a knight, were returned. Both had plotted to restore Charles Stuart in 1657. Woodcock proved a full-blooded Monarchist, Stapley a more ambiguous one. The circumstances of their election are unknown. Did Rivers stand again? Did the Borough Puritans field a candidate? - especially as the nature of any restored State Church was still undecided. Perhaps not. Maybe - despite the fate of Nathaniel Jones - they believed the king's vague promise that no one who lived 'peaceably' would suffer for 'religion'. At the county election Sir John Pelham was again chosen, but so was the dogged royalist, John Ashburnham, who attended Charles I on the scaffold - his descendants still own the shirt the king wore, the watch he carried. The Cavalier zeal of his new Parliament persuaded Charles II, closet Catholic though he was, to restore an ultra-Anglican State Church - Arminian in doctrine, Laudian in ritual, and committed to the Divine Right of 'sacred majesty'. Some two thousand Puritan ministers, who would not conform, were ejected from their livings during the summer of 1662 - among them Edward Newton and Walter Postlethwaite. Puritans boycotting the restored services, or worshipping in their own 'conventicles', soon faced fines or imprisonment - they became 'Dissenters'.[50]

here lieth ye **Bodie of Marie ye wife of Richard** Dikes of ye Clift

September anno 1632 |

She was in life a vertuous wife
a frend and mother deare
Now lies in dust hoping with trust
in Christ for to appeare

grocer who died ye xx[th]iii day of

148 A Cliffe housewife trusts in Christ

The Weighing Machine near Eastgate

318

11

A resilient economy
1662-1714

Lewes seated on the Ouse River; a place of good antiquity; large, well-built, and well inhabited, containing six parish churches, and esteemed the best borough-town of the county. 'Tis beautified with divers handsome streets, and has a good trade, with a well-frequented market on Saturdays. The opinion of John Ogilby in 1675.

The election in 1661 of a Cavalier Parliament wedded to 'sacred majesty', and eager to criminalize Puritans for dissenting from an Anglican State Church, ushered in three decades of bitter civil strife, till the flight of James II cleared the way for a limited Toleration. But even after 'the Glorious Revolution', new conflicts between Whigs and Tories were fuelled by the wars with Louis XIV waged till 1713. Yet though Lewes experienced the political turmoil, and though the French wars disrupted sea-borne trade, its economy remained resilient. Its shops displayed an ever richer variety of merchandise, some from Asia or the Caribbean. This furthered the decline of rival retail centres at Seaford and Eastbourne, at Cuckfield and Hailsham, and consolidated thereby the town's commercial hinterland. Its markets and fairs continued to channel corn and wool, cattle and hops, towards a burgeoning London. Its quarter sessions and Church courts still summoned litigants and jurors. Lawyers and physicians flourished, along with 'gentlemen' living off rents, interest or government patronage - a sphere much expanded by war finance. In 1713 John Macky noted that the town's 'cheapness' - and its being 'governed by Gentlemen', not by a vulgar Corporation - made it 'the best Retreat' he knew for half-pay officers. The townsfolk immersed in this commerce - probably there were about two thousand all told - had best be introduced before the ideological tensions that beset them are explored.[1]

An opportunity to chart how commercial space along the Borough's High Street was used in the 1660s is afforded by the hearth-tax returns. (An assessment for five or more hearths will be shown in brackets.) Busiest was the level market area reaching westward from the public well

11.1 Householders in Lewes High Street in the 1660s

Some locations conjectural

Town Wharf
1 Edw Fitzherbert
2 *The Friars*
3 Ri Page
4 Ri Kidder
5 Sam White
6 Edw Greene
7 J Holney
8 Ri Belson
9 J Brooker
10 J Seawar
11 J Dalby
12 Geo Whirrell
   The Unicorn
13 Amb Galloway
14 H Bodle
15 W Goring
Almshouse
16 T Harris
17 H Bill
   Benj White
18 W Bryan
   White Lion
19 Edm Middleton
20 J Cornford
21 H Rose
22 Ro Baker
23 Wid Garland
24 W Alcock
25 W Marshall
26 T Russell
27 J Coote
28 W Calchin
29 Laun Mitchell
30 Ph Moone
31 Ri Knight
32 Sam Catellus
33 Chas Goodwin
   (White Hart)
34 T Hopkins
35 Edw Bailey

36 Ro Martin
37 T Norton
38 J Draper
39 Jos Dabson
40 Benj Wood
41 Mary Shoulder
42 Wa Brett
43 T Harrison
44 J Henty
45 J Apps
46 Ri Dodson
47 Sam White
48 Edw Brinkhurst
49 P Barton
50 P Ray
51 Edw Erridge
52 J Devale
53 J Knapp
54 Cornelius Tinsley
55 Ro Legatt
56 Ri Russell
57 Ro Swan
58 St Snatt
59 W Claggett
60 T Matthews
61 J Raynes
62 Hercules Courtney
63 Wid Russell
64 Geo Farncombe
65 Ri Stearnes
66 Ri Grisebrook
67 Ferdinando Bryan
   The Bull
68 Geo Goldham
69 W Stapley
70 W Thurgood
71 Eliz Beecher
72 T Crouch
73 Eliz Michell
74 Edw Holmewood
75 Ri Boughton
   (Antioch House)
76 Leon & Nich
   Grasbrook
77 Ant Holman
78 H Thurman
79 Wa Rowe
80 J Eager
81 H Owden
82 T Harman
The Pound
St Mary Westout

83 Edw Kennard
84 J Pannell
    (The Dog)
85 T Payne
86 Edw Wiskey
87 Jas Eager
88 Sir T Woodcock
89 T Waller
90 Sam Button
91 Edw Tipton
92 Wid Tipton
93 J Stonestreat

94 J Whitpaine
    The King's Head
95 St French
96 W Swan
97 Sam Postlethwaite
98 Chris Yokehurst
99 Ri Bennett
100 St Botting
101 Sam Rose
102 T Henshawe
103 Rog Fillery
104 Sam Sternes

105 Edw White
106 Sim Prickavance
     The White Horse
106 W Newton
107 J Crouch
108 Rog Godman
     (Barbican House)
109 Greg Combes
110 Ri Savage
111 J Lopdell
112 Ri Barnard
113 T Elphick
114 Ellis Midmore
115 Sam Cruttenden Jr
116 J Gearing
117 Nich Curle
118 Edw Barrett
119 Sir T Nutt
     (Newcastle House)
120 Edw Henty
121 Fran Challoner
122 Sam Cruttenden Sr
123 T Tourle
124 Abraham Vine
125 Edw Bristowe
126 Ralph Richardson
     The Star
127 T Fissenden
128 Ro Stuckle
129 H Townsend
     The Black Lion
130 Edw Burkin
131 Jos Bailey
132 Ri Isted
133 W Humphrey
134 Mary Panton
135 T Novis
136 Ri Styles
137 Ri Reade
138 Wid Anne Isted
     (The Turks Head)
139 H Hopkins
140 T James
141 Mistress Relfe
142 Amb Trayton
143 J Stone
144 Ro Rossam
     Town Ditch
145 T Oliver
146 W Peake
The Bridge

70
69
68
95
96
97
WEST GATE
67
La.
98
66
99
65
64
63 **ST MICHAEL'S**
62
61
60 100
59 101
    102
58 103
57 104
    105
54 106
53 107
H
I **CASTLE**
G
H
50
Market La. Market House
49
48 108
46
45 109
44 110 **BARBICAN**
43 111
42 112
    113
41 114
40
39 115
38 116
37 117
36 118
Andrew's La.
35
34 119
    120
33 121
    122
32 123
31 124
30
St Mary's La. Fisher St
S
T
R
E
E
T
ergate La.
Sessions
House

**ST MARY
WESTOUT** ✝
**Bounder
stone**
Bucketwyn
83
84
The
Pound
82
81
80 85
79
    86
    87
78 88
77 89
Site of
St Peter's 90
76 91
75 92
74 93
73
72 94
71
70 95
Keere St Westgate La.
WEST GATE

by the clock-house, past the sessions-house and the market-house, to the west gate - along it William Foory was whipped at the cart's tail in January 1664. An aid to market trading was the clock which the Borough authorities had installed in the tower of the Broken Church - in October 1658 a white buck ferret changed hands close by. In 1690 the Borough paid Thomas Barrett twenty shillings to mend the clock, and in 1695 spent nearly £26 on repairing the tower. By then the Borough also maintained a bell and a clock at the market-house. That structure had been replaced in 1648, perhaps by the wooden one pulled down in 1793, and it probably sheltered the stocks and the pillory, the whipping-post and the proclamations-board, which the Borough also repaired. In 1661 Susan Elliot was 'openly' whipped at the post 'until her body be bloody', and in 1654 Edward Jenner, convicted of wilful perjury, was nailed by his ears to the pillory 'in the market place'. Also publicized there, in 1668, were the names of parvenus falsely claiming to be 'gentlemen' - doubtless the shaming details were avidly absorbed by the many folk converging there from across mid Sussex. The Borough sold 'the Nails' of the west gate for twenty shillings in 1673-4, though the archway and bastions survived.[2]

Dealing in sheep, cattle and horses within the market area was perhaps busiest near the public well. Certainly blacksmiths, butchers and leather workers were clustered between the Broken Church and the sessions-house - amid the ubiquitous victuallers, inn keepers and clothiers . On the south side of the High Street, west of Walwers Lane and the *White Lion*, whose landlord, William Bryan (11 hearths), left £650 to his wife Mary in 1670, lived Edmund Middleton (5) mercer, John Cornford butcher, Henry Rose saddler, Robert Baker butcher, Widow Garland grocer, William Alcock, the former Clerk of the Peace (10), William Marshall mercer, Thomas Russell (5) grocer, John Coote tailor and victualler, William Calchin butcher, Launcelot Mitchell victualler. The butchers here enjoyed back-access to yards and slaughter-houses. Indeed John Cornford was obstructing St Nicholas Lane with a pig-sty in 1668, besides keeping 'the dead flesh of Beasts till it be rotten, by which the Air is infected'. Down St Mary's Lane [Station Street] were John Partridge (5) baker and victualler, and Henry Hutchins currier - there were tanneries near Watergate and Green Wall. Between St Mary's Lane and the Pelhams' former town-house [now the *White Hart*], opposite the sessions-house, traded three victuallers, Philip Moone (4), Richard Knight (5) and Samuel Cattellus (6) who doubled as a carrier.[3]

Mercer Middleton sold to the rector of Horsted Keynes, Giles Moore, seven yards of Devonshire cloth, and mercer Marshall, 'over against the Star', sold him the fabrics needed by a parson busily conforming to the Restored Anglican Church: scarlet serge and four dozen red silk buttons for a waistcoat; Spanish cloth for a doublet and two pairs of breeches; '10 yards of haire Prunella' for a cassock. When he returned to purchase '30 yards and 3 quarters of Serge Seraphico' to make 'a Canonical coat, a vest [and] a pair of trousers', and more scarlet serge and scarlet silk buttons for a waistcoat, he complained that the colour made the buttons 'as dear again as any other silk that is not of scarlet dye'. But Marshall protested he had paid as much at London to 'within 4d' - at London too the parson himself bought 'a Levitical girdle'. In 1669 at Newhaven a William Marshall also loaded 'draperies', thread and ready-made shoes onto a Brighton vessel bound for Virginia.[4]

On the north side of the High Street, near the public well, by the turning to Green Wall [Market Street], traded Edward Burkin blacksmith, 'the last male' of his line. Alexander Outton locksmith worked for him and was buried at the 'west end' of his grave in 1688. His neighbour, Joseph Bailey, being a shoemaker, was perhaps the man who shipped oxbones and leather through Newhaven to Dieppe and imported herringnets. Between the Green Wall turning and Fisher Street lived Henry Townsend (9), landlord of the *Black Lion* [the Crown], Robert Stuckle blacksmith, Thomas Fissenden (4) apothecary, Ralph Richardson (15) at the *Star*, and Edward Bristowe (5) tailor. A parlour, a west chamber, two kitchens and a brew-house were noted at the *Black Lion* in 1710, also 42 plates and 11 pewter dishes, several casks of beer worth £15, hay worth £7, two horses, and three pigs in a pound. David Penny, a 'sea surgeon' from Tavistock, expired there in 1717. As for the *Star*, Ralph Richardson bought it for £372 in 1657, soon after John Taylor praised its good 'Diet' and good Wine. After the Restoration local clergy dined there with the archdeacon. In 1687 Sir John Ashburnham deemed it 'the best Inn' The landlord in 1717, John Lidgitter, offered Thomas Marchant sixpence per pound for carp a foot long and upwards. Maybe too he bought rabbits, pigeons and wheatears - Southdown delicacies to be had at the *Lamb* in Eastbourne. Evidently affluent, Lidgitter was buried beneath 'a handsome raised monument of Portland stone'.[5]

Affluent too was Thomas Fissenden who in 1667 sold Giles Moore 'as many Physical ingredients towards the making of a Diet Drink as cost Me 4s 10d'. After the parson suffered six bouts of a quotidian ague, the apothecary supplied him with six ounces of *Syrrop lychores cum Rheubarbaro*, and subsequently with jaundice powder, *Saffron & Mithridate*, a cephalic plaster and a small pot of *Aloes Rosatum*. His reputation as a druggist became such that a bill for physic sent to the Pelhams at Halland topped £100 in January 1684 - the year he bequeathed £750 in cash, a farm at Funtington and stock in the East India Company. His massive iron pestle and bronze mortar, dated 1669, are preserved by the Sussex Archaeological Society, and some plants he pounded probably came from Earls Garden near St John's. His son, Thomas II, later occupied a physic garden near the bottom of Watergate Lane, formerly tended by the Cluniacs, and was left medical notebooks in 1689 by a brother-in-law, Dr Henry Panton.[6]

West from Fisher Street Corner traded Abraham Vine bellows maker and Thomas Tourle (4) butcher, with a back access in Fisher Street. In 1668 along with his cleavers and blocks, knives and ropes, Tourle left over £300 and copyhold land at Westmeston. His son, Thomas II, later occupied cattle pastures at Firle, at Arlington (his wife's parish), and at Westham in Pevensey Level - the 'Goschen' of Sussex - and his lease of Landport farm was taken over in 1708 by Thomas Tourle III, who bought barren heifers and 300 wether sheep at Birling near Eastbourne. The family was still leasing Landport in 1810 when John Tourle was reckoned 'the richest man on the South Downs'. In 1687 marshland near Rye and a farm at Wittersham were owned by John Tufton, a butcher whose hogs roamed 'at large' in St Michael's parish.[7]

Doubtless the Borough's butchers preserved their close links with Wealden farmers whose husbandry remained livestock-centred. At Barcombe William Heasman planted ten acres of wheat, seven of barley, six of peas, four of tares and eleven of oats, some of which fed four oxen, six cows and seven calves, four runts, seven two-yearlings and seven year-lings, three horses, one colt and nine pigs, 48 ewes and 48 'couples' of ewes and lambs. He also owned a cheese press and 10,000 hop poles, and used chalk to improve the soil - to that end Henry Bingham at Ardingly bought clover-seed in 1712. Such Wealden farms supplied oats and eggs, butter and cheese, to the Borough market, as well as cattle and sheep. Ned Penfold was bringing butter from Hurstpierpoint when blown off his horse in 1714. The Whitsun livestock fair held in the High Street, where runts were bought by the Halland estate steward, was becoming a popular local holiday - on 10 May 1694 'the shewmen' were rounded up by a press gang, taken to the *White Horse* and escorted to Shoreham har-bour. As for hops grown in mid Sussex, most were carried directly to London through East Grinstead and Croydon, though some 'bags' were shipped from Newhaven to Dartmouth and Plymouth.[8]

Presumably livestock trading overflowed into Fisher Street which tradition also links with the fish market - John Blaber was elected its clerk in 1686 - and with fishwives from Brighton. A local dealer was Mrs Dabson of Lewes; in 1714 Thomas Marchant removed 244 live carp in three dung-carts from a stew-pond she stocked near Homewood Gate in Streat. Householders at Fisher Street in the 1660s included Stephen Inskipp currier, William Britten tailor, John Blunden victualler, and close to the *Star*'s side-entrance, Stephen Apps carrier and victualler. John Apps, also a carrier, was based near the market-house, while William Apps scrivener lived at Southwark, where in 1667 letters could be left at the *Talbot* on Thursday before noon for a carrier plying to and from Lewes. In 1681 three carriers using the inn were haphazardly listed as John Alsop senior [Apps], and Thomas Rawlinson and Thomas Talbott [Tabrett], both of Cliffe. In 1603-4 William 'Addis' had carried 196 pigeons from the Lord's Place to London and in 1651 'Apps' had been

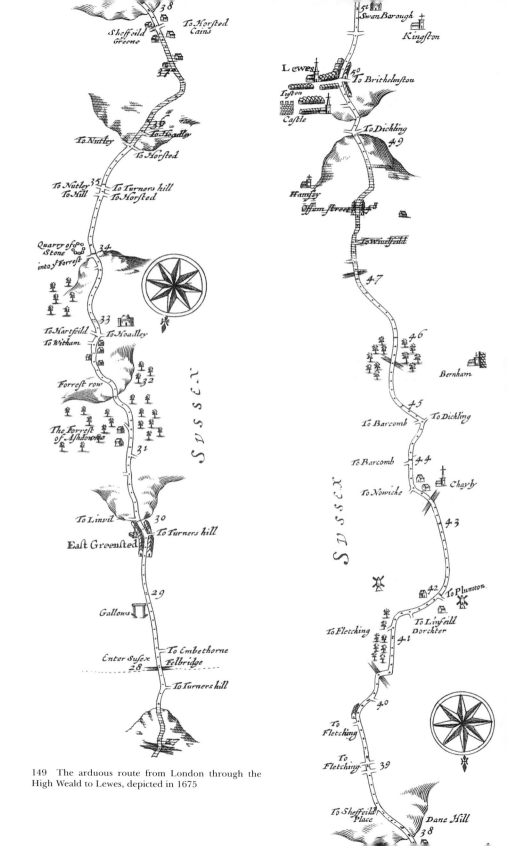

149   The arduous route from London through the
High Weald to Lewes, depicted in 1675

150 The horrid 'murther'
impartially related

hired with eight horses to convey there the cash gathered in Sussex by the Commonwealth's tax collectors. More sensationally, in 1679 John Apps brought down the yellow arsenic Robert Brinkhurst used to poison a local draper's apprentice. Being detected, Brinkhurst killed himself. Whereupon his corpse was conveyed - in a dung-cart like Mrs Dabson's carp - to the Spital crossroads at Westout, and buried 'North-South' with a stake through the heart; his remains were discovered in 1897. When John Hanning was interred at the cross roads near St John's in 1798 , after stabbing a press-ganger at Newhaven and then hanging himself in North Street gaol, a stake was dispensed with.[9]

Despite the carriers, the Lewes-London road was 'inconsiderably frequented'. Though a public coach ran from London to Tunbridge Wells by 1682 and to Reigate by 1703, the arduous uplands of Ashdown Forest long delayed even an official letter-post between Lewes and the metropolis. One that started about 1662 lapsed within months - indeed in 1666 the lack of up-to-date news from London was blamed for over-heated political gossip at Lewes. In 1675 the town was linked, very circuitously, with the capital, through Brighton and Shoreham, Arundel and Midhurst. A direct postal link, through East Grinstead, was achieved in 1685; Jonas Wayth was the 'postman' in 1695. But this ceased soon after 1705.[10]

Just west of Fisher Street Corner stood the sessions-house on its island site. In 1620 George Randoll had depicted an upper chamber resting on stumpy arcades and reached by a ladder-like stairway. Though the county's JPs ordered the Borough to repair it in 1665, they agreed in 1668 that 'no precedent' had been created, and accepted in 1696 that the Borough should maintain the inside, the three eastern rapes the exterior. Some customers in the High Street, of course, were there because they had been summoned to a variety of official business - to quarter or petty sessions, to ecclesiastical visitations or the archdeacon's court, to militia musters or county elections. A commercial setback, therefore, was the Borough's continuing failure to capture the assizes. Doubtless hopes were raised when the floor of the Nisi Prius Court in the sessions-house at East Grinstead collapsed in March 1684, tumbling 'all the jury, gentlemen, counsel and lawyers into the cellar'. But the local burgesses paid very promptly paid for its repair. Lewes did welcome the royal judges in July 1687 - a time of acute political crisis - but not thereafter till 1713. Some profit, though, stemmed from the Triennial Act passed in 1694, for this required a general election to be held at least once every three years. Thereafter freeholders from Sussex congregated the more frequently at Lewes or Chichester to elect knights of the shire, a process often spread over several days. In May 1705 2914 electors converged on the Borough; in September 1713 2780 voted, 'in the upper and lower courts' of the sessions house and in four wagons parked for the purpose. Because 'the distance and the badness of the roads' impeded them venturing to Chichester, freeholders in Hastings rape fruitlessly petitioned in 1707 that the venue be fixed at Lewes.[11]

Westward from the sessions-house, as far as the west gate, the balance of trading shifted somewhat. There were no blacksmiths or curriers, fewer butchers, more mercers and drapers, haberdashers and tailors. Half way along, moreover, near the market-house, a cluster of two goldsmiths, two scriveners and two basket makers suggests that the focus of 'the corn market' was there. An increase in trading by sample, rather than in bulk, perhaps accounted for barns in and around Fisher Street becoming obsolete. One had made way for a side-entrance to the *Star*. John Matthews butcher owned another in 1660, along with an orchard 'lying to Primrose Hill' west of Watergate Lane. 'The tithe-barn' belonging to Malling Deanery survived till 1732.[12]

As John Ogilby observed, the Saturday corn market, unlike the Lewes-London road, was 'well-frequented' in 1675. Its hinterland stretched eastward along the South Downs to Pevensey Level and northward to the headwaters of the Cuckmere and the Ouse. A miller from Heathfield bought wheat at Lewes in 1695, allegedly 'before market time', and though a Friday market was resurrected at Cuckfield, it was dismissed in 1673 as 'small', the town as 'indifferent', the vicinity as 'dirty'. Beyond the headwaters folk resorted to Battle, to East Grinstead with 'a good market on Thursday', and to Horsham where London higglers bought chickens in bulk. To the south-west, of course, was the market at Brighton. But as already noted, the town's plebeian character restricted its outreach, and though its mariners were shifting resourcefully from sea-fishing to freight-carriage, great damage was done by 'the raging and swelling of the sea', which in November 1703 left it looking 'bombarded'. Another storm in August 1705 destroyed every house in the Lower Town below the cliff, concealing its site 'beneath a mound of beach'. To combat the port's growing destitution, a county rate was levied. Punier still was the market at Seaford, deemed in 1743 a 'poor miserable village'.[13]

Respice finem

151 A FINIS for smugglers?

Most of the wheat and barley harvested in the South Downs, marketed in the Borough and shipped coastwise through Newhaven, went to London, where the population perhaps rose from 400,000 in 1650 to 575,000 in 1700. Local grain also reached the royal dockyards at Portsmouth and Plymouth. From 1670, moreover, corn could be shipped overseas without a licence. Cargoes from Newhaven mostly went to populous Holland and Zeeland - Rotterdam received over 24,000 bushels in 1676. The English garrison at Tangiers was supplied in 1663, Lisbon in 1707, Bilbao in 1712. Shipments to France, though, were impeded by embargo and war. Perhaps some to Ostend and Dunkirk in 1712, and to Boulogne and Dieppe in 1713, fed the duke of Marlborough's advancing army and also a famished hinterland. The Borough remained too a market for local wool. Short-stapled Southdown fleeces were becoming almost as valued as Spanish ones, and were increasingly smuggled overseas from the Sussex coast and Romney Marsh. Indeed a corps of 'riding-officers' was set up in 1698 to combat this. Meanwhile, as weaving in the Weald of Kent declined, so doubtless much Southdown wool was carried overland to the capital. John Benton of London paid £147 4s for the clip from Birling near Eastbourne in September 1697.[14]

Between the sessions-house and the market-house, on the sunny north side of the High Street, clothiers were especially entrenched. The householders included Samuel Cruttenden (6) hatter, Francis Challoner (8) mercer, Edward Henty shoemaker, Sir Thomas Nutt (15) [Newcastle House], Edward Barrett clock maker, Nicholas Curle haberdasher, John Gearing butcher, with back-access to Castle Ditch Lane, Samuel Cruttenden junior (5) hatter, Ellis Midmore (5) linen draper, Thomas Elphick shoemaker, Richard Barnard (7) woollen draper, John Lopdell (7) woollen draper, Richard Savage (5) saddler, Gregory Combes (6) surgeon and Roger Godman (5) physician [Barbican House]. Five of the hatters, haberdashers and drapers bequeathed Wealden tenements, as far afield as Fletching and Hellingly, Stone Cross and Speldhurst, a likely source of timber, wool and hides. Shoemaker Elphick owned land at Ringmer and cottages 'under one roof' by St John's, near the tannery at Green Wall. In 1674 draper Barnard's successor, Richard II, built a smart rear extension [behind 173]; its walls of thin red brick were adorned with

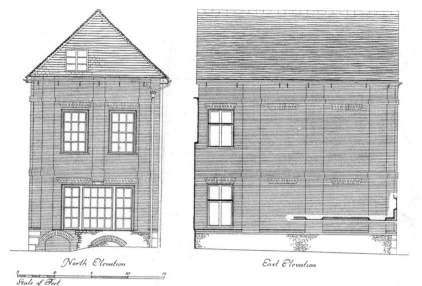

North Elevation   *East Elevation*

Scale of Feet

152 Richard Barnard's extension

wide pilasters on a moulded plinth, an Artisan Mannerism also deployed at the Friars, the new mansion by the bridge. Richard II bought lambs' wool at Birling in September 1697.[15]

By the market-house, at Castlegate Corner opposite Roger Godman, traded John Crouch, tailor and goldsmith, father of the Independent preacher and son-in-law of the deceased goldsmith, William Dodson. By the 1670s Crouch's own son-in-law, Robert Colgate goldsmith, resided there, in all likelihood 'a very active' maker of silver spoons. Westward from Crouch were William Newton tailor, Simon Prickavance (8) innkeeper, Edward White (4) basket maker, Samuel Sternes joiner, Roger Fillery (4) hosier, Thomas Henshawe attorney, Samuel Rose (5) saddler, Stephen Botting (6) baker. Beyond St Michael's church lived Richard Bennett tailor and Christopher Yokehurst shoemaker, and beyond the west gate, pastor Samuel Postlethwaite (8), ejected from St Michael's in 1662, and William Swan maltster. Hosier Fillery's tenement [164] included an acre below the castle-keep, ideal for drying or bleaching cloth. Prickavance kept the *White Horse* [166] where local clergy dined with the bishop in 1675. He was accused of keeping a Gallon measure 'which wants one pint'.[16]

On the south side, opposite the sessions-house, in the Pelhams' former town-house, resided Charles Goodwin (13) attorney, a receiver of the county's assessed taxes. In 1665 he compiled and engrossed on vellum a meticulous rental of the manor of Brighton owned by the earls of Thanet. But an affidavit in his own hand, attached to its final page, affirmed he was 'most unkindly' turned out of his stewardship, without

329

153 Lawyers' signatures

any just cause assigned - prompting Paul Dunvan to speculate that 'gilded lies of sepulchral flattery' were doubtless chiselled on the tomb of the heartless seigneur. Goodwin, nothing daunted, was steward in 1696 of copyholds at Willingdon and Wilmington held by his neighbour, Thomas Erridge shoemaker. He himself owned pastures at Langney and a timber yard at South Street in Cliffe.[17]

West of Goodwin lived Thomas Hopkins tailor and Edward Bailey shoemaker, a Searcher of Leather in 1670, who held half of Hedgelands, a tenement in Chailey. Between St Andrew's Lane and Market Lane [St Martin's Lane] traded Robert Martin haberdasher, Thomas Norton draper, John Draper scrivener and victualler (his trade token survives), Joseph Dabson, a 'poor' glover, Benjamin Wood mason, who paved Keere Street in 1682, Mary Shoulder (5), a scrivener's widow, Walter Brett (5) grocer, Thomas Harrison grocer, John Henty pewterer, John Apps carrier, Richard Dodson (5) goldsmith, Samuel White (4) brazier, Edward Brinkhurst (4) cutler and victualler, and facing the market house, Peter Barton (4) baker. From Walter Brett, a leading Dissenter, bailiffs seized two barrels of sugar in 1670, after finding a butt of currants too heavy to shift. The goldsmith, Dodson II, probably made an extant silver spoon dated 1661 and marked with a D beneath a crown, the stem and bowl stamped with the Borough coat-of-arms. Till his death in 1710 he went on using the same marks as his father William, 'often striking a very worn punch'. He also owned the *Unicorn* on School Hill, that mythical beast being an emblem of his profession.[18]

Between Market Lane and St Swithun's Lane traded Peter Ray victualler - a Peter Ray had been a surgeon in Herbert Morley's regiment - Edward Erridge shearman, John Devale felt maker, John Knapp barber, Cornelius Tinsley basket maker, Robert Legatt upholsterer, Richard Russell (6) apothecary, who owned 'lands in Ireland', Robert Swan (5) barber and Stephen Snatt (7) woollen draper. Giles Moore suspected Snatt of overcharging him, for ten yards of 'Haire Prunello' and for mending four pairs of stockings. Legatt, however, obligingly journeyed to Horsted Keynes to sell him a pair of fine blankets, a green woollen rug, and enough ticking for two 'pillow coats'. The upholsterer left his daughter a silver bowl and asked William Longuir, a citizen of London, to appraise his stock. Itinerants from Douglas and Dumfries sold linen cloth and worsted stockings at Horsted Keynes in the 1670s. Mungus Muray, a 'scotch pedlar', resided at Lewes in 1699, and Scotsmen 'with large packs of linen goods' later lodged at the *Wheatsheaf* in Malling. The Borough draper, James Charters, had clients spread between Steyning, Godstone and Battle in 1694, so he too travelled in pursuit of custom.[19]

Between St Swithun's Lane and the west gate resided William Claggett (8) haberdasher, Thomas Matthews (10) woollen draper, John Raynes (6) attorney, Hercules Courtney (5) tailor, Widow Russell (5), George Farncombe tailor, Richard Stearnes tailor, Richard Grisebrook (4), a butcher with an orchard and pigeon house down Bull Lane, and Ferdinando Bryan (10) at the *Bull*. He was a nephew of William at the *White Lion* and raised a handsome monument of Portland stone to his wife Mercy.

154 The *Bull*

Beyond the west gate traded George Goldham tailor and William Stapley (6) glover and victualler. Matthews, Claggett and Snatt, like several clothiers nearer the sessions house, owned tenements in the Weald, at Plumpton, Barcombe and Framfield. Hercules Courtney occupied the Tenter Garden off St Andrew's Lane. Giles Moore employed him to stitch 'a Canonical Coat' from ten yards of 'Italiano', with buckram buttons, also a 'mourning' gown and a doublet, re-using a cloak Moore had bought in London and 'pieces found in my Boxes'.[20]

The father of the attorney living opposite St Michael's was Edward Raynes, 'a great conveyancer and court-keeper', who married John Rowe's daughter, followed him as Principal of Clifford's Inn and bought the Coneyborough estate in Barcombe for £720. Doubtless John shared the paternal practice which included oversight of the earl of Dorset's estates in Sussex. Edward died in 1677 and John in 1687. Whereupon Coneyborough passed to a brother-in-law, Thomas Medley, whose portrait shows him as every inch a steward, with a rental of Brede manor in his hand and a bookcase bulging with estate records, neatly labelled. Yet in 1702 it was claimed that, while steward of Southover manor and tenant of its demesne lands, he tampered with court rolls, illicitly sold timber, and removed stone from the priory precinct, wainscot from the manor-house, 'mould' from the garden, cattle cribs from the yard.

Medley counter-claimed that he planted 100 ash trees on the site of the Pad Pool, removed stone only to build flood defences round the Upper Rise, preserved 'heirlooms' in the manor-house and planted the garden with fruit trees. In 1704 he bought the Friston estate from the heirs of Sir Edward Selwyn.[21]

A contrast to the bustling market area between the clock-house and the west gate was School Hill. Its householders were gentlefolk or professional men, or traders not seeking a hectic commercial location. On the north side, ascending from Eastgate, lived Ambrose Trayton (13

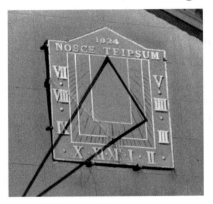

hearths) gentleman, Mistress Relfe (7), Thomas James (6) gentleman, who owned property at Cliffe Corner and in the City of London, Henry Hopkins (5) surgeon, James's brother-in-law, Anne Isted (6), an attorney's widow - in the former town-house of the Dobells [Albion Street] - Mary Panton (7), a physician's widow whose son Henry continued the practice, and William Humphrey surgeon, her tenant. Dispersed near them were Robert Rossam brewer, John Stone cooper, Richard Reade glover, Richard Styles cooper and Thomas Novis, brazier and

155 The sundial

victualler. Above Humphrey resided Widow Isted's eldest son, Richard, (10), a Framfield-born attorney and member of Clifford's Inn. His 'gardens, orchards and lands' reached almost to the top of the hill [194-200], and possibly his mansion carried the sundial with the Isted motto that now adorns Dial House.[22]

In 1671 Isted encountered John Bargrave, a strong-willed ecclesiastic from Canterbury who had ransomed 162 captive Christians in the market at Algiers, 'buying them slave by slave as one buys horses in Smithfield'. He arrived in Lewes seeking three years' back-rent for his Dean and Chapter from their tenant at Wootton farm in East Chiltington. When Isted advised him to distrain livestock if need be, he took the 'dirty hard way' to Wootton with Tipton, the Lewes bailiff, and seized six fat oxen, seven runts, six cows and a bull. Isted also owned the *Turks Head* by 1696. Located in the former Dobell town-house, its sign alluded perhaps to the Lincoln-born landlord, John Tooke, who in 1678 offered twenty shillings for news of a 'reddish roan Mare' stolen from the inn. She was meticulously described as 'about 14 hands; six years old; has a white blaze down her face; three white feet; with a white speck on the stifle bone on the far side, and a white streak on her near side from the flank downwards'. A tapster there, Charles Forde, was buried in 1683, an ostler, James Head, in 1688, and a guest of doubtful status, Thomas Dawe, 'commonly called Sponge', in 1690.[23]

On the south side of School Hill in the 1660s, up to the almshouses at Brooman's Lane Corner, the tone was more commercial, but still low-key. At the bottom, well positioned for broken axles, lived Richard Page wheelwright and his landlord, Richard Kidder wheelwright, also Samuel White joiner and Edward Greene tailor. Then came John Holney (4) apothecary, who displayed in his house [17] the horns of a large moose. He died in 1707, leaving lands at Selmeston and in West Sussex. Above him were Richard Belson - perhaps the mason who repaired the House of Correction in 1651- John Brooker victualler, John Seawar labourer, John Dalby thatcher, and George Whirrell, a shoemaker, victualler and parish clerk - his house had become the *Unicorn* in 1679, owned by Dodson the goldsmith. Higher up lived Ambrose Galloway tailor, Henry Bodle tailor and William Goring, locksmith and gunsmith.[24]

Above Brooman's Lane [at Lewes House] resided Thomas Harris (6), the bishop's registrar. And School Hill was to remain, it seems, an address favoured by officials of the restored archdeacon's court. The heavy cost of proving her husband's will at Lewes was noted in 1700 by Elizabeth Cowper of Squibbs Farm at Salehurst: 'for transcribing a Copy of the will to be kept for a Guide for the overseers, the Original being left in Court, and for Copying out the Inventory, and for writing of a Bond; in all £3 2s 6d'. The issuing of marriage licences at Lewes caused many couples from elsewhere to be wedded in its churches. And church-wardens converged there after Easter to be sworn in by the visiting archdeacon or his surrogate, and to deliver cash collected in church for authorized good causes: Streat managed £2 2s 8d for Irish Protestants in 1689, 20s for the Vaudois in 1699. The churchwardens returned at Michaelmas to report on defective church fittings and churchyard fences, on midwives and loose livers, and until 1685 on Dissenters. Restored too in 1660 were tenths, synodals and procurations - archaic dues paid to the bishop by the parish clergy. Each year at Lewes Giles Moore settled with John Simes, their collector - the 'green wax' involved cost 5s 8d. Moore also paid James Clarke for 'getting my Orders of Priest & Deacon, my Institution & Induction, entered'. Clarke was a deputy-registrar, and local Quakers denounced him as 'a sot, much addicted to wine and brandy'. There was, of course, conviviality when Moore and his fellow parsons dined at the *Star* or the *White Horse* during a visitation - in 1668 archdeacon Hardy footed the bill himself, a Red Letter Day indeed. In 1669 the clergy also savoured a sermon by Dr Malachi Conant from Beeding; entitled *Urim and Thummim*, it expounded the Dignity and the Duty of the clergy.[25]

In 1662 Benjamin White physician bought the mansion [School Hill House] below the *White Lion*, though he shared it perhaps with Henry Bill (10) gentleman, the son of a King's Printer and county Treasurer for Charitable Purposes in 1666. School Hill was now to consolidate as a Mecca for those in search of a cure, with White as its rising star - his copy

156 Gerarde's *Herbal*

of Gerarde's *Herbal* survives. He was fortunate that Robert Moncke, who treated Giles Moore for a lingering quartan ague (£1), was buried at All Saints in 1660, and that Henry Panton, who supplied him with 'a Diet drink' (13s) in May 1661, embraced Dissent soon after. Young White it was, a steady Anglican, fresh from his studies at Leyden, who called at Horsted Keynes in December 1662 (10s). In 1671 he wedded the sister of Peter Courthope of Danny Park. By 1674 he was writing to the Court physician, Hugh Chamberlain, giving the ingredients of a pill to act as 'a true corrector of opium and all vegetable poisons', and lightly alluding to the passing of 'Madame' Juliana Gage at Bentley: 'she was so happy as to be out of misery'. In 1686 his black mare was 'covered' at Firle by Sir John Gage's brown bay. By then forty guineas was his annual fee for attending Lady Pelham at Halland. When he charged £2 to visit Timothy Burrell's wife at Cuckfield in 1689, 'Jude' of Lewes got ten shillings for bleeding her. Massive too was White's prowess as a usurer along the South Downs - £200 lent to Sackville Graves at Firle, £400 to Henry Bridger at Southwick, £550 to Captain William Scrase at Annington. His successor on School Hill, his son Peter, married a granddaughter of Nicholas Tattersal, the captain who conveyed Charles Stuart to France. In 1713-14 Peter's far-flung patients included a boy near Westham subject to violent fits, and a woman from Poynings, severely bruised 'at the election for knights of the shire'. Henry Panton died at School Hill in 1688, leaving property at Ditchling and £200 in the East India Company. By then Dr William Rose resided just above White, and in 1702 Dr John Tabor bought the mansion [Lewes House] just below him. Tabor extended its grounds and studied antiquities, hobbies facilitated perhaps by a marriage to Elizabeth Board which brought him Howbourne manor in Buxted.[26]

Hopkins, the surgeon on School Hill, who married a daughter of the merchant Samuel Towers, was clearly a cut above 'Jude'. Twice in 1682 he was summoned to bleed Lady Pelham and in 1687 'to make an issue' for Betty, Sir John Ashburnham's daughter. Of course there were rustic blood-letters and bone-setters, like William Batchelour of Lindfield who bled Giles Moore, made his 'suppositours', washed his teeth and supplied pills if they ached. Nonetheless when Anne Geale of Horsted Keynes was afflicted by 'Lanions', she chose to consult surgeons at Lewes, - where she died, at John Wicker's house on School Hill. Nathaniel Welch charged five shillings in 1678 for treating Jane Pringgs at the House of Correction; the ointments, salves and poultices cost nine shillings. His bill for 'the cure' of a boy there, the tips of whose toes had 'mortified', came to £1 10s 1d - one big toe remained 'very sore'. Thomas Stonestreat petitioned the Lewes bench to pay his expenses while treating a man from Hampshire who developed 'a distemper' in the legs when mowing at Piddinghoe - such was the smell, 'scarce anybody would come near him'. St Michael's parish paid John Walter thirty shillings for setting a pauper's thigh; his lancets with their case were valued at five shillings in 1711, his other instruments and two 'plaster boxes' at £1. Low in the medical hierarchy was 'Mistress Holman the midwife', buried at All Saints in 1689 aged 84 years, and even lower, Jane Hudson, excommunicated in 1688 for practising surgery without a licence.[27]

Lewes escaped the plague in 1666. Four JPs gallantly attended quarter sessions there in October, despite 'the pestilence spread in divers places within the County'. They instructed parish officers to ensure that 'all Travellers and Beggars and other idle persons' were sent to their legal place of settlement, and hired a Bishopstone man to 'watch' an infected hoy anchored off Newhaven. That it was the last outbreak in Sussex has been credited to the grey rat displacing the plague-carrying black rat, seen locally as 'much inferior in Sagacity'. But smallpox did recur - with little regard for social status. At the *Star* it killed the under-sheriff's clerk in 1652, the landlord's wife in 1674 and the landlord in 1691. It struck down Mr Studley's servant in 1675, Mr Studley's son in 1684 and Mr Thomas Pellatt at the Friars in 1680. In 1673 the nursing of a sick prisoner at the House of Correction cost £1 7s 6d. In 1701 the Borough rented premises in St Michael's to isolate 'Veraull's family'. Lacking a permanent 'pest house', it paid the diocesan registrar to search (in vain) for the will of Richard Kykherste who left four houses in Rotten Row for charitable uses in 1586. Though long since embezzled, they could not have coped with the epidemic that broke out in October 1710. Because of 'the distemper now reigning' at Lewes, JPs met at Battle in February 1711; probate business at the archdeacon's court was disrupted, and the opening of Mr Pelham's charity school was delayed till 28 May. The Borough hired a scavenger to scour the streets, and paid the manorial poundkeeper to clear them of stray hogs. It was said that '1000 people' - perhaps half the town's population - were infected and that 'about 120' died - a mortality largely confirmed by the parish burial registers.[28]

Even more than on School Hill, householders in Westout were distanced from intensive retailing. It was already muted in Keere Street where lived William Pilbeame glazier, Thomas Brad tailor, John Crips shoemaker, Edward Ward cooper, John Brinkhurst gardener and at 'Caprons' the affluent George Stonestreat (7). There John Virgoe owned the *Cock* in 1677, and Thomas Matthew draper, the *Bottle* in 1685. According to local Quakers, William Thurgood, the butcher at its northwest corner, employed Edward 'Scripps', a cobbler who once tried to make 'red herring' of them, by smoking them out of their Meeting House, and duly perished driving a cow from Ditchling through heavy snow in 1677; the Friends also alluded to his over-familiarity with a mare.[29]

West of Thurgood lived Elizabeth Beecher (5), a tailor's widow, and her son Anthony, a pastor ejected in 1662 from Kingston, who kept a school. Next door was Thomas Crouch tailor whose Tenter Garden lay

157 The arched
chimney-beam

on the south-facing slope behind. Beyond him resided Widow Elizabeth
Michell (7) and Edward Holmewood (6) woollen draper - perhaps
retired; his dwelling [103 High Street] retains an arched oak chimney-
beam with leaves carved on the spandrels. Then came Richard Boughton
(13) barrister and former Borough MP [at Antioch House]. On the island
between Rotten Row and Antioch Street perhaps stood a smithy, worked
by Leonard and Nicholas Grasbrook. Beyond this, Anthony Holman (4)
'gent' leased the rectory, whereas Westout's parson, Henry Thurman (6),
lived just above [St Anne's House] in spacious premises with a barn and
malt-house, a croft and orchard. Above Thurman, the slope of the hill
allowed space for workshops, yards and saw-pits - indeed a large barn
abutted the road just below the house 'by the church gate', near the
manor pound. Thereabouts lived the carpenters Thomas Harman and
Henry Owden, and probably the sawyers John Eager and Walter Rowe.
The hill was well placed for timber carted from the Low Weald, from
Balneath and Homewood. And probably, just beyond the Borough
'bounder stone' [in Western Road], traded William Bauldy blacksmith,
William Gill (4) wheelwright and victualler, and Richard Saunders carpenter, who helped rebuild the grammar school in 1661.[30]

Perhaps Harman the carpenter had a second trade, for in 1657 a
Thomas Harman of Westout, pipe maker, stood surety for William Tyler
of Westout, a pipe maker accused of fathering Rose Beard's bastard child.
Though pipe making had spread from London to Canterbury and
Southampton by 1618, Harman and Tyler are among the earliest practi-
tioners known in Sussex. 'Harman senior', a pipe maker in Westout, was
denounced in 1685 as 'ill affected' to the government. A Thomas

Harman, buried there in 1706, possibly made the pipe, with a bowl bearing the long serif initials 'T/H', found at a fulling-mill site in Ardingly. 'J' and 'H' were stamped on fragments of pipe dug up near the tannery at Green Wall, amid a mass of cattle-horn cores; the initials stand upright at the sides of a flat-based

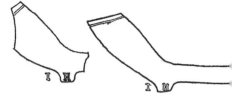

158 The pipe fragments

spur and the bowls are 'London style', rather long, narrow and outward-leaning. Possibly the maker was John Holcombe who kept the *Ship* in St Mary's Lane and was buried at St John's in 1699 'aged 66 or more'. His daughter Rebecca married Richard Briant, a pipe maker interred there in 1707. By 1680 demand for the weed was such that Richard West, 'tobacco cutter', was at work in Cliffe.[31]

On the north side of the hill spacious living again mingled with low-key trading. Beyond Westgate Lane, at the bottleneck [143], resided Stephen French (11) 'gent', also a landowner at Stream in Chiddingly. Next came John Whitpaine (7) at the *King's Head*, with its malt-house and orchard, and John Stonestreat (8), the pastor ejected from Lindfield in 1662, who had bought the inn next door for £175 in 1654. Above him were Widow Tipton (4), Edward Tipton (4), the Senior Bailiff of Lewes Rape, and Samuel Button (4) attorney, described as of Staple Inn in 1682 - the premises were acquired to re-house the grammar school about 1715. At 'the Chauntry House' [*Shelleys Hotel* car park] lived Thomas Waller mason, and at the former *Vine* Sir Thomas Woodcock (11), the Cavalier MP. Just above [135-6] traded James Eager (4) baker - impressive ovens still survive; Richard Eager, a baker at Westout in 1713, owned wheat and meal worth £20, a kneading trough and six gingerbread moulds. At the *Rose* was Edward Wiskey victualler - perhaps the barber-surgeon, 'lately' in Parliament's army, granted a county pension in 1659, and above him, Thomas Payne sawyer, a tenant of baron Bergavenny's [at St Peters Place]. The house of John Pannell victualler [now the *Pelham Arms*] later bore the sign of the *Dog* in 1708 - perhaps harriers hunted on the adjacent Downs. In that year, a sailor, fallen sick there, was carried in Tapsfield's wagon to London. Edward Kennard, at Irelands Lane Corner, worked a mill in Westout, perhaps Inkersoll's mill just beyond the 'bounder stone'.[32]

Inkersoll's mill commanded a noble panorama of the South Downs, whose sheep-corn husbandry supplied most of the grain traded in the Borough - the yields now enhanced still further by the growing of clover and turnips. The resources of local farmers were often impressive. Henry Shelley, residing at the *Vine* in 1691, had 24 plough oxen at Houndean, 720 sheep 'upon the hills' and fifty more at Southover on 'the Rises'. In May 1713 William Marchant, a yeoman in Westout, owned 477 sheep and lambs and sowed 76 acres with wheat and barley, peas and tares.

Head shepherds, like John Ward at Landport, were highly regarded - his headstone in the churchyard at St John's showed the angel proclaiming to shepherds in the Holy Land the message: 'Glory to God on high'. Because family-farmers were few and the corn land not 'well peopled', outside help was needed with the harvest - the reason militia men resident at Waldron in the Weald were away 'in the South Downs' in August 1672.[33]

159 The headstone

Wealden militia men, though, resorted to the Lewes Downs outside the harvest season. A mile or so north-west of the bounder stone was 'Henrys mount', noted in April 1676 as the normal 'Muster Place' for the three eastern rapes of Sussex. Thomas Seaman from Horsted Keynes spent twelve days soldiering at 'Lewes' in May 1664, and four days in September 'when the whole Regiment mustered'. Parson Giles Moore paid for his sword and bandoleer, his musket and rest. When Sussex was 'threatened by [the] Dutch and French' in June 1666, Seaman was again mobilized - repairs to the stock of his musket costing the parson four pence. William Goring, the gunsmith on School Hill, received £3 6s from the militia tax in April 1673 for cleaning and mending muskets. In June 1700 Richard Stapley at Twineham paid William Peckham to exercise at 'Lewes' for two days.[34]

Quite apart from the diversity of trades and professions pursued by householders in its High Street, the resilience of the Borough's economy also reflected the ever wider range of choice offered to customers there. As for grocers, whereas George Norton, it seems, was the only one to join the Elizabethan Fellowship, by the 1660s Walter Brett, Thomas Harrison, Thomas Russell and Widow Garland were in business. Moreover, delicacies from the Far East and the West Indies were percolating through to the provinces - a Borough butcher, John Miles, owned a coffee pot in 1710. About then Susan Tourle was selling coffee and tobacco, Fine Bohea Tea, Imperial Green Tea and Refined Loaf Sugar, also anchovies, Gloucester cheese and New Thin cheese, Crown soap, playing cards and gunpowder. Notice was taken maybe of the standard set at sybaritic Tunbridge Wells - 'A very sweet place, private and refreshing', it seemed to John Evelyn, lodging at a cottage in 1652 to drink the waters. But forty years on, Celia Fiennes observed two bustling coffee-houses there, also rooms 'for the lottery and hazard board', and shops full of toys, silver and china. And Daniel Defoe noted that a wheatear cost far more than at Lewes, where Giles Moore bought sixty for 14 pence in August 1662. Trapped at harvest time by Southdown shepherds, Defoe lauded them as English ortolans, smaller than 'a Lark or Sparrow', but a delicious

160 The Pantiles at sybaritic Tunbridge Wells

161 Plaster work at Barbican House

mouthful. John Taylor agreed that if well roasted, 'bones, flesh, and all' would 'lusciously' dissolve'.[35]

The Borough could satisfy too an incessant demand for fashionable adornment. In 1645 Anthony Stapley from Hickstead Place bought £20-worth of clothes there. In 1683 his son Richard bought silver buttons, and in 1716 Richard's brother, Anthony, anxious to cut a dash at the assizes, sent there a silver-mounted bridle, saddle and spurs to be renewed and a saddle-cloth to be re-embroidered - though sadly they were not ready in time. In 1688 the draper William Hurst sold 'marble' and printed calicoes, 'Norridge' crepe, Irish frieze, French sarsenet, Persian silk, Indian stripe and 'bengawle' remnants. In 1696 Anne Rose 'seamstress' traded scarves and children's frocks, silk caps for men, ribbons of every hue and 'Alla mode Hoods'. In 1711 Ann Colgate stocked ivory combs, horn needles and silk handkerchiefs, Bibles and bobbins, writing paper and 372 pieces of lace and purl. The enterprising spinster had assumed 'the burden of the shop' in 1693 from her cousin, Susan Crouch, who bequeathed property on London Bridge. In 1706, however, bankruptcy befell a draper too strenuously responding to consumer choice. In 1702 James Lopdell was dabbling in 'the starch trade' with two Huguenots, John Thiery and James Hallee, a 'refugee' from Caen. He also owned a paper-mill on the Ouse, just north of Barcombe mill, where Richard Henton paper maker worked in 1701, and the source, presumably, of 248 reams shipped by Ambrose Galloway through Newhaven to London in 1702. Maybe, too, it was Lopdell who installed at his residence [Barbican House] the oak staircase with fine spiral balusters, and the plaster work which cases the ceiling beams on the first-floor landing, adorned with a guilloche pattern enclosing small flowers.[36]

Like coffee and calicoes, tuition in the social graces was becoming readily available. In 1672 a quarrel erupted between Robert Colgate, the Presbyterian goldsmith whose daughter assumed 'the burden' of Susan Crouch's boutique, and a French fencing master, Robert Verron, a friend of Thomas Wright, a dancing master. Gentleman boarders at the grammar school, like Timothy Burrell from Cuckfield who entered St John's College Cambridge in 1682, were expected to receive a fashionable polish. The 'Enlarged Conversation' of its headmaster, Thomas Peirce, was attributed in 1713 to the sons of 'Considerable Gentlemen' residing with him. Peirce received £22 5s 4d for a year's schooling of Nicholas Gilbert, an attorney's son from Eastbourne. Also reimbursed were Mr Keeler writing master, James Lunn dancing master, Thomas Friend draper (£10) and Francis Saunders shoemaker. Moreover, Peter Marchant charged thirty shillings for shaving Gilbert's head and fitting a wig. His attire and deportment, like his ten shillings annual pocket-money, safely set him apart from the 'free boys'. Most tradesmen's sons were taught by the likes of Charles Comyrlon, 'a writing Master' from London who 'kept his school at Henry Rose's in St Michael's, but boarded at William Rose's in All Saints', where he was buried in 1680. Tuition for young ladies was also available in the Borough by 1717. On 10 January Thomas Marchant delivered his daughter Bett to Mrs Atkinson who charged £13 per annum; three years later, to the day, he bore her back to Hurstpierpoint.[37]

As for the Borough's wig makers, John Wallis in 1699 received from Twineham in a pasteboard box a periwig of Richard Stapley's, to be changed for one larger 'in the head and cowl'. Peter Marchant, who fitted Master Gilbert, attended Walter Dobell at Folkington Place in 1708. Three ounces of hair (worth 4s 6d) were stolen in 1713 from Daniel Fabre, a Huguenot periwig maker and barber who mingled socially with John Thieary starch trader and Isaac Guepin clock maker. The shop of Samuel Driver in 1711 contained a barber's chair, 15 razors in a leather case - four of them silver-topped, ten pewter 'blood porringers', and to beguile his customers, a Bible, 24 old books and 18 pictures.[38]

Borough clock makers also served an affluent clientele with ever-increasing skill. In 1656 Giles Moore carried home a clock (£2 10s) and a roasting jack (£1 5s) made by Edward Barrett, who regularly cleaned 'the Jack Clock' at Halland in the 1680s. Thomas Rotherham, a clock and watch maker, resident by 1670, mended Lady Pelham's clock there in 1681. 'The Lewes clock maker' was paid 15 shillings 'for old work' at Ashburnham in 1679. Barrett's son, Thomas, agreed in 1690 to mind the Borough clock and to ring Gabriel at 4 a.m. and 8 p.m., receiving for these unsocial hours £4 a year. He also minded Walter Dobell's clocks at Folkington, and was a skilled maker of lantern clocks and of thirty-hour long-case clocks with single hands, an expertise matched by Abraham Weston - a bracket clock of his, in a black lacquer case, is 'of London quality'. He also fitted the Borough clock with a pendulum and in 1709 made a large brass badge, 'gilt with gold' and adorned with the Town Arms, to be set on the crier's coat. Barrett and Weston also traded as gun makers. The local pioneer, William Goring, was buried at All Saints in 1681, 'aged 78 or more'. His informing against local Quakers in 1670 was goaded perhaps by their pacifism. His son Richard, gun maker, was something of a loose cannon - armed with horse-pistols, he rode through Denton to the 'great terror' of its parishioners; at Seaford he wrestled a musket from Thomas Elphick.[39]

There was also a rising demand for books. From Thomas Norman in 1708 the Borough bought Mr Nelson's volume relating to the *Office & Authority of a Justice of the Peace &c. and also showing the Duty of Constables*. Norman also bound 'the Town book of Records', and supplied Acts of Parliament to the Clerk of the Peace and a *Lex Testamentaria* to Thomas Marchant at Hurstpierpoint. Quite probably too he secured for parson Grave at Westout some of the volumes -148 folios, 109 quartos, 146 octavos and 120 duodecimos or sextodecimos - which he bequeathed to 'benefit' the Borough. Among them were tomes by such Low Church or Presbyterian theologians as Baxter, Clarkson and Flavel, Burnet and Tillotson; also *De Imitatione Christi* by Thomas a Kempis, and ground-breaking works by Grotius, Descartes, Robert Boyle and William Wiston. More popular with Lewesians, perhaps, were Camden's *Britannia* (1657 edition), Speed's *Survey of London*, Sir Francis Bacon's *Henry VII* and Glanville's *Of Witches*. Local pride drew them maybe to John Evelyn's *De Sylva*, even to Brian Twine's *Antiquitatis Academiae Oxoniensis Apologia*, and sheer wonderment perhaps to Brian Walton's *Biblia Polyglota* (five folio volumes) and to Thomas Tomkin's *Musica Deo Sacro et Ecclesiae Anglicanae* (six folio volumes).[40]

As shopping became more satisfying, and social life more relaxed, visitors to the Borough needing refreshment and a night's lodging probably increased. At Chichester in queen Anne's time, after the weekly market - so it was said - some local farmers spent several days in 'revellings and Night Freaks' at its 45 public houses. Such disorder might, of course, provoke official action. The six alehouses trading at Southover in 1685, a 'small' place and on 'no great road', attracted 'many idle and lewd people' and caused the poor to squander 'time and money', so the JPs reduced them to three. In 1686 a national survey allotted Chichester 84 'guest beds', Lewes 99 - with stabling for 245 horses - East Grinstead 103 and Salisbury, on the Great South-West Road, 548. As already noted, the assizes met at East Grinstead, and in 1676 its 'many beds', and the spaciousness of its Common, were urged as reasons to hold militia musters there.[41]

In the late 1690s there was some relocation of hospitality in the Borough. The *Turk's Head*, the *White Lion* and the *Bull* closed down. Samuel Snashall of Southover, a Dissenting maltster, bought the *Lion* for

£265 and shared the premises with a rising carpenter, Robert Burstow. The *Bull* was sold for £210 to a Dissenting minister, Thomas Barnard, who gutted the Elizabethan range at the rear, leaving its outer shell to encase a meeting-house for his Presbyterians. After William Read, landlord of the *Kings Head*, died in 1696 worth over £1000, William Stonestreat sold it for £140 to Jacob Mabb carpenter, who changed its use before 1713. These four inns were somewhat distanced from market trading, whereas three houses west of St Mary's Lane, in the thick of it, and occupied by victuallers in 1662, had emerged by the mid-1680s as the *Crown*, the *Pelicans* - a tribute to the Pelhams - and the *George,* where a soldier from a Marine Regiment died in 1691.[42]

The Borough's economy was also nourished by residents who drew solid incomes from a variety of assets. Two were Cavalier activists who arrived with the Restoration; but Sir Thomas Woodcock departed soon after Henry Shelley bought the former *Vine* from the Sackville estate in 1663, and Sir Thomas Nutt quitted [Newcastle House] in 1673. An abiding Cavalier, however, an Anglican praised for his 'piety', was Ambrose Trayton, buried at All Saints in 1679 aged 87 years. His son predeceased him, and his grandson, Ambrose, died in May 1686, just short of his 27th birthday, leaving Dobell's Field, Greenwall tannery and houses on School Hill to a brother Nathaniel, a barrister at Clement's Inn whose clients included the duke of Norfolk. Nathaniel bought Southover manor and its demesne from the Tuftons in 1709, and being a fervent Tory, he largely funded the rebuilding of the church tower.[43]

It was after the affluent John Oliver died in 1686 that the *White Lion* and the *Bull* were sold - a nephew, Thomas Browne, inherited his lands at Firle and Framfield and the mansion [Dial House] at Bridgefoot. Oliver had married Mary, a sister of Peter Courthope at Danny Park. As already noted, another sister, Dorothy wedded Dr Benjamin White. Henry Bill, moreover, White's friend on School Hill, married their sister Jane, and then, after Jane's death, John Oliver's sister Frances. These close-knit nuptial alliances allowed the eminent naturalist, John Ray, when writing to Courthope in 1673, to offer his 'humble service' to 'Mr Oliver & Mrs Oliver, Mr Bill, Mr White & his lady' - all 'known to me as though I had named them'. At Cambridge in the 1650s Ray had tutored Courthope, and his cousin, Timothy Burrell of Cuckfield. In 1662 he inquired of Courthope, on behalf of a friend, if the 'free school' at Lewes still lacked a master. During his visits to them in Sussex the cousins encouraged his search for rare ferns and hairy wood-grass, and to them he dedicated his *Synopis animalium quadrupedum et serpentini generis* (1693). Courthope also persuaded him to compile *A collection of English words, not generally used, with their significations and origin*; Burrell's brother bore the cost of its printing in 1674 - an appendix described how Wealden iron was made. Such was Ray's affection for the Lewes Downs that the view from Plumpton Plain [close to 'Boxholte' where Montfort re-grouped his

HERE LYES THE BODY
OF ROBERT HEATH SON OF
ROBERT HEATH & GRANDSON
OF WILLIAM HEATH ALL OF THIS
TOWNE OF LEWIS ESQVIRES HE
DYED THE 10TH DAY OF IANVARY
ANNO DNI

MDCLXXXL

ÆTAT XXIIII

162 The memorial brass

army] was commended in his most popular work, *The Wisdom of God in the works of Creation*, as equal to any he knew of in Europe.[44]

Increasingly affluent was Henry Shelley, the eldest son of the Civil War MP. He bought the former *Vine* for £210 in 1663 and installed a stone tablet of Tudor date displaying the family coat-of-arms buttressed by amorini. Mention has been made of his ambitious sheep-corn husbandry, thereafter, at Houndean and 'the Rises'. He acquired Telscombe manor in 1686 and died in 1691 worth over £3000. Also wealthy, with several estates in eastern Sussex, was his cousin, Robert Heath, who acquired, after Lady Margaret Pelham's death, her mansion in St Andrew's Lane. His memorial brass in St Mary Westout recorded his own untimely demise in 1682. His widow, Frances, bore him a posthumous heir, Robert II, and then married Henry, the younger son of Sir John Pelham of Laughton. Henry settled at St Andrew's Lane, though he was 'gone to Holland' when Sir John Ashburnham called, hoping to dine, in June 1687. In her will, made in 1703, Frances allowed Henry the use of the mansion rent-free, if he remained a widower, till Robert II came of age, and Robert leased it to him, after wedding Arabella Trevor in 1707 and settling at Glyndebourne. Henry became Clerk of the Office of Pells for life in 1698, a lucrative sinecure at the Exchequer secured by his family's influence in Whig circles.[45]

The considerable property acquired by William Alcock while serving as Clerk of the Peace - a more strenuous post than Pelham's - was to anchor two other gentlemen in the Borough. His daughter Hannah took the Friars estate by the bridge to Thomas Pellatt of Bignor in West Sussex. In 1673 he replaced the Tudor pile depicted by George Randoll with a smart brick box of six bays - already the Artisan Mannerism of its bold angle-quoins, string-course and two-tier pilasters had been deployed at draper Barnard's High Street extension. Pellatt died at the Friars of smallpox in 1680 and was buried in All Saints, despite owning Bignor Park, as well as lands at Isfield and Firle, and a London wharf off Thames Street, shared with his brother, a City ironmonger. By her marriage Alcock's other daughter, Elizabeth, took lands at Ovingdean to Richard Paine from East Grinstead. He moved into Richard Boughton's former residence [Antioch House], possibly about 1671 - the date on a rainwater-head there. He also bought an adjacent garden from butcher

163 The smart brick box

Thurgood. And he opted to be interred at St Mary Westout in 1693, despite owning Gravetye manor and Burstow Park, both near East Grinstead.[46]

During and after the 1680s the Paines and Pellatts cemented by marriage their ties with each other, and with the Shelleys and the Newtons. Richard Paine's son, Richard II, wedded Thomas Pellatt's daughter Mary, and her sister Hannah, Henry Shelley's son Richard. Pellatt's son William, married Apsley Newton's daughter Grace, and Paine's daughter Anne, married Newton's son William. Since all were Anglican Whigs, their network had political, as well as social, consequence in the Borough. In 1658 Apsley Newton had inherited the Grange (11 hearths) at Southover, also extensive property in the Weald. Like his grandfather, Evelyn's Puritan mentor, he was a barrister at Gray's Inn. His wife was Elizabeth Caldicott from Selmeston, a granddaughter of Matthew who served the prodigal third earl of Dorset. Her sister had married Henry Shelley. During sixty years Apsley made few structural changes to his ancestral home, though a stone mantel piece in a second-floor bedroom is inscribed 'A E 1675'. But like his father William, he extended the grounds by acquiring tenements beyond the Winterbourne fronting onto Eastport Lane.[47]

The partiality for Lewes shown by the Pellatts and the Paines, the Shelleys and the Newtons, despite their lands elsewhere, was matched by the sons-in-law of Stephen French, the owner of Stream in Chiddingly. He died in 1666 and two years later so did his only son, John, whose alabaster memorial in Wadham College chapel is adorned with bay-wreaths and borne up by two sturdy dolphins. In 1678 Stephen's widow, Susan, the daughter of a Lord Chief Justice, settled the house at the bot-

345

tleneck [143] on her daughter Charity, whose husband, Thomas Newdigate, a barrister at Gray's Inn, often resided there till his death in 1720. In 1687 Susan bought another house a few doors up [138-139], which her daughter Anne's husband, Thomas Bromfield, often used, though he inherited the manors of Brede and Udimore in 1690.[48]

In the 1660s well-to-do householders also resided in Southover, especially in sunny, spacious, well-drained Westport (See map 5.2). At Southover End [Brookside] was William Coby (7) attorney, who bought the manor of Balsdean in 1679. Widow Grace Caldicott (7), Apsley Newton's mother-in-law, lived just across Juggs Lane. The freehold of William Russell (5) [the Old Brewery House] encompassed a malt-house, orchards and four acres of pasture; his bequests included Piddinghoe 'rectory' and marshland at Pevensey. Next door was John Tichborne (6) gentleman, the son of an ironmaster at Cowden , and east of him [at Fairhall] resided affluent William Lane (10), a barrister at the Middle Temple who inherited 'rebels lands in Ireland'. Lane died in 1688 owning the manors of Plumpton-Piddinghoe and Meeching, ferries at Stock and Newhaven, and a garden 'environed with a wall', opposite Fairhall, which descended with it till 2001. Further east lived Frances Pickering (6), widow of Benjamin, the Presbyterian rector, and next door [at the Croft] was William Russell junior (7), who married John Vinall's granddaughter, and inherited the *Swan* from Richard Kidder.[49]

South of the High Street stood the spacious but redundant Lord's Place, which accounted for most of the 33 hearths credited to the earl of

164 The Old Brewery House

Thanet. In 1664 ten pounds of lead were stolen from its roof. William Lane and others contracted to demolish the mansion in 1668 and maybe he removed to Fairhall the stone door-case carved with Renaissance detail, already noted there. Moreover, the precinct water-mill, leased by Francis Verrall in 1636, had ceased to turn by 1702 when Thomas Medley claimed to have planted its pond-head, the Pad Pool, with a hundred ash trees. The demesne farmhouse to the west of Cockshut Lane [Southover Manor] was occupied by Mr Goodwin (6), acting presumably as the earl of Thanet's steward. West of the *Swan* lived John Boult (4), the non-resident parson of Telscombe. He sold the house soon after to Henry Sheppard, newly reinstated as vicar of Iford. Richard Burdett (8), the former Borough grocer and Puritan activist, had bought the premises next door [Southover Old House] in 1661; he also acquired an adjacent walled garden 'where a house had lately stood'.[50]

165 Gables Cottage

Like spacious living, malting, brewing and the drink trade remained well entrenched at Westport. Thomas Combes, maltster and victualler, owned a horse-mill and lived a few doors west of Edward Auger (6), a weaver and innkeeper at the corner of 'Potters Lane'. A decade or so later, their premises bore the sign of the *Spread Eagle* (an emblem of the earl of Thanet) and of the *Three Mariners*, and between them stood the *Red Lion*. Across Potters Lane [at Anne of Cleves House] was Richard Dunke (4), a maltster and 'grain factor' who exported 5120 bushels of malt to London in 1668. Next door [at Gables Cottage] traded Richard Gill (4) maltster. The *Swan* [17-19] was kept by James Carver (6), a brewer accused of sup-

166 The former *Swan*

347

plying six barrels of strong beer to an unlicensed alehouse at Hamsey; a native of Brighton, he was doubtless related to Dirck Carver, the brewer martyred under Mary. A patron of the *Swan*, approached there to pay his poor rate in 1665, threatened to throw the collector down the stairs and spit on the JP who authorized it. If anything, malting in Westport was to intensify. In 1691-3 John Verrall [at the Old Brewery House] bought barley in bulk from Richard Shelley, and in 1687 his eastern neighbour, William Auger brewer, owned a malt-house, 3200 bushels of malt worth £360, 216 bushels of sea-coal, and 19 runts in Pevensey Level - at some date columns and bases of Caen stone were removed from the priory precinct to underpin buildings on the site [32-33]. By 1697 there was a malt-house too in the grounds of Fairhall.[51]

Probably most of the six alehouses, denounced in 1685 as havens of the idle, the lewd, and the profligate poor, were in Westport, for though Southover was but a 'small suburb' and 'no great road', traffic from Newhaven and from Brighton did mingle at Juggs Lane Corner. It continued eastward, past the premises David Wood blacksmith shared in the 1660s with Mary Auger, a weaver's widow, and past 'the foot way for foot passengers' [Bell Lane], to turn north [down St Pancras Lane], past a forge worked by William Parcel and Thomas Deane, to cross the bridge, haphazardly prefixed in a post-Catholic era as Pancras, Pankeridge, Panchurst and Penticost. Because it had been 'altogether unpassable for three weeks', tenants of lands 'late belonging to the priory of Saint

167 The smithy at Southover End

Pancras' were ordered to repair it in January 1651. Once across, traffic could ascend to the Borough with relative ease up Rotten Row. The bridge further downstream, called Bowiers Bridge in 1512, the stone bridge in 1635 and Leopard's Bridge in 1657 and 1682, was less used, for it led to Keere Street, a precipitous ascent to the Borough. Apart from the blacksmiths and sellers of drink, this road traffic provoked little commerce in Westport in the 1660s. East of Thomas Combes lived Henry Chitty weaver and John Burgess, bailiff of Southover; west of the *Swan* was Richard Augur weaver, east of it, Seth Turner shoemaker, Thomas Kennard clothier and William Dunn haberdasher and petty chapman. - in the 1650s the Turners falsely accused the Dunns of poisoning their home-brewed beer.[52]

At the east corner of St James's Street [the Red House] resided pastor Edward Newton (7), rector till August 1662 of Southover and Westout. (See map 5.3) A later occupier, perhaps, was Richard Mantle gardener; his inventory in 1720 included turnip, carrot and cabbage plants, also a dozen 'old Turkey worked chairs'. Horticulture, it seems, flourished in Southover. In 1679 clusters of grapes were stolen from a garden there. Thomas Medley - so he said - established a host of bushes around the manor house - apricot, peach, nectarine and plum, grape, gooseberry, currant and raspberry - as well as 'a small knot bed'. In 1711 Thomas Hunt gardener stocked 14 cucumber glasses and some 2500 grafted trees. And Apsley Newton [at the Grange] supplied the 'excellent' grafts of 'the wardens and pear royal' sent to John Evelyn by William Snatt, the curate at Malling. Possibly Apsley also planted the [now threatened] North American tulip tree. There were well tended gardens too in the Borough. John Macky noted the 'Gentlemen's Seats, joining to one another with their Gardens up Hill and down Hill'. Benjamin White on School Hill sent 'very good' grafts of 'popperings' [a pear from Flanders] to William Snatt. Local 'ladies' found the grapes on their vines tasted of salt after the great storm on 26 November 1703 which sank Admiral Shovell off the Scillies. As for retailing at 'Lewes', cherries were carried from 'the fruiterer' there to viscount Montague at Poynings Place in September 1657, and Giles Moore bought garden seeds there - as well as a thousand 'bowler' stones at Brighton for his knot garden.[53]

168 The tulip tree

169 The 'old freehold house'

170 The massive table-tomb

In St James's Street in the 1660s lived Robert Belson mason and John Heaver shoemaker. Belson's descendent, the builder John Latter Parsons, fondly described the mason's premises [12] in 1885 as an 'old freehold house' owned by his family since 'the time of the Commonwealth'. Masons, bricklayers and carpenters mostly clustered, however, in the workaday cul-de-sac of Eastport. John Pannett carpenter and John Cole glover remained as tenants when Zachery Smith, ejected from Glynde parsonage in 1662, bought the corner-house opposite Newton [the *King's Head*] in 1663. Next door [at 36-38 Priory Street] lived Thomas Swane (4) bricklayer, who with Saunders the carpenter received £10 to rebuild the free school in 1661; his massive table-tomb survives. Between Swane and 'Copthall', the parish poor-house, was Thomas Hunter weaver. At the south-east corner of The Island [in Garden Street] resided Robert Harwood mason, and along Eastport Lane [at Dale House] Robert Holford (5) mason, who owned the *Chequer* at the Lane's south-west corner. In 1657 the swine of Thomas Tidy mason, his tenant maybe, foraged along 'the twitten'. By 1687 the *Chequer* was a disorderly alehouse where William, 'a stranger', expired. As already noted, the seven or so tenements lying between Eastport Lane and the Winterborne in the 1660s, were all to be absorbed into the Grange estate by the early 18th century; already annexed were a house and orchard 'late Darington's'. One occupier, William Gaston carpenter, refused to assist a rate collector in 1667; another, Thomas Waller bricklayer, also used the Chauntry House on the hill at Westout.[54]

John Crampe miller had lived near The Island in 1611, when 'the little mill' below Watergate was still turning. However Edward Cornford of Southover, tanner, was accused in 1654 of buying a 'rough' hide direct from a butcher, and by then his tannery had probably replaced the mill. In 1657 his house - later he was assessed for 3 hearths - stood near 'the common well or spring in Nithingale Lane' - a name perhaps for Garden Street. Possibly it was the house and orchard called Otelands, with a

'Pond Garden', described in 1620 as facing [across Garden Street] to the free school, which stood near the corner of Eastport Lane - its site now part of the Grange gardens. By the mill pond a footbridge over the Winterbourne gave boys from the Borough access to the school. Maybe John Cotmot had this low-lying location in mind when he bequeathed 6s 8d in 1559 'for making of high ways for children to go to school'. On the east, the mill site and Pond Garden abutted water-meadows along the Winterbourne, so perhaps building materials were delivered thereabouts by water. A wharf at Southover End, approached from the tortuous Cockshut stream, was later occupied by the Barcombe timber-merchant, Nicholas Longley, who owned another at Sharpsbridge in Newick. He supplied wood for the repair of Keere Street in 1682.[55]

As for the wharfs along the Ouse, a few were clustered at Bridgefoot. South of the bridge lay the Town Wharf, eighty-feet-long, the 'legal quay' for the conduct of foreign trade, and the site perhaps of the Borough's ducking-stool. West of it lived Edward Fitzherbert (4) who supplied iron in the 1650s for a 'pier' projected at Newhaven harbour. His successors were James Reade, a major dealer in ordnance, and Ambrose Galloway II, a remarkably versatile merchant. William Peake (10) had bought the house and wharf north of the bridge for £249 in 1658. He traded with Normandy, Ostend and Holland; he also sent hops to Dublin and wheat to the Canaries, and received tobacco, ebony and fustic wood from Jamaica; in 1671 he purchased the manor of Seaford. His Bridgefoot premises passed in 1684 to a nephew, Simon Snell, who traded to Dieppe, Bordeaux and Portugal and shipped wine to London. Next to

171 Bridgefoot: looking west past the Friars

172 The Weighing Machine

Peake was John Oliver (10), owner of the *White Lion* and the *Bull*, whose freehold bordered the riverbank north of Peake. Near Eastgate, beside the Town Ditch, Gideon Mantell was to sketch a massive and venerable Public Weighing Machine in 1810. John Reddington, a Supervisor of his Majesty's Customs, was buried at All Saints in 1680, and near him in 1690 a colleague, Francis Cooke.[56]

East of Lewes Bridge at Cliffe the commercial layout cannot be charted in any detail because its householders were jumbled up, with little regard for street order, in the single surviving hearth tax return, made in 1662. (See map 5.4) To identify householders listed, the hearths assessed will, in all cases, be given in brackets. North of the bridge [at 1-8 High Street] Widow Judith Stevenson (11) owned spacious premises and wharfs, occupied in 1650 by her father Samuel Towers, who traded with Dieppe and Flushing, Cork and Kinsale; they were used also that year by a cutler, a basket maker and a dyer. Sometime between 1645 and 1685 the premises were partly rebuilt [4-8] as a series of 'multi-roomed lodgings' linked by wide corridors; a plaster frieze also survives. Other householders in West Street [now High Street] had access to wharfs adjoining the Ouse or the Great Sewer. On the south side were Ralph Akehurst (9), the merchant who shackled his wife, the pioneering Friend, and also Simon Everenden (6), the grocer who cast iron shot for the Commonwealth and sent 70 pounds of beeswax to Dieppe in 1662 - unless it was his son, Simon II. At that date another son, Walter, owned Copped Hall opposite the Combe in North Street [Malling Street]. But Walter probably resided at West Street by 1674 when his 'company' imported from London groceries, spinach and pickles, alum, starch and lead, madder and glass, brandy, vinegar and tobacco, Rhenish and Spanish wine - he received £8 3s for a hogshead of wine supplied to Glynde Place. Walter also shipped hops, wrought iron and osier 'basket rods' to West Country ports. John Vandike plumber, painter and glazier, had followed his father as Master of the House of Correction in West Street by 1672 when his 'company' unloaded from London lead, tin and pewter, nails and hemp, soap and oil, pitch and tar, tobacco, brandy and Canary wine, sugar and ginger bread, oranges, raisins and walnuts. Vandike cast bullets for the local militia and 'coloured' the doors and windows in the 'withdrawing room' at Glynde Place.[57]

352

Wharfs also abutted South Street. Charles Goodwin, the Borough attorney, owned a timber yard there, occupied by Stephen Gunn in 1687. Maybe an earlier occupier, called 'Taylor', was the Thomas Taylor of Cliffe who bequeathed timber at Heathfield in 1649. Storer Bythwood, owner of an adjacent yard, sent 1360 bushels of wheat to London in 1688. Simon Edmonds fellmonger, assessed for 6 hearths in 1662, embezzled seven tenements in South Street, parish property of which he was a feoffee - so perhaps it was there that in 1668 he stockpiled wool, 'by a navigable river', with intent to smuggle it abroad. Doubtless South Street was home to some of the ten 'reputed seamen' listed at Cliffe in 1672: John Giner had served in the *Monke* and others were 'at Yarmouth' - probably with Brighton's fishing fleet. Between 1697 and 1719 Cliffe boys were apprenticed to mariners at Whitby and Rochester, Brighton and Fowey, and to an anchor-smith at Wapping.[58]

Beyond South Street, on the riverbank near Southerham, timber was stacked in the 1680s by John Farley, a bargeman who built a 'good tenantable house' in South Street [the Old Ship], and in 1679 by Christopher Cole from Pulborough whose 'Company' shipped 24 loads of timber through Newhaven to London in 1682, and by John Best from Wivelsfield and John Ford from Framfield - Wealden parishes with immense reserves of oak. Riding southwards from Tunbridge Wells, Daniel Defoe saw specimens of 'prodigious' size, destined for the royal shipyards at Chatham, but dumped by the road till drier weather would allow a 'tug' pulled by 22 oxen to move them further. Great piles of wood fuel 'designed for London' were stacked on a wharf at Pevensey in 1686, but whether much was sent down the Ouse is uncertain.[59]

As for wrought iron, shipments through Newhaven drifted lower as Wealden manufacture continued to decline - 65 tons in 1663, 48 in 1674, 126 in 1683, 50 in 1693, 42 in 1702, 13 in 1713. Most went to London, a little till the 1680s to Kings Lynn, Chichester and Bristol. Shippers included Sir John Pelham who owned forges at Brightling and Mayfield; the iron masters Sir Thomas Dyke and Thomas Western; the local dealers James Reade, Walter Everenden and Ambrose Galloway. Wealden producers now faced competition from abroad. Indeed in 1664 a Sussex petition denounced sweated labour in Sweden, where men worked as Slaves, without 'that liberty which the meanest of Your Majesty's subjects comfortably enjoy'. 'Foreign' iron was unloaded at Newhaven from Spain via London in 1663, from Sweden via Cowes in 1674, from Flanders via Rotterdam in 1677. William Fry at Bristol sent English iron, nails and scythes in 1702; and in 1708 sweated Swedish iron arrived direct from Fredrikstad near Oslo, along with Norwegian deals and barrel staves.[60]

The export of iron guns through Newhaven, however, was boosted by the wars with the Dutch in 1664-7 and 1672-4. Wealden roads were torn up in 1669 by their carriage to the riverside at Cliffe and Southerham from furnaces at Pounsley and Maresfield. Walter Norman, a Quaker engaged in the 'Boring of Guns' at Maresfield in 1674, was visited by emissaries from the Lewes Meeting who fruitlessly pressed him to refrain. Both these furnaces, it seems, were worked by John Newnham, a major shipper of guns to London between 1668 and 1674. The 300 tons he sent in 1672 included nine 'murderers' - small cannon that could be used to clear Dutch boarding parties from English decks. And 'very dangerous to passengers', apparently, was Newnham's habit, noted in 1677, of 'laying and [test] firing' his guns by the river at the Malling end of South Street - the wood broker, John Ford, 'tried' his in Southerham chalk pit. Abetting Newnham was James Reade, his partner perhaps. Reade was the sole shipper of ordnance to London between 1675 and 1677, dispatching 200 or 300 tons a year, as well as small consignments to Ostend, Dunkirk and Dieppe. Perhaps he invested too heavily - while serving as Junior Constable in 1681 he died insolvent, 'not able to satisfy his debts'. William Peake and John Garland, his neighbours at Bridgefoot, also dabbled in guns, maybe more cautiously.[61]

Shipments, mostly to London but a few to Bristol, were boosted afresh by the wars with Louis XIV between 1689 and 1713. Indeed new furnaces were built in the hinterland of Lewes at Pippingford on Ashdown Forest and at Heathfield. In 1743 the Heathfield to Lewes road was still being torn up by guns - 'nothing' could follow them and 'the Country' cursed heartily. From his Waldron furnace in 1693 Sir John Pelham dispatched 84 tons of 'Grenado shells' and guns, via Lewes, to Newhaven. Yet the busiest dealer was Ambrose Galloway II, a cradle Quaker whose father had reproved Walter Norman for 'Boring' at Maresfield. Each year between 1684 and 1704 and in 1713-14 he shipped up to 300 tons of ordnance, as well as a galaxy of artefacts cast by skilled mould-makers at furnaces upstream: anvils, weights and anchors, bolts, hinges and saws, pans and 'poison' pots, kettles and fire-backs, plates and braces, furnaces and stoves, 'elbows', 'knees' and 'crooks', rollers to grind sugar. Galloway himself worked Ardingly forge by 1696, and to supply it maybe, he imported 'old ballast iron' from Rotterdam. Among small dealers in guns, shot (and grain) were Thomas Akehurst at West Street Cliffe, a Quaker like his shackled mother; John Farley, the bargeman at South Street, and Abraham Vine, possibly the bellows maker at Fisher Street Corner.[62]

In 1685 four patten woods - moulds used for casting iron artefacts - were stolen from Benjamin Court at Cliffe, where George Trelpha was employed in making them in 1688; some indeed were shipped through Newhaven to London. Court, an ironmonger, supplied nails to repair the House of Correction in 1702. (Anthony Tompkins 'caster maker' died at Cliffe in 1700; but he probably retired there to be near his Quaker son-in-law, Thomas Beard.)[63] By then the casting of bells locally had ceased. John Palmer, at the bottom of St Mary's Lane, who feuded in 1661 with the Pursers at Pinwell and whose widow was buried at All Saints in 1670, had supplied them to Friston, Horsted Keynes and Woodmancote. By 1676 William Hull, who trained under John Hodson, a leading London founder, had settled at Malling, where he cast at least 18 bells for churches in eastern Sussex, among them a treble and a tenor for St Mary Westout. In 1687 he bequeathed his bell-metal, a large silver cup and the use of his workshop, to his son John, who perhaps cast a bell for Kingston. Possibly the workshop was near the Combe in North Street where the *Five Bells* stood in the mid 18th century.[64]

Much merchandise unloaded at Newhaven was destined for Lewes and offered a widening choice to customers there. Cargoes from London could include sherry, walnuts and port wine, Virginia tobacco, Canary wine, 'florence' wine and mum (a German beer), pantiles, brass kettles and stool pans, German linen, aniseed, oranges and anchovies, copperas and indigo, whalebone and wainscot boards. Tobacco-pipe clay arrived from Cowes and Poole, along with Newfoundland fish and train-oil, and Hampshire salt from Southampton and Lymington. Prunes, brandy and Portuguese wine were unshipped from Portsmouth; 'prize wine' from Plymouth; tin from Penryn; and bottles and glasses, iron ware and buttons, serge blankets and cheese, cider and spirits from Bristol. Possibly carried overland to London were the large quantities of French silks, unloaded between 1662 and 1664, along with glass necklaces and hair powder, hats and fans, Seneca gum, white coral and Sarsaparilla root. Locally distributed were occasional cargoes of silks and brandy, glass and canvas, prunes and paper, coral beads, walnuts and orange-flower ointment from Dieppe and St Valery, of stone from Caen, and salt from the Bay of Biscay. However an embargo placed on French imports, between 1678 and 1685, caused canvas, copy-paper and brandy to be shipped from Ostend, and wine and cherry brandy, linen and window glass, toy snuff boxes and whistles, salt and two asses from Portugal. After the Dutch Wars ended in 1674, there was also a brisk import from Rotterdam of bricks and brandy, pantiles and Delft ware, Rhenish wine, kettles and tea tables, spinning wheels and iron chimney-backs, bulrushes, tin roasting boxes and earthenware stew pans.[65]

Demand was rising too for Baltic softwoods. Direct from Norway came the 2600 deals unloaded at Newhaven by John Best of Wivelsfield in 1680, also the 2200 deals and middle baulks, spars and handspikes, imported in 1687 by Stephen Gunn, the occupier of Goodwin's yard at South Street. Edward Meads, a Borough carpenter, stocked Norway 'oak', English oak and Irish boards in 1710. Swedish and Polish timber was used to build a farm house at Kingston in 1711, Norwegian deals - 'Christiany', 'dram' and 'long sound' - to floor Peter White's new house on School Hill in 1715. Whether there was a more urgent demand for the coal from Newcastle and Sunderland, delivered to Newhaven by local shipmasters, is unclear. In 1687 the brewer William Auger stocked 216 bushels at Southover; but Peter White's new fire-places were designed to burn wood. Unusual was a cargo of coal from Swansea in 1672.[66]

The carriage of merchandise by barge to and from Newhaven was still hampered, of course, by eastward-drifting shingle at the harbour mouth, which also caused flooding along the lower Ouse. Various attempts were made to stem the shingle. A 'pier' at the harbour was projected sometime before April 1652 when a blacksmith's widow at Southover asked the Lewes bench to repay her £17 which he had spent in their employ, making ironwork for it. More grandiose in scope was a licence granted in 1664 to a syndicate of courtiers. Besides a pier they envisaged lighthouses, fortifications and slaughter-houses. Yet in September 1671 flood water was swirling waist high at West Street in Cliffe, and by 1677 Andrew Yarranton - no enemy of Improvement - was claiming that at least £4000 had been wasted on building a useless 'northern' pier, whereas a 'western' one, costing £6000, would have created a deep-water anchorage, ideal for trade and strategically sited 'over against the Naval of France'. The northern pier was in any case a wreck by 1689, prompting Lewesians to petition fruitlessly for new harbour works in 1693, 1715 and 1724.[67]

Beyond the harbour lay the hazards of Seaford Bay, where many vessels were wrecked, especially near Cuckmere Haven and Birling Gate: the *Adventure* from Plymouth, the *Humility* from Milford, the *Albany* from Scotland, the *Saint Andrew* from Bruges. Merchandise washed ashore included French wine, brandy and silk, Irish tallow, freize and goats' hair, Brazil wood and indigo, molasses and tobacco, beaver furs, sperm oil and New England fish oil. A Lymington boat, carrying 500 bushels of salt, foundered near the harbour mouth in 1701. By then government warehouses, spaced between Telscombe and East Dean, stored salvaged wine, brandy and Portuguese oil, anchors and masts, sails and cordage, cannon and muskets. Rough seas could also precipitate commerce. When the *Saint Anne* of Middelburg was 'forced in by the weather', brandy loaded at Nantes was sold, and Purbeck marble when a Waterford vessel bound for Ostend lost its anchor. But despite a reputation for 'wrecking', fifty local men with boats rescued a Hamburg vessel 'off the rock' in 1672.[68]

The wars with the Dutch also disrupted Newhaven's trade. In January 1665 three of their warships lurking in Brighton Bay provoked 'great fear' at Lewes. In 1672 Sir John Pelham asked the government to supply some small frigates as protection against 'the Hollanders' - when they chased a French ship into Newhaven, the master traded a tarred rope for provisions. But far more damaging to Channel commerce were the wars with Louis XIV between 1689 and 1713. Though in 1700 Thomas Pelham secured a government cutter, the *Lion*, to patrol the port's approaches, privateering was rife. Ambrose Galloway II lost 550 bushels of salt when the *John and Margaret* of Lymington was captured off Selsey in 1708. Newhaven's trade was much reduced. Indeed corn and guns were probably sent to London overland, despite the often appalling state of Wealden roads - Daniel Defoe noted the carriage of 'a lady of very good quality' being drawn through the mud to church by six oxen.[69]

The fleet of freighters at Newhaven was always small compared with those at Brighton and Hastings. In 1687-8 eight vessels based there appeared in local ports books. The *George* voyaged to Dieppe; the *Lewes Adventure* and the *Lewes and Cliffe* to London; the *Plain Dealing* and the *John and Thomas* to London and Newcastle; the *Happy Return* to London and Plymouth, Dieppe and Boulogne; the *Blessing* to London and Plymouth, Morlaix and Rotterdam; the *Susan and Mary* to London, Newcastle and Plymouth, Morlaix, Croisic and Bordeaux. Possibly other vessels were on long voyages by-passing the home port. Captain John Hesilgrove, ashore at Bethnal Green in 1665, had asked that his frigate, the *Lewes*, be freighted with victuals for Tangiers, so she could 'sail thence to Turkey, where he has assurance of a full lading homewards'. A rarity was the *Rejoice*, a vessel based at Seaford, which carried grain to Rotterdam in 1676. By 1701 Newhaven mustered a mere 13 sailors and its fleet had dwindled to four ships, compared with 35 at Hastings and 77 at Brighton. The *Elizabeth*, the *John and Thomas*, the *Lewes Adventure* and the *Plain Dealing* voyaged to London that year; the *Plain Dealing* also to Bristol and Newcastle, and the *Lewes Adventure* to Rotterdam.[70]

By 1685 a focus of river traffic at Cliffe, south of the bridge and opposite the Town Wharf, was the *Bear*, owned by Dr William Harrison, vicar of Little Horsted, and kept by John Farley. An 18th-century tankard shows an animal on all fours, with a collar and length of chain, so maybe the premises included a bear pit - in 1598 John Stow noted the kennels for mastiffs at the *Bear* by London Bridge in Southwark. The landlord at Cliffe was perhaps the John Farley who stacked timber at Southerham, exported guns, and supplied boards when flints and 'small chalk' were laid on the bridge in 1681. This wooden structure, much battered by traffic and a turbid Ouse, needed constant repair. In 1667 £10 were spent, and £20 in 1671, after folk had waded waist-deep along West Street. A rebuilding was mooted in 1686 and in 1711, and finally in 1726 a robust arch of Portland stone, designed by Nicholas Dubois, was set in place. Just east of the *Bear*, about 1685, William Austen butcher occupied a house 'late the *Lamb*'; its earlier history, like the *Bear*'s, is unknown.[71]

Craftsmen at Cliffe still took advantage of the wetland along the Ouse. John King dyer (2 hearths) occupied ground on the rim of Wood Brooks in 1663. John Holmwood (3) itemized a dye house and furnace, a press and a pair of shears in his shop at West Street. Richard Adams (2), glover and fell-

173 The bear on all fours

monger, owned a house and rose garden 'under the chalk rock', separated by North Street from his orchards, workshop and water-meadow - in 1652 a man riding a brown bay horse had sold him some sheep skins stolen from Anthony Stapley MP. Thomas White (2), basket maker, occupied an osier bed called Fishers Plot on an island in the Ouse opposite South Street. Edward Dawley thatcher had owned the house and water-meadow near the Combe in North Street, used in 1662 by John West (3) blacksmith - a site well placed for in-coming horse traffic. On the Borough bank, Ralph Pope (4) worked the tannery at Green Wall, from which Richard Puxty shipped leather to Ostend in 1716 and supplied cow-hair to plasterers at Stanmer House. Near the tannery, perhaps, laboured John Foule soap boiler, whose wife was buried at St John's in 1673. John Gibson glover had a workshop in meadow land near the Friars in 1725.[72]

Ditches crossing the Wood Brooks probably allowed boats to approach the quarry just south of the Combe. Recorded in 1508, the working became a burial ground in 1846 - local Quakers chronicled a rock fall at Cliffe in 1681 because it killed John Coppard, a chalk-digger who greatly harassed them when a court bailiff. Near the Combe in 1662 probably lived Edmund Whitebread (2) mason, and earlier, perhaps, Foster Whitebread slate layer, and Francis Whitebread 'stone healer', who erected a cottage without the legally-required four acres of ground attached in 1654. Also adjacent to the Wood Brooks at North Street, by 1718, resided the timber shippers and carpenters, John and William Gasston. By then too, west of the Wood Brooks, two notable mansions had been re-built in brick. The seven bays of Malling Deanery were sturdily bonded by angle quoins and pilasters. Malling House was more chastely classical, 'stretching comfortably' across nine bays - tradition credits its re-fashioning to John Spence in 1710. Maybe neither had been

174 Malling Deanery and Malling House

altered by June 1687: Sir John Ashburnham merely noted they were 'very near one the other'.[73]

In 1662 brewers and maltsters at Cliffe still tapped the spring water below 'the sea-sand and slub'. Thomas James owned a malt-house south-east of Cliffe Corner. Edmund Goldham (2) probably leased one opposite the *Dorset Arms* in North Street. 'Grains and other filthiness' were thrown into West Street [from numbers 12-13] by John Palmer (5) maltster and Nicholas Hartley (3) brewer in 1667. Mercy Palmer (5), John's widowed mother, and William Cooper (2) shoemaker owned malt-houses on its south side. By 1686 there were others too on John Oliver's premises at Bridgefoot, and one on Trayton property above Eastgate Corner. Thereabouts in 1662 lived the coopers, John Stone and Richard Styles, and Robert Rossam brewer.[74]

Though inextricably linked to the commerce of Lewes borough, Cliffe remained a market 'town' in its own right. Its market-house was still in West Street, near the east entrance to the Fair Place. The upper room was rented out from 1695 and an 18th-century sketch shows what may be its sturdy finial. In 1670 a Ditchling blacksmith charged £5 10s to replace the mechanism of a nearby clock, usefully sited in the church tower. By the 1690s livestock trading in September was especially busy. On the 21st - the day of saint Matthew's fair - and 'on every market day' that month, 'great quantities of sheep of all sorts' were sold. Purchasers included 'farmers and countrymen' from Ashburnham, just north of Pevensey Level. Also bought, in 1698, was a spring lock for Richard Stapley at Twineham. Thomas Marchant and his wife from Hurstpierpoint attended in 1720. But Ashburnham folk chose to purchase their 'milch cows and steers' at Nutley fair held two days before the saint Mark's cattle fair at Cliffe on 25 April. So trading there was probably less hectic than in September, though the Pelham steward at Halland occasionally bought oxen.[75]

175 The finial silhouetted east of the chancel of St Thomas's

Facing the market-house was the *Swan* with its orchard and closes. In North Street, beyond the parsonage house (9), with access to the Fair Place, stood the *Dorset Arms*, perhaps kept in 1662 by George Vandyke (6) victualler - and in 1632 by George Shelton. Its alias, the *Cats*, was provoked by the ounces, the wild cats supporting the arms of the earls of Dorset, manorial lords of Cliffe. Also in North Street, opposite the *Cats*, John Hodge opened the *King and Queen*, probably in 1693 - its sign a tribute to the Protestant rulers, William and Mary. From his time may date the present four-bay street range and carriage arch [Pastorale Antiques]. Some tankards from the inn, made of London stoneware, were broken at the Fair Place. Hodge stood surety in 1694 for a labourer charged with 'beating off' a customs officer searching a barn in Ovingdean where 16 bales of French silks and laces lay hidden. Just west of the church [24-25] William Faulkner kept the *Greyhound* in 1686. The premises had been an alehouse in 1652, with a baker, James Eager, next door [22-23].[76]

In 1662 others traders clustered near the market-house. Richard Saxby (2) butcher was accused of slaughtering animals during Lent. So was Richard Paine (2) who rented Mill Field above East Street. Richard White (2/3) brazier had a married daughter living in New England. Richard White (2/3) basket maker was suspected of unlawfully 'destroying the young fry' in the Ouse. The assets of Thomas Ridge (5) draper were valued at £436 16s 5d in 1678. James Emery (2) goldsmith was the son of a maltster at Malling. Apprenticed to a London goldsmith in 1644, he sold to Sir John Stapley of Patcham in 1668 a silver salver engraved with the name and initials of Herbert, Stapley's eleven-year-old son. In 1670 Giles Moore paid him 'for exchange of my gold ring, being 2s 2d and for fashion 1s'. Half his working tools Emery left in 1675 to his son James who, besides domestic tumblers and spoons, made a communion cup for Alfriston in 1683. Simon Grover (3) blacksmith and Adrian Vandike (3) glazier traded north-east of Cliffe Corner in 1659, and Thomas Rawlinson carrier, north-west of it in 1681 when his wagons trundled to the *Talbot* at Southwark. John Tabret (4) carrier had bought premises west of the church in 1653.[77]

Traders further along West Street tapped traffic funnelling towards the bridge. Seemingly they included, on the north side, John Hanson (3) saddler, Thomas Winchester (2) butcher, who rented Church Wish at Wood Brooks, Valentine Tyler (2), hatter and felt maker, John Wade (2) tailor, and Nathaniel Newington (3) grocer who supplied the militia with four barrels of gunpowder in 1666. On the south side traded Simon Everenden (6) grocer, William Cooper (2) shoemaker, Richard Wickersham (3) draper, who leased premises by the House of Correction, and the landlord of the *Red Lion*.[78]

Despite its commercial vitality, lawyers, physicians and men with private means still avoided Cliffe. House-sites in North Street and South Street were cramped and overhung. West Street was founded on 'sea-sand' and subject to floods. The sewers crossing it were covered with iron gratings or with planks bored with auger holes. In the 1790s Paul Dunvan was to bewail its air and water supply, 'as bad as a narrow, crowded street and a swampy, dirty situation can make them'. Because of 'extreme inattention to the sewers' the well water tended to be 'impregnated with noisome and disgusting particles'; residents, not relishing 'the filtration of a jacques', resorted to the spring at Chapel Hill. In 1687, moreover, Sir John Ashburnham, familiar with malaria in Pevensey Level, had been quick to observe that 'the wet grounds' near Lewes 'must needs be great annoyances', rendering the air 'none of the best'. And indeed fevers were locally rife. William Spence at Malling complained in 1671 of a 'quartan ague going and coming all this winter'. John Clifton recalled in 1718 the medical bills he incurred while his family sickened at the parsonage amid 'the unwholesome air in the Cliffe' - more lethal even than the cutting winds on the South Downs. John Mills, a 'practitioner in physic', did settle there, but died unmarried in 1710, leaving property at Lindfield to his father.[79]

The wetlands, though, were still ideal for shooting wildfowl. 'From this town to the Sea is the best Winter Game for a Gun that can be imagined', John Macky observed in 1713. 'Several Gentlemen', he added, kept packs of dogs, but 'you must follow up Hill and down Hill, at the hazard of your neck, or you are thrown out of the Sport'. It was from a windmill high above the town that he admired its 'Romantick' situation, a 'Prospect' exceeding 'that of Cleves, Nimeguen, the Castle of Nuremberg'. Was the mill in question the one at Malling, worked in 1662 by Cornelius Fox (2), or Cliffe mill, then occupied by John Baldy (4), or the one at Cranedown, used by John Vinall in 1655, and by Richard Pescod who shipped grain and alder poles to London in 1683?[80]

Yet despite the a 'Romantick' prospect, and a solid broadly-based economy, Lewes in 1713 was rife with religious and political discord. The Restoration of Charles II had settled neither the complexion of the State Church nor the balance between Crown and Parliament. Even after the Glorious Revolution in 1688-9 Whigs and Tories, Dissenters and Anglicans, were still in conflict, the nation a prey to rumour and discontent. The turmoil must now be examined.

176 The Dorset arms

Overleaf: the Popish Pedlar

12

The shadow of the Great Rebellion 1662-1714

They [the bailiffs] now approach the Town of Lewes, the Constable and Headborough of that Borough assisting them, but a far greater number of Children gazing and wondring after them .From Richard Thomas, a butcher, they take his weights for five shillings. They approach the house of Edward Henly, a shoemaker, and though they saw five pair of shoes hanging out of his stall worth double his fine, yet they fall a breaking open his door, which they split in sunder, and had one blow been given more, they had made the lock fly, but at length they better bethought themselves, and took the other shoes without entering. At Richard Benets, a Taylor, they stoutly battered his door till opened to them from withinside, there for his and his wives fine, being ten shillings, they took goods of several sorts, such as the kitchen would afford. At Nicholas Grisbrooks, a Blacksmith, they brake open his doors, and now the poor man can now no longer save his Bacon, they take amongst other things a good part of a flitch; one would not think they wanted a Rasher, that saw how rashly they acted.

John Ayres's NARRATIVE of the late proceedings of some Justices and others, pretending to put in execution the late Act, against Conventicles, against several peaceable people in and about the town of Lewes, in Sussex, only for their being quietly met to worship God [printed in 1670].

Just before the Pope marched Guy Faux with his dark Lanthorn, being booted and spurred after the Old Fashion and wearing a Vizard with a wonderful long Nose. Next comes the Pope with his Cross keys, Crosier staff and other Fopperies, having his Train borne up by several of his Clergy, being saluted as he passed by with a Copy of Verses. Next followed the Cardinals in their Caps, with the rest of the Clergy, Secular and Regular, having wonderful long beards and a string of beads about their middle, which they told as they went by. Behind these went the Nuns. But last of all comes the Ghost of Sir Edmund Berry Godfrey represented by a Person in black Clothes and a Shirt all Bloody, and his Face painted so white that he seemed rather Dead than Alive; before whom went a person carrying a Bloody Sword in his hand, who sometimes looking back would seem to be greatly affrighted at the sight of him.

The Domestick Intelligence no. 39, Tuesday 18 November 1679.

The solid prosperity of Lewes in the later Stuart period was achieved despite political and religious strife which the Glorious Revolution of 1688-9 by no means entirely dispelled. An avidly 'Cavalier' Parliament, elected in April 1661, was not dissolved till 1679. The MPs for Lewes borough, Sir John Stapley and Sir Thomas Woodcock, were both Monarchists and both were sweetened with official rake-offs, from the customs of London and from the excise. Yet neither flourished overmuch. Stapley sold his family estate at Patcham; Woodcock quitted his rented house at Westout and laid dubious claim to a niece's property at Newtimber. The Cavalier Parliament promptly alienated Puritans of every complexion by restoring a State Church, Arminian in doctrine and Laudian in ritual. Its priests saw themselves as 'the successors of the Apostles'. They also taught that Passive Obedience was owed to the king's 'sacred majesty' and sponsored a cult of his deceased father - a new church at fashionable Tunbridge Wells was dedicated to King Charles the Martyr. In 1665 Monarchists at Lewes 'strictly kept' the anniversary of his execution, January 30th.[1]

Over a thousand Puritan clergy rejected so 'Catholic' a State Church and vacated their livings in August 1662. Among them were Edward Newton (Southover and St Mary Westout) and Walter Postlethwaite (St Michael's). Soon after, the Cavalier Parliament imposed penalties - fines or imprisonment - on Puritans who boycotted the restored Anglican services, or worshipped in 'conventicles' of their own. In Lewes borough - an important regional capital - the policing of these 'Dissenters' depended on there being Monarchist High Constables ready to report them to quarter sessions and assizes. But in October 1663 only three members of the Fellowship, which elected the Constables, were firmly Monarchist: Richard Grisbrook butcher, Henry Rose saddler and William Brian who kept the *White Lion*. All three were new, recruited perhaps as a sop to Monarchists, along with a Puritan, Samuel Cruttenden haberdasher. Most of the other 19 members, relics of the Interregnum, were embracing Dissent. Because the Fellowship was prescriptive, the Crown could

177 Communion plate at St Michael's

not purge it by calling in and re-drafting a royal charter, a device used to pack the Corporations at Rye and Arundel with Monarchists. So radical political surgery was resorted to: on 5 October 1663 the Monarchist JPs who dominated the Lewes bench took the drastic step of themselves appointing Thomas James gentleman and John Holney apothecary as High Constables, and a year later Richard Grisbrook and Ralph Richardson who kept the *Star*. This action in effect ended the Borough's civic autonomy, for only Grisbrook was a member of the Fellowship. Because non-attenders at church had also to be reported to the restored Church courts, the Lewes bench intervened, in January 1664, to impose two Monarchist churchwardens on St Michael's - a strongly Puritan parish. William Thorgood butcher and John Brinkhurst gardener promptly purchased a silver communion cup and paten cover, to make good the plate sold in 1650.[2]

The neutered Fellowship also lost control of the Borough's rate income and property, causing some members to attempt passive resistance. In January 1664 Ralph Pope, junior Constable in 1662-3, was refusing 'to deliver over the weights and measures and other things in his custody of public use to the present Constables'. In July 1667 the County Commissioners for Charitable Uses demanded that Ralph Pope, Stephen Snatt and Edward Holmwood surrender bonds and money belonging to the Borough. Direct rule by the Lewes bench ended in October 1665 when Constables and Headboroughs were chosen - not by the Fellowship - but 'at the Law Day holden for the Town and Borough of Lewes'. An order made by the bench in October 1668, however, shows that selection of Constables at the Law Day was a regression to direct seigneurial control. Because the serving Constables had been in office for over a year, and no others were 'likely to be chosen by the Lords of the Leet or their Steward', the bench appointed Henry Hopkins surgeon and Ferdinando Bryan who kept the *Bull*, to act until the Lords of the Leet 'shall duly elect and make choice of others'. All three 'Lords', whose stewards presided over the court leet in rotation, were Monarchists. Richard Sackville, earl of Dorset, became Lord Lieutenant of Sussex in 1670 with his son Charles, who succeeded him in 1677. George Nevill, baron Bergavenny, and Thomas Howard, duke of Norfolk, were Catholics. Bergavenny died in 1666, but his heir grew up in the faith. And though Norfolk was insane, his brother, also a Catholic, acted for him till inheriting the title in 1677. The selection itself was perhaps convoluted, for in 1733, and probably in 1686, the steward chose the two Constables from four 'senior' jurors nominated by the leet jury. But since the steward selected the jury from the customary tenants, he could ensure a Monarchist majority within it. Certainly most jurors between 1666-7 and 1671-2 were Monarchists - 15 served as Constables, two more as Headboroughs. Of the 34 Constables in office between 1663-4 and 1688-9, only two were Dissenters. John Knapp, chosen in October 1673, died in office, and the Lewes bench ordered Walter Brett junior to succeed him. Brett served again in 1684-5, the year a Monarchist Grand Jury denounced him as 'dangerous and ill affected'. Why they were chosen is obscure.[3]

The Monarchist High Constables duly harassed Dissenters who refused to attend church, reporting 99 to the Lewes bench between 1663 and 1665, and 133 to the assizes at Horsham in 1670. They also accused them of trading offences: selling wool without a licence, buying butter and eggs out of market hours, using false bread-weights. Churchwardens too reported non-attenders to the Church courts. Moreover, in November 1662 weapons were confiscated from 'factious persons'. Yet the truculence of local Dissenters in October 1663 shocked a government informer, John Hetherington. Their conventicles were as crowded 'as in Oliver's time'. Their preachers were 'Fellows no way qualified and obstinate opposers of His Majesty's government'. Some had been fined for non-attendance, yet 'five times as many' were guilty. The caution of local JPs was due to their 'fear of a turn' - indeed there was talk of 'a plot for this town to have risen, but nothing was made out'. There was a need for JPs, and militia officers, to buttress the 'honest party' [the Monarchists]. In December 1663 Hetherington's outrage remained unabated. The town continued 'much at the old rate'; twenty shops traded 'in contempt' on Christmas Day, and parson Henry Thurman had been molested in a churchyard tussle. Hearing that Dissenters planned to bury a 'saint' at dead of night, he emerged from the shadows to read the Anglican burial service. The corpse was duly hurried away, but he lurked till the bearers returned two hours later, whereupon the 'rogues grew so insolent that they were very like to throw him into the grave'. 'Fair means', fumed Hetherington, 'will do no good upon these stubborn rascals' - pessimism echoed in February 1666 by bishop King of Chichester writing to archbishop Sheldon: 'Lewis is a place full of fanatics and dis-affected people (as indeed is Chichester & divers eminent places in Sussex)'.[4]

Monarchist concern at the scale of local Dissent was doubtless sustained by an episcopal survey of conventicles made in 1669. 'About 500' Presbyterians met in South Malling under the pastoral care of Edward Newton and John Earle. 'Numerous' Independents assembled in All Saints parish, shepherded by Walter Postlethwaite. 'Sixty' Quakers gathered in Cliffe. Such estimates probably included fringe sympathizers, and apprentices, servants and older children, as well as householders. In 1670 two informers testified that '500 common followers' attended an open-air Presbyterian service at Henge Lane, 'a private By-lane' in South Malling below Mount Caburn. John Ayres, the schoolmaster who wrote the NARRATIVE already quoted, was unperturbed by the two infiltrators, for 'the Captain of our Salvation, amongst but twelve Select Disciples, found one treacherous Judas'. In 1673 the Borough's High Constables and soldiers from Captain Littleton's troop in the earl of Oxford's regiment disturbed 'about 150' Independents gathered to hear John Crouch preach at Thomas Fissenden's barn in All Saints. In 1675 at least 39 Quakers were observed at Mary Galloway's house on School Hill. Informers also reported the presence of three townsfolk at Baptist meetings in and around Ditchling. The Quakers' own records reveal that, conversely, Lewes was resorted to by Friends from villages in its vicinity.

Similarly, William Ridge from Iford was at Henge Lane, and men from Ringmer and Westmeston, Plumpton and Mayfield were at Fissenden's barn. Various sources also suggest that the householders in the town indicted for non-attendance in the mid-1670s were equivalent, very roughly, to 325 Presbyterian 'hearers', 190 Independents, 50 Quakers and ten Baptists. So, all in all, Dissent probably mustered at least 600 followers in a town with perhaps 2000 inhabitants, a swarm of 'fanatics' probably unequalled in Sussex for size and diversity.[5]

The 1669 survey also claimed that they were largely from 'the middle sort'- self-employed tradesmen, ranking above wage-earners but below 'gentlemen'. And indeed the almost 200 males, identified as Dissenters between 1663 and 1686, seemed well entrenched in the town's commerce, especially in textiles and clothing. There were 30 shearmen, weavers and feltmakers, dyers and tailors, hosiers and hatmakers, glovers and collarmakers, 24 drapers and haberdashers, 15 shoemakers. Few, though, were butchers, and none, innkeepers, the drink trade being a Monarchist bastion. The self-esteem of this 'middle sort' shaped John Ayres's comment on the informers at Henge Lane - 'persons who like the unjust Steward cannot dig, and to beg they are ashamed, and therefore fit to live like the drone, upon the substance that the industrious bee hath gathered'; the hearers there, by contrast, were 'honest, peaceable and industrious people'.[6]

The commercial weight of Dissent was very apparent in St Michael's, a parish encompassing much of the market area. Because 23 householders elected two Puritans, John Crouch and John Geering, as churchwardens in April 1663, the Lewes bench intervened to impose Thorgood the butcher and Brinkhurst the gardener. Dissenters there formed over half the fifty or so householders rated at three hearths or more in 1665, and nine of the 16 assessed at six or more - the others were the Dowager Lady Margaret Pelham; Stephen Snatt draper, whose wife and daughters were non-attenders; two attorneys; the keepers of the *White Horse* and the *Bull*, and Sir Thomas Nutt JP. The parish also harboured refugee Puritan ministers: Nathaniel Jones from Westmeston, John Earle from Tarring Neville and Edward Beecher from Kingston, who kept a school outside the west gate. Lewes borough not being a corporate town, they could legally reside, despite the Five Mile Act.[7]

Charles II knighted Thomas Nutt for a fitful royalism displayed in 1658. Though a landowner at Berwick and Buxted, he acquired the former town-house of the Springetts [Newcastle House] and his daughter Catherine was baptized at St Michael's in 1665. He braved the bustle of the market, partly it seems, to further the Monarchist cause. As a JP he harassed the hearers observed at Henge Lane. Indeed he contrived, so John Ayres alleged, that seven cows distrained from them were bought by his brother at knock-down prices. Yet Nutt sold his town-house in 1673 to William Spence of Malling - discouraged perhaps by U-turns in

Shelley

royal policy. For in March 1672 Charles II disconcerted his 'Cavalier' Parliament by issuing a Declaration of Indulgence granting freedom of worship to Dissenters and Catholics. Edward Newton was licensed by the Crown to preach to Presbyterians in Widow Swan's house, John Crouch to Independents in Thomas Fissenden's 'back house', his barn presumably. However the king's avidly Anglican parliament blocked money to finance a war with the Dutch till he withdrew the Declaration. Indeed it also passed a Test Act which confined the holders of any state office, civil or military, to Anglicans receiving Holy Communion. So it was to a re-criminalized conventicle that Crouch preached in September 1673. During this brief U-turn, however, William Spence at Malling and Henry Shelley at Westout, both sympathetic to Dissent, had joined the Lewes bench. They proved eager, for instance, to refund fines levied on local Quakers if legally possible. Spence was a veteran of the 1654 Nominated Parliament. Shelley's father had been a Borough MP during the Civil War, and his sister Martha and her husband, Robert Coby, were Independents.[8]

The influence of 'gentlemen' paying lip-service to a Restored Anglican Church could explain why Constables at Southover failed to report Dissenters, even though in 1676 parson Isaac Wright estimated that 24 out of 67 adults there were non-conformists. Not till 1684 did a Grand Jury, composed of Monarchist county freeholders, cobble together for quarter sessions a brief list of non-attenders. Earlier, in 1676, the inertia of the churchwardens, Seth Turner and John Chitty, had been reported to the Lewes bench. Turner, in any case, was an awkward cuss: when Constable in 1668 he allegedly boasted 'I do not care a fart for the justices of the peace, for I am a justice of peace myself in my own liberty and have power to hang and draw etc.' - a gross inflation of any residual 'liberties' enjoyed by his ex-Cluniac parish. Affluent resident Anglicans, well disposed to Dissent, probably included Apsley Newton and William Coby, William Lane and John Tichborne. Newton, the grandson of Evelyn's Puritan mentor, was a brother-in-law of Henry Shelley. The attorney, William Coby, was the half-brother of Robert who wedded Martha, Shelley's sister. William Lane, like Apsley Newton, was of Puritan stock and his widow in 1689 became the second wife of Edward Newton, the ejected minister. John Tichborne, the son of a Cowden ironmaster, was a cousin of the regicide, Roger Tichborne. (Near him, in the 1660s, lived Anne Tillinghurst 'spinster', quite possibly his niece. Her father had quitted Streat rectory to preach Fifth Monarchism in Essex.)[9]

More explicit Dissenters at Southover in the 1660s were pastor Edward Newton; Richard Burdett, the grocer and Commonwealth administrator; three Presbyterian masons, Robert Harwood, Robert Holford and Thomas Swane; two Baptists, John Coles glover and

William Parsell blacksmith; a militant Quaker, John Wenham tailor, who died in Horsham gaol, and James Carver at the *Swan*, descended perhaps from the Brighton brewer martyred under Mary. Zachary Smith, the minister ejected at Glynde, also bought a house in Eastport. And a Monarchist bastion in the parish bit the dust when the Lord's Place, which the earl of Thanet had planned to fortify for king Charles in 1643, was pulled down. William Lane, Henry Shelley and Edward Trayton paid £375 for a ten-year lease in 1668, on condition they demolished the 'great old house', the great barn and great stable, but left standing to a height of eight feet the wall of the mansion east of the churchyard, the north part of the great gateway, and the wall of the stable and barn beside Cockshut Lane and the High Street - which a Buck print suggests they did. Evidence of demolition perhaps are the pieces of clay-pipe, 'Restoration' in date, found at the site, and slates discoloured maybe by fire.[10]

178 The walls remaining, eight feet high

Dissenters in Cliffe were also less harassed than in the Borough. Along with Malling it lay within a Hundred of Ringmer dominated by gentry families of Puritan stock, by Morleys and Hays, Springetts and Spences. Nor was William Kempe at Malling Deanery a zealous Anglican, for in 1671 he was denying the curate the £20 stipend instituted by John Stansfield. The Constable of the Hundred was loath to act against the 'hearers' at Henge Lane, the landlord of the *Cats* to store goods distrained from them. Not till 1683 were non-attenders at Cliffe reported to quarter sessions. They were mostly Quakers, so were half of the sixteen listed by churchwardens in 1676. Yet Cliffe tradesmen present at Henge Lane in 1670 included Simon Grover blacksmith, Richard Lancaster victualler, Thomas Ridge draper, John Tabrett carrier, Richard Tyler hatmaker and Richard White brazier. Moreover, Roger Fillery hosier and John Palmer maltster were Presbyterian 'professors' there. Several of these were trustees of Cliffe charities, as were the merchants, John and

Walter Everenden, whose brother-in-law, Henry Godman, was the minister, ejected from Rodmell, who preached at Henge Lane.[11]

The cluster of Quaker tradesmen might itself suggest that at Cliffe they were sheltered somewhat from official harassment. Resident by 1682 were Thomas Beard grocer, Thomas Robinson feltmaker, John Ellis draper, Benjamin Moseley draper and Thomas Moseley, a mercer who in 1689 bequeathed over £800, a house at Hailsham and land 'on the bank at Newhaven'. Much earlier, of course, Mary Akehurst had been chained up by her husband for interrupting sermons. A widow by 1672, she briefly lodged William Penn. If he was the William Penn who imported through Newhaven twelve cushions and two quernstones from Rotterdam in 1687, maybe he was advised by Mary's sons, Ralph and Thomas, who traded in grain and iron

179 A trade token struck in 1667 for Mary Akehurst

shot, wine, flax and pantiles, glasses, brandy and blacking. On the Borough bank at Bridgefoot (arguably outside the Borough's jurisdiction) the Quaker merchant, Ambrose Galloway II, zestfully pursued a many-sided commerce which included Wealden guns.[12]

Of the Dissenters in the town, the Presbyterians remained the more conservative, as well as the most numerous. Their pamphleteer, John Ayres, had no wish 'to embitter the spirits of any against lawful superiors'. They were, he claimed, men 'peaceable and faithful in the Land. In matters of the Kingdom malice itself can find nothing wherewith to accuse them, only in this matter of their God'. Edward Newton gave strong clerical leadership, aided at first by John Earle, a minister 'outed' from Tarring Neville, who suffered official harassment and died in 1670, and then by James Bricknell, outed from Beddingham, who preached 'occasionally' and taught grammar with 'little encouragement'. Briefly absorbed into the congregation, having been expelled from Oxford fellowships at All Souls and Magdalen, were John Panton and John Brett. Panton's brother Henry was the physician on School Hill, Brett's father Walter the grocer near the market-house. Walter oversaw the finances of William, Herbert Morley's heir at Glynde, and of the widow of Thomas Grundy, a 'melancholy thinking' minister outed from Denton. Barrels of sugar were distrained from Brett's son, Walter II, after he refused to pay fines for being at Henge Lane. When six cows at Northease, owned by Richard and Thomas Barnard, the Borough drapers, were also seized, a nimble-minded milkmaid remarked - it is alleged - that the bailiffs 'would have store of sillibubs ... having gotten so much sugar of Mr Brett'. As already noted, Richard built a smart brick extension behind his High Street premises; his brother Thomas became a Presbyterian minister in 1688. Thomas Matthew draper bequeathed £60 in 1690 to assist 'outed' ministers, also a house in Keere Street to shelter poor widows - nine Dissenters were appointed its trustees.[13]

Independents in the town were fewer in number, for their tolerance of (almost) any Protestant belief was not shared by most Puritans. Their first pastor, Walter Postlethwaite, the millenarian preacher relished by Major-General Goffe, died in 1672. His watch and his books, he left to a local tailor's son, John Crouch, a former chorister of Magdalen College Oxford, outed before he could graduate. He was licensed to preach in Fissenden's barn in May 1672. But Joseph Whiston, licensed at Mayfield that year, superceded him at Lewes soon after. As a former chaplain to Major-General Harrison, a leading advocate in the New Model Army of approaching Apocalypse, Whiston doubtless shared Postlethwaite's millenarian expectations. Certainly his political radicalism was unflinching. His nephew William, Isaac Newton's successor as Lucasian Professor of Mathematics at Cambridge, tried many times to convince him of 'the unlawfulness' of the Civil War, but 'in vain'. Doubtless many among his hearers were equally obdurate. Thomas Fissenden, Jeremy Tomkins and George Stonestreat had administered the estates of 'delinquent' royalists in 1650, with Thomas Crouch as their agent - in 1673 Fissenden, Tompkins and George's widow Martha were in Fissenden's barn when Crouch's nephew preached. So were the widow of Edward Bailey, a Captain like Fissenden in Herbert Morley's regiment, and Martha Coby, the daughter of Henry Shelley, the Puritan MP. Independency did not preclude affluence. George Stonestreat, brother of John outed from Lindfield, bequeathed an eighth of Houndean manor and over £900 in 1669, Thomas Fissenden over £1500 in 1684. Richard Russell apothecary owned lands in Ireland, John Lopdell draper, tenements at Hellingly and Westham.[14]

Prosecution did not greatly deter local Presbyterians and Independents, but it eased any tension between them. The preacher at Henge Lane in 1670 was Henry Godman, an Independent, who shepherded a conventicle at Deptford soon after. Widow Elizabeth Gunn left money to the ministers of both congregations in 1670, and Joseph Whiston was always eager to promote 'unanimity'. Puritan animosity towards local Quakers also slackened. Whereas most Dissenters endured only fitful financial penalties, the Friends courted severe punishment, including months, even years, in Horsham gaol, where the Southover tailor, John Wenham, died in 1668. Many Anglicans were outraged by their contempt for 'mass-priests' and 'steeple-houses', their refusal to swear oaths of allegiance, serve as parish officers, pay militia taxes or recognize courts of law. Moreover, clean contrary to Statute, local Friends built a Meeting House in 1675 at Puddlewharf [in Friars Walk]. Promptly the High Constables raided it, reinforced by militia men and 'a great number of rude people of the baser sort', who beat and kicked the worshippers. A week later, the Quakers were violently ejected, a guard set at the door and seventeen deal forms removed. Thereafter harassment abated - indeed in 1681 their Monthly Meeting reproved Widow Akehurst for allowing her children to 'scoff at people on the fast day as they went to the Steeplehouse'. The few Baptists in the town were artisans. In 1670 Thomas Brad tailor, and John and Joshua Coles, both glovers, resorted to Ditchling to worship. Brad's daughter Mary married an 'Anabaptist' yeoman Peter Terry, at whose house in Clayton William Parsell, the Southover blacksmith, preached.[15]

Despite their exclusion from civic office, many Dissenters did vote in bitterly fought parliamentary elections held between 1679 and 1681. Politics in the provinces were especially inflamed by rumours of a Popish Plot to kill the king and extirpate the Protestant faith, a fiction elaborated by the Hastings-born Titus Oates and lent credence by the murder of a London JP, Sir Edmund Berry Godfrey. The panic tempted enemies of 'prerogative' royal government, led by the earl of Shaftesbury - then and later labelled Whigs - to demand the exclusion from the throne of James, the Catholic duke of York, the king's brother and heir. The Whigs' Monarchist opponents, then and later, were labelled Tories. Playing for time, Charles II called general elections, in February 1679, August 1679 and March 1681. The crisis precipitated a Whig triumph at Lewes borough. Its Monarchist MPs, Woodcock and Stapley, had been close to the duke of York - indeed Stapley's business agent, a Catholic lawyer, was executed for complicity in 'the Plot'. (Yet, Janus-like, the regicide's son also cultivated Dissent, a house of his at Hove being licensed for Presbyterian worship in 1672.) Both Monarchists were replaced in February 1679, by William Morley and Richard Bridger, men endorsed by Shaftesbury. Morley had inherited the Glynde Place estate from his father Herbert in 1668. He sheltered Zachary Smith as his chaplain, paid Edward Newton £2 for a sermon and patronized Dissenting tradesmen. Once elected, he voted for an Exclusion Bill, but died of smallpox soon after. In August 1679 the vacancy was filled by Thomas Pelham of Laughton, the grandson of Herbert Morley's chief collaborator in Sussex during the Civil War. Already endorsed by Shaftesbury while MP for East Grinstead, Pelham was to sit for Lewes borough till elected a knight of the shire in 1702. Richard Bridger of Hamsey, a JP since July 1660, bought the Coombe Place estate at Hamsey in 1657. Re-elected in August 1679 and in March 1681, he was noted soon after, like Pelham, as a candidate acceptable to the 'Dissenting' party. He held the seat till 1695. Sir John Ashburnham, the Whig son of a Monarchist father, succinctly described him as 'a very honest gentleman of about £1000 per annum'. Tradition asserts his campaigns never cost him more than a hogshead of cider - whereas Pelham's election in August 1679 set his father back £40 15s 6d.[16]

Whether contested or not, the election of Morley, Bridger and Pelham in the Whig interest owed much in 1679-81, and thereafter, to a coalition in the Borough of Dissenters and affluent Anglicans. Its dynamic can be glimpsed in 1682 when Walter Brett, Stephen Snatt and Thomas Holmwood 'gent', all linked with Dissent and the redundant Fellowship, chose nineteen additional trustees for Blunt's Charity. Seemingly the only Tory was Ambrose Trayton. The rest included four Anglican Whigs - Henry Shelley and his son Richard, William Pellatt at the Friars and his son Thomas - a phalanx of Dissenting tradesmen, and an Independent 'gent', Joseph Studley, plus his son Nathaniel.[17]

The hysteria excited by the Popish Plot fuelled an elaborate 'No-Popery' parade in the town on 5 November 1679. A London newspaper, the *Domestick Intelligence*, reported in detail the 'extraordinary Solemnity'.

In the first place went a company of young men armed with Swords and Muskets, pikes etc., like a company of Soldiers; next several Pictures were carried upon long Poles; the first being a Jesuit represented with a bloody Sword and a Pistol, with this inscription, *Our Religion is Murder, Rapine and Rebellion*. The second was the Picture of a Friar and a Jesuit wantonly dallying with a Nun, the Devil looking from behind a Curtain and saying *I will spoil no sport my dear Children*. The third was the picture of two Devils bringing a Triple Crown to the Pope with the words *Hail Holy Father*. To every one of these were verses spoken as they passed by. Just before the Pope marched Guy Faux with his dark Lanthorn, being booted and spurred after the Old Fashion and wearing a Vizard with a wonderful long Nose. Next comes the Pope with his Cross keys, Crosier staff and other Fopperies, having his Train borne up by several of his Clergy. Next followed the Cardinals in their Caps, with the rest of the Clergy, Secular and Regular, having wonderful long beards and a string of beads about their middle, which they told as they went by. Behind these went the Nuns. But last of all comes the Ghost of *Sir Edmund Berry Godfrey* ... a Person in black Clothes and a Shirt all Bloody, and his Face painted so white that he seemed rather Dead than Alive; before whom went a person carrying a Bloody Sword in his hand, who sometimes looking back would seem to be greatly affrighted at the sight of him. There were between twenty and thirty boys with Vizards, and two or three who had their faces painted after an Antick manner, one whereof carried Holy Water in a Tin Pot, sprinkling the People with a Bottle-Brush. In this manner they, having carried his Holiness through the Town and Streets adjacent, at Night, after they had first degraded him, they committed him to the Flames.

Amid the hysteria Catholic recusants at Firle were reported to the Lewes bench, also four at Cliffe: Martin Kestar joiner, Joan Cobham widow, William Eaton 'gent' and his wife. Hysteria too informed the images on a tobacco-pipe stopper found at Southover: when reversed, the head of a pope with a triple tiara becomes a devil, and a cardinal's head, a fool with cap and bells.[18]

Yet the frenzy prompted a backlash. In April 1681 Charles II dissolved his fourth parliament, a month after its election, and thenceforth he pursued the Whigs as enemies, relying heavily on French cash and avidly Monarchist Tories. In September 1681 'Presbyterians' in Lewes were reported as keeping 'a very strict fast' to mourn the execution of Stephen College, a Whig activist in London. Many Tories, for their part, feared a new Civil War. In January 1682 bishop Carleton of Chichester assured his Primate, 'the dissenters in this county carry themselves with such insolence and speak so boldly as if they were just drawing their swords and every day expected the hoped-for command to stand to their arms. God preserve the whole church from the malicious designs of those bloodthirsty Presbyterians'. Tory panic intensified when the Rye House Plot by Whig extremists to murder the king was uncovered in June 1683. The government ordered all 'ill affected persons' in Sussex to be disarmed. Seven muskets and two swords, seized in the Borough, were stored in the sessions-house. Elsewhere in Sussex the search was limply conducted. His deputy-lieutenants informed the earl of Dorset, 'we cannot find any number of arms, though we have reason to suspect there are many'. Bishop Carleton, however, did secure Henry Shelley's removal from the Lewes bench in 1683 - hoping that his 'being disgracefully turned out for neglect of his duty' might deter JPs 'of the same stamp', prone to 'faction and schism and disobedience to the Government'. Shelley's shielding of local Quakers had caused especial outrage. When parson Eresby and Samuel Astie, a proctor of the Church court, urged him to summons them in 1682, he refused to be 'a journeyman for idle fellows' and instead berated Eresby for pastoral negligence, for merely reading a few prayers before 'dismissing the people'.[19]

Carleton's fears were fanned afresh in September 1683 when Thomas Barrett, his registrar in Lewes, bewailed the strength of local Dissent, the inertia of JPs, the damage done by Anglican Whigs. 'This part of your diocese, as it is far remote from your palace, so is [it] filled with a sort of men who are remote from loyal principles, especially that part [Lewes] in which your consistory [court] is appointed, for here is a contempt of the King's command and all Acts of Parliament. We have still conventicles held, schism maintained, and the preachers of it defended by those pretended officers of justice who, for fear of being thought too active in prosecution, have totally neglected what lay in their own way for promoting the loyal cause'. Indeed they take 'all occasions to blacken the credit of informers' and 'show at all times the Dissenters more favour than their cause could claim'. One JP indeed - doubtless Henry Shelley - had urged people to complain to quarter sessions about 'extortions in ecclesiastical officers' and 'errors in their proceedings as to excommuni-

cations'. 'The continuance of this moulded faction here', Barrett concluded, 'is not owing so much to the professed Separatists as to others,
who go to church [and] being really private favourers of the factious
party, under the disguise of churchmen, take all opportunities of serving
their turns'.[20]

Nonetheless the county sheriff and the Clerk of the Peace did assemble at successive quarter sessions Grand Juries packed with Tory freeholders from the shire very willing to denounce 'faction'. In January
1684 they declared it their 'bounden duty to present such persons as are
not conformable to the laws established, or through an Atheistical or
Phanatical zeal obstruct the same, finding by long and woeful experience
[that] an introduction to Rebellion took its rise from like pretences to
Religion'. The Jurors listed seven persons, so dangerous to the government, they should give security for good behaviour. Two were townsmen
- Thomas Fissenden, a former Captain in Parliament's army, and far less
predictably, Joseph Grave, rector of St Mary Westout. A student at
Wadham College in the 1650s, he was a steady collector of Puritan and
Low Church theology - books he left to the Borough. The Crown had
appointed him rector in October 1679 - before the king finally broke with
the Whigs. Clearly he became as detested by local Tories as his neighbour
Henry Shelley.[21]

In April and October 1684 - 'notwithstanding the discouragement
we have hitherto met with', the Tory Grand Jurors boldly lengthened
their list of persons steeped in 'Antimonarchical principle', 'dangerous
and ill affected'. Now included were sixteen townsmen: parson Grave
and the 'disgraced' Henry Shelley; five Presbyterians - Samuel Watts who
'allowed a conventicle in his house', Henry Panton, Walter Brett I, Walter
Brett II and Roger Fillery; five Independents - Joseph Whiston, 'a
Conventicle preacher', Thomas Fissenden II, John Lopdell, Thomas
Read and Thomas Botting; three Quakers - Ambrose Galloway, Richard
Stephens and Benjamin Moseley; and Edward Henty, a Baptist perhaps.
Moreover the Grand Jurors also named, as 'favourers of the factious
party', three landed magnates: Sir John Fagge, John Hay of Little
Horsted and - most intrepidly perhaps - Thomas Pelham, the Borough
MP. Prudently the Lewes bench decided such charges were not 'particular' enough. But the Grand Jurors felt free to denounce these magnates
because, in the aftermath of the Rye House Plot, the king's government
was itself striking down Whig grandees, such as the earl of Essex, lord
John Russell and Algernon Sidney whose families in the 1640s had
stoked Civil War. Sidney (Pelham's uncle) was executed for arguing, in an
unpublished manuscript, that it might be justifiable to resist the powers
that be.

Sidney's fate perhaps encouraged the Grand Jurors in April 1685 to
accuse John Hay of having distributed a 'scandalous and seditious' libel
at Lewes in March 1681. The petition, from 'the freeholders of Sussex',

had urged their knights of the shire to continue the campaign 'to bar the door against all Popish Successors to the Crown and in particular against James duke of York and [against] Arbitrary Government'; and to ensure that 'exemplary justice' was meted out to 'those execrable villains [like Woodcock and Stapley] that, by receiving the cursed Pensions, betrayed their trust and our liberties in the late Long ['Cavalier'] Parliament. The 'freeholders' also promised to defend the knights of the shire, if 'any hazard' befell them, 'as worthy Patriots with our lives and fortunes' - envisaging, it seems, an armed Rebellion. The Grand Jurors also denounced the Presbyterian draper, Thomas Matthew, for declaring that 'every good Protestant or good Christian would be for the Bill of Exclusion'.[22]

But by April 1685 'Exclusion' at least was a dead issue, for in February the duke of York had become James II. At an election in March Richard Bridger and Thomas Pelham were again returned for Lewes borough, despite a challenge from Sir John Stapley. However, Tories dominated the parliament and their Monarchism reached fever pitch after the defeat at Sedgemoor in July 1685 of the rebel duke of Monmouth. Grand Jurors at Lewes were provoked to demand draconian safety-measures. Having 'taken into our serious Consideration the late horrid Invasion and Rebellion of James Scott, late duke of Monmouth, and all his traitorous and bloody Associates, who were abetted and assisted by the whole body of the Malcontent, dissenting and Phanatical Party, or those pretending to tender Consciences, [in order that] the Publique peace of this County for the future may be by our fellow subjects kept inviolable, we do desire that all ill affected persons to the Government, and dissenters from the discipline of the Church of England, may give security for their Peace and Good behaviour'. Among those listed were fifty townsfolk, women as well as men; they included four pastors - Newton, Barnard, Bricknell and Whiston.[23]

All fifty had cause for alarm, for seemingly James II could command the allegiance of a victorious army, a Tory parliament and a State Church endorsing Passive Obedience to a sanctified monarchy. Yet Monarchists soon had cause for dismay. Their anointed king began appointing Catholics to key posts in the government and the army. He purged Magdalen College Oxford of Anglican fellows who resisted his choice of a Catholic as their President. Worse still, on 14 April 1687, he granted Catholics, and Dissenters, full liberty of worship and access to public office. Clearly the king hoped to mobilize them, if need be, against Tory Monarchists aghast at his assault on their Anglican citadel. On 18 April bishop Lake of Chichester informed archbishop Sancroft that Dissenters at Lewes, Arundel and Brighton, 'like men stirring with a Tarantula, must have their old loud music of the pulpit, to influence their madness'. In July the king added a Catholic, Sir John Gage of Firle, to the Lewes bench, and made him sheriff of Sussex in November. The earl of Dorset was replaced as Lord Lieutenant in February 1688 by another Catholic, viscount Montague.[24]

Chaos now enveloped English politics. Anglican bells at Cliffe rang out in June 1688 to celebrate queen Mary of Modena giving birth to a son, the future Old Pretender. A few days later they pealed to rejoice that a London jury had acquitted Sancroft, Lake and five other bishops of sedition - a charge brought by the king because they doubted the legality of his Declaration of Indulgence. Many Tories now set Passive Obedience aside; many Dissenters would not accept Toleration from a Papist king. The scene was set for James's Protestant nephew, William of Orange, the ruler of the Dutch United Provinces, to intervene. (Henry Pelham was in 'Holland', perhaps on political business, when Sir John Ashburnham called at St Andrew's Lane in June 1687.) With William poised to 'invade' England in October 1688, only five JPs attended the quarter sessions at Lewes, to signal thereby their support for the king's offer of Toleration. Four were new-comers to the bench: John Spence of Malling and John Hay of Little Horsted, both Radical Whigs, and Henry Plummer and Sir John Shelley both Catholics. Yet though support for James was eroding, his army was intact. Indeed two troops of 'King James' soldiers - one with a German trumpeter - were billetted in the Borough, at the *Black Lion* and the *Pelicans*. However, on 20 December 1688, the king fled abroad, and during a virtual interregnum, at New Year and at Easter 1689, no quarter sessions were held at Lewes.[25]

When a Settlement came, it ended the grip on civic office in the Borough that seigneurial tinkering with the leet jury had secured for Cavaliers and Tories since October 1663. As already noted, Monarchists commanded so constricted a commercial base that Whigs had been returned as MPs from February 1679. Only one High Constable, Joshua Curle haberdasher, had defected from the Puritan families dominating local trade in the 1650s. Indeed four Constables in the bruising years between 1663 and 1669 were incomers, with strong Anglican connections: Thomas James gentleman, Henry Hopkins surgeon, John Holney apothecary and Edmund Middleton haberdasher. James and Hopkins each married a daughter of Samuel Towers merchant. His father, a prebendary of St Paul's, was related to John Towers, a Laudian bishop impeached in 1641, whose son published in 1660 a timely treatise on the *Obedience Perpetually Due To Kings*. Holney owned land at West Grinstead and his father-in-law was rector of Shermanbury, both in west Sussex. Middleton, a citizen of London in 1658, was related to Thomas Middleton,

Towers

the crypto-royalist MP who sat for Horsham in the 1640s. Anglican too was the ambience of Thomas Russell grocer and Henry Rose saddler, High Constables born in the Borough. Russell's father had clung on as rector of St John's in the 1640s; as well as the apostate Joshua Curle, his kin included a parson at Hollington, a parson at Ripe, and James Clarke, a registrar at the Church Court, vilified by local Quakers as 'a fat man who sweated much when abusing Friends' and died 'senseless', a sot, addicted to wine and brandy. Henry Rose in 1677 was singled out in the All Saints burial register as 'a very honest, just and good man'. In March 1655 Herbert Morley had ordered a watch to be kept for any ship carrying his brother, Samuel Rose, who often crossed to France and was thought to be a Papist. Samuel was awarded £8 from the county fund for Maimed Soldiers in 1662, and caused an anchor to be impounded at Brighton in 1667, suspecting it had been stolen from Portsmouth dockyard. 'There has been much of this trade in the town', he assured the Navy Commissioners, and offered to be 'diligent' if they deputed him to suppress it.[26]

Between 1663 and 1669 three High Constables, Ralph Richardson, Ferdinando Bryan and George Tye, were recruited from a commercial sector largely shunned by Puritans. Richardson was keeping the *Bull* when the Woodcock brothers assailed 'a saint' with a beer mug in 1657. That year he paid £372 for the *Star*, which he bequeathed in 1688 to his nephew Conyers Richardson, a staunchly Tory parson elected to Convocation in 1708 by the clergy in Chichester archdeaconry. Ferdinando Bryan owned the *Swan* in Southover and his daughter married Samuel Astie, the Church court official who complained about Henry Shelley shielding Quakers. George Tye was landlord of the *White Lion*. While churchwarden at All Saints, he tricked Ambrose Galloway I into parting

180 A trade token struck in 1667 for Ambrose Galloway I

with two thin cheeses, after the Quaker refused to pay a rate to repair the 'steeplehouse'. Also a Tory High Constable then was Anthony Holman 'gent', a son-in-law of Henry Townsend who 'lived and died' at the *Black Lion*. From a trade allied to inn-keeping came Richard Grisbrook and William Thurgood butchers.[27]

New Constables recruited between 1669 and 1689 do not suggest much widening of Monarchism's commercial base. John Tooke from Lincoln was landlord of the newly launched *Turk's Head*. William Read, aptly enough, kept the *King's Head* - his trade token bore the royal image with crown and sceptre. Other Constables, moreover, were of very doubtful calibre. William Weston, possibly a sievemaker, was illiterate. James Read, the ordnance-shipper, died in office, 'unable to satisfy his debts'. Robert Phipps cook kept an alehouse, and Thomas Harrison grocer - according to John Ayres the Presbyterian - was both a renegade Puritan who had 'served against His Majesty by Sea and Land', and an inept tradesman who returned dead drunk from Horsham assizes in 1670 riding the wrong horse, though it had a 'long flick tail'. Perhaps they can be identified as the Thomas Harrison and Robert Phipps, both of Lewes and 'poor', later granted a county pension by the Lewes bench in the early 1680s. More respectable maybe was John Delves, a draper from Isfield, who held office in 1675-6, 1683-4 and 1688-9.[28]

Clearly affluent, though, was William Pellatt, a merchant from Arundel who in 1678 bought from William Spence's executors his mansion in St Michael's [Newcastle House]. Pellatt's daughter Mary married Thomas Barrett, the Church registrar who denounced Henry Shelley to bishop Carleton. His bequests in 1691 included tithes at Piddinghoe, 'Sharpes' wharf in Newick, and silver boxes for sugar, pepper and mustard. His son Thomas, baptized at Southover in 1672, became President of the College of Physicians and edited Isaac Newton's *Chronology of Ancient Kingdoms*. And it was William maybe who gave his St Michael's mansion a smart, pedimented, seven-bay facade of Caen stone. Sir John Ashburnham described the house in 1687 as the best in the town 'after Mr. Pelhams', and the newels of its staircase, 'turned in a spiral with a vase-like pedestal', date perhaps from Charles II's time. In 1682 Nathaniel Henty was cautioned for peering into the windows when 'many Gentry' were inside.[29]

181 'Newcastle House' as later subdivided

The veteran Tory High Constables, John Holney, Edmund Middleton and Ralph Richardson, served on the Grand Juries that denounced the 'Malcontent, dissenting and Phanatical Party' between January 1684 and August 1685. Acting with them were three local gentlemen, Philip Bennett from Southover, Henry Campion from Westout and Ambrose Trayton. Bennett's father-in-law, Thomas More, patron of the living at Wivelsfield, had clashed in the 1660s with Puritans intent that 'an unlearned and unordained maltman' should occupy the pulpit there. His son, Walter More, also a Grand Juror, sold a farm at Wivelsfield to Middleton's son John. Campion's father, it seems, was the strenuous royalist, Sir William of Combwell in Kent, who defended Boarstall House in Buckinghamshire and was killed at Colchester in 1648. His sons were brought up by the Parkers at Willingdon, his widow's family. Though Ambrose Trayton's grandfather, Ambrose I, had co-ordinated the Borough's defence in November 1642, he abstained from public life in the 1650s and when he died in 1679, aged eighty-seven, his 'never omitting the public worship of God', was thankfully noted in the All Saints register. In 1682 Ambrose II joined with John Holney, John Tooke at the *Turks Head*, and the Church officials, Clarke, Astie and Barrett, to oversee the will of John Sewer labourer, their neighbour on School Hill - the backbone of the Borough's most Monarchist parish. Ambrose died in 1686, aged twenty-six, leaving his brother Nathaniel to nurture the Tory cause.[30]

Doubtless the meagre revenues of the town's Anglican rectories hindered the Monarchist cause - money allocated in the 1640s had been restored to the cathedral at Chichester in 1660. Indeed bishop Carleton conceded in 1682 that the 'maintenance' at St Michael's and at All Saints, 'two lesser things of mine', would be inadequate, even if the stipends were united - yet they were both populous parishes. The advowson of St John's, the best endowed rectory, was briskly traded by its patrons. Francis Challoner bought it for £143, but bishop King refused to institute him as rector in 1666, claiming he tailored the Prayer Book to suit local Puritan 'Fanaticks'. Installed at Telscombe instead, Challoner suffered hogs to root in the churchyard. The advowson of St John's he sold to Henry Thurman, the new rector at Westout, who owned pastures in Pevensey Level. Said to be 'a common drunkard', Thurman scuffled at night with local Dissenters intent on privately burying 'a saint', and accused his neighbour, Anthony Holman, (a fellow Monarchist) of maliciously invading his premises. In 1668 his executors sold the advowson to Richard Clarke, a London apothecary who nominated Thomas Clarke as rector. After Thomas died in 1673, Philip Shore, a distiller, bought it. He appointed John Shore, who served there, and at Hamsey, till 1708.[31]

One consequence of meagre stipends was pluralism, and a conspicuous holder of several local benefices was William Snatt, a graduate of Magdalen College Oxford, the son of John Evelyn's schoolmaster. While languishing at Malling as its curate in 1668, he assured Evelyn that 'If the dead have any knowledge of affairs here below, your greatly obliging kindness to the necessitous son cannot but be hugely acceptable to the defunct father' - the excellent grafts he procured Evelyn, from Mr Newton at Southover and Dr White on School Hill, have already been noted. These gifts bore fruit, for though in 1671 he bewailed having preached 'every Lord's day' for three years at Malling without promotion, Evelyn's brother secured him a living at Denton in 1672. By 1674, moreover, he was rector of Cliffe and of 'those lesser things', All Saints and St Michael's. Resolving to 'root out' Quakers, he invaded their meeting-house and sent names to the Lewes bench. They in turn alleged that he caroused 'with the wickedest men in the town' and kept a crucifix and other 'Popish Reliques' in his house. His patron, bishop Carleton, however, assured the archbishop in 1682 that 'worthy Mr Snatt' had found his three parishes 'deeply infected by phanaticisms', yet his preaching a sound sermon 'every day in the week' had rendered them 'the only good pattern' in the town and its vicinity. The bishop, though, was prone to extreme judgements. While brawling in public with his diocesan chancellor, Thomas Briggs, he dislodged the Doctor's periwig and vowed to make him so hated that 'every man who sees him should piss on him'. Snatt, moreover, in his returns for an episcopal census in 1676, understated the strength of 'phanaticism'. Whereas Isaac Wright totalled 24 adult Dissenters (36%) in Southover and 27 (31%) in Westout, and John Shore 32 (25%) in St John's, Snatt returned 16 (6%) in Cliffe, 23 (9%) in All Saints and 67 (21%) in St Michael's. Yet in Cliffe Quakers alone accounted for at least 12 adults in 1676; in All Saints forty non-attenders at Anglican services were listed one year, and in St Michael's at least eighty.[32]

Before removing to Cuckfield in 1682, a rich living in the bishop's gift, Snatt ensured that Richard Jones of All Saints painted the King's Arms on cloth for Cliffe church and 'beautified' its chancel. He also recommended as his successor 'ingineous and orthodox' John Eresby, an usher at the grammar school, fresh from Magdalene College Cambridge. Besides coping with three busy parishes, he was entrusted, it seems, with Southover, displacing Joseph Grave the Whig 'Malcontent', who clung on at St Mary Westout. John Shore, meanwhile, proved a sturdily Tory rector at St John's between 1674 and 1708. He was left money in 1679 by Thomas Stafford, headmaster of the grammar school, who was followed by Thomas Whalley, Snatt's brother-in-law, 'a solid scholar and divine'.[33]

The accession of William and Mary in 1689 - celebrated by the sign at John Hodge's new public house, the *King and Queen* - finally ended disproportionate Tory control of local government in Lewes borough and in Sussex. Above all, the Revolution Settlement transformed English politics by giving Protestant Dissenters freedom to assemble for public worship, unless they were 'Socinians' - Unitarians who denied the divinity of Christ. Business at Church courts shrank accordingly. The Presbyterian, Edward Newton, could now 'officiate' legally at a house in St Michael's owned by Isaac Butler [possibly the former Music School in Watergate Lane], and the Independent, Joseph Whiston, at premises 'adjoining' the residence on School Hill [Lewes House] of Joseph Studley, a landowner at Mayfield and Lindfield, whose father had attended the Nominated Parliament in 1654. The Quakers continued at their meeting-house in Friars Walk, once the scene of kickings and 'smokings'. In October 1697 local Anabaptists registered John Henty's house near the north-east corner of Eastport Lane. Its garden probably bordered the Winterbourne, which offered 'living water' for baptism by total immersion and for the ritual washing of feet. And possibly for them, in October 1706, William Wood certified premises at Southover 'built' for religious worship [at 40-2 High Street].[34]

Toleration raised still higher the profile of local Dissent. As for the Presbyterians, Edward Newton agreed in August 1695 that Thomas Barnard should become joint-pastor with him - a regime justified by Titus 1: 5, 6 & 7, Philippians 1: 1 and Acts 20: 17 & 28. In his register, citing Isaiah's command, 'Look unto the Rock whence ye are hewen', Barnard noted his father, the draper in St Michael's, his ordination at Glyndebourne in 1688, and his early ministry at Brighton, Hastings, Cranbrook and Benenden. He noted too his dislike of 'immersion', even of 'partial dipping' - he baptised 21-year-old Frances Charman, lying fatally ill at Cliffe, by just pouring water on her face. Afterwards she revealed to him that an Angel 'in human shape, white and very illustrious' had told her that he [the Angel] would soon be accompanying her 'to the Land of desire'. Barnard, uneasy about the 'supposed Apparition', advised her to rely on 'the surer word of prophesy'.[35]

In 1695 the 13 townsmen, who as full members of this Presbyterian 'Church' were admitted to its Sacrament, formed a robust cross-section of local commerce - apart from George Salter 'gent'. They were Richard Barnard and Samuel Watts drapers, Nathaniel Russell apothecary, Abraham Vine bellows maker, John Ridge tanner, Robert Colgate goldsmith, John Palmer and Edmund Goldham maltsters, Richard Paine shoemaker, Samuel Swane and Joseph Swane bricklayers and Thomas Norman bookseller. Admitted by 1701 were Samuel Yorkton mercer, Edward Henty shoemaker, and two men possibly at Henge Lane in 1670, Robert Harwood mason and John Wood blacksmith. Among 26 townswomen, members in 1695, were Elizabeth, wife of Walter Brett II grocer; Widow Banks who owned 'Mr Carryll's books upon Job'; the widow of Francis Daranda, former pastor to the Huguenots at Canterbury; and the widow of William Wallace, a Scotsman who 'spake English very ill', outed from East Dean in 1662 - he later eluded detection when a conventicle at Brighton was raided because 'several women big with child stood about him'. During the Toleration in 1672-3 he preached at a house in Hove owned by Sir John Stapley, and that opportunist's sister-in-law, Widow Douglas Stapley, became a hearer at Lewes. Indeed in 1695 she left £5 to pastor Newton, a guinea to pastor Barnard, and to Sibella Stapley her 'china' in the parlour chamber of Mr Russell, her lodging in the High Street. Another hearer, it seems, was John

Spence. Residing with him at Malling about 1693 was Mr Bradshaw, formerly a Presbyterian pastor at Brighton, and in 1698 Barnard baptised Spence's son Trevor, born to his third wife, Anne Trevor of Glynde Place - in October 1688 Spence's deceased father, John, had joined Catholics on the Lewes bench.[36]

In 1696 George Salter bequeathed Barnard and Newton a guinea each, to buy a mourning ring, and Mrs Newton a box of tobacco, 'being about 12 lbs'. Yet despite Titus 1: 5,6 & 7 etc., their joint pastorate was soon to fly asunder. In 1698 Barnard bought the *Bull* and gutted the rear premises to form a meeting-house; big new windows were inserted, re-using stone mullions and transoms; octagonal posts supported the framework. Barnard believed this 'suitable enlargement' would cater for a 'greatly increased and increasing Auditory', the 'vast majority' of whom were in favour; it was also 'a matter of Conscience', strengthening 'the Gospel interest of our Lord Jesus Christ'. Yet pastor Newton, so Barnard complained, mounted an 'unreasonably obstinant Opposition'. The rift became such that 'the Church stood like a tottering house ready to drop on our heads; for a year and a quarter many stood looking on, but not one offered to enter into our communion'. Barnard first preached at 'Westgate' on 5 November 1700. But on 30 March 1701 Newton 'invaded' his turn in the pulpit and a week later 'sealed the Schism with an opposite Sacrament' - presumably at the old meeting-place in Watergate Lane.

And there he stayed put, with only a 'few Adherents', according to Barnard.[37]

After the Schism 'large' additions were made to Barnard's Westgate congregation. By 1711 recruits from the town included John Mills surgeon, Thomas Barrett and Abraham Weston clockmakers, James Reeves currier, John Peckham dyer, James Daw bricklayer. By then, too, almost fifty members were resident elsewhere in mid-Sussex, scattered from Streat and Chailey to Newhaven, Seaford and Alfriston, Chiddingly, Hailsham and Westham. Some probably attended the Saturday corn market and then lodged overnight. Membership to the south-west was curtailed by the outreach of a Presbyterian meeting at Brighton. Before becoming a pastor there in 1698, John Duke was

182 Westgate chapel

briefly at Lewes. In a register book, given him by pastor Newton, he noted a 'recipe' for consumption, using raisins, honey, springwater and a 'Lickerishstick'.[38]

The Schism of 1701 issued from a clash of personalities, not of doctrine. Indeed when George Humphrey, a local tailor, left money in 1706 to the congregations of Mr Newton, Mr Barnard and Mr Starr (by then the Independent pastor), his even-handedness reflected a slackening of doctrinal tension. Pastor Whiston, 'a man of great wisdom and moderation', had promoted 'an Association of Ministers of both Sorts', Independent and Presbyterian, and though in 1691 it 'died with him', pastors of both sorts, in and around London, started a Common Fund to assist men to train for either ministry. Also promoting unity was Joseph Studley on School Hill. Though he acted as Whiston's executor, he had allowed his Mayfield house to be licensed in 1672 for the Presbyterian preacher, John Brett, the former fellow of All Souls. Moreover, Whiston's successor in August 1693, the aged Dr George Porter - outed decades earlier from the Vice-Presidency of Magdalen College - agreed to officiate at Barnard's inauguration as pastor in 1695. Porter, though, was a depressive, prone to derive 'little Comfortable Enjoyment of his Friends, himself or his God', and he moved to Clare in Suffolk before 1697. His successor, the equally venerable Comfort Starr, had migrated to New England in 1635 with his father, a surgeon from Cranbrook,and became a trustee of Harvard university in 1650, before returning to a Puritan Republican England.[39]

Starr made way for John Olive in July 1709 and died in November 1711, leaving his books in Latin, Greek and Hebrew to Joseph, his son 'beyond the sea at Bermuda'. While a student, Olive had drawn on the Common Fund in 1700, so probably he encouraged the Union consummated when his Independents quitted their meeting-house and joined Barnard's Presbyterians at Westgate on 6 November 1711. His members included John Olive, Samuel Snashall and William Langford maltsters, Thomas Botting baker, Stephen Weller tallow-chandler, William Read hatter, Thomas Fissenden apothecary, Christopher Yokehurst shoemaker; also the wives of George Starr upholsterer, John Maynard grocer and Henry Owden, a carpenter who 'vilified' the local Church court in 1685, refusing to doff his hat. In 1700, the congregation was left £20 by Nathaniel Garland, a wealthy merchant at Bridgefoot, who unloaded canvas from Ostend, mussels and mackerel nets from Dieppe, wine and figs from Bordeaux, cherry brandy from Portugal, and shipped away guns, beeswax, calf-skins, coney-hair and woollen stockings. As with the Presbyterians, some members in 1711 were resident outside the towm, scattered as far as Angmering, Beeding, Portslade and Ditchling, Lindfield, Seaford, Selmeston, Heathfield and Cranbrook.[40]

Toleration was of especial benefit to local Quakers, though they still chronicled petty harassment. A crowd 'of loose persons', led by a tinker, 'spoiled' the wares of Richard Stephens when he opened his grocer's shop on Christmas Day in 1689. A 'rabble' broke the windows of Benjamin Moseley for trading his drapery on 14 February 1690, a 'Thanksgiving day for the [advent] of the Prince of Orange'. Their refusal to pay tithes and militia rates still exposed their goods to distraint. Moreover, after Ambrose Galloway II withheld the cost of 'one quarter part of a musket charged on him', the soldiers of Major Monk took him to the *Turk's Head* and tried to 'entangle' him 'about the lawfulness of Government'. At Cliffe in 1713, to satisfy parson Whalley's executors, hops were seized from Thomas Beard, silverware from Thomas Robinson and hardware from Elias Ellis. Friends claimed the value of chattels taken far exceeded the money withheld, but perhaps no lasting damage was done to the dozen families, mostly tradesmen and farmers, from Cliffe and Lewes borough, Kingston and Rottingdean, who met at Friars Walk. Ambrose Galloway II at Bridgefoot still conducted a farflung commerce with Chatham, London, Hull and Norway, with Holland, Dunkirk, Bristol and San Sebastian. In 1697 the congregation bought from John Newnham of Barcombe, as a site for a burial ground, a thousand-year lease of a 'quarter' of a field called Bugates abutting Friars Walk, which it holds today. Fifty pounds for its 'poor' were left in 1699 by Anthony Tompkins at Cliffe, the owner of malt houses at Ware and premises near St Clement Danes. Thomas Rowland and his wife at Cliffe were allowed wheat in 1712 and rent aid in 1713, though their surplus chattels, mostly old husbandry tackle, were sold to help pay for this.[41]

As well as granting Toleration to Dissenters, the Revolution Settlement gave Whig politicians reasonably steady access to official posts in the gift of the Crown. Their leader in eastern Sussex was Sir John Pelham of Laughton. Re-elected a knight of the shire in 1689, he diligently advanced loans to the new regime and supplied it with ordnance. Thomas, his elder son, remained an MP for Lewes borough till returned for the county in 1702. Made a Lord of the Treasury in 1697, Thomas secured the Clerkship of the Pells for his brother Henry. Doubtless this sinecure in the Exchequer, worth £2000 a year, helped to fund Henry's purchase of the Stanmer estate for £7500 in 1713. But Henry was still at St Andrew's Lane when elected in 1695 to replace the ailing Richard Bridger as a Borough MP. In January 1701 he made way for a fellow Whig, Sir Thomas Trevor, whose brother John had inherited the Morley estate at Glynde in 1679. But when Sir Thomas resigned the seat to become Chief Justice of the Common Pleas, Henry was again returned in November 1701.[42]

After a Triennial Act was passed in 1694 general elections were held at least every three years. Yet maybe there was no challenge to Whig candidates at Lewes borough till after queen Anne's accession in 1702. Local Dissenters and Anglican Whigs could collaborate in the 1690s unharassed by a hostile Court or Tory Grand Jurors. Dissenters indeed were often chosen as High Constables. Richard Barnard and Thomas Fissenden served in 1691 and picked two Presbyterians as their Headboroughs. The three reigning 'Lords of Lewes', the earl of Dorset, the duke of Norfolk and baron Bergavenny, were themselves Whigs - indeed the baron led a large posse of freeholders to the county election at Chichester in 1695. If needed, their stewards could secure juries at the Borough's court leet favourable to the Whig cause.[43]

The Revolution Settlement, moreover, provoked deep disarray among erstwhile Monarchists. Archbishop Sancroft, bishop Lake and William Snatt were among 400 Anglicans who resigned their benefices rather than break their oath of allegiance to James II by swearing one to William and Mary. Few of these 'non-jurors' became Jacobites, anxious to restore 'the king over the water'. But William Snatt did mount the scaffold at Tyburn in 1696 to give spiritual comfort to Sir John Friend and Sir William Parkyns, convicted for plotting to kill king William at Turnham Green. Snatt prayed with them, heard their confessions and gave absolution - for which he was briefly imprisoned. Quietly conforming, though, were John Eresby, who accepted the living at Firle vacated by the non-juring Lewis Roberts, and Snatt's brother-in-law, Thomas Whalley, the grammar school master, who pliantly replaced Eresby at Cliffe, All Saints and Southover.[44]

Yet the non-jurors' departure did not restore Anglican unity. 'High Churchmen', still resolutely Tory, feared Dissenters would mobilize to dismantle the State Church and end the Anglicans' monopoly of Public Office - with dire consequences, they deemed, for political and social stability. John Shore at St John's, in a sermon on the day of queen Mary's funeral in 1695, entitled *The Threnody of the Bow; or The Country's Lamentation*, did indeed denounce Jacobites as men 'that fight against God who by a miraculous Revolution has set our present Prince [king William] upon the Throne', a Deliverance as great as that of the Israelites from Pharoah. Yet in 1712, mindful of militant Dissent and of Anglican afflictions during the Great Rebellion, he wrote 'We were on the brinks of the same precipice very lately; we are yet scarcely safe - God deliver me from the tender mercies of that Enthusiastical Brood that has once already sacrificed Church and State'. 'Low Churchmen', however, enjoyed relaxed relations with Dissent and still inclined to the Whigs. When one of them, George Barnsley, rector of Sedlescombe, offered himself to the clergy in Lewes archdeaconry as their spokesman at Convocation in 1695, Sir John Pelham sent venison to his supporters. Joseph Grave at St Mary Westout, the erstwhile 'Malcontent', was friendly with Simon Patrick, a Low Church bishop of Chichester. He probably had few qualms when entrusted, after Eresby's departure, with St Michael's parish, that vortex of well-heeled Nonconformity. In 1717 he left to local Whig trustees an annuity of £10 so that his library, replete with works by Low Church and Dissenting divines, could be housed and replenished for the benefit of townsfolk.[45]

Though queen Anne's accession in 1702 installed a sovereign devoted, indeed Bounteous, to the Anglican church, Whigs dominated her government till 1710. By then, though, High Church Tories were gaining ground. They alleged that Toleration had encouraged Unitarians, despite their exclusion from the Act. And indeed, before baptizing Frances Charman at Cliffe, pastor Barnard had confirmed that she believed Jesus Christ 'to be God', in case Matthew Caffyn, a 'Socinian' preacher famous as 'the Battle Axe of Sussex', had infected her Anabaptist parents at Horsham. Tories also benefited from popular anger at the Whig government's ill-advised impeachment of Dr Sacheverell in 1709 for preaching High Church sermons. By then too the war with France was becoming an electoral liability for the ministers conducting it. Marlborough's victories were thwarting Louis XIV's bid for supremacy in Europe, but the cost was heavy. In 1706 the 'slowness' of Sussex folk to subscribe to the Society for Promoting Christian Knowledge was blamed on 'scarcity of money' in 'these taxing times'. Many landowners resented a land tax being the mainstay of war finance, and denounced the profits made by City men, mostly Whigs, from the new-fangled Bank of England and National Debt. The state bureaucracies spawned by the war also gave Whig ministers a rich source of patronage - adeptly exploited, for instance, by the Pelhams.[46]

Thomas Pelham, a Whig, and Henry Lumley, a Tory, were elected knights of the shire for Sussex in 1702, and John Morley Trevor of Glynde, a Whig, and Sir George Parker of Willingdon, a Tory, in 1705. That year the shire contest was held at Lewes, where columns of 'western' freeholders arrived, headed by the Whig dukes of Richmond and Somerset. But the sheriff excluded both grandees from the sessions-house because they were Lords of Parliament, so they killed time watching a puppet show in the High Street. In 1708 Tory support in Sussex was somewhat eroded by panic along the coast because the Old Pretender was assembling an invasion army at Dunkirk. Some pregnant women miscarried - it was said - when a Lewes butcher, John Apted, rode through Brighton blowing a post horn and shouting that 30,000 Frenchman had landed at Shoreham. The anti-Gallicanism aided the return of two Whigs, Sir Henry Peachey of Petworth and Peter Gott of Stanmer. The son of a Presbyterian ironmaster, and a director of the Bank of England, Gott had bought the Stanmer estate in 1700. In Sussex, however, as elsewhere, the tide turned decisively for the Tories in 1710. Robert Harley formed a Tory government intent on making peace, and in the election that followed Sir George Parker and Charles Eversfield of Horsham, both Tories, were returned for Sussex. After being appointed by the Crown to an office of profit in 1712, Eversfield was re-elected - perhaps without opposition, for according to the Tory *Post Boy*, crowds of 'substantial freeholders' and 'above 150 of the clergy' swarmed into Lewes 'crying peace, peace'.[47]

Harley's ministry concluded a Peace with France in 1713 and a treaty to reduce trade tariffs. It also ended the 'occasional conformity' whereby Dissenters had evaded the Test and Corporation Acts excluding them from Public Office. Extreme Tories, however, members of an October Club, were now intent on closing down Dissenting schools, denying citizenship to refugee Protestants, and securing the Old Pretender as successor to the childless queen Anne. John Fuller of Brightling and Henry Campion, elected knights of the shire for Sussex in 1713, were both members. Campion, a nephew of his namesake, the Tory Grand Juror, had married Barbara Courthope, heiress to Danny Park at Hurstpierpoint. His Jacobitism was such that after George of Hanover's accession, he left Sussex to serve 'the Chevalier St George, commonly called the Pretender'. Before the 1713 election, doubtless bitterly fought, the Whig candidates, John Morley Trevor of Glynde and James Butler of Warminghurst in West Sussex, proclaimed their zeal for 'a Protestant succession' vested to 'the illustrious House of Hanover' - also the need to protect 'the woollen manufactures' of Great Britain, an attack on the tariff treaty.[48]

Yet despite their triumph in the county, Tories in Lewes borough made little headway. Quite probably the Tory *Post Boy* was accurate when it reported that the crowds of freeholders and clergy, who invaded the town crying 'peace, peace' in 1712, 'gave great disturbance to the inhabitants who are, most of them, Dissenters, or those who delight in war'. Hatred of France was fuelled there by Louis XIV's support for the Pretender's invasion, and by fears that smugglers worked hand in glove with Jacobite agents. Lewes was also a haven for Huguenots fleeing Louis's persecution. James Hallee, born in Caen, but 'refugeed in England upon the account of religion', died there in 1702. Also of Gallic origin were his fellow starch maker, John Thieary, Daniel Fabre barber and Isaac Guepin clockmaker. In 1709 local collections were made to relieve 'the poor Palatines', German Protestants savaged by a pitiless French war-machine.[49]

As for the town's Dissenters, the county poll books show that the more affluent, who qualified as forty shilling freeholders, almost always voted for both Whig candidates, giving them comfortable majorities in the Borough, Southover and Cliffe. As for known Anglicans, some voted Whig, some (rather fewer) Tory, and some cross-voted - in 1705, 1708 and 1710 mostly for the 'eastern' Tory, Sir George Parker of Willingdon, and for an 'eastern' Whig. At the hard-fought 1713 election Whig support was especially strong. Of the 121 voters in the town, 80 polled for Trevor and Butler, 19 for Fuller and Campion; 21 split their votes, and John Sweetlove, the miller at Cliffe, plumped for Trevor. To the Whigs rallied such affluent Anglicans as Henry Pelham, Richard Paine, Richard Shelley, John Apsley, Apsley Newton and William Lane. The only Tory of substance was Nathaniel Trayton. Cross-voters included Benjamin White, Peter White and John Tabor - physicians with a foot in each camp.[50]

Reliance on these county poll books would suggest, therefore, that the return of two Whigs at each Borough election between 1702 and 1713 had resulted from a formidable alliance of Dissenters and affluent Anglicans. In 1702 Thomas and Henry Pelham made way for Sir Nicholas Pelham of Catsfield, a step-brother of their father, and for Richard Paine, a landowner resident in Westout already noted as related to Richard Shelley, William Pellatt at the Friars and William Newton at Southover. In 1705 Paine was re-elected, along with Nicholas Pelham's son Thomas. Thereafter Thomas was to sit without interruption till 1741. Richard Paine was followed in 1708 by Samuel Gott whose father Peter was elected a knight of the shire that year. Samuel made way in 1710 for Peter, but he hanged himself in April 1712, whereupon John Morley Trevor of Glynde was elected, and re-elected in 1713. Trevor's sister, Arabella, had married Robert Heath II, the step-son of Henry Pelham, and from 1711 twenty local boys were 'cloathed at the charge of Mr Pelham who finds them Books & gives the Master 20 pounds per annum to teach them to Read, Write, Cast Accounts, the Catechism and to Sing Psalms'.[51]

However, a Borough poll book for the 1705 election, the only one to survive for this period, reveals that the alliance of Dissenters and Anglican Whigs was far from straight-forward. Thomas Pelham and Richard Paine polled 147 and 125 votes. Ninety-nine out of the 215 electors polled for both of them, including such leading Anglicans as parson Joseph Grave, the gentlemen Henry Pelham, William Pellatt, Richard Shelley and Thomas Browne, the lawyers Thomas Isted and Samuel Isted - also the government postman, Jonas Wyath. Their wealth swelled the resources available to 'treat', bribe or browbeat electors. Also voting for them were the High Constables, Thomas Waterman and Nicholas Stent, which suggests the Borough's manorial machine was in Whig hands. Ten of the 15 jurors, who nominated Waterman and Stent at the court leet in October 1704, also voted for Pelham and Paine. As returning officers, they resolved doubtful or disputed votes: in 1734 these involved 48 electors and caused an angry exchange of pamphlets, the last 93 pages long.[52]

Yet the poll book also reveals a powerful challenge from an Ultra-Whig. Thomas Fagg received votes from 107 townsmen, almost half of those who polled. His father, Sir John Fagg of Wiston, had been a brother-in-law and close ally of Herbert Morley, and supported James II's grant of Toleration to Dissenters and Catholics. Educated at a Dissenting academy in Steyning, Thomas encouraged Presbyterians to worship in his mansion at Glynleigh near Westham. He became a member of pastor Newton's Lewes meeting in 1695 and bought the former Springett mansion in St Michael's [Newcastle House] in 1700. Previously MP for Rye, he was a fuller-blooded champion of Dissent than either Pelham or Paine, at a time when Tories in Parliament were seeking to end 'occasional conformity'. And indeed - apart from Ambrose Galloway II and Thomas Norman the bookseller, who opted for Pelham and Paine - his support among leading Dissenters was solid. They cast a single vote for Fagg - he attracted 44 plumpers - or gave him one vote, and Pelham or Paine the other. His only affluent Anglican supporter, Thomas Bromfield, was something of an outsider. Fagg's powerful Ultra-Whig challenge might explain why some apparent Tories rallied to a pair of moderate Whigs - among them the former High Constables, John Holney, Henry Hopkins and John Tooke; the Church lawyer Thomas Barrett, and Edward Inskipp and Henry Rose who voted Tory in the county election.

Two other candidates also stood. John Spence at Malling House was a landowner with strong Presbyterian links, who had married Fagg's sister and was presumably his ally. Nathaniel Trayton, the barrister on School Hill, headed the Borough's most prominent Tory family. Yet Trayton received only four votes and Spence only six - one from pastor Barnard's brother, another from pastor Newton's future executor. Perhaps they both joined the fray after polling began, or retired from it early on. Either way, Trayton's truncated showing offers no guide to Tory support in the Borough, modest though it must have been.[53]

Whether Ultra-Whig champions stood again for Lewes borough before 1714 is uncertain. Fagg died in 1705 - his widow Elizabeth becoming a member at Westgate in 1709. Nathaniel Trayton did stand again in 1710, the year the earl of Thanet sold him Southover manor. In a subsequent petition he claimed a majority of the votes legally cast, alleging Peter Gott had resorted to bribery and other nefarious practices. But given the strength in 1705 of the Pelham-Paine coalition, and of Fagg's challenge to it, any such majority seems implausible. As a faithful Tory

Trayton funded in 1714 the first stage of a new church tower at Southover, his initials being lusciously carved on a plaque. Possibly too he paid for the 'ruinous' chancel to be shortened - glass in its east window displayed the Trayton coat of arms.[54]

Amid this tumult of High Politics there were attempts in 1698 and 1709 to revive the 'Fellowship called the Twelve', the body neutered by Monarchist JPs in October 1663. Since then the High

183 Trayton's plaque

Constables had answered to the court leet jury for their disbursement of a Town rate. The 'necessary expenses' can be glimpsed from 1694 onwards. The salary of Edward Tipton, their clerk, was ten shillings a year. They paid for drums and trumpets at queen Anne's proclamation, for beer, tobacco and the ringing of the Town Bell at her coronation and for beer when a coroner's jury deliberated on the death of William Winkton's son. They detained a 'suspicious' person who came from France; funded a hue and cry; repaired the pillory and stocks, and bought a proclamations' board. They supplied green baize for the justices's table in the sessions-house - red cloth for the rail and seats, scarlet cloth for the cushions. They hired men to whip vagrants, gypsies and Jarvis Murray, 'our parish boy' who absconded from his master at Fletching - Palmer's cart was used to pace such punishment. They arranged the billeting of soldiers and their horses - in 1692 the landlord of the *White Lion* was owed over £38 by officers since departed. The Constables facilitated the impressment for the Navy of 'showmen' at a Whitsun fair, and of a man staying at the *Star*, lodging him in their lock-up at the west gate. In 1708 they sent the indenture confirming Samuel Gott's election as their MP to the under-sheriff's chambers at Cliffords Inn in London, 'at number X up two pairs of stairs'. Embarassing was 'the indictment' of their deficient Market Bushel at the assizes in July 1712; they bought a new one in August.

Advertising their authority was the town crier or 'bellman' who also 'tended' the lower court of the sessions-house. He broadcast details of town rates and town meetings, parliamentary elections, militia musters and courts leet, the 'pressing' of wagons and the closure of the bridge for repair; he publicized campaigns to expel beggars, to impound stray hogs, and to require householders to set basins of water at their doors when smallpox was rife. In December 1708 he was bought a blue coat, a pair of hose and trimming for his hat. Abraham Weston made a large brass

badge, 'with the Town Arms and guilt with Gold', to be set on his coat. The silver cup that Thomas Blunt had given in 1611 was soldered in 1703, and other town property kept in repair. Carpenters and masons viewed the clock-house. The 'dungeon' at the west Gate was paved. A room was built for the fire engines - there were three by 1681. Thomas Barrett was paid to oil the market clock and the town clock. The sessions-house was glazed and leaded in 1694, though it was agreed in 1696 that the Borough should maintain the inside only.[55]

184 The large brass badge

The powers of the High Constables, and their role as returning offi-
cers, could explain an attempt to wrestle their election from a court leet
answerable to the Lords of Lewes and to vest it in a revived 'Society or
Fellowship of the Town and Borough of Lewes Commonly called the
Twelve'. As recorded in the Town Book, this was enacted on Whitsun
Monday in 1698 by Ralph Pope 'aged 82' and Stephen Snatt 'aged 85'.
In 1664 both had fought a rear-guard action on behalf of the Twelve -
Pope hung on to 'the weights and measures in his custody', Snatt to
bonds and money in his. Claiming now to be 'the surviving society or fellowship', pursuing 'the usual and Ancient custom', they recruited into it
the serving High Constables, 14 previous Constables, three former headboroughs and Samuel Watts. A second entry in the Town Book reveals
that 14 of these, the 'Surviving Society', met on 13 June 1709, 'being
Whitsun-Monday', 'to revive the ancient custom' and elect 'several persons' into the Fellowship. But clearly the resurrected Fellowship did not
claw back the election of Constables from the court leet, for John Austen
(1699-1700) and others were not among those recruited in 1698. Both
entries in the Town Book were intruded unofficially and the venue in
1709 was at the *Star*, not the town-house. Moreover, the space for listing
new members in 1709 remained blank. So doubtless, as Paul Dunvan
assumed, the Fellowship expired with the death, about 1720, of Samuel
Watts, last survivor of those recruited in 1698.[56]

Possibly this revived Fellowship was 'the societie of this town' which
placed in the town-house in 1709 'a tablet' celebrating nine worthy bene-

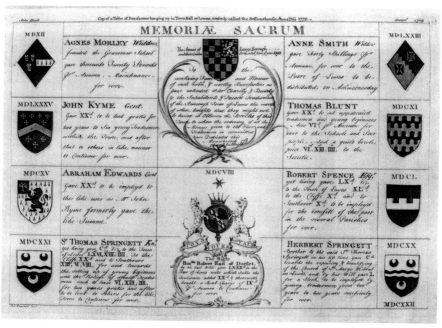

185 The 'tablet'

factors of the Borough, 'a Monument of thankfulness' to ensure their charity was not 'buried in Oblivion'. The tablet also credited 'the societie' with 'the ordering of all the Moneys given to the Poor and Tradesmen'. Yet it was from the Borough rate - surely not under the control of any 'society' - that Benjamin Couley was paid to paint seven coats of arms upon the board. Moreover the High Constables were still accounting to the court leet jury for the 'bonds' associated with the 'Moneys'. Earlier, in the 1660s, the abeyance of the Fellowship had complicated a bequest of houses in the High Street by the Reverend George Steer. Intending that their rents should fund at the university a son of 'Godly poor Parents' in or near Lewes, 'especially of a Godly poor Minister', he entrusted them to 'the Chief Officers and four others of the most able inhabitants'. But a Commission under the Great Seal of England, finding that the inhabitants were not 'a Body' capable 'to take' any such bequest, entrusted them to feoffees instead.[57]

The members of the resurrected Fellowship were mostly Whigs, and mostly Dissenters, but not all were. So maybe their pursuit of a lost autonomy was not primarily inspired by faction. That it languished is not surprising. An enclave of local government, however puny, controlled by a co-opted oligarchy of tradesmen and based on prescriptive right, would hardly have suited the landowners, however Whiggish, who controlled the Lewes bench and the court leet of the manor of Lewes borough.

186 Malling House: the seat of John Spence, the advanced Whig   **Overleaf:** School Hill House

Postscript

The legacy

The town of Lewes, though small indeed if compared with some we have, is prosperous, and has abundance of all things contributing to the necessities, uses, or even pleasure of life. And who would not admire the street leading down to the river! Standing on the ridge, you see on the right and the left a well-peopled valley, vessels going up and down, well-watered meadows, and workshops for whatever is needed for navigation. I observe that the public buildings, being very old, are quite decayed and dirty, with nothing venerable or ornamental in them, but very many of the houses of individuals are well-designed and handsome.
The Reverend John Burton (about1730).

During the reign of George I (1714-27) the English achieved a political consensus by resolving conflicts which had inflamed politics for a century or more. Earlier, the New Monarchy constructed a Nation State firmly based on the shire - on assizes, quarter sessions and militia musters; a State relying on a royal navy, augmented by merchant ships, as a first line of defence. The standing army and the full-time bureaucracy remained small, and taxation was reduced to a minimum. But during the Great Rebellion this decentralized regime fell apart, because Ship Money and 'Popish' altar rails were seen as threats to Liberty, local and national. When a Puritan Republic proved impossible, a constitutional Monarchy was restored. But not till the Glorious Revolution was the autonomy of Parliament ensured and the Toleration of Dissent enshrined in statute. Thereafter, though, the extent of Toleration was still contested, and politics further bedevilled by Jacobitism and the burden of war finance.

These were tensions that the reign of George I resolved. The king formed the keystone of a parliamentary system acceptable to most men of property - its stability further bolstered by low taxation and buoyant commerce stemming from the Peace made with France in 1713. Whig statesmen and Low Church bishops now dominated an Anglican ruling class which guaranteed to mainstream Dissenters freedom to worship, to educate their children and 'occasionally' conform. Radicals like Comfort Starr, Edward Newton and Joseph Grave, men shaped by a Puritan republic and Cavalier repression, had no successors. And High Toryism withered under a German dynasty very lacking in 'sacred majesty' - Anne was the last monarch to touch for the King's Evil, though after 1714 a few

die-hard monarchists did resort to Ashburnham to revere the relics of
Charles the Martyr. The Tory paladin, Nathaniel Trayton, died in 1715,
and the erstwhile Jacobite, Henry Campion, grudgingly accepted the
new regime in September 1720, returning to Danny Park from the
Continent, 'having been away 5 years and 6 weeks'.[1]

Dissent was now firmly buttressed by statute. An estimated 670
Presbyterians, Independents and Baptists worshipped at Lewes in 1715.
The town was 'miserably overrun' by them, complained the bishop of
Chichester, and parsons held in 'great contempt'. The very fabric of its
Anglican churches decayed. The collapsed 'steeple' at Southover was
rebuilt up to 'the first loft' in 1713-14, as a result of Nathaniel Trayton's
munificence - and 5s 4d collected at Maresfield. But it remained in that
'half-raised state' - the bells grounded - till 1738. When the south aisle at
'ruinous' St Michael's was restored in 1747, the cost was mostly borne by
the bishop and the Pelham family.[2]

The Pelhams at Laughton, Catsfield and St Andrew's Lane had
formed the local hub of the alliance between Whig politicians and
Dissenters which withstood a Cavalier onslaught under Charles II and
welcomed the House of Hanover in 1714. The alliance was maintained
by Thomas Pelham-Holles who followed his father as baron Pelham of
Laughton in 1713. Through his mother, Lady Grace Holles, he also
acquired the dukedom of Newcastle-upon-Tyne and great tracts in the
Midlands. By February 1715 the fledgling Whig grandee was wooing
freeholders at the county election held at Chichester. Thomas Marchant,
a Tory who arrived in a tilt-wagon, sourly blamed his 'indirect practices',
as 'their grand patron', for the victory scored by the Whigs. In 1717 he
became Lord Chamberlain and in 1724 a Secretary of State. At the
Borough election in 1715 Thomas Pelham of Catsfield and John Trevor
of Glynde were returned, and in 1722 Thomas Pelham and Henry
Pelham of Stanmer, whose father had been Clerk of the Pells. Henry
employed Nicholas Dubois, the king's Master Mason, to design an austere seven-bay mansion at Stanmer, and sold his house in St Andrew's
Lane in 1725 to Thomas Pelham, whose gift of a fire-engine to the
Borough caused Benjamin Couley to add his name to its benefactors'
board in 1726.[3]

To further increase their influence in an affluent Borough with a
large electorate, the Pelhams bought up houses, spent heavily in the
shops and subsidized education. From 1711 the Clerk of the Pells had
funded a charity school, and in 1715, as a trustee of the grammar school,
he released £100 for a new 'schoolroom' at Westout - Mrs Mary Jenkins
had bequeathed the money and the site. By 1717, moreover, as a base for
their supporters, Richard Verrall had turned their former town-house
into the *White Hart* - in 1682, at an alehouse bearing that sign, elsewhere
in St Michael's parish, men had played cards all night in flat defiance of
the watch. The new hostelry soon eclipsed its neighbours, the *Pelicans*

and the *Running Horse* (previously the *George*). In its Great Room were four tables, 25 chairs and 15 sconces, in the club-room a billiard table and 11 prints, in the best bedrooms 'china' furniture (green, blue and yellow), in the stables 120 halters. Revellers could use 33 decanters and 20 punch bowls, eight Delft plates and 30 wheatear pots, 82 pewter dishes and a cohort of chamber pots, pewter and 'white'. During the Borough election in 1727 the Pelhams spent £137 16s 10d on 'entertainment' there.[4]

Doubtless too they promoted the robust arch of stone which in 1727 replaced the battered wooden frame that had served as Lewes Bridge. The design was by Nicholas Dubois, the architect of Stanmer House. In 1715, moreover, a town meeting in the Borough authorized 'the getting of hands' for a petition, to persuade the government to build 'a Pier' at Newhaven harbour. Resolute action, though, was delayed. Indeed in December 1730 thirteen ships laden with Southdown corn were trapped by eastward-drifting shingle choking the harbour mouth. But in 1731 a Harbour Commission was set up and two effective breakwaters built.[5]

187 The bridge designed by Dubois

And maybe the Pelhams secured the summer assizes for the Borough - another step to county town status. As already noted, only in July 1687 and July 1713 had the circuit judges by-passed East Grinstead and toiled through a 'deep and dirty' Weald to Lewes. Indeed the High Constables spent £36 10s 7d 'altering' the sessions-house in 1713: Couley cleaned a coat-of-arms, Kennard turned '30 banisters', and a brass pin was bought 'for the judges hat'. The judges, however, returned in July 1716 when the Borough happily paid for a cart 'to draw the men to the Gallows' - and they reappeared most summers till 1731. Their 'entertainment' by Benjamin Court ironmonger - presumably at his palatial High Street showrooms - cost the Borough £8 7s 9d in 1724, an expense partly met in 1726 by public subscription.[6]

The courting by the Pelhams of a Borough electorate with a powerful Dissenting component reveals how thoroughly the instinct for Liberty had permeated English politics - in part due to a Great Rebellion driven by the Puritan conscience, and in part to the long-established presence of Lord Lieutenants, JPs and deputy-lieutenants at the assizes, the quarter sessions and the militia musters - the apparatus of a decentralized State. John Burton contrasted the Borough's decayed public buildings with its handsome private houses, and indeed towns in Whiggish Low-Church England lacked the flamboyantly Baroque facades, advertising the royal barracks, the Governor's residence and the prelate's palace, so conspicuous in provincial capitals throughout the autocracies of Europe.

The affluent elite of the shire also gathered at Lewes for the Plate Race, which Will Marchant from Hurstpierpoint attended in May 1718. By 1727 the two-day meeting was held in August, to dovetail with the assizes, thereby enhancing the town as a focus of Fashion. The duke of

Newcastle became its Steward and mounted 'the hill' each year with a bevy of Whig supporters 'in the most sumptuous style'. When races were first held there is uncertain. But in 1706 local JPs named George Wattle, 'a horse courser' from Reigate, as the father of a bastard child born in St Michael's parish. An amateur 'courser' perhaps was Benjamin Ellis who died in August 1747 aged 89. His headstone at Westout describes him as 'litle Benjamin the Ruler'; while a 'diligent' servant of the attorney Charles Goodwin, he was robbed of a riding-coat in 1692; later he leased Spital Farm near the racecourse.[7]

Local commerce - the supplying of 'all things contributing to the necessities, uses, or even pleasure of life' - benefited from political stability and the Peace with France, from Pelhams purchasing votes and JPs mixing shire business with recre-

188 The headstone

398

ation. Businesses now took very firm root. William Brett inherited the ancestral grocery at Watergate Corner in 1735 and bought a share in the Bridge coffee-house; his son-in-law, Francis Whitfield, became a founding partner of Lewes New Bank in 1789. Thomas Friend [at Barbican House] sold a communion cloth to St Mary Westout in 1716, and being also a wool dealer with London contacts, arranged bills of credit for Henry Campion. His extensive landed property passed by descent to Thomas Read Kemp who developed the Brighton estate as Kemp Town. In 1707 Benjamin Court had opened new showrooms [at Newcastle House] where Burton admired his 'magazine of ironmongery' - the sundial survives. He supplied locks to Horsham Gaol, a stove to Danny Park and a kitchen-jack chain to Compton Place at Eastbourne. His goodwill passed in 1734 to Joseph Molineux who probably built a six-bay shop-front opposite [61 High Street] - the stately doorcase remains.[8]

189 The sundial

190 The stately doorcase

The town also consolidated as a base for builders. In 1714 William Stephens used red and grey bricks in a chequer pattern on the first stage of the church tower at Southover. In 1723 Thomas Morris laid out a 'Walk' in Westout churchyard, planted with 12 lime trees - a tribute perhaps to the House of Hanover. When Arthur Morris was made a 'foreign member' of the London Masons' Company in 1712, he probably occupied a riparian stone-yard in Cliffe, north of the bridge. Before 1730 he moved to the west bank, near the south end of Green Wall. In 1714 he charged almost £300 to re-build Dr Peter White's residence [School Hill House] as a five-bay mansion. (See chapter opener) A London relative of White supplied wainscot and Baltic deals, advised on the making of sash windows, and worried that the entrance, 'so very near one corner', rendered the facade 'very irregular'. Morris, whose brickwork was faultless, was later used by Colen Campbell at Compton Place and by Nicholas Dubois at Stanmer House, though the 'intolerably saucy and unruly' Morris apparently called the King's Master Mason 'the French son of a bitch'. About 1800 the Eastgate yard passed to the Parsons family whose forbears, all builders, had lived in St James Street 'since the Commonwealth'.[9]

191 The panel

Faultless too was Dr White's staircase, crafted by Robert Burstow, a carpenter with a yard behind the defunct *White Lion*. At Stanmer House he installed three wide elliptical arches for the inner hall 'with open Pilasters and Keys in the Center'; also a cantilevered staircase with '31 steps made of right wainscot' and with 'rails and balusters twisted and ramped'. As for herald painters, Robert Smith moved from New Shoreham, a ship-building town, to execute a King's Arms for St Michael's in 1720, for St Mary Westout in 1723, and possibly for Cliffe church, where a robustly fluent panel superseded the cloth painted by Richard Jones in 1681. Later on, the Lamberts combined heraldry with more ambitious artistic endeavour.[10]

Lewes also remained a focus of Physic. Indeed Richard Russell, the son of a Dissenting High Street apothecary, established sea-bathing at Brighton. An enterprising youth, he measured a Roman mosaic at Eastbourne in 1712 and notified the Royal Society; he married Mary Kempe, heiress to Malling Deanery, in 1719; he studied at Leiden, where his thesis on epilepsy satisfied the eminent Herman Boerhaave, whose prescriptions Dr Peter White collected; and while building a fashionable practice in mid Sussex, he publicized sea water as Nature's defence against all bodily 'putrefaction', instancing the firm gums and radiant teeth of fish-wives at Brighton. Once his 'cure' grew popular, he erected a house at the Steine to receive his patients in 1753. A line from Euripides, translating as 'The sea washes away all the ills of mankind', adorns his modest memorial in Malling church.[11]

192 The memorial

John Tabor, the School Hill physician, shared Russell's interest in the Eastbourne villa. He excavated the bath there in 1716 and his report was the first relating to Sussex to be printed, by the Royal Society. He also measured 18 earthworks on the South Downs between Belle Tout and the Trundle, believing they were built by the Romano-Britons, to combat king Aelle's invasion: 'the ground was disputed inch by inch … the pick-axe and spade were as much made use of as the sword'. His knowledge of Wealden terrain near his manor of Howborne in Buxted was perhaps the source of Stukeley's strangely accurate surmise that a Roman road from Lewes to London passed 'by Isfield' and crossed the Ouse 'by Sharnbridge' [Shortbridge]. As for the

Eastbourne mosaic, only a bed of plaster was left by 1743 - 'everybody that came to see it took away pieces of it'. More enduring was the antiquarian research pursued at Lewes by Robert Austen, John Elliot and Thomas Woollgar, Paul Dunvan, Gideon Mantell and Thomas Horsfield.[12]

Whereas commercial prosperity at Lewes lasted for a century after 1714, along with shire government by the gentry, the ideological truce brokered under George I dissolved in the 1760s. Religious Enthusiasm erupted when Calvinistic Methodists arrived from Brighton, dispatched by Selina countess of Huntingdon. And political consensus had collapsed by August 1770 when, amid pealing bells and crowds crying 'Wilkes and Liberty', the 'great patriot' rested at the *Star* and then toured the castle. Observing him maybe was an excise officer, Thomas Paine, a lodger at Bull House since 1768. His pamphlets were to fuel an 'Atlantic Revolution', which engulfed America and France and caused William Pitt's government to resort to repression in the 1790s. Most local Dissenters espoused the cause of Liberty, along with such Low Church gentlemen as Thomas Read Kemp and Henry Shelley - replicating the coalition forged against Cavalier repression after 1660. Shelley indeed was a descendant of the Civil War MP and of his parson-baiting 'Malcontent' son. And Thomas Mantell, a Dissenting shoemaker, named his first-born Gideon Algernon, to salute the champion of Israel and the Whig aristocrat executed in 1683. Paul Dunvan's *History of Lewes* (1795), moreover, identified Sir Thomas Nutt as 'a malign retailer of penal law who accelerated the glorious revolution eighteen years later'. Dunvan also relished the fate of the *Royal Escape* which carried the fugitive Charles Stuart to France: she was moored in the Thames, opposite Whitehall, 'to receive the veneration of a besotted multitude' but the conduct of Charles II proved 'a bitter restorative from political insanity'. So she was moved to Deptford and steadily decayed till 1791 when 'her mouldering remains were broke up for fuel'.[13]

One Friend of Liberty enlisted Lewes castle in its cause. Elizabeth Hitchener attended an academy for young ladies on School Hill, before becoming the soul-mate of Percy Bysshe Shelley. The ivy wreathing the ruined keep was for her

> *An emblem as of Liberty's green flag,*
> *Which seems o'er tyranny and gothic strength*
> *Triumphantly its standard thus to rear.*

In grim reality, of course, the castle had several times received men at war with 'tyranny and gothic strength'. It was occupied by soldiers of Simon of Montfort, fresh from capturing a King of the Romans at Westout. Folk from mid Sussex looted it to avenge the crass cupidity of an earl of Arundel. Protestants, martyred for their faith, were probably imprisoned there. Its guns consumed a barrel of powder firing salvoes rejoicing at the defeat of the Spanish Armada. Into its bailey swarmed forty-shilling freeholders determined to elect knights of the shire unwelcome to the Lord Protector Cromwell. Pioneer Quakers were kicked and beaten while testifying on its 'green'. And its walls echoed the cheers on 5 November 1679 when an effigy of 'the Pope, with his Cross keys, Crosier staff and other Fopperies, was first degraded and then committed to the flames'. Crude, sometimes bigoted, though this pursuit of Liberty may have been, it laid a foundation for English Democracy - a precious legacy of pre-Georgian Lewes.[14]

Saxon freemen had built and guarded the burh into which the Norman castle intruded. They farmed the South Downs and exploited the forested Weald; they fished and sailed the Ouse and the English Channel. Their little world of mid Sussex - a microcosm of Lowland England - with its richly varied soils, abundant timber and cheap fish, nourished peasant communities difficult to terrorize. Yet William the Conqueror managed to, and thereby divided the folk from its rulers, side-lined its culture and pillaged its resources to fund Continental feuds. But the Norman Police State slowly fell apart: the battle of Lewes shook it; the Peasants' Revolt and Cade's Rebellion signalled its terminal decline. When the New Monarchy based a decentralized State on assizes, quarter sessions and shire militias - and augmented a royal navy with merchant ships - the JPs and officers came from the gentry, but the jurors, soldiers and sailors from the folk. All spoke English, identified with England and were proud of it - in being was the nation which Elizabeth governed and Shakespeare adored. This nation survived a Great Rebellion and a Cavalier Restoration, and partly thanks to Puritan Dissent, and to London its great bastion, the kingdom then settled for a Parliamentary Monarchy, in which Property and Conscience were tolerably safe, and Power was hedged by Liberty.

In this story pre-Georgian Lewes had played several parts, as a hub of commerce, of decentralized government, of intellectual debate, and by 1714 its emergence as a county town was complete.

An emblem as of Liberty's green flag

Overleaf: a crouching satyr at the former *Bull* inn

403

References

Details of published works are to be found in the Bibliography. Frequently cited documents do not state the Record Offices in which they are held but can be identified by consulting the list of repositories and document prefixes below.

British Library: Add Ch, Add MS, Harleian MS.
Centre for Kentish Studies: U.
East Sussex Record Office: ABE, ACC, ADA, AMS, ASH, BMW, CHR, DAN, DYK, FRE, GIL, GLY, HBR, HIC, HOW, KIR, LAN, LEW, MOB, NU, PAR, PDA, QDS, QI, QM, QO, QR, R/C, ROB, RYE; SAS/A, ACC, C, CH, CO, D, DN, E, F, G, HC, I, JC, L, M, PN, RF, SH, SM, WH, WS; SAU, SHR, SOF, SRA, SRL, TD, W, XE.
National Archives (formerly Public Record Office): ASSI, C, DL, E, JUST, LR, LP, PROB, SC, SP, WARDS, WO.
West Sussex Record Office: Ep, Lavington MS., Wiston MS.

1 Before the burh: mounds and minsters
Epigraph. Dunvan 6.
1. Rudling 1992 238; Green 1980 69-86.
2. Cunliffe 15; Lysons plate 3 facing p. 20.
3. Rudling 1998 41-65; Rudling & Butler 6-7; Margary 204-7; Brodribb 183-96; Tebbutt 1979 47-56; Biggar 149-50; Bedwin 1978 241-54.
4. Margary 93-203; Marsden 1979 229-30; Norris 1956 10-12; Scott 59.
5. Bleach 131-42; Greatorex 15; Figg 1861 2-3.
6. Dunvan 5-10; Horsfield Lewes 1: 51-74; Green 1980 84; Lewis 30; Freke 1975 70-3.
7. Salzman 1921 201; Rudling 1998 46.
8. Barker 1947 43-5; Welch 81-3; Rudling 1998 52-9; Bell 36-53; Coates 1980 324-5.
9. Lower 1846 96; Mantell 1940 76; Thomas 2002 4-5; Craddock 85-102.
10. Barker 1947 43-5; Coates 1980 310; Drewett & Hamilton 1999 29-33.
11. Drewett & Hamilton 1999 7-37, 2001 256-62; Curwen 1954 270-2.
12. Horsfield Lewes 1: 74-6; Bleach 135-7.
13. Torr 1964 98.
14. Bleach 135; Town Book 2: 116; ADA 160/209; Reynolds 1999 105-9.
15. Coates 1990-1 5-15, 1997 141-2, 1998 18-20; Forsberg 1997 passim; Horsfield Lewes 1: 9-11.
16. Morris 63-76 255-8; Kirby 167-8.
17. Whatmore 1-54; Povey 285; Anon 1856 322.
18. Sawyer 1968 312-13 444; VCHS 7:101; Mawer & Stenton 2: v 29; Mayr-

Harting 1981 1-17; Morris 14 20 110-11 128-38; Lyne 1997 14-19.
19. Barker 1947 43-9, 1948 126-32; Gardiner 1989 39-42.
20. Barker 1948 131-2; Domesday f. 16; Du Boulay 1966 25 31-2; Sawyer 1968 403-4; Turner 1852 128-9.
21. Domesday f. 16v; Du Boulay 1966 126-7; Holgate 1929 183; Sawyer 1968 83.
22. Farmer 1992 220-1; Town Book 1: 29; Rowe 16; ABE ACC 560/1; Brighton History Centre, (S9) LEW EL5.
23. Blair 1998 124-30; Freke 1975 66-84; ADA 50/46; Domesday f. 21v; VCHS 7: 33; Round 1888 11-14.
24. Hodges 105; Blair 1997 173-92; Welch 79-81; Dunvan 6.

2 A Saxon stronghold c890-1066
Epigraphs. Dunvan 33; Domesday f. 26.
1. Biddle 99-150; Hill 179-89; Hill & Rumble passim; Dunvan 353.
2. Dunvan 300; SAS Library Woollgar's *Spicilegia* 1:148 (henceforth Woollgar); SRA 6/13/2; Arundel Castle MS A 1871; *Sussex Weekly Advertiser* 17 Nov. 1823; Spokes 1932 208; VCHS 7: 8.
3. Gardiner 1996a 75-8 99; Darby & Campbell 453-5; Domesday f. 26; VCHS 1: 366-7 382; Allcroft 45-6.
4. Hill & Rumble 142-3; Combes & Lyne 213-24; Domesday ff. 16-29v.
5. Round 1899 75-80; Williams 1981 171-86; Domesday 5-9.
6. Biddle 99-150; Hill & Rumble 143-4; Hooke 201-12.

7. Domesday ff. 26-7; Mason 1964 68-93.
8. Hill & Rumble 160-72; Dudley 70-5;
Stewart 89-137; King 518-36; Domesday
f. 26; Rudling 1989 245-6.
9. Domesday f. 17v; Brent 1993 7 11.
10. Domesday f. 27v; Nairn & Pevsner
584; McCarthy 42; Round 1888 11-14;
Chartulary 1: 4.
11. Brandon 1978 138-59; Domesday f.
22v; Chartulary 1: 119.
12. Domesday ff. 20v 22 22v 26; Darby &
Campbell 453-5; Freke 1976a 176-193.
13. Hooke 201-12; Gardiner & Greatorex
154-5; Freke 1976a 176-93, 1979 134-49;
Domesday 8.
14. Godfrey 1927a 171-5; Domesday ff. 17
20v 23 26; Brandon & Short 37; Salzman
1923 138.
15. Morris 141 169 213; Godfrey 1927a
171-5; Round 1888 11-14; Peckham 1941
14-15; VCHS 7: 38 40 41; Chartulary 1:
14-15 20-1.
16. Peckham 1946 14; Domesday ff. 16v
17; EpVI/1/1/5/139; Chartulary 2: 23-4;
Mantell 1846a 26-7; ADA 160/426; Bleach
137; VCHS 7: 37-8.
17. VCHS 7: 41; Domesday f. 16v.
18. Phillips 1894a 216; E40/A14180;
Chartulary 2: 24-5; Nairn & Pevsner 551-
2; VCHS 7: 39-40; Brent & Brent 200-1.
19. Johnston 1919 76; Nairn & Pevsner
552; Pye 181-4; Rowe 16; Torr 1964 98;
Brighton History Centre (S9) LEW EL5;
Gilbert 1974 44-7.
20. Pye 181-4; Godfrey 1942a 25-8;
Horsfield Lewes 1: 274-5; Mantell 1846a
115-6.
21. Domesday f. 21v; ADA 50/46; Round
1888 11-14; VCHS 7: 33.
22. Godfrey 1927a 171-7.
23. Figg 1861 9 11 12 15; Horsfield Lewes
1: 164; VCHS 7: 7 11; Rowe 13; ADA 156;
LAN 287/164.
24. Dunvan 332-3 341-2; Town Book 2:
116; ADA 156 158 160-1; SAS/ACC 3746.
25. Dunvan 332-3; Salzman 1934 98;
Rowe 122; LEW/C2/3/1; ADA 156 159-60
162; SP 13/A6; Eastbourne Library, Elliot
notebook 429; ADA 159-60; Mantell 1846a
29-30.
26. Thomson 337-9; Freke 1975 66-73;
Hill & Rumble 76 195-6 208.
27. Hill & Rumble 208.
28. AMS 5753; Figg 1861 30; Rowe 9 122.

29. Chartulary 2: 23; QR 297/21;
EpVI/1/1//5/139; Coates 2001 6;
E40/A4190; Rowe 122. John Houghton
has argued for an east gate somewhat
lower down School Hill: see Houghton
1997 18-24.
30. Gardiner 1996a 73 80 95 99; Rowe 9
121; ADA 160/334; LAN 2/66.
31. Chartulary 2:27; Rice 1902 120-1;
ACC 2327/3/1/1 (1657); Add Chs 30560
30696; W/A1/179; Dunvan 335; Town
Book 2: 115; LEW/C3/1/2.
32. Brandon & Short 22; Brighton
History Centre (S9) LEW EL5; Chartulary
2: 4; Salzman 1934 99; Freke 1976a 176-9;
ADA 156.
33. Biddle 129-31; Hill & Rumble 123.
34. Arundel Castle MS A1871; Add Ch
30552; Chartulary 2: 22; Add Ch 30575;
SAS Library, Elliot ACC 3717; Rowe 122;
E40/A4193; PROB 11/16/36.
35. Houghton 1986 119-28, 1997 27-31.
36. Chartulary 1: 21; Searle 1974 81-2.
37. Rowe 8-10.
38. Rowe 15-16; Woollgar 1: 530.
39. EpII/5/4/62 65-71; Figg 1861 44.
40. Freke 1978a 183; Rudling 1983a 54;
Greatorex 14-15; Locke 227-34;
EpVI/1/1/3/150.
41. ADA 50/46; Dunvan 268; Add MS
33338; SAS/C133; Rowe 5 207-8 236; ADA
184; DAN 1126/206.
42. Rowe 3-8; VCHS 7: 58; Wiston MS
5210; Domesday f. 27v; SHR 2852.
43. Mawer & Stenton 2: 322.
44. Rowe 3-8; DAN 1126/150-4; Brandon
1998 50-1; Mawer & Stenton 2: 321-2.
45. VCHS 7: 35; Domesday ff. 22v 26 26v.
46. ADA 45-6; Wiston MS 1870; VCHS 7:
33; SHR 384 -9; BMW/C4/2; AMS 4871.
47. Domesday f. 22v; ADA 239; Rowe 5-8;
SHR 384 -9; W/A6/278; Chartulary 1: 14
29.
48. Taylor 1939 69-70; SAS/PN 165; ADA
186-92; Thorburn passim; Sawyer 1968
83; ACC 2327/1/9/6-8.
49. VCHS 7: 104; Rowe 16 40-56; Holgate
1926 20.

3 The Warennes 1066-1304

Epigraphs. Blaauw 1849b 28 36.
1. Lucas 1869 219-20; Brandon & Short
26-9; Domesday ff. 17v 26; Dudley 73;
Allen 1995 29.

2. Brandon & Short 29-39.
3. Clay 1-6; Anderson 1986 20-4; Mantell 1846b 433; Salzman 1942a 20-5.
4. Clay 1-6; Houts forthcoming; Anderson 1986 21-2; Hollister 101; Blair 1980 99-100 112.
5. Searle 1974 207-18; Thompson 1997 209-13.
6. Clay 7-12 87; DNB Warenne, 831-2, Hugh 163-4; Hollister 93-107; Chartulary 2:15.
7. Greenway 77; Coad & Streeten 178-96; Jones 1999 6; Wilson 195-6; Drewett & Hamilton 1999 31-3; Freke 1975 70-6; Blair 1998 124-30.
8. Clay 12-13 93-4; VCHS 7: 40; Chartulary 1: 20-4.
9. DNB Warenne 832; Chartulary 2: 15; Mantell 1846b 434; Drewett 1992 88-9.
10. Drewett 1988 3-4; Brent 1993 17; Coad & Streeten 178-96.
11. VCHS 7: 21-3; Byng 126; Drewett 1992 74-5; Thomas 2001 224-7; SAS/ACC 3746.
12. VCHS 7: manorial descents.
13. Domesday 23-4; VCHS 7: manorial descents; ADA 184-5; DAN 1126/206; Rowe 207-8 236. As for the sites of these 'town-houses', Plumpton's occupied 103-4 High Street, outside the west gate (Rowe 236), Portslade's, the west side of Keere Street (Rowe 207-8), Hamsey's, 5 Station Street and the former Wesleyan chapel (VCHS 7: 15) and Hurstpierpoint's, two acres called 'Bugates' between Pinwell Street and Brooman's Lane (ADA 7: Oct. 1658).
14. Searle 1974 49 53-4 201-6 407; Chartulary 1:12 34; SAS/WS 149; Town Book 1:111, 2: 116.
15. Clay 13-18.
16. Clay 13-14 18-20; Barlow 106; DNB Warenne 819-21; Anderson 1992 112-21.
17. DNB Warenne 819-21; Clay 26-32; Barlow 114 223-7 257; Salzman 1925a 63-4 68.
18. Pevsner 1967 167-9; VCHS 7: 23.
19. Drewett 1992 75-83 103-5; VCHS 7: 21.
20. Clay 14 18-23; Chartulary 2: 18; Power 207.
21. VCHS 9: 2; Clay 24-5; Blaauw 1849a 133-6; Salzman 1943 49-50 54; Warren 82-3 99 107-8; VCHS 6 (2): 107.

22. DNB Warenne 833; VCHS 1: 494; Malden 9; CPR 1216-25: 87.
23. DNB Warenne 833-4; Clay 24-5; Thompson 214-16; Cokayne Surrey 502; CLibR 1226-40: 483; Cokayne Pembroke 364; Chartulary 2: 18.
24. CLibR 1226-40: 483; DNB Warenne 821 825; Cokayne Surrey 503; Chartulary 2: 18; Prestwich 4 22-3 25 41.
25. Blaauw 1849b 27; Prestwich 43-4; Carpenter 1987 12-18.
26. Carpenter 1987 19-34; Taylor 1939 26; Prestwich 43; Beamish 149 156; Powicke 115-16; Figg 1861 6; Arundel Castle MS M 529; W/C4/20; Drewett 1992 95-8; Lower 1845 317-19.
27. Carpenter 1987 22-3 34-6; Blaauw 1849b 28; *Sussex Weekly Advertiser* 23 July 1770; Dunvan 370-1; Gardiner 1994 9; Beamish 155-6 200-2; Johnston 1956 169-71.
28. Cooper 1896 190-1; Prestwich 53-4 68; Chartulary 1: 52-3; DNB Warenne 822-3.
29. DNB Warenne 823; Prestwich 89 91 204 216; Hubbard 182-3.
30. Blaauw 1849b 36; Chartulary 2: 17-18; VCHS 7: 49; Figg 1848 43-4; Cokayne Braose 302; Salzman 1964 109-11; Blaauw 1849a 148.
31. DNB Warenne 823-5; Prestwich 478-9 489.
32. Salzman 1942a 20-32; Taylor 1939 passim; Salzman 1943 49 50-3; DNB Warenne 823.
33. Horsfield Lewes 1: 162-3; Anon 1932 115-17; Salzman 1943 51.
34. Salzman 1943 49-53; VCHS 7: 226 283; Meekings 196-7; Salzman 1938 54-8.
35. Green 1991 110; Salzman 1943 50 53, 1945 67.
36. Saul 1986 40; Hunnisett 1960 48; CCR 1253-4: 18; Salzman 1942a 28.
37. Hunnisett 1960 44-8 55 57; Salzman 1943 50; Hudson 1909 51; Chartulary 1: 208, 2: 154.
38. Searle 1974 227; VCHS 7: 15; CCR 1227-31: 379, 1247-51: 120, 1259-61: 172-3; CPR 1266-72: 380-1.
39. Salzman 1943 50; VCHS 7: 24 29; Searle 1974 85-8.
40. VCHS 7: 15; Blaauw 1849a 137-55, 1849b 32-3.
41. DNB Warenne 825; Salzman 1968a 189-90; Chartulary 1: 52-3, 2: 16-17.

4 Cluniacs, prelates and Franciscans
1066-1300

Epigraphs. Dunvan 42; Blaauw 1849b 29 33-4.

1. Chartulary 1: 1-7, 2: xix-xx; Lyne 1997 5-7; Hunt 2-3 20-1 39 130 152; Knowles 1950 107 280; Bates 376-7; Houts forthcoming.

2. Lyne 1997 19-23.

3. Knowles & Hadcock 100; Knowles 1950 151-2 156; Clarke 13 58.

4. Lyne 1997 23-7 71-80 124-31; Tudor-Craig 4-5; Milner-Gulland 2-3.

5. Anderson 1989a 6 8 16-28 33; Lyne 1997 18-19. My thanks to Eric Fernie for casting doubt on a Saxon date for the wall.

6. Lyne 1997 33-9; Chartulary 1: 16; Gem 411-12; Houts 2004 113.

7. Knowles, Brooke & London 119; DNB Hugh 163-4; Knowles 1950 172 174 280-2; Salzman 1925a 62-3; Galbraith 1954 289-302.

8. Knowles 1950 277-8 282-3 286-93; Clarke 58 138; Knowles & Hadcock 96-102.

9. Knowles, Brooke & London 119-20; Crook 1940a 77-8 84; Chartulary 2: 110-11; Holgate 1937 2-6 82-4 221, 1938 91-2; Blaauw 1849b 24-9; Peckham 1941 56-77; Salzman 1942b 127; Blaauw 1850 197; Charvin 1: 300.

10. Chartulary 1: 20-3; Lyne 1997 7-13 27-8; Anderson 1989a 9 33-4; Pevsner 1962 113; Anderson 1986 59-61 266.

11. Hunt 110 181-3; Conant 200-8; Anderson 1986 92-8 102-8 120-1.

12. Lyne 1997 27-8.

13. Anderson 1986 177 209-10 275, 1989b 49-60; Lyne 1977 136-7; Nairn & Pevsner 44 427-8; Godfrey 1927b 202; Harrison 24; Chartulary 1: 180.

14. CPRL 1198-1304: 186; Anderson 1986 124-6 151 166 222 265, 1984 92-5 99-100, 1992 112-20; Godfrey 1929a 196.

15. Anderson 1989a 34; Lyne 1997 38 41-53.

16. Anderson 1989a 9-13; Lyne 1997 35 40 55-65 107-8.

17. Willis 158-65; Dunvan 417; Figg 1854 150-7.

18. Hope 1906 70-2; Anderson 1989a 29-32, 1986 47; Blaauw 1849b 24; Anderson 1986 47; Horsfield Lewes 1: 248.

19. Chartulary 1: 166-8 173.

20. VCHS 7: 46; Mantell 1846a 31 57; Lower 1846 39; Anderson 1986 10 13 59-60; Spurrell 263-5.

21. Knowles 1950 406 615-16, 1962 270-9, 1955 282-4 325-7; JUST 1/921/14; Blaauw 1849b 33-4; Chartulary 1: 144 166-8; Saul 1986 14-15.

22. Chartulary 1: 129-30; Redwood & Wilson 60; Dugdale 5: 18; GLY 996/4; J[ohnston] 1969 74.

23. Harrison 22 52; Chartulary 1: 52-3, 2: 86-7; Carlin 25-6 62 276; Schofield 231-2; Gwilt 604-6: Blair 1980 113.

24. Blaauw 1849b 29; Knowles 1950 148-50.

25. Blaauw 1850 199; Mayr-Harting 1964 178; Holden 1963 62; Chartulary 1: 173; GLY 998/3; E40/A15602.

26. Jones 1993 17-18 32-3; Peckham 1941 8; Deedes 1910 372 415-18; CPRL 1396-1404: 301; VCHS 7: 32; FRE 520/131; VCHS 9: 13-14.

27. Godfrey 1939 139; Chartulary 1: 61-2, 2: 66-7; Blaauw 1849b 27; Meekings 196-7; E40/ A15622.

28. Salzman 1925a 64; Blaauw 1849a 146; Godfrey 1939 140.

29. Godfrey 1939 139; E40/A 4192 4218 15603-11; Daniel-Tyssen 1873 146; Blaauw 1849b 25; Backhouse & others 124-5.

30. Hunt 69 139; Knowles 1950 28-9; Anderson 1992 112-21 127, 1995 14; Chartulary 1: 99.

31. Searle & Ross 7-8; Saul 1986 152-3; Knowles 1950 475-6, 1955 282-3 286; Chartulary 1: 12 32-3 41 55 107 135 150 161, 2: 37 50 52 63 118; Salzman 1922 180; Duckett 1888 1: 72.

32. Hunt 57 62-4 109; Blaauw 1849b 36; Knowles 1950 429-30; Crook 1940a 94; Dalton 33.

33. Hunt 62-4 120; Knowles 1950 88 428, 1955 334-41; Watson 1984 1: 76; E[sdaile] 156-8; Chartulary 2: 6-7; Anderson 1992 116-17; Archives Nationales Paris, AE 11-138 (1.966, no. 4).

34. Lieberman 61-9; Blaauw 1849b 22-37.

35. Hunt 65-6; Knowles 1950 431; Dugdale 5: 19; Clarke 138; Mayr-Harting 1964 173-4; Lieberman 87; Harrison 18.

36. VCHS 7: 48; Godfrey 1927b 201-3; Chartulary 1: 99; Godfrey 1936a 50-2.

37. Dugdale 5: 19; Blaauw 1849b 24; Lower & Cooper 143; Chartulary 1: 36-7;

Nairn & Pevsner 173-4; Grose 5: 158-9; PROB 11/64/20; ADA 45/27. Andrew Rudebeck alerted me to the column base and David Godfrey to the measurements of the hall and to the wall at number 12.
38. Dugdale 5:19; SC6 HEN VIII/ 3529; Gardiner 1994 9; Figg 1861 3-6; Newman 1969a 326-7; ABE 18R/2 (14); QDS 2/1.
39. Gardiner 1994 9; Chartulary 1: 94; Knowles 1950 279; Salzman 1925b 236.
40. Knowles 1950 430-3 456; Chartulary 1: 9 12 48-9 98-9 169-70 173, 2: 103; VCHS 2: 66; Lyne 1997 171-3 178; Chartulary 1: 80 167 173-4; Blaauw 1849b 29.
41. Chartulary 1: 117, 2: 46-7; Crook 1940a 84.
42. Chartulary 2: 66-7; Clarke 111; Knowles 1959 248 473; Dugdale 5: 16-20.
43. Clarke 111 121; VCHS 7: passim; Norris & Hockings 222-5; Nairn & Pevsner 44; Knowles 1955 289-92; Mayr-Harting 1964 57 62-9 172-3; Blaauw 1849b 25-6; Peckham 1941 359; Jones 1993 19 37-9.
44. Golding 71; CCR 1318-23: 658.
45. Knowles 1950 156-8, 1955 157-8; Hunt 171-4; Crook 1940a 80.
46. Knowles 1955 158, 1950 155; Charvin 1: 300; Knowles & Hadcock 96-102; Knowles, Brooke & London 120; Blaauw 1849b 37; Charvin 2: 238.
47. Crook 1940a 88-90; Royal Library Copenhagen, Ny kgl. S. 172 8 150 (henceforth Copenhagen).
48. Knowles 1950 156-7; Chartulary 1: 41 44-6; Crook 1940b 15-21 67-9; Clay 1949 119-23; VCHS 2: 66; CPRL 1198-1304: 119.
49. Crook 1940a 85-6 90; VCHS 2: 66 70; Charvin 1: 275 390 422 451; CPRL 1198-1304: 186; CCR 1259-61: 43.
50. Ancient correspondence 27/5; Saul 1986 42; Crook 1940a 78-80 86-7; Graham 1929 102-5; VCHS 2: 70; Charvin 2: 58 67 73 133 176.
51. Knowles 1955 158-9; CCR 1288-96: 460.
52. Knowles 1955 127-45 180-8; CLibR 1240-45: 85; CCR 1237-42: 426-7, 1242-7: 207, 1302-7: 249; VCHS 2: 95-6; SC6 HENVIII/3518-20; Anon 1929a 145-6; Blaauw 1849a 146 148.
53. Gardiner 1996a 71-96; Rudling 1983

66-9; Figg 1861 34.
54. Knowles 1942 3-4, 1962 232; Du Boulay 1966 248-9; Martin 1882-5 passim; Blaauw 1849b 32 36.
55. Du Boulay 1966 100-3 138 167 237-8 269; Redwood & Wilson passim; Graham 1952 xxviii-xlii.
56. Round 1888 11-14; Salzman 1925a 63-4; Turner 1865 45; AMS 5775; SRA 6/13/2; Anderson 1986 67; *Lewes News* May 1984 no. 28; Turner 1852 140.
57. ADA 45; SRA 6/13/2; GLY 84; Du Boulay 1966 125 136-7 173 195; Redwood & Wilson 35-7 86 88-91 106-11.
58. AMS 5775; Du Boulay 1966 286 299-300; Redwood & Wilson 60; QR 55/24; Allen 1995 29.
59. Du Boulay 1966 50-1; Dunkin 1875 15; Mayr-Harting 1964 54; Daniel-Tyssen 1869 162.
60. Dunkin 1875 85-6; Martin 1882-5 3: 1033; Daniel-Tyssen 1869 172; Turner 1856 270; Godfrey 1955a 156-7.
61. Knowles 1950 139-42 174-5; Knowles & Hadcock 418 439; Turner 1852 130-1; Du Boulay 1966 203; Godfrey 1931a 247, 1928a 89; Nairn & Pevsner 608-9; AMS 6008/3/6/2.
62. Mayr-Harting 1964 51; Domesday f. 16v; EpVI/1/1/3/150, 5/139; Peckham 1941 14.
63. Mayr-Harting 1964 48-50; Chartulary 1: 82-3; Jones 1993 13 44-5; Peckham 1941 62-3; CLibR 1226-40: 6, 1245-51: 275.
64. Knowles 1950 374; Jones 1993 5 8 21 67-8 70 189 204 211 214-16 234; Lawrence 35-55.
65. VCHS 7: 9 38 40-1; Round 1888 11-14; Godfrey 1926a 4-6; Anon 1947 xli; Gilbert 1974 44-7.
66. Phillips 1894a 216; Godfrey 1928b 159-69; Page 1853 26; PAR 411/31/1/2.
67. Brent & Brent 200-01; Slocock 9 15; AMS 5510/3; Chartulary 2: 23; Pugin 121; QR 44/18.
68. Chartulary 2: 23-4; ACC 2327/3/1/1; SC6 HENVIII/3532.
69. VCHS 7: 39-40; Godfrey 1928b 165-8.

5 A market and port serving mid Sussex 1066-1300

Epigraphs. Chartulary 2: 45, 1: 80-81; CPR 1258-66: 590.

1. Domesday ff. 20 23 26-7v; VCHS 1: 382-4; Brandon & Short 37; Dulley 1966 39-40.

2. Dudley 70-8; Gardiner 1996a 113.

3. Drewett 1992 87; Blaauw 1849a 146-9.

4. Drewett 1992 95-6 98-100; Pelham 1933a 129-31; CLibR 1340-45: 196; Freke 1976a 189-90; Gardiner 1996a 115.

5. Gardiner 1995 209-10; VCHS 7: 3; SAS/WS 149; ACC 3412/387; Rowe 4-5; MOB 1699; Blaauw 1848 62.

6. Chartulary 1: 18-19; Drewett 1992 98; VCHS 1: 366; Gardiner 1999 91; Rowe 3-5; SAS/WS 149; ACC 3412/387; ABE 22R; Dunvan 1795 34; Blaauw 1849c 80-98; Farrant & others 1991 130.

7. Cooper 1896 191-2; Chartulary 1: 9; CCR 1302-7: 257; DYK 1123; Arundel MS A1871; Shelley 42; ACC 3412/400; SC6 HENVIII/3525.

8. Pelham 1931 178-84; Margary 134-64 188; Chartulary 1:116; Wood 1976 5-6 10; Blaauw 1849a 152.

9. Hudson 1980 11-29; Gardiner 1996a 75-8 99; VCHS 7: 9; Woollgar 2: 247; Rudling 1991 165-81; Godfrey 1955a 156-7; Anon 1947 xlii; Spokes 1929 222.

10. Domesday f. 26.

11. Round 1930 102; Arnold 235; Chartulary 1: 9; Salzman 1943 49; JUST 1/941A mm. 3 23 33; Gardiner 1995 189-92; Taylor 1937 2-3; Farrant & others 130.

12. Lyne 1997 133-4 139; VCHS 7: 21; Lower & Cooper 143; Salzman 1906 12.

13. Anderson 1984 85-100; Lyne 1997 133-4 138 139; Gardiner 1996a 114-15.

14. Lyne 1997 101-7; Drewett 1992 85-7 91 100; Gardiner 1996a 71-109 116; Holden 1965a 67-78; Murray 79-82; Holden 1989 73-88.

15. Lyne 1997 110-18; Rudling 1983a 69; Gardiner 1996a 104-7; Drewett 1992 91.

16. Gardiner 1996a 104 114; Lyne 1997 55 133-4 149-50 179; Freke 1978a 183-94; Chartulary 1: 21; Redwood & Wilson 134; Drewett 1992 91.

17. Brandon & Short 21-2 61-2 66-9; Round 1930 101; Pelham 1931 168-70; Gardiner 1995 190; Lower 1854 77.

18. Round 1888 11-14; Chartulary 1: 12; Figg 1861 6; W/SM/C4/20, W/A8/259.

19. Brandon 1998 62-70; Pelham 1934a 128-35; Salzman 1943 49; Saul 1986 134; Melville 95-8.

20. Lyne 1997 143-6; TD 46 49 61; ADA 46; LR 3/198; SAS/C139; Dugdale 5: 18; Chartulary 1: 44-5; VCHS 7: 230; Chartulary 2: 45; University College London, Field Archaeology Unit, Newsletter 5, 1996-7; VCHS 2: 66.

21. Pelham 1933b 131-9, 1935a 137-41, 1935b 166-71; CCR 1296-1302: 111; VCHS 7: 34 209 212; E122/135/2A.

22. Freke 1976a 178 185, 1978 196; Pelham 1929 109; Chartulary 2: 2-3; Rothwell 1975 881-2; Chartulary 1: 18.

23. Chartulary 1: 122-4 157-8 169; DL/42/112; Silvester 109-15.

24. Searle 1974 46; Brandon & Short 14-15 20-5 49-56; Gardiner 1996b 125 130-1; Blaauw 1853 44; VCHS 2: 263.

25. Round 1930 102; Arnold 235; Salzman 1906 14-15; Pelham 1928 170-82; Redwood & Wilson 32 37 75 138; VCHS 2: 242; Cleere & Crossley 87.

26. TD 7 103; ADA 203; W/A6/36; Chartulary 1:14; AMS 1016; ACC 7633/5; Chartulary 2: 131.

27. AMS 5909/11 12; Straker 1934 47-56.

28. Domesday f. 22v; Chartulary 1: 17 72-5 119-20 131-2.

29. Chartulary 1: 79-81 83-4 119-20; Straker 1934 51; Wood 1976 5-6 10.

30. ADA 203; ACC 7633/5; Straker 1934 47; Chartulary 1: 12 36; AMS 1016; Blair 1980 109-14.

31. Pelham 1931 172-4; ACC 7633/5; ADA 250; Chartulary 1: 113; Holden 1989 74-5.

32. Chartulary 1: 8-9 96 104-5, 2: 5-6; E40/A15507 15605 15607; VCHS 2: 259, 7: 32; Searle 1974 199-303.

33. Drewett 1992 91 98; Gardiner 1996a 113; Freke 1978a 181 195-7; Godfrey 1940 232-6; CLibR 1260-67: 264; Straker 1931 33; Schubert 142.

34. Hadfield 89-106; Lyne 1997 82-96; Drewett 1992 85; Gardiner 1996a 102-4 107 111-13; Gregory 8.

35. VCHS 7: 104 145 156; Brandon & Short 91; Leppard 1991 29-32; Salzman 1901 31; Redwood & Wilson 95; Jones 1993 189; Arundel MS A1871; Houghton 1997 31.

36. Freke 1976a 190; Rudling 1983a 61; Blaauw 1849a 140; Drewett 1992 100-2; Gardiner 1996a 115-17; Lyne 1997 167-8.

37. Holden & Hudson 126-7 136;

Chartulary 1: 73; Round 1888 11-14; Wiston MS 5988.

38. Gardiner 1996a 104 107; Freke 1976a 178 185, 1978b 203 222; Figg 1848 45; Gardiner 1995 204-5; Salzman 1906 11; Holden 1963 179.

39. Lyne 1997 171-3; Chartulary 1: 12 105; SC6 HENVIII/3521 3525; VCHS 2: 66; CLibR 1226-40: 476; Gardiner 1995 197-9.

40. Hurst 119-24; Freke 1976a 178 181; Lyne 1997 85-6 91; Rudling 1983a 56 58; Gardiner 1996a 102-4; Drewett 1992 87; JUST 1/811 m. 7.

41. Pelham 1929 107-11; Freke 1976a 178, 1978a 197; O'Shea 370; Drewett 1992 91; Gardiner 1996a 114; Holden 1965b 187-90; Lyne 1997 155.

42. CPR 1258-66: 590.

43. Chartulary 1: 22 28-9 37 45 55 176-7; Rowe 211-17; LR 3/198/67; E315/414/54-5; ADA 172.

44. B[udgen] 1941 153-4; Gardiner 1995 189-212; CCR 1296-1302: 473.

45. Jones 1983 79-86, 1993 67-8; Blaauw 1849a 139-40 151; Turner 1865 11-12; Searle 1974 352; Farmer 1992 55-6 218-19 224 272 446; Blair 1997 173-92; Johnston 1915 151; Salzman 1928a 135-7.

46. Lower & Cooper 143; Salzman 1945 73; Glover 19-20; Whitley 1919 143.

47. Hudson 1909 35-7 50-1 66-7; Redwood & Wilson 135-7; Pelham 1934b 18-19; Saul 1986 134; Hills 4; Hunnisett 1960 57; Chartulary 1: 96 103-5, 2: 2 24 38.

48. Rudling 1983a 53-62; Freke 1978a 179-97; Greatorex 3-8; E40/A 4172 4183 4186 4190-1; Chartulary 2: 23-4; EpVI/I/I/3/150, 5/139.

49. SAS Library, Elliot ACC 3717; E40/A 4127 4193; Anon 1940 58; E40/A 4160 15622; AMS 2705/2.

50. Brighton History Centre (S9) LEW EL5; Chartulary 2: 4; SAS Research Committee Minutes, 9 Jan. 1963; Freke 1976a 176-93; Page 1973 113-14.

51. Searle 1974 72-9 88-90 352-3.

52. E40/A 10958 15615; U269/E66/2/110-12; E40/A 14585.

53. Chartulary 1: 8-9 21 96; SC6 HENVIII/3526-8; GLY 998/3; E40/A 15596; WARDS 7/314/119; SAS/C 157.

54. SC6 HENVIII/3526-8; Harleian Roll D21; Craddock 85-102.

55. Hudson 1905 23; E40/A 4124 4218 15545-6 15589 15602-4 15606 15611 15613 15615; Add Ch 8090; Harleian Roll D21; E40/A 4099 4126 4128 4137 4148 15507 15605 15607 15609; Chartulary 2: 95; ACC 2327/3/1/1(c1634); Chartulary 1: 92.

56. E40/A 15615; Rice 1903 139; QR280/9.

57. ADA 45; U269/E66/3; E40/A 4091 4098 4138; Chartulary 1: 96.

58. Rudling 1991 165-81; Redwood & Wilson 61 74 115-7 133-4; CCR 1272-9: 345.

59. Redwood & Wilson 106-15 131-3 135-7; Rowe 136; JUST 1/811 m. 7.

6 Converging calamities: pillage, commotion and plague 1300-1461

Epigraphs. Dobson 93; Cooper 1866 17-36; Ziegler 168.

1. Blaauw 1849 155-60, 1849c 80-98; DNB Warenne 825-9; Cokayne Surrey 508-11; Fairbank 193-264; Salzman 1968a 160-1 171-2.

2. Saul 1986 29-30; Cooper 1896 193.

3. Coad & Streeten 141-2; VCHS 7: 15; Hope 1915 180-4.

4. Saul 1986 35 37-8 73-4; VCHS 7: 176 207; CPR 1345-8: 58; Godfrey 1931b 131-6; Thomas-Stanford 1921 71-6; Round 1921 1-20; E40/A4186.

5. CCR 1333-7: 679; Godfrey 1929b 9-18; Lower 1862a 268; Drewett 1992 105; Saul 1986 89.

6. VCHS 7: 10; Godfrey 1928c 234; Arundel MS A1871; Phillips 1894b 223-4; W/A10/300; Rowe 14; ADA 156/10.

7. VCHS 7: 11-12; CPR 1330-4: 517; Brent 1993 110-11.

8. Testamenta 1836 41-5; Saul 1986 35 56.

9. Davidson-Houston 1937 108-9; Mantell 1846a 104; CCR 1339-41: 18 82; CPRL 1342-62: 12, 1362-1404: 6-7.

10. Saul 1986 35 42 67, 1998 123-32; CPR 1350-4: 103 267 322 426, 1354-8: 33 212 322, 1358-61: 562, 1361-4: 5; Nairn & Pevsner 501-2; Peckham 1941 267; Fairbank 219 261-4; Bond 453-69.

11. Blaauw 1848 62-3; VCHS 9: 40; Gardiner 1995 190-1; Saul 1986 134; Melville 57; CCR 1327-30: 397, 1340-9: 195, 1349-60: 268-9; CPR 1343-5: 279.

12. Brandon & Short 81-5; Searle 1974 341-4; Saul 1986 29 56; Salzman 1906 21-2, 1916 153, 1953 32-5; VCHS 1: 511.
13. Saul 1986 42 189 192; Salzman 1953 35-6; VCHS 1: 510-11, 4: 168, 7: 114 231 233 237, 9: 202; E179/189/41/25; Lower & Cooper 147; CPR 1358-61: 444; CCR 1381-5: 432.
14. VCHS 1: 511; Saul 1986 81-2; Salzman 1934 65, 1953 35-6; CPR 1381-5: 259; Searle 1974 339-46; Du Boulay 1966 185-9.
15. Salzman 1942c 94, 1968b 49-52; CPR 1396-9: 110-1; CCR 1389-92: 373.
16. Saul 1986 35; Salzman 1953 44-50; Tierney 1: 270-7.
17. Roskell 1: 657-9, 2: 540-1, 3: 163 214 403-4 698-9; Saul 1997a 221-39.
18. DNB Fitzalan 100-3; Cokayne Arundel 245-6; Anon 1863 211-13; Roskell 3: 849, 4: 832.
19. VCHS 7: 3-5.
20. DNB Pelham 693-5; Saul 1986 70-2; Pelham & Mclean 72; Salzman 1928b 53-70; Roskell 1: 643-7
21. Walker 1983 87-94; Nairn & Pevsner 534; Saul 1986 7-13.
22. Harvey 1991 passim; VCHS 1: 513; Cooper 1866 23-30; Lower & Cooper 145-6.
23. Wedgwood 60 783; Salzman 1934 97.
24. Bindoff, 1: 205-6; Wedgwood 72 267; SC6 HENVIII/3502; Chartulary 1: 103 129.
25. Harvey 1991 39-40 78-9 154-7 168; VCHS 1: 513-14; Hunnisett 1955 116-20; Cooper 1866 35-6; Lower 1854 84.
26. Knowles 1955 158-9 284; VCHS 2: 66-7 70; Blaauw 1850 198-9; CCR 1302-7: 18 58, 1313-18: 101 460, 1318-23: 116, 1323-7: 310, 1339-41: 273 447; Charvin 2: 475.
27. VCHS 2: 67; Blaauw 1850 199-200; CCR 1318-23: 358, 1323-7: 34 235 310 534; CPR 1313-17: 570, 1324-7: 41 149.
28. VCHS 2: 67 70; Blaauw 1850 200; Clarke 1995 171; Charvin 3: 186; CPR 1317-22: 120, 1338-40: 23; CCR 1337-9: 111-2, 1339-41: 651.
29. VCHS 2: 67-8; Blaauw 1850 201; CCR 1341-4: 462, 1346-9: 359; CPR 1345-8: 272 362 533.
30. Blaauw 1850 207-8; Charvin 2: 357, 3: 186 435 437; CPR 1317-21: 261-2.
31. Knowles 1955 159; VCHS 2: 68;

Blaauw 1850 201-2; CPR 1343-5: 360, 1350-4: 47-8, 1370-4: 286; Copenhagen MS 151.
32. VCHS 2: 69-71; Copenhagen MS 151-2; CPRP 1342-1419: 285, 536; CPR 1350-4: 103 267 322 426, 1361-4: 447-8; CPRL 1362-1404: 2 25; Ancient correspondence 42/17; CCR 1364-8: 100.
33. Knowles 1955 159-61 167-8; Graham 1923 484 486-8.
34. VCHS 2: 68 70; Copenhagen MS 151; Saul 1986 88-9; CPRL 1396-1404: 564; National Library of Scotland Adv MS 18. 4.2; CPR 1396-9: 248, 1408-13: 143-4, 1413-16: 199; Knowles 1955 160-1; Graham 1923 493-5, 1929 64-72.
35. Jacob 1947 334-5; VCHS 7: 225; Graham 1929 72-5; Knowles 1955 161.
36. Godfrey 1939 138, 1936b 56-7; Harvey 1944 32-3; Brighton 14-35.
37. VCHS 7: 58; Wiston MS 5210; Godfrey 1939 139; Chartulary 2: 15-19.
38. Godfrey 1939 138-9 141; Daniel-Tyssen 1873 146-9.
39. Godfrey 1939 138 140-2.
40. VCHS 2: 70; Nairn & Pevsner 88; Saul 1986 1-7 144-54, 1997b 454; Anon 1950 77-9; Godfrey 1939 139.
41. Baker 1966 1-5; Holden 1963 54-181; Brandon 1971a 80; Pelham 1929 104; Freke 1975 74; Lyne 1997 65: VCHS 1: 510.
42. Chartulary 2: 6-7; Godfrey 1927a 171-7.
43. Hudson 1909 109 183 185 197; Pelham 1937 211-23.
44. Chartulary 1: 113 149; Salzman 1916 35 60 ; Godfrey 1927a 177; VCHS 7: 13; CCR 1318-23: 236, 1349-54: 344; CPR 1350-4: 142, 1396-9: 236; HBR 1/1394.
45. Nairn & Pevsner 48 633-4; Anderson 1986 60-1; Lyne 1997 29 119-22 140 146-7; VCHS 7: 45.
46. Gardiner 1996a 104-7 109-11.
47. VCHS 7: 48-9; *East Sussex News* 27 Feb. 1885; PDA/L49; ABE ACC 560/1; SAS Library, ACC 9089; Torr 1964 99-100.
48. Brent 1968 91 93; Brandon & Short 93-4; VCHS 1: 68, 2: 14 68; Pelham 1929 103; E40/A15573.
49. Brandon & Short 101-8; Brent 1973 255-8; Saul 1986 107-16 130-1; Brandon 1971a 69-93, 1971b 94-106; CCR 1405-9:

78; SC6 HENVIII/3526.

50. Taylor 1939 61-6.

51. Searle 1974 233-65 355-66; CPRL 1362-1404: 396; Knowles 1959 248 473; SC6 1023/30.

52. Godfrey 1939 144; CPRL 1396-1404: 417 546; SC6 HENVIII/3529; DNB Philpot 1045-7; Peckham 1941 370-1; VCHS 2: 68; Searle 1974 265; SAS/A610-11.

53. Brandon & Short 92; Searle 1974 265; CCR 1429-35: 318; Schofield 231-2; Carlin 46-7 62; Wheatley 264.

54. CPR 1422-9: 392, 1429-36: 263; Blaauw 1850 203-4; Graham 1929 72-4; Davidson-Houston 1936 149-52; Charvin 5: 105.

55. Anon 1931 551-5.

56. VCHS 2: 69-70; Copenhagen MS 152; Graham 1929 74-6; CPRL 1427-47: 586-7; Galbraith 1924 196-205; Chartulary 1: xviii; Blaauw 1850 203-4.

57. Godfrey 1955b 88; Mantell 1846b 431-2; Horsfield Lewes 1: 247-8; Sawyer 1896 270-1; *Sussex Weekly Advertiser* 13 Aug. 1804; VCHS 7: 45.

58. Godfrey 1936c 3-14; Nairn & Pevsner 544-5; Toy 125-33; Searle 1974 253-4 267; Dugdale 5:18; Harrison 21; LP HVIII: 13(1) 389.

59. Gardiner 1996a 94-5; GLY 1001/5 1075; SAS/G44/10; Anon 1929 145; AMS 2181.

60. Nairn & Pevsner 566; Jacob 1937-47 passim; Du Boulay 1957 passim; Newman 1969b 342-9; Lambeth Palace archives, ED 690/1 690A.

61. Saul 1986 5-6; Dunkin 1875 81; Jacob 1937-47 42: 595-6; Way 2-4.

62. Turner 1852 140-1; Daniel-Tyssen 1869 159-63; SRA 6/13/2; Woollgar 2: 142-9 441; Spokes 1929 207.

63. Taylor 1939 50-61; Roskell 1: 658; Saul 1986 93; CCR 1377-81: 67 72.

64. Saul 1986 47 76 101-3 163 177; CPR 1401-5: 94-5; Hunnisett 1960 62 64; Fenwick 2: 625; Salzman 1916 163-98; SAS/G8/34; GLY 996/1-2; VCHS 2: 411-12; Chartulary 2: 67; Godfrey 1939 152.

65. Pelham 1929 116-17, 1931 160 166-7 171-2, 1934c 33-4; Cooper 1865 116; Gardiner 1996b 134.

66. CCR 1337-9: 562, 1349-54: 339-40, 1385-9: 222; CPR 1452-61: 256.

67. Melville 44-5; Saul 1986 134; SAS/G44/9 10; Pelham 1934a 133.

68. Pelham 1930 171-80; Salzman 1935a 163-5, 1953: 37-9 45; Fairbank 1907 238-9; Roskell 1: 657-60, 3: 232; CCR 1364-8: 130, 1371-81: 426; CPR 1391-6: 584, 1396-9: 350.

69. Melville 110-13 xix-xxiii; Salzman 1934 66, 1968b 49-52; Fenwick 2: 625; Hills 6 7; VCHS 7: 229; Roskell 2:167-8, 3: 846; PROB 11/6/9; CPR 1396-9: 350; Chartulary 1: 92.

70. Melville 17 116 121; CCR 1396-9: 100 516, 1399-1402: 55, 1405-9: 428, 1409-13: 22, 1413-19: 45 325, 1441-7: 239; CPR 1416-22: 417 442, 1452-61: 117 344; E122/17-18; Roskell 4: 11-12.

71. Pelham 1928 173-4, 1929 110; CPR 1367-70: 437; Roskell 2: 540-4; Add Ch 30560; Holden & Hudson 128.

72. CPR 1361-4: 436, 1385-9: 271, 1391-6: 485, 1416-22: 24 97; Arundel Castle MS A1871; Roskell 2: 246; Hills 9; CCR 1327-30: 558, 1413-19: 223; Pelham 1929 107-11.

73. Horsfield Lewes 1: 163; CPR 1330-4: 571.

74. Lyne 1997 107 112-7; Holden 1965a 67-78; Gardiner 1995 197 206; Beswick 17.

75. CPR 1367-70: 437; E122/33/18; Chartulary 1: 113, 2: 12; Roskell 3: 196; CPR 1416-22: 24; ADA 250; PAR 496/26/8; E179/189/41/25; SRA /C1/1/15; Holden 1989 74-5.

76. Taylor 1939 62; AMS 5775; Cockburn 1975a 55; CChR 1341-7: 38; PAR 415/26/1.

77. Hunnisett 1957 50; Arundel Castle MS A1871; GLY 998/3 5; VCHS 7: 32; CPRL 1396-1404: 301; Deedes 1910 372; GLY 996/1, 998/3-5, 999, 1000/3 5, 1075; CPR 1370-4: 222.

78. Searle & Ross 74; Harvey 1991 15; SAS/G1/45; SAS/CH 265; SAS/G44/31 34 74 97-8; Salzman 1911 86-100; Lambeth Palace archives ED 1302/1; Hudson 1910 229; CCR 1429-35: 65; CPR 1370-4: 44; Salzman 1942b 137; CPR 1429-36: 537-62; E179/189/35/1; SAS/G8/29 36; CCR 1409-13: 184.

79. Searle 1974 355-64; E40/A 4172 4183 4186 4190-1; DAN 1126/206; EpVI/1/1/5/139, 2/1/1; Brighton History

Centre (S9) LEW EL5; E40/A 4193; Rowe
122.
80. Brighton History Centre (S9) LEW
EL5; Freke 1976a 179; Salzman 1934 99;
Lambeth Palace archives ED 1081;
E40/A15586-7; Chartulary 1: 4; Arundel
Castle MS A1871; Rowe 16; Torr 1964 98.
81. Arundel Castle MS A1871.
82. Godfrey 1927a 171-7; Deedes 1911
312; Town Book 1: 20; Deedes 1908 148,
1911 359-60; Salzman 1942b 138; CPR
1441-6: 259; VCHS 7: 37-8; PAR
410/1/1/1.
83. VCHS 7: 38-41; ABE/ACC 560/1.
84. Salzman 1968b 49-52.
85. Dunkin 1875 24; Nairn & Pevsner
553-4.
86. Harvey 1991 183; Gardner 3: 126 303.

7 The impact of a 'New Monarchy' 1461-1558

Epigraph. Kitch 1981 88-92.
1. DNB Norfolk 1119-22, Bergavenny
248-50 257-8; Cokayne Bergavenny 30-1,
Norfolk 612-15; VCHS 7: 3-5; Godfrey
1939 140; Lower 1866 70; Perry 3-6.
2. DNB Dudley 100-02; Lower 1865 331;
Wedgwood 285-6; VCHS 7: 84-5; Rowe
156-8; Lancashire Record Office DD Cl
298. My thanks to C. Whittick for the link
with Ernley.
3. DNB Nevill 257-8; Goring 1978 1-10;
Cokayne Norfolk 615-20; Swales 51;
Bindoff 1: 397-8 490-2.
4. Bindoff 2:179-82; Clough 1964 xxiii-
xxvii; Searle 1974 422; Davidson-Houston
1936 175-6.
5. Wedgwood 35 360 542 763-4; AMS
6326/119-20; CPRL 1455-64: 167.
6. Add MS 5672 f. 5; Torr 1964 98.
7. Whittick 213-15; Roskell 1: 658;
Hunnisett 1964 40.
8. Figg 1861 28; Hunnisett 1965 52;
Whitley 1902 46; CPR 1476-85: 191;
Hunnisett 1964 45.
9. VCHS 7: 245-6; Cornwall 1956 xxvii
166; Kitchen 183.
10. Cleere & Crossley 111-25; Awty
115-23.
11. Knowles 1955 161, 1950 711; Graham
1929 81-2; VCHS 2: 69; CPRL 1471-84:
85 272; Copenhagen MS 152.
12. SC6 1023/30; E40/A4214; Cornwall
1956 96; Salzman 1935b 178-9; SC6

HENVIII/3530.
13. Knowles 1955 248 473.
14. SC6 HENVIII/3518-24, 3529-30;
SAS/JC 3; SP1/126/172-5; Green 1886
219-242; Searle & Ross 20-1; Whitley 1919
143.
15. SC6 1023/30, HENVIII/3530; Godfrey
1939 142-4; PROB 11/11/31, 22/15.
16. Blaauw 1850 204; Knowles 1955 14;
Graham 1923 487; Brooke 1 4 7; Ancient
deeds 3: 196 (5580); CPR 1354-8: 103;
Foster 1: 35; Venn 1: 23; Venn & Venn 1:
45 175 421, 3: 283, 4: 43; Leadham-Green
1992 67 79 114-15; Hunt 117.
17. Knowles 1955 295-6; Copenhagen MS
150-2.
18. Knowles 1962 284, 1955 245 325-7;
Searle 1974 251; SC6 HENVIII/3520
3529; SP1/126/172-5; W/A1/46 47, A2/16;
Harleian Roll D21.
19. SC6 HENVIII/3521, 3525, 3530.
20. SC6 HENVIII/3521, 3525.
21. SC6 HENVIII/3518-20.
22. SAS/WH 191; SAS/ACC 1244; ROB
2/1/1; Town Book 2: 279-280; SC6
1023/30, HENVIII/3520, 3522-5; Knowles
1962 281.
23. SC6 HENVIII/3526-8.
24. SC6 HENVIII/3502-03, 3510-12,
3516; SAS/E 234; AMS 5897/68.
25. PROB 11/11/13, 13/16; Norman 7-8;
AMS 6326/19; Sadler 134; SP1/126/172-5;
VCHS 7: 67 100; Lloyd 44-6; CSPD 1547-
80: 448.
26. SC6 HENVIII/3526-28; Kitch 1981
89; Reynolds 1997 11-17; C66/693 m. 24;
ACC 2187; Elphick 340.
27. Goring 2003 25; Anon 1860a 198-9;
Kitch 1981 88-92; Searle 1974 439-40.
28. VCHS 2: 96, 7: 55; Salzman 1935b
178-82, 1954 32-4.
29. SP1/241/243; LP HVIII 13 (1): 277
389 470; Stevens 1911 268; LP HVIII 13
(2): 79 85 92.
30. Hope 1906 74-88; Pevsner 1957 91;
Lyne 1997 31; LP HVIII 14 (2): 317-45.
31. Dunvan 393-4; Anderson 1989b 49-
60; Kay 1982 28-36; VCHS 7: 40 48 72;
Nairn & Pevsner 551; Godfrey 1938 44.
32. VCHS 2: 96; LP HVIII 12 (2): 418
448, 13 (2): 452; Gardiner 1996a 94-5 97-
9 112-13; Ker 115; AMS 6326/19; Goring
2003 28; PROB 11/18/30.
33. Goring 1996 141-4; Hudson 1901 199-

201; PAR 414/9/1/1a; Jones 1983 79-86; Brent & Brent 200-01; AMS 5510.
34. PAR 414/9/1/1a.
35. LP HVIII 13 (2): 278; VCHS 7: 39 41; Rowe 197-9; PAR 414/9/1/1a.
36. Elphick 64-9 341-2; Davidson-Houston 1935 49-54.
37. Kitch 1981 94-5; Mayhew 1983 38-58; Goring 1996 144-6 152; Godfrey 1939 97; PAR 414/9/1/1a.
38. Salzman 1935b 180; Du Boulay 1966 262; Kitch 1978 283; Way 2-4.
39. Way 2-4; Turner 1852 136-7; Byng 126; Daniel-Tyssen 1869 179 182; CPR 1413-16: 182; Blencowe 1851 251.
40. Daniel-Tyssen 1869 178-85; Dunkin 1875 77 81; PROB 11/24/22 26/2; SAS Library, ACC 3717; AMS 5775.
41. DNB Fiennes 1296-7, Nevill 250.
42. Bindoff 2: 179-82; VCHS 7: 48.
43. Town Book 1: 1- 2; Bindoff 2: 485; Challen 1962 111 114; AMS 5510; VCHS 7: 36-7.
44. VCHS 7: 42 217; Ray 1930 27-8 57 126-7; Challen 1962 135; Rowe 16; Phillips 1894a 216; SAS/C133 139.
45. Goring 1996 146; PROB 11/18/21; Dunvan 314; Woollgar, 2: 248; Salzman 1925a 76-7; Godfrey 1939 111.
46. Rice 1903 134-44.
47. VCHS 2: 412-14; Rowe 156-9; Ray 1930 138.
48. LP HVIII 13(1): 131, 13(2): 518; SC6 EVI/453; U269/A1/8; W/A4/298, A9/57; PAR 411/31/1/1, 413/1/1/1; Brent 1993 104.
49. Goring 1996 147-8 150-2; Mayhew 1983 38-58; Kitch 1981 87-8; Godfrey 1939 95-134; PAR 414/9/1/1a.
50. Swales 54-7; Bindoff, 1: 205-6 689-91, 2: 243 601-2, 3: 350-1; Harleian Roll D21; Norman 7-8; Town Book 1: 5.
51. Town Book 1: 5-6; Salzman 1935b 180; PAR 414/9/1/1a; Daniel-Tyssen 1869 159-90; Hudson 1905 22; W/A6/100.
52. Swales 57-60; Bindoff, 1: 205-6, 2: 19-20 40 179 182 243 422-3 635, 3: 90 381; Hasler 1: 259-60, 3: 344.
53. Town Book 1: 1-14; Mayhew 1982 139-60; Goring 1996 152.
54. Rice 1902 114-27.
55. Ray 1930 138-9; Pullein 375-8; W/A1/12/53, A3/170.
56. Goring 1996 148-52, 2003 33-4; Kitch 1981 94-7; Gratwick & Whittick 228-31 239; Stoneham passim; Cattley & Townsend 7: 321-6.
57. Horsfield Lewes 1: 161; Lower 1858 186.
58. Lower 1865 142-3.

8 A thirst for Order 1558-1625

Epigraph. Town Book 1: 130-3
1. Gratwick & Whittick 230; Hudson 1905 22-3; PAR 414/9/1/1a.
2. Hasler 1: 255, 3: 316-71; VCHS 7: 35 48 55 58; Horsfield Lewes 2: 169.
3. Webb & Wilson passim; Phillips c1927 1: 197 231 234; Sackville-West 1859a xxxvii-xxxviii; Cooper 1852 192-3; Straker 1935 193-5; Town Book 1: 33; SRL 7/3; AMS 2588.
4. 26 tons of Caen stone were unloaded at Newhaven in March 1574; E739/21. Norris 1955 xxxvi; SAS/WH 191; Anderson 1983 48 68 69 79 278 283 284; British Museum, MAGUS. RG. 1839 1029.106-7. On Cuilfail in Cliffe a sandstone piece adorned with shallow fluting also survives, along with medieval stonework; information from A. Rudebeck.
5. U269/A2/1/49; Wiston MS 1870; Taylor 1988 41-59; Batho 1-27; Turner 1868 175-9; Sackville-West 1923 31; Marsden 1983 69-73.
6. Gilbert 1963 196; Phillips c1927 1: 242-4; PAR 410/1/1/2.
7. PROB 11/111/9; U269/E341; Martin & Martin 1997 passim.
8. U269/E66/2/110-12, A1/1/49; E755/2 20; DNB Browne 64-72; Williams 1904 109-13.
9. VCHS 7: 45; EpII/5/4/124; PROB 11/33/6; U269/E341; Noyes 323-4; Kay 1982 28-36.
10. Challen 1962 119-20; DNB John & Thomas Twyne 1329-31; Godfrey 1926b 9.
11. Davidson-Houston 1937 105-7.
12. DNB Brian Twyne 1328-9; Godfrey 1929 197-201 229-33, 1930 40-2 82-4.
13. ADA 156; DNB Yonge 1244-5; Sadie 27: 664-5; PROB 11/26/2 33/6.
14. Gratwick & Whittick 230; McCann 1981 99-115; Cockburn 1975a 254 334 353 369, 1975b 12 18 21 24; SAS/G/ACC 917; Anon 1929b 175-7; Fletcher 102; Abercrombie 129.

15. Hasler 1: 533; Manning 103-12
16. Hasler 1: 426, 2: 112 209, 3: 103 378; VCHS 7: 230.
17. Hasler 3: 378; Turner 1866 128-32; Challen 1962 111-37.
18. VCHS 7: 9-10 35 172 175; Godfrey 1928d 21-2, 1926c 21-2, 1960 2.
19. Manning 1968 108; Hasler 1: 260 502-3, 2: 196-7 209-10 265, 3: 196 315 344; PROB 11/64/20.
20. Hasler 3:193-5; Horsfield Lewes 1: 279; Kitchen 183.
21. Hasler 3: 375-6; Add Chs 30603 30608-9 30624 30627; VCHS 7: 9; Norris 1951-69.
22. Hasler 2: 209-10; Godfrey 1924 260, 1926c 21-2, 1943 122; Horsfield Lewes 1: 280; Lambarde 79-80.
23. Town Book 1: 14; Hasler 3: 125; Cleere & Crossley 172.
24. Hasler 3: 315-16; Rowe 169-70; Sackville-West 1923 30 76 92-3; ACC 2187.
25. Turner 1870 42-3; Godfrey 1955c 17; Sackville-West 1923 35; Baker 1984 496; Fletcher 9 42; PROB 11/161/61.
26. DNB Goring 248-51.
27. Goring 1981 160-1 164; Town Book 1: 27; W/A8/309, A28/165; U269/A1/1/32, Al/3; ADA 45; Godfrey 1929-30 40-2, 1931 251.
28. Town Book 1: 33 36; Cockburn 1975a 183 222 235 381.
29. Goring 1996 151; Town Book 1: 14; Torr 1920 114-18; Bindoff 2: 635, 3: 381-2; SAS/ACC 1244.
30. Goring 1981 166-7, 1996 151; Ellis 1858b 53-6; Lower 1865 345; Sawyer 1879 191-5; W/A7/79.
31. Goring 1981 166, 2003 3-39; Ellis 1860 260; Challen 1962 119-20; Lower 1862b 246, 1865 179.
32. Jenkins 164; Sackville-West 1859b 227; Renshaw 1910 3; Rowe 16; Figg 1861 12; VCHS 7: 40; AMS 5775; Du Boulay 1966 317 324-7; CPR 1558-60: 440-2.
33. Fletcher 71-4; Smart 45-7.
34. Fletcher 63-4; Noyes 323 335; Foster 1066.
35. Renshaw 1906 47-65, 1907 41-6, 1909 192; Blencowe 1851 284-5; Lower 1865 46 48; Ross 106-7; EpII/5/6/63-4; Cooper 1853 225-7.
36. Goring 1981 157; Clywd Record Office D/HE/732 735; Thomas-Stanford 1910 18, 1918 116-20; ADA 45/130.
37. Cockburn 1975a 31-8 81 99 152-7, 1975b 1 5 13-14 44; Town Book 1: 16.
38. Leppard 1980 388-9; QR 1/10 7/59 9/114 18/32; Cockburn 1975a 5 10, 1975b 55; Rowe 152-5; Fletcher 164.
39. Cockburn 1975a 352; QR 19 cover; Town Book 1: 11 13 26 28 45-6.
40. Courthope 87; Cockburn 1975a 20 73 413, 1975b 28 64; Historical Manuscripts Commission Reports 7 (1879): 634; PAR 414/9/1b/16.
41. Goring 1981 160-1 163; Turner 1872 85-98; Dunvan 363-4; Rowe vii-xiv 16 17 112-15 120-5 136-7 155-85; U269/E66/3.
42. Daniel-Tyssen 1871 231-6; ADA 156; DYK 1122-3; Rowe 16.
43. Rowe 120.
44. Goring 1981 157-72; Caldecott 1940 25; VCHS 7: 24 29; QR 30/65.
45. Town Book 1: 4 18 25 45-6 51 133; Rowe 124; VCHS 7: 25.
46. Town Book 1: 10 19 24 36 131.
47. Town Book 1: 33-4 36 44.
48. Town Book 1: 3 10-11 18 20 24-5 31 39-40: Rowe 177-83.
49. Rowe 124; Town Book 1: 21 36; Hasler 1: 260.
50. Town Book 1: 8 20-2, 2: 192; LEW/C8/4/1; Rowe 124; VCHS 7: 25; Town Book 2: facing p. 144; Salzman 1964 109-11.
51. Town Book 1: 15-17 25; ACC 3746; W/A6/102; Rowe 125.
52. Town Book 1: 4 13-14 18 19 29-30 43 56 130; W/A5/144; Rowe 121 123-4 177.
53. Goring 1981 157-72; SAS/ACC 2953/1 (17 June 1598); U269/E184.
54. Town Book 1: 4-5 43-8 130-4.
55. Fletcher 234; Mason 1990 157-75; Goring 1981 157-72; Challen 1962 129; W/A14/192 A28/74; Venn 2: 465.
56. LEW/C1/1/205; Town Book 1: 43-8.
57. Town Book 1: 1-48 132.
58. Town Book 1: 46-52 134; LEW/C1/1/199 205; W/A28/91.
59. Town Book 1: 48-9; VCHS 7: 284; Rowe 177-83.
60. Godfrey 1933 216-17.

9 A focus of economic recovery 1461-1625

Epigraphs. Straker 1931 v; SAS/M 757.

1. Young 348; Camden 30; SC6 HENVIII/3510-12; AMS 5775; SAS/E 234; SAS/G11/18, G35/13; Figg 387; Cockburn 1975a 22; Renshaw 1916 197; Brent 1993 106-7 110.

2. Warne 1989 189-210; VCHS 2: 257; W/A15/45; SAS/G8/49; Brent 1973 118-20 256-8; CSPD 1638-9: 52-3; Rowe 139; QR 27 cover; EpII/5/6/263-4, 11/61-2; QR 72/120 86/100; Cockburn 1975a 10; QR 212/5.

3. Add. MS 33142/73; W/A6/363; Straker 1931 120; Town Book 1: 13; Cornwall 1955 86; QR 83/9 11; RYE 47/16 (113).

4. Brent 1976 38-48; Thomas-Stanford 1910 7-8; QR 123/85.

5. Brent 1976 41-55; Wilde 233; Davidson-Houston 1936 190; PAR 498/1/1/2; Attree 1888 52; Tate 134; Cornwall 1960 129.

6. AMS 5775; Lower 1865 79; Cockburn 1975b 55; QR 101/11; APC 1591: 4; Salzman 1901 34; Fletcher 5; QR 135/110; XE 6.

7. Turner 1867 164; Brent 1976 43 45; PROB 11/42A/17; Town Book 1: 15 62 72-3.

8. QR 67/72; Cockburn 1975b 55; RYE 47/78; Brent 1973 78-85; APC 1639-40: 100; W/A12/251; E190/755/2.

9. Phillips c1927 234; Woollgar 1: 433; Fletcher 148-50; QR 41/21-2.

10. Fletcher 150; QR 83/9 11; SAS/A1454; W/U1/390; SRA/C1/1/29; SAS/DN 184.

11. Harvey 1991 21-2; Brandon & Short 122 152 203; PAR 422/1/1/1; AMS 4596/7; ADA 45/29; Brent 1973 94-6.

12. SC6 HENVIII/3518-20; SAS/WH 182-3; U269/E66/3; QR 16/6 41/21-2; W/A8/162; PROB 11/93/24, 72/27; QR 16/6; PROB 11/101/134; QR 83/9; PROB 4/13093; PAR 410/1/1/1; W/A3/231.

13. Brent 1973 51-60 98-104; Cockburn 1975a 240; PAR 414/9/1a/98; FRE 520/131; ACC 8189/76; PAR 415/9/1a; Add MS 33144; QR 72/57 73/64; W/U1/70; E190/757/9.

14. PROB 11/19/23; Cornwall 1956 97-9; W/A4/523 A3/122 A11/189 A10/110; SAS/A 90; W/A21/59; Rowe 226; SAS/D 150; EpII/5/12/83.

15. SAS/E 234; DYK 1122/17; Add MS 33142; E190/739/8; CSPD 1619-23: 434.

16. Brandon & Short 186; LP HVIII 13 (1): 100; W/A16/117; PROB 11/162/88;

ACC 4299 (NRA 77/50); *Sussex Weekly Advertiser* 27 Feb. 1769; E190/739/20 740/6 755/20 763/4; QR 85/67; EpII/5/4/172; W/A17/23.

17. QR 86/102 104; Godfrey 1950a 130-1; ADA 156/45 90; QR 95/15-16 106/10; APC 1630-1: 161 165; E190/762/8.

18. Cockburn 1975a 388; ADA 156/4-5; Cockburn 1975a 114; W/A 4/370 A7/189 A24/148 A10/300; Sawyer 1880 245; W/U1/81; QR 7/98; Cockburn 1975a 218; E190/739/20; W/A15/58 A20/100; Hunnisett 1998 76; SAS/G8/15; W/SM/D44.

19. Add. MS 33142/39-73; U269/E15; SC6 HENVIII/3526-8; Rowe 125; W/SM/B7; W/A11/54 A3/265; PROB 11/179/47; Turner 1857 128; W/A8/263 A11/227.

20. Straker 1931 114-21; Cornwall 1955 85-91; Brent 1973 116-17 170-3; APC 1571-5: 124; DYK 1122/17; W/SM/F129; W/A17/18; SC6 HENVIII/3518-20.

21. Cleere & Crossley 111-25; Awty 115-23; RYE 60/6/106, Budgen 1929 147; W/A3/58.

22. Cleere & Crossley 126 130-2; Brent 1973 133-48.

23. Berkshire Record Office D/EN/0/23 (thanks to Tim.Cornish for this reference); SAS/G8/49 34/72; Teesdale 74-86; APC 1577-8: 338; Lavington MS 832; Cleere & Crossley 148 157-8 332; Lower 1849 184; E190/739/20; Straker 1931 151-2 389; VCHS 2: 247-8; Goring 1981 157-72.

24. E190/764/19 760/1; Crake 278-83; Clwyd RO RHVAC MS D(HE) 732 15-16; Cleere & Crossley 173-5 179-80; E190/758/11; SAS/G11/11-24 G5/41; Challen 1958a 158-9; Lower 1860 270.

25. Daniel-Tyssen 1864 156-70, 1915 81; Davidson-Houston 1935 81 85; PROB 11/72/6; Lower 1867 43; KIR 32/11; PAR 415/9/1a/5 34, QR 89/1.

26. Brandon & Short 190; E190/745/13 23; Cockburn 1975a 208; QR 6/19; W/A14/108; E190/754/12.

27. SC6 HENVIII/3521 3525; DYK 1123/14; Figg 1861 26; Brent 1993 41; W/A5/497; QR 37/62 66/84; 268/4; U269/A2/1/49 50; SAS/G 8/5; QR 36/26; W/SM/G3; QR 67/7; Curwen 1942 81-2.

28. SC6 HENVIII/3526-8; Dugdale 5:18; SAS/G8/50; Brandon 1971b 97-9; Ellis 1858b 96-9; Salzman 1910 54-5.

29. Town Book 1: 29; Rice 126; PAR 419/7/4/1-4; Cockburn 1975a 202; EpV/5/1/73-4; ADA 45/140; U269/A1/1/17 A2/1/31; SAS Library, Budgen notebook 38/38; W/A14/144 A5/427.

30. Camden 30; APC 1629-30: 87; Town Book 1: 58-9; SRA/C1/1/1; Johnston 1958 305; PAR 490/1/1/1.

31. E190/813/4, 754/18, 745/13, 745/23, 755/20, 762/2, 764/19, 766/23; Brent 1973 293-335; CSPD 1619-23: 349-50; Lower & Cooper 149-50.

32. SRA/C1/1/15; Clwyd Record Office RHVAC MS D(HE) 732 23; Cockburn 1975b 11; QR 62/2; Blencowe & Lower 183; Blencowe 1851 256; QR 103/4; Wilde 232-3; Turner 1867 154-64; SC6 HEN VIII/3525; W/A5/102; Cooper 1851 25; E190/741/28, 741/31; ACC 4113.

33. Brent 1993 3; PAR 414/9/1/1c; ASH 933; Fletcher 7 165; ASH 931/1.

34. Godfrey 1947 102-3; Town Book 1: 13 29 77; Rowe 121; Fletcher 226-7; Cockburn 1975b 30 41.

35. Larwood & Hotten 94 96 293-4; W/A3/122; VCHS 7: 13; Phillips 1892a 225; Salzman 1942d 92; U269/E66/3; Godfrey 1955b 17; AMS 5735; Lower 1851 309-15; Pevsner & Nairn 397; Searle 1974 409.

36. PROB 11/18/34; Morris 265-6; Daniel-Tyssen 1864 138-232; Andre 222; Godfrey 1950b 164-5; Anon 1930 116; Salzman 1911 85; Johnston 1915 151; AMS 5753; Homan 207-8; Deedes 1: 54-5; VCHS 3: 75.

37. E190 passim; Brent 1973 168-70; W/A11/55.

38. PROB 11/85/29 156/79 191/12; De Beer 1955 2: 2-3 7-8; Rowe 202; PROB 11/151/26; Mosse 126.

39. E190/737/2, 738/2, 738/24, 740/6; W/A10/200; Lower 1857 100; EpII/5/17/56-7; W/A9/15; Dale 246-9: Lower 1867 38.

40. Caldecott 1938 61-73; Sawyer 1880 246-7; Godfrey 1960 2; E190/754/12, 755/2, 755/20, 757/9, 761/18.

41. Cockburn 1975a 104 382 219 321 212; De Beer 1955 2: 27; QR 11/7 49, 42/59 71.

42. Cockburn 1975a 427; QR 7/59; Cockburn 1975a 308; QR 28/4; VCHS 2: 258; W/A1a/38; PROB 11/157/25; Godfrey

1942b 3-9; SAS/PN 134; PROB 11/157/25; W/A7/153 A9/324.

43. Gardiner 1996a 113; Hudson 1905 23; Town Book I: 20-1; SC6 HENVIII/3518-20 3526-8; Tyler 10 24 31; QR 22/18 36/112 51/27; Dunkin 1902 227; W/A8/259 A24/148.

44. E190/738/2; W/A10/8; SAS/WH 184; QR 16/70; W/U1/62; T.S. 85.

45. Fletcher 144; Cooper 1853 225-7; W/A18/89; SAU 660; SAS/M 757; W/A28/50; QR 2/17.

46. PROB 11/161/61; Turner 1872 85-98; Rowe 88; W/A12/42 A10/187; DYK 1122; ADA 156; SAS/ACC 2953/1; Rowe 178 180; Attree 1912 212; PROB 11/135/47; AMS 5930; Noyes 312-42.

47. Goring 1981 160-3 165; W/A7/308 A14/192; PROB 11/145/27; ADA 156; W/A20/111; PROB 11/134/99; De St Croix 50; PROB 11/138/99.

48. Fletcher 41; PROB 11/191/12; Foster 1112; Raach 49; Attree 1888 41;W/A17/23; Venn & Venn 4: 34; EpV/3/1/60; Rowe 24; Challen 1955 73-8; PROB 11/161/53; W/A23/167; Thomas-Stanford 1910 200.

49 W/A10/206 A18/196; Horsfield Lewes 1: 276; Cockburn 1975a 360; Daniel-Tyssen 1871 243.

50. C1/445/33; De Beer 1955 2: 8; W/A15/153 A14/153; Town Book 1: 56 61-2; PAR 412/7/4; Sackville-West 1923 105.

51. E190/813/4 738/2; Challen 1962 129; W/A28/74 A18/125; Lower 1868 34-46; Rowe 183-4; VCHS 7: 74 11.

52. W/A12/12; Rowe 40 57; W/A16/218; PROB 11/129/4; W/A13/104 A28/20; ADA 45/46; PROB 11/161/53; W/A18/84; Rowe 139; W/A19/91; PROB 11/113/12; VCHS 7: 45; Godfrey 1930 58-9; Challen 1943 137-8.

53. Rowe 5 9; Radcliffe 124-6; VCHS 7: 114 117 224; Blaauw 1851 93-5; Nairn & Pevsner 611; VCHS 9: 181; SAS/A 86; Add Ch 30643; W/A28/121 A1/33 A5/102 A14/211 A22/33.

54. Thirsk 558-60; W/A3/122; PROB 11/84/62; ADA bundle 860; PROB 11/151/5; Rowe 11; DL/D145/1/3; SAS/ACC 2953/1; W/A33/31; U269/A2/1/31; Whitley 1902 49; Sawyer 1880 245-7; W/A7/270 276; QR 27/15.

55. Godfrey 1960 1-11; Cockburn 1975a 290; QR 29/89; PROB 11/167/146; AMS

5753; Rowe 15; W/A10/300; SAS/ACC
2953/1; EpII/5/17/51; W/U1/81.
56. Rowe 9 15; W/A21/59; ADA 156;
PROB 11/72/6; EpII/5/17/51; PROB
11/79/8 157/25; QR 83/9 11; W/A20/171.
57. QR 121/63; SAS/L 21; QR 45/33; Rowe
152; Woollgar 2: 453; U269/E66/3; ACC
2933; EpII/5/12/57; ACC 2327/3/1/1/31;
Sussex Express 7 Apr. 2000.
58. VCHS 7 11-12; Reader 221-62; PAR
414/9/1/1b; W/A6/348 A8/425.
59. W/A19/87; Cockburn 1975b 40; QR
28/3; PROB 11/212/106; Louis xlii-xliv
xlviii 30-4 41 97 203; Town Book 1: 7 10;
PAR 309/1/1/1.
60. Louis xl; Cockburn 1975a 117-18 220;
Hunnisett 1996 33 73-84; W/A8/259; QR
6/18; VCHS 2: 197; QR 44/1; Hunnisett
1966 217-21; Blencowe 1859 18.
61. E179/191/410, 416, 258/15 [taxpayers
at Cliffe in 1524 were lumped into the
hundred of Ringmer; a total of fifty has
been estimated]; Brent 1973 336; Louis
xxv; SP1/126/172-5; ACC 4299 (NRA
77/50); W/A13/104; Rowe 122; W/SM/D44;
PROB 11/121/43.
62. Cornwall 1956 96-101 127-9, 1976 1-
27; PROB 11/21/27; W/C4/24; W/A1/155;
W/C4/12 106; W/A1/114.
63. Cornwall 1976 15; Farrant 1996 169
172; Whitley 1902 46; SP13/A6; Arundel
MS A 1871; Salzman 1934 69 97-8 100;
Searle 1974 365.
64. Cornwall 1976 16; Brent 1973 276
279-80 293-333; McCann 1979 182;
Godfrey 1929-30 42; Salzman 1925 76-7;
LP HVIII 13(1): 389; Phillips 1: 192;
W/A1/43.
65. SC6 HENVIII/3526-8; Cornwall 1956
45; PAR 414/9/1/1c; Anderson 1989b 49-
60; columns: information from C.
Whittick; Figg 1861 19; Gardiner 1996a
97; Martin 1997 passim.
66. AMS 6433/1; W/A11/54; QR 71 cover;
PROB 11/121/43; SAS/ACC 1244; PAR
413/12/2/18 19; ACC 2327/3/1/1 (1638);
W/A25/3.
67. AMS 5753; PAR 419/7/4/4; Town Book
1: 27; W/A25/171 A9/60 A7/29 A18/129.
68. Fletcher 9; VCHS 7: 11; HBR 1/1233;
SAS/ACC 2953/1; ADA 156; W/A17/117;
Farrant 1996 172.
69. PAR 309/1/1/1; ACC 3412/ 387;
SAS/WS 148; ACC 2187; ADA 45/132;

Rowe 12; PAR 414/30/1/1; W/A20/142;
SAS/ACC 3746; Smail 34 37.
70. Rowe 8-16; Godfrey 1955b fig. 5.

10 The Great Rebellion and its aftermath 1625-1662

Epigraphs. W/A19/150; Dixon 365-74;
Figg 1864 66-7.
1. Fletcher 188 193-200 211-12; PAR
414/9/1/1c; De Beer 1955 2: 8 .
2. PAR 415/9/1a; Fletcher 102; Clwyd
Record Office RHVAC MS D/HE/732/28-
9; W/A19/150-4; Radcliffe 126 132; DNB
Barton 348.
3. Fletcher 24 42 71-2 232; ACC 4113.
4. Fletcher 56 240; Harleian MS 2313.
5. Sackville-West 1923 92-3; U269/A1/8;
VCHS 7: 35 74; PROB 11/161/61; Rowe
202; SAS /C 247; Budgen 1950 32;
U455/T283; PROB 11/178/174; ADA
45/124 131.
6. Fletcher 90-1; Woollgar 2: 287;
EpII/9/23/21 56-7, 15/1/4 49 50; PAR
414/9/1/1c; Thomas-Stanford 1910 29.
7. PAR 415/9/1a; Cooper 1902 21 25; QR
33/20 23; QO 2/46-7.
8. EpV/3/1/65, 3/109-11 148; PROB
11/307/19 156/79; Fletcher 40;
E190/763/4, 764/19, 764/79, 766/12,
PROB 11/151/26; ACC 4216; W/SM/F28;
PROB 11/25/26.
9. SAS/COc 72; EpV/8/1; Radcliffe 132;
EpV/3/3/92; Ladipo no. 67; Cooper 1909
26; EpV/3/3/72; Dunkin 1875 82-3; Torr
1964 100-1; Couchman 232.
10. Christchurch College Oxford, Evelyn
MSS 1043-4.
11. Fletcher 62; Rowe 184; VCHS 7: 40;
Dixon 365-74.
12. Fletcher 92-3 191 205-9; RYE 47/130;
Rowe 241; PAR 414/9/1/1c; QR 44/1; RYE
47/130.
13. Fletcher 49 55 92-3 241-2; DNB
Lunsford 281-3; Blaauw 1852 80-3.
14. Fletcher 221 243 248-9: VCHS 7: 217;
W/A23/207; Add MS 32683/9; ACC
2327/3/1/1 (1650).
15. Town Book 1: passim; QR 53/152;
Thomas-Stanford 1910 286-7; Bodleian
Library, Rawlinson MS A25/553 557.
16. PAR 414/9/1/1c, 415/9/1a; Fletcher
255-7.
17. Town Book 1: 64 66 68-9; QR 56/115;
Fletcher 255-6 262-4; Thomas-Stanford

1910 40-1 48.

18. Fletcher 105 264-9 328; Thomas-Stanford 1910 64-5; PAR 415/9/1a; Horsfield Lewes 1: 199-200.

19. Dixon 365-74; Lower 1868 45; Fletcher 68.

20. Thomas-Stanford 1910 158-61; Hampshire Record Office 15M84/23/3.

21. Fletcher 269-70; Thomas-Stanford 1910 162-4 179-85 245-6.

22. Fletcher 223-4 325-9; Thomas-Stanford 1910 156; SP28/181; Green 1889 264; W/U1/154; PROB 11/322/157 377/105.

23. Fletcher 143-4 340; QR 34/1; PROB 11/258/361; AMS 5996/3/4.

24. EpII/9/24; Renshaw 1906 47-65, 1907 41-6; Fletcher 79 106 108 112-16 153 159-60 167 279-80; QO 2/20; Matthews 1988 358.

25. Sawyer 1888b 145; Thomas-Stanford 1910 137; Fletcher 73 116; PROB 11/267/351.

26. Blencowe 1851 288; Thomas-Stanford 1910 245; PAR 414/9/1/1c, 415/9/1a.

27. Fletcher 291; SAS/SM 147.

28. Fletcher 272-3 284 292-3; Thomas-Stanford 1910 196-203 214-16 246.

29. Fletcher 72-3 294 299-300 339 352-3; Thomas-Stanford 1910 227 259 273-5 285; QR 102/2; Salzman 1914 199; PAR 414/9/1/1c; D'Elboux 123; QR 107/68; PROB 11/283/601.

30. Town Book 1: 72-3; Fletcher 23 32 333; Thomas-Stanford 1910 124; Woollgar 4: appendix 342-3.

31. Fletcher 117 120; Matthews 1988 396; Sawyer 1888b 157; PROB 11/330/75; PAR 414/9/1/1c; PROB 11/230/280; QR 83/47.

32. Fletcher 111 283 328; SP/28/135; Sawyer 1881 191; Brent 1985 210; Blaauw 1852 97; PAR 414/9/1/1c; QO 60; Anon 1860c 260.

33. Cleere & Crossley 173-80 184; SAS/G13/100; QR 85/64 77/63; CSPD 1651-2: 228; E190/763/11; Straker 1931 251; PROB 11/267/323.

34. Fletcher 144 331-2 337-8; Green 1889 172 181 198 264; Brent 1985 209-11; PROB 11/420/114.

35. Town Book 1: 56-85; Brent 1985 208-11.

36. Fletcher 110; QO 2/62; Sawyer 1881 184; Brent 1985 211; Blaauw 1852 39.

37. Brent 1985 195-206.

38. Brent 1985 208-11; Challen 1958b 61; Woollgar 4: 326-7; Salzman 1924 46; QO 3/78; VCHS 2: 414; FRE 520/59; Thulesius 12.

39. QO 57; PAR 415/9/1a; PROB 11/288/153; St. Croix 83.

40. Caldecott 1940 24-5; QO 3/9 2/34 38; QR 94/15 123/30 148/12 149/69.

41. Davies 194-5; Brent 1985 211-12; Fletcher 120-1 316; SOF 5/1; Figg 1864 66; QR 41/21; E190/761/6, 763/4, 763/11; PROB 11/322/139.

42. Fletcher 295 299-302; Thomas-Stanford 1910 288.

43. DNB Goffe 71-3; Fletcher 120 302-11; Thomas-Stanford 1910 284-8; PROB 11/267/351.

44. Fletcher 310 312-14; Courthope 87; Thomas-Stanford 1910 296-303 326-9.

45. Fletcher 223 296 302-3 308; Thomas-Stanford 1910 252; PROB 11/358/121; W/A42/30; ADA bundle 860.

46. Fletcher 312 315-18; Thomas-Stanford 1910 305-6 311-12; Blaauw 1852 95-100.

47. De Beer 1937 177-83; Christchurch College Oxford, Evelyn MSS 1046-8; Fletcher 318-19. In 1648 Evelyn sold Malling Deanery to its occupier, William Kempe; AMS 5763/97.

48. Brent 1983 95-7; Henning 1: 417-18 424, 3: 335 477-8; Fletcher 321.

49. De Beer 1955 3: 246; Fletcher 320; DNB Ludlow 255-61; Thomas-Stanford 321-2.

50. Matthews 1934 302; QO 4/5; Henning 1: 552-3, 3: 757.

11 A resilient economy 1662-1714

Epigraph. Turner 1867 164.

1. Andrews 1640 58.

2. E179/191/410, 258/15, 258/18; QR 140/72, 121/63; LEW/C2/1/1; Daniel-Tyssen 1864 180-1; Town Book 1: 73; QR 132/61; QO 2/70; Blencowe 1859 13-14; Town Book 1: 96.

3. W/A32/4; QI 3/104.

4. Moore 120-1 124-5; E190/770/35.

5. E190/768/16; QR 83/9 11; W/INV/55; ADA bundle 860; Caldecott 1940 24; Moore 230-5; ASH 933; PAR 414/7/4; Marchant 179.

6. Moore 139-43; Add MS 33146/32; PROB 11/377/113, 394/35; Add Ch 30696.

7. W/A30/386; SAS/G31/49; SAS/WS 225; SHR 1608; AMS 2177; GIL 289; Brent 1993 8; W/A38/141; QR 236/1.
8. W/INV/256, 789; QR 140/11 29; Marchant 172; Add MS 33146; LEW/C2/1/1.
9. ADA 158; Marchant 16-18; DL/D145/4 ; Greenwood 56; De-Laune 419; U269/A2/1/31; SP/28/181; Dunvan 254-7; Sawyer 1899 22; Salzman 1947 110-11.
10. Turner 1867 162; Cooper 1852 193; Blencowe 1860 55; Greenwood 56-8; CSPD 1665-6: 493-4; QR 267/33.
11. QO 5/27 93; Dunvan 268; Stenning 1868 132-3; ASSI 35/128/9; Horsfield Sussex 2: appendix 3 23-4.
12. Town Book 1: 72-3; W/A29/35; Dunvan 268.
13. Turner 1867 163-4; Brandon & Short 164; QR 265/3; Cooper 1903 105; QO 7/100; VCHS 7: 245; HOW 34/16; QO 12; Farrant 2001 97.
14. Brandon & Short 152 223 228-9; Cooper 1858 76-80; GIL 289.
15. PROB 11/ 322/157, 363/114, 409/50; W/A30/297 359, A39/98; Godfrey 1927c 67-78; GIL 289 .
16. QR 140/3 20; King 30-2; ABE 17L; QI 3/76.
17. Lefevre 28; Dunvan 351-2; W/A42/185, A45/70.
18. QO 5/131; W/A33/16; Figg 1859 177; QR 186/55, 214/52; Horsfield Lewes 1: appendix xxviii; T.S. 85; King 24; SAS/PN 439.
19. QO 360; PROB 11/377/105; Moore 18 19 122; W/A34/104; QR 281/20; Brent 1993 54; PROB 4/21523.
20. Add Ch 30669; PAR 412/7/4; PROB 11/455/63, 401/167; Moore 132.
21. Dodson 55-7; SAS/PN 138; Hawkesbury 102; Lefevre 62-3; AMS 38485/84 101.
22. PROB 11/323/15; Godfrey 1955b 32-3.
23. Woodruff 192-7; PROB 11/435/225; PAR 412/7/4; Lower 1872 140.
24. W/A47/63; Farrant 2001 20; QR 90/98; SAS/PN 439.
25. Hodson 62; Huzel 4-5; Fitzhugh 135; Moore 228-35; Lower 1865 332.
26. SAU 663; Lower 1854 137; QO 5/48; Moore 137-8; Challen 1946 58-61; AMS 6458; Lefevre 47; Add MS 33146/44; Blencowe 1850 124; SHR 1608 1613a;

PROB 11/394/35; SAS/HC 591 592.
27. Add MS 33146/28; ASH 933; Moore 137-41; QR 201/49, 217/29, 335/22; QO 9/13; W/INV/248; EpII/9/31.
28. QO 5/50 67; PAR 347/7/1; QR 178/109; LEW/C2/1/1; W/INV/134; Caffyn 157.
29. SOF 5/1; W/A34/268; ADA 50/36.
30. W/A29/63; SAS/WH 184; VCHS 7: 11; Godfrey 1955b 14; W/A31/146; AMS 5745/87; QR 130/63.
31. QR 116/39; Atkinson 1977 3; Bedwin 1976 52-54; Tebbutt 1975 52; Freke 1975 68; Atkinson 1965 170; W/A43/206; QR 204/38.
32. AMS 2019; QR 97/34; Add Ch 30654; W/INV/431; QO 3/60; LEW/C2/1/1; W/A45/69; PAR 411/10/2.
33. Brandon & Short 220-1; AMS 3066; W/INV/425; PAR 412/7/4; ASH 933; U269/C46/13.
34. U269/C46/7; Moore 95-8; QR 182/109; Stapley 1849 125.
35. Goring 1981 160; W/INV/110; Anon 1896 276-7; Thomas-Stanford 1910 267-8; Brandon & Short 160; Rhys 1: 127; Moore 228; Caldecott 1940 27.
36. Turner 1871 50; HIC 1166; PROB 5/4720, 4/6038; W/INV/118; PROB 11/414/64; W/A45/72; ACC 4113; E190/797/28; QR 287/9; Shorter 169-70; Godfrey 1942b 9-11.
37. QR 173/25; VCHS 2: 414; GIL 4/9/4/41; Caffyn 157; Marchant 179 188.
38. Stapley 1849 122 124; QR 284/10; Blaauw 1851 98-9; QR 337/6 13; PAR 412/1/1/3; W/INV/247.
39. Moore 22; Add MS 33146/18 39 48; ASH 1630/48; Figg 1861 31; Blaauw 1851 99; LEW/C2/1/1; Tyler passim; QR 170/30-31, 214/10, 246/2 8, 259/33.
40. LEW/C2/1/1; Town Book 2: 10 23-4; QO 16; Marchant 173;Woollgar 1: 247-53.
41. Haines 228; QO 8/188; QR 224/130; WO 30/48; U269/C46/7.
42. Sawyer 1880 247; W/A48/238; Godfrey 1960 5; W/A41/94; SAS/ RF7/2; ADA 50/35; W/A36/186.
43. East Sussex County Council current deeds T300.3.181/3 (henceforth T300); Godfrey 1955 17-18, 1931c 250-2; PROB 11/383/65; ABE 34C (13); VCHS 7: 48
44. W/A37/114; Farrant 2001 20 23; Blencowe 1858 13-33; DAN 355-6.

45. AMS 3007; Godfrey 1955c 17-18;
VCHS 7: 67-8 76; PROB 11/371/153;
Davidson-Houston 107; ASH 933; SAS/A
345 363; GLY 824a.

46. Phillips 1892 124-6; Woollgar 2: 248-9;
PROB 11/364/153; Comber 1932 290-2;
W/A42/30; VCHS 7: 11.

47. Comber 1933 200-1;
PROB11/283/601; Flack 15 17; ACC
2327/3/1/1-2.

48. Lower 1862 229 244; Butler 275;
CHR 3/2/1-2; SAS/F 190; VCHS 9: 169
173.

49. E179/258/15, 258/18; ACC 4299 (NRA
77/7/14); VCHS 7: 235; W/A35/422; CHR
4/2/1; W/U1/154; W/A38/105; Field 173;
SAS/I 42.

50. QR 144/25; SAS/WH 191; W/A28/144,
A31/154; SAS/I 8-19.

51. SAS/D 275; W/A34/287; ACC
2327/3/1/2; W/B9/114; QR 167/22;
E190/770/18; W/A32/322; QR 135/6;
W/A20/128; QR 146/64; AMS 3066; PROB
4/13093; SAS/ACC 1244.

52. QO 8/176; QR 224/130, 99/57; ACC
2327/3/1/1 (1650); QR 230/11 33;
W/A34/325; QR 90/57; Rice 1903 134-44;
ACC 2327/3/1/1 (1635, 1657); QR 212/21;
SAS/ACC 1244; QR 159/56, 145/25, 107/6
34.

53. W/INV/1286; QR 203/17; W/INV/127;
Christchurch College Oxford, Evelyn MS
1165; Flack 15 17; Andrews 1940 58;
Horsfield Lewes 1: 207; Holland 50-1;
Moore 199.

54. QO 5/29; A2327/3/1/1 (1664); 12 St
James's Street: deeds in private hands;
ACC 2327/3/1/1 (1663); QR 130/63; ACC
2327/3/1/1 (1653, 1657); QR 234/6, 153/1.

55. ACC 2327/3/1/1 (c1635); QR 106/12;
ACC 2327/3/1/1 (1657); Woollgar 2: 412;
W/A17/138, 5/144; Woollgar 2: 65; ADA
250; QR 214/52.

56. VCHS 7: 9; Andrews 1954a 2; QR
91/1; PROB 11/116/140; National Library
of New Zealand qMS 1292.

57. E179/256/16; ACC 4113; SAS/FA 807;
HBR 1/1262; ADA 50/45-6; PROB
11/315/1118; SAS/BR 337-77; GLY 2933;
QO 6/63; QR 169/33; GLY 2932.

58. ADA 50/45; W/A45/70; E190/784/1;
PROB 11/192/8; Dunvan 317-19; QR
158/4 8; U269/029; PAR 415/33/3 18 23-4
32.

59. SOF 5/1/194-6; SAS/G34/66; QI 5/79;
Defoe 1: 128-9; ASH 931/1.

60. Straker 1931 61-3.

61. QI 4/8; QO 6/18; SOF 30/1; Cleere &
Crossley 342; QI 5/36; SAS/G34/72A;
Town Book 1: 103.

62. Cleere & Crossley 168 194-5 392;
VCHS 2: 248-9.

63. QR 227/61; Challen 1951 180-2;
QR 295/32; AMS 6433; PROB 4/6564,
11/454/41.

64. Daniel-Tyssen 1864 162-5 170, 1915
84-5; Hoare 213; QR 131/36 37;
W/SM/D1/131.

65. E190/768/16 to 809/5, passim.

66. W/INV/113; Straker 1933 249; SHR
1642 1645; PROB 4/13093.

67. QR 95/1; CSPD 1663-4: 656; Woollgar
2: 342; Lower 1857 99-101; Brent 1993
18-19.

68. E190/770/14, 771/19, 785/3; QO 12;
E190/768/16.

69. Smart 1881 134; CSPD 1672: 450-51;
E190/773/5, 771/19; QR 319/22; Defoe 1:
129.

70. E190/784/1 21, 785/3, 785/10; CSPD
1664-5: 485; E190/796/39, 797/8; Andrews
1954b 47.

71. ADA 50/45; W/A36a/50; Wheatley 360;
QR 213/40; QO 5/66, 6/63; QO 9 (Apr.
1686), 12 (July 1711); Brent 1993 5.

72. Woollgar 2: 314; W/SM/D2/111; AMS
5569; QR 97/34-5; W/SM/G3; SM/F129;
ADA 50/45; Brent 1993 37; ACC 4113.

73. SC6/206/34/84; PAR 415/16/26; SOF
5/1; AMS 6433/1-2; ADA 50/44; QR 71/52,
107/32; Woollgar 2: 328; Nairn & Pevsner
609; ASH 933.

74. PROB 11/323/15, 307/19; ADA 50/45;
LAN 236; QI 3/86; W/SM/G4; PROB
11/362/17; W/A37/114; PROB 11/383/65.

75. Woollgar 2: 327 332-7; Phillips 1890
37; ASH 1178/259-60; HIC 1166;
Marchant 187; Add MS 33146/15 18 25.

76. Horsfield Lewes 1: 288-9; PROB
11/213/121; Daniel-Tyssen 1871 241-2;
SAS/ PN 652; Woollgar 2: 316; Rudling
1991 169-170 172; HBR 1/1278; QR
264/13; ACC 380/9; QR 95/57.

77. QR 134/1 48; PROB 11/323/15; ADA
50/46; PROB 11/363/101; QI 5/53;
EpV/1/2/24; Kent 28-31; QR 25/16; PROB
11/273/81, 387/67; De-Laune 419; ACC
380/9.

78. ACC 380/9; Woollgar 2: 314; PROB 11/331/149; DL/D145/20; PROB 11/336/65; QR 169/33; PROB 11/ 362/17; SOF 5/1; QO 4/14.
79. QR 415 (Jan. 1733); Dunvan 320-1; ASH 933; QR 168/69; Chamberlain 25; W/SM/D5/103.
80. Andrews 1940 58; A2327/3/1/1 (1655); SAS/C 776; PROB 11/315/118.

12 The shadow of the Great Rebellion 1662-1714

1. Henning 1: 417-18 424, 3: 477-8 757; Chamberlain 103-25; Dunkin 1894 180; FRE 4410.
2. Brent 1983 95-7; QI 3/37; Couchman 230.
3. Brent 1983 97-8.
4. Brent 1985 195-7 199-201; QI 3/64 103, 5/36, 6/116, QR 186/4; Brent 1983 96 102; Alnwick Castle MS Y. iv 4a.4; Hobbs 146-7.
5. Brent 1985 195; Lyon-Turner 1: 32-3, 2: 1033.
6. Brent 1985 195-6 201 203.
7. Brent 1985 201; PAR 414/9/1/1c.
8. Brent 1983 103; Horsfield Lewes 1: appendix xxix; Lyon-Turner 1: 305, 3: 397-400; Brent 1985 199; QR 168/69.
9. Brent 1985 196 199-200; QI 3/103; AMS 3065; W/A36/46, A45/132; Matthews 1934 364; Ewing 98-103; Burchall 1974 86.
10. Brent 1985 208-12; SAS/I 8-19; ACC 2327/3/1/1; EpII/9/27/55; SAS/WH 191; Norris 1951-69.
11. Brent 1985 196 199-200 208-9; Christ Church College Oxford, Evelyn MS 1167; Horsfield Lewes 1: appendix xxv-xxxii; ACC 4216.
12. Brent 1985 206 212; E190/784/1.
13. Brent 1985 201-3 208-9.
14. Brent 1985 203-5 209-11; Lyon-Turner 1: 305 533; Matthews 1934 150-1.
15. Brent 1985 205-7; Rector 33 35.
16. Henning 1: 719, 3: 106 220-1; Lyon-Turner 3: 788; Brent 1983 102; VCHS 7: 84; ASH 933.
17. AMS 5996/3/5; W/A39/40.
18. British Library, *The Domestick Intelligence*, no. 39, 18 Nov. 1679; QI 5/61-4; Curwen 1934 11-12.
19. SP 29/416/166; Bodleian Library, Tanner 36(222); Town Book 1: 105; SP 29/427/104, 421/154, 432/19.
20. SP 29/431/87.
21. QR 220/28; Renshaw 1912 239.
22. QR 221/2, 225/117 118.
23. QR 226/48-50.
24. Duckett 1881 1-24; Bodleian Library, Tanner 29/9; Miller 220 224; Stapley 113.
25. Lefevre 84; QR 239; PAR 410/1/1/3.
26. Brent 1983 99-100.
27. Brent 1983 100-1; ADA bundle 860; Chamberlain 213.
28. Brent 1983 101-2; PAR 412/7/4; Horsfield Lewes 1: appendix xxxi.
29. T300.3.181/3; W/A40/192; Phillips 1893 64-6; ASH 933; Godfrey 1954 3-11; QR 214/10.
30. Warne 1994 39-42 62; ADA 50/38; Henning 2: 5; Fletcher 262 339; W/A36/65.
31. Bodleian Library, Tanner 148/3; Hobbs 146-7; Lefevre 1989 223; QI 3/78, QR 139/18; W/A31/146; VCHS 7: 41.
32. Cooper 1903 108-10; Christ Church College Oxford, Evelyn MSS 1165-7; SOF 5/1; Bodleian Library, Tanner 148/3; Lefevre 219; Brent 1985 199.
33. PAR 415/9/1a, 410/1/1/3; Bodleian Library, Tanner 148/3; Brent 1983 99; EpII/10/6; W/B9/33; Sawyer 1880 134.
34. Chamberlain 44; QO 9 (July 1689); Caplan 1961 45; A2327/3/1/1; QR 310/9; Goring 2003 70.
35. NU1/1/1.
36. NU1/1/1; PROB 11/449/36; Caplan 1961 37-8; Lyon-Turner 2: 788; Matthews 1934 157 524; W/A41/101, A42/90.
37. PROB 11/432/126; Godfrey 1960 5; NU1/1/1; Caplan 1961 37-45; Dunvan 349; Horsfield Lewes 1:304; R/C4/378.
38. NU/1/1/1; Caplan 1961 37-45.
39. W/A46/245; Matthews 1934 524; Caplan 1961: 2; W/A40/111; Lyon-Turner 1: 533; Matthews 1934 395.
40. PROB 11/524/267; NU1/1/1; QR 225/119; PROB 11/455/73; E190/774/12, 781/18, 782/26, 784/1.
41. SOF1/1, 5/1; Brent 1993 50; Rector 33-4 36; PROB 11/454/41.
42. Henning 3: 218-19 220-1; Hayton 2: 594-8 610-11, 3: 326, 5: 120-5 687-90; Lefevre 34-5; VCHS 7: 239; PROB 11/371/153.
43. Beddard 153.
44. Cooper 1903 111-12.

45. Chamberlain 178-9 184; Sawyer 1881 179; Beddard 156; Horsfield Lewes 1: 315.
46. NU1/1/1; Goring 2003 71; Chamberlain 32.
47. Hayton 2: 594-8 610-11; QR 318/2; VCHS 7: 239.
48. Hayton 2: 597-8; Wooldridge xvi-xvii; Marchant 173 187.
49. Hayton 2: 596-7; Chamberlain 208-9; Cooper 1858 77-80; W/A45/72; Blencowe 1850 159.
50. Renshaw 1905 43 47 55; Brighton History Centre S324; DAN 2189; Add MS 32,290.
51. Hayton 2: 51, 4: 52-3, 5: 117-18 122 125-6 687; GLY 824a; Caffyn 157.
52. Woollgar 2: 14-16; ADA 158 (Oct. 1704); Brent 1993 176-7.
53. Henning 1: 417-18, 2: 289-91; Hayton 3:1009; QR 181/27; NU1/1/1; T300.3.181/3.
54. Horsfield Lewes 1: 296, 2: appendix 3 46; VCHS 7: 48-9.
55. LEW/C2/1/1; QM 3 (July 1692); QO 10 (Easter 1696).
56. Town Book 1: 120-1, 2: 11; Dunvan 211-17.
57. Button 39-40; Town Book 2: 120-6.

Postscript. The Legacy
Epigraph. Blaauw 1856 262.
1. Whistler 161-71; Marchant 187 .
2. Cooper 1908b 13; Caplan 1977 116-17; Chamberlain 200-1; Turner 1869 214; Horsfield Lewes 1: 294; Brent 1993 151.
3. Watkin 68-70; Marchant 171-2; Brent 1993 168-72 210; Town Book 2: 25; LEW/C2/1/1.
4. Caffyn 157; SAS/WH 206; QR 214/10; Brent 1993 16 94; Godfrey 1928e 58.
5. LEW/C2/1/1; Brent 1993 18-19 210.
6. Stenning 1868 132-3; Stapley 113; LEW/C2/1/1; Brent 1993 67.
7. Blaauw 1856 262; Brent 1993 129-30; Cooper 1868 227; Marchant 183; QR 309/1, 255/27; W/A45/70; GLY 2769.
8. Brent 1993 33-4 46 51 56 57; GIL 4/9/4/41; PAR 411/9/1.
9. Brent 1993 208-10; SHR 1613a 1617 1641-5.
10. SHR 1617; Brent 1993 211-13.
11. Brent 1993 86; Farrant 2001 13.
12. Farrant 2001 13 210-11; Margary 124 147; QO 16 (Jan. 1724).
13. Brent 1993 153 157 181-202; Dunvan 251 480.
14. Brent 1993 102.

193 The squint at Cliff church

Bibliography

Abbreviations used:
SAC Sussex Archaeological Collections
SAS Sussex Archaeological Society
SNQ Sussex Notes & Queries
SRS Sussex Record Society

Abercrombie, N.J. 1981. From Counter-Reformation to bourgeois Catholicism. In *Studies in Sussex Church History*, ed. M.J. Kitch, 125-40.

Ade, C. 1848. The discovery of Anglo-Saxon coins at Milton Street, near Alfriston. *SAC* 1: 38-42.

Allcroft, A.H. 1917. The first castle of William de Warenne. *Archaeological Journal,* 74: 36-78.

Allen, M.J. 1995. The prehistoric land-use and human ecology of the Malling-Caburn Downs. *SAC* 133: 19-43.

Ancient correspondence. *Ancient correspondence of Chancery and Exchequer.* List & index society 15.

Ancient deeds. *A descriptive catalogue of ancient deeds in the Public Record Office.*

Anderson, F.E.M. 1983. *Lewes priory sculptures: catalogue.* 4 volumes. Typescript in SAS Library.

—— 1984. The Tournai marble sculptures of Lewes Priory. *SAC* 122: 85-100.

—— 1986. *The Romanesque sculptures of Lewes priory.* London University Ph.D.

—— 1989a. Saint Pancras Priory, Lewes: its architectural development to 1200. *Proceedings of the Battle Conference* 11:1-35.

—— 1989b. Two Romanesque capitals from Lewes priory. *SAC* 127: 49-60.

—— 1992. 'Uxor Mea': the first wife of the first William of Warenne. *SAC* 130:107-29.

—— 1995. The hunt for the black Tournai tomb slab. *Sussex Past & Present* 75: 14.

Andre, J.L. 1900. Mural paintings in Sussex churches. *SAC* 43: 220-51.

Andrews, C.B. ed. 1940. A letter from Sussex in queen Anne's reign. *Sussex County Magazine* 14: 57-9.

Andrews, J.H. 1954a. The customs ports of Sussex 1680-1730. *SNQ* 14: 1-3.

—— 1954b. The trade and ships of Brighton in the second half of the seventeenth century. *SNQ* 14: 46-8.

Anon. 1856. Catalogue of antiquities exhibited ... at Chichester, July 1853. *SAC* 8: 281-344.

—— 1860a. Sussex religious houses and recusants temp. Hen. VIII and Elizabeth. *SAC* 12: 199-202.

—— 1860b. Leonard's furnace, Brede. *SAC* 12: 270.

—— 1860c. Troops in Sussex at the close of the Commonwealth. *SAC* 12: 260.

—— 1863. Proofs of age of Sussex families: Selwyne. *SAC* 15: 211-14.

—— 1896. Some 17th and 18th century Sussex tradesmen's accounts. *SAC* 40: 274-7.

—— 1929a. Tithes belonging to Lewes friars 1547. *SNQ* 2: 145-6

—— 1929b. The Gage monuments, Firle. *SNQ* 2: 175-7.

—— 1930. Church of St Mary the Virgin, Ringmer: Sussex church plans no xi. *SNQ* 3: 116.

—— 1931. The funeral of prior Nelond. *Sussex County Magazine* 5: 551-5.

—— 1932. Sussex lands held by English religious houses situated outside the county: III The lands of Hyde abbey. *SNQ* 4: 115-17.

—— 1940. Report of Lewes Secretary. *SNQ* 8: 58.

—— 1947. Additions to museum to July 1947. *SAC* 86: xxxix-xlii.

—— 1950. Will of Richard Weyvile 1417. *SNQ* 12: 77-9.

—— 1955. Report of Council: museum. *SAC* 94: xxxvi.

APC. *Acts of the privy council of England*.

Arnold, F.S. 1870. The carriage of timber to Lewes. *SAC* 22: 235.

Atkinson, D.R. 1965. Clay pipes made at Lewes. *SNQ* 16: 170-2.

—— 1977. *Sussex Pipes and the Pipemakers*.

Attree, F.W.T. 1888. Wivelsfield. *SAC* 36: 19-74.

—— ed. 1912. *Notes of post mortem inquisitions taken in Sussex, 1 Henry VII to 1649 and after*. SRS 14.

Awty, B. 1987. A cast-iron cannon of the 1540s. *SAC* 125:115-23.

Backhouse, J. & others 1984. *The Golden Age of Anglo-Saxon art*.

Baker, A.R.H. 1966. Some evidences of a reduction in the acreage of cultivated lands in Sussex during the early fifteenth century. *SAC* 104: 1-5.

Baker, J.H. 1984. *The order of serjeants at law*. Selden Society, supplementary series 5.

Barker, E. 1947, 1948. Sussex Anglo-Saxon charters. *SAC* 86: 42-101, *SAC* 87:112-63.

Barlow, F. 1987. *Thomas Becket*.

Bates, D. ed. 1998. *Regista Regum Anglo-Normanorum*.

Batho, G. 1957. The Percies at Petworth, 1514-1632. *SAC* 95: 1-27.

Beamish, T. 1965. *Battle Royal: a new account of Simon de Montfort's struggle against king Henry III*. .

Beddard, R.A. 1968. The Sussex general election of 1695. *SAC* 106: 145-57.

Bedwin, O. 1976. The excavation of Ardingly fulling mill and forge 1975-6. *Post-Medieval Archaeology* 10: 34-64.

—— 1978. The excavation of a Romano-British site at Ranscombe Hill, South Malling, East Sussex, 1976. *SAC* 116: 241-54.

Bell, M. 1978. Saxon settlements and buildings in Sussex. In *The South Saxons*, ed. P. Brandon, 36-53.

Beswick, M. 1993. *The history of brick making in Sussex*.

Biddle, M. 1976. Towns. In *The archaeology of Anglo-Saxon England*, ed. D. M. Wilson, 99-150.

Biggar, J. 1978. A field survey of Houndean-Ashcombe and other downland fields west of Lewes 1972-75. *SAC* 116: 143-53.

Bindoff, S.T. 1982. *The history of Parliament: the House of Commons, 1509-58*. 3 volumes.

Blaauw, W.H. 1848. Remarks on the Nonae of 1340 as relating to Sussex. *SAC* 1: 58-64.

——1849a. Royal journies in Sussex from the Conquest to king Edward I. *SAC* 2: 132-60.

—— 1849b. On the early history of Lewes priory and its seals. *SAC* 2: 7-38.

—— 1849c. Letters of Edward, Prince of Wales, written in Sussex in the year 1305. *SAC* 2: 80-98.

—— 1850. On the Cluniac priory of Saint Pancras, at Lewes, its priors and its monks. *SAC* 3: 185-210.

—— 1851. On Streat Place, the ancient mansion of the Dobells. *SAC* 4: 93-100.

—— 1852. Passages of the Civil War in Sussex. *SAC* 5: 29-104.

—— 1853. Visit of Edward the Second to Battle and other parts of Sussex in 1324. *SAC* 6: 41-53.

—— 1856. Extracts from the *Iter Sussexiense* of Dr. John Burton. *SAC* 8: 250-65.

Blair, J. 1980. The Surrey endowments of Lewes priory before 1200. *Surrey Archaeological Collections* 72: 97-126.

—— 1997. Saint Cuthman, Steyning and Bosham. *SAC* 135: 173-92.

—— 1998. Bampton: an Anglo-Saxon minster. *Current Archaeology* 14 (4): 124-30.

Bleach, J. 1997. A Romano-British (?) barrow cemetery and the origins of Lewes. *SAC* 135: 131-42.

Blencowe, R.W. 1848. Extracts from the journal and account book of the Reverend Giles Moore. *SAC* 1: 65-127.

—— 1850. Extracts from the journal and account book of Timothy Burrell esq. *SAC* 3:

117-72.

—— 1851. Extracts from the parish registers. *SAC* 4: 243-90.

—— 1858. Extracts from manuscripts in the possession of William John Campion. *SAC* 10: 1-33.

—— 1859. Paxhill and its neighbour hood. *SAC* 11:1-49.

—— 1860. Extracts from the memoirs of the Gale family. *SAC* 12: 45-60.

—— & M.A. Lower. 1859. Extracts from the diary of a Sussex tradesman. *SAC* 11: 179-220.

Bond, E. 1853. The last days of Isabella, queen of Edward the Second. *Archaeologia* 35: 453-69.

Brandon, P.F. 1971a. Agriculture ... at Barnhorne, Sussex, during the late Middle Ages. *SAC* 109: 69-93.

—— 1971b. The origin of Newhaven and the drainage of the Lewes and Laughton levels. *SAC* 109: 94-106.

—— 1978. The South Saxon *Andredesweald*. In *The South Saxons*, ed. P. Brandon, 138-59.

—— 1998. *The South Downs*.

—— & B. Short. 1990. *A regional history of England: the South East from A.D.1000.*

Brent, C. 1973. *Employment, Land Tenure and Population in Eastern Sussex 1540-1640.* Sussex University Ph.D..

—— 1975. Urban employment and population in Sussex between 1550 and 1660. *SAC* 113: 35-50.

—— 1976, 1978. Rural employment and population in Sussex between 1550 and 1640. *SAC* 114: 27-48, *SAC* 116: 41-55.

—— 1983. The neutering of the Fellowship and the emergence of a Tory Party in Lewes, 1663-1688. *SAC* 121: 95-107.

—— 1985. Lewes Dissenters outside the Law, 1663-1686. *SAC* 123: 195-214.

—— 1993. *Georgian Lewes.*

—— 1995. *Historic Lewes.*

—— & J. Brent. 1993. The dedication of Saint Anne's church, Lewes. *SAC* 131: 200-1.

Brent, J. 1968. Alciston manor in the later Middle Ages. *SAC* 106: 89-102.

Brighton, T. 1987. An Arundel tomb: the monument. *Otter Memorial Paper* 1: 14-35.

Brodribb, G. 1980. A further survey of stamped tiles of the Classis Britannica. *SAC* 118: 183-96.

Brooke, C. 1985. *History of Gonville and Caius College.*

B[udgen], W. 1929. Guns bought for Eastbourne, 1550. *SNQ* 2: 146-7.

—— 1941. Sussex ports in 1204. *SNQ* 8: 153-4.

—— 1950. The manor of Chalvington. *SNQ* 13: 25-32.

Burchall, M.J. 1973-4. A Tillinghast genealogy. *Sussex Family Historian* 1: 57-9, 85-8.

Butler, C. 1999. The Romans at Barcombe. *Sussex Past & Present* 18: 7.

Butler, G.S. 1861. The vicars of Rye and their patrons. *SAC* 13: 270-6.

Button, J.V. 1805. *The Brighton and Lewes guide.*

Byng, J. 1954. A tour into Sussex 1788. In *The Torrington diaries: a selection from the tours of the Hon. John Byng between the years 1781 and 1794*, ed. C. B. Andrews, 111-34.

Caffyn, J. 1998. *Sussex schools in the 18th century.* SRS 81.

Caldecott, J.B. 1938. Sussex taverns in 1636. *SAC* 79: 61-73.

—— 1939-40. Sussex 17th century tokens. *British Numismatic Journal* 23: 301-20.

—— 1940. John Taylor's tour of Sussex in 1653. *SAC* 81: 19-30.

Camden, W. 1610. *Britannia* - Surrey and Sussex portion, ed. P. Holland, reprinted Reigate 1905.

Caplan, N. 1961. *An outline of the origins and development of Nonconformity in Sussex.* Part 1 1603-1803. Part 2, 1689-1724. Typescript in SAS Library.

—— 1977. Religious Dissent in Sussex in 1717. *SAS Newsletter* 21: 116-17.

Carlin, M. 1996. *Medieval Southwark.*

Carpenter, D. 1987. *The battles of Lewes and Evesham.*

—— 1996. *The reign of Henry III.*

Cattley, S.R. & Townsend, G. eds. 1837-42. J. Foxe, *Acts and Monuments.*

CChR. *Calendar of charter rolls.*

CCR. *Calendar of close rolls.*

Challen, W.H. 1943, 1946, 1958a. Sussex entries in London parish registers. *SNQ* 9: 135-9, *SNQ* 11: 57-62, *SNQ* 14: 157-62.

—— 1951. Court family. *SNQ* 13: 179-82.

—— 1955. Richard Russell, M.D. *SNQ* 14: 73-8.

—— 1958b. Edward Snatt. *SNQ* 15: 61.

—— 1962. The Kyme family of Lewes. *SAC* 100: 111-37.

Chamberlain, J.S. 1992. *'The Changes and Chances of this Mortal Life' ... High Churchmanship and politics among the clergy of Sussex, 1700-1745.* Chicago University Ph.D.

Chartulary 1: Salzman, L.F. ed. 1932. *The chartulary of the priory of St Pancras of Lewes.* SRS 38.

Chartulary 2: Salzman, L.F. ed. 1938. *The chartulary of the priory of St Pancras of Lewes.* SRS 40.

Charvin, G. ed. 1965-72. *Statutes, chapitres generaux et visites de l'ordre de Cluny.* 6 volumes.

Clarke, M. 1995. *The early endowments of Lewes priory ..., c1077-c1200.* Reading University M.Phil.

Clay, C.T. 1949. *Early Yorkshire charters: vol 8 The Honour of Warenne.* Yorkshire Record Society, extra series 6.

Clayton, C.E. 1892. Portions of old walls found at Lewes. *SAC* 38: 200-1.

Cleere, H. & D.W. Crossley, 1985. *The iron industry of the Weald.*

CLibR. *Calendar of Liberate Rolls.*

Clough, M., ed. 1964. *The Book of Bartholomew Bolney.* SRS 63.

—— 1969. *Two Fitzalan Surveys.* SRS 67.

Coad, J.G. & A.D.F. Streeten, 1982. Excavations at Castle Acre castle, Norfolk, 1972-77. *Archaeological Journal* 139: 138-301.

Coates, R. 1980. Studies and observations in Sussex place-names. *SAC* 118: 309-29.

—— 1990-1. The name of Lewes: some problems and possibilities. *The English Place-Name Society Journal* 23: 5-15.

—— 1997. The name of Lewes. *SAC* 135: 141-2.

—— 1998. Review of Forsberg (1997). *Locus Focus* 2, (2): 18-20.

—— 2001. Walwer's Lane, Lewes. *Locus Focus* 5, (5): 6.

Cockburn, J.S. ed. 1975a. *Calendar of assize records:Sussex indictments Elizabeth I.*

—— 1975b. *Calendar of assize records: Sussex indictments James I.*

Cokayne, G.E. 1910-98. *The complete peerage of England, Ireland , Great Britain and the United Kingdom, extant, extinct or dormant.* 14 volumes.

Comber, J. 1931. *Sussex genealogies (Horsham Centre).*

—— 1932. *Sussex genealogies (Ardingly Centre).*

—— 1933. *Sussex genealogies (Lewes Centre).*

Combes, P. & M. Lyne, 1995. Hastinge, Haestingaceaster and Haestingsport. *SAC* 133: 213-24.

Conant, K. J. 1959. *Carolingian and Romanesque architecture, 800 to 1200.*

Connell, J. M. 1916. *The story of an old Meeting House.*

Cooper, C. no date [1970s]. *Kingston open fields* (unpublished survey).

Cooper, G.M. 1853. Berwick parochial records. *SAC* 6: 223-43.

Cooper, J.H.1896. Cuckfield from the 11th to the 15th centuries. *SAC* 40: 173-210.

—— 1899. Cuckfield families. *SAC* 42: 19-53.

—— 1902-3. The vicars and parish of Cuckfield. *SAC* 45: 1-33, *SAC* 46: 94-113.

—— 1908. The manor of Cuckfield from the fourteenth to the nineteenth centuries. *SAC* 51: 79-94.

—— 1909. Cuckfield briefs. *SAC* 52: 24-31.

Cooper, W.D. 1851. Extracts from account books of the Everenden and Frewen families.

SAC 4: 22-30.

—— 1852. Queen Elizabeth's visits to Sussex. *SAC* 5: 190-7.

—— 1858. Smuggling in Sussex. *SAC* 10: 69-94.

—— 1865. Produce of and supplies from Sussex. *SAC* 17: 115-22.

—— 1866. Participation of Sussex in Cade's Rising, 1450. *SAC* 18:17-36.

—— 1867. Royalist compositions in Sussex during the Commonwealth. *SAC* 19: 91-120.

—— 1868. Racing in Sussex in 1727. *SAC* 20: 227-8.

Cornwall, J.C.K. ed. 1956. *The lay subsidy rolls for the county of Sussex, 1524-25.* SRS 56.

—— 1955. Forestry and the timber trade in Sussex, 1560-1640. *SNQ* 14: 85-91.

—— 1960. Agricultural improvement, 1560-1640. *SAC* 98: 118-132.

—— 1962. English country towns in the fifteen twenties. *Economic History Review*, second series, 1: 54-69.

—— 1976. Sussex wealth and society in the reign of Henry VIII. *SAC* 114: 1-27.

Couchman, J.E. 1911. Sussex church plate. *SAC* 54: 183-258.

Courthope, F.G. 1908. Extracts from the memoirs of Sir George Courthope, 1616-1685. *SAC* 51: 65-98.

CPR. *Calendar of patent rolls.*

CPRL. *Calendar of entries in the papal registers relating to Great Britain and Ireland: papal letters.*

CPRP. *Calendar of entries in the papal registers relating to Great Britain and Ireland: petitions.*

Craddock, J. 1979. The Anglo-Saxon cemetery at Saxonbury, Lewes, East Sussex. *SAC* 117: 85-102.

Crake, W.V. 1912. A notice of Maresfield Forge in 1608. *SAC* 55: 278-83.

Crook, B.M. 1940a. General history of Lewes priory in the twelfth and thirteenth centuries. *SAC* 81: 68-96.

—— 1940b. *The history of Lewes priory in the twelfth and thirteenth centuries.* Oxford University B.Litt..

Crossley, D.W.C. 1974. Ralph Hogge's ironworks accounts, 1576-81. *SAC* 112: 48-79.

CSPD. *Calendar of state papers domestic.*

Cunliffe, B. 1999. Togidubnus again. *Sussex Past & Present* 87: 15.

Curwen, E.C. 1934. Pipe stoppers. *SNQ* 5: 11-12.

—— 1942. An eel-spear from Lewes. *SNQ* 9: 81-2.

—— 1954. *The archaeology of Sussex.*

Dale, J. 1853. Extracts from churchwardens' accounts ... belonging to the parish of Bolney. *SAC* 6: 244-52.

Dalton, O.M. 1912. *Franks Bequest: catalogue of finger rings.*

Daniel-Tyssen, A. 1864. The church bells of Sussex. *SAC* 16: 138-232.

—— J.R. 1869. Survey of the church of the college of South Malling, near Lewes. *SAC* 21: 159-90.

—— 1871. The Parliamentary surveys of the county of Sussex, 1649-1653. *SAC* 23: 217-313.

—— 1873. Documents relating to Lewes priory. *SAC* 25: 136-51.

—— 1915. Sussex church bells. *SAC* 57: 1-118.

Darby, H.C. & E.M.J. Campbell. 1962. *The Domesday geography of South-east England.*

Davidson-Houston, C.E.D. 1935-7. Sussex monumental brasses. *SAC* 76: 46-114, *SAC* 77: 130-94, *SAC* 78: 63-125.

Davies, G. 1945. *The early Stuarts, 1603-1660.*

De Beer, E.S. 1937. Evelyn and colonel Herbert Morley in 1659 and 1660. *SAC* 78: 177-83.

—— ed. 1955. *The diary of John Evelyn.* 6 volumes.

De St Croix, W. 1868. Parochial history of Glynde. *SAC* 20: 47-90.

Deedes, C. ed. 1908, 1910. *Episcopal register of Robert Rede.* Parts 1 and 2, SRS 8 and 11.

Defoe D. 1927. *Daniel Defoe, A tour through England and Wales* , ed . E. Rhys. 2 volumes.

D'Elboux, R.H. 1947. Sussex monumental brasses: addenda. *SAC* 86: 118-25.

De-Laune, T. 1681. *The present state of London.*

Dell, R.F. 1964. *The Glynde Place archives*.

Dixon, H. 1851. An original account of the Springett family. *Gentleman's Magazine*, 365-74.

DNB: 1885-1901. *The dictionary of national biography*. 66 volumes.

Dobson, R.B. 1970. *The Peasants' Revolt of 1381*.

Dodson, F.H. 1880. St Mary's church, Barcombe. *SAC* 30: 52-62.

Domesday. James, S. & D.A. Seal, eds. 1990. *The Sussex Domesday*.

Drewett, P. 1988. Digging up Lewes castle. *Sussex Past & Present* 56: 3-6.

—— 1992. Excavations at Lewes Castle, East Sussex, 1985-1988. *SAC* 130: 69-106.

—— & S. Hamilton. 1999. Excavations and landscape studies at the Caburn hill fort, East Sussex, 1996-98. *SAC* 137: 7-37.

—— 2001. Caburn: sacred mount and classic hill fort. *Current Archaeology* 174: 256-62.

Du Boulay, F.R.H. 1952. Archbishop Cranmer and the Canterbury temporalities. *English Historical Review* 67: 19-36.

—— ed. 1957. *Registrum Thome Bourgchier Cantuariensis Archiepiscopi*. The Canterbury and York Society 54.

—— 1966. *The lordship of Canterbury: an essay on medieval society*.

Duckett, G.F. 1881. The Test and Penal Statutes in 1688. *SAC* 31: 1-24.

—— ed. 1888. *Charters and records among the archives of the ancient abbey of Cluni 1077-1534*. 2 volumes.

Dudley, C. 1978. Saxon and medieval mints and moneyers in Sussex. In *CBA Research Report* 29, ed. P. Drewett, 70-8.

Dugdale, Sir W. ed. 1849. *Monasticon Anglicanum*. 5 volumes.

Dulley, A.J.F. 1966. The level and port of Pevensey in the Middle Ages. *SAC* 104: 26-45.

—— 1967. Excavations at Pevensey. *Medieval Archaeology* 11: 209-32.

Dunkin, E.H.W. 1875. Contributions towards the ecclesiastical history of the deanery of South Malling. *SAC* 26: 9-96.

—— 1890, 1894. A Calendar of the deeds and other documents in the possession of the Sussex Archaeological Society. *SAC* 37: 39-110, *SAC* 39: 179-96.

—— ed. 1902. *Calendar of Sussex marriage licences recorded in the consistory court of the bishop of Chichester for the archdeaconry of Lewes*. SRS 1.

[Dunvan, P.] 1795. *Ancient and modern history of Lewes and Brighthelmston*.

Ellis, H. 1858a. Commissioners of sewers for the Lewes Levels. *SAC* 10: 95-9.

—— 1858b. Notices of Richard Curteys, bishop of Chichester 1570 to 1582. *SAC* 10: 53-6.

—— 1860. Notices of Crown presentations to rectories and vicarages in Sussex during the reign of queen Elizabeth. *SAC* 12: 256-60.

Ellis, W.S. 1859. The descent of the manor of Hurstpierpoint and its lords. *SAC* 11: 50-88.

Elphick, G.P. 1970. *Sussex bells and belfries*.

Emden, A.B. 1974. *Register of the University of Oxford, 1501-40*.

E[sdaile], A. 1941. A breviary-missal of Lewes priory. *SNQ* 8: 156-8.

Evans, J. 1931. *Monastic life at Cluny, 910-1157*.

Ewing, G. n.d. [c1927]. *A history of Cowden*.

Fairbank, F.R. 1907. The last earl of Warenne and Surrey. *Yorkshire Archaeological Journal* 19: 193-264.

Faraday, L. 1950. Sussex relics on exhibition in London. *Sussex County Magazine* 24: 61-6.

Farmer, D.H. 1992. *The Oxford dictionary of saints*.

Farmer, P.J. & N.C. 1979. *An introduction to Scarborough ware and a re-assessment of knights' jugs*.

Farrant, J. 1996. 'A garden in a desert place and a palace among the ruins': Lewes castle transformed, 1600-1850. *SAC* 134: 169-77.

—— 2001. *Sussex Depicted*. SRS 85.

—— , M.Howard, D.Rudling, & others. 1991. Laughton Place: a manorial and architectural history. *SAC* 129: 99-164.

Farrer, W. c1926. *Honors and knights fees,* volume 3.

Fenwick, C.C. 2001. *The poll taxes of 1377, 1379 and 1381.* 2 volumes.

Field, L.F. 1925. Meeching ferry and Stockferry. *SNQ* 5: 171-4.

Figg, W. 1848. On two relics found at Lewes. *SAC* 1: 43-5.

—— 1854. On *The Lantern* in the Cluniac priory of St Pancras Lewes. *SAC* 7: 150-7.

—— 1859. On Sussex tradesmens' tokens in the seventeenth century. *SAC* 11: 171-8.

—— 1861. Some memorials of Old Lewes. *SAC* 13: 1-48.

—— 1864. Extracts from documents illustrative of the Quakers in Lewes. *SAC* 16: 65-125.

Fitzhugh, M.C. 1873. Streat. *SAC* 25: 126-35.

Flack, A.M. 1948. *Southover Grange: a brief history.*

Fletcher, A. 1975. *A county community at peace and war: Sussex 1600-1660.*

Forsberg, R. 1997. The place-name Lewes. *Studia Anglistica Upsaliensia* 100.

Foster, J. ed. 1887-92. *Alumni Oxonienses.* 4 volumes.

Freke, D.J. 1975 Excavations in Lewes, 1974. *SAC* 113: 66-84.

—— 1976a. Further excavations in Lewes, 1975. *SAC* 114: 176-93.

—— 1976b. Further excavations in Lewes, East Sussex. In *Rescue Archaeology in Sussex 1975,* ed. P. Drewett, Bulletin of the Institute of Archaeology 13: 90-5.

—— 1978a. Excavations in Friar's Walk, Lewes, 1976. *SAC* 116: 179-97.

—— 1978b. Excavations in Church Street, Seaford. *SAC* 116: 199-224.

—— 1979. Excavations in Tanyard Lane, Steyning, 1977. *SAC* 117: 135-49.

Gage, J. 1831. Letter accompanying drawings of remains of the prior of Lewes' hostelry, in the parish of St. Olave, Southwark. *Archaeologia* 23: 299-308.

Galbraith, V.H. 1924. Press marks in the deeds of Lewes priory. *SAC* 65: 196-205.

—— 1954. Osbert Dean of Lewes. *English Historical Review* 69: 289-302.

Gardiner, M. 1989. Some lost Anglo-Saxon charters and the endowment of Hastings College. *SAC* 127: 39-48.

—— 1994. St Nicholas hospital: 100 bodies at medieval hospital, Sussex. *Sussex Past & Present* 73: 9.

—— 1995. Aspects of the history and archaeology of medieval Seaford. *SAC* 133: 189-212.

—— 1996a. Excavations at Lewes friary, 1985-6 and 1988-9. *SAC* 134: 71-123.

—— 1996b. The geography and peasant rural economy of the eastern Sussex High Weald, 1300-1420. *SAC* 134: 125-39.

—— 1999. Shipping and trade between England and the Continent during the eleventh century. *Anglo-Norman Studies* 22: 71-93.

—— & C. Greatorex, 1997. Archaeological excavations in Steyning, 1992-95. *SAC* 135: 143-71.

Gardner, J. ed. 1986. *Paston letters.*

Gem, R. 1998. Review of Lyne (1997). *The Archaeological Journal* 155: 411-12.

Gilbert, R. 1963. Lewes priory in 1772. *SNQ* 16: 194-8.

—— 1974. Evidence for tower transepts at the old church of St. John-sub-castro, Lewes. *SAC* 112: 44-7.

Glover, H.J. 1940. Fifteenth century glass in Westham church. *SNQ* 8: 19-20.

Godfrey, W.H. 1924. Reports of local Secretaries: Lewes. *SAC* 65: 260.

—— 1926a. *Notes on Lewes castle and other ancient buildings in Lewes.*

—— 1926b. *Some Lewes townsfolk of the Past.*

—— 1926c. The estate of George Goring. *SNQ* 1: 21-2.

—— 1927a. The parish churches of Lewes in the fourteenth century. *SAC* 68: 171-7.

—— 1927b. Lewes priory hospital and Southover church. *SNQ* 1: 201-3.

—— 1927c. No. 173 High Street, Lewes. *SAC* 68: 67-78.

—— 1928a. South Malling church. *SNQ* 2: 89.

—— 1928b. The church of St. Anne, Lewes; an anchorite's cell and other discoveries. *SAC* 69: 159-69.

—— 1928c. Reports of local Secretaries. *SAC* 69: 234.

—— 1928d. A carved figure from Lewes. *SNQ* 2: 21-2.

—— 1928e. Election expenses, Lewes, 1727. *SNQ* 2: 58-60.

—— 1929a. Review of *English Ecclesiastical Studies* by Rose Graham. *SNQ* 2: 196.

—— 1929b. The barbican, Lewes castle. *SAC* 70: 9-18.

—— 1929c. The family of Kyme in Lewes. *SNQ* 2: 182-3.

—— 1929-30. Thomas and Brian Twine. *SNQ* 2: 197-201, 229-33, *SNQ* 3: 40-2, 82-4.

—— 1930. Effigies and arms of Hassard, All Saints, Lewes. *SNQ* 3: 58-9.

—— 1931a. Sussex church plans ... South Malling. *SNQ* 3: 247.

—— 1931b. A fourteenth century hall at Hamsey. *SNQ* 3: 131-6.

—— 1931c. Trayton of Lewes, sketch pedigree. *SNQ* 3: 250-2.

—— 1933. St Thomas-at-Cliffe, Lewes. *SNQ* 4: 216-17.

—— 1936a. The parish church of St John the Baptist Southover. *SNQ* 6: 50-2.

—— 1936b. Tombs of the earl of Arundel and Eleanor his wife. *SNQ* 6: 56-7.

—— 1936c. Swanborough manor house. *SAC* 77: 2-14.

—— ed. 1938. *Transcripts of Sussex wills... by the late R. Garraway Rice*, vol. 2. SRS 42.

—— ed. 1939. *Transcripts of Sussex wills... by the late R. Garraway Rice*, vol. 3. SRS 43.

—— 1940. A Lewes man as king's smith in the thirteenth century. *SNQ* 8: 25-6.

—— 1942a. St John-Sub-Castro, church and site, Lewes. *SNQ* 9: 25-8.

—— 1942b. Barbican House, Lewes. *SAC* 82: 3-19.

—— 1943. The church of St Michael, Lewes. *SNQ* 9: 121-3.

—— 1947. St Mary's and Priory Cottage, Bramber. *SAC* 86: 102-17.

—— 1948 Review of *Southover Grange: A brief history*, by A. M. Flack. *SNQ* 12: 68-70.

—— 1950a. Letter from William Newton of Southover, 26 November, 1598. *SNQ* 12: 130-1.

—— 1950b. The White Hart and the Parker family. *SNQ* 12: 164-5.

—— 1953. *Lewes castle*. (4th edition).

—— 1954. Newcastle House, Lewes. *SAC* 92: 3-23.

—— 1955a. Sussex church plans: St Thomas at Cliffe, Lewes. *SNQ* 13: 156-7.

—— 1955b. Fifteenth-century sculpture from Lewes priory. *Antiquarians Journal* 35: 88.

—— 1955c. The High Street, Lewes. *SAC* 93: 1-33.

—— 1960. At the sign of the Bull, Lewes. *SAC* 98: 1-11.

Golding, B. 1980. The coming of the Cluniacs. *Proceedings of the Battle Conference* 3: 65-77.

Goodman, A. 1971. *The Loyal Conspiracy: the Lords Appellant under Richard II.*

Goring, J. 1978. The riot at Bayham Abbey, June 1525. *SAC* 116: 1-10.

—— 1981. The Fellowship of the Twelve in Elizabethan Lewes. *SAC* 119: 157-72.

—— 1996. Reformation and reaction in Sussex, 1554-1559. *SAC* 134: 141-54.

—— 2003. Burn Holy Fire: Religion in Lewes since the Reformation.

Graham, R. 1922. The Cluniac order and its English province. *Journal of the British Archaeological Association* 28: 169-73.

—— 1923. The Papal Schism of 1378 and the English province of the order of Cluny. *English Historical Review* 38: 481-95.

—— 1929. The English province of the order of Cluny in the fifteenth century. *English Ecclesiastical Studies.*

—— 1939. The history of the alien priory of Wenlock. *Journal of the British Archaeological Association*, series 4, 3: 117-40.

—— ed. 1952. *Registrum Roberti Winchelsey, Cantuariensis archiepiscopi*. The Canterbury and York Society 51.

Gratwick, A.S. & C. Whittick, 1995. The Loseley list of martyrs. *SAC* 133: 225-40.

Greatorex, C. 2000. *An archaeological field evaluation of the Lewes House site, High Street, Lewes, East Sussex*. Archaeology South-East, project no. 1240.

Green, C. 1980. Handmade pottery and society in late Iron Age and Roman Sussex. *SAC* 118: 69-86.

Green, E. 1886. On the words 'O Sapientia' in the Kalendar. *Archaeologia* 49: 219-42.

Green, J. 1991. Financing Stephen's War. *Proceedings of the Battle Conference* 14: 91-114.

Green, M.A.E. ed. 1889. *Calendar of the proceedings of the committee for compounding, 1643-1660,* part 1.

Greenway, D., ed. 2002. *Henry of Huntingdon: the history of the English People 1000-1154.*

Greenwood, J. 1973. *The posts of Sussex: the Chichester branch 1250-1840.*

Gregory, D. 1993. Ringmer pottery dig. *Sussex Past & Present* 71: 8.

Grose, F. 1772-87. *The antiquities of England and Wales.* 6 volumes.

Gunnis, R. no date [c.1964]. *Dictionary of British sculptors, 1660-1851.*

Gwilt, C.E. 1834. Letter addressed to John Gage. *Archaeologia* 25: 604-6.

Hadfield, J.I. 1981. The excavation of a medieval kiln at Barnett's Mead, Ringmer. *SAC* 119: 89-106.

Haines, W. & F.H. Arnold. 1879. Spershott's memoirs of Chichester (18th century). *SAC* 29: 219-31.

Harrison, D., ed. 1935. The Surrey portion of the Lewes chartulary. *Surrey Archaeological Collections* 43.

Harvey, I.M.W. 1991. *Jack Cade's rebellion of 1450.*

Harvey, J.H.H. 1944. *Henry Yevele.*

Hasler, P.W. 1981. *The history of Parliament: the House of Commons 1558-1603.* 3 volumes.

Hawkesbury (Lord). 1904. Catalogues of portraits at Compton Place and at Buxted Place. *SAC* 47: 82-108.

Hayton, D.W. & others. 2002. *The history of Parliament: the House of Commons 1690-1715.* 5 volumes.

Henning, B.D. 1983. *The history of Parliament: the House of Commons 1660-1690.* 3 volumes.

Hill, D. 1978. The origins of the Saxon towns. In *The South Saxons*, ed. P. Brandon, 179-89.

—— & Rumble, A.R. 1996. *The defence of Wessex: the burghal hidage and Anglo-Saxon fortifications.*

Hills, W.H. 1908. *The parliamentary history of Lewes Borough 1295-1885.*

Hoare, H.R. 1857. Notes on the church of St Margaret, Buxted. *SAC* 9: 208-22.

Hobbs, M. 1987. The Restoration correspondence of bishop Henry King. *SAC* 125: 139-53.

Hodges, R. 1989. *Dark Age economics: the origins of towns and trade AD 600-1000.*

Hodson, L.J. 1920. A seventeenth century account book. *SAC* 61: 61-4.

Holden, E.W. 1963. Excavations at the deserted medieval village of Hangleton. *SAC* 101: 54-181.

—— 1965a. Slate roofing in medieval Sussex. *SAC* 103: 67-78.

—— 1965b. Lava quern stones from Selmeston and Lewes. *SNQ* 16: 187-90.

—— 1989. Slate roofing in medieval Sussex - a reappraisal. *SAC* 127: 73-88.

—— & T. Hudson 1981. Salt-making in the Adur valley, Sussex. *SAC* 119: 117-48.

Holgate, M.S. 1926. Rivers in Ardingly. *SNQ* 1: 19-20.

—— 1929. The canons' manor of South Malling. *SAC* 70: 183-95.

—— 1931. The Sussex manors of Francis Carewe. *SNQ* 3: 173-5, 201-3.

—— 1937-8. The mutilated effigy in West Walton Church, Norfolk. *SNQ* 6: 2-6, 82-4, 221, *SNQ* 8: 91-2.

Holland, T.A. 1863. Poynings. *SAC* 15: 1-56.

Hollister, C.W. 1979. Henry I and the Anglo-Norman magnates. *Proceedings of the Battle Conference* 2: 93-107.

Homan, W.M. 1938. The marshes between Hythe and Pett. *SAC* 79: 199-223.

Hooke, D. 1988. *Anglo-Saxon settlements.*

Hope, W.H. St John. 1895. Castleacre priory. *Norfolk Archaeology* 12:105-57.

—— 1906. The Cluniac priory of St Pancras at Lewes. *SAC* 49: 66-88.

—— 1915 A Palatinate seal of John earl of Warenne, Surrey and Stratherne. *SAC* 57: 180-4.

Horsfield Lewes. Horsfield, T.J. 1824, 1827. *The history and antiquities of Lewes and its vicinity.* 2 volumes

—— supplement. 1832.

Horsfield Sussex. Horsfield, T.J. 1835. *The history, antiquities and topography of the county of Sussex.* 2 volumes.

Houghton, J. 1986. Burgage tenure and topography in Lewes, East Sussex. *SAC* 124: 119-28.

—— 1997. *Unknown Lewes.*

Houts, E. van. Forthcoming, The epitaph of Gundrada of Warenne. *Nova de Veteribus. Festschrift fur Paul Gerhard Schmidt.*

—— 2004. The Warenne view of the past 1066-1203. *Anglo-Norman Studies* 26: 103-21.

Hubbard, E. 1986. *The buildings of Wales: Clwyd.*

Hudson, T.P. 1980. The origins of Steyning and Bramber. *Southern History* 2: 11-29.

Hudson, W. 1901. The hundred of Eastbourne and its six 'Boroughs'. *SAC* 44: 199-201.

—— 1905. Extracts from the first book of the parish of Southover. *SAC* 48: 16-37.

—— ed. 1909. *The three earliest subsidies for the county of Sussex.* SRS 10.

Hunnisett, R.F. 1955. Treason by words. *SNQ* 14: 116-20.

—— 1957, 1960. Sussex coroners in the Middle Ages. *SAC* 95: 42-58. *SAC* 98: 44-70.

—— 1964-5. The last Sussex abjurations. *SAC* 102: 40-51. A postscript. *SAC* 103: 49-52.

—— 1966. Early Sussex cricket. *SNQ* 16: 217-21.

—— ed. 1985. *Sussex coroner's inquests 1485-1558.* SRS 74.

—— ed. 1996. *Sussex coroners' inquests 1558-1603.*

—— ed. 1998. *Sussex coroners' inquests 1603-1688.*

Hunt, N. 1967. *Cluny under saint Hugh.*

Hurst, J.G. 1980. Medieval pottery imports in Sussex. *SAC* 118: 119-24.

Huzel, J.P. 1971. Population change in an East Sussex town: Lewes 1660-1800. *Sussex Industrial History* 3: 2-19.

Jacob, E.F. ed. 1937-47. *The register of Henry Chichele, Archbishop of Canterbury.* The Canterbury and York Society 42, 45-47. 4 volumes.

Jenkins, P.R. 1982. The rise of a graduate clergy in Sussex 1570-1640. *SAC* 120: 161-9.

Johnston, G.D.J. 1956. The crossing of the Ouse after the battle of Lewes. *SNQ* 14: 169-71.

—— 1958. Ferries in Sussex: Stock Ferry (Ouse). *SNQ* 16: 305-11.

J[ohnston], G.D.J. 1969. Perambulations of the parish of Ringmer. *SNQ* 17: 73-8.

Johnston, P.M. 1915. Steyning church. *SAC* 57: 149-61.

—— 1919. Poling and the Knights Hospitallers. *SAC* 60: 67-91.

Jones, D.J. 1983. The cult of Saint Richard of Chichester in the Middle Ages. *SAC* 121: 79-86.

—— ed. 1993. *Saint Richard of Chichester.* SRS 79.

Jones, R. 1999. Anarchy in Sussex. *Sussex Past & Present* 89: 6.

Kay, J. 1982. Clayhill House. *Ringmer History Newsletter* 1: 28-36.

—— 1984. William Penn's visit to Ringmer. *Ringmer History Newsletter* 19: 2-3.

Kent, T. 2002. Sussex silver and its makers.

Ker, N.R. ed. 1964. *Medieval libraries of Great Britain.*

King, H.H. 1955-7. The coins of the Sussex mints: part 3: Lewes. *British Numismatic Journal* 28: 516-36.

Kirby, D.P. 1978. The Church in Saxon Sussex. In *The South Saxons*, ed. P. Brandon, 160-73.

Kitch, M.J. 1978. The Chichester cathedral chapter at the time of the Reformation. *SAC* 116: 277-92.

—— 1981 The Reformation in Sussex. In *Studies in Sussex Church History*, ed. M. J. Kitch, 77-98.

Kitchen, F. 1986. The ghastly war-flame. *SAC* 124: 179-91.

Knowles, D. 1942. Some aspects of the career of archbishop Pecham. *English Historical*

Review 57: 1-18.

—— 1950. *The monastic order in England 943-1216.*

—— 1962. *The religious orders in England.* Volume 1.

—— 1955. *The religious orders in England.* Volume 2.

—— 1959. *The religious orders in England.* Volume 3.

—— & Hadcock, R.V. 1971. *Medieval religious houses: England and Wales.*

—— & others. 1972. *The heads of religious houses in England and Wales 940-1216.*

Ladipo, S. 2000. *The memorial inscriptions of South Malling parish church, Lewes.*

Lambarde, F. 1927. Notes on the history of Goring and Covert. *SAC* 68: 79-88.

Larwood, J. & J.C. Hotten. 1951. *English inn signs.*

Lawrence, C.H. 1981. Saint Richard of Chichester. In *Studies in Sussex Church History,* ed. M. J. Kitch, 35-55.

Leadham-Green, E. & others. 1992. *Garett Godfrey's accounts, c1527-1533.*

Lefevre, P. 1989. *Justices and administration: the political development of Sussex 1660-1714.* Brighton University Ph.D.

Legg, L.G.W. ed. 1936. *Relation of a short survey of the western counties.* Camden Society, third series, 52.

Lennard, T.B. 1905. Extracts from the household account book of Herstmonceux Castle. *SAC* 48: 104-37.

Leppard, M.J. 1980. Quarter sessions in Elizabethan Sussex. *SAC* 118: 388-9.

—— 1991. East Grinstead before the town. *SAC* 129: 29-32.

Leroquais, V. 1935. *Le breviare-missal du prieure Clunisien de Lewes.*

Lewis, R. 1972. Archaeology and Lewes. *Sussex Archaeological Society Newsletter* 8: 30-1.

Lieberman, F. 1902. The annals of Lewes priory. *English Historical Review* 17: 61-9.

Lloyd, E. 1911. Leedes of Wappingthorne. *SAC* 54: 44-6.

Locke, A. 2001. Excavations at Clothkits warehouse extension, Brooman's Lane, Lewes. *SAC* 139: 227-34.

Louis, C. ed. 2000. *Records of early English drama - Sussex.*

Lower, M.A. 1845. *Curiosities of heraldry.*

—— 1846. *A handbook of Lewes.*

—— 1849. Iron works of the county of Sussex. *SAC* 2: 169-220.

—— 1851. On the Star Inn at Alfriston. *SAC* 4: 309-15.

—— 1854. Memorials of the town, parish and Cinque Port of Seaford. *SAC* 7: 73-150.

—— 1857a. Notices of the family of Miller of Burghill and Winkinghurst. *SAC* 9: 33-40.

—— 1857b. Notes on the churches of Newhaven and Denton. *SAC* 9: 89-101.

—— 1858. Inns and inn-signs in Sussex. *SAC* 10: 181-92.

—— 1860. Richard Leonard: Brede furnace 1636. *SAC* 12: 270.

—— 1862a. The De Warenne 'chequy' in architecture. *SAC* 14: 268.

—— 1862b. Parochial history of Chiddingly. *SAC* 14: 207-52.

—— 1865. *The Worthies of Sussex.*

—— 1866. The antiquities preserved in the museum of Lewes Castle. *SAC* 18: 60-73.

—— 1867. On some old parochial documents relating to Lindfield. *SAC* 19: 36-52.

—— 1868. Sir William Springett and the Springett Family. *SAC* 20: 34-46.

—— 1870. *A compendious history of Sussex.*

—— 1872. Newspaper cuttings relating to Sussex. *SAC* 24: 139-44.

—— & W.D. Cooper, 1865. Further memorials of Seaford. *SAC* 17: 141-63.

LP HVIII. *Letters and Papers of Henry VIII.*

Lucas, J.C. 1869. Anglo-Saxon coins found in Sussex. *SAC* 21: 219-20.

Lyne, M. 1995. *The pottery from Beddingham Roman Villa.* Typescript in SAS Library.

—— 1997. *Lewes priory: excavations by Richard Lewis 1969-82.*

Lyon-Turner, G. 1911-14. *Original records of Nonconformity under Persecution and Indulgence.* 3 volumes.

Lysons, S. 1815. *The remains of a Roman villa discovered at Bignor in Sussex.*

435

McCann, T. J. 1979. William Bullaker, 1531-1608, Grammarian and Phonetician. *SAC* 117: 174-84.

——— 1981. The clergy and the Elizabethan Settlement in the diocese of Chichester. In *Studies in Sussex Church History*, ed. M.J. Kitch, 99-123.

McCarthy, E. & M. 1979. *Sussex River*.

Malden, H.E. 1926. Old roads from the Sussex coast. *SNQ* 1: 7-10.

Manning, R.B. 1968. Anthony Browne, 1st viscount Montague. *SAC* 106: 103-12.

Mantell. Curwen, E. C. ed. 1940. *The journal of Gideon Mantell*.

Mantell, G.A. 1846a. *A day's ramble in Lewes*.

——— 1846b. A few remarks on the discovery of the remains of William de Warren and his wife Gundrad. *Archaeologia* 31: 430-7.

Marchant. Turner, T. ed. 1873. The Marchant diary, 1714-1728. *SAC* 25: 163-203

Margary, I.D. 1949. *Roman ways in the Weald*.

Marsden, F. 1979. Roman pewter plate from Glynde. *SAC* 117: 229-30.

——— 1983. Lewes priory mount. *SAC* 12: 69-73.

Martin, C.T. 1882-1885. *Registrum Epistolarum Fratris Johannis Peckham, Archiepiscopi Cantuariensis*. Rolls Series. 3 volumes.

Martin, D. & B. 1997. *Fairhall, High Street, Southover, Lewes, East Sussex*. Archaeology South-East, project report 604.

Mason, I. 1990. Arundel borough 1586-1677. *SAC* 128: 157-75.

Mason, J.F.A. 1964. The rapes of Sussex and the Norman conquest. *SAC* 102: 68-93.

Matthews, A.G. 1934. *Calamy Revised*.

——— 1988. *Walker Revised*.

Mawer, A. & F.M. Stenton. 1929-30. *The place-names of Sussex*. 2 volumes. English Place-Name Society 6, 7

Mayr-Harting, H. ed. 1964. *The Acta of the Bishops of Chichester 1075-1207*. The Canterbury and York Society 56.

——— 1981. Saint Wilfrid in Sussex. In *Studies in Sussex Church History*, ed. M. J. Kitch, 1-17.

Mayhew, G. 1982. Religion, faction and politics in Reformation Rye, 1530-59. *SAC* 120: 139-60.

——— 1983. The progress of the Reformation in east Sussex, 1530-1559. *Southern History* 5: 38-67.

Meekings, C.A.F. ed. 1979. *The 1235 Surrey eyre*. Surrey Record Society 31.

Melville, A.M.M. 1931. *The pastoral custom and local wool trade of medieval Sussex 1085-1485*. London University MA.

Miller, J. 1973. *Popery and politics in England 1660-1688*.

Milner-Gulland, R. 2003. Clayton, Coombes, Plumpton. *Friends of Sussex Churches Trust Newsletter* 2-3.

Moore. Bird, R. ed. 1971. *The journal of Giles Moore 1656-1679*. SRS 68.

Morris, R. 1989. *Churches in the landscape*.

Mosse, H.R.1933. *The monumental effigies of Sussex (1250-1650)*.

Murray, J.W. 1965. The origin of some medieval roofing slates from Sussex. *SAC* 103: 79-82.

Nairn, I. & N. Pevsner 1965. *The buildings of England: Sussex*.

Newman, J. 1969a. *The buildings of England: north east and east Kent*.

——— 1969b. *The buildings of England: west Kent and the Weald*.

Norman, M. 1989. *Marlipins Museum*.

Norris, N. 1951-69. *Archeological papers and plans*. Working papers in the SAS Library.

——— 1955. Excavations on the site of the Lords Place, Southover. *SAC* 94: xxxvi.

——— 1956. Miscellaneous researches 1949-56. *SAC* 94: 1-12.

——— & E. Hockings 1951. The early Norman chapel at Balsdean. *Sussex County Magazine* 25: 222-5.

Noyes, T.H. 1857. Some notices of the family of Newton. *SAC* 9: 312-42.

O'Shea, E.W. 1980. Further finds from Lewes excavations 1974-7. *SAC* 118: 369-73.

Page, T.B. 1973. Excavations at Edward Street, Lewes, 1971. *SAC* 111: 113-14.

Page, W. 1853. *Guide to Lewes*.

Peckham, W.D. 1929. The first and last heraldic visitation of Sussex. *SNQ* 2: 202-7.

—— ed. 1941. *The chartulary of the High Court of Chichester*. SRS 46.

Pelham, A. & D. Mclean. 1931. *Some early Pelhams*.

Pelham, R.A. 1928. Timber exports from the Weald during the 14th century. *SAC* 69: 170-82.

—— 1929. The foreign trade of Sussex 1300-1350. *SAC* 70: 93-118.

—— 1930. Some further aspects of Sussex trade during the fourteenth century. *SAC* 71: 171-204.

—— 1931. Studies in the historical geography of medieval Sussex. *SAC* 72: 157-84.

—— 1932. The distribution of wool merchants in Sussex c1330. *SNQ* 4: 65-7.

—— 1933a. Further evidence of the methods of transporting produce in mediaeval Sussex. *SNQ* 4: 129-31.

—— 1933b. Exportation of wool from Sussex in the early 14th Century. *SAC* 74: 131-9.

—— 1933. The distribution of wool merchants in Sussex in 1296. *SNQ* 4: 161-3.

—— 1934a. The distribution of sheep in Sussex in the early fourteenth century. *SAC* 75: 128-35.

—— 1934b. Further evidence of the distribution of wealth in medieval Sussex: the ship-masters. *SNQ* 5: 18-19.

—— 1934c. Sussex provision for the siege of Calais 1346. *SNQ* 5: 33-4.

—— 1935a-b. Sussex wool ports in the thirteenth century: 2 Shoreham. *SNQ* 5: 137-41, 3 Seaford. *SNQ* 5: 166-71.

Perry, M. 1998. *Sisters to the King*.

Pevsner, N. 1957. *The buildings of England: Northumberland*.

—— 1962. *The buildings of England: north-west and south Norfolk*.

—— 1967. *The buildings of England: Yorkshire the West Riding*.

Phillips, C.J. no date [c1927]. *The history of the Sackville family*.

Phillips, C.T. 1890. Local presentations to the Society's museum. *SAC* 37: 199.

—— 1892. Relics of ancient Lewes. *SAC* 38: 225.

—— 1894a. Relics of the church of St Peter Westout, Lewes. *SAC* 39: 216.

—— 1894b. 'La Peryne', St Michael's, Lewes. *SAC* 39: 223-4.

Phillips, M. 1892, 1893. Pedigree and genealogical memoranda relating to the family of Pellatt. *SAC* 38: 99-128, *SAC* 39: 55-93.

Povey, K. 1928. Saint Lewinna, the Sussex martyr. *Sussex County Magazine* 2: 280-91.

Power, D. 2002. The French interests of the marshal earls of Striguil and Pembroke, 1189-1234. *Anglo-Norman Studies* 25: 199-225.

Powicke, M. 1964. *The battle of Lewes*.

Prestwich, M. 1988. *Edward I, king of England*.

Prince, C.L. 1882. List of Sussex nobility and gentry in 1673. *SAC* 32: 223-8.

Pugin, A.W.N. 1836. *Contrasts*. Reprint Leicester University Press 1969.

Pullein, C. 1928. *Rotherfield*.

Pye, D.W. 1965. The Magnus inscription. *SNQ* 16: 181-4.

Raach, J.H. 1962. *A directory of English country physicians, 1603-1643*.

Radcliffe, A.F. 1925. Dobell of Streat. *SAC* 66: 123-35.

Ray, J.E. ed. 1930. *Sussex Chantry Records*. SRS 36.

Reader, F.W. 1936. Tudor domestic wall-paintings. *Archaeological Journal* 93: 221-62.

Rector, W.K. 1978. Lewes Quakers in the seventeenth and eighteenth centuries. *SAC* 116: 31-40.

Redwood, B.C. & A.E. Wilson eds. 1958. *Custumals of the Sussex manors of the archbishop of Canterbury*. SRS 57.

Renshaw, W.C. 1905. *Miscellaneous records for the county of Sussex*. SRS 4.

—— 1906. Notes from the act books of the archdeaconry court of Lewes. *SAC* 49: 47-65.

—— 1907. Notes from the act books of the court for the deanery of South Malling. *SAC* 50: 41-6.

—— 1909. Alleged witches at Hove. *SAC* 52: 192.

—— 1910. East Sussex churches in 1586. *SAC* 53: 1-4.

—— 1912. Some clergy of the archdeaconry of Lewes and South Malling deanery. *SAC* 55: 220-77.

—— 1916. A pigeon-house at Rodmell. *SAC* 58: 197.

Reynolds, A. 1999. *Late Anglo-Saxon England: life and landscape.*

Reynolds, P.K.B. 1997. *Castle Acre priory.*

Rice, R.G. 1902. The household goods etc. of Sir John Gage of West Firle, Sussex, 1556. *SAC* 45: 114-27.

—— 1903. The testament and will of Agnes Morley. *SAC* 46: 134-44.

—— ed. 1924. *Sussex Apprentices and Masters, 1710-1752.* SRS 28.

Roskell, J.S. & others. 1992. *The history of Parliament: the House of Commons 1386-1431.* 4 volumes.

Ross, T. 1871. Hastings documents. *SAC* 23: 85-118.

Rothwell, H. ed. 1975. *English historical documents, 1189-1327.*

Round, J.H. ed. 1888. *Ancient charters.* Pipe Roll Society 10.

—— 1896. Some early grants to Lewes Priory. *SAC* 40: 58-78.

—— 1899. Some early Sussex charters. *SAC* 42: 75-86.

—— 1921. The Lords Poynings and St John. *SAC* 62: 1-20.

—— 1930. Sussex in the pipe rolls under Henry II. *SAC* 71: 97-105.

Rouse, J. 1825. *The beauties and antiquities of the county of Sussex.*

Rowe. Godfrey, W.H. ed. 1928. *The Book of John Rowe ... 1597-1622.* SRS 34.

Rudling, D. 1983a. Trial excavations in Brooman's Lane, Lewes, 1979. *SAC* 121: 53-62.

—— 1983b. A trial excavation on the site of the Grey Friars, Lewes. *SAC* 121: 66-9.

—— 1989. Continental coins in medieval Sussex. *SAC* 127: 245-6.

—— 1991. Excavations at Cliffe, Lewes. *SAC* 129: 165-81.

—— 1992. An Iron Age gold coin from South Malling. *SAC* 130: 238.

—— 1998. The development of Roman villas in Sussex. *SAC* 136: 41-65.

—— & C. Butler. 2001. Barcombe Roman villa. *Sussex Past & Present* 95: 6-7.

Sackville-West, R.W. ed. 1859a. *The works of Thomas Sackville, lord Buckhurst.*

—— 1859b. 'A rolle of the severall Armors and furniture'. *SAC* 11: 225-7.

Sackville-West, V. ed. 1923. *The diary of the Lady Anne Clifford.*

Sadie, S. ed. 2001. *The new Grove dictionary of music and musicians.*

Sadler, A.G. 1988. *The lost monumental brasses of Sussex.*

Salzman, L.F. 1901. *History of Hailsham.*

—— 1906. Documents relating to Pevensey Castle. *SAC* 49: 1-30.

—— 1910. The inning of Pevensey Levels. *SAC* 53: 32-60.

—— 1911. Early churchwardens' accounts, Arlington. *SAC* 54: 85-112.

—— 1914. Plumpton and the Springett family. *SAC* 56: 199-200.

—— ed. 1916. *An abstract of feet of fines relating to the county of Sussex....* SRS 23.

—— 1921. Roman coins found at Newhaven. *SAC* 62: 201.

—— 1922. Sussex Domesday tenants III: William de Cahagnes and the family of Keynes. *SAC* 63: 180-202.

—— 1923. The castle of Lewes. *SAC* 64:134-9.

—— 1924. *The parish register of Glynde, Sussex.* SRS 30.

—— 1925a. Some Sussex miracles. *SAC* 66: 62-82.

—— 1925b. The family of Chesney. *SAC* 66: 236-7.

—— 1928a. A litigious anchorite. *SNQ* 2: 135-7.

—— 1928b. The early heraldry of Pelham. *SAC* 69: 53-70.

—— 1934. The borough of Lewes in 1498. *SNQ* 5: 65-70, 97-101.

—— 1935a. Officers of the Staple at Chichester. *SNQ* 5: 163-5.

—— 1935b. The last prior of Lewes. *SAC* 76: 178-82.

—— 1938. The family of Aguillon. *SAC* 79: 45-60.

—— 1942a. The hundred roll for Sussex, part 1. *SAC* 82: 20-34.

—— 1942b. Sussex excommunicates. *SAC* 82: 124-40.

—— 1942c. The Sacking of Lewes castle, 1381. *SNQ* 9: 94.

—— 1942d. Pottery from the site of the Star Inn, Lewes. *SNQ* 9: 92.

—— 1943, 1945. The Hundred Roll for Sussex. *SAC* 83: 35-54, *SAC* 84: 60-81.

—— 1947. A strange coincidence. *SNQ* 11: 110-11.

—— 1953. The property of the earl of Arundel, 1397. *SAC* 91: 32-52.

—— 1954. Sussex religious at the Dissolution. *SAC* 92: 24-36.

—— 1960-1. Early taxation in Sussex. *SAC* 98: 29-43, *SAC* 99: 1-19.

—— 1964. The Arms of Lewes. *SNQ* 16: 109-11.

—— 1968a. *Edward I.*

—— 1968b. Poll tax in Lewes, 1378. *SNQ* 17: 49-52.

Saul, N. 1986. *Scenes from provincial life: knightly families in Sussex, 1280-1400.*

—— 1997a. The Sussex gentry and the oath to uphold the acts of the Merciless Parliament. *SAC* 135: 221-39.

—— 1997b. *Richard II.*

—— 1998. The rise of the Dallingridge family. *SAC* 136: 123-32.

Sawyer, F.E. 1879. The ecclesiastical history of Brighton. *SAC* 29: 191-5.

—— 1880. The White Lion: an extinct inn at Lewes. *SAC* 30: 245-7.

—— 1880-1, 1888b. Proceedings of the committee of plundered ministers relating to Sussex. *SAC* 30: 112-136, *SAC* 31: 169-200, *SAC* 36: 136-59.

—— 1887. East Sussex population and sects in 1724. *SAC* 35: 191-2.

—— 1888a. Sussex markets and fairs. *SAC* 36: 180-92.

Sawyer, F.J. 1896. The 'great pigeon-house' of the Cluniac Priory of St. Pancras, Lewes. *SAC* 40: 270-1.

Sawyer, J. 1899. *Guide to Lewes.*

Sawyer, P.H. 1968. *Anglo-Saxon charters: an annotated list and bibliography.*

Schofield, J. 1994. *Medieval London houses.*

Schubert, H.R. 1957. *History of the British iron and steel Industry.*

Scott, E. 1993. *A gazetteer of Roman villas in Britain.*

Searle, E. 1974. *Lordship and community: Battle abbey and its banlieu.*

—— 1980. The abbey of the Conqueror. *Proceedings of the Battle Conference* 2: 154-64.

Searle, E. & B. Ross eds. 1967. *The cellarers' rolls of Battle abbey.* SRS 65.

Shorter, A.H. 1951. Paper-mills in Sussex. *SNQ* 13: 169-74.

Silvester, R.J. 1985. West Walton: the development of a siltland parish. *Norfolk Archaeology* 39: 101-17.

Slocock, G. ed. 1999. *Saint Anne in history and art.*

Smail, H. 1949. *The Worthing map story.*

Smart, T.W.W. 1857. Extracts from the MSS of Samuel Jeake. *SAC* 9: 45-7.

—— 1881. A notice of the Reverend John Allin, vicar of Rye. *SAC* 31: 123-56.

Spokes, S. 1929, 1932. Reports of local Secretaries: Lewes. *SAC* 70: 221-2, *SAC* 73: 207-8.

Spurrell, F. 1853. Architectural relics of Lewes priory. *SAC* 6: 253-64.

Stapley. Turner, T. ed. 1849. Diary of Richard Stapley. *SAC* 2: 102-28.

Stenning, A.H. 1887. A Return of the Members of Parliament for ... Sussex. *SAC* 35: 127-64.

Stenning, J.C. 1868. Notes on East Grinstead. *SAC* 20: 132-74.

Stevens, F.B. 1911. The dedication of St. Anne's church, Lewes. *SAC* 54: 268.

—— 1958. Manors of Meeching and Plompton-Piddinghoe. *SNQ* 15: 39-42.

Stewart, I. 1978. The Sussex mints and their moneyers. In *The South Saxons,* ed. P. Brandon, 89-137.

Stoneham, E.T. 1967. *Martyrs of Jesus.*

Straker, E. 1931. *Wealden iron.*

—— 1933. Building costs in 1711. *SNQ* 4: 248-9.

—— ed. 1934. *The Buckhurst terrier 1597-1598*. SRS 39.

—— 1935. Old Sussex farm leases. *SNQ* 5: 193-5.

Swales, R.J. 1976. The Howard interest in Sussex elections, 1529 to 1558. *SAC* 114: 49-60.

Tate, W.E. 1949. Sussex inclosure acts and awards. *SAC* 88: 115-56.

Taylor, A.J., ed. 1939. *Records of the barony and honour of the rape of Lewes*. SRS 44.

Taylor, C.1988. *The archaeology of gardens*.

Taylor, J.G. 1937. *The parish church of saint Leonard, Seaford*.

Tebbutt, C.F. 1975. Old Buxted Place. *SAC* 113: 51-3.

—— 1979. Three Roman bloomery furnaces at Hartfield. *SAC* 117: 47-56.

Teesdale, E. 1984. *The Queen's gunstonemaker*.

Testamenta Eborasensia. 1836. *Surtees Society Publications* 4, 41-5.

Thirsk, J., ed. 1967. *The agrarian history of England and Wales, 1500-1640*.

Thomas, G. 2001. An archaeological discovery on Brack Mount, Lewes. *SAC* 139: 224-7.

—— 2002. Teeth worn down like Iguanadons. *Sussex Past & Present* 96: 4-5.

Thomas-Stanford, C. 1910. *Sussex in the Great Civil War and the Interregnum*.

—— 1918. The Sussex musters of 1618. *SAC* 59: 116-25.

—— 1921. The manor of Radynden. *SAC* 62: 71-6.

Thompson , K. 1997. Lords, castellans, constables and dowagers: the rape of Pevensey. *SAC* 135: 209-20.

Thomson, D. 1967. Green Wall (Lewes). *SNQ* 16: 337-9.

Thorburn, M. 2001. *An account of the manor of Hyde*.

Thulesius, O. 1992. *Nicholas Culpeper*.

Thurlby, M. 1982. A twelfth-century figure fragment from Lewes priory. *SAC* 120: 215-22.

Tierney, M.A. 1834. *The history and antiquities of the castle and town of Arundel*.

Torr, V.J. 1920. The Elizabethan return of the state of the diocese of Chichester. *SAC* 61: 114-18.

—— 1964. Sir Stephen Glynne's notes on churches. *SNQ* 16: 96-101.

Town Book 1. Salzman, L. F. ed. 1945. *The Town Book of Lewes, 1542-1701*. SRS 48.

Town Book 2. Smith, V. ed. 1972. *The Town Book of Lewes, 1702-1837*. SRS 70.

Toy, S. 1953. Langney Grange, Westham. *SAC* 91: 125-33.

T.S. 1938. A Lewes spoon. *SNQ* 7: 85-6.

Tudor-Craig, P. 2003. The angels displaying the unveiled Cross. *Friends of Sussex Churches Trust Newsletter* 4-5.

Turner, E. 1852. The college of Benedictine canons at South Malling. *SAC* 5: 127-42.

—— 1856. Seal of South Mallyng College. *SAC* 8: 270.

—— 1857. The Kidders of Maresfield. *SAC* 9: 125-37.

—— 1865. Battel Abbey. *SAC* 17: 1-56.

—— 1866. Isfield Place, with notes respecting the family of Shurley. *SAC* 18: 124-40.

—— 1866. The Stapley diary. *SAC* 18: 151-62.

—— 1867. High roads in Sussex. *SAC* 19: 153-69.

—— 1868. Saint Anne's Hill, Midhurst. *SAC* 20: 175-9.

—— 1869. Briefs. *SAC* 21: 207-17.

—— 1870. Memoir of Henry Smith. *SAC* 22: 30-49.

—— 1871. On the domestic habits and mode of life of a Sussex gent. *SAC* 23: 36-72.

—— 1872. A brief sketch of the history of John Rowe. *SAC* 24: 85-98.

Tyler, E.J. 1994. *The clockmakers of Sussex*.

VCHS. *Victoria County History of Sussex*. 1 1905, 2 1907, 6(1) 1980, 6(2) 1986, 7 1940, 9 1937.

Venables, E. 1851. The castle of Herstmonceux and its lords. *SAC* 4: 125-202.

Venn, J. 1897-1901. *History of Gonville and Caius College Cambridge*. 3 volumes.

Venn, J. & J.A. 1922-54. *Alumni Cantabrigienses*. 10 volumes.

Walker, S. 1983. Lancaster v. Dallingridge: a franchisal dispute in the fourteenth century.

440

SAC 121: 87-94.

Warne, H. 1989. Stanmer: a restructured settlement. *SAC* 127: 189-210.

—— ed. 1994. *Wivelsfield: the history of a Wealden parish.*

Warren, W.L. 1961. *King John.*

Watkin, D. & others. 1984. *A house in Town: 22 Arlington Stree: its owners and builders.*

Watson, A.G. 1984. *Catalogue of dated and datable manuscripts c. 435-1600 in Oxford libraries,* volume 1.

Watson, J. 1782. *Memoirs of the ancient Earls of Warren and Surrey.*

Way, T. 2000. *Deans of the college of canons, South Malling.*

Webb, C. & A.E. Wilson eds. 1952. *The Ancient Customs of Brighthelmston 1580.*

Wedgwood, J.C. 1936. *History of parliament: biographies of the members of the Commons House 1439-1509.*

Welch, M. 1989. The kingdom of the South Saxons: the origins. In *The origins of Anglo-Saxon kingdoms,* ed. S. Bassett, 75-83.

Whatmore, L.E. 1979. *Saint Lewinna: East Sussex martyr.*

Wheatley, H.B. ed. 1956. *Stow's survey of London.*

Whistler, R.F. 1883. The Ashburnham registers. *SAC* 33: 49-68.

—— 1888. The relics of king Charles I at Ashburnham Place. *SAC* 36: 161-71.

Whitley, H.M. 1902. The churchwarden's accounts of St Andrew's and St. Michael's, Lewes. *SAC* 45: 40-61.

—— 1919. Relics at Wisborough Green church. *SAC* 60:143.

Whittick, C. 1983. R. v. Walson: new light on a medieval mugging. *SAC* 121: 213-15.

Wilde, S.D. 1851. Fletching parish and church. *SAC* 4: 231-42.

Willett, M. 1916. Old Sussex iron. *SAC* 58: 197-8.

Williams, A. 1981. Land and power ... the estate of Harold Godwinson. *Proceedings of the Battle Conference* 3: 171-87.

Williams, C. 1904. The pedigree of Sir Thomas Browne. *Norfolk Archaeology* 15: 109-13.

Willis, R. 1868. The architectural history of ... Christ Church in Canterbury. *Archaeologia Cantiana* 7: 158-199.

Wood, P.D. 1976. East Grinstead borough in the Middle Ages. *East Grinstead Society Bulletin* 19: 5-6,10.

—— 1996. East Grinstead in the Domesday survey. *East Grinstead Society Bulletin* 58: 3-23.

Woodruff, C.E. 1910. A survey of the estates of the dean and chapter of Canterbury. *SAC* 53: 192-7.

Wooldridge, J.A. ed. 1966. *The Danny archives.*

Young, Rev. A. 1813. *A general view of the agriculture of the county of Sussex.*

Ziegler, P. 1998. *The Black Death.*

Persons index

Inclusive of Lewesians c1500-1714;
otherwise selective

Nath, 382; Nich, 274 276; Ri, 274 302 308 330 371; T, 322 339 377; W, 346; W II, 346
Russinoll, W, prior, 79

Sackville, earls of Dorset, Alice (nee Colson), 221; Anne Ldy Clifford, 231-3 292-3; Chas, 365; Edw, 290 293 297 306; Ri, 209 232-3 237-8 275 280-1 286 291-3 345; Ri II, 365 374 376 386; Ro, 221 224 229 232 245; T, 218-19 221-2 224 226-33 237-9 242 245 248 255 279; -- H, invalid, 221 274 293; Sir Ri, 218 222 238; (Chiddingly), J, 133
St John, Edw, 166; Ldy Joan, 166
Salter, Geo, 382-3
Samboyce, Mary, 271 291
Sampson, Ri, bishop, 204
Sancroft, W, archbishop, 316-17 386
Sanderford, W, 279
Saunder(s), Fra, 341; Ri, 337; T, 97 212 229
Savage, J, 308; Ri, 328
Saverie, the lyneter, 142
Saxby, Ri, 360
Saxpes, J, 276
Scot, Warren, wool-dealer, 127
Scotson, J, 304; T, 274
Scras, Alan, auditor, 198
Scripps, Edw, 336
Seager, Geo, 275 298
Seaman, T, 339
Se(a)war, J, 333, 380
Seffrid, bishop, 96
Selverleg, W, MP, 138
Senock, Dr J, monk, 195 199 200
Serle, J, legal advisor, 138
Sermerye [St Mary], Geof atte, 93
Sexbyrht, 22
Shareshulle, Ri, goldsmith, 182
Sharp, J (Sharpsbridge), 132 180
Sheldon, Gilb, archbishop, 366
Shelley (Southover & Westout), Hannah (nee Pellatt), 345; H, MP, 298 305-6 312 314 371; H II, 343-5 368-9 373-5 378-9; Martha (nee Coby), 368 371; Ri, 345 348 373 388-9; -- Nich, 310
Shelton, Geo, 360
Sheppard, H, parson, 347
Sherman, als Baker, Joan, 190; J, 190 275; J II, 190; T, 190
Shore, J, parson, 380-1 386; Ph, 380
Shoulder, Dan, 255; Geo, 284; Mary, 330
Shurley, Edw, 227; J, 227-8 232-3 239 275; Sir J, 266; T, 228
Sikelfoot, Gilb, coroner, 69 138 145

Simes, J, 333
Slade, J, 355 358
Slutter, T, 242 278; Wid, 278
Smith, Smyth, Emma, 257; J, 132 180; Ro, 400; W, cloth merchant, 179; Zachery, minister, 350 369 372
Smither, Geo, 281
Snashall, Sam, 342-3 384
Snatt, Edw, 309; Ri, 298; St, 308 331 365 367 373 392; T, 247; W, 349 380-1 386
Snelingius, fisherman, 141
Snell, Simon, 351
Southcote, J MP, 210
Southease, W of, wool-dealer, 127
Southwell, J, (MP), 161
Sparkes, H, 280
Spence, Anne (nee Trevor), 383; J I, 383; J II, 358 377 382-3 390; Trevor, 383; W, 305 312 361 367 379
Spencer, Agnes, 234
Springett, Gulielma Maria Posthuma, 300 310; Harbert, 273-4 276 287 296 301 305; Katherine, 296; Ldy Mary (nee Proude), 296 300; Sir T, 276 292 296 305; Sir W, 296, 300-1
Stafford, J, archbishop, 190; T, 381
Standen, Ro, 284 298
Standing, J, 296
Stanimough, W, 308-9
Stansfield, Eleanor, 271; Jane, 271 295; J, 258 270-1 275 287 292-5 298
Stapley, Patcham, Ant, regicide, 291-2 294 297-9 300 305-6 312 315 358; Ant II, 312-13; Douglas, 382; Herb, 360; Sir J, 277 286 312-13 315-16 360 364 372 376 382; -- Twineham, Ant, 340; Ant II, 340; Ri, 339-41 359; -- Ro, butcher, 257; St, regis-trar, 273; W, glover, 331
Starr, Comfort, minister, 384; Geo, 384; Jos, 384
Steer, Geo, parson, 393
Stempe, J, 161 177; J II, 197-8; J III, 211-12 218 234-5 245-6 282; W, 246
Stent, Nich, 389
Stephen of Rouen, prior, 79
Ste(a)rnes, Ri, 331;Sam, 329
Stevens, Stephens, Geo, 214; Ri, 375 385; W, 399
Stevenson, Judith, 352
Stone, And, 256; J, 332 359; P, 270
Stonestreat, Stonestreet, Geo, 307-8 336 371; H, 272; H II, 272; J, 307-8 338 371; Martha, 371; Mary (nee Claggett), 272; T, 335; W, 343
Storer, W, 310
Stowell, T, 241

Alcock

Subject index

194 A massive gold ring found in the remains of Southover priory